MASTERING VISUAL BASIC .NET

BY EVANGELOS PETROUTSOS

ISBN 0-7821-2877-7 $49.99

1,184 pages

This book offers comprehensive coverage of all the major aspects of programming with this revolutionary release of VB: new object-oriented language features, advanced graphics controls, Web Forms, database programming with ADO.NET, and building interactive Web applications and Web Services with ASP.NET and XML. Special information for upgraders from VB6 is highlighted throughout the book. The companion CD-ROM includes all the code from the book, sample applications and databases, and a fully searchable electronic edition of the book.

ADO AND ADO.NET PROGRAMMING

BY MIKE GUNDERLOY

ISBN 0-7821-2994-3 $59.99

1,040 pages

This book covers both ADO and ADO.NET in one volume, allowing a programmer to select the appropriate technology for their database application. The material is good for not only VB.NET and C# programmers but also for those using VBA, Access, and older versions of the Microsoft programming tools. It includes numerous examples showing various combinations of servers and clients, including SQL Server, Jet, and Oracle on the server side, and VB, Access, ASP.NET, and VB.NET on the client side. It also covers more advanced topics, such as disconnected recordsets, XML integration, schema modification, and multidimensional aggregation. The companion CD-ROM includes all the sample code and applications from the book, plus a collection of third-party ADO utilities.

D0937506

VISUAL BASIC® .NET
COMPLETE

Associate Publisher: Richard Mills

Acquisitions and Developmental Editor: Denise Santoro Lincoln

Compilation Editor: Gregory Beamer

Editor: Kathy Grider-Carlyle

Production Editor: Mae Lum

Technical Editor: Greg Guntle

Book Designer: Maureen Forys, Happenstance Type-o-Rama

Electronic Publishing Specialists: Stacey Loomis, Bill Clark, Interactive Composition Corporation

Proofreaders: Nanette Duffy, David Nash, Yariv Rabinovitch, Nancy Riddiough

Indexer: Nancy Guenther

Cover Designer: Design Site

Cover Illustrator: MaryBeth Thielhelm, PhotoDisc

Library of Congress Card Number: 2002101980

ISBN: 0-7821-2887-4

CONTENTS AT A GLANCE

CONTENTS

Chapter 14 □ A First Look at ADO.NET   549

Part VI ▶ Building Real-World Applications   835

Chapter 20 ▫ Planning Applications   837

INTRODUCTION

Visual Basic .NET Complete is a one-of-a-kind computer book—valuable both for the breadth of its content and for its low price. This thousand-page compilation of information from five Sybex books provides comprehensive coverage of VB .NET, ASP.NET, database programming with ADO and ADO.NET, and XML integration. This book, unique in the computer book world, was created with several goals in mind:

- ▶ To offer a thorough guide covering all the important user-level features of VB .NET at an affordable price

- ▶ To acquaint you with some of our best authors, their writing styles and teaching skills, and the level of expertise they bring to their books—so that you can easily find a match for your interests and needs as you delve deeper into VB .NET

Visual Basic .NET Complete is designed to provide you with all the essential information you'll need to get the most from VB .NET. At the same time, *Visual Basic .NET Complete* will invite you to explore the even greater depths and wider coverage of material in the original books.

If you have read other computer "how to" books, you have seen that there are many possible approaches to effectively using the product and technologies. The books from which *Visual Basic .NET Complete* was compiled represent a range of teaching approaches used by Sybex and Sybex authors. The source books range from our Mastering series books, which are designed to bring beginner and intermediate level readers to a more advanced understanding, to the Developer's Handbook series, which is intended as an essential resource for experienced VB .NET programmers. As you read through various chapters of *Visual Basic .NET Complete*, you will be able to choose which approach and which level of expertise works best for you. You will also see what these source books have in common: a commitment to clarity, accuracy, and practicality.

In these pages, you will find ample evidence of the high quality of Sybex's authors. Unlike publishers who produce "books by committee," Sybex authors are encouraged to write in their individual voices, voices which reflect their own experience with the software at hand and with the evolution of today's personal computers, so you know you are getting the benefit of their direct experience. Nearly every book represented here is the work of a single writer or a pair of close collaborators. Similarly, all of the chapters here are based on the individual experience of the authors, their first-hand testing of pre-release software, and their subsequent expertise with the final product.

In adapting the various source materials for inclusion *in Visual Basic .NET Complete*, the compilation editor preserved these individual voices and perspectives. Chapters were edited to minimize duplication, omit coverage of non-essential information, update technological issues, and cross-reference material so you can easily follow a topic across chapters. Some sections may have been edited for length in order to include as much updated, relevant, and important information as possible.

Who Can Benefit From This Book?

Visual Basic .NET Complete is designed to meet the needs of a wide range of programmers working with the newest version of Visual Basic. VB .NET provides an extraordinarily rich development environment, enabling programmers to write both Windows applications and robust web solutions using ADO.NET, ASP.NET, and XML. Therefore, while you could read this book from beginning to end, all of you may not need to read every chapter. The table of contents and the index will guide you to the subjects you're looking for.

How This Book Is Organized

Here's a look at what *Visual Basic .NET Complete* covers in each part:

Part I: Visual Basic .NET Essentials This section covers the history of Visual Basic, introduces .NET, and gets you started creating your first Visual Basic .NET project.

Part II: Advanced Visual Basic .NET Part Two is where the real fun begins. You'll explore the Visual Basic .NET language, learn to write and use procedures, explore error handling and debugging, and develop Windows forms. By the time you're finished with this part, you'll have a sound foundation of the Visual Basic language and be able to create some Windows applications.

Part III: ASP.NET Essentials In this section, you'll learn all about Web Forms, get up to speed with XML Web Services, and learn to develop web applications with ASP.NET.

Part IV: Database Programming   Part Four goes through the basics of relational databases and gives you your first look at ADO.NET. You will also learn to retrieve and edit data and explore how to use WinForms and ADO.NET.

Part V: XML and VB .NET   In this section you'll learn to use XML with VB .NET and also how to build web applications using XML.

Part VI: Building Real-World Applications   Now it's time to put everything you've learned to work. This section pulls it all together by walking you through the process of planning your applications and teaching you how to deploy your web projects. You'll also build components for the middle tier and actually build an online store.

On the Sybex website (`www.sybex.com`), you'll find all the code in the book. Search for the book by its ISBN number, 2887, or its title, *Visual Basic .NET Complete*. You can download the code from the download button.

A Few Typographic Conventions

When an operation requires a series of choices from menus or dialog boxes, the ➤ symbol is used to guide you through the instructions, like this: "Select Programs ➤ Accessories ➤ System Tools ➤ System Information." The items the ➤ symbol separates may be menu names, toolbar icons, check boxes, or any place you can make a selection.

`This typeface` is used to identify code and Internet URLs. **Boldface type** is used whenever you need to type something into a text box.

You'll find these types of special notes throughout the book:

TIP
Denotes quicker and smarter ways to accomplish a task, as well as any helpful tidbits you should know.

NOTE
Notes usually offer some additional information that needs to be highlighted.

WARNING

In some places, you'll see a Warning like this one. These appear when there is a possibility of goofing something up. If you see one, read it carefully to make sure you don't get into trouble.

YOU'LL ALSO SEE "SIDEBAR" BOXES LIKE THIS

These boxed sections provide added explanations of special topics, examples of how certain people or companies might handle a situation, or ways to perform a special function. Each sidebar has a heading that announces the topic so you can quickly decide whether it's something you need to know about.

For More Information

See the Sybex website, www.sybex.com, to learn more about all the books that went into *Visual Basic .NET Complete*. Also on the Sybex website is all the code in the book. Search for the book by its ISBN number, 2887, or its title, *Visual Basic .NET Complete*. You can download the code from the download button. On the Sybex website's Catalog page, you'll find links to any book you're interested in.

We hope you enjoy this book and find it useful. Good luck!

Part I
VISUAL BASIC .NET
ESSENTIALS

Chapter 1

ESSENTIAL SKILLS FOR VISUAL BASIC .NET

Everybody has to start somewhere. Right? Software development is an acquired skill, similar to building a house. The master carpenter has to build up his craft from basic skills, such as using a drill and choosing the correct materials. This section will help introduce the novice software developer to the tools he will use in writing Visual Basic .NET software.

We will begin with an introduction to the integrated development environment (IDE)—the program within which you will design your applications and write your code. You will then write a complete, simple program from start to finish, to see how the process of developing a piece of software is carried out. While authoring this program, you will learn about the primary components of programming objects—properties, events, and methods.

The next portion of this Essential Skills section will teach you how to code for the eventuality of runtime errors. Runtime errors are a fact of life when writing any program, and the graceful handling of them is essential to delivering a robust application.

Written expressly for *Visual Basic .NET Complete*
by Matt Tagliaferri

Next, you will be presented with the most basic visual controls available to you as you design your programs and the most common members that make up these controls. This should give you a good running start in developing more full-featured applications.

We'll cover *control docking* and *anchoring,* which allow controls to automatically resize themselves as the forms upon which they sit are resized. The ability to dock and/or anchor controls on forms eliminates the need to manually write resizing code for every form.

You'll learn about the Visual Studio Help system, which is much more than just a simple help file. Tools like Statement Completion, Procedure Parameter Information tooltips, and the Class View of your project all assist you in learning the new structures of Visual Basic .NET programs and classes.

After you have learned the previous programming basics, the text will guide you through the authoring of a reusable component. Creating reusable objects is equivalent to the master carpenter crafting a tool that can be used for a specific purpose.

Finally, you'll learn some basic data-binding techniques, because so many applications require the functionality of reading and writing to some form of data source.

The IDE

The Visual Studio integrated development environment (IDE) employs a tabbed document interface. This allows multiple types of windows to be available on the screen at the same time. The arrangement of the tabbed documents is entirely up to you as the developer. If you want to keep all of your help windows together at the bottom of the screen, for example, you can do that by clicking the desired tab and dragging it to a new location. Documents can float freely or be docked in tabbed document locations, as shown in Figure 1.1.

You can see tabs at the bottom of the screen (with names like Task List and Output). The bottom-right contains tabs such as Properties and Dynamic Help.

One of the first menus you should start to explore is the View menu, as shown in Figure 1.2. It contains options and keyboard shortcuts for opening up most of the important windows in the IDE.

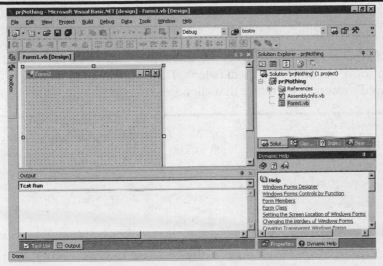

FIGURE 1.1:   Documents can float freely or be docked in a tabbed document.

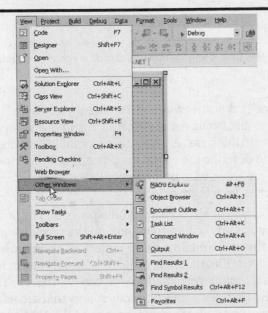

FIGURE 1.2:   The View menu with the Other Windows submenu opened

The design area is where you will lay out your forms and also where you will write most of your code. Figure 1.3 shows the layout, two tabs, design window, and code window for a class named Form1. The design window is where you visually add controls to your forms and make them look the way you want them to look. The code window is similar to a word-processing interface that allows you to type code for your classes.

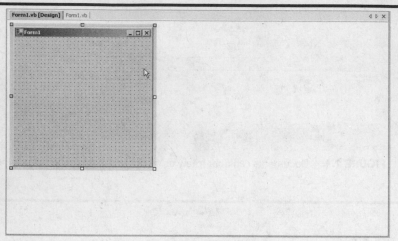

FIGURE 1.3: The layout, two tabs, design window, and code window for a class named Form1

The Properties tab (or "Properties window") is where you assign design-time properties to all of your visual elements. Figure 1.4 shows the Properties tab for the Form1 designs. A property is a variable "attached" to an object that helps to describe the object's position, location, appearance, or behavior. Like variables, each property has its own type. The figure shows the properties for a Form object.

A *solution* is a group of one or more Visual Studio projects. The Solution Explorer window shows all the files that make up the projects in your solution. Simple solutions contain a single project, as shown in Figure 1.5. The project in the illustration is made up of a single form file, Form1.vb, and the Visual Studio–generated file AssemblyInfo.vb. The References portion of the tree view shows the *namespaces* that are referenced in this project. You can think of a namespace as a DLL that contains collections of classes that you can use in your project. The .NET Framework is a collection of namespaces.

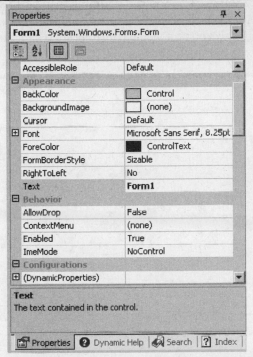

FIGURE 1.4: The Properties window for the form named Form1 in the design area

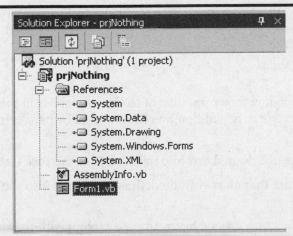

FIGURE 1.5: Solution Explorer window showing a simple solution for a single project named prjNothing

Figure 1.6 shows the Toolbox. The Toolbox contains the controls you can add to your project. Many of these controls are visual in nature, such as Buttons or ListBoxes. However, non-visual controls, such as Timers and EventLog classes, exist in the Toolbox as well.

FIGURE 1.6:   The Toolbox

The Task List window shows you a list of all the code errors in your application as you code it. In addition, you can add your own tasks in one of two ways:

▶ Manually type the desired text into the top line of the Task List.

▶ Add comments that start with predefined keywords into your application.

Figure 1.7 shows a task created by starting a comment with the keyword TODO ("to do"). Adding this comment to the project automatically creates a corresponding task in the Task List. This allows you to set up a list of items you want to get back to and complete later.

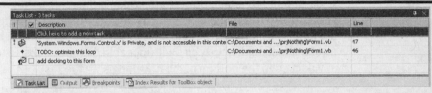

FIGURE 1.7: The Task List window

There are several types of help windows that you can arrange into the IDE. The newest type of help is called Dynamic Help, which is shown in Figure 1.8. This window dynamically changes content as you click various other items in your project. If you add a button to a form, you will see help topics like the ones shown in the illustration.

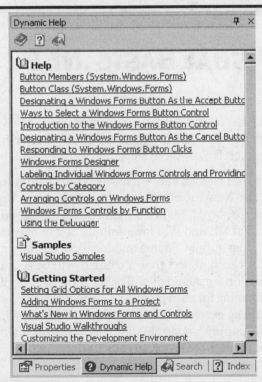

FIGURE 1.8: Dynamic Help

EXPERT ADVICE

▶ In addition to Dynamic Help, there is also a Search window for searching help topics for keywords and an index for looking alphabetically through the help topics. After performing a search, all of the matching help topics will appear in their own tabs, usually docked to the bottom of the IDE along with the Task List.

▶ The View menu is a good place to start learning about all the frequently used areas of the IDE.

▶ The Solution Explorer window is where you'll manage all of the files in your project(s). (A group of projects is called a *solution*.)

▶ Use the Task List to organize your project and denote places in your program that you want to come back to and continue working on later.

YOUR FIRST VISUAL BASIC .NET APPLICATION

Now that we've taken a brief tour of the IDE, let's build our first VB .NET application. This application will take two numbers from the user and add those numbers together. Follow these steps:

1. The first step is to choose File ≻ New ≻ Project from the main menu. The New Project dialog box, as shown in Figure 1.9 will be displayed. Make sure that Visual Basic Projects is selected at left and Windows Application is selected on the right. Then supply a name and location for the project. The files for each project that you create will be kept in their own folder on your hard disk. The location you specify will remain the same for each project that you create (unless you change it). The new project will be stored in a folder with the name you supply under this location. In the dialog shown, we are about to create a project named myFirstApp in the folder C:\vbNet\myFirstApp.

2. Figure 1.10 shows the Solution Explorer after the starting information for the project was specified. You can see that the files named AssemblyInfo.vb and Form1.vb already exist

as part of your project. The *assemblies* under the References node of the Explorer are also listed. An assembly is a collection of .NET Framework classes grouped into one or more files (usually a .DLL). The assemblies listed in this project are part of the .NET Framework, and you'll probably become very familiar with them. As an advanced user, you'll learn how to make your own assemblies so that you can share common functionality in multiple projects.

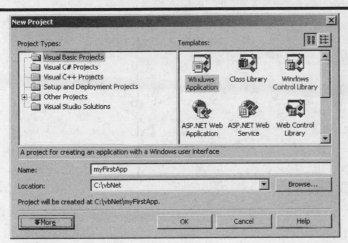

FIGURE 1.9: The New Project dialog box

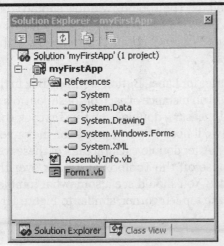

FIGURE 1.10: The Solution Explorer with the myFirstApp project loaded

3. If you have been following along, you should be able to see the Form1.vb [Design] tab shown in Figure 1.11. If the form is not visible, double-click Form1.vb in the Solution Explorer to bring up the designer for the form. You should see a blank, square form in the designer.

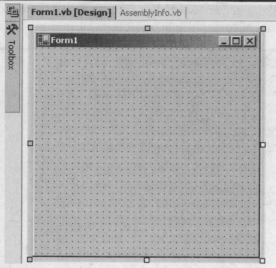

FIGURE 1.11: The Form1.vb [Design] tab

4. Move your mouse over the crossed hammer-and-wrench icon to the left of the Toolbox. The Toolbox window should come into view. Figure 1.12 shows the Toolbox on the left side of the screen. Make sure Windows Forms is the current visible page on the Toolbox.

5. Double-click the entries for Label, Button, and TextBox in the Toolbox. This will add an instance of each of these controls to your form. For good measure, double-click the TextBox control a second time (we'll need two text boxes for the project we're going to write). After double-clicking each of these controls, move the mouse off the Toolbox and back over the design view of Form1. You should see a somewhat jumbled mess of controls in the top-left corner, similar to Figure 1.13.

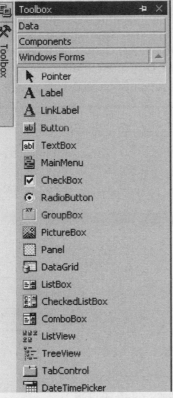

FIGURE 1.12:   The Toolbox on the left side of the screen

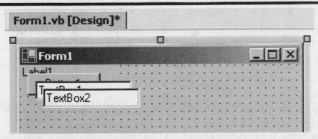

FIGURE 1.13:   Form1 design area showing various controls added from the Toolbox

Part I

6. Click one of the individual controls on Form1 to select it. You can move the control into place by dragging it around on the surface for the form. You can also drag on the sizing handles surrounding the controls to change their length and width. Arrange the controls so your form looks similar to the one in Figure 1.14.

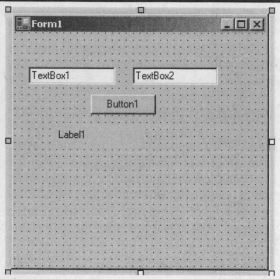

FIGURE 1.14:   Form1 after arranging the individual controls

7. Click a blank area of the form to select it. Make sure the Properties window, as shown in Figure 1.15, has Form1 as the selected item in the drop-down box at the top of the control. In the Properties window, find the Font property. Select it by clicking anywhere on the row. A small box with an ellipsis will appear on the far right of the row.

8. Click the button with the ellipsis. The standard Windows Font dialog box will be displayed. Change the font to Tahoma, 8 pt. After selecting OK, the controls on your form should be displayed in the new font, as shown in Figure 1.16.

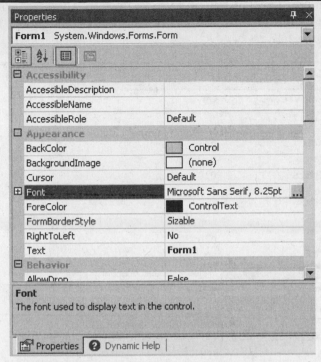

FIGURE 1.15: Form1 Properties window

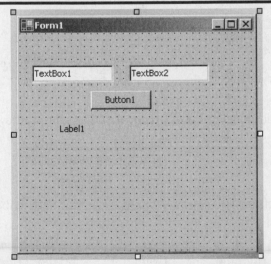

FIGURE 1.16: The controls on your forms should be displayed in the new font.

9. Find the StartPosition property for the form. Change it from WindowsDefaultLocation to CenterScreen, as shown in Figure 1.17.

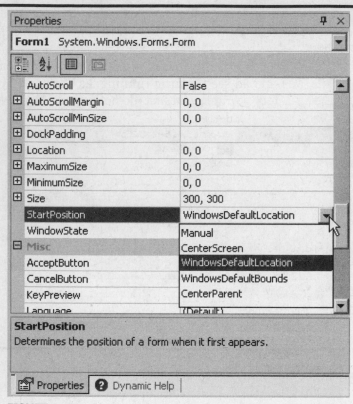

FIGURE 1.17:   Changing the StartPosition property for Form1 through the Form1 Properties window

10. Set these additional properties using the Properties window:

Control	Property	Setting
Button	(Name)	cbGo
	Text	Add
The first (leftmost) TextBox	(Name)	tbFirstNumber
	Text	[*none—remove*
The second (rightmost) TextBox	(Name)	Textbox1]
		tbSecondNumber

Label	Text	[*none—remove*
	(Name)	Textbox1]
		lbOut
	Text	Sum:

The parentheses around the (Name) property are correct; this is how it's actually displayed in the Properties window.

11. Press the F5 key to run your program. After a short compile, you should see the form running, as shown in Figure 1.18. You've written your first (do-nothing-yet) Windows program!

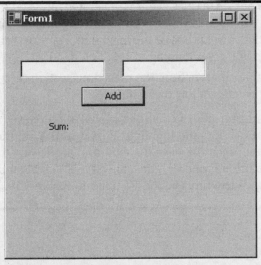

FIGURE 1.18:   Your form running!

EXPERT ADVICE

▶ The visual elements of forms are designed using the Toolbox. Controls can be dragged off the Toolbox onto the form, or the control in the Toolbox can be double-clicked to add an instance of it to the form. You arrange the controls on the form by dragging them around, and you size them using the sizing handles.

▶ Using the Properties window, you can modify the name, appearance, and behavior of controls by setting their properties.

CONTINUED ➠

> ► Run your program by pressing F5. (You can also run the program by selecting Start in the Debug menu.)

EVENT CODING

Windows programs are *event-driven,* which means that code is written to respond to important things that happen in the program. For example, when the user clicks a button, a Click event is generated, and you (as the developer) write code to respond to that event. Learning what events can be generated from each control is one of the most important first steps in learning Visual Basic .NET programming.

Let's make our sample program from the preceding section do something by adding some events. Follow these steps:

1. Open up your project in Visual Basic .NET if you have not done so already. Find and highlight Form1 in the Solution Explorer. Then, click the View Code button, at the very top-left of the Solution Explorer. The main area of Visual Studio will display a code-editing window similar to Figure 1.19.

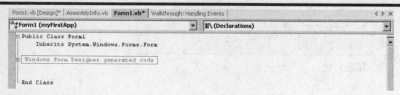

FIGURE 1.19:   The code-editing window for Form1

2. Find and select tbFirstNumber in the code window's leftmost drop-down list. The rightmost drop-down list will then be populated with all of the available events that can be fired by this TextBox control. Find and select Enter in the drop-down. Visual Studio will create the skeleton of the Enter event code for you:

```
Private Sub tbFirstNumber_Enter(ByVal sender As Object, _
                ByVal e As System.EventArgs) _
                Handles tbFirstNumber.Enter

End Sub
```

3. Inside the Enter event procedure, add the three lines of code as shown next. These lines of code highlight whatever text is in the TextBox when the user tabs into it. This causes the current text in the text box to be automatically deleted if the user tabs into the text box and starts typing. If the user wants to keep the text currently in the text box, they simply have to hit the Home or End key to move the cursor.

```
Private Sub tbFirstNumber_Enter(ByVal sender As Object, _
                    ByVal e As System.EventArgs) _
                    Handles tbFirstNumber.Enter
    Dim t As TextBox
    t = sender
    t.SelectAll()
End Sub
```

4. Note that instead of referring to the TextBox directly by its name, tbFirstNumber, we instead set up a local variable named *t* and set it equal to the value of the parameter *sender*. What this allows us to do next is use the same Enter event for more than one TextBox control. To link up the second TextBox to the same event, we manually add it to the Handles clause in the procedure declaration, as shown here:

```
Private Sub tbFirstNumber_Enter(ByVal sender As Object, _
                    ByVal e As System.EventArgs) _
                    Handles tbFirstNumber.Enter, _
                    tbSecondNumber.Enters
    Dim t As TextBox
    t = sender
    t.SelectAll()
End Sub
```

5. Next, go back to the left drop-down list and select the cbGo control (a button, if you'll recall). Then, select the Click event in the right drop-down list. Again, a Click event procedure will be started for you in the code editor. Place the following code in this procedure:

```
Private Sub cbGo_Click(ByVal sender As System.Object, _
                ByVal e As System.EventArgs) _
                Handles cbGo.Click
    Dim i As Integer
    Dim j As Integer
    Dim s As Integer
    i = tbFirstNumber.Text
    j = tbSecondNumber.Text
```

```
        s = i + j
        lbOut.Text = "Sum: " & s
End Sub
```

This is the code that adds the two numbers input into the text boxes. First, variables i and j are declared and initialized to contain whatever text is currently in the two TextBoxes. Then, variable s is declared, and its content is set to be the sum of variables i and j. Finally, the text property on the label control lbOut is set to display the calculated sum.

The code, as shown in this section, is not the only way to accomplish the task of adding two input variables together and displaying the result. There are literally hundreds of ways to get the same job done (this is why some say that writing code is as much an art as a science). Some people strive to write fewer lines of code, at the expense of readability. Others make it their goal to have the most readable code, while others attempt to write code that will execute in the shortest possible time. There are unlimited shades of gray between these extremes, as well.

Press F5 to try your program. You should be able to tab into the text box and type some text. Note that you never had to write any code that allowed the user to type text into a text box; the Visual Basic .NET TextBox control handles all of this automatically. You should also be able to tab out of the text boxes, and any text in that box should be highlighted when you tab back in (because of the SelectAll methods we put in the Enter event of the controls). Finally, clicking the button should display the sum of the two numbers in the input text, as shown in Figure 1.20.

EXPERT ADVICE

▶ Use the two drop-down boxes at the top of the code window to select the control and the event for which you want to write event code.

▶ Learning about the available events for each type of control is one of the most important parts of learning Windows programming.

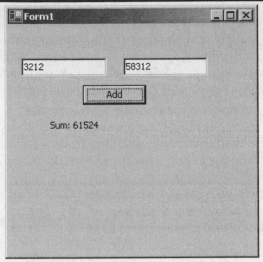

FIGURE 1.20:   Running your new application and adding two numbers

SIMPLE ERROR HANDLING

Our simple calculator is pretty impressive, to be sure, but there's a problem. Our TextBox controls can take any values that the user decides to enter. What if some smart-aleck user tries to add the values **Cow795** and **xf4ee5&^**? You can try this for yourself and see: try entering garbage into the TextBox controls and clicking the Add button. You should be presented with an error message similar to the following:

```
An unhandled exception of type
    'System.InvalidCastException' occurred in
    microsoft.visualbasic.dll.
    Additional information: Cast from String "Cow795")
    to type 'Integer' is not valid.
```

What this message is telling you is that Visual Basic .NET can't successfully store the garbage characters into an Integer variable. If you click the Break button, the code window will display the line of code that's causing the error. These are called runtime errors, because there aren't any problems in the code that the compiler could detect—the error occurs because of some conditions caused by the data the program is handling.

Runtime errors are often much more difficult to track down than design-time errors, because you often don't anticipate the types of data that might choke the program. Harder still is trying to anticipate and protect against these types of errors before you've even see them. In this case, however, we've seen the error at least once, and now we'll change our code to handle the input of garbage characters into the text boxes.

```
Private Sub cbGo_Click(ByVal sender As System.Object, _
          ByVal e As System.EventArgs) Handles cbGo.Click
    Dim i As Integer
    Dim j As Integer
    Dim s As Integer
    Dim bErrorFound As Boolean = False
    Try
        i = tbFirstNumber.Text
    Catch
        i = 0
        bErrorFound = True
    End Try
    Try
        j = tbSecondNumber.Text
    Catch
        j = 0
        bErrorFound = True
    End Try
    s = i + j
    lbOut.Text = "Sum: " & s
    If bErrorFound Then
        lbOut.Text &= Environment.NewLine
        lbOut.Text &= "(non-numeric entries treated as 0)"
    End If
End Sub
```

The big change here is that the transfer from the value of each text box to the integer variables *i* and *j* is wrapped within a Try...Catch block. This is called an *exception-handling block*. What happens here is that the code under the Try statement runs normally, but if an error (also known as an *exception*) is generated, then the code under the Catch command runs instead. In this case, the variable in question is set to value 0, and a flag variable named *bErrorFound* is set to True, which signals to us that an error has occurred.

At the end of the procedure, if the flag variable is indeed set to True, then the output string is modified to tell the user that we took the liberty of assuming the garbage data was 0 when we took our sum. Figure 1.21 shows how the program responds to nonnumeric entry.

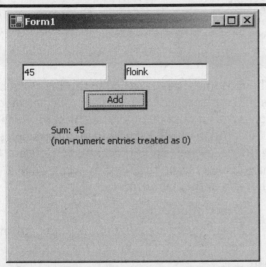

FIGURE 1.21:   The program responding to a nonnumeric entry

EXPERT ADVICE

▶ Use Try...Catch exception blocks to gracefully handle and trap for runtime errors that might occur in your code.

▶ A Try...Finally block (not demonstrated here) can also be used to guarantee blocks of code to run, regardless of errors found. This type of exception handler is good for making sure that resources like database connections are properly released.

METHODS

Let's go back to the event-handling code that we wrote for the two text boxes.

```
Private Sub tbFirstNumber_Enter(ByVal sender As Object, _
                       ByVal e As System.EventArgs) _
                       Handles tbFirstNumber.Enter, _
                             tbSecondNumber.Enters

        Dim t As TextBox
        t = sender
        t.SelectAll()
    End Sub
```

Notice the SelectAll procedure that's attached to the TextBox object variable *t*. Procedures that are attached to objects are called *methods*. Methods usually do some type of work on or for the object to which they're attached. The SelectAll method that we called, for example, did the task of highlighting all of the text in the text box. Here are some of the other common methods on the TextBox control and a brief description of what action they perform:

Method	Description
Cut	Places the current text in the Clipboard, and removes the text from the TextBox
Copy	Places the current text in the Clipboard, and keeps the text in the TextBox
Paste	Places text in the Clipboard into the TextBox
Undo	Undoes the last edit operation in the TextBox
ClearUndo	Re-performs the last undone edit operation in the TextBox

EXPERT ADVICE

► Methods are procedures attached to object classes. They typically perform some type of work on the control or its data.

CONTINUED ➡

▶ Use the IntelliSense feature to get a list of all the available methods for a control as you type.

▶ The Object Browser is yet another good study tool for learning about the available methods on a control.

Part I

BASIC CONTROL SUMMARY

The following tables list the most common Windows controls and the most-frequently used properties, events, and methods (collectively called *members*) that are special to each control. This should serve as a good starting place for designing most common Windows forms and dialog boxes. As always, complete listings of all the members of a control with descriptions can be found in the online help. (This is especially useful for common events such as MouseUp, MouseDown, Enter, Leave, etc.) In some cases, there really aren't common members of a particular type (that isn't to say that there aren't any members of this type, just no common ones), so <none> is listed in those spots.

Button

The button is the standard "clickable doohickey" on a form. Figure 1.22 shows an example of a button. Buttons are primarily used to close dialog boxes or to start actions. (An OK and a Cancel button are provided so the user can either save changes made on the dialog box or cancel them.)

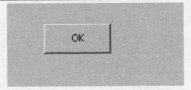

FIGURE 1.22:   An example of a button

Here are a few of the most widely used properties, events, and methods for a button:

Properties	Events	Methods
DialogResult	Click	<none>
Image		
TextAlign		

TextBox

Text boxes are used to allow the user to enter text. They can be single-line TextBoxes, as shown in Figure 1.23, or multiline TextBoxes that allow large quantities of text to be entered.

FIGURE 1.23:   Single-line TextBoxes

Here are a few of the most widely used properties, events, and methods for a textbox:

Properties	Events	Methods
Lines	Change	AppendText
MultiLine	Validating	Copy
PasswordChar		Cut
Text		Paste
WordWrap		Select
		SelectAll
		Undo

RadioButton

The RadioButton (sometimes known as the OptionButton) is used to provide a list of mutually exclusive choices to the user, like Yes and No when only one item can be selected. Figure 1.24 shows an example with two RadioButtons.

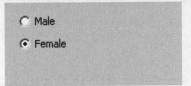

FIGURE 1.24: An example with two RadioButtons

Here are a few of the most widely used properties, events, and methods for a RadioButton:

Properties	Events	Methods
AutoCheck	CheckChanged	<none>
CheckAlign		
Checked		
Text		

CheckBox

CheckBoxes are used to provide a series of options to the user. The answers to the questions are independent of each other—the user can check all boxes, uncheck all boxes, or check as many boxes as needed. Figure 1.25 shows an example with three options.

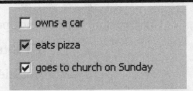

FIGURE 1.25: An example with three CheckBoxes

Here are a few of the most widely used properties, events, and methods for a CheckBox:

Properties	Events	Methods
AutoCheck	CheckChanged	<none>
CheckAlign		

Checked

CheckState

Text

ThreeState

ListBox

A ListBox provides a list of choices to the user. Figure 1.26 shows an example of a ListBox with five items available. The ListBox allows for the selection of some combination of items therein. The ListBox can be configured to allow for only a single item or multiple items.

To learn how to add and remove items from the ListBox, consult additional help on the Items property.

FIGURE 1.26:   An example of a ListBox with five items available

Here are a few of the most widely used properties, events, and methods for a ListBox:

Properties	Events	Methods
HorizontalScrollBar	SelectedIndexChanged	BeginUpdate
Items		EndUpdate
MultiColumn		FindString
SelectedIndex		GetSelected
SelectionMode		SetSelected
Sorted		

ComboBox

A ComboBox combines an editable TextBox with a hidden ListBox that drops down and allows the user to select a single item from the list. Figure 1.27 shows an example of a ComboBox. In this example, the drop-down list box has been opened to show all the possible selections. The ComboBox can be configured to either allow editing in the TextBox or force the user to select an item from the list.

To learn how to add and remove items from the ComboBox, consult additional help on the Items property.

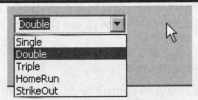

FIGURE 1.27: An example of a ComboBox

Here are a few of the most widely used properties, events, and methods for a ComboBox:

Properties	Events	Methods
DropDownStyle	DropDown	BeginUpdate
Items	SelectedIndexChanged	EndUpdate
MaxDropdownItems		FindString
Sorted		Select
		SelectAll

DOCKING AND ANCHORING

Arranging controls on your forms is an important part of making easy-to-use, intuitive interfaces. This task becomes more challenging when you try to keep your forms looking good even after the user starts resizing them. After all, the user is in control of his own desktop, and if he wants to maximize your application's main form, that's his prerogative. Some users almost certainly run in different screen resolutions than you do. Your perfectly arranged form designed on a 1024×768 screen resolution may be all but unusable on the 640×480 resolution that your accounting department uses.

One solution to this type of problem is to have the controls on your form size themselves automatically as the form resizes. VB .NET controls have two properties (the Dock and the Anchor properties) that allow them to quickly resize to their parent form.

The Dock Property

Setting the Dock property causes the control to "hang onto" one or more edges of its parent control. This allows the control to automatically resize itself as the form it's on resizes. Follow these steps to see the Dock property in action:

1. Create a new project named prjDock.

2. Use the Toolbox to add a TreeView control by double-clicking the control. Do not bother sizing the control. You should see something that looks similar to Figure 1.28.

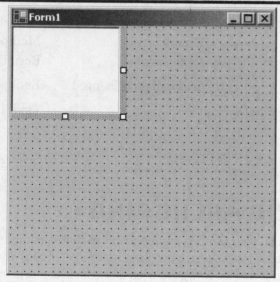

FIGURE 1.28:   Adding a TreeView control

3. Select the TreeView control by clicking it. Locate the Properties window in the IDE. Scroll down until you see the Dock property. Click the down arrow on the far right of the Dock property. You will be presented with the small window, as shown in Figure 1.29.

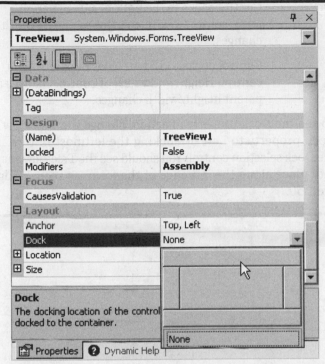

FIGURE 1.29: The Dock property options appearing in a drop-down list.

The six buttons inside the Dock selection control represent the six different Dock settings a control can take. These settings are None, Left, Right, Top, Bottom, and Fill. Each setting performs as follows:

Dock Setting	Description
None	Docking is not done. Control remains in place as form resizes.
Left	Control docks to the left side of parent form/control. Height changes as parent height changes.
Right	Control docks to the right side of parent form/control. Height changes as parent height changes.
Top	Control docks to the top side of parent form/control. Width changes as parent width changes.

Bottom   Control docks to the bottom side of parent
                form/control. Width changes as parent width
                changes.

Fill   Control docks to all four sides of parent form/
                control. Height and width of control changes as
                parent height/width changes.

4. To see the Dock property in action, change the TreeView's
   Dock property to Left by clicking the leftmost button in
   the Dock selection control. You should see the TreeView snap
   into place along the left edge of the form, as seen in Figure 1.30.

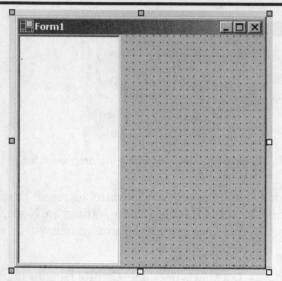

FIGURE 1.30: The TreeView is snapped into place along the left edge of the
form.

You can experiment with different controls and the six different settings for the Dock property to see how to make your forms look their best
as the form is resized.

The Anchor Property

Sometimes you want a control to resize as the parent form resizes, but you don't necessarily want the control to be smashed right up to the parent control's edge. In this event, the property that you're looking for is the Anchor property. To see a demonstration of the Anchor property, perform the following steps on the same project that you started with the Dock property example:

1. Resize the form in the project to make it a bit wider. Add a Panel control to the form, and move it into place so that it lies on the upper part of the form, to the right of the Tree-View control, as seen in Figure 1.31.

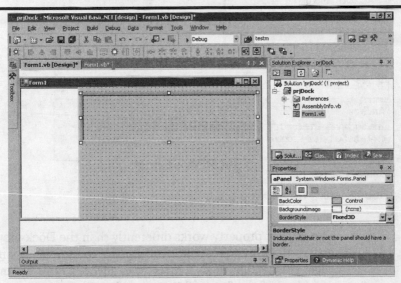

FIGURE 1.31: The resized form with an added panel control

2. Set the BorderStyle property on the Panel control to Fixed3D, so that you can see the control when the project is running.

3. Find the Anchor property in the Properties window, and click the down arrow on the far right of the Anchor property. You will be presented with a drop-down picture that looks like Figure 1.32.

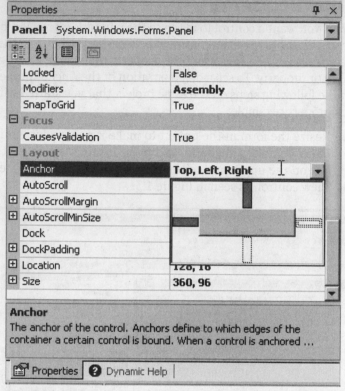

FIGURE 1.32:   The Anchor property for the Panel control

4. The Anchor property works differently than the Dock property in that you can anchor the control to more than one edge. The default for all controls is to anchor to the left and top edges of the form. This means that when the form is resized, the controls will maintain an equal relative distance to the left and top edges. Change the Anchor property of the Panel control by adding the right side. The Properties window should read Top, Left, Right after you change the setting.

5. Run the project, and resize the form. You should see the panel's width change as the form resizes. Note how the distance between the panel and the left, right, and top edges of the form remain constant, while the distance between the

panel and the bottom edge of the form changes as the form resizes.

EXPERT ADVICE

▶ Use the Dock property to snap controls up against the edge of a form or parent control. You can dock against any one edge or against all four edges by using the Fill setting on the Dock property.

▶ Use the Anchor property to allow a control to dynamically resize as the form resizes. Specify the edges whose distance you want to remain fixed.

▶ Not all controls may have a form as their parent container. For example, you can put controls inside the Panel control that you used in the Anchor example. The Dock and Anchor properties always do their docking and anchoring against the parent control of the control in question.

USING HELP

Whether you're an experienced programmer new to the .NET world or a complete novice programmer using Visual Basic .NET as your first foray into the world of software development, you have a large set of choices before you when you need help with a certain topic. Visual Studio .NET has a comprehensive set of tools and ways of providing help to all levels of developers.

Dynamic Help

Dynamic Help, as shown in Figure 1.33, is the most "in your face" of all the forms of help because, by default, it's always visible and changes as you work. Dynamic Help is usually located on a tab behind the Properties window. It takes the form of a series of hyperlinks that you can click to get more information about whatever you're working on at the time. If you add a control to a form, for example, the Dynamic Help will change to display hyperlink topics about the control, form layout, and any special topics that are related to the control you've just created.

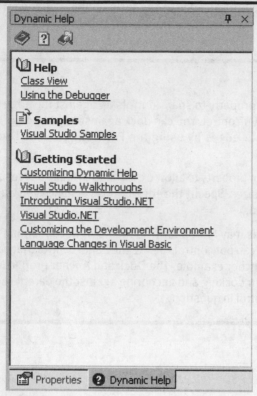

FIGURE 1.33:   The Dynamic Help window

Index

The Help Index is the best way to get help on a specific topic when you can describe the topic by name. It displays an alphabetical list of topics that can be scanned by typing text in the drop-down box at the top of the Index window, as shown in Figure 1.34. The drop-down saves the last several topics that you've searched for, in case you need to consult the same help text again. (You may often find yourself flipping between two or three help topics, and the drop-down provides an easy way to do this.)

FIGURE 1.34:   Shows the Help Index for XML Web Services, UDDI

In addition, you can filter the index to contain help topics that fall under certain areas, such as the .NET Framework, Visual Basic, or Visual Studio. Beginners should leave the filtering off, because they may not know if a help topic falls under a .NET Framework topic or a language topic.

Search

When topic searches are not quite enough, you can use the Search capability to perform full-text searches on the entire body of help topics. As with all keyword search engines, try and keep your search keywords as specific as possible to avoid returning hundreds of candidate topics. As you did with the Help Index, you can filter your searches on specific subsets of the help system. Figure 1.35 shows an example of the Search window.

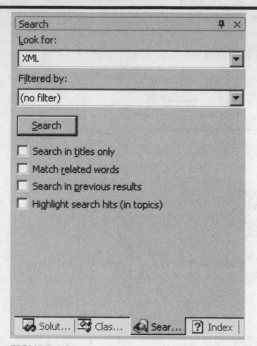

FIGURE 1.35:   An example of the Search window

After performing the search, Visual Studio will display the search results in a tabbed window at the bottom of the environment. Figure 1.36 shows the result of the XML search shown in Figure 1.35. Double-clicking any of the items in the Search Results window will display that topic.

Search Results for XML - 500 topics found			旱 ×
Title	Location	Rank	
XML for Analysis Specification	XML for Analysis Spec	1	
XML for Analysis Specification	XML for Analysis Spec	2	
Audience	XML for Analysis Spec	3	
Design Goals	XML for Analysis Spec	4	
Design Summary	XML for Analysis Spec	5	
Part I: XML for Analysis	XML for Analysis Spec	6	
Introduction to XML for Analysis	XML for Analysis Spec	7	

☑ Task List ▦ Output 🗐 Index Results for XML Web services, UDDI 🔍 Search Results for XML

FIGURE 1.36:   The result of the search for XML topics

Statement Completion

Statement Completion might be one of the best help tools available because it assists you as you write your code. Statement Completion is a magical list that appears after you type the period on any object. The available properties, events, and methods appear in the list. As you begin to type the desired member name, the list auto-scrolls to match what you type. Figure 1.37 shows an example of Statement Completion in action. Once the list has the member selected that you are putting in your code, you can hit the Tab key and the completed member will be placed into your code.

Statement Completion can be a huge timesaver as you learn how many keystrokes it takes to get to certain members. For example, once you type a TextBox name and a period, you can choose its SelectAll method by pressing **S**, **E**, down arrow, and then the Tab key. That's four keystrokes instead of nine. A savings of five keystrokes might not seem like a big deal in a single example, but a professional coder typing eight or more hours per day can make small keystroke savings add up to a large productivity gain.

```
Private Sub Button1_Click(ByVal sender As System.Object,

    aPanel.rese
End Sub       PreProcessMessage
Class         RectangleToClient
              RectangleToScreen
              Refresh
              ResetText
              ResumeLayout
              RightToLeft
              Scale
              ScrollControlIntoView
              ScrollStateAutoScrolling
```

FIGURE 1.37:   An example of Statement Completion in action

Parameter Info

Parameter Info comes into play when you type the left parenthesis on a method call. A tooltip, as shown in Figure 1.38, is displayed that shows one possible list of parameters for the method you have just typed. Pressing the up or down arrow at this point will display another parameter list for the method in question. As you type the commas between each parameter, the parameters in the tooltip will change, showing you the current parameter that you're working on in a bold font.

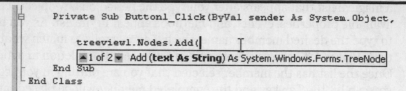

```
Private Sub Button1_Click(ByVal sender As System.Object,
    treeview1.Nodes.Add(
    ▲ 1 of 2 ▼  Add (text As String) As System.Windows.Forms.TreeNode
End Sub
End Class
```

FIGURE 1.38: As you enter parameters for a function, the Parameter Info box appears to help with each parameter.

Object Browser

The Object Browser window can be called up from the View, Other Windows menu, or with the keyboard shortcut Ctrl+Alt+J. The Object Browser displays a large hierarchical structure of the classes and members that make up your project and the .NET Framework assemblies referenced by your project.

Figure 1.39 shows the tree structure of the Object Browser, which is somewhat inverted compared to a true class layout.

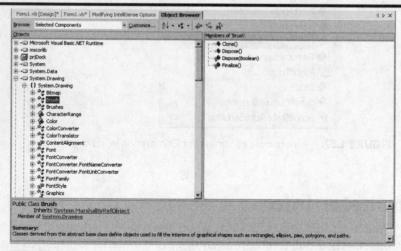

FIGURE 1.39: The tree structure of the Object Browser

In a traditional hierarchical view of the class structure of the entire .NET Framework, the abstract class Object would be at the root of the tree. In the Object Browser, the roots are assembly names, and individual classes lie under each root node. From each class, you can expand the tree until you eventually reach the base Object class.

Class View

The Class View of your project provides the logical class structure of your project. It is somewhat similar in layout to the Object Browser, except that the hierarchical relationship, shown in Figure 1.40, is the true nested structure of the classes and members within your code. It also focuses on displaying only those members that you have currently written code for, as opposed to showing you all the available members in the objects that make up your project.

Many developers find that the Class View is a much more useful view of their project than the Solution Explorer, which provides more of a physical, file-based view of the current project. Clicking a node in the Class View will bring you to that location in the code, making this an excellent navigation tool as well.

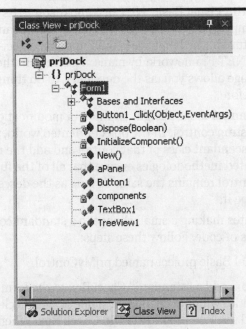

FIGURE 1.40: The Class View for your project represents the hierarchical relationship of the classes and members within your code.

EXPERT ADVICE

▶ Numerous sources of help to developers of all skill levels are built into the Visual Studio IDE.

▶ Dynamic Help provides an ever-changing list of context-sensitive help topics as you construct your project.

▶ Statement Completion and Parameter Info are tools built into the IDE that help you construct code on a line-by-line basis.

▶ The Class View is an excellent logical view into the class structure of your project, and can be a fine navigation tool when your projects grow larger.

YOUR FIRST CONTROL

One of the big features of the Visual Basic .NET in comparison to its predecessors is that it is a complete object-oriented language. This means that every control and feature in the language is built upon an object-oriented framework—the .NET Framework, by name. This shift in the very skeleton of the language allows you, as the developer, to do things that you could never do before.

For example, say you want to make a slight addition or modification to the functionality of an existing control. In the object-oriented world, you simply need to create a descendant class of that control and add the new functionality. Object-oriented methodologies ensure that all of the functionality in the original control remains the same as long as the descendant control doesn't change it.

This section demonstrates making a small change to a standard control in only two dozen lines of code. Follow these steps:

1. Start a new Visual Basic project named prjMyControl.

2. Using the Toolbox, add a "standard" CheckBox to the form. Using the Properties window, change the name of the CheckBox to **cbOld** and the Text property to **Old Check Box**. When completed, the form should look similar to Figure 1.41.

3. In the Solution Explorer, right-click the name of the project and choose Add ≻ Add Class from the menu, as shown in Figure 1.42. Select the default filename of Class1.vb.

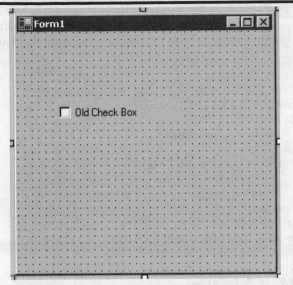

FIGURE 1.41:   A CheckBox added to the form

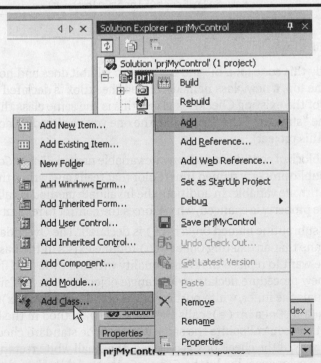

FIGURE 1.42:   Adding a class

4. If the code window does not open automatically, double-click
    Class1.vb in the Solution Explorer to open up the code win-
    dow. Type the following lines of code into the code window:

```
Public Class ColoredCheckBox
    Inherits CheckBox
    Private FInnerColor As Color = Color.DarkBlue
    Property InnerColor() As Color
        Get
            Return FInnerColor
        End Get
        Set(ByVal Value As Color)
            FInnerColor = Value
            Invalidate()
        End Set
    End Property
    Protected Overrides Sub OnPaint( _
            ByVal e As PaintEventArgs)
        Dim r As New Rectangle(2, 11, 9, 9)
        MyBase.OnPaint(e)
        If Me.Checked Then
            e.Graphics.FillRectangle( _
                New SolidBrush(FInnerColor), r)
        End If
    End Sub
End Class
```

Let's study this code for a bit and try to learn what it does and how it
does it. At the top, a new class named ColoredCheckBox is declared as a
descendant of the existing CheckBox class (this is the same class that
makes up the "standard" check box, like the one you've already placed on
the form of this project).

The next block of code declares a private variable named *FInnerColor*
and then a public property named InnerColor that reads and writes the
value of this private variable. In addition, the Invalidate method is called
whenever the property is changed, which forces the control to repaint itself.

Finally, a subroutine named OnPaint() is declared. The Overrides
keyword means that an existing OnPaint() routine exists in the base
class, and we want to replace that functionality with our own. The first
line of this new procedure declares a Rectangle object of a specific size
(this size equals the inner, white portion of the standard check box). The
next line, MyBase.OnPaint(e), calls the OnPaint() method in the base
class, so that the control paints the same way that the standard check
box does. Finally, if the check box is checked, the small white rectangle is
filled with the color specified by the *FInnerColor* variable. Note that the

black check was indeed drawn in the previous step; we are painting over that check with the colored rectangle.

The final effect is that this new type of check box displays its checked state as a solid colored block and its unchecked state as a solid white block. The fill color is specified as a property.

5. Now that the new check box is coded, we need to write some code to create an instance of one so we can see it in action. To do this, go back to the Solution Explorer and select Form1.vb. Click the View Code button at the top of the Solution Explorer to get to the code window. Using the two drop-down boxes, locate and open the Form1_Load event, and add the following code:

```
Private Sub Form1_Load(ByVal sender As System.Object, _
        ByVal e As System.EventArgs) Handles MyBase.Load
    Dim cbNew As New ColoredCheckBox()
    With cbNew
        .Text = "New Check Box"
        .InnerColor = Color.Yellow
        .Left = cbOld.Left
        .Top = cbOld.Top + cbOld.Height
        .Size = cbOld.Size
        .Visible = True
    End With
    Controls.Add(cbNew)
End Sub
```

This code creates an "on the fly" instance of our new ColoredCheck-Box and prepares it on the form by setting the following properties:

Property	Setting
Text	The caption of the check box.
InnerColor	The new property that we defined, which is the fill color of our filled check box.
Left	The horizontal location on the form is set to be the same as that of the original, "standard" check box.
Top	The vertical position is set to be just below the original, "standard" check box.
Size	The size is set to be exactly equal to the original, "standard" check box.
Visible	The new CheckBox control is set to be visible on the form.

6. You should now be able to run the project and see your new control in action. Figure 1.43 shows what the application looks like when it is started. When the application first starts, the two check boxes should look identical except for their captions. However, if you check the lower box, it should fill with the color specified in the previous code.

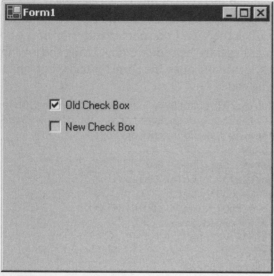

FIGURE 1.43: What the application looks like when it is started

EXPERT ADVICE

▶ Object-oriented programming allows you to create classes with different behavior in only a few lines of code. You gain all the functionality of the original class "for free" by inheriting from it.

▶ Keep your classes in separate files from your form objects, so that you can reuse them in multiple projects later.

▶ Although the previous example did not do this, you can add your new controls to the Toolbox so that you can add them to a form the same way you add the standard controls. Consult the full text to learn how to do this.

DATA BINDING

Most applications need to read and write some form of data. Several database back-ends are available on the market, from Microsoft SQL Server and Oracle to MySQL or FoxPro. You can also connect to databases on other systems such as DB2 (running on an AS/400).

The .NET Framework uses a series of classes to connect to databases that are collectively called ADO.NET. In the past few versions of their database connectivity, Microsoft has gotten very good at making all of the connectivity work the same. This means that you access data the same way no matter what type of database back-end you're accessing.

This sample program connects to a Microsoft SQL Server named taglius and to the Northwind database, which is the sample database included in all SQL Server installations. The server name, taglius, is the name of the machine. As long as you have SQL Server loaded, you should be able to follow along with this example. The program shows you how to use a connection to bind a table in the database to a control named a DataGrid. Follow these steps:

1.   Start a new Visual Basic .NET project. Name the project **prjData**.

2.   Find the DataGrid control in the Toolbox, and drag an instance of it onto the default form. Resize the form and the DataGrid to make each wider. (If you're really adventurous, you can try setting the Dock or Anchor properties on the DataGrid so that it will grow as the form grows.) Your form should look something like Figure 1.44.

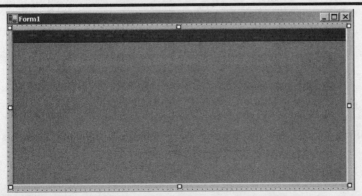

FIGURE 1.44:   New Form with a resized DataGrid control

3. Locate the Server Explorer. The icon for this window is located either just below or just above the Toolbox icon on the far left of the Visual Studio IDE. If you have trouble finding it, you can also use the menu option under the View menu to bring it up.

After locating the Server Explorer, scroll down the list, opening the + symbol(s) until you find the Northwind database. You'll need to know the name of that server to do so. After connecting to the server, open the tree all the way down to the Customers table in the Northwind database, as shown in Figure 1.45.

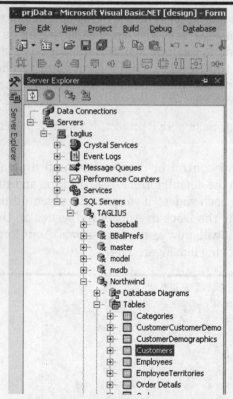

FIGURE 1.45:   Opening the Server Explorer tree and locating the Customers table in the Northwind database

4. After locating the Customers table, drag the word *Customers* in the Server Explorer TreeView onto the form of your project and drop it there. You should see two new objects created in the area below your form: a SQLConnection1 and a SQL-DataAdapter1. Figure 1.46 shows what your screen should look like at this point.

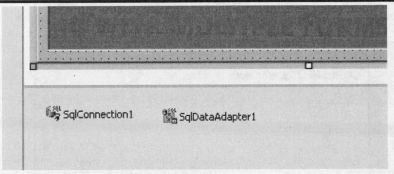

FIGURE 1.46:   Two new SQL Server objects created from the Server Explorer

5. From the main menu, choose Data ➢ Generate Dataset. You will be prompted with a dialog box similar to Figure 1.47. In this figure, the instance has already been added. In your case, you will need to accept the default. This means a new dataset labeled DataSet1. Accept the defaults for all of the options shown by clicking OK. This will create a DataSet object instance in the same area as the SQLConnection1 and SQL-DataAdapter1 objects created in the last step.

6. Select the DataGrid control on the form. Using the Properties window, change the DataSource property to DataSet11 .Customers. Once you successfully do this, the DataGrid should show you the column headers of the Customer table, as shown in Figure 1.48.

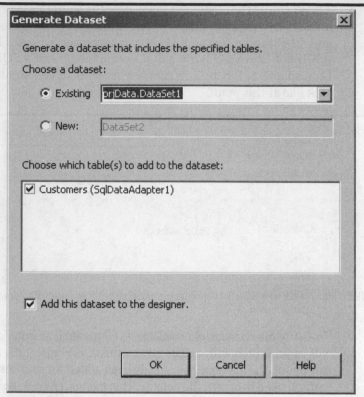

FIGURE 1.47:   Generating the DataSet for a new SQL Server connection

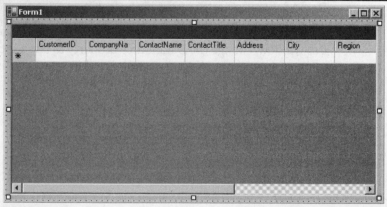

FIGURE 1.48:   The DataGrid showing you the column headers of the Customer
table

7. Add the following single line of code to the Form_Load event of the form:

```
Private Sub Form1_Load(ByVal sender As System.Object, _
        ByVal e As System.EventArgs) Handles MyBase.Load
    SqlDataAdapter1.Fill(DataSet11)
End Sub
```

8. Run the project. You should see the data filling the grid, as shown in Figure 1.49.

CustomerID	CompanyNa	ContactName	ContactTitle	Address	City	Region
ALFKI	Alfreds Futter	Maria Anders	Sales Repres	Obere Str. 57	Berlin	(null)
ANATR	Ana Trujillo E	Ana Trujillo	Owner	Avda. de la C	México D.F.	(null)
ANTON	Antonio More	Antonio More	Owner	Mataderos 2	México D.F.	(null)
AROUT	Around the H	Thomas Hard	Sales Repres	120 Hanover	London	(null)
BERGS	Berglunds sn	Christina Ber	Order Admini	Berguvsväge	Luleå	(null)
BLAUS	Blauer See D	Hanna Moos	Sales Repres	Forsterstr. 57	Mannheim	(null)
BLONP	Blondesddsl	Frédérique Ci	Marketing Ma	24, place Klé	Strasbourg	(null)
BOLID	Bólido Comid	Martín Somm	Owner	C/ Araquil, 67	Madrid	(null)
BONAP	Bon app'	Laurence Leb	Owner	12, rue des B	Marseille	(null)
BOTTM	Bottom-Dollar	Elizabeth Lin	Accounting M	23 Tsawasse	Tsawassen	BC
BSBEV	B's Beverage	Victoria Ashw	Sales Repres	Fauntleroy Ci	London	(null)
CACTU	Cactus Comi	Patricio Simp	Sales Agent	Cerrito 333	Buenos Aires	(null)

FIGURE 1.49:   The data filling the grid

EXPERT ADVICE

▶ Use the Server Explorer to make connections to different types of data sources.

▶ Binding a table's contents to a DataGrid is a simple matter of dragging that table onto your form, generating a DataSet, and adding a line of code to fill the DataSet.

▶ DataSets are the primary feature of ADO.NET. They allow for disconnected recordsets on the client, which are very good in Internet programming environments.

WHAT'S NEXT

This first chapter presented a quick highlight of Visual Basic .NET. We covered the new IDE, writing your first application, and the main controls used within most Visual Basic .NET applications.

Now that the essentials have been covered, in the next chapter you are given an overview of the new features that Visual Basic .NET offers.

Chapter 2

WHAT'S NEW IN VISUAL BASIC .NET?

Although most existing Visual Basic code will port without major changes to Visual Basic .NET, there are also many changes to the language. Understanding the new capabilities of Visual Basic .NET will help you write efficient .NET programs. Here's a list of some of the most significant language changes:

- Inheritance
- Shared members
- Overloading and overriding
- Explicit constructors and destructors
- Declaring and implementing interfaces
- Structured exception handling
- Delegates
- Namespaces

Adapted from *ADO and ADO.NET Programming*
by Mike Gunderloy
ISBN 0-7821-2994-3 $59.99

In addition to these changes, there are many other enhancements and improvements to the Visual Basic language and to the various graphical designers in the product. For example, you can now write multithreaded code with Visual Basic .NET. For a complete list of all the changes, refer to the Visual Studio .NET documentation.

INHERITANCE

Inheritance is a simple but powerful idea (and one that has been missing from Visual Basic for years, much to the dismay of object-oriented purists). It's based on the notion that classes of things come in natural hierarchies, based on "is a" relationships. For example, in the natural world, you might observe that:

A horse is an animal.

A sheep is an animal.

If you know the general rules about how animals behave, you know something about how horses and sheep behave. On the other hand, there are specific things about horses and sheep (for example, their diets) that distinguish them from other animals.

In the business world, you also run into inheritance hierarchies. For example, in a sales application, you might notice that:

A preferred customer is a customer.

A suspended customer is a customer.

Here again, knowing how customers behave in your system tells you most of what you need to know about preferred customers and suspended customers, but not everything.

Visual Basic .NET includes new keywords for implementing inheritance. Listing 2.1 shows some code for three simple classes, named Animal, Horse, and Sheep.

NOTE

You'll find all the code from this chapter on www.sybex.com. Search for the book by its ISBN number, 2887, or its title, *Visual Basic .NET Complete*. You can download the code from the download button.

Listing 2.1: Using Inheritance in Classes

```
Public Class Animal

    Private mstrName As String

    Public Property Name() As String
        Get
            Name = mstrName
        End Get
        Set(ByVal Value As String)
            mstrName = Value
        End Set
    End Property

    Public Function Move() As String
        Move = mstrName & " walked across the farm."
    End Function

    Overridable Function Eat() As String
        Eat = mstrName & " ate."
    End Function

End Class

Public Class Horse
    Inherits Animal

    Sub New()
        MyBase.Name = "The horse"
    End Sub

    Overrides Function Eat() As String
        Eat = MyBase.Name & " ate some oats."
    End Function

End Class

Public Class Sheep
    Inherits Animal
```

```
Sub New()
    MyBase.Name = "The sheep"
End Sub

Overrides Function Eat() As String
    Eat = MyBase.Name & " ate some grass."
End Function
```

```
End Class
```

You should notice a few things as you inspect this code:

▶ You don't have to do anything special to define a class (such as Animal in this example) as a *base class* (one that other classes can inherit from) in Visual Basic .NET. Any class is, by default, inheritable. You can use the NotInheritable modifier when defining a class to prevent it from being a base class. On the other hand, you can use the MustInherit modifier to specify that a class can be used only as a base class, with no instance ever being declared directly.

▶ The Inherits keyword specifies the base class for a class. A class can have only a single base class. If you like, you can build hierarchies, where class *A* is inherited by class *B*, which in turn is inherited by class *C*, and so on.

▶ The Overridable modifier declares a base class member to be one that a derived class can override—that is, the derived class can implement its own version of that member.

▶ The MyBase keyword, when used within a derived class, refers to the underlying base class.

Figure 2.1 shows the result of calling these classes from the btnInheritance button in this chapter's sample project:

```
Private Sub btnInheritance_Click _
    (ByVal sender As System.Object, _
     ByVal e As System.EventArgs) _
     Handles btnInheritance.Click

    Dim h As New Horse()
    Dim s As New Sheep()
```

```
lboResults.Items.Add(h.Move)
lboResults.Items.Add(s.Move)
lboResults.Items.Add(h.Eat)
lboResults.Items.Add(s.Eat)

    End Sub
```

Note the difference between the Move method, which isn't overridden in the derived classes, and the Eat method, which is overridden.

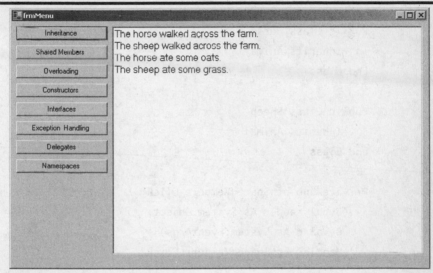

FIGURE 2.1:   Using derived classes

TIP

There is no need to set object variables to Nothing in .NET when you've finished using them. The Common Language Runtime (CLR) will take care of cleaning things up for you, whether you do this or not.

SHARED MEMBERS

Sometimes it's convenient to have a single instance of a property shared among all instances of a class. If the shared property belongs to a base class, it will be shared among all instances of any class derived from that base class. For example, in my imaginary world of animals, I might specify a location for my farm. If I were to change that location, I would want to change it once and have the change apply to all the animals on the farm.

Visual Basic .NET uses the Shared keyword to indicate a shared member. The sample project uses this code to demonstrate this keyword:

```
Public Class Animal
    Public Shared Location As String
End Class


Public Class Horse
    Inherits Animal
End Class


Public Class Sheep
    Inherits Animal
End Class


Private Sub btnSharedMembers_Click
   (ByVal sender As System.Object, _
    ByVal e As System.EventArgs) _
    Handles btnSharedMembers.Click

    Dim h As New Horse()
    Dim s As New Sheep()

    h.Location = "Oregon"
    lboResults.Items.Add(h.Name & " lives in " _
                       & h.Location)
    lboResults.Items.Add(s.Name & " lives in " _
                       & s.Location)

End Sub
```

Figure 2.2 shows the result of calling the code from the btnShared-Members button in the sample project. You can see that setting the

Location property for the Horse object also sets the property for the Sheep object.

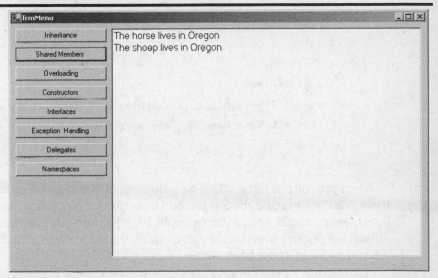

FIGURE 2.2:   Using a shared property

OVERLOADING AND OVERRIDING

Overloading and *overriding* are two ways to provide different behavior for the same method applied to two different objects. Basically, overriding applies within a class, while overloading applies to methods external to a class.

You've already seen overloading in the discussion of inheritance. If a base class method is overridable, the derived classes can use the Overrides keyword to provide their own implementation of the class. For example, the Eat methods of the Horse and Sheep objects override the Eat method of the Animal base class:

```
Public Class Animal
    Overridable Function Eat() As String
        Eat = mstrName & " ate."
    End Function
End Class
Public Class Horse
```

```
        Inherits Animal
        Overrides Function Eat() As String
            Eat = MyBase.Name & " ate some oats."
        End Function
    End Class
    Public Class Sheep
        Inherits Animal
        Overrides Function Eat() As String
            Eat = MyBase.Name & " ate some grass."
        End Function
    End Class
```

When you call the Eat method on a Horse or Sheep object, Visual Basic .NET will execute the Eat method from the corresponding class. If you declare another class (for example, Pig) that also inherits from Animal but doesn't override the Eat method, the class will use the Eat method declared in the base class.

Overloading, on the other hand, allows you to define a single function name that can be called with different sets of parameters. This is useful, for example, in cases where you need two types of objects to be treated differently. For instance, the sample project contains these definitions of a Feed function:

```
    Private Overloads Function Feed(ByVal h As Horse) As String
        Feed = "You give the horse some oats."
    End Function
    Private Overloads Function Feed(ByVal s As Sheep) As String
        Feed = "You turn the sheep loose to graze."
    End Function
```

Both of these definitions are in the code behind frmMenu, not in any class. When you call the Feed function, Visual Basic .NET compares the arguments you supply with the various overloaded function definitions, and executes the one that matches (or returns an error if there is no match). In the sample project, btnOverloading uses this code to demonstrate both overriding and overloading:

```
    Private Sub btnOverloading_Click_
        (ByVal sender As System.Object, _
        ByVal e As System.EventArgs) _
```

```
Handles btnOverloading.Click

Dim h As New Horse()
Dim s As New Sheep()


lboResults.Items.Add(Feed(h))
lboResults.Items.Add(h.Eat)
lboResults.Items.Add(Feed(s))
lboResults.Items.Add(s.Eat)


End Sub
```

Figure 2.3 shows the results of executing this code.

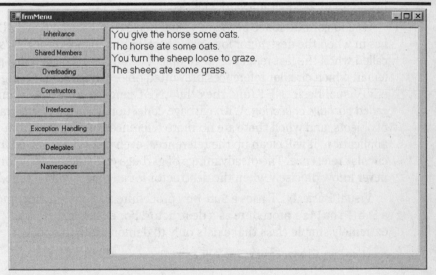

FIGURE 2.3: Overriding and overloading methods

Overloading is much more flexible than this simple example demonstrates:

▶ You can have as many different versions of the same procedure as you like, as long as each one has a distinct argument list.

▶ You can have a different order of arguments between different overloaded versions of a procedure.

▶ Overloaded versions of a procedure can have different return datatypes (although they must also have different argument lists).

EXPLICIT CONSTRUCTORS AND DESTRUCTORS

A *constructor* is a procedure that is called when an object is first created, and a *destructor* is a procedure that is called when an object is destroyed. Visual Basic 6 allowed you to write explicit constructors and destructors in a class module by using the Initialize and Terminate procedures. Visual Basic .NET goes a step further by providing constructors and destructors for all objects, including system objects such as WinForms and other instances of .NET Framework classes.

One major difference between Visual Basic 6 and Visual Basic .NET lies in when the destructor for a class is called. In Visual Basic 6, it's called when the last reference to an object is dropped. This led to a problem in which circular references prevented objects from terminating properly. Visual Basic .NET (and the other .NET languages) uses a scheme called *garbage collection*. With garbage collection, the CLR keeps track of objects, and when there are no more references to an object from your application, it will clean up the references, even if they're involved in a circular reference. The disadvantage of garbage collection is that you never know precisely when the destructor for an object will be called.

Visual Basic .NET uses a Sub New procedure as a constructor, and a Sub Finalize procedure as a destructor. For example, here's an extremely simple class that exists only to demonstrate this code:

```
    Public Class EmptyClass


        Sub New()
            MyBase.New()
            MsgBox("The constructor has been called")
        End Sub

        Protected Overrides Sub Finalize()
            MsgBox("The destructor has been called")
```

```
        MyBase.Finalize()
    End Sub
End Class
```

NOTE

In a derived class, you should call the New and Finalize methods of the base class, as shown in this example. Because all classes are derived from System.Object if they're not otherwise declared, you should always do this.

This class is used from the Constructors button on the sample form:

```
Private Sub btnConstructor_Click _
    (ByVal sender As System.Object, _
    ByVal e As System.EventArgs) _
    Handles btnConstructor.Click

    Dim EC As New EmptyClass()
    MsgBox("Click OK to end the procedure" & _
        " and destroy the EmptyClass")
End Sub
```

If you run this code, you'll find that the constructor for EmptyClass is called as soon as you click the button, but the destructor is not called until you close the form. That's because EmptyClass uses so few resources that the CLR garbage collection mechanism doesn't waste time cleaning it up until the project is closing down.

NOTE

If you have resources in a class that you'd like to free when you're done with the class, you should write a Sub Dispose procedure in that class and call it explicitly, rather than wait for the Finalize to be called.

DECLARING AND IMPLEMENTING INTERFACES

An *interface* defines a set of methods, properties, and events that can be used by multiple classes. Visual Basic 6 includes the Implements keyword so that Visual Basic classes can use interfaces defined by other components. Visual Basic .NET adds the `Interface` keyword, which allows you to define interfaces directly within Visual Basic .NET.

The sample project includes an interface definition in `Main.vb`:

```
Module Main


    Interface Care
        Function Groom() As String
        Function Deworm() As String
    End Interface


End Module
```

Like a base class definition, an interface represents a contract on the part of your code to adhere to a certain structure. But interfaces have advantages in some situations over using base classes and inheritance. First, interfaces tend to be less complex than base classes, and therefore more easily maintained. Second, a single class can implement multiple interfaces, which allows you to simulate inheritance from multiple base classes simultaneously.

Both the Horse and the Sheep class implement the Care interface:

```
Public Class Horse
    Inherits Animal
    Implements Care


    Function Groom() As String Implements Care.groom
        Groom = "You brush the horse."
    End Function


    Function Deworm() As String Implements Care.Deworm
        Deworm = "You give the horse a dose of dewormer."
    End Function


End Class
Public Class Sheep
    Inherits Animal
```

```
Implements Care

Function Groom() As String Implements Care.groom
    Groom = "You shear the sheep."
End Function

Function Deworm() As String Implements Care.Deworm
    Deworm = "You give the sheep a dose of dewormer."
End Function

    End Class
```

When you implement an interface, the return type of all properties and methods must exactly match the definition in the interface itself. Also, interfaces must be implemented completely. For example, if you left the Deworm function out of the Sheep class after declaring that the class would implement the Care interface, you would get an error while trying to run the code.

The menu form in the sample project contains code to call the implemented interface members:

```
Private Sub btnInterfaces_Click _
    (ByVal sender As System.Object, _
    ByVal e As System.EventArgs) _
    Handles btnInterfaces.Click

    Dim h As New Horse()
    Dim s As New Sheep()

    lboResults.Items.Add(h.Groom)
    lboResults.Items.Add(s.Groom)
    lboResults.Items.Add(h.Deworm)
    lboResults.Items.Add(s.Deworm)

    End Sub
```

Figure 2.4 shows the result of running this code.

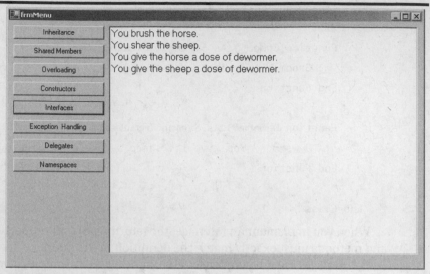

FIGURE 2.4:   Calling implemented interfaces

STRUCTURED EXCEPTION HANDLING

Visual Basic .NET adds a number of improvements to error handling, compared with previous versions. Chief among these is *structured exception handling,* implemented in a Try...Catch...Finally block. The Try keyword tells Visual Basic .NET that this is the beginning of a structured exception-handling block. The Catch keyword indicates a point where code execution should be transferred if an error occurs. The Finally keyword marks a block of code that will always be executed, whether or not an error occurs.

The sample project includes a very simple structured exception-handling example:

```
Private Sub btnExceptionHandling_Click _
    (ByVal sender As System.Object, _
    ByVal e As System.EventArgs) _
    Handles btnExceptionHandling.Click


    Dim b As Byte
```

```
' Set up a structured exception handling block
Try
    b = 255
    b = 3 * b
Catch ex As Exception
    lboResults.Items.Add(ex.Message)
    lboResults.Items.Add(ex.StackTrace)
Finally
    lboResults.Items.Add("Executing the Finally block")
End Try


End Sub
```

Any error within the Try...End Try markers will cause execution to resume at the Catch line. The Finally block is executed regardless. Figure 2.5 shows the result of running this code.

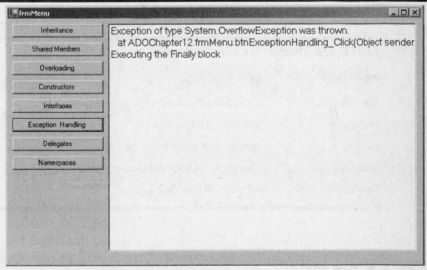

FIGURE 2.5: Structured exception handling

A great deal of flexibility is built into the Catch keyword beyond what is shown here. The Catch block can open with a *filter* to catch only specific exceptions, and it can be repeated. For example, the following is the skeleton of a valid structured exception-handling block.

```
Try

    …

Catch e As System.IO.EndOfStreamException

    …

Catch When ErrNum = conErrMyError

    …

Catch e As Exception

    …

Finally

    …

End Try
```

As you can see, a filter can be either a particular type of exception (all exceptions are subclasses of the Exception class) or a Boolean expression. When an error occurs, the CLR inspects all Catch blocks until it finds the first one that matches the current exception.

The Exception class has a number of useful properties. Table 2.1 summarizes them.

TABLE 2.1:   Properties of the Exception Class

PROPERTY	EXPLANATION
HelpLink	Link to a help file explaining the exception
Message	Text of the error message
Source	Application or object that caused the error
StackTrace	Trace of the call stack that led to this exception
TargetSite	Method that threw the exception

DELEGATES

Delegates provide Visual Basic .NET with a way to refer to procedures at runtime (delegates are sometimes called *type-safe function pointers*). You can use delegates in any situation where you want to decide at runtime which procedure to call in response to a particular event. Although delegates are a general-purpose concept, they are most useful in Visual Basic .NET as a way to handle events dynamically at runtime. Visual Basic .NET includes the AddHandler and RemoveHandler statements. The former connects an event to a procedure by creating a new delegate; the latter removes an existing connection between an event and a procedure.

The sample project contains some code to demonstrate changing event handlers at runtime:

```
Private Sub btnDelegates_Click _
    (ByVal sender As System.Object, _
    ByVal e As System.EventArgs) _
    Handles btnDelegates.Click

    lboResults.Items.Add("In btnDelegates_Click")
    AddHandler btnDelegates.Click, AddressOf EH1
    RemoveHandler btnDelegates.Click, _
                AddressOf btnDelegates_Click

End Sub

Private Sub EH1(ByVal sender As System.Object, _
            ByVal e As System.EventArgs)

    lboResults.Items.Add("In EH1")
    AddHandler btnDelegates.Click, AddressOf EH2
    RemoveHandler btnDelegates.Click, AddressOf EH1

End Sub

Private Sub EH2(ByVal sender As System.Object, _
            ByVal e As System.EventArgs)

    lboResults.Items.Add("In EH2")
    AddHandler btnDelegates.Click, AddressOf EH1
    RemoveHandler btnDelegates.Click, AddressOf EH2

End Sub
```

Each of these three procedures has the right argument list to be an event handler for a button Click event. The first is the default event handler that the Windows Forms package creates for btnDelegates' Click event. This procedure uses the AddHandler statement to add the EH1 procedure to the list of handlers for the event, and then uses RemoveHandler to remove itself from the list. Note that both AddHandler and RemoveHandler take two parameters:

▶ The name of an event

▶ A pointer to a procedure to handle that event, obtained with the AddressOf operator

The other two procedures also use AddHandler and RemoveHandler to alternate handling the event.

Figure 2.6 shows the result of repeatedly clicking the Delegates button.

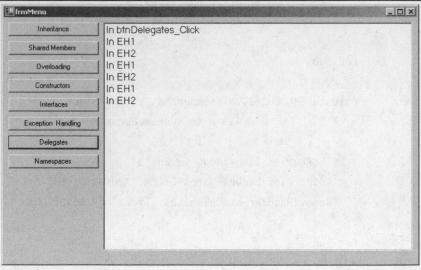

FIGURE 2.6:   Using AddHandler and RemoveHandler statements

NAMESPACES

The next chapter, "Introduction to .NET," will introduce you to the concept of *namespaces:* groups of objects that perform similar functions. Namespaces are also useful for avoiding name collisions. That is, two classes may have the same class name without causing an error, as long as they are located in different namespaces.

In addition to being able to use the namespaces of the .NET Framework class library, in Visual Basic .NET, you may also declare your own namespaces. Here's a small bit of sample code from the `Namespaces.vb` file, which can be downloaded from the Sybex website:

```
Namespace Farm
    Public Class Fork
        Public Length As String = "7 feet"
    End Class
End Namespace


Namespace Kitchen
    Public Class Fork
        Public Length As String = "6 inches"
    End Class
End Namespace
```

Just like a `Class` declaration statement, a `Namespace` declaration statement must be matched to a corresponding `End Namespace` statement. This particular bit of code declares two namespaces, Farm and Kitchen, each of which contains a Fork class. The fully qualified names of the classes are `Farm.Fork` and `Kitchen.Fork`, and you can use those names elsewhere in your code:

```
Private Sub btnNamespaces_Click _
    (ByVal sender As System.Object, _
    ByVal e As System.EventArgs) _
    Handles btnNamespaces.Click

    Dim Fork1 As New Farm.Fork()
    Dim Fork2 As New Kitchen.Fork()

    lboResults.Items.Add(Fork1.Length)
    lboResults.Items.Add(Fork2.Length)

End Sub
```

Even though the classes have the same unqualified name, they can both be used in the same program without conflict because they are in different namespaces.

You can nest Namespace statements to create a hierarchy of namespaces, as in this example:

```
Namespace Vehicle
    Namespace Passenger
        Class Sedan

        End Class
        Class StationWagon

        End Class
    End Namespace
End Namespace
```

This declares two classes, Vehicle.Passenger.Sedan and Vehicle.Passenger.StationWagon.

WHAT'S NEXT

This chapter introduced the new features and components of Visual Basic .NET. Visual Basic .NET is still just a component of the overall .NET strategy. In the next chapter, we will begin to delve into the .NET component and how to build .NET applications using Visual Basic .NET.

Chapter 3

INTRODUCTION TO .NET

In the preceding two chapters, you were given an overview of the skills needed and a quick glance as to what is new in Visual Basic .NET. In this chapter, you are presented with an introduction to the framework that provides Visual Basic .NET with additional flexibility and power: the .NET Framework. It's clear that .NET represents a major shift in the way that many software applications will be designed and written.

.NET is a huge subject—and a new one to many developers. The sheer amount of documentation that ships with the .NET Framework and Visual Studio .NET can be overwhelming and even frightening. This chapter will provide an overview of .NET. I'll teach you the basics of the .NET architecture, discuss the .NET languages, and show you how you can still use your existing ADO code from .NET. Part IV of the book will provide more details about using ADO.NET.

Adapted from *ADO and ADO.NET Programming*
by Mike Gunderloy
ISBN 0-7821-2994-3 $59.99

NOTE

The .NET content in this book is based on Microsoft's beta 2 release. Although this version is stable and usable, it's not the final software. Be sure to check the book's web page for any last-minute changes that affect my .NET coverage. (Go to Sybex's website, www.sybex.com. In the Search box, type the book's ISBN code, **2887**, or the book's title.)

.NET ARCHITECTURE

Microsoft describes the .NET Framework variously as "a new computing platform designed to simplify application development in the highly distributed environment of the Internet" and as "an XML Web Services platform that will enable developers to create programs that transcend device boundaries and fully harness the connectivity of the Internet." While such descriptions give you some sense of *what* .NET can do, you, as a working developer, are probably more interested in *how* it can do those things. In this section, I'll describe some of the features and innovations that are the underpinnings of the .NET Framework:

The Common Language Runtime (CLR)

Managed execution

The Common Type System (CTS)

Cross-language interoperability

The .NET Framework class library

Namespaces

Assemblies

Application domains

Security

Deploying and configuring .NET applications

Web Services

Windows Forms

ASP.NET

The Common Language Runtime

The Common Language Runtime (CLR) is the core of the .NET Framework. All code written in the .NET languages is executed via the CLR. In that respect, the CLR is similar to previous runtimes such as the Visual Basic runtime. Visual Basic code is executed via the Visual Basic runtime, which translates the VB language into low-level Windows API calls.

The CLR is a much more active component of applications than the VB runtime is. In fact, the CLR takes such an active role in the execution of code that code written for the CLR is referred to as *managed code*. That's because, in addition to executing code, the CLR provides services. For example, the CLR takes care of all memory management and garbage collection (reusing memory occupied by objects that are no longer in use) for .NET applications.

The CLR is responsible for enforcing various rules that are designed to make .NET applications robust. These include constraints on datatypes, memory usage, and application security. Because all of this management is taking place in the CLR, it's impossible for even poorly written .NET code to contain many common types of errors. For example, memory leaks (where an object is instantiated and never destroyed) are impossible in managed code. And this protection comes at no cost to the developer. You don't have to write a single line of code to be assured that your application won't contain memory leaks.

Managed Execution

The entire process of turning your source code into a running application in the .NET Framework is referred to as *managed execution*. This process consists of four steps from start to finish:

1. You create your program's source code using a specialized development environment such as Visual Studio .NET or a general-purpose tool such as a text editor.

2. You use a .NET compiler to turn the source code into a form known as Microsoft Intermediate Language (MSIL). MSIL files typically have the file extension .dll or .exe. They look like executable files to the operating system, although they cannot run without the CLR. The MSIL format is independent of any particular operating system or hardware architecture.

3. When you run a .NET executable, the .NET Framework uses a just-in-time (JIT) compiler to translate the MSIL instructions into actual hardware-specific instructions that can be executed by your computer's CPU.

4. The CLR passes the compiled code to the CPU, monitoring its execution to perform management services such as memory management, security checking, and versioning support.

Figure 3.1 shows the managed execution process schematically.

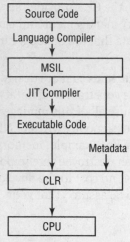

FIGURE 3.1: The managed execution process

As Figure 3.1 shows, the MSIL version of your application contains information other than the code to perform the application's functions. This *metadata* is a separate section of the MSIL file that describes the contents of the file. This metadata is used by the CLR to ensure proper operation of the code. For example, the metadata contains descriptions of the datatypes exposed by your application; the CLR can use these descriptions to make sure it properly interoperates with other applications.

The .NET Framework includes a tool that you can use to examine the contents of an MSIL file. This tool is the IL disassembler, or ILDASM. To run ILDASM, follow these steps:

1. Choose Start ➤ Programs ➤ Microsoft Visual Studio .NET 7.0 ➤ Visual Studio .NET Tools ➤ Visual Studio .NET Command Prompt.

2. At the command prompt, type **ILDASM**.

3. Choose File ➤ Open to load an MSIL file into ILDASM.

Figure 3.2 shows a simple "Hello, World" program written in Visual Basic .NET and opened in ILDASM. The treeview shows the information contained in the metadata, while the separate window shows the actual MSIL code for the selected component.

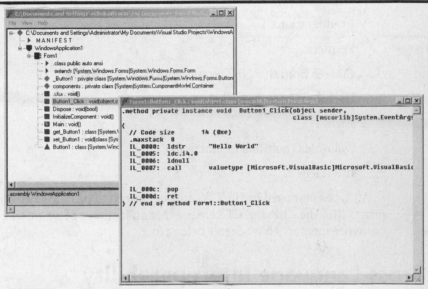

FIGURE 3.2:   Examining MSIL with ILDASM

The Common Type System

The CLR defines the Common Type System (CTS). At its most basic level, you can think of the CTS as defining all the datatypes that managed code is allowed to use. It also defines rules for creating, persisting, using, and binding to types.

Because the CTS includes rules for creating new types, you're not limited to a small set of datatypes. In particular, you can define your own values (for example, Visual Basic .NET enumerations) or your own classes such that they will be acceptable to the CTS. Indeed, as long as you're using a .NET language, the operation of defining CTS-acceptable types is transparent to the developer. The compiler will take care of following the CTS rules.

The CTS manages many categories of types, including these:

> Built-in value types such as byte or Int32 (a 32-bit signed integer)

> User-defined value types (for example, you could write code to define a complex number type)

> Enumerations

> Pointers

> Classes from the .NET Framework class library

> User-defined classes

> Arrays

> Delegates (pointers to functions)

> Interfaces

All types managed by the CTS are guaranteed to be *type safe*. That means that the CLR and CTS ensure that an instance of a type cannot overwrite memory that doesn't belong to it.

Cross-Language Interoperability

Because the CLR manages all .NET code, regardless of the language in which it's written, the .NET Framework is an ideal environment for cross-language interoperability. That is, code written in one .NET language can be easily used from another .NET language. This interoperability is pervasive. For example, you can define a class in VB .NET and then call the methods of that class, or even derive a new class from the original class, in C# code.

The key to interoperability is the metadata contained in MSIL files. Because this metadata is standardized across all .NET languages, a component written in one language can use the metadata to figure out the proper way to call a component written in another language.

However, not every .NET language can use all the features of the CLR. For example, the CTS defines a 64-bit unsigned integer datatype, but not all languages allow you to define variables using that type. To ease this problem, .NET defines the Common Language Specification, or CLS. The CLS is a set of rules that dictate a minimum core set of .NET constructs that every .NET language must support. If you write components that conform to the CLS, you can be sure that they will be usable by components written in other .NET languages.

The .NET Framework Class Library

The other major component of the .NET Framework, besides the CLR, is the .NET Framework class library. A *class library* is a set of predefined classes that can be used to access common functionality. By supplying a class library, the .NET Framework keeps developers from having to "reinvent the wheel" in many cases.

If you've used Visual Basic 6, you're already familiar with the notion of a class library, although you may not recognize it by that name. Built-in Visual Basic objects, such as the Err and Debug objects, are part of the class library that ships with Visual Basic.

The .NET Framework class library is exceptionally rich, containing several hundred classes. These classes encapsulate functionality such as the following:

Defining data with the CLR datatypes

Defining data structures, including lists, queues, and hash tables

Installing software

Debugging applications

Globalizing software

Reading and writing data

Interoperating with unmanaged code

Managing threads

Handling security

WARNING
If you're not comfortable with concepts such as classes, objects, properties, and methods, you'll need to remedy this before you start working with .NET.

Namespaces

Classes within the .NET Framework class library are arranged in *namespaces*, groups of objects that perform similar functions. Namespaces also contain other .NET entities, such as structures, enumerations, delegates, and interfaces. Namespaces, in turn, are arranged into a hierarchy. For example, one class you'll see used in ADO.NET code is named System.Data.OleDb.OleDbConnection. An object instantiated from this class represents a single connection to an OLE DB database. This is the OleDbConnection class within the System.Data.OleDb namespace (a collection of classes dealing with access to OLE DB data), which is, in turn, contained within the System.Data namespace (a collection of classes dealing with data access), which is, in turn, contained within the System namespace (which is the root namespace for almost all the .NET Framework class library namespaces).

The .NET Framework class library contains nearly 100 namespaces. A complete listing would be exhausting and (because such a listing already appears in the .NET Framework SDK documentation) pointless. Table 3.1 lists some of the namespaces that you'll see in this book as you dig into ADO.NET.

TABLE 3.1:   Selected .NET Framework Namespaces

NAMESPACE	CONTENT
System.Collections	Abstract data structures, including lists, hash tables, queues, and dictionaries
System.Data	The root namespace for the ADO.NET classes
System.Data.Common	Classes shared by all .NET data providers
System.Data.OleDb	The OLE DB .NET data provider
System.Data.SqlClient	The SQL Server .NET data provider
System.Data.SqlTypes	Implementations of the SQL Server native datatypes
System.Diagnostics	Debugging and tracing aids
System.DirectoryServices	An interface to the Windows Active Directory
System.Drawing.Printing	Printer functionality
System.Globalization	Classes useful in globalizing an application
System.IO	Classes for reading and writing streams and files

TABLE 3.1 continued: Selected .NET Framework Namespaces

NAMESPACE	CONTENT
System.Messaging	Inter-application messaging support
System.Net	Network protocol support
System.Resources	Resource file support
System.Runtime.Remoting	Support for distributed applications
System.Runtime.Serialization	Support for saving objects to files or streams
System.Security	Security and permissions functionality
System.Web	Support for communication with web browsers
System.Windows.Forms	Stand-alone user interface components
System.XML	Classes for using XML

Assemblies

.NET groups code into units called *assemblies*. An assembly can consist of a single file or can consist of components distributed across multiple files. In all cases, there is one file that contains the *assembly manifest*, a part of the metadata that lists the contents of the assembly.

When you're writing .NET code, you can designate which files will go into an assembly, and which other assemblies a particular assembly is designed to work with. The CLR uses assemblies as a fundamental unit of management in many respects:

- ▶ Permissions are requested and granted on an assembly as a whole.

- ▶ A type retains its identity within an assembly. That is, if you declare a type named CustomType within an assembly, that type will be identical in all files contained in the assembly. But different assemblies may contain two different types named CustomType.

- ▶ The assembly manifest specifies which types may be used by code outside the assembly.

- ▶ Version tracking is done on the assembly level. An assembly can specify the version of another assembly that it requires, but it cannot specify a version for an individual file within an assembly.

Part I

▶ Assemblies are deployed as a unit. When an application requests code contained in an assembly, it must install the entire assembly.

.NET also allows "side-by-side" assemblies. That is, you can have two versions of the same assembly installed on the same computer, and different applications can use them simultaneously.

Application Domains

Application domains provide a second level of code grouping in .NET. An application domain is composed of a group of assemblies loaded together. The CLR enforces isolation between application domains, such that code running in one application domain cannot directly manipulate objects in another application domain.

NOTE

The CLR provides services for allowing cross-domain calls. You can manipulate objects across application domain boundaries by copying them between application domains or by constructing a proxy to forward the calls.

Application domains are not the same as Windows processes. On the Windows level, all of the code within a single application (such as Internet Explorer) runs in a single operating system process. But on the .NET level, multiple application domains can be contained within a single process. This allows, for example, several .NET-developed controls to be used on the same ASP.NET web page without any risk that one will corrupt the other.

Security

.NET is the first of Microsoft's development environments to be designed with serious attention to security. It's a fact of life that security holes have become more critical as more applications are connected to the Internet, where a wide variety of people with bad intentions can attempt to exploit any holes.

The .NET Framework implements both *code access security* and *role-based security*. Code access security is designed to protect the operating system from malicious code by granting permissions to resources based on the source of code and the operations that the code is attempting to perform. You can mark various classes and their members within your application to deny unknown code from using those resources.

Role-based security allows you to grant or deny access to resources based on credentials supplied by users. In role-based security, a user's identity determines the roles to which the user belongs, and permissions are granted to roles. The identity can be determined either by the user's Windows login credentials or by a custom scheme used only by your application.

Deploying and Configuring .NET Applications

The .NET Framework is designed to make deploying applications simple and less likely than current models to cause conflicts with existing applications. Because assemblies contain metadata that describes their contents, there is no need to make Registry entries or transfer files to the system directory in order to use an assembly. In fact, the simplest possible deployment is often appropriate for a .NET application: Just use XCOPY or FTP to move the application's files to a directory on the target machine, and then run the application. The CLR in conjunction with the metadata will take care of the rest.

The .NET Framework also supports version 2 of the Windows Installer. By using this installer to package and deploy your application, you can offer a wider variety of options to the user, including the option to install only portions of the application.

The .NET Framework also supports a mechanism for changing the behavior of applications after they are deployed. This mechanism is the *configuration file*, which is a file of settings stored as XML that the CLR can parse. Such files can include information on local security settings, on the location of particular assemblies, and on performance-related settings. You can also use configuration files to hold parameters for your own applications.

Web Services

As .NET catches on, you're going to hear a lot (if you haven't heard enough already!) about *Web Services*. You may also read a lot of complex, confusing explanations of the architecture of these Web Services. But at their most basic level, Web Services are simple: They are a means for interacting with objects over the Internet.

The key to Web Services is that they are built with common, pervasive Internet protocols: All communication between Web Services clients and servers is over HTTP and XML by default (although developers may use other protocols if they want). For this to work, there has to be a way to translate objects (as well as their methods and properties) into XML. That way is called SOAP, the Simple Object Access Protocol. SOAP is a way to encapsulate object calls as XML sent via HTTP.

There are two major advantages to using SOAP to communicate with Web Services. First, because HTTP is so pervasive, it can travel to any point on the Internet, regardless of intervening hardware or firewalls. Second, because SOAP is XML-based, it can be interpreted by a wide variety of software on many operating systems.

There are two other important acronyms you'll run into when learning about Web Services in .NET. UDDI stands for Universal Discovery, Description, and Integration; it's a method for finding new Web Services by referring to a central directory. WSDL stands for Web Services Description Language, a standard by which a web service can tell clients what messages it accepts and which results it will return.

Using the .NET tools, you can take any data and define it as a web service. For example, you could develop a Customer object that retrieves address information from a database via ADO.NET, and wrap it as a web service. Once you've done that, client programs will be able to create new Customer objects and retrieve addresses from anywhere on the Internet.

Windows Forms

.NET also includes a new visual programming model called Windows Forms. Windows Forms is based on the MFC and Visual Basic forms models, and it provides a powerful way to design the user interface for .NET applications. Windows Forms was designed to fit well with the rest of the .NET universe: It includes easy connections to ADO.NET data as well as support for CLR features such as versioning, licensing, and security.

I'll show you some simple Windows Forms code later in this chapter.

ASP.NET

.NET was designed from the ground up to run code on web servers as well as on stand-alone and networked computers. ASP.NET is Microsoft's server-based framework for running .NET code on web servers. ASP.NET still uses the CLR to execute and manage .NET code, but it's tightly integrated into the web development process.

Conceptually, the ASP.NET processor is very similar to the existing ASP processor that you'll find in Internet Information Server (IIS). The user sends, via a web browser, a request to open a page—in this case, one with the extension .aspx. The ASP.NET process on the server executes the .NET code that is contained within the requested page and sends only the results of the execution back to the client.

Because ASP.NET is layered on top of the CLR, the entire spectrum of .NET code is available for ASPX web pages. The distinction between scripting languages (such as VBScript) and "real" languages (such as Visual Basic) found in previous server-side development systems is gone in .NET.

ASP.NET also includes a new visual programming model called Web Forms. These forms are very similar in appearance to Windows Forms and share many of the same controls. Web Forms provide an easy way to handle such tasks as data input, validation, and display.

You'll learn more about ASP.NET in Part III, "ASP.NET Essentials."

BUILDING A .NET APPLICATION

Windows Forms are text files, just like any other source files in .NET. You can, if you like, write a Windows Form in a text editor, compile it into your .NET application, and have it work perfectly. However, most developers are unlikely to do so. That's because Visual Studio .NET includes a Windows Forms designer that provides a graphical design surface. This designer translates the graphical design into the textual source code for you.

In this section, I'll show you the Windows Forms designer as part of the process of designing a simple .NET application. You'll see that the built-in tools in .NET make using ADO.NET to display and edit data a very simple task. But don't be fooled by the power of the design tools—there's still a lot to understand in ADO.NET. In this example, I'll let the tools write the code; however, in Part IV, "Database Programming," I'll show you how to write your own data access code using ADO.NET.

This and the other examples in this book use Visual Basic .NET as their language. I've chosen this language because it's most likely to be familiar to the majority of the readers, who will probably recognize the Visual Basic underpinnings of this language. It's important to remember, though, that none of the functionality I demonstrate is specific to Visual Basic .NET. All of the .NET Framework is available to any .NET language.

Creating a New Application

To create a new application that uses Visual Basic .NET and Windows Forms, follow these steps:

1. Choose Start ➢ Programs ➢ Microsoft Visual Studio .NET ➢ Microsoft Visual Studio .NET.

2. If this is your first time to launch Visual Studio .NET, the Start page will open to the My Profile section, shown in Figure 3.3. If you're an experienced Visual Basic developer, or you just want to make your screen look the same as it does in my screen shots, you should use the settings shown in Figure 3.3.

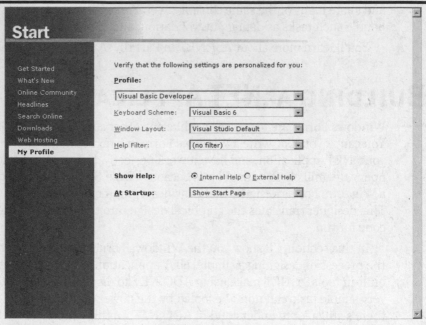

FIGURE 3.3:   Visual Studio .NET Start page

3. Click Get Started on the left side of the Start page.

4. Click the New Project button. This will open the New Project dialog box shown in Figure 3.4.

5. Select Visual Basic Projects as the project type, and Windows Application as the template for the project.

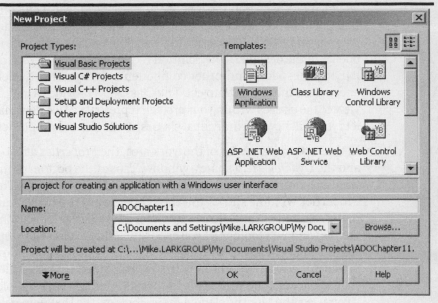

FIGURE 3.4: New Project dialog box

6. Name the new project **ADOChapter3**; then click OK to create the project.

NOTE

The source code for this project can be found at Sybex's website (www . sybex . com). Search for the book by its ISBN number, 2887, or its title, *Visual Basic .NET Complete*. You can download the code from the download button.

The Visual Basic .NET Design Environment

When you first open a Visual Basic .NET project, you may be overwhelmed by the sheer number of windows and buttons available. Here's what you'll find in the default set of Visual Basic .NET windows:

▶ In the center of the work area is the *designer*. This is the portion of Visual Basic .NET where you can design forms and write code, as well as design other specialized objects.

▶ In the upper-right corner of the work area, the *Solution Explorer* and *Class View* share a window. Tabs at the bottom of the window let you move back and forth between these two tools. The Solution Explorer provides a file-based view of the components within your Visual Basic .NET project. You can double-click a file here to open it in the designer. The Solution Explorer also shows you the .NET namespaces and other components that you have referenced from the current project. The Class View provides a logical view of the classes within your project. It presents a treeview that lets you drill down to individual classes, methods, and properties.

▶ In the lower-right corner of the work area, the *Properties window* and the *Dynamic Help* share a window. Tabs at the bottom of the window let you move back and forth between these two tools. The Properties window shows you the properties of the object currently selected in the Solution Explorer or the designer. Buttons on this window's toolbar let you choose whether to view the properties alphabetically or by category. The Dynamic Help window provides you with hyperlinks to the Visual Studio .NET help files that match what you're doing in the design interface. For example, if you select the MonthCalendar in the Toolbox, the Dynamic Help window will show you topic titles related to the MonthCalendar. If you click one of these titles, the corresponding help topic will open in the main designer window.

▶ At the bottom of the work area, you'll see the *Output Window*. Visual Basic .NET uses this window to send you informational messages. For example, when you run a Visual Basic .NET project, this window will tell you exactly which .NET assemblies are loaded, to provide functionality for the project.

▶ The *Toolbox* is to the left of the design surface. It contains controls and other components that you can add to your project. Some of these are Windows Forms controls, while others (for example, those on the Data tab) are nongraphical controls. The tabs on the Toolbox (Data, Components, Windows Forms, Clipboard Ring, and General, by default) allow you to keep components sorted into various categories. You can right-click the Toolbox and select Add Tab to add your own custom categories to the list.

▶ At the far left of the design surface, you'll see a tab for the Server Explorer. If you hover over this tab, the Server Explorer window will slide out and cover the Toolbox. You can control this sliding behavior by clicking the tiny pushpin icon in the Server Explorer's title bar. The Server Explorer lets you explore databases and other system services that are available to your application.

Of course, the entire Visual Basic .NET interface is customizable. You can drag windows around, leave them free-floating or dock them, and hide or display them. The View menu offers options to display the default windows as well as some other useful windows like the Object Browser and the Command Window.

Connecting to Data

In this example, I'll develop a project that allows you to edit data from a table in the SQL Server Northwind sample database.

NOTE
Before proceeding, you need to be able to connect to and log in to a SQL Server that has the Northwind sample database installed. If you don't already have SQL Server installed on your network, you can install the SQL Server Desktop Edition (MSDE) from the Visual Studio .NET CD-ROMs.

To connect your application to the Customers table in the SQL Server Northwind database, follow these steps:

1. Hover the mouse cursor over the Server Explorer tab. This will cause the Server Explorer window to slide out from the left-hand edge of the screen. Click the pushpin icon to anchor the Server Explorer window while you're working with it.

2. Expand the Servers node in the treeview. This will show you the servers that Visual Studio .NET knows about on your network. To start, it will show only the computer where you are actually running Visual Studio .NET. If this is the same computer where you have SQL Server installed, you can continue with Step 4. Otherwise, you'll need to add a server.

3. Right-click the Servers node and select Add Server. In the Add Server dialog box, enter the computer name or the IP address of the computer where SQL Server is installed. Click OK to add the server.

4. Expand the node for the server where SQL Server is installed, and then expand the SQL Servers node. Continue expanding

to drill into the SQL Server, then the Northwind database, and then the tables in Northwind. Figure 3.5 shows the fully expanded tree in Server Explorer.

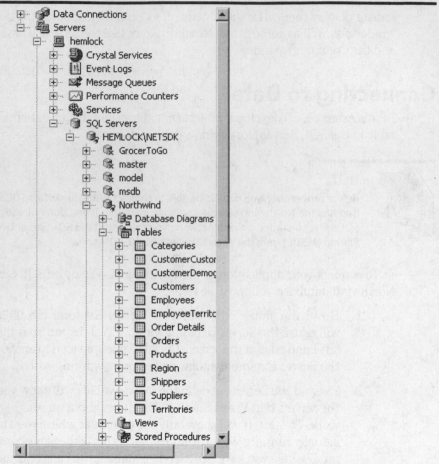

FIGURE 3.5:   Locating a database table in Server Explorer

5. Drag the Customers table from the Server Explorer to the designer, and drop it on the design surface of the default Form1. Visual Basic .NET will create two objects for you when you do this: SqlConnection1 and SqlDataAdapter1. These will appear in a window at the bottom of the designer.

6. Click the pushpin icon in Server Explorer again, and move your cursor elsewhere to allow the Server Explorer window to slide back off-screen.

7. Click SqlDataAdapter1 in the designer. The Properties window will show you the properties of the DataAdapter object, as well as some hyperlinks for working with the object. Click the Generate Dataset link. This will open the Generate Dataset dialog box, shown in Figure 3.6. Accept the default choices in this dialog box and then click OK. This will add a third item, DataSet11, to the designer.

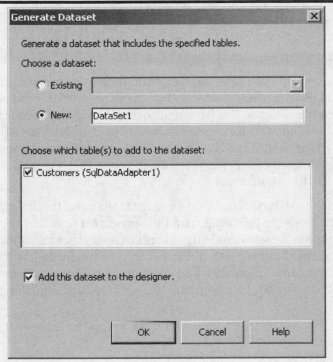

FIGURE 3.6:   Generating a DataSet

The Connection, DataAdapter, and DataSet objects are ADO.NET objects that handle the task of moving data from a database to a local cache. You'll learn more about these objects in Part IV.

Creating the User Interface

Now you can create a user interface for the data and bind the data in the DataSet to the user interface. To finish the project, follow these steps:

1. In the designer, use the sizing handle at the lower-right corner of Form1 to resize it to fill most of the available space.

2. Click the DataGrid control in the Toolbox. Click and drag the mouse on Form1 to create an instance of the DataGrid control that fills most of the available area.

3. In the Properties window, locate the DataSource property for the DataGrid control. When you click this property, it becomes a drop-down list. Use the list to set the property to DataSet11.Customers (the Customers table that has been retrieved into the DataSet).

4. Now you need to write just a little code to glue everything together. Choose View ➢ Code to open the code for Form1.vb in the designer. You'll see that there is already some code in the window. In fact, there's quite a bit of code. If you click the + sign next to the box that says, "Windows Form Designer generated code," you'll see all the code that Visual Basic .NET has written for you so far.

5. In the Method Name drop-down list at the top of the designer, select New. This will expand the generated code and show you the New procedure that's executed every time an instance of this form is created. You'll find a comment telling you where to add your own initialization code. Add three lines of code after the comment that Visual Basic .NET supplies, as follows:

```
'Add any initialization after the InitializeComponent() call
SqlConnection1.Open()
SqlDataAdapter1.Fill(DataSet11)
SqlConnection1.Close()
```

This code will open a connection to the SQL Server and retrieve the Customers data whenever you open the form.

6. Select (Base Class Events) in the Class Name drop-down list at the top of the designer, and then select Closing in the Method Name drop-down list. This will create a blank Closing

event procedure (which is executed whenever you close the form). Add one line of code to the empty procedure:

```
Private Sub Form1_Closing(ByVal sender As Object, _
  ByVal e As System.ComponentModel.CancelEventArgs) _
  Handles MyBase.Closing
    SqlDataAdapter1.Update(DataSet11)
End Sub
```

This code will save any changes to the bound DataSet whenever you close the form.

Running the Project

Now you're ready to run the project. Select Release from the Solution Configurations combo box on the toolbar. This defaults to Debug. For this test, though, you don't need to capture debugging information, and the project will run faster in Release mode. Then click the Start button on the toolbar or press F5 to start the project. You should see a form similar to the one shown in Figure 3.7, displaying the data from the Customers table in the Northwind database.

FIGURE 3.7:   Customers data on a Visual Basic .NET form

You'll find that you can edit the data on this form by typing in the cells, and you can add records via the blank row at the end of the grid.

You can also delete records by highlighting them and pressing the Delete key. If you make some changes, close the form, and run the project again, you'll see that your changes have been saved back to the database.

If you think about previous data access solutions, this example should convince you that ADO.NET is a powerful alternative that's well integrated with the Visual Studio .NET user interface. It takes very little effort to write an application to edit data. There's also an interesting feature hidden in the few lines of code that you added: The code closes the connection to the SQL Server database as soon as the DataSet has been retrieved. This demonstrates that ADO.NET is designed from the start for disconnected data access—a useful feature for distributed databases.

UNDERSTANDING NAMESPACES

As mentioned earlier in the chapter, a namespace is a group of objects that perform similar functions. But as you start investigating .NET namespaces in search of the functionality that you need for your applications, you'll find a confusing variety of objects. In this section, I'll explore a bit of the System.Data namespace to introduce you to the types of built-in objects you can expect to find in .NET namespaces.

The *System.Data* Namespace

The System.Data namespace contains the fundamental classes for representing data in ADO.NET. Namespaces are designed to hold a group of related classes, and they may also contain other namespaces that provide additional functionality. System.Data is the root of a hierarchy of namespaces:

System.Data: classes for representing data

System.Data.Common: classes shared by all data providers

System.Data.OleDb: the OLE DB data provider

System.Data.SqlClient: the SQL Server data provider

System.Data.SqlTypes: SQL Server datatypes

Typically, you'll use classes from several namespaces together in your applications. For example, to retrieve data from a SQL Server database to a DataSet in memory, you'll need to use classes from the System.Data, System.Data.Common, and System.Data.SqlClient namespaces.

Some namespaces also have links to other namespaces in different parts of the .NET Framework class library. For example, if you're using XML to transmit the structure of a DataSet to another computer over an Internet connection, you'll need to work with the System.Xml.Schema namespace as well as the System.Data namespaces.

Classes

Of course, one thing that you'll find in a namespace is a set of *classes*. The System.Data namespace contains a total of 44 classes. You'll use some of these more often than others. For example, any data access with ADO.NET will probably use the DataSet class, while you won't need to use the ReadOnlyException class unless your code might try to change the value of a read-only column.

Each class in .NET represents a particular entity. An instance of the DataSet class (part of the System.Data namespace), for example, represents an in-memory cache of data from some data source. Classes have members (constructors, methods, properties, and events). Table 3.2 lists the members of the DataSet class.

TABLE 3.2: Members of the *System.Data.DataSet* Class

	PUBLIC	PROTECTED
Constructor	DataSet Constructor	DataSet Constructor
Properties	CaseSensitive	Events
	Container	
	DataSetName	
	DefaultViewManager	
	DesignMode	
	EnforceConstraints	
	ExtendedProperties	
	HasErrors	
	Locale	
	Namespace	
	Prefix	
	Relations	
	Site	
	Tables	

TABLE 3.2 continued: Members of the *System.Data.DataSet* Class

	PUBLIC	PROTECTED
Methods	AcceptChanges	Dispose
	BeginInit	Finalize
	Clear	GetSchemaSerializable
	Clone	GetSerializationData
	Dispose	HasSchemaChanged
	EndInit	MemberwiseClone
	Equals	OnPropertyChanging
	GetChanges	OnRemoveRelation
	GetHashCode	OnRemoveTable
	GetService	RaisePropertyChanging
	GetType	ReadXmlSerializable
	GetXml	ShouldSerializeRelations
	GetXmlSchema	ShouldSerializeTables
	HasChanges	
	InferXmlSchema	
	Merge	
	ReadXml	
	ReadXmlSchema	
	Reset	
	ToString	
	WriteXml	
	WriteXmlSchema	
Events	Disposed	
	MergeFailed	

As you can see in Table 3.2, the members of a class are divided into public members and protected members. Public members can be called by code that's external to the class; protected members can be called only by code within the class, or within a class that inherits from the class. That is, in .NET, you can create your own class that inherits all the members of the DataSet class; within your own class, you are free to use the protected members. For the most part, your ADO.NET code will be concerned with only the public members of the ADO.NET classes.

Classes have four types of members:

Constructors These are the special methods that are called when you create a new instance of a class. A class can have multiple constructor methods. For example, in Visual Basic .NET, you can create a DataSet using a constructor with or without a string parameter, as shown in these two examples:

```
Dim dsNew As DataSet
dsNew = New DataSet
```

```
Dim dsNew As DataSet
dsNew = New DataSet("DataSetName")
```

In both cases, the New keyword represents the constructor. In the second case, the code uses a form of the constructor that takes a name for the new DataSet object as a parameter.

Properties   Properties are the members that describe the class. They can return simple values (for instance, the System.Data.DataSet.Name property returns a string containing the name of the DataSet), or they can return other classes (for example, the DataSet.Relations property returns a System.Data.DataRelationCollection object).

Methods   Methods are the members that represent actions that a class can perform. Members can return output (for example, the Copy method returns a new DataSet object that is a copy of the current DataSet), but they are not required to do so. (The Clear method, which clears the contents of a DataSet, has no return value.)

Events   Events are things that can happen within a class that your code can monitor. For example, the DataSet.MergeFailed event is raised whenever you call the Merge method on a pair of DataSets, the EnforceConstraints property is set to True, and two rows have the same primary key.

Interfaces

Many namespaces also define *interfaces*. An interface resembles a class, in that it is a piece of functionality that can have properties, methods, and events. The big difference is that application code never creates instances of interfaces directly. Instead, your application code can create an instance of a class that implements an interface. Interfaces are normally pieces of functionality that are common across several classes. The interface resembles a contract that guarantees that the functionality will work the same way in all the classes that implement the interface.

An example may make this clearer. The System.Data namespace defines an interface named IDbTransaction. This interface represents a database transaction. The IDbTransaction interface defines three members: an IsolationLevel property, a Commit method, and a Rollback method.

The SqlTransaction class (part of the System.Data.SqlClient namespace) represents a transaction against a SQL Server database. This class implements the IDbTransaction interface. As a result, the SqlTransaction class includes an IsolationLevel property and Commit and Rollback methods. It also includes other methods, such as Save, that are not part of this interface.

The OleDbTransaction class (part of the System.Data.OleDb namespace) represents a transaction against an OLE DB database. This class also implements the IDbTransaction interface. As a result, the OleDbTransaction class includes an IsolationLevel property and Commit and Rollback methods. It also includes other methods, such as Begin, that are not part of this interface.

Because both SqlTransaction and OleDbTransaction implement that IDbTransaction interface, you can write code that expects an instance of this interface that will work equally well when passed an instance of either class.

Delegates

Namespaces can also include *delegates*. Like interfaces, delegates represent a sort of code contract. In this case, they define a method that you can write in your code that will be called from within a class (as opposed to interfaces, which define methods within classes that you can call from within your code).

In the .NET Framework class library, the primary use of delegates is defining the parameters that event-handling functions must implement. For example, the System.Data namespace defines a delegate named DataRowChangeEventHandler. This delegate has this programming signature:

```
Public Delegate Sub DataRowChangeEventHandler( _
  ByVal sender As Object, _
  ByVal e As DataRowChangeEventArgs)
```

Any function that has these parameters can be used to respond to the DataRowChange event of the DataTable object (which is what this delegate represents). In Visual Basic .NET, you use the AddHandler keyword to add a delegate. The following block of code will create a DataTable object and set up a delegate to handle its DataRowChange event:

```
Private dtMain As DataTable

Private Sub Setup
    dtMain = New DataTable("Customers")
    AddHandler dtMain.RowChanged, AddressOf dtMain_Changed
End Sub

Protected Sub dtMain_Changed _
(sender As Object, e As System.Data.DataRowChangeEventArgs)
    ' code to handle event goes here
End Sub
```

Enumerations

Finally, a namespace may contain *enumerations*. An enumeration is a set of constants that are defined for a particular purpose. For example, the System.Data namespace includes an enumeration named DataRowState. As you might guess from the name, this enumeration includes the possible values for the RowState property of the DataRow class:

Added

Deleted

Detached

Modified

Unchanged

If you retrieve the DataRow.RowState property for a particular row in your code, you're guaranteed to get back one of these values.

WHAT'S NEXT

In this chapter, you saw some of the basic underpinnings of the .NET Framework. Some parts of .NET, such as objects with interfaces, Windows Forms, and XML, may look very familiar. Other areas, including the Common Language Runtime and the .NET deployment model, are new to Windows programming. Overall, the .NET Framework includes a great deal of innovation, and you'll need to work with it for some time before you feel comfortable with all of the new concepts.

Now that you have a solid base understanding of Visual Basic .NET and the .NET Framework, it's time to start creating Visual Basic projects. In the next chapter, we will begin utilizing some of this base knowledge to create Visual Basic .NET projects.

Chapter 4

VISUAL BASIC PROJECTS

The previous chapters introduced the basic skills that you need to understand before you jump into Visual Basic .NET. In this chapter, we begin to build on that basic knowledge by building some "real" applications. Among other topics, we'll look at how to write applications that validate user input and how to write error-handling routines. We'll also look at several techniques you'll need as you work through the applications we develop in the rest of the book. In the last part of the chapter, you'll learn how to distribute your application with a proper Windows installer (a program that installs your application to the target machine).

The bulk of this chapter demonstrates very basic programming techniques, such as building user interfaces, event programming, validating user input, and handling errors. The goal is to show you how to write simple applications using the most basic elements of the language. This chapter will explain the methodology for building applications. Although the code of the applications will be rather simple, it will demonstrate the basics of validating data and trapping errors.

Adapted from *Mastering Visual Basic .NET*
by Evangelos Petroutsos
ISBN 0-7821-2877-7 $49.99

If you're a beginner, you may be thinking, "All I want now is to write a simple application that works—I'll worry about data validation later." It's never too early to start thinking about validating your code's data and error trapping. As you'll see, making sure that your application doesn't crash may require more code than the actual operations it performs! If this isn't quite what you expected, welcome to the club. A well-behaved application must catch and handle every error gracefully, including user errors.

BUILDING A LOAN CALCULATOR

One easy-to-implement, practical application is a program that calculates loan parameters. Visual Basic provides built-in functions for performing many types of financial calculations, and you only need a single line of code to calculate the monthly payment given the loan amount, its duration, and the interest rate. Designing the user interface, however, takes much more effort.

Regardless of the language you use, you must go through the following process to develop an application:

1. Decide what the application will do and how it will interact with the user.

2. Design the application's user interface according to the requirements of Step 1.

3. Write the actual code behind the events you want to handle.

How the Loan Application Works

Following the first step of the process outlined above, you decide that the user should be able to specify the amount of the loan, the interest rate, and the duration of the loan in months. You must, therefore, provide three text boxes where the user can enter these values.

Another parameter affecting the monthly payment is whether payments are made at the beginning or at the end of each month, so you must also provide a way for the user to specify whether the payments will be early (first day of the month) or late (last day of the month). The most appropriate type of control for entering Yes/No or True/False type of information is the CheckBox control. This control is a toggle: If it's checked, you can clear it by clicking it. If it's cleared, you can check it by clicking again. The user doesn't enter any data in this control (which means you need not anticipate user errors with this control), and it's the simplest method for specifying values with two possible states. Figure 4.1 shows a user interface that matches our design specifications. This is the main form of the LoanCalculator project.

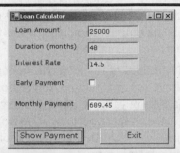

FIGURE 4.1:   LoanCalculator is a simple financial application.

NOTE

You'll find all the code from this chapter on www.sybex.com. Search for the book by its ISBN number, 2887, or its title, *Visual Basic .NET Complete*. You can download the code from the download button.

After the user enters all the information on the form, they can click the Show Payment button to calculate the monthly payment. The program will calculate the monthly payment and display it in the lower TextBox control. All the action takes place in the button's Click subroutine. The function for calculating monthly payments is called Pmt() and must be called as follows:

```
MonthlyPayment = Pmt(InterestRate, Periods, Amount, _
                     FutureValue, Due)
```

The interest rate (argument *InterestRate*) is specified as a monthly rate. If the interest rate is 16.5%, the value entered by the user in the Interest Rate box should be 16.5, and the monthly rate will be 0.165 / 12. The duration of the loan *(Periods)* is specified in number of months, and *Amount* is the loan's amount. The *FutureValue* of a loan is zero (it would be a positive value for an investment), and the last parameter, *Due*, specifies when payments are due.

The value of *Due* can be one of the constants DueDate.BegOfPeriod and DueDate.EndOfPeriod. These two constants are built into the language, and you can use them without knowing their exact value. In effect, this is the essence of using named constants: you type a self-descriptive name and leave it to VB to convert it to a numeric value. As you will see, .NET uses numerous constants, all of which are categorized in groups called *enumerations*. The constants that apply to the *Due* argument of the Pmt() function belong to the DueDate enumeration, which has two members, the BegOfPeriod and EndOfPeriod members.

The present value of the loan is the amount of the loan with a negative sign. It's negative because you don't have the money now. You're borrowing it; it's money you owe to the bank. Future value represents the value of something at a stated time—in this case, what the loan will be worth when it's paid off. This is what one side owes the other at the end of the specified period. So the future value of a loan is zero.

Pmt() is a built-in function that uses the five values in the parentheses to calculate the monthly payment. The values passed to the function are called *arguments*. Arguments are the values needed by a function (or subroutine) to carry out an action or calculation. By passing different values to the function, the user can specify the parameters of any loan and calculate its monthly payment.

You don't need to know how the Pmt() function calculates the monthly payment. The Pmt() function does the calculations and returns the result. To calculate the monthly payment on a loan of $25,000 with an interest rate of 14.5%, payable over 48 months, and due the last day of the payment period (which in our case is a month), you'd call the Pmt() function as follows:

```
Console.WriteLine(Pmt(0.145 / 12, 48, -25000, 0, _
    DueDate.EndOfPeriod))
```

The value 689.448821287218 will be displayed in the Output window (you'll see later how you can limit the digits after the decimal point to two, since this is all the accuracy you need for dollar amounts). Notice the negative sign in front of the *Amount* argument in the statement. If you specify a positive amount, the result will be a negative payment. The payment and the loan's amount have different signs because they represent different cash flows. The loan's amount is money you *owe* to the bank, while the payment is money you *pay* to the bank.

The last two arguments of the Pmt() function are optional. If you omit them, Visual Basic uses their default values, which are 0 for the *FutureValue*

argument and DueDate.BegOfPeriod for the *Due* argument. You can
entirely omit these arguments and call the Pmt() function like this:

```
Console.WriteLine(Pmt(0.145 / 12, 48, -25000))
```

Calculating the amount of the monthly payment given the loan parameters is quite simple. What you need to know or understand are the
parameters of a loan and how to pass them to the Pmt() function. You
must also know how the interest rate is specified, to avoid invalid values.
What you don't need to know is how the payment is calculated—Visual
Basic does it for you. This is the essence of functions: They are "black
boxes" that perform complicated calculations on their arguments and
return the result. You don't have to know how they work, just how to
supply the values required for the calculations.

Designing the User Interface

Now that you know how to calculate the monthly payment, you can
design the user interface. To do so, start a new project, name it
LoanCalculator, and rename its form to **LoanForm**.

Your first task is to decide the font and size of the text you'll use for
most controls on the form. Although we aren't going to display anything
on the form directly, all the controls we place on it will have, by default, the
same font as the form. The form is the container of the controls, and they
inherit some of the form's properties, such as the Font. You can change
the font later during the design, but it's a good idea to start with the right
font. At any rate, don't try to align the controls if you're planning to change
their fonts. This will, most likely, throw off your alignment efforts.

TIP

Try not to mix fonts on a form. A form, or a printed page for that matter, that
includes type in several fonts looks like it has been created haphazardly and is
difficult to read. However, you can use different sizes for some of the controls
on the form.

The loan application you'll find on the Sybex website uses the 10-point
Verdana font. To change it, select the form with the mouse, double-click
the name of the Font property in the Properties window to open the Font
dialog box, and select the desired font and attributes. When the form is
selected, its name appears in the ComboBox at the top of the window, as
shown in Figure 4.2.

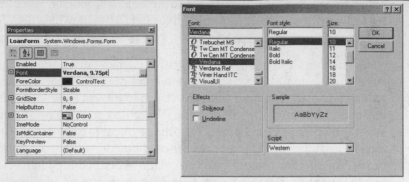

FIGURE 4.2: Setting the form's Font property

To design the form shown previously in Figure 4.1, follow these steps:

1. Place four labels on the form and assign the following captions to them:

Label	Caption
Label1	Loan Amount
Label2	Duration (in months)
Label3	Interest Rate
Label4	Monthly Payment

    The labels should be large enough to fit their captions. You don't need to change the default names of the four Label controls on the form because their captions are all we need. You aren't going to program them.

2. Place a TextBox control next to each label. Set their Name and Text properties to the following values. These initial values correspond to a loan of $25,000 with an interest rate of 14.5% and a payoff period of 48 months.

TextBox	Name	Text
TextBox1	txtAmount	25,000
TextBox2	txtDuration	48
TextBox3	txtRate	14.5
TextBox4	txtPayment	

3. The fourth TextBox control is where the monthly payment will appear. The user isn't supposed to enter any data in this box, so you must set its ReadOnly property to True. You'll be able to change its value from within your code, but users won't be able to type anything in it. (We could have used a Label control instead, but the uniform look of TextBoxes on a form is usually preferred.)

4. Next, place a CheckBox control on the form. By default, the control's caption is Check1, and it appears to the right of the check box. Because we want the titles to be to the left of the corresponding controls, we'll change this default appearance.

5. Select the check box with the mouse (if it's not already selected), and in the Properties window, locate the Check-Align property. Its value is MiddleLeft. If you expand the drop-down list by clicking the Arrow button, you'll see that this property has many different settings and each setting is shown as a square. Select the square in the middle row, the right column. The string MiddleRight will appear in the property's box when you click the appropriate button. The first component of the CheckAlign property's value indicates the vertical alignment of the check box, and the second component of the value indicates the horizontal alignment. MiddleRight means that the check box should be centered vertically and right-aligned horizontally.

6. With the check box selected, locate the Name property in the Properties window, and set it to chkPayEarly.

7. Change the CheckBox's caption by entering the string **Early Payment** in its Text property field.

8. Place a Button control in the bottom-left corner of the form. Name it **bttnShowPayment**, and set its caption to Show Payment.

9. Finally, place another Button control on the form, name it **bttnExit**, and set its Text property to Exit.

Aligning the Controls

Your next step is to align the controls on the form. First, be sure that the captions on the labels are visible. Our labels contain lengthy captions, and if you don't make the labels long enough, the captions may wrap to a second line and become invisible.

TIP

Be sure to make your labels long enough to hold their captions, especially if you're using a nonstandard font. A user's computer may substitute another font for your nonstandard font, and the corresponding captions may increase in length.

The IDE provides commands to align the controls on the form, all of which can be accessed through the Format menu. To align the controls that are already on the LoanForm, follow these steps:

1. Select the four labels on the form with the mouse and left-align them by choosing Format ➤ Align ➤ Left. The handles of all selected controls will be white, except for one control whose handles will be black. All controls will be left-aligned with this control. To specify the control that will be used as reference point for aligning the other controls, click it after making the selection. (You can select multiple controls either by drawing a rectangle that encloses them with the mouse, or by clicking each control while holding down the Ctrl button.)

2. With the four text boxes selected, choose Format ➤ Align ➤ Left. Don't include the check box in this selection.

TIP

When you select multiple controls to align together, use the control with black handles as a guide for aligning the other controls.

3. With all four text boxes still selected, use the mouse to align them above and below the box of the CheckBox control.

Your form should now look like the one in Figure 4.1. Take a good look at it, and check to see if any of your controls are misaligned. In the interface design process, you tend to overlook small problems such as a slightly misaligned control. The user of the application, however, instantly spots such mistakes. It doesn't make any difference how nicely the rest of the controls are arranged on the form; if one of them is misaligned, it will attract the user's attention.

Programming the Loan Application

Now run the application and see how it behaves. Enter a few values in the text boxes, change the state of the check box, and test the functionality already built into the application. Clicking the Show Payment button won't have any effect because we have not yet added any code. If you're happy with the user interface, stop the application, open the form, and double-click the Show Payment Button control. Visual Basic opens the code window and displays the definition of the ShowPayment_Click event:

```
Private Sub bttnShowPayment_Click _
        (ByVal sender As System.Object, _
        ByVal e As System.EventArgs) _
        Handles bttnShowPayment.Click


End Sub
```

NOTE
I've broken all the lines with an underline character, because it wouldn't fit on the page. The underscore character is the line-continuation character, which allows you to break a long code line into multiple text lines.

This is the declaration of the Button's Click event handler. This subroutine will be invoked when the user clicks the Show Payment button. Above the definition of the event handler, you will see the following two statements:

```
Public Class LoanForm
    Inherits System.Windows.Forms.Form
```

The first statement creates a new class for the project's form; the second inherits the functionality of the Form object. These statements are placed there by the IDE, and you shouldn't change them. When you learn more about classes and inheritance in the second part of the book, you'll be able to better understand the role of these statements.

Place the pointer between the lines `Private Sub` and `End Sub`, and enter the rest of the lines of Listing 4.1 (you don't have to reenter the first and last lines that declare the event handler).

Listing 4.1: The Show Payment Button

```
Private Sub bttnShowPayment_Click _
    (ByVal sender As System.Object, _
     ByVal e As System.EventArgs) _
     Handles bttnShowPayment.Click

     Dim Payment As Single
     Dim payEarly As DueDate
     If chkPayEarly.Checked Then
         payEarly = DueDate.BegOfPeriod
     Else
         payEarly = DueDate.EndOfPeriod
     End If
     Payment = Pmt(0.01 * txtRate.Text / 12, _
                   txtDuration.Text, _
                   -txtAmount.Text, 0, payEarly)
     txtPayment.Text = Payment.ToString("#.00")

End Sub
```

The code window should now look similar to the one shown in Figure 4.3. Notice the underscore character at the end of the first part of the long line. The underscore lets you break long lines so that they will fit nicely in the code window. I'm using this convention in this book a lot to fit long lines on the printed page. The same statement you see as multiple lines in the book may appear in a single, long line in the project.

You don't have to break long lines manually as you enter code in the editor's window. Open the Edit menu, and select Advanced ➤ Word Wrap. The editor will wrap long lines automatically at a word boundary. While the word wrap feature is on, a check mark appears in front of the Edit ➤ Advanced ➤ Word Wrap command. To turn off word wrapping, select the same command again.

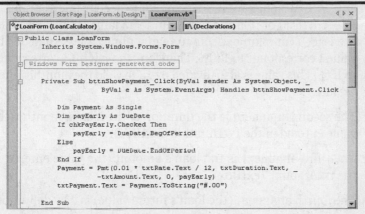

```
Object Browser | Start Page | LoanForm.vb [Design]* | LoanForm.vb* |                    ◁ ▷ ×
LoanForm (LoanCalculator)                      ▼ | (Declarations)                        ▼
Public Class LoanForm
    Inherits System.Windows.Forms.Form

 Windows Form Designer generated code

    Private Sub bttnShowPayment_Click(ByVal sender As System.Object, _
                     ByVal e As System.EventArgs) Handles bttnShowPayment.Click

        Dim Payment As Single
        Dim payEarly As DueDate
        If chkPayEarly.Checked Then
            payEarly = DueDate.BegOfPeriod
        Else
            payEarly = DueDate.EndOfPeriod
        End If
        Payment = Pmt(0.01 * txtRate.Text / 12, txtDuration.Text, _
                  -txtAmount.Text, 0, payEarly)
        txtPayment.Text = Payment.ToString("#.00")

    End Sub
```

FIGURE 4.3:   The Show Payment button's Click event subroutine

In Listing 4.1, the first line of code within the subroutine declares a variable. It lets the application know that *Payment* is a placeholder for storing a *floating-point number* (a number with a decimal part)—the Single datatype. The second line declares a variable of the DueDate type. This is the type of the argument that determines whether the payment takes place at the beginning or the end of the month. The last argument of the Pmt() function must be a variable of this type, so we declare a variable of the DueDate type. As mentioned earlier in this chapter, DueDate is an enumeration with two members: BegOfPeriod and EndOfPeriod. In short, the last argument of the Pmt() function can be one of the following values:

DueDate.BegOfPeriod

DueDate.EndOfPeriod

The first really executable line in the subroutine is the If statement that examines the value of the chkPayEarly CheckBox control. If the control is checked, the code sets the *payEarly* variable to DueDate.BegOfPeriod. If not, the code sets the same variable to DueDate.EndOfPeriod. The ComboBox control's Checked property returns True if the control is checked at the time, False otherwise. After setting the value of the *payEarly* variable, the code calls the Pmt() function, passing the values of the controls as arguments:

▶ The first argument is the interest rate. The value entered by the user in the txtRate TextBox is multiplied by 0.01 so that the value 14.5 (which corresponds to 14.5%) is passed to the Pmt() function as 0.145. Although we humans prefer to specify interest rates as integers (8%) or floating-point numbers larger than 1 (8.24%), the Pmt() function expects to read a number less than 1. The value 1 corresponds to 100%. Therefore, the value 0.1 corresponds to 10%. This value is also divided by 12 to yield the monthly interest rate.

▶ The second argument is the duration of the loan in months (the value entered in the txtDuration TextBox).

▶ The third argument is the loan's amount (the value entered in the txtAmount TextBox).

▶ The fourth argument (the loan's future value) is 0 by definition.

▶ The last argument is the *payEarly* variable, which is set according to the status of the chkPayEarly control.

The following two statements convert the numeric value returned by the Pmt() function to a string and display this string in the fourth TextBox control. The result is formatted appropriately with the following expression:

```
Payment.ToString("#.00")
```

The *Payment* variable is numeric, and all numeric variables provide the method ToString, which formats the numeric value and converts it to a string. The character # stands for the integer part of the variable. The period separates the integer from the fractional part, which is rounded to two decimal digits. Because the Pmt() function returns a precise number, such as 372.2235687646345, you must round and format it nicely before displaying it. Because the bank can't charge you anything less than a penny, you don't need extreme accuracy. Two fractional digits are sufficient. For more information on formatting numeric (and other) values, see the section "Formatting Numbers" in Chapter 5, "Visual Basic .NET: The Language."

To display the result returned by the Pmt() function on the *txtPayment* TextBox control, use the following statement:

```
txtPayment.Text = Pmt(0.01 * txtRate.Text / 12, _
        txtDuration.Text, -txtAmount.Text, 0, payEarly)
```

This statement assigns the value returned by the Pmt() function directly to the Text property of the control. The monthly payment will be displayed with four decimal digits, but this isn't a proper dollar amount.

TIP

You almost always use the ToString method (or the `Format()` function) when you want to display the results of numeric calculations, because most of the time you don't need Visual Basic's extreme accuracy. A few fractional digits are all you need. In addition to numbers, the ToString method can format dates and time. The ToString method's formatting capabilities are discussed briefly in the next chapter.

The code of the LoanCalculator project, found on the Sybex's website (www.sybex.com), is different and considerably longer than what I have presented here. The statements discussed in the preceding text are the bare minimum for calculating a loan payment. The user may enter any values on the form and cause the program to crash. In the next section, we'll see how you can validate the data entered by the user, catch errors, and handle them gracefully (that is, give the user a chance to correct the data and proceed), as opposed to terminating the application with a runtime error.

Validating the Data

If you enter a nonnumeric value in one of the fields, the program will crash and display an error message. For example, if you enter **twenty** in the Duration text box, the program will display the error message shown in Figure 4.4. A simple typing error can crash the program. This isn't the way Windows applications should work. Your applications must be able to handle most user errors, provide helpful messages, and in general, guide the user in running the application efficiently. If a user error goes unnoticed, your application will either end abruptly or produce incorrect results without an indication.

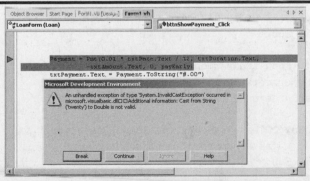

FIGURE 4.4:   The Cast Exception message means that you supplied a string where a numeric value was expected.

Click the Break button, and Visual Basic will take you back to the application's code window, where the statements that caused the error will be highlighted in green. Obviously, we must do something about user errors. One way to take care of typing errors is to examine each control's contents; if they don't contain valid numeric values, display your own descriptive message and give the user another chance. Listing 4.2 is the revised Click event handler that examines the value of each text box before attempting to use it in any calculations.

Listing 4.2: The Revised Show Payment Button

```
Private Sub bttnShowPayment_Click _
   (ByVal sender As System.Object, _
   ByVal e As System.EventArgs) _
   Handles bttnShowPayment.Click

   Dim Payment As Single
   Dim LoanIRate As Single
   Dim LoanDuration As Integer
   Dim LoanAmount As Integer
' Validate amount
   If IsNumeric(txtAmount.Text) Then
      LoanAmount = txtAmount.Text
   Else
      MsgBox("Please enter a valid amount")
      Exit Sub
   End If
' Validate interest rate
   If IsNumeric(txtRate.Text) Then
      LoanIRate = 0.01 * txtRate.Text / 12
   Else
      MsgBox("Invalid interest rate, please re-enter")
      Exit Sub
   End If
' Validate loan's duration
   If IsNumeric(txtDuration.Text) Then
      LoanDuration = txtDuration.Text
   Else
      MsgBox("Please specify the loan's duration " & _
             "as a number of months")
      Exit Sub
   End If
```

```
' If all data were validated, proceed with calculations
    Dim payEarly As DueDate
    If chkPayEarly.Checked Then
        payEarly = DueDate.BegOfPeriod
    Else
        payEarly = DueDate.EndOfPeriod
    End If
    Payment = Pmt(LoanIRate, LoanDuration, _
                    -LoanAmount, 0, payEarly)
    txtPayment.Text = Payment.ToString("#.00")

End Sub
```

First, we declare three variables in which the loan's parameters will be stored: *LoanAmount, LoanIRate,* and *LoanDuration*. These values will be passed to the Pmt() function as arguments. Each text box's value is examined with an If structure. If the corresponding text box holds a valid number, its value is assigned to the numeric variable. If not, the program displays a warning and exits the subroutine without attempting to calculate the monthly payment. The user can then fix the incorrect value and click the ShowPayment button again. IsNumeric() is another built-in function that accepts a variable and returns True if the variable is a number, False otherwise.

If the Amount text box holds a numeric value, such as 21,000 or 21.50, the function IsNumeric(txtAmount.Text) returns True, and the statement following it is executed. That following statement assigns the value entered in the *Amount* TextBox to the *LoanAmount* variable. If not, the Else clause of the statement is executed, which displays a warning in a message box and then exits the subroutine. The Exit Sub statement tells Visual Basic to stop executing the subroutine immediately, as if the End Sub line were encountered.

You can run the revised application and test it by entering invalid values in the fields. Notice that you can't specify an invalid value for the last argument; the CheckBox control won't let you enter a value. You can only check or clear it and both options are valid. The LoanCalculator application, which can be found at www.sybex.com, contains this last version with the error-trapping code.

The actual calculation of the monthly payment takes a single line of Visual Basic code. Displaying it requires another line of code. Adding the code to validate the data entered by the user, however, is an entire program. And that's the way things are.

WRITING WELL-BEHAVED APPLICATIONS

A well-behaved application must contain data-validation code. If an application such as LoanCalculator crashes because of a typing mistake, nothing really bad will happen. The user will try again or else give up on your application and look for a more professional one. However, if the user has been entering data for hours, the situation is far more serious. It's your responsibility as a programmer to make sure that only valid data are used by the application and that the application keeps working, no matter how the user misuses or abuses it.

NOTE

The applications in this book don't contain much data-validation code because it would obscure the "useful" code that applies to the topic at hand. Instead, they demonstrate specific techniques. You can use parts of the examples in your applications, but you should provide your own data-validation code (and error-handling code, as you'll see in the following section).

Now run the application one last time and enter an enormous loan amount. Try to find out what it would take to pay off the national debt with a reasonable interest rate in, say, 72 months. The program will crash again (as if you didn't know). This time the program will go down with a different error message. Visual Basic will complain about an "overflow." The exact message is "Arithmetic operation resulted in an overflow," and the program will stop at the line that assigns the contents of the *txtAmount* TextBox to the *LoanAmount* variable. Press the Break button, and the offending statement in the code will be highlighted (see Figure 4.5).

TIP

An overflow is a numeric value too large for the program to handle. This error is usually produced when you divide a number by a very small value. When you attempt to assign a very large value to an Integer variable, you'll also get an overflow exception.

Actually, in the LoanCalculator application, any amount greater than 2,147,483,647 will cause an overflow condition. This is largest value you can assign to an Integer variable; it's plenty for our banking needs, but not nearly adequate for handling government budgets. As you'll see in the next chapter, Visual Basic provides other types of variables, which can store enormous values (making the national debt look really small). In the meantime, if you want to use the loan calculator, change the declaration of the *LoanAmount* variable to:

```
Dim LoanAmount As Single
```

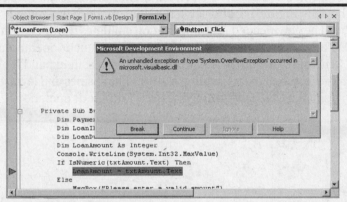

FIGURE 4.5:   Very large values can cause the application to crash with this error message.

The Single datatype can hold much larger values. Besides, the Single datatype can also hold non-integer values. I'm assuming you won't ask for a loan of $25,000 and some cents, but if you want to calculate the precise monthly payment for a debt you have accumulated, then you should be able to specify a non-integer amount. In short, we should have declared the *LoanAmount* variable with the Single datatype in the first place (but then I wouldn't have been able to demonstrate the overflow exception).

An overflow error can't be caught with data-validation code. There's always a chance your calculations will produce overflows or other types of math errors. Data validation isn't going to help here; you just don't know the result before you carry out the calculations. We need something called *error handling*, or *error trapping*. This is additional code that can handle errors after they occur. In effect, you're telling VB that it shouldn't stop with an error message. This would be embarrassing for you and wouldn't help the user one bit. Instead, VB should detect the error and execute the proper statements that will handle the error. Obviously, you must supply these statements, and you'll see examples of handling errors at runtime in the following section.

BUILDING A MATH CALCULATOR

Our next application is more advanced, but not as advanced as it looks. It's a math calculator with a typical visual interface that demonstrates how Visual Basic can simplify the programming of fairly advanced operations. If you haven't tried it, you may think that writing an application such as this one is way too complicated, but it isn't. The MathCalculator application is shown in Figure 4.6, and you'll find it in on the Sybex website where it can be downloaded. The application emulates the operation of a hand-held calculator and implements the basic arithmetic operations. It has the structure of a math calculator, and you can easily expand it by adding more features. In fact, adding features like cosines and logarithms is actually simpler than performing the basic arithmetic operations.

FIGURE 4.6:   The Calculator application window

Designing the User Interface

The application's interface is straightforward, but it takes quite a bit of effort. You must align buttons on the form and make the calculator look as much like a hand-held calculator as possible. Start a new project, the MathCalculator project, and name its main form **CalculatorForm**.

Designing the interface of the application isn't trivial, because it's made up of many buttons, all perfectly aligned on the form. To simplify the design, follow these steps:

1. Select a font that you like for the form. All the Command buttons you'll place on the form will inherit this font. The Math-Calculator application on the CD uses 10-point Verdana font.

2. Add the Label control, which will become the calculator's display. Set its BorderStyle property to Fixed 3D so that it will have a 3-D look, as shown in Figure 4.6. Change its ForeColor

and BackColor properties too, if you want it to look different from the rest of the form.

3. Draw a Button control on the form, change its caption (Text property) to 1, and name it **bttn1**. Size the button carefully so that its caption is centered on the control. The other buttons on the form will be copies of this one, so make sure you've designed the first button as best as you can, before you start making copies of it.

4. Place the button in its final position on the form. At this point you're ready to create the other buttons for the calculator's digits. Right-click the button, and select Copy. The Button control is copied to the Clipboard, and now you can paste it on the form (which is much faster than designing an identical button).

5. Right-click somewhere on the form and select Paste to create a copy of the button you copied earlier. The button you copied to the Clipboard will be pasted on the form, on top of the original button. The copy will have the same caption as the button it was copied from, and its name will be Button1.

6. Now set the button's Name to bttn2 and its Text property to 2. This button is the digit 2. Place the new button to the right of the previous button. You don't have to align the two buttons perfectly now; we'll use later the Format menu to align the buttons on the form.

7. Repeat Steps 5 and 6 eight more times, once for each numeric digit. Each time a new Button control is pasted on the form, Visual Basic names it Button1 and sets its caption to 1; you must change the Name and Text properties. You can name the buttons anything you like; their Click event will be handled by the same subroutine, which will read the button's Text property to find out which digit was clicked.

8. When the buttons of the numeric digits are all on the form, place two more buttons, one for the C (Clear) operation and one for the Period button. Name them bttnClear and bttnPeriod, and set their captions accordingly. Use a larger font size for the Period button to make its caption easier to read.

9. When all the digit buttons of the first group are on the form and in their approximate positions, align them with the commands of the Format menu.

a. First, align the buttons of the top row. Start by aligning the 1 button with the left side of the lblDisplay Label. Then select all the buttons of the top row and make their horizontal spacing equal (select Format ≻ Horizontal Spacing ≻ Make Equal). Then do the same with the buttons in the first column, and this time, make sure their vertical distances are equal (Format ≻ Vertical Spacing ≻ Make Equal).

b. Now you can align the buttons in each row and each column separately. Use one of the buttons you aligned in the last step as the guide for the rest of them. The buttons can be aligned in many ways, so don't worry if somewhere in the process you ruin the alignment. You can always use the Undo command in the Edit menu. Select the three buttons on the second row and align their Tops using the first button as reference. Do the same for the third and fourth rows of buttons. Then do the same for the four columns of buttons.

Now, place the buttons for the arithmetic operations on the form—addition (+), subtraction (−), multiplication (∗), and division (/). Use the commands on the Format menu to align these buttons as shown earlier in Figure 4.6. The control with the black handles can be used as a reference for aligning the other controls into rows and columns. The form shown in Figure 4.6 has a few more buttons, which you can align using the same techniques you used to align the numeric buttons.

The Equals button at the bottom is called bttnEquals, and you must make it wide enough to cover the space of the three buttons above it.

Programming the MathCalculator App

Now you're ready to add some code to the application. Double-click one of the digit buttons on the form, and you'll see the following in the code window:

```
Private Sub bttn1_Click _
    (ByVal sender As System.Object, _
    ByVal e As System.EventArgs) _
```

```
Handles bttn1.Click


End Sub
```

This is the Click event's handler for a single-digit button. Your first attempt is to program the Click event handler of each digit button, but repeating the same code 10 times isn't very productive. We're going to use the same event handler for all buttons that represent digits. All you have to do is append the names of the events to be handled by the same subroutine after the Handles keyword. You should also change the name of the event handler to something that indicates its role. Because this subroutine handles the Click event for all the digit buttons, let's call it Digit_Click(). Here's the revised declaration of a subroutine that can handle all the digit buttons:

```
Private Sub Digit_Click _
    (ByVal sender As System.Object, _
    ByVal e As System.EventArgs) _
    Handles bttn1.Click, bttn2.Click, _
    bttn3.Click, bttn4.Click, bttn5.Click, bttn6.Click, _
    bttn7.Click, bttn8.Click, bttn9.Click


End Sub
```

When you press a digit button on a hand-held calculator, the corresponding digit is appended to the display. To emulate this behavior, insert the following line in the Click event handler:

```
lblDisplay.Text = lblDisplay.Text + sender.Text
```

This line appends the digit clicked to the calculator's display. The *sender* argument of the Click event represents the control that was clicked (the control that fired the event). The Text property of this control is the digit of the button that was clicked. For example, if you have already entered the value 345, clicking the digit 0 displays the value 3450 on the Label control that acts as the calculator's display.

The expression sender.Text is not the best method of accessing the Text property of the button that was clicked, but it will work as long as the Strict option is off. You should convert the *sender* object to a TextBox object and then access its Text property with the following statement:

```
CType(sender, TextBox).Text
```

The CType() function is discussed in the following chapter. For now, keep in mind that it converts an object to an object of a different type. You will also notice that after typing the period following the closing parenthesis, all the members of the TextBox control will appear in a list, as if you had entered the name of a TextBox control followed by a period.

The code behind the digit buttons needs a few more lines. After certain actions, the display should be cleared. After pressing one of the buttons that correspond to math operations, the display should be cleared in anticipation of the second operand. Actually, the display must be cleared as soon as the first digit of the second operand is pressed. Revise the Digit_Click event handler as shown in Listing 4.3.

Listing 4.3: The Digit_Click Event

```
Private Sub Digit_Click _
    (ByVal sender As System.Object, _
     ByVal e As System.EventArgs) _
     Handles bttn1.Click, bttn2.Click, _
     bttn3.Click, bttn4.Click, bttn5.Click, bttn6.Click, _
     bttn7.Click, bttn8.Click, bttn9.Click

    If clearDisplay Then
        lblDisplay.Text = ""
        clearDisplay = False
    End If
    lblDisplay.Text = lblDisplay.Text + sender.text

End Sub
```

The *clearDisplay* variable is declared as Boolean, which means it can take a True or False value. Suppose the user has performed an operation and the result is on the calculator's display. The user now starts typing another number. Without the If clause, the program would continue to append digits to the number already on the display. This is not how calculators work. When a new number is entered, the display must clear. And our program uses the *clearDisplay* variable to know when to clear the display.

The Equals button sets the *clearDisplay* variable to True to indicate that the display contains the result of an operation. The Digit_Click() subroutine examines the value of this variable each time a new digit button is pressed. If the value is True, Digit_Click() clears the display and then prints the new digit on it. The subroutine also sets *clearDisplay* to False so that when the next digit is pressed, the program won't clear the display again.

What if the user makes a mistake and wants to undo an entry? The typical hand-held calculator has no backspace key. The Clear key erases the current number on the display. Let's implement this feature. Double-click the C button, and enter the code in Listing 4.4 in its Click event.

Listing 4.4: The Clear Button

```
Private Sub bttnClear_Click _
  (ByVal sender As System.Object, _
   ByVal e As System.EventArgs) Handles bttnClear.Click

   lblDisplay.Text = ""

End Sub
```

Now we can look at the Period button. A calculator, no matter how simple, should be able to handle fractional numbers. The Period button works just like the digit buttons, with one exception. A digit can appear any number of times in a numeric value, but the period can appear only once. A number like 99.991 is valid, but you must make sure that the user can't enter numbers such as 23.456.55. Once a period is entered, this button mustn't insert another one. The code in Listing 4.5 accounts for this.

Listing 4.5: The Period Button

```
Private Sub bttnPeriod_Click _
  (ByVal sender As System.Object, _
   ByVal e As System.EventArgs) Handles bttnPeriod.Click

   If lblDisplay.Text.IndexOf(".") > 0 Then
      Exit Sub
   Else
      lblDisplay.Text = lblDisplay.Text & "."
   End If

End Sub
```

IndexOf is a method that can be applied to any string. The expression lblDisplay.Text is a string (the text on the Label control), so we can call its IndexOf method. The code IndexOf(".") returns the location of the first instance of the period in the caption of the Label control. If this number is positive, the number entered contains a period already, and another can't be entered. In this case, the program exits the subroutine. If the method returns 0, the period is appended to the number entered so far, just like a regular digit.

Check out the operation of the application. We have already created a functional user interface that emulates a hand-held calculator with data-entry capabilities. It doesn't perform any operations yet, but we have already created a functional user interface with only a small number of statements.

Math Operations

Now we can move to the interesting part of the application: considering how a calculator works. Let's start by defining three variables:

Operand1   The first number in the operation

Operator   The desired operation

Operand2   The second number in the operation

When the user clicks one of the math symbols, the value on the display is stored in the variable *Operand1*. If the user then clicks the Plus button, the program must make a note to itself that the current operation is an addition and then clear the display so that the user can enter another value. The symbol of the operation is stored in the *Operator* variable. The user enters another value and then clicks the Equals button to see the result. At this point, our program must do the following:

1. Read the *Operand2* value on the display.

2. Add that value to *Operand1*.

3. Display the result.

The Equals button must perform the following operation:

```
Operand1 Operator Operand2
```

Suppose the number on the display when the user clicks the Plus button is 3342. The user then enters the value 23 and clicks the Equals button. The program must carry out the addition:

```
3342 + 23
```

If the user clicked the Division button, the operation is

```
3342 / 23
```

In both cases, when Equals is clicked, the result is displayed (and it may become the first operand for the next operation).

Variables are local in the subroutines where they are declared. Other subroutines have no access to them and can't read or set their values. Sometimes, however, variables must be accessed from many places in a program. If the *Operand1*, *Operand2*, and *Operator* variables in this application must be accessed from within more than one subroutine, they must be declared outside any subroutine. The same is true for the *clearDisplay* variable. Their declarations, therefore, must appear outside any procedure, and they usually appear at the beginning of the code with the following statements:

```
Dim clearDisplay As Boolean

Dim Operand1 As Double

Dim Operand2 As Double

Dim Operator As String
```

Let's see how the program uses the *Operator* variable. When the user clicks the Plus button, the program must store the value "+" in the *Operator* variable. This takes place from within the Plus button's Click event. But later, the Equals button must have access to the value of the *Operator* variable in order to carry out the operation (in other words, it must know what type of operation the user specified). Because these variables must be manipulated from within more than a single subroutine, they were declared outside any subroutine.

The keyword Double is new to you. It tells VB to create a numeric variable with the greatest possible precision for storing the values of the operators. (Numeric variables and their types are discussed in detail in the next chapter.) The Boolean type takes two values, True and False. You have already seen how the *clearDisplay* variable is used.

The variables *Operand1*, *Operand2*, and *Operator* are called *Form-wide*, or simply *Form*, variables, because they are visible from within any subroutine on the form. If our application had another form, these variables wouldn't be visible from within the other form(s). In other words, any subroutine on a form on which the variables are declared can read or set the values of the variables, but no subroutine outside that form can do so.

With the variable declarations out of the way, we can now implement the Operator buttons. Double-click the Plus button and, in the Click event's handler, enter the lines shown in Listing 4.6.

Listing 4.6: The Plus Button

```
Private Sub bttnPlus_Click _
   (ByVal sender As System.Object, _
    ByVal e As System.EventArgs) Handles bttnPlus.Click

   Operand1 = Val(lblDisplay.Text)
   Operator = "+"
   clearDisplay = True

End Sub
```

The variable *Operand1* is assigned the value currently on the display. The Val() function returns the numeric value of its argument. The Text property of the Label control is a string. For example, you can assign the value "My Label" to a label's Text property. The actual value stored in the Text property is not a number. It's a string such as "428," which is different from the numeric value 428. That's why we use the Val() function to convert the value of the Label's caption to a numeric value. The remaining buttons do the same, and I won't show their listings here.

So far, we have implemented the following functionality in our application: When an operator button is clicked, the program stores the value on the display in the *Operand1* variable and the operator in the *Operator* variable. It then clears the display so that the user can enter the second operand. After the second operand is entered, the user can click the Equals button to calculate the result. When this happens, the code of Listing 4.7 is executed.

Listing 4.7: The Equals Button

```
Private Sub bttnEquals_Click _
   (ByVal sender As System.Object, _
    ByVal e As System.EventArgs) Handles bttnEquals.Click

   Dim result As Double
   Operand2 = Val(lblDisplay.Text)
   Select Case Operator
      Case "+"
         result = Operand1 + Operand2
      Case "-"
         result = Operand1 - Operand2
      Case "*"
         result = Operand1 * Operand2
```

```
        Case "/"
            If Operand2 <> "0" Then _
                  result = Operand1 / Operand2
    End Select
    lblDisplay.Text = result
    clearDisplay = True

  End Sub
```

The *result* variable is declared as Double so that the result of the operation will be stored with maximum precision. The code extracts the value displayed in the Label control and stores it in the variable *Operand2*. It then performs the operation with a Select Case statement. This statement compares the value of the *Operator* variable to the values listed after each Case statement. If the value of the *Operator* variable matches one of the Case values, the following statement is executed.

- ▶ If the operator is "+", the *result* variable is set to the sum of the two operands.

- ▶ If the operator is "−", the *result* variable is set to the difference of the first operand minus the second.

- ▶ If the operator is "*", the *result* variable is set to the product of the two operands.

- ▶ If the operator is "/", the *result* variable is set to the quotient of the first operand divided by the second operand, provided that the divisor is not zero.

NOTE

Division takes into consideration the value of the second operand because if it's zero, the division can't be carried out. The last If statement carries out the division only if the divisor is not zero. If *Operand2* happens to be zero, nothing happens.

Now run the application, and check it out. It works just like a hand-held calculator, and you can't crash it by specifying invalid data. We didn't have to use any data-validation code in this example because the user doesn't get a chance to type invalid data. The data-entry mechanism is foolproof. The user can enter only numeric values because there are only numeric digits on the calculator. The only possible error is to divide by zero, and that's handled in the Equals button.

Debugging Tools

Our application works nicely and is quite easy to test—and to fix, if you discover something wrong with it. But that's only because it's a very simple application. As you write code, you'll soon discover something that doesn't work as expected, and you should be able to find out why and repair it. The process of eliminating errors is called *debugging,* and Visual Studio provides the tools to simplify the process of debugging. These tools are discussed in Chapter 7, "Error Handling and Debugging." There are a few simple operations you should know, though, even as you work with simple projects like this one.

Open the MathCalculator project that was just created, or download the code from www.sybex.com. Place the cursor in the line that calculates the difference between the two operands. Let's pretend there's a problem with this line and we want to follow the execution of the program closely, to find out what's going wrong with the application. Press F9 and the line will be highlighted in brown. This line has become a *breakpoint:* As soon as it is reached, the program will stop.

Press F5 to run the application and perform a subtraction. Enter a number, then click the minus button, then another number, and finally the equals button. The application will stop, and the code editor will open. The breakpoint will be highlighted in yellow. Hover the pointer over the *Operand1* and *Operand2* variables in the code editor's window. The value of the corresponding variable will appear in a small box or tooltip. Move the pointer over any variable in the current event handler to see its value. These are the values of the variables just prior to the execution of the highlighted statement.

The *result* variable will most likely be zero, because the statement hasn't been executed yet. If the variables involved in this statement have their proper values (if not, you know that the problem is prior to this statement, and perhaps in another event handler), then you can execute this statement by pressing F10. By pressing F10, you're executing the highlighted statement only. The program will stop at the next line. The next statement to be executed is the End Select statement.

Find an instance of the *result* variable in the current event handler, rest the mouse over it, and you will see the value of the variable after it has been assigned a value. Now you can press F10 to execute another statement or F5 to return to normal execution mode.

You can also evaluate expressions involving any of the variables in the current event handler by entering the appropriate statement in the

Command window. The Command window appears at the bottom of the IDE. If it's not visible, then from the main menu, select View ➢ Other Windows ➢ Command Window. The current line in the Output window is prefixed with the greater than symbol (reminiscent of the DOS days). Place the cursor next to it, and enter the following statement:

```
? Operand1 / Operand2
```

The quotient of the two values will appear in the following line. The question mark is just a shorthand notation for the Print command. If you want to know the current value on the calculator's display, enter the following statement:

```
? lblDisplay.Text
```

This statement requests the value of a property of a control on the form. The current value of the Label control's Text property will appear in the following line. You can also evaluate math expressions with statements like the following:

```
? Math.Log(3/4)
```

Log() is the logarithm function, and it's a method of the Math class. To create a random value between 0 and 1, enter the statement:

```
? Rnd()
```

With time, you'll discover that the Command window is a very handy tool in debugging applications. If you have a statement with a complicated expression, you can request the values of the individual components of the expression and thereby make sure they can be evaluated.

Now move the pointer off the breakpoint and press F9 again. This will toggle the breakpoint status, and the execution of the program won't halt the next time this statement is executed.

If the execution of the program doesn't stop at a breakpoint, it means that the statement was never reached. In this case, you must search for the bug in statements that are executed before the breakpoint. If you didn't assign the proper value to the *Operator* variable, the Case "-" statement will never be reached. You should place the breakpoint at the first executable statement of the Equal button's Click event handler to examine the values of all variables the moment this subroutine starts its execution. If all variables had the expected values, you will continue testing the code forward. If not, you'd have to test the statements that lead to this statement—the statements in the event handlers of the various buttons.

Another simple technique for debugging applications is the Output window. Although this isn't a debugging tool, it's very common among VB programmers (and very practical, may I add). Many programmers print the values of selected variables after the execution of some complicated statements. To do so, use the statement:

```
Console.WriteLine
```

followed by the name of the variable you want to print, or an expression:

```
Console.WriteLine(Operand1)
```

This statement sends its output to the Output window, which is displayed next to the Command window—click the Output tab at the bottom of the IDE to view this window. Alternatively, you can select the command by choosing View ➢ Other Windows ➢ Output. This is a very simple technique, but it works. You can also use it to test a function or method call. If you're not sure about the syntax of a function, pass an expression that contains the specific function to the `Console.WriteLine` statement as argument. If the expected value appears in the Output window, you can go ahead and use it in your code.

Let's consider the `DateDiff()` function, which contains the difference between two dates. The simplest syntax of this function is

```
DateDiff(interval, date1, date2)
```

I never know whether it subtracts *date1* from *date2* or the other way around—if you don't get it right the first time, then every time you want to use this function, there's always a doubt in your mind. Before using the function in my code, I insert a statement like:

```
Console.WriteLine(DateDiff(DateInterval.Day, _
                  #1/1/2000#, #1/2/2000#))
```

The value printed on the Output window is 1, by the way, indicating that the first date is subtracted from the second.

You will find more information on debugging in Chapter 7. I've just shown you a few simple techniques that will help you take advantage of the simpler debugging tools of Visual Studio as you write your first applications.

Adding More Features

Now that we have implemented the basic functionality of a hand-held calculator, we can add more features to our application. Let's add two more useful buttons:

▶ The +/−, or Negate, button, which inverts the sign of the number on the display

▶ The 1/x, or Inverse, button, which inverts the display number itself

Open the code window for each of the Command buttons, and enter the code from Listing 4.8 in the corresponding Click event handlers. For the +/− button, enter the event handler named bttnNegate_Click, and for the 1/x button, enter the one named bttnInverse_Click.

Listing 4.8: The Negate and Inverse Buttons

```
Private Sub bttnNegate_Click _
  (ByVal sender As System.Object, _
  ByVal e As System.EventArgs) Handles bttnNegate.Click

    lblDisplay.Text = -Val(lblDisplay.Text)
    clearDisplay = True

End Sub


Private Sub bttnInverse_Click _
  (ByVal sender As System.Object, _
  ByVal e As System.EventArgs) Handles bttnInverse.Click

    If Val(lblDisplay.Text) <> 0 Then _
        lblDisplay.Text = 1 / Val(lblDisplay.Text)
        clearDisplay = True
    End If

End Sub
```

As with the Division button, we don't attempt to invert a zero value. The operation (1 / 0) is undefined and causes a runtime error. Notice also that I use the value displayed on the Label control directly in the code. I could have stored the Display.Text value to a variable and used the variable instead:

```
TempValue = Val(lblDisplay.Text)
If TempValue <> 0 Then lblDisplay.Text = 1 / TempValue
```

This is also better coding, but in short code segments, we all tend to minimize the number of statements.

You can easily expand the Math application by adding Function buttons to it. For example, you can add buttons to calculate common functions, such as Cos, Sin, and Log. The Cos button calculates the cosine of the number on the display. The code behind this button's Click event is a one-liner:

```
lblDisplay.Text = Math.Cos(Val(lblDisplay.Text))
```

It doesn't require a second operand, and it doesn't keep track of the operation. You can implement all math functions with a single line of code.

Of course, you should add some error trapping, and in some cases, you can use data-validation techniques. For example, the Sqr() function, which calculates the square root of a number, expects a positive argument. If the number on the display is negative, you can issue a warning:

```
If lblDisplay.Text < 0 Then
    MsgBox("Can't calculate the square root " & _
           "of a negative number")
Else
    lblDisplay.Text = Math.Sqr(Val(lblDisplay.Text))
End If
```

All math functions are part of the Math class; that's why they're prefixed by the name of the class. You can also import the Math class to the project with the following statement and therefore avoid prefixing the math functions:

```
Imports System.Math
```

The Log() function can calculate the logarithms of positive numbers only. If you add a button to calculate logarithms and attempt to calculate the logarithm of a negative number, the result will be the string "NaN." This value is similar to infinity, and it says that the result is not a valid number (NaN stands for *not a number* and is discussed in detail in the following chapter). Of course, displaying a value like NaN on the calculator's display isn't the most user-friendly method of handling math errors. I would validate the data and pop up a message box with the appropriate description, as shown in Listing 4.9.

Listing 4.9: Calculating the Logarithm of a Number

```
Private Sub bttnLog_Click _
  (ByVal sender As System.Object, _
   ByVal e As System.EventArgs) Handles bttnLog.Click
```

```
If Val(lblDisplay.Text) < 0 Then
    MsgBox("Can't calculate the logarithm " & _
        "of a negative number")
Else
    lblDisplay.Text = Math.Log(lblDisplay.Text)
End If
clearDisplay = True

End Sub
```

One more feature you could add to the calculator is a limit to the number of digits on the display. Most calculators can only display a limited number of digits. To add this feature to the Math application (if you consider this a "feature"), use the Len() function to find out the number of digits on the display and ignore any digits entered after the number has reached the maximum number of allowed digits.

Exception Handling

Crashing this application won't be as easy as crashing the Loan application. If you start multiplying very large numbers, you won't get an overflow exception. Enter a very large number by typing repeatedly the digit **9**, then multiply this value with another, equally large value. When the result appears, click the multiplication symbol and enter another very large value. Keep multiplying the result with very large numbers, until you exhaust the value range of the Double datatype (that is, until the result is so large, that it can't be stored to a variable of the Double type). When this happens, the string "infinity" will appear in the display.

Our code doesn't include statements to capture overflows, so where did the string "infinity" come from? As you will learn in the following chapter, it is possible for numeric calculations to return the string "infinity." It's Visual Basic's way of telling you that it can't handle very large numbers. This isn't a limitation of VB; it's the way computers store numeric values: they provide a limited number of bytes for this. You will find out more about oddities such as infinity in the following chapter.

You can't create an overflow exception by dividing a number with zero either, because the code will not even attempt to carry out this calculation. In short, the Calculator application is pretty robust. However, we can't be sure that users won't cause the application to generate an exception, so we must provide some code to handle all types of errors.

Errors are now called *exceptions*. You can think of them as exceptions to the normal (or intended) flow of execution. If an exception occurs, the program must execute special statements to handle the exception—statements that wouldn't be executed normally. I think they're called exceptions because "error" is a word none of us likes, and most people can't admit they wrote code that contains errors. The term *exception* can be vague. What would you rather tell your customers: that the application you wrote has errors, or that your code has raised an exception? You may not have noticed it, but the term *bug* is not used as frequently any more; bugs are now called "known issues." The term *debugging,* however, hasn't changed yet.

VB6 programmers used the term *error* to describe something wrong in their code, and they used to write error-trapping code. With VB .NET, your code is error-free—it just raises exceptions every now and then. Both the error-trapping code of VB6 and the exception-handling features of VB .NET are supported. The error-trapping code of VB6 could get messy, so Microsoft added what they call *structured exception handling*. It's a more organized method to handle runtime errors—or exceptions. The basic premise is that when an exception occurs, the program doesn't crash with an error message. Instead, it executes a segment of code that you, the developer, provide.

TIP

By the way, if you have a hard time admitting it's a bug in your code, use the expression "mea culpa." It's Latin, and it sounds so sophisticated, most people won't even ask what it means.

How do you prevent an exception raised by a calculation? Data validation isn't going to help. You just can't predict the result of an operation without actually performing the operation. And if the operation causes an overflow, you can't prevent it. The answer is to add a structured exception handler. Most of the application's code is straightforward, and you can't generate an exception. The only place that an exception may occur is the handler of the Equals button, where the calculations take place. This is where we must add an exception handler. The outline of the error structure is the following:

```
Try
    { statements block }
Catch Exception
    { handler block }
Finally
```

```
{ clean-up statements block }
```
  End Try

The program will attempt to perform the calculations, which are coded in the statements block. If it succeeds, it continues with the clean-up statements. These statements are mostly clean-up code, and the Finally section of the statement is optional. If missing, the program execution continues with the statement following the End Try statement. If an error occurs in the first block of statements, then the Catch Exception section is activated and the statements in the handler block are executed.

The Catch block is where you handle the error. There's not much you can do about errors that result from calculations. All you can do is display a warning and give the user a chance to change the values. There are other types of errors, however, which can be handled much more gracefully. If your program can't read a file from a CD drive, you can give the user a chance to insert the CD and retry. In other situations, you can prompt the user for a missing value and continue. In general, there's no unique method to handle all exceptions. You must consider all types of exceptions your application may cause and handle them on an individual basis.

The error handler for the Math application must inform the user that an error occurred and abort the calculations—not even attempt to display a result. If you open the Equals button's Click event handler, you will find the statements detailed in Listing 4.10.

Listing 4.10: The Revised Equals Button

```
Private Sub bttnEquals_Click _
  (ByVal sender As System.Object, _
  ByVal e As System.EventArgs) Handles bttnEquals.Click

  Dim result As Double
  Operand2 = Val(lblDisplay.Text)
  Try
    Select Case Operator
      Case "+"
        result = Operand1 + Operand2
      Case "-"
        result = Operand1 - Operand2
      Case "*"
        result = Operand1 * Operand2
      Case "/"
```

```
                If Operand2 <> "0" Then _
                    result = Operand1 / Operand2
            End Select
            lblDisplay.Text = result
        Catch exc As Exception
            MsgBox(exc.Message)
            result = "ERROR"
        Finally
            clearDisplay = True
        End Try

    End Sub
```

Most of the time, the error handler remains inactive and doesn't interfere with the operation of the program. If an error occurs, which most likely will be an overflow error, the error-handling section of the Try...Catch...End Try statement will be executed. This code displays a message box with the description of the error, and it also displays the string "ERROR" on the display. The Finally section is executed regardless of whether an exception occurred or not. In this example, the Finally section sets the *clearDisplay* variable to True so that when another digit button is clicked, a new number will appear on the display.

NOTE

The *exc* variable represents an exception; it exposes a few properties in addition to the Message property, which is the description of the exception. For more information on the members of the Exception class and how to handle exceptions, see Chapter 7.

TAKING THE LOANCALCULATOR TO THE WEB

In this section, we're going to build a new project that is a loan calculator just like the one we built earlier. This time, though, the application will run on the browser, and any user who can connect to your server will be able to use it without having to install it on their computer. As you can understand, you're about to convert the LoanCalculator from a Windows application to a web application. It's a little early in the book to discuss web applications, but I wanted to show you that building a web application is quite similar to building a Windows app.

Web applications are discussed in detail in Part III, "ASP.NET Essentials," but since they're among the hot new features of the .NET platform, let me demonstrate why they are so hot. In a sentence, Visual Studio .NET is the first attempt to make the development of web applications as easy as VB applications. You will see shortly that you can create the interface of a Web Form (an HTML page with controls that interact with the user) just as you create a Windows Form. As for the application's code, it's just like writing VB code to handle the events of a Windows Form.

To write and test web applications, you must have Internet Information Server (IIS) installed and running on your computer. IIS is distributed with Windows 2000, and you must make sure it's running. Open the Start menu and select Settings ➢ Control Panel. Double-click the Administrative Tools, then double-click the icon of the Internet Services Manager tool. When the Internet Services Manager window appears, expand the node of your computer, right-click the Default Web Site item, and from the context menu, select Start. This will start the web server.

Start a new project and, on the New Project dialog box, click the ASP.NET Web Application icon. Then enter the name of the application in the Name box—call it **WebLoanCalculator**. When you close the New Project dialog box, you will see a window with a grid as usual, which represents the web page, or Web Form. This document is called WebForm1.aspx (the default name of the Web Form). The Web Form is equivalent to the Windows Form, but it's displayed as HTML on a browser such as Internet Explorer, as you see in Figure 4.7.

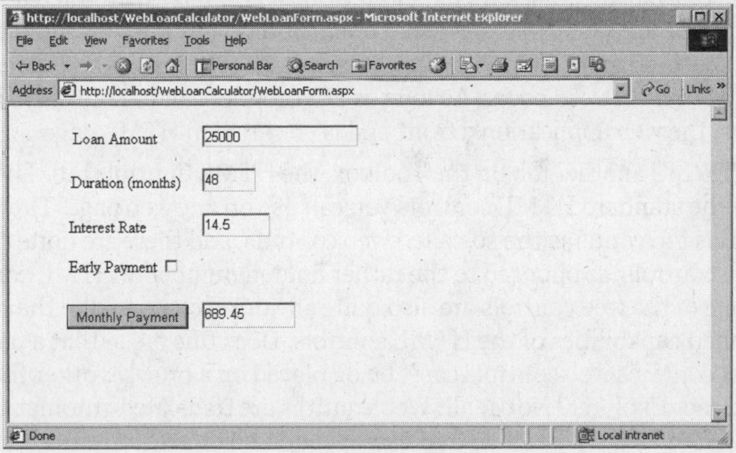

FIGURE 4.7: The WebLoanCalculator Web application

A new Windows project is stored in its own folder under the folder specified in the Location field on the New Project dialog box. Web applications are also stored in their own folder, but this folder is created under the web server's root folder (usually the C:\Inetpub\wwwroot folder).

Opening a web project is not as simple as double-clicking the icon of a Solution file. I suggest you follow the steps described in this chapter to create the project. If you want to open the WebLoanCalculator project, first go to www.sybex.com and download the source code, and copy the entire WebLoanCalculator folder into the web server's root folder. Then start Visual Studio .NET and open the WebLoanCalculator solution file. The text describes how to create the project from scratch. The application's main form is called WebLoanForm.aspx (it's equivalent to a Windows Form). You can open the application by starting Internet Explorer and enter the following URL in its Address box:

```
http://localhost/webloancalculator/webloanform.aspx
```

Let me describe the process of building the web application from scratch. Change the name of WebForm1 to WebLoanForm. Open the Toolbox, and you see that the Web Forms tab is activated, instead of the Windows Forms tab. The Web Forms tab contains the icons of the controls you can place on a Web Form, which are similar to the Windows controls but not as elaborate or as rich in functionality. As you already know, web pages use a much simpler user-interaction model. The viewer can enter text on certain controls, check or clear a few options, and click a button to submit the form to the server. The server reads the values on the controls, processes them, and returns a new page with the results. In the future, you can expect that applications running over the Internet will become more and more elaborate, but for now no one questions the HTML model used so far. As long as the browser can handle only HTML files, the web application's front end is confined to HTML pages.

There's another tab on the Toolbox, the HTML Controls tab. These are the standard HTML controls you can use on any web page. The Web Forms tab contains the so-called web controls, and there are quite a few web controls, as opposed to the rather limited number of HTML controls. Some of the web controls are also quite advanced compared to the really limited capabilities of the HTML controls. Does this mean that a page that contains web controls can't be displayed on a browser other than Internet Explorer? Not at all. Web controls are translated automatically into standard HTML code that can be rendered on any browser. For example, on the Web Forms tab you'll find some very elaborate controls, such as the TreeView control. HTML doesn't provide any controls that come even near the functionality of TreeView. Yet, a Web TreeView control can be rendered on any browser. The Web Forms Designer will insert the appropriate HTML tags to create something that looks and behaves like the TreeView control—but it's not a TreeView control. There's a lot to be said about web controls, but you'll have to wait until Part III. For now, we'll build a simple application that uses web controls to prompt the user for the parameters of a loan and that will display the monthly payment on the same page, just like a Windows application.

Start by placing four Label controls on the Web Form. (Double-click the Label control's icon on the Toolbox four times, and four labels will be placed on the Web Form for you.) Change their placement on the form by arranging them with the mouse, just as you would do with the controls on a Windows Form. You don't have to align them perfectly now; you'll use the commands of the Format menu to align the controls on the form. Just place them roughly at the positions shown in Figure 4.7. Then select each Label with the mouse and, in the Properties window, locate the Text property of the control.

As you can see, most of the basic properties of the web controls have the same name as the Windows controls. Change the captions of the four labels to "Loan Amount," "Duration (in months)," "Interest," and "Monthly Payment." Notice that the Label Web control is resized automatically to accommodate the string you assign to its Text property.

Now place four TextBox controls on the Web Form, each next to one of the Labels. By default, all TextBox controls are empty (they have no initial content). Change their size with the mouse and align them roughly to their corresponding Label controls. Then select them one at a time and change their ID property to txtAmount, txtDuration, txtRate, and txtPayment, respectively. The ID property of a web control is the unique identifier of the control, similar to the Name property of a Windows control. You'll use the ID property to access the control's members from within your code.

Then place a CheckBox control, set its Text property to Early Payment, and name it **chkPayEarly**. Set its TextAlign property to Left, so that its check box will be placed to the right of the text. The check box will be drawn immediately after the text, so you have to append a few spaces to the control's caption to clearly separate it from the check box.

The last control to place on the form is the Button control, whose Text property will be "Show Payment" and Name property will be bttnShow-Payment. This button will submit the loan parameters entered on the form to the server, where the appropriate code will calculate the monthly payment and return it to the client. This is a good point to align the controls on the Web Form. Select the Label controls and align them left with the Format ➤ Align ➤ Left command. While the labels are selected, use Format ➤ Vertical Spacing ➤ Make Equal to space them equally from one another. Once the labels are in place, you can align each text box to the corresponding label, with the Format ➤ Align ➤ Middles command. Select one pair of Label and TextBox controls at a time and align them. When selecting a pair of controls (a label and its textbox control) just make sure that the Label control is selected first as the main control in which the textbox should be aligned.

At this point, you're done designing the interface of the application. The interface is quite similar to the interface of the equivalent Windows application, only this one was designed on a Web Form with web controls. Other than that, the process was the same; even the tools for aligning the controls on the Web Form are the same as those for the Windows Form. Our next task is to program the application.

Double-click the button on the Web Form, and the editor window will open. The Web Form Designer has selected the Click event of the button and inserted its definition. All you have to do is insert the same code for this event that we used in the LoanCalculator application at the very beginning of this chapter.

You can switch to the Windows application and copy the code (which was shown back in Listing 4.2). Just paste the code behind the Show Payment button of the LoanCalculator Windows application in the Click event handler of the same button of the web application, and there won't be a single error. You can reuse the code as is!

Press F5 to run the application. It will be several seconds before the Internet Explorer window will pop up, displaying the page you've designed. Enter the parameters of a loan and then click the Show Payment button. A few seconds later, the monthly payment will appear on the form. As you will notice, a totally new page will arrive in the browser; this page contains the parameters of the loan (the values you've entered on the form) and the result of the calculations.

If you look at the source code of the document shown on Internet Explorer, you will see straight HTML code. The interface of the WebLoan-Calculator application looks fine, but not quite like a web page. There's none of the color or graphics we're so accustomed to seeing on web pages. Our Web Form contains only controls, but it's an HTML page and you can add any element that could appear on a web page. In other words, the Web Form can be edited as an HTML document. Not only that, but the

Part I

IDE allows you to edit your page either visually or in HTML mode. Let's add a colored caption and change the page's background color.

Select the Web Form by clicking somewhere on the form. In the Properties window, locate the property pageLayout. Its setting is `GridLayout`, which explains why you were able to place the controls anywhere on the page and align them in all possible ways. Those of you familiar with HTML know that aligning controls on a Web Form is anything but trivial. Change the pageLayout property from `GridLayout` to `FlowLayout`. Now you're in normal HTML editing mode. Place the cursor at the top of the page and start typing. Enter the string **Easy Loan Calculator** and then select it with the mouse. You will notice that the text-formatting buttons on the toolbar have been enabled. Set the text's size to 6 and set its foreground and background colors. To set these properties, use the two buttons next to the Bold/Italic/Underline group of buttons. The string is flush-left on the form, so enter a few spaces in front of the string to center it above the controls.

NOTE

A quick comment for readers familiar with HTML: Browsers ignore multiple spaces, but the editor silently converts the spaces you enter into ` ` codes, which are the HTML equivalent of "hard"—that is, nonbreaking—spaces.

You can also change the color of the page. Locate the page's bgColor property in the Properties window and set it to a light color. When the Color Picker dialog box appears on the form, you will see the tab with the web colors. These are the colors than can be displayed by all browsers, the so-called *safe colors*. (See Figure 4.8.)

FIGURE 4.8:   The WebLoanCalculator as a web page

To see how the Web Form Designer handles the HTML elements of the page, click the HTML button at the bottom of the Designer. The Web Form can be viewed and designed either in Design view (which is the default view) or in HTML view. The Web Form Designer inserted the following statement in the HTML document to generate the header of the page:

```
<FONT style="BACKGROUND-COLOR: #ffff66" _
            color="#996666" size="6">
<STRONG>Easy Loan Calculator</STRONG></FONT>
```

This is straight HTML code that could appear in any web page, and it doesn't use any web controls. Select the <FONT> tag and delete it. Then switch to the Design view to see that the header has disappeared. Switch back to the HTML view and insert the following statement right after the <body> tag and before the <form> tag, as shown in Figure 4.9:

```
<h1>Easy Loan Calculator</h1>
```

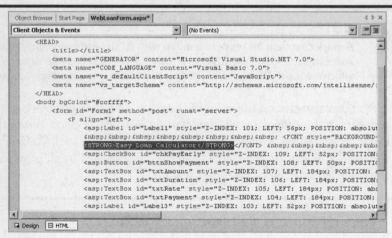

FIGURE 4.9: Editing the Web Form's HTML code

Click F5 to run the application. When Internet Explorer appears, enter some values in the text boxes and check out the application. The web application is functionally equivalent to the Windows loan application you developed at the beginning of this chapter. Yet, its user interface runs in the browser, but the calculations take place on the server (the machine to which the clients connect to request the WebLoanForm.aspx web page). Every time you click the Monthly Payment button on the page, the page is *posted* to the server. The browser transmits the values on the various controls back to the server. The server processes these values (actually, it executes the event handler you wrote) and creates a new page, which is sent to the client. This page includes the value of the monthly payment. Web applications are discussed in Part III; with this example I wanted to demonstrate the similarities between Windows Forms and Web Forms and how the same code works with both types of applications.

WORKING WITH MULTIPLE FORMS

Let's return to Windows applications. Few applications are built on a single form. Most applications use two, three, or more forms that correspond to separate sections of the application. In this section, we are going to build an application that uses three forms and lets the user switch among them at will. You'll see how to write an application that opens multiple windows on the Desktop. In this chapter, we'll build a simple example of a multiform application by combining the math and financial calculators we built earlier in the chapter.

The way to combine the two applications is to create a new form, which will become the switching point for the two calculators. The user will be able to invoke either of the two calculators by clicking a button on the new form. Let's design an application that combines the forms of the two projects.

Start a new project and call it Calculators. The project's form will become the switching point between the other two forms, and it's shown in Figure 4.10. Start by renaming the new form from Form1 to Calculators-Form. To design it, add two Button controls and name them **bttnMath** and **bttnLoan**. Then set their Text properties to Simple Math and Simple Loan, respectively. As you can guess, all you have to do now is add the code to invoke each of the existing forms from within each button's Click event handler. Add a third button on the form, call it bttnGame, and later you can add an action game to the Calculators project.

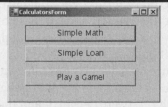

FIGURE 4.10:   The main form of the Calculators application

Part I

At this point, we must add the forms of the MathCalculator and Loan-Calculator projects into the new project. Right-click the name of the project, and select Add Existing Item from the context menu. In the dialog box that appears, select the item MathForm.vb in the MathCalculator project's folder. Do the same for the LoanForm of the LoanCalculator project. The Calculators project now contains three forms.

If you run the project now, you will see the Calculators form, but clicking its button won't bring up the appropriate form. Obviously, you must add a few lines of code in the Click event handler of each button to invoke the corresponding form. To display one form from within another form's code, you must create an object that represents the second form and then call its Show method. The code behind the Simple Math button is shown in Listing 4.11.

Listing 4.11: Invoking the Math Calculator

```
Private Sub bttnMath_Click _
    (ByVal sender As System.Object, _
    ByVal e As System.EventArgs) Handles bttnMath.Click

    Dim calcForm As New CalculatorForm
    calcForm.Show()

End Sub
```

The *calcForm* variable is an object variable that represents the CalculatorForm form of the Calculators application. The name of the form is actually used as a datatype, and this requires some explanation. The form is implemented as a Class and therefore you create objects of this type.

The Dim statement creates a new instance of the form, and the Show method loads and displays the form. If you run the project now, you'll see the main form, and if you click the first button, the math calculator's form will appear. If you click the same button again, another instance of the form will appear. What can we do to prevent this? We would like to display the CalculatorForm initially and then simply show it, but not load another instance of the form. The answer is to move the declaration of the *calcForm* variable outside the event handler, into the Form's declaration section. The variable is declared once, and all the procedures in the form can access its members. Variables declared in an event handler take effect only in the event handler in which they were declared, and that's why at this point, every time you click a button, a new instance of the corresponding form is created and displayed. If the variable *calcForm* points to a single instance of the CalculatorForm, then the form will be displayed every time we click the Easy Math button, but no new instance of it will be created. You'll find out more about the scope of variables in the following chapter.

When one of the two calculators is displayed, it doesn't automatically become the active form. The active form is the one that has the focus, and this is the main form of the application. To work with a calculator, you must click the appropriate form to make it active. To activate the most recently displayed form from within another form's code, we'll use the Activate method of the Form object. Rewrite the Click event handlers of the two buttons on the form as shown in Listing 4.12 (the listing shows the entire code of the form, so that you can see the declarations of the two variables that represent the forms of the application).

Listing 4.12: The Calculators Project

```
Public Class CalculatorsForm
    Inherits System.Windows.Forms.Form
    Dim calcForm As New CalculatorForm()
    Dim loanForm As New loanForm()

    Private Sub bttnMath_Click _
        (ByVal sender As System.Object, _
         ByVal e As System.EventArgs) Handles bttnMath.Click

        calcForm.Show()
        calcForm.Activate()

    End Sub

    Private Sub bttnLoan_Click _
        (ByVal sender As System.Object, _
         ByVal e As System.EventArgs) Handles bttnLoan.Click

        loanForm.Show()
        loanForm.Activate()

    End Sub

End Class
```

Notice the statement that declares the *loanForm* variable: the variable has the same name as the datatype, but this is not a problem. It goes without saying that the name of the variable can be anything. Our next task is to specify which form will be displayed when we start the application. Right-click the Calculators project name and, in the context menu, select Properties. On the Calculators Property Pages dialog box is a ComboBox named StartUp Object. Expand it and you will see the names of all the forms in the project. Select the name of form you want to appear when the program starts, which is the CalculatorsForm. (See Figure 4.11.)

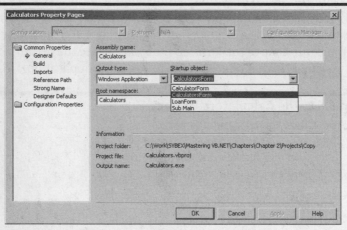

FIGURE 4.11:   Open the Project Properties dialog box to specify the startup object.

The code behind the Play A Game button should also call the Show method of another form, but it doesn't. I regret not developing a game for your enjoyment, but I did implement a fun feature. When you click this button, it jumps to another place on the form. The button's Click event handler is shown next:

```
Private Sub bttnGame_Click _
    (ByVal sender As System.Object, _
     ByVal e As System.EventArgs) Handles bttnGame.Click


    bttnGame.Left = Rnd() * Me.Width * 0.8
    bttnGame.Top = Rnd() * Me.Height * 0.8


End Sub
```

This subroutine manipulates the Left and Top properties of the control to move the button to a different position. The Rnd() function returns a random value between 0 and 1. To calculate the horizontal position, the code multiplies the random value by the width of the form (actually, 80 percent of the width). The vertical position is calculated in a similar manner.

Each Visual Basic project is made up of files that are all listed in the Solution Explorer window. Each project contains quite a few files in addition to the Form files, and they're all stored in a single folder, which is named after the project. If you open the Calculators folder, you will see that it contains the CalculatorForm and LoanForm forms. These are copies of the original forms of their corresponding applications. When you add an existing item to a project, VB makes a copy of this item in the project's folder. (See Figure 4.12.)

FIGURE 4.12:   The components of the Calculators project

To move a project to another location, just move the project's folder there. To create a copy of the project, just copy the project's folder to a different location.

Working with Multiple Projects

As you have noticed, every new project you create with VB is a so-called *solution*. Each solution contains a project, which in turn contains one or more files, references to .NET or custom components, and other types of items, which will be discussed in the following chapters. Both solutions and projects are containers—they contain other items. A solution may contain multiple projects. Each project in a solution is independent of the other projects, and you can distribute the projects in a solution separately. So, why create a solution? Let's say you're working on several related projects, which are likely to use common components. Instead of creating a different solution for each project, you can create a single solution to contain all the related projects.

Let's build a solution with two related projects. The two related projects are the two calculators we built earlier in this chapter. The two projects don't share any common components, but they're good enough for a demonstration, and you will see how VB handles the components of a solution.

VB .NET at Work: The Calculators Solution

Create an Empty Project, and name it **Calculators** by selecting File ➢ New ➢ Blank Solution. In the Solution Explorer window, you will see the name of the project and nothing else, not even the list of references that are present in any other project type. To add a project to the solution, choose File ➢ Add Project ➢ Existing Project. (You can also right-click the solution's name in the Solution Explorer, select Add Existing Item ➢ Project, and, in the dialog box that pops up, select the Calculator project.) Do the same for the LoanCalculator project. When the Add Existing Project dialog box appears, navigate to the folders with the corresponding projects and select the project's file.

You now have a solution, called Calculators, which contains two projects. If you attempt to run the project, the IDE doesn't know which of the two projects to execute and will generate an error message. We must decide how to start the new project (that is, which form to display when the user runs the Calculators application). When a solution contains more than a single project, you must specify the startup project. Right-click the name of one of the projects and, from the context menu, select Set As StartUp Project. To test a different project, set a different StartUp project. Normally, you will work for a while with the same project, so switching from one project to another isn't really a problem. It is also possible that different developers will work on different projects belonging to the same solution.

Let's say you're going to design a documentation file for both projects. A good choice for a short documentation file is an HTML file. To add an HTML file to the solution, right-click the solution's name and select Add New Item. In the dialog box, select the HTML Page template, and then enter a name for the new item. An HTML page will be added to the project, and an empty page will appear in the Designer. This is the newly added HTML page, and you must add some content to it.

Place the cursor on the design surface and start typing. Figure 4.13 shows a very simple HTML page with an introduction to the application. To format the text, use the buttons on the toolbar. These buttons embed the appropriate tags in the text, while you see the page as it would appear in the browser. This is the Design view of the document. You can switch to the HTML view and edit the document manually, if you're familiar with HTML. The HTML page can be used by either project—at the very least, you can distribute it with the application.

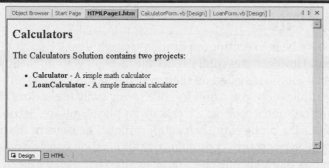

FIGURE 4.13: Adding an HTML Document to a solution

If you open the folder created for the project, you'll find that it contains an unusually small number of files. The projects reside in their respective folders. Make a change to one of the project's files. You can change the background color of the three TextBox controls on the Loan-Form to a light shade, like Bisque. Then open the LoanCalculator project, and you will see that the changes have taken effect. VB doesn't create new copies of the forms (or any other component) added to the Calculators solution. It uses the existing files and modifies them, if needed, in their original locations. Of course, you can create a solution from scratch and place all the items in the same folder. Each project is a separate entity, and you can create executables for each project and distribute them.

To create the executables, open the Build menu and select Build Solution or Rebuild Solution. The Build Solution command compiles the files that have been changed since the last build; Rebuild Solution compiles all the files in the project. The executables will be created in the Bin folder under each project's folder. The file Loan.exe will be created under the \Loan\Bin folder and the Calculator.exe file under the \Calculator\Bin folder.

The solution is a convenience for the programmer. When you work on a large project that involves several related applications, you can put them all in a solution and work with one project at a time. Other developers may be working with other projects belonging to the same solution. A designer may create graphics for the applications, you can include them in the solution, and they'll be available to all the projects belonging to the solution.

The Calculators project we built earlier contains copies of the forms we added to the project. The Calculators solution contains references to external projects.

Executable Files

So far, you have been executing applications within Visual Basic's environment. However, you can't expect the users of your application to have Visual Studio installed on their systems. If you develop an interesting application, you won't feel like giving away the code of the application (the *source code*, as it's called). Applications are distributed as executable files, along with their support files. The users of the application can't see your source code, and your application can't be modified or made to look like someone else's application (that doesn't mean it can't be copied, of course).

NOTE

An *executable file* is a binary file that contains instructions only the machine can understand and execute. The commands stored in the executable file are known as *machine language*.

Applications designed for the Windows environment can't fit in a single file. It just wouldn't make sense. Along with the executable files, your application requires *support files,* and these files may already exist on many of the machines on which your application will be installed. That's why it doesn't make sense to distribute huge files. Each user should install the main application and only the support files that aren't already installed on their computer.

The executable will run on the system on which it was developed, because the support files are there. Under the project's file, you will find two folders named Bin and Obj. Open the Obj folder, and you will see that it contains a subfolder named Debug. This is where you will find the executable, which is named after the project and has the extension `.exe`. Make sure that no instance of VS is running on your computer and then double-click the icon of the MathCalculator.exe or LoanCalculator.exe file. The corresponding application will start outside the Visual Studio IDE, and you can use it like any other application on your PC. You can create desktop shortcuts to the two applications.

The folder Debug contains the Debug version of the executable. Normally, after you're done debugging the application, you should change the default configuration of the project from Debug to Release. To change the project's configuration, select Build ➤ Configuration Manager. The Configuration Manager dialog box will pop up, as shown in Figure 4.14.

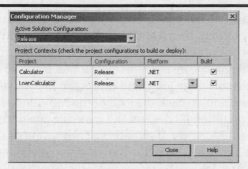

FIGURE 4.14:   The Configuration Manager window

The default configuration for all projects is Debug. This configuration generates code optimized for debugging. The other possible setting for the configuration is Release. Change the configuration to Release and close the dialog box. If you build the project or the solution again, a Release folder will be created under the Obj folder and will contain the new executable. The difference between the two versions of the executable files is that Debug files contain symbolic debug information. The Release configuration executes faster because it doesn't contain any debugging information.

DISTRIBUTING AN APPLICATION

Distributing just an EXE file isn't going to be any good, because the executable requires support files. If these files aren't installed on the target system (the computer on which your application will be installed), then the EXE file isn't going to work. The file will be executed only on a system that has Visual Studio .NET on it. Distributing a large number of files and installing them on the target computer is quite a task. You must create an installation program that (almost) automatically installs your application and the required support files on the target computer. If some of those files are already installed, they will not be installed again.

NOTE

Eventually, all the support files will become part of the operating system, and then you'll be able to distribute a single EXE file (or a small number of files). This hasn't happened with Windows 2000 or Windows XP and won't for some time. Until it does, you must provide your own installer.

A Setup project creates a Windows installer file (a file with extension .msi), which contains the executable(s) of the application and auxiliary files that are necessary for the application, Registry entries (if the application interacts with the Registry), installation instructions, and so on. The resulting MSI file is usually quite long, and this is the file you distribute to end users. They must double-click the icon of the MSI file to install the application on their computer. If they run the same file again, the application will be removed. Moreover, if something goes wrong during the installation, the installation will be rolled back and any components that were installed in the process will be removed.

The topic of creating and customizing Windows installers is huge, and there are already a couple of books on this topic alone—for example, *VB/VBA Developer's Guide to the Windows Installer* by Mike Gunderloy (Sybex, 2000). As you can understand, in this chapter we'll only scratch the surface. I will show you how to create a simple Setup project for installing the Calculators project on another machine. Your main priority right now is to learn to write .NET applications and master the language. You should be able to distribute even small applications, so the topic of creating Setup projects shouldn't be missing from this book. Yet, you aren't going to use the more advanced features for a while—not before you can write elaborate applications that require a customized installation procedure. In this section, I'll show you how to create a Setup project for the Calculators project. It's a simple project that demonstrates the basic steps of creating a Windows installer using the default options, and you'll be able to use this application to install the Calculators application to a target computer.

VB .NET at Work: Creating a Windows Installer

To create a Windows installer, you must add a Setup project to your solution. The Setup project will create an installation program for the projects in the current solution. Open the Calculators solution and add a new project (File ➤ Add Project ➤ New Project). In the dialog box that appears (see Figure 4.15), click the Setup and Deployment Projects item. In the Templates pane, you will see five different types of Setup and Deployment projects. The simplest type of Setup project is the Setup Wizard. This wizard takes you through the steps of creating a Setup project, which is another wizard that takes the *user* through the steps of installing the application on the target computer. Select this template and then enter the project's name in the Name box; name the project SimpleCalculators. Click OK, and the first screen of the wizard will appear. This is a welcome screen, and you can click the Next button to skip it.

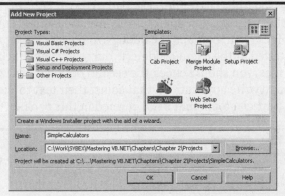

FIGURE 4.15:   Adding a Setup and Deployment project to your solution

On the next screen, you'll be prompted to choose a project type. You can create a project that installs an application or one that adds components to an existing installation. We want to create a project that installs an application for the first time, and we have two options: to create a setup for a Windows application or to create a setup for a web application. Select the first option, as shown in Figure 4.16, and click Next to move to the next screen of the wizard.

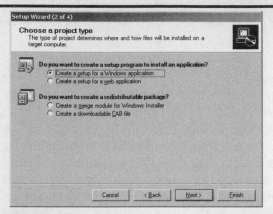

FIGURE 4.16:   The Project Type screen of the wizard

On the next screen, you'll be prompted to select any files you want to add to the installation program. Here you must click the items checked in Figure 4.17. The Primary Output is the executable file, and the Content Files include things like the HTML file we added to the project. In the release version of the program, you don't usually want to include debug symbols or source files (well, perhaps the debug symbols for large projects that are also tested at the client's side). If your application includes localized resource files, you should check the second option. Localized resources allow you to write applications that adjust their text to the end user's culture. It's a special topic that's not covered in this book.

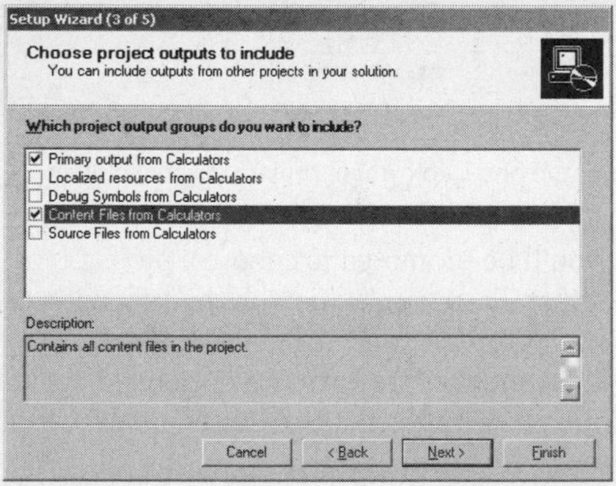

FIGURE 4.17:   Specifying the items you want to install

The Setup project we're creating here is part of a solution with the project you want to install on the target machine. I've included the Setup project in the same solution for convenience only. You can also create a Setup project and specify any executable file you want to install. The Setup project takes a while to compile, so you should add it to the solution only after you have debugged the application. Or remove the Setup project from the solution after you have created the Setup file.

Click Next again to see another screen, where you can specify additional files that are not part of the project. You can add text files with installation instructions, compatibility data, registration information, and so on. Click Next again, and the last screen of the wizard displays a summary of the project you specified. Click Finish to close the wizard and create the Setup project.

The wizard adds the Setup project to your solution. Select the new project with the mouse and open the Properties window to see the properties of the new project. The Solution Explorer and the new project's Properties window should look like the ones shown in Figure 4.18. The good news is that you don't have to write any code for this project. All you have to do is set a few properties and you're done.

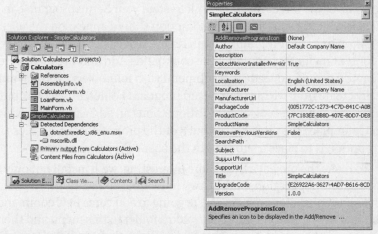

FIGURE 4.18: The Setup project's Properties

The AddRemoveProgramsIcon property lets you specify the icon of the installation and removal programs—yes, VB will also create a program to uninstall the application. You can specify whether the Setup project will detect newer versions of the application and won't overwrite them with an older version. The DetectNewerInstalledVersion property is True by default. You can also specify your company's name and URL, support line, the title of the installation window, and so on.

The Manufacturer property will become the name of the folder in which the installation will take place. By default, this folder will be created in the user's Program Files folder. Assign a name that reflects either your company or the project type—a string like "The Math Experts" for the Calculators example. The Author property is where your name should appear. The ProductName property is by default the name of the Setup project; change it to "The EasyCalc Project." The Title property is the title of the installer (what users see on the installation wizard's title bar while the application is being installed).

The Solution Explorer Buttons

You will notice that the usual buttons on the Solution Explorer have been replaced by six new buttons, which are described in the following sections.

File System Editor Button   Click this button and you will see the four sections of the target machine's file system your Setup program can affect. Decide whether your application's action should appear on the user's Desktop or in the Programs menu. Right-click either item and you will see a context menu that contains the commands Add and Create Shortcut. The Add command leads to a submenu with four objects you can automatically create from within your Setup program: Folder, Project Output, File, and Assembly. For typical applications, you can add a folder (in which you can later place the project's output), or the project output. The less intruding option is to place a shortcut in the user's Programs menu.

To make the project a little more interesting, we'll install not only the Calculators application, but the two individual applications: the Calculator and LoanCalculator projects. We're going to add three new commands to the user's Programs menu, so let's add a folder to this menu and then the names of the applications in this folder. Right-click the item User's Programs Menu and select Add Folder. A new folder will be added under the User's Programs Menu item. Change its name to Demo Calculators, as shown in Figure 4.19. Select the new folder and look up its properties. The AlwaysCreate property should be True—if not, the wizard will not add the folder to the user's Programs menu.

Then right-click the newly added folder and select Add ≻ File. A dialog box will pop up where you can select the executables that must appear in the Demo Calculators folder on the Programs menu. Browse your disk and locate the Calculators, Calculator, and LoanCalculator executables in the \Obj\Release folder under the corresponding project's folder (all three files have the extension EXE).

After adding the items you want to appear in the Demo Calculators folder of the Programs menu, the File System Editor should be like the one in Figure 4.19.

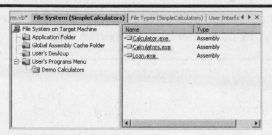

FIGURE 4.19:   Specifying how the installation program will affect the user's file system

Registry Editor Button   Click this button to add new keys to the user's Registry. You don't *have* to add anything to the user's Registry, especially for this project. But you can place special strings in the Registry, like an encoded date to find out when a demo version of your application may expire. You must first familiarize yourself with the Registry and how to program it with Visual Basic, before you attempt to use it with your applications.

File Types Editor Button   If your application uses its own file type, you can associate that type with your application, so that when the user double-clicks a file of this type, your application starts automatically. This is a sure way to ruin the user's file associations. If your application can handle GIF images or HTML files, don't even think of taking over these files. Use this option *only* with files that are unique to your application.

To add a new file type on the user's machine, click the File Types Editor button on the Properties window. On the Designer's surface, you will see a single item: File Types On Target Machine. Right-click the item and select Add File Type. This command will add a new file type and the verb **&Open** under it. Click the new file type and you will see its properties in the Properties window. You can assign a description to the new file type, its extension, and the command that will be used to open the files of this type (the name of your application's EXE file).

User Interface Editor Button   Click this button and you will see the steps of the installation on the Designer's surface, as shown in Figure 4.20. Each phase of the installation process has one or more steps, and a different dialog box is displayed at each step. Some of the dialog boxes contain messages, like a short description of the application or a copyright message. These strings are exposed as properties of the corresponding dialog box, and you can change them. Just click a dialog box in the User Interface Editor and then look up its properties in the Properties window.

FIGURE 4.20:   The outline of the installation process

The wizard inserts all the necessary dialog boxes, but you can add custom dialog boxes. If you do, you must also provide some code to process the user's selections on the custom dialog box. For our simple example, we don't need any customized dialog boxes. I will repeat here that the topic of creating a customized Windows installer is one of the major aspects of Visual Studio .NET, and when you're ready to build an installer for a large application, you will have to consult the documentation extensively.

Custom Actions and System Requirements Buttons   The last two buttons on the Properties window allow you to specify custom actions and requirements for the target machine. For example, you may specify that the application be installed only on systems on which a specific component has already been installed. You can ignore these buttons for a simple installation project.

Part I

Finishing the Windows Installer

OK, we're almost there. Select Build ➤ Build Solution, and VB will create the installation program. First, it will create a new project folder, the SimpleCalculators folder. This is where the Setup project's files will be stored and where the executable file of the installation program will be created. The process of building the executables and creating the Setup program will take several minutes. The output of the build process is the `SimpleCalculators.msi` file. This is an executable file (known as Windows Installer Package), and it will be created in the `\SimpleCalculators\Release` folder. Its size will be approximately 15MB. If you're wondering what's in this file, take a look at the Output window of the IDE and you will see a large list of components added to the package.

Running the Windows Installer

Now you're ready to install the Calculators project to your computer. If you have access to another computer that doesn't have Visual Studio installed, you should copy the `SimpleCalculators.msi` file there and install the application there. The components required for your application to run properly are already installed on the development machine, and you can test the Setup project better on another machine.

Go to the folder `\SimpleCalculators\Release` and double-click the icon of the Windows Installer Package (or the folder to which you have copied this file on another machine). The MSI file is represented by the typical installation icon (a computer and a CD). The following figures show the installation steps. Please notice where the captions you specified in the Setup project's properties appear in the screens of the installation wizard. Consult these figures as you build a Setup application to make sure the proper messages are displayed during the installation on the target computer.

1. This dialog appears while the Windows installer starts.

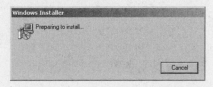

2.   The welcome screen of the wizard will guide the user through the installation procedure. The messages on this screen are the properties CopyrightWarning and WelcomeText of the Welcome dialog box in the User Interface Editor.

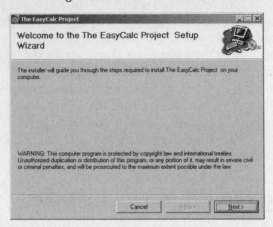

3.   This screen lets the user change the default path of the application to be installed. Notice how the default path is formed. You can control the default installation path by setting the appropriate properties of the Setup project. The installer will create a folder, under the Program Files folder, named after the Manufacturer and ProductName properties of the Setup project.

4. This screen asks the user to confirm the installation—which can be cancelled later as well.

5. The application is being installed, and this screen displays a progress indicator. The user can terminate the installation by clicking the Cancel button.

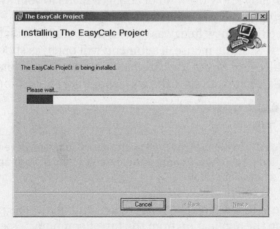

6. The last screen of the installer confirms the successful installation of the application. Click Close to end the program. If there was a problem installing the application, a description of the problem will be displayed on this last screen. In this case, all the components installed in the process will be automatically removed as well.

Verifying the Installation

You already know the kind of changes made to your system by an installation program. If you open the Programs menu (Start ➤ Programs), you will see that a new item was added, the Demo Calculators item. If you select it with the mouse, a submenu will open, as shown in Figure 4.21. You can select any of the three commands (Calculators, Calculator, or LoanCalculator) to start the corresponding application.

TIP

All three items in the Demo Calculators submenu have the default application icon. You should change the default icons of your applications for a more professional look.

The Windows installer has created and installed a program for uninstalling the application from the target computer. Open Control Panel and double-click the Add/Remove Programs icon. The dialog box that appears contains an item for each program you can remove from your computer. The newly installed application is the item The EasyCalc

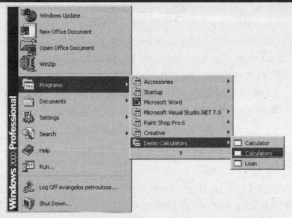

FIGURE 4.21: The new items added to the Programs menu by the Windows installer

Project, as shown in Figure 4.22. Click its Remove button to uninstall the application or the Change button to repair an existing installation.

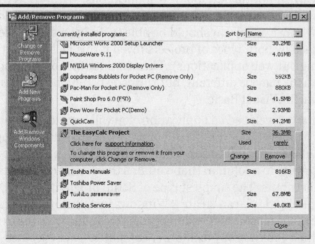

FIGURE 4.22: Use the Add/Remove Programs utility to remove or repair an application installed by the Windows installer.

As for the location of the executables and their support files, they're in the EasyCalc Project folder under the \Program Files\CompanyName folder. If the same customer installs another of your applications—say, the ProCalc Project—it will also be installed in its own folder under \Program Files\CompanyName. Just make sure all the Setup projects have the same value for the Manufacturer property, and the support files won't be installed in multiple folders.

WHAT'S NEXT

This chapter introduced you to the concept of *solutions* and *projects*. You learned how to build a simple solution with a single project, as well as a solution with multiple projects. Use solutions to combine multiple related projects into a single unit, so that your projects can share components. Each project in a solution maintains its individuality, and you can either edit one from within the solution or open it as a project and edit independently of the other projects in the solution.

You also learned how to develop web applications. With VB .NET, developing web applications is as easy as developing Windows applications. In a few short years, you should be able to design a single interface that can be used by both types of projects (even if this means that there will be nothing but web applications). The user interface of web and Windows applications may be different, but the code behind both types of projects is straight Visual Basic.

After you have developed an application, you will have to distribute it. Distributing Windows application isn't a trivial process, but building a Setup program for your application with VB .NET is. All you have to do is add a Setup project to a solution that contains the project or projects that you want to distribute. The simplest type of Setup program doesn't require any code, and you can create a Windows installer by just setting a few properties. The output of the Setup program is a file with the extension .msi, which you can copy to another computer. Once executed on the target computer, the MSI file will install the application, create a shortcut to the application in the user's Programs menu, and even create an entry in Add/Remove Programs for repairing or uninstalling the application.

By now, you have a good idea about the environment and how Windows applications are built. This chapter concludes Part I. In Part II, "Advanced Visual Basic .NET," you will learn more about the Visual Basic .NET language and writing procedures. You will study error handling in more depth, and you will learn more about window forms.

Part II
ADVANCED VISUAL
BASIC .NET

Chapter 5

VISUAL BASIC .NET: THE LANGUAGE

This chapter and the next discuss the fundamentals of any programming language: variables, flow-control statements, and procedures. A *variable* stores data, and a *procedure* is code that manipulates variables. To do any serious programming with Visual Basic .NET, you must be familiar with these concepts. To write efficient applications, you need a basic understanding of some fundamental topics, such as the datatypes (the kind of data you can store in a variable), the scope and lifetime of variables, and how to write procedures and pass arguments to them.

NOTE
In order to save space, some of the material in this chapter has been modified slightly or omitted from the original.

Adapted from *Mastering Visual Basic .NET*
by Evangelos Petroutsos
ISBN 0-7821-2877-7 $49.99

This chapter explores in greater depth how variables store data and how programs process variables. If you're familiar with Visual Basic, you might want to simply scan the following pages and make sure you're acquainted with the topics and the sample code discussed in this chapter. I would, however, advise you to read this chapter even if you're an experienced VB programmer.

VB6 TO VB .NET

Experienced Visual Basic programmers should pay attention to these special sidebars with the "VB6 to VB .NET" title, which calls your attention to changes in the language. These sections usually describe new features in VB .NET or enhancements of VB6 features, but also VB6 features that are no longer supported by VB .NET.

VARIABLES

In Visual Basic, as in any other programming language, variables store values during a program's execution. Let's say you're writing a program that converts amounts between different currencies. Instead of prompting the user for the exchange rates all the time—or even worse, editing your code to change the currency rates every day—you can store the exchange rates into variables and use these variables to perform the conversions. If the current exchange rate between the U.S. dollar and the euro is 0.9682, you can store this value to a variable called *USD2Euro*. If you change the value of this variable once in your code, all the conversions will be calculated based on the new rate. Or you can prompt the users for the exchange rate when they start the program, store the rate to the *USD2Euro* variable, and then use it in your code.

A variable has a name and a value. The variable *UserName,* for example, can have the value "Joe," and the variable *Discount* can have the value 0.35. *UserName* and *Discount* are variable names, and "Joe" and 0.35 are their values. "Joe" is a *string* (that is, text or an alphanumeric value), and 0.35 is a numeric value. When a variable's value is a string, it must be enclosed in double quotes. In your code, you can refer to the value of a variable by the variable's name. For example, the following statements calculate and display the discount for the amount of $24,500:

```
Dim Amount As Single
Dim Discount As Single
Dim DiscAmount As Single
Amount = 24500
Discount = 0.35
DiscAmount = Amount * (1 - Discount)
MsgBox("Your price is $" & DiscAmount)
```

Single is a numeric datatype. It can store both integer and non-integer values. There are other types of numeric variables, which are discussed in the following sections. I've used the Single datatype because it's the most commonly used datatype for simple calculations that don't require extreme accuracy.

The message that this expression displays depends on the values of the *Discount* and *Amount* variables. If you decide to offer a better discount, all you have to do is change the value of the *Discount* variable. If you didn't use the *Discount* variable, you'd have to make many changes in your code. In other words, if you coded the line that calculated the discounted amount as follows:

```
DiscAmount = 24500 * (1 - 0.35)
```

you'd have to look for every line in your code that calculates discounts and change the discount from 0.35 to another value. By changing the value of the *Discount* variable in a single place in your code, the entire program is updated.

VB6 TO VB .NET

In VB6, amounts of money were usually stored in Currency variables. The Currency datatype turned out to be insufficient for monetary calculations and was dropped from the language. Use the Decimal datatype, discussed later in this chapter, to represent money amounts.

Variables in VB .NET are more than just names, or placeholders, for values. They're intelligent entities that can not only store but also process

Part II

a value. I don't mean to scare you, but I think you should be told: VB .NET variables are objects. And here's why:

A variable that holds dates must be declared as such with the following statement:

```
Dim expiration As Date
```

Then you can assign a date to the *expiration* variable, with a statement like this:

```
expiration = #1/1/2003#
```

So far, nothing out of the ordinary. This is how you use variables with any other language. In addition to holding a date, however, the *expiration* variable can process it. The expression

```
expiration.AddYears(3)
```

will return a new date that's three years ahead of the date stored in the expiration variable. The new date can be assigned to another Date variable:

```
Dim newExpiration As Date

newExpiration = expiration.AddYears(3)
```

The keywords following the period after the variable's name are called *methods* and *properties*, just like the properties and methods of the controls you place on a form to create your application's visual interface. The methods and properties (or the *members*) of a variable expose the functionality that's built into the class that represents the variable itself. Without this built-in functionality, you'd have to write some serious code to extract the month from a *Date* variable, to figure out whether a character is a letter, a digit, or a punctuation symbol, and so on. Much of the functionality you'll need in an application that manipulates dates, numbers, or text has already been built into the variables themselves, and you will see examples of other properties and methods exposed by the various datatypes later in this chapter.

Declaring Variables

In most programming languages, variables must be declared in advance. Historically, the reason for doing this has been to help the compiler. Every time a compiled application runs into a new variable, it has to create it. Doing so doesn't take a lot of statements, but it does produce a delay that could be avoided. If the compiler knows all the variables and their types that are going to be used in the application ahead of time, it can produce the most compact and efficient, or optimized, code. For example, when you tell the compiler that the variable *Discount* will hold a number, the compiler sets aside a certain number of bytes for the *Discount* variable to use.

When programming in VB .NET, you should declare your variables, because this is the default mode and Microsoft recommends this practice strongly. They've been recommending it with previous versions of VB, but up to VB6 the language was accepting undeclared variables by default. If you attempt to use an undeclared variable in your code, VB .NET will throw an exception. It will actually catch the error as soon as you complete the line that uses the undeclared variable, underlining it with a wiggly red line. It is possible to change the default behavior and use undeclared variables the way most people did with earlier versions of VB (you'll see how this is done in the section "The Strict and Explicit Options," later in this chapter), but nearly all the examples of the book declare their variables. In any case, you're strongly encouraged to declare your variables.

VB6 TO VB .NET

Although not an absolute requirement, VB .NET encourages the declaration of variables. By default, every variable must be declared. Moreover, when you declare a variable, you must also specify its type. One of the new terms in the VB .NET documentation is *strictly typed*, which simply means that a variable has a specific type and you can't store a value of a different type to the variable. See the discussion of Option Explicit and Option Strict statements later in this chapter for more information on using variables without declaring them, or declaring them without a specific type.

VB .NET recognizes the type identifier characters. A variable name like *note$* implies a String variable, and you need not supply a datatype when you declare the variable. The Defxxx statements (DefInt, DefDbl, and so on), however, are not supported by VB .NET. The Defxxx statements were already obsolete, and they were rarely used even with older versions of Visual Basic.

In VB .NET you can declare multiple variables of the same type without having to repeat each variable's type. The following statement,

CONTINUED ➡

Part II

for instance, will create three Integer variables:

```
Dim width, depth, height As Integer
```

The following statement will create three Integer and two Double variables:

```
Dim width, depth, height As Integer, area, volume As _
Double
```

Another convenient shortcut introduced with VB .NET is that now you can initialize variables along with their declaration. Not only can you declare a variable with the Dim statement, you can also initialize it by assigning a value of the proper type to it:

```
Dim width As Integer = 9
Dim distance As Integer = 100, time As Single = 9.09
```

When you declare variables in your code, you're actually telling the compiler the type of data you intend to store in each variable. This way, the compiler can generate code that handles the variables most efficiently. A variable that holds characters is different from a variable that holds numbers. If the compiler knows in advance the type of data you're going to store in each variable, it can not only optimize the executable it will produce, it can also catch many mistakes as you type (an attempt to store a word to a numeric variable, for instance).

To declare a variable, use the Dim statement followed by the variable's name, the As keyword, and its type, as follows:

```
Dim meters As Integer
Dim greetings As String
```

We'll look at the various datatypes in detail in the next section. In the meantime, you should know that a variable declared As Integer can store only integer numbers, and a variable declared As String can only store text (strings of characters, or simply strings).

The first variable, *meters,* will store integers, such as 3 or 1,002, and the second variable, *greetings,* will store text, such as "Thank you for using Fabulous Software". You can declare multiple variables of the same or different type in the same line, as follows:

```
Dim Qty As Integer, Amount As Decimal, CardNum As String
```

When Visual Basic finds a Dim statement, it creates one or more new variables, as specified in the statement. That is, it creates a structure in the memory where it can store a value of the specified type and assigns a name to it. Each time this name is used in subsequent commands, Visual Basic accesses this structure to read or set its value. For instance, when you use the statement

```
meters = 23
```

Visual Basic places the value 23 in the structure reserved for the *meters* variable. When the program asks for the value of this variable, Visual Basic reads it from the same structure.

To use the *meters* variable in a calculation, reference it by name in a statement in your code. The statement

```
inches = meters * 39.37
```

multiplies the value stored in the *meters* variable and assigns the result to the *inches* variable. The equal sign is the assignment operator; it assigns the value of the expression that appears to its right, to the variable listed to its left. Only the variable to the left of the equal sign changes value.

One good reason for declaring variables is so that Visual Basic knows the type of information the variable must store and can validate the variable's value. Attempting to assign a value of the wrong type to a declared variable generates an error. For example, if you attempt to assign the value "Welcome" to the *meters* variable, Visual Basic won't compile the statement because this assignment violates the variable's declaration. The *meters* variable was declared as Integer, and you're attempting to store a string in it. It will actually underline the statement in the editor with a red wiggly line, which indicates an error. If you hover the pointer over the statement in error, a box with an explanation of the error will appear.

You can use other keywords in declaring variables, such as `Private`, `Public`, and `Static`. These keywords are called *access modifiers*, because they determine what sections of your code can access the specific variables and what sections can't. We'll look at these keywords in later sections of this chapter. In the meantime, bear in mind that all variables declared with the `Dim` statement exist in the module in which they were declared. If the variable *Count* is declared in a subroutine (an event handler, for example), it exists only in that subroutine. You can't access it from outside the subroutine. Actually, you can have a *Count* variable in multiple procedures. Each variable is stored locally, and they don't interfere with one another.

Variable-Naming Conventions

When declaring variables, you should be aware of a few naming conventions. A variable's name:

▶ Must begin with a letter.

▶ Can't contain embedded periods. Except for certain characters used as datatype identifiers (which are described later in this chapter), the only special character that can appear in a variable's name is the underscore character.

▶ Must not exceed 255 characters.

▶ Must be unique within its scope. This means that you can't have two identically named variables in the same subroutine, but you can have a variable named *counter* in many different subroutines.

Variable names in VB .NET are case-insensitive: The variable names *myAge, myage,* and *MYAGE* all refer to the same variable in your code. Conversely, you can't use the names *myage* and *MYAGE* to declare two different variables.

TIP

In fact, as you enter variable names, the editor converts their casing so that they match their declaration.

Variable Initialization

You can also initialize variables in the same line that declares them. The following line declares an Integer variable and initializes it to 3,045:

```
Dim distance As Integer = 3045
```

This statement is equivalent to the following statements:

```
Dim distance As Integer
distance = 3045
```

It is also possible to declare and initialize multiple variables, of the same or different type, on the same line:

```
Dim quantity As Integer = 1, discount As Single = 0.25
```

If you want to declare multiple variables of the same type, you need not repeat the type. Just separate all the variables of the same type with commas and set the type of the last variable:

```
Dim length, width, height As Integer, volume, area As Double
```

This statement declares three Integer variables and two Double variables. Double variables hold fractional values (or *floating-point* values, as they're usually called) similar to the Single datatype, only they can represent non-integer values with greater accuracy.

VB6 TO VB .NET

Another interesting new feature introduced with VB .NET is the shorthand notation of common operations, such as the addition of a value to a variable. The statement

```
counter = counter + 1
```

can now be written as

```
counter += 1
```

The symbols += form a new VB operator (there's no space between the plus and the equal sign), which adds the value to its left to the value of the variable to its right and assign the result to the initial variable. Only a variable may appear to the left of this operator, while on the right you can type either a variable or a value. The statement

```
totalCount = totalCount + count
```

is equivalent to

```
totalCount += count
```

The same notation applies to other operators, like subtraction (-=), multiplication (*=), division (/=), integer division (\=), and concatenation (&=). All these operators are new to VB .NET. I will not overuse this notation in the book for the sake of current VB programmers; most of them consider this notation one of the trademarks of the C language.

Types of Variables

Visual Basic recognizes the following five categories of variables:

- ▶ Numeric
- ▶ String

▶ Boolean

▶ Date

▶ Object

The two major variable categories are numeric and string. *Numeric variables* store numbers, and *string variables* store text. *Object variables* can store any type of data. Why bother to specify the type if one type suits all? On the surface, using object variables may seem like a good idea, but they have their disadvantages. Integer variables are optimized for storing integers, and date variables are optimized for storing dates. Before VB can use an object variable, it must determine its type and perform the necessary conversions, if any. If an object variable holds an integer value, VB must convert it to a string before concatenating it with another string. This introduces some overhead, which can be avoided by using typed variables.

Numeric Variables

You'd expect that programming languages would use a single datatype for numbers. After all, a number is a number. But this couldn't be farther from the truth. All programming languages provide a variety of numeric datatypes, including the following:

▶ Integers (there are several integer datatypes)

▶ Decimals

▶ Single, or floating-point numbers with limited precision

▶ Double, or floating-point numbers with extreme precision

NOTE
Decimal, Single, and Double are the three basic datatypes for storing floating-point numbers. The Double type can represent these numbers more accurately than the Single type, and it's used almost exclusively in scientific calculations. The integer datatypes store whole numbers.

The datatype of your variable can make a difference in the results of the calculations. The proper variable types are determined by the nature of the values they represent, and the choice of datatype is frequently a trade-off between precision and speed of execution (less-precise datatypes are manipulated faster). Visual Basic supports the numeric datatypes shown in Table 5.1.

TABLE 5.1: Visual Basic Numeric Datatypes

DATATYPE	MEMORY REPRESENTATION	STORES
Short (Int16)	2 bytes	Integer values in the range −32,768 to 32,767.
Integer (Int32)	4 bytes	Integer values in the range −2,147,483,648 to 2,147,483,647.
Long (Int64)	8 bytes	Very large integer values.
Single	4 bytes	Single-precision floating-point numbers. It can represent negative numbers in the range −3.402823E38 to −1.401298E−45 and positive numbers in the range 1.401298E−45 to 3.402823E38. The value 0 can't be represented precisely (it's a very, very small number, but not exactly 0).
Double	8 bytes	Double-precision floating-point numbers. It can represent negative numbers in the range −1.79769313486232E308 to −4.94065645841247E−324 and positive numbers in the range 4.94065645841247E−324 to 1.79769313486232E308.
Decimal	16 bytes	Integer and floating-point numbers scaled by a factor in the range from 0 to 28. See the description of the Decimal datatype for the range of values you can store in it.

Part II

VB6 TO VB .NET

The Short datatype is the same as the Integer datatype of VB6. The new Integer datatype is the same as the Long datatype of VB6; the VB .NET Long datatype is new and can represent extremely large integer values. The Decimal datatype is new to VB .NET, and you use it when you want to control the accuracy of your calculations in terms of number of decimal digits.

Integer Variables There are three different types of variables for storing integers, and the only difference is the range of numbers you can represent with each type. As you understand, the more bytes a type takes, the larger values it can hold. You should choose the type that can represent the largest values you expect to come up in your calculations. You can go for the Long type, to be safe, but Long variables are four times as large as Short variables, and it takes the computer longer to process them.

Single- and Double-Precision Numbers The names Single and Double come from single-precision and double-precision numbers. Double-precision numbers are stored internally with greater accuracy than single-precision numbers. In scientific calculations, you need all the precision you can get; in those cases, you should use the Double datatype.

The result of the operation $1 / 3$ is 0.333333... (an infinite number of digits "3"). You could fill 64MB of RAM with "3" digits, and the result would still be truncated. Here's a simple, but illuminating, example:

In a button's Click event handler, declare two variables as follows:

```
Dim a As Single, b As Double
```

Then enter the following statements:

```
a = 1 / 3
Console.WriteLine(a)
```

Run the application and you should get the following result in the Output window:

```
.3333333
```

There are seven digits to the right of the decimal point. Break the application by pressing Ctrl+Break and append the following lines to the end of the previous code segment:

```
a = a * 100000
Console.WriteLine(a)
```

This time the following value will be printed in the Output window:

```
33333.34
```

The result is not as accurate as you might have expected initially—it isn't even rounded properly. If you divide a by 100,000, the result will be:

```
0.3333334
```

which is different from the number we started with (0.3333333). This is an important point in numeric calculations, and it's called *error propagation*. In long sequences of numeric calculations, errors propagate. Even if you can tolerate the error introduced by the Single datatype in a single operation, the cumulative errors may be significant.

Let's perform the same operations with double-precision numbers, this time using the variable *b*. Add these lines to the button's Click event handler:

```
b = 1 / 3
Console.WriteLine(b)
b = b * 100000
Console.WriteLine(b)
```

This time, the following numbers are displayed in the Output window:

```
0.333333333333333
33333.3333333333
```

The results produced by the double-precision variables are more accurate.

NOTE

Smaller-precision numbers are stored in fewer bytes, and larger-precision numbers are stored in more bytes. The actual format of the floating-point numeric types is complicated and won't be discussed in this book. Just keep in mind that fractional values can't always be represented precisely in the computer's memory; they produce more accurate results, but using more precision requires more memory.

Why are such errors introduced in our calculations? The reason is that computers store numbers internally with two digits: zero and one. This is very convenient for computers, because electronics understand two states: on and off. As a matter of fact, all the statements are translated into bits (zeros and ones) before the computer can understand and execute them. The binary numbering system used by computers is not much different than the decimal system we humans use—computers just use fewer digits. We humans use 10 different digits to represent any number, whole or fractional, because we have 10 fingers. Just as with the decimal numbering system some numbers can't be represented precisely, there are numbers that can't be represented precisely in the binary system. Let me give you a more illuminating example.

The Decimal Datatype   Variables of the last numeric datatype, Decimal, are stored internally as integers in 16 bytes and are scaled by a power of 10. The scaling power determines the number of decimal digits to the right of the floating point, and it's an integer value from 0 to 28. When the scaling power is 0, the value is multiplied by 10^0, or 1, and it's represented without decimal digits. When the scaling power is 28, the value is divided by 10^{28} (which is 1 followed by 28 zeros—an enormous value), and it's represented with 28 decimal digits.

The largest possible value you can represent with a Decimal value is an integer: 79,228,162,514,264,337,593,543,950,335. The smallest number you can represent with a Decimal variable is the negative of the same value. These values use a scaling factor of 0.

VB6 TO VB .NET

The Decimal datatype is new to VB .NET and has replaced the Currency datatype of previous versions of VB. The Currency type was introduced to handle monetary calculations and had a precision of four decimal digits. It was dropped from the language because it didn't provide enough accuracy for the types of calculations for which it was designed. Most programmers wanted to be able to control the accuracy of their calculations, so a new, more flexible type was introduced, the Decimal type.

When the scaling factor is 28, the largest value you can represent with a Decimal variable is quite small, actually. It's 7.9228162514264337593543950335 (and the largest negative value is the same with the minus sign). The number zero can't be represented precisely with a Decimal variable scaled by a factor of 28. The smallest positive value you can represent with the same scaling factor is 0.00...01 (there are 27 zeros between the decimal period and the digit 1)—an extremely small value, but still not quite zero.

NOTE

The more accuracy you want to achieve with a Decimal variable, the smaller the range of available values you have at your disposal—just as with the other numeric types, or just like about everything else in life.

When using Decimal numbers, VB keeps track of the decimal digits (the digits following the decimal point) and treats all values as integers. The value 235.85 is represented as the integer 23585, but VB knows that it must scale the value by 100 when it's done using it. Scaling by 100 (that is, 10^2) corresponds to shifting the decimal point by two places. First, VB multiplies this value by 100 to make it an integer. Then, it divides it by 100 to restore the original value. Let's say you want to multiply the following values:

```
328.558 * 12.4051
```

First, you must turn them into integers. You must remember that the first number has three decimal digits and the second number has four decimal digits. The result of the multiplication will have seven decimal digits. So you can multiply the following integer values:

```
328558 * 124051
```

and then treat the last seven digits of the result as decimals. Use the Windows Calculator (in the Scientific view) to calculate the previous product. The result is 40,757,948,458. The actual value after taking into consideration the decimal digits is 4,075.7948458. This is how VB works with the Decimal datatype. If you perform the same calculations with decimals in VB, you will get the exact same result. Notice that the Decimal datatype doesn't introduce any rounding errors. It's capable of representing the result with the exact number of decimal digits. This is the real advantage of decimals, which makes them ideal for financial applications. For scientific calculations, you must still use Doubles. Decimal numbers are the best choice for calculations that require a specific precision (like four or eight decimal digits).

Infinity and Other Oddities

VB .NET can represent two very special values, which may not be numeric values themselves but are produced by numeric calculations: NaN (not a number) and Infinity. If your calculations produce NaN or Infinity, you should confirm the data and repeat the calculations, or give up. For all practical purposes, neither NaN nor Infinity can be used in everyday business calculations.

Part II

VB6 TO VB .NET

VB .NET introduces the concepts of an undefined number (NaN) and infinity to Visual Basic. In the past, any calculations that produced an abnormal result (i.e., a number that couldn't be represented with the existing datatypes) generated runtime errors. VB .NET can handle abnormal situations much more gracefully. NaN and Infinity aren't the type of result you'd expect from meaningful numeric calculations, but at least they don't produce run-errors.

Some calculations produce undefined results, like infinity. Mathematically, the result of dividing any number by zero is infinity. Unfortunately, computers can't represent infinity, so they produce an error when you request a division by zero. VB .NET will report a special value, which isn't a number: the Infinity value. If you call the ToString method of this value, however, it will return the string "Infinity." Let's generate an Infinity value. Start by declaring a Double variable, *dblVar*:

```
Dim dblVar As Double = 999
```

Then divide this value by zero:

```
Dim infVar as Double
infVar = dblVar / 0
```

and display the variable's value:

```
MsgBox(infVar)
```

The string "Infinity" will appear on a message box. This string is just a description; it tells you that the result is not a valid number (it's a very large number that exceeds the range of numeric values that can be represented in the computer's memory).

Another calculation that will yield a non-number is when you divide a very large number by a very small number. If the result exceeds the largest value that can be represented with the Double datatype, the result is Infinity. Declare three variables as follows:

```
Dim largeVar As Double = 1E299
Dim smallVar As Double = 1E-299
Dim result As Double
```

NOTE

The notation 1E299 means 10 raised to the power of 299, which is an extremely large number. Likewise, 1E-299 means 10 raised to the power of -299, which is equivalent to dividing 10 by a number as large as 1E299.

Then divide the large variable by the small variable and display the result:

```
result = largeVar / smallVar
MsgBox(result)
```

The result will be Infinity. If you reverse the operands (that is, you divide the very small by the very large variable), the result will be zero. It's not exactly zero, but the Double datatype can't accurately represent numeric values that are very, very close to zero.

NOT A NUMBER (NAN)

NaN is not new. Packages like Mathematica and Excel have been using it for years. The value NaN indicates that the result of an operation can't be defined: It's not a regular number, not zero, and not Infinity. NaN is more of a mathematical concept, rather than a value you can use in your calculations. The Log() function, for example, calculates the logarithm of positive values. By default, you can't calculate the logarithm of a negative value. If the argument you pass to the Log() function is a negative value, the function will return the value NaN to indicate that the calculations produced an invalid result.

The result of the division 0 / 0, for example, is not a numeric value. If you attempt to enter the statement "0 / 0" in your code, however, VB will catch it even as you type and you'll get the error message "Division by zero occurs in evaluating this expression."

To divide zero by zero, set up two variables as follows:

```
Dim var1, var2 As Double
Dim result As Double
var1 = 0
var2 = 0
```

```
result = var1 / var2
MsgBox(result)
```

If you execute these statements, the result will be a NaN. Any calculations that involve the *result* variable (a NaN value) will yield NaN as a result. The statements:

```
result = result + result
result = 10 / result
result = result + 1E299
MsgBox(result)
```

will all yield NaN.

If you make *var2* a very small number, like 1E-299, the result will be zero. If you make *var1* a very small number, then the result will be Infinity.

Testing for Infinity and NaN   To find out whether the result of an operation is a NaN or Infinity, use the IsNaN and IsInfinity methods of the Single and Double datatype. The Integer datatype doesn't support these methods, even though it's possible to generate Infinity and NaN results with Integers. If the IsInfinity method returns True, you can further examine the sign of the Infinity value with the IsNegativeInfinity and IsPositiveInfinity methods.

In most situations, you'll display a warning and terminate the calculations. The statements of Listing 5.1 do just that. Place these statements in a Button's Click event handler and run the application.

Listing 5.1: Handling NaN and Infinity Values

```
Dim var1, var2 As Double
Dim result As Double
var1 = 0
var2 = 0
result = var1 / var2
If result.IsInfinity(result) Then
    If result.IsPositiveInfinity(result) Then
        MsgBox("Encountered a very large number. " & _
               "Can't continue")
    Else
        MsgBox("Encountered a very small number. " & _
               "Can't continue")
```

```
      End If
   Else
      If result.IsNaN(result) Then
          MsgBox("Unexpected error in calculations")
      Else
          MsgBox("The result is " & result.ToString)
      End If
   End If
```

This listing will generate a NaN value. Change the value of the *var1* variable to 1 to generate a positive infinity value, or to −1 to generate a negative infinity value. As you can see, the IsInfinity, IsPositiveInfinity, IsNegativeInfinity, and IsNaN methods require that the variable be passed as argument, even though these methods apply to the same variable. An alternative, and easier to read, notation is the following:

```
   System.Double.IsInfinity(result)
```

This statement is easier to understand, because it makes it clear that the IsInfinity method is a member of the System.Double class.

This odd notation is something you will have to get used to. Some methods don't apply to the object they refer to, and they're called *shared* methods. They act on the value passed as argument and not the object to which you apply them.

The Byte Datatype   In some situations, however, data is stored as bytes, and you must be able to access individual bytes. The Byte type holds an integer in the range 0 to 255. Bytes are frequently used to access binary files, image and sound files, and so on.

To declare a variable as a Byte, use the following statement:

```
   Dim n As Byte
```

The variable *n* can be used in numeric calculations too, but you must be careful not to assign the result to another Byte variable if its value may exceed the range of the Byte type. If the variables *A* and *B* are initialized as follows:

```
   Dim A As Byte, B As Byte
   A = 233
   B = 50
```

the following statement will produce an overflow exception:

```
   Console.WriteLine(A + B)
```

The same will happen if you attempt to assign this value to a `Byte` variable with the following statement:

```
B = A + B
```

The result (283) can't be stored in a single byte. Visual Basic generates the correct answer, but it can't store it into a Byte variable. If you do calculations with Byte variables and the result may exceed the range of the Byte datatype, you must convert them to integers, with a statement like the following:

```
Console.WriteLine((CInt(A) + CInt(B)))
```

The `CInt()` function converts its argument to an Integer value. You will find more information on converting variable types later in this chapter, in the section "Converting Variable Types." Of course, you can start with integer variables and avoid all the conversions between types. In rare occasions, however, you may have to work with bytes and insert the appropriate code to avoid overflows.

TIP

The operators that won't cause overflows are the Boolean operators AND, OR, NOT, and XOR, which are frequently used with Byte variables. These aren't logical operators that return True or False. They combine the matching bits in the two operands and return another byte. If you combine the numbers 199 and 200 with the AND operator, the result is 192. The two values in binary format are 11000111 and 11001000. If you perform a bitwise AND operation on these two values, the result is 11000000, which is the decimal value 192.

In addition to the Byte datatype, VB .NET provides a Signed Byte datatype, which can represent signed values in the range from −128 to 127.

Boolean Variables

The Boolean datatype stores True/False values. Boolean variables are, in essence, integers that take the value −1 (for True) and 0 (for False). Actually, any nonzero value is considered True. Boolean variables are declared as:

```
Dim failure As Boolean
```

and they are initialized to False.

Boolean variables are used in testing conditions, such as the following:

```
If failure Then MsgBox("Couldn't complete the operation")
```

They are also combined with the logical operators AND, OR, NOT, and XOR. The NOT operator toggles the value of a Boolean variable. The following statement is a toggle:

```
running = Not running
```

If the variable *running* is True, it's reset to False, and vice versa. This statement is a shorter way of coding the following:

```
Dim running As Boolean
If running = True Then
    running = False
Else
    running = True
End If
```

Boolean operators operate on Boolean variables and return another Boolean as their result. The following statements will display a message if one (or both) of the variables *ReadOnly* and *Hidden* are True (presumably these variables represent the corresponding attributes of a file):

```
If ReadOnly Or Hidden Then
    MsgBox("Couldn't open the file")
Else
    { statements to open and process file }
End If
```

You can reverse the logic and process the file if none of these variables are set to True:

```
If Not (ReadOnly Or Hidden) Then
    { statements to process the file }
Else
    MsgBox("Couldn't open the file")
End If
```

String Variables

The String datatype stores only text, and string variables are declared with the String type:

```
Dim someText As String
```

You can assign any text to the variable *someText*. You can store nearly 2GB of text in a string variable (that's 2 billion characters and is much more text than you care to read on a computer screen). The following assignments are all valid:

```
Dim aString As String
aString = "Now is the time for all good men to come " & _
          "to the aid of their country"
aString = ""
aString = "There are approximately 29,000 words " & _
          "in this chapter"
aString = "25,000"
```

The second assignment creates an empty string, and the last one creates a string that just happens to contain numeric digits, which are also characters. The difference between these two variables:

```
Dim aNumber As Integer = 25000
Dim aString As String = "25,000"
```

is that they hold different values. The *aString* variable holds the characters "2", "5", ",", "0", "0", and "0", and *aNumber* holds a single numeric value. However, you can use the variable *aString* in numeric calculations and the variable *aNumber* in string operations. VB will perform the necessary conversions, as long as the Strict option is off (its default value).

VB6 TO VB .NET

Another feature not supported by VB .NET is the fixed-length string. With earlier versions of VB, you could declare variables of fixed length with a statement like the following, to speed up string operations:

```
Dm shortText As String * 100
```

This is no longer needed, as the Framework supports two powerful classes for manipulating strings: the String class and the String-Builder class.

Character Variables

Character variables store a single Unicode character in two bytes. In effect, characters are unsigned short integers (UInt16); you can use the CChar() function to convert integers to characters, and the CInt() function to convert characters to their equivalent integer values.

VB6 TO VB .NET

Character variables are new to VB .NET, and they correspond to the `String * 1` type so often used with previous versions of VB.

To declare a Character variable, use the `Char` keyword:

```
Dim char1, char2 As Char
```

You can initialize a Character variable by assigning either a character or a string to it. In the latter case, only the first character of the string is assigned to the variable. The following statements will print the characters "a" and "A" to the Output window:

```
Dim char1 As Char = "a", char2 As Char = "ABC"
Console.WriteLine(char1)
Console.WriteLine(char2)
```

The integer values corresponding to the English characters are the ANSI codes of the equivalent characters. The statement:

```
Console.WriteLine(CInt("a"))
```

will print the value 65.

If you convert the Greek character alpha (α) to an integer, its value is 945. The Unicode value of the famous character π is 960.

Character variables are used in conjunction with strings. You'll rarely save real data as characters. However, you may have to process the individual characters in a string, one at a time. Because the Char datatype exposes interesting methods (like IsLetter, IsDigit, IsPunctuation, and so on), you can use these methods in your code. Let's say the string variable *password* holds a user's new password, and you require that passwords contain at least one special symbol. The code segment of Listing 5.2 scans the password and rejects it if it contains letter and digits only.

Listing 5.2: Processing Individual Characters

```
Dim password As String, ch As Char
Dim i As Integer
Dim valid As Boolean = False
While Not valid
    password = InputBox("Please enter your password")
    For i = 0 To password.Length - 1
```

Part II

```
            ch = password.Chars(i)
            If Not System.Char.IsLetterOrDigit(ch) Then
                valid = True
                Exit For
            End If
        Next
        If valid Then
            MsgBox("You new password will be activated " & _
                "immediately!")
        Else
            MsgBox("Your password must contain at least " & _
                "one special symbol!")
        End If
    End While
```

NOTE

If you are not familiar with the If...Then, For...Next, or While...End While structures, you can read their description in the "Flow-Control Statements" section of this chapter and then return to check out this example.

The code prompts the user with an input box to enter a password. (Later in the book, you'll find out how to create a form that accepts the characters typed but displays asterisks in their place, so that the password isn't echoed on the screen.) The *valid* variable is Boolean, and it's initialized to False (you don't have to initialize a Boolean variable to False, because this is its default initial value, but it makes the code easier to read). It's set to True from within the body of the loop, only if the password contains a character that is not a letter or a digit. We set it to False initially, so that the While...End While loop will be executed at least once. This loop will keep prompting the user until a valid password is entered.

The loop scans the string variable *password*, one letter at a time. At each iteration, the next letter is copied into the *ch* variable. The Chars property of the String datatype is an array that holds the individual characters in the string (another example of the functionality built into the datatypes).

The IsLetterOrDigit method of the Char datatype returns True if a character is either a letter or a digit. If the current character is a symbol, the program sets the *valid* variable to True, so that the outer loop won't be executed again, and it exits the For...Next loop. Finally, it prints the appropriate message and either prompts for another password or quits.

Date Variables

Date and time values are stored internally in a special format, but you don't need to know the exact format. They are double-precision numbers: the integer part represents the date and the fractional part represents the time. A variable declared as *Date* can store both date and time values with a statement like the following:

```
Dim expiration As Date
```

The following are all valid assignments:

```
expiration = #01/01/2004#
expiration = #8/27/2001 6:29:11 PM#
expiration = "July 2, 2002"
expiration = Now()
```

The Now() function returns the current date and time. The pound sign tells Visual Basic to store a date value to the *expiration* variable, just as the quotes tell Visual Basic that the value is a string. You can store a date as string to a Date variable, but it will be converted to the appropriate format. If the Strict option is on, you can't specify dates using the long date format (as in the third statement of this example).

The Date datatype is extremely flexible; Visual Basic knows how to handle date and time values, so that you won't have to write complicated code to perform the necessary conversions. To manipulate dates and times, use the members of the Date type, or the Date and Time functions. The difference between two dates, for example, is calculated by the function DateDiff(). This function accepts as argument a constant that determines the units in which the difference will be expressed (days, hours, and so on) as well as two dates, and it returns the difference between them in the specified interval. The following statement returns the number of days in the current millennium:

```
Dim days As Long
days = DateDiff(DateInterval.Date, #12/31/2000#, Now())
```

You can also call the Subtract method of the Date class, which accepts a date as argument and subtracts it from a Date variable. The difference between the two dates is returned as a TimeSpan object.

The Nothing Value

The Nothing value is used with Object variables and indicates a variable that has not been initialized. If you want to disassociate an Object variable from the object it represents, set it to Nothing. The following statements create an Object variable that references a Brush, use it, and then release it:

```
Dim brush As System.Drawing.Brush
brush = New System.Drawing.Brush(bmap)
{ use brush object to draw with }
brush = Nothing
```

The first statement declares a Brush variable. At this point, the *brush* variable is Nothing. The second statement initializes the *brush* variable with the appropriate constructor. After the execution of the second statement, the brush variable actually represents an object with which you can draw. After using it to draw something, you can release it by setting it to Nothing.

VB6 TO VB .NET

The Set statement is obsolete in VB .NET. You can initialize Object variables just like any other type of variable, with the assignment operator.

If you want to find out whether an Object variable has been initialized, use the Is keyword, as shown in the following example:

```
Dim myPen As Pen
{ more statements here }
If myPen Is Nothing Then
    myPen  = New Pen(Color.Red)
End If
```

The variable *myPen* is initialized with the New constructor only if it hasn't been initialized already. If you want to release the *myPen* variable later in your code, you can set it to Nothing with the assignment operator.

Datatype Identifiers

Finally, you can omit the As clause of the Dim statement, yet create typed variables, with the variable declaration characters, or *datatype identifiers*. These characters are special symbols, which you append to the variable name to denote the variable's type. To create a string variable, you can use the statement:

```
Dim myText$
```

The dollar sign signifies a string variable. Notice that the name of the variable includes the dollar sign—it's *myText$*, not *myText*. To create a variable of a particular type, use one of the data declaration characters in Table 5.2 (not all datatypes have their own identifier).

TABLE 5.2:   Datatype Definition Characters

Symbol	Datatype	Example
$	String	*A$, messageText$*
%	Integer (Int32)	*counter%, var%*
&	Long (Int64)	*population&, colorValue&*
!	Single	*distance!*
#	Double	*ExactDistance#*
@	Decimal	*Balance@*

Using type identifiers doesn't help produce the cleanest and easiest to read code. If you haven't used them in the past, there's no really good reason to start using them now.

The Strict and Explicit Options

Previous versions of Visual Basic didn't require that variables be declared before they were used. VB .NET doesn't *require* that you declare your variables either, but the default behavior is to throw an exception if you attempt to use a variable that hasn't been previously declared. If an undeclared variable's name appears in your code, the editor will underline the variable's name with a wiggly red line, indicating that it caught an error. Rest the pointer over the segment of the statement in question to see the description of the error.

To change the default behavior, you must insert the following statement at the beginning of the file, above the Imports statements:

```
Option Explicit Off
```

The Option Explicit statement must appear at the very beginning of the file. This setting affects the code in the current module, not in all files of your project or solution.

The sample code in this section assumes that Option Explicit has been set to Off. For all other examples in the book, I will assume that this option is set to On.

You can also specify the settings of the Strict and Explicit options from the Property Pages dialog box of the current project, as shown in Figure 5.1. To open this dialog box, right-click the name of the project in the Solution Explorer and, from the context menu, select Properties. The settings you specify here take effect for all the components of the current project.

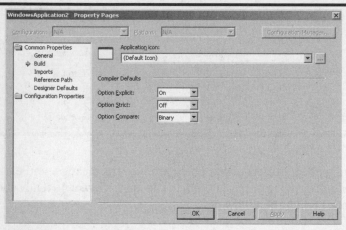

FIGURE 5.1: Setting the Strict and Explicit options on the project's Property pages

The default value of the Option Explicit statement is On. Most programmers familiar with previous versions of VB will not like having to declare their variables, but using variants for all types of variables has never been a good idea. In the later section "Why Declare Variables?" you will see an example of the pitfalls you'll avoid by declaring your variables.

By setting the Explicit option to Off, you're telling VB that you intend to use variables without declaring them. As a consequence, VB can't make any assumption as to the variable's type, so it uses a generic type of variable that can hold any type of information. These variables are called Object variables, and they're equivalent to the old variants.

When Visual Basic meets an undeclared variable name, it creates a new variable on the spot and uses it. The new variable's type is Object, the generic datatype that can accommodate all other datatypes. Visual Basic adjusts its type according to the value you assign to it. Create two variables, *var1* and *var2*, by referencing them in your code with statements like the following ones:

```
var1 = "Thank you for using Fabulous Software"
var2 = 49.99
```

The *var1* variable is a string variable, and *var2* is a numeric one. You can verify this with the GetType method, which returns a variable's type. The following statements print the types shown below each statement, in bold:

```
Console.WriteLine "Variable var1 is " & _
                    var1.GetType().ToString
```

Variable var1 is System.String

```
Console.WriteLine "Variable var2 is " & _
                    var2.GetType().ToString
```

Variable var2 is System.Double

Later in the same program you can reverse the assignments:

```
var1 = 49.99
var2 = "Thank you for using Fabulous Software"
```

If you execute the previous Print statements again, you'll see that the types of the variables have changed. The *var1* variable is now a double, and *var2* is a String.

Another related option is the Strict option, which is Off by default. The Strict option tells the compiler whether the variables should be *strictly typed*. A strictly typed variable can accept values of the same type as the type with which it was declared. With the Strict option set to Off, you can use a string variable that holds a number in a numeric calculation:

```
Dim a As String = "25000"
Console.WriteLine a / 2
```

The last statement will print the value 12500 on the Output window. Likewise, you can use numeric variables in string calculations:

```
Dim a As Double = 31.03
a = a + "1"
```

If you turn the Strict option on by inserting the following statement at the beginning of the file, you won't be able to mix and match variable types:

```
Option Strict On
```

If you attempt to execute any of the last two code segments while the Strict option is On, the compiler will underline a segment of the statement to indicate an error. If you rest the pointer over the underlined segment of the code, the following error message will appear in a tip box:

```
Option strict disallows implicit conversions from String to _
    Double
```

(or whatever type of conversion is implied by the statement).

When the Strict option is set to On, the compiler doesn't disallow *all* implicit conversions between datatypes. For example, it will allow you to assign the value of an Integer to a Long, but not the opposite. The Long value may exceed the range of values that can be represented by an Integer variable. You will find more information on implicit conversions in the section "Widening and Narrowing Conversions," later in this chapter.

Moreover, with `Option Strict On`, you can't late-bind an expression. *Late binding* means to call a method or a property of an object, but not be able to resolve this call at design time.

When you declare an object, like a Pen or a Color object, and then you call one of its properties, the compiler can verify that the member you call exists. Take a look at the following lines:

```
Dim myPen As Pen
myPen = New Pen(Color.Red)
myPen.Width = 2
```

These three statements declare a Pen object and initialize it to red color and a width of two pixels. All the shapes you'll draw with this pen will be rendered in red, and their outlines will be two pixels wide. This is *early binding,* because as soon as the variable is declared, the compiler can verify that the Pen object has a Width and the Color object has a Red property.

Now let's use an Object variable to store our Pen object:

```
Dim objPen As Object
objPen = New Pen(Color.Red)
objPen.Width = 2
```

This is called late binding, and it will work only if the Strict option is turned off. The *objPen* variable is an Object variable and can store anything. The compiler has no way of knowing what type of object you've stored to the variable, and therefore it can't verify that the *objPen* variable exposes a Width property. In this short segment, it's pretty obvious that the *objPen* variable holds a Pen object, but in a larger application the *objPen* variable may be set by any statement.

Early binding seems pretty restricting, but you should always use it. Notice that you don't have to turn on the Strict option to use early binding—just declare your variables with a specific type. Early-bound variables display their members in a drop-down list when you enter their name, followed by a period. If you enter *myPen* and the following period in the editor's window, you will see a list of all the methods supported by the Pen object. However, if you enter *objPen* and the following period, you will see a list with just four members—the members of any Object variable.

Converting Variable Types

In some situations, you will need to convert variables from one type into another. Table 5.3 shows the Visual Basic functions that perform data-type conversions. Actually, you will have to convert between datatypes quite often now that VB doesn't do it for you.

TABLE 5.3:   Datatype Conversion Functions

FUNCTION	CONVERTS ITS ARGUMENT TO
CBool	Boolean
CByte	Byte
CChar	Unicode character
CDate	Date
CDbl	Double
CDec	Decimal
CInt	Integer (4-byte integer, Int32)
CLng	Long (8-byte integer, Int64)
CObj	Object
CShort	Short (2-byte integer, Int16)
CSng	Single
CStr	String

Part II

To convert the variable initialized as:

```
Dim A As Integer
```

to a Double, use the function:

```
Dim B As Double
B = CDbl(A)
```

Suppose you have declared two integers, as follows:

```
Dim A As Integer, B As Integer
A = 23
B = 7
```

The result of the operation *A / B* will be a double value. The following statement:

```
Console.Write(A / B)
```

displays the value 3.28571428571429. The result is a double, which provides the greatest possible accuracy. If you attempt to assign the result to a variable that hasn't been declared as Double, and the Strict option is On, then VB .NET will generate an error message. No other datatype can accept this value without loss of accuracy.

As a reminder, the Short datatype is equivalent to the old Integer type, and the CShort() function converts its argument to an Int16 value. The Integer datatype is represented by 4 bytes (32 bits), and to convert a value to Int32 type, use the CInt() function. Finally, the CLng() function converts its argument to an Int64 value.

You can also use the CType() function to convert a variable or expression from one type to another. Let's say the variable *A* has been declared as String and holds the value "34.56." The following statement converts the value of the *A* variable to a Decimal value and uses it in a calculation:

```
Dim A As String = "34.56"
Dim B As Double
B = CType(A, Double) / 1.14
```

The conversion is necessary only if the Strict option is On, but it's a good practice to perform your conversions explicitly. The following section explains what may happen if your code relies to implicit conversions.

Widening and Narrowing Conversions

In some situations, VB .NET will convert datatypes automatically, but not always. Let's say you have declared and initialized two variables, an integer and a double, with the following statements:

```
Dim count As Integer = 99
Dim pi As Double = 3.1415926535897931
```

If the Strict option is On and you attempt to assign the value of the *pi* variable to the *count* variable, the compiler will generate an error message to the effect that you can't convert a double to an integer. The exact message is

```
Option Strict disallows implicit conversions from Double to _
   Integer
```

VB6 TO VB .NET

You will probably see this message many times, especially if you're a VB6 programmer. In the past, VB would store the value 3 to the *count* variable and proceed. If you weren't careful, you'd lose significant decimal digits and might not even know it. This implicit conversion results in loss of accuracy, and VB .NET doesn't perform it by default. This is a typical example of the pitfalls of turning off the Strict option.

When the Strict option is On, VB .NET will perform conversions that do not result in loss of accuracy (precision), or magnitude. These conversions are called *widening* conversions, as opposed to the *narrowing* conversions. When you assign an Integer value to a Double variable, no accuracy or magnitude is lost. On the other hand, when you assign a Double value to an Integer variable, then some accuracy is lost (the decimal digits must be truncated). Normally, you must convert the Double value to an Integer value and then assign it to an Integer variable:

```
count = CInt(pi)
```

This is a narrowing conversion (from a value with greater accuracy or magnitude to a value with smaller accuracy or magnitude), and it's not performed automatically by VB .NET. Table 5.4 summarizes the widening conversions VB .NET will perform for you automatically.

TABLE 5.4: VB .NET Widening Conversions

ORIGINAL DATATYPE	WIDER DATATYPE
Any type	Object
Byte	Short, Integer, Long, Decimal, Single, Double
Short	Integer, Long, Decimal, Single, Double
Integer	Long, Decimal, Single, Double
Long	Decimal, Single, Double
Decimal	Single, Double
Single	Double
Double	none
Char	String

If the Strict option is off (the default value), the compiler will allow you to assign a Long variable to an Integer variable. Should the Long variable contain a value that exceeds the range of values of the Integer datatype, then you'll end up with a runtime error. Of course, you can avoid the runtime error with the appropriate error-handling code. If the Strict option is on, the compiler will point out all the statements that may cause similar runtime errors, and you can re-evaluate your choice of variable types. You can also turn on the Strict option temporarily to see the compiler's warnings, then turn it off again.

User-Defined Datatypes

In the previous sections, we assumed that applications create variables to store individual values. As a matter of fact, most programs store sets of data of different types. For example, a program for balancing your checkbook must store several pieces of information for each check: the check's number, amount, date, and so on. All these pieces of information are necessary to process the checks, and ideally, they should be stored together.

A structure for storing multiple values (of the same or different type) is called a *record,* or *structure.* For example, each check in a checkbook-balancing application is stored in a separate record, as shown in Figure 5.2. When you recall a given check, you need all the information stored in the record.

Record Structure

Check Number	Check Date	Check Amount	Check Paid To

Array Of Records

275	04/12/01	104.25	Gas Co.
276	04/12/01	48.76	Books
277	04/14/01	200.00	VISA
278	04/21/01	430.00	Rent

FIGURE 5.2: Pictorial representation of a record

To define a record in VB .NET, use the `Structure` statement, which has the following syntax:

```
Structure structureName
    Dim variable1 As varType
    Dim variable2 As varType
    ...
    Dim variablen As varType
End Structure
```

varType can be any of the datatypes supported by the framework. The `Dim` statement can be replaced by the `Private` or `Public` access modifiers. For structures, `Dim` is equivalent to `Public`.

After this declaration, you have in essence created a new datatype that you can use in your application. *structureName* can be used anywhere you'd use any of the base types (integers, doubles, and so on). You can declare variables of this type and manipulate them as you manipulate all other variables (with a little extra typing). The declaration for the record structure shown in Figure 5.2 is

```
Structure CheckRecord
    Dim CheckNumber As Integer
    Dim CheckDate As Date
    Dim CheckAmount As Single
    Dim CheckPaidTo As String
End Structure
```

This declaration must appear outside any procedure; you can't declare a `Structure` in a subroutine or function. The `CheckRecord` structure is a new datatype for your application. To declare variables of this new type, use a statement such as this one:

```
Dim check1 As CheckRecord, check2 As CheckRecord
```

To assign a value to one of these variables, you must separately assign a value to each one of its components (they are called *fields*), which can be accessed by combining the name of the variable and the name of a field separated by a period, as follows:

```
check1.CheckNumber = 275
```

Actually, as soon as you type the period following the variable's name, a list of all members to the CheckRecord structure will appear, as shown in Figure 5.3. Notice that the structure supports a few members on its own. You didn't write any code for the Equals, GetType, and ToString members, but they're standard members of any Structure object and you can use them in your code. Both the GetType and ToString methods will return a string like "ProjectName.FormName+CheckRecord."

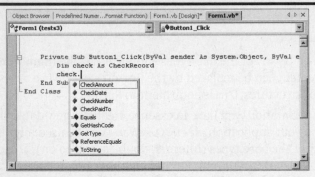

FIGURE 5.3:   Variables of custom types expose their members as properties.

You can think of the record as an object and its fields as properties. Here are the assignment statements for a check:

```
check2.CheckNumber = 275
check2.CheckDate = #09/12/2001#
check2.CheckAmount = 104.25
check2.CheckPaidTo = "Gas Co."
```

You can also create *arrays of records* with a statement such as the following (arrays are discussed later in this chapter):

```
Dim Checks(100) As CheckRecord
```

Each element in this array is a `CheckRecord` record and holds all the fields of a given check. To access the fields of the third element of the array, use the following notation:

```
Checks(2).CheckNumber = 275
Checks(2).CheckDate = #09/12/2001#
Checks(2).CheckAmount = 104.25
Checks(2).CheckPaidTo = "Gas Co."
```

All datatypes expose the Equals method, which compares an instance of a datatype (a integer variable, for example) to another instance of the same type. This is a trivial operation for simple datatypes, as you can compare the two variables directly. The Equals method can also compare two Structure variables and return True if all of their fields match. If a single field differs, the two objects represented by the variables are not identical. Use this method to compare variables declared as custom structures to avoid comparing all their members. Let's say you have created two variables of the `CheckRecord` type:

```
Dim c1, c2 As CheckRecord
{ assign values to the c1 and c2 variables }
If c1.Equals(c2) Then
    MsgBox "Same"
Else
    MsgBox "Different"
End If
```

Examining Variable Types

Besides setting the types of variables and the functions for converting between types, Visual Basic provides two methods that let you examine the type of a variable. They are the `GetType()` and `GetTypeCode()` methods. The `GetType()` method returns a string with the variable's type ("Int32", "Decimal", and so on). The `GetTypeCode()` method returns a value that identifies the variable's type. The code for the Double datatype is 14. The values returned by the `GetType()` and `GetTypeCode()` methods for all datatypes are shown in Table 5.5.

TABLE 5.5: Variable Types and Type Codes

GetType()	GetTypeCode()	Description
Boolean	3	Boolean value
Byte	6	Byte value (0 to 255)
Char	4	Character
DateTime	16	Date/time value
Decimal	15	Decimal
Double	14	Double-precision floating-point number
Int16	7	2-byte integer (Short)
Int32	9	4-byte integer (Integer)
Int64	11	8-byte integer (Long)
Object		Object (a non-value variable)
SByte	5	Signed byte (–127 to 128)
Single	13	Single-precision floating-point number
String	8	String
UInt16	8	2-byte unsigned integer
UInt32	10	4-byte unsigned integer
UInt64	12	8-byte unsigned integer

Any variable exposes these methods automatically, and you can call them like this:

```
Dim var As Double
Console.WriteLine "The variable's type is " & _
    var.GetType.ToString
```

These functions are used mostly in If structures, like the following one:

```
If var.GetType() Is GetType(System.Double) Then
    { code to handle a Double value }
End If
```

Notice that the code doesn't reference datatype names directly. Instead, it uses the value returned by the GetType() function to retrieve the type of the class System.Double and then compares this value to the variable's type with the Is keyword.

Is It a Number or a String?

Another set of Visual Basic functions returns variables' datatypes, but not the exact type. They return a broader type, such as "numeric" for all numeric datatypes. This is the type you usually need in your code. The following functions are used to validate user input, as well as data stored in files, before you process them.

> **IsNumeric()**   Returns True if its argument is a number (Short, Integer, Long, Single, Double, Decimal). Use this function to determine whether a variable holds a numeric value before passing it to a procedure that expects a numeric value or process it as a number. The following statements keep prompting the user with an InputBox for a numeric value. The user must enter a numeric value, or click the Cancel button to exit. As long as the user enters nonnumeric values, the Input Box pops up and prompts for a numeric value:

```
Dim strAge as String = "$"
Dim Age As Integer
While Not IsNumeric(strAge)
    strAge = InputBox("Please enter your age")
End While
```

The variable *strAge* is initialized to a nonnumeric value so that the While...End While loop will be executed at least once. You can use any value in the place of the dollar sign, as long as it's not a valid numeric value.

> **IsDate()**   Returns True if its argument is a valid date (or time). The following expressions return True, because they all represent valid dates:

```
IsDate(#10/12/2010#)
IsDate("10/12/2010")
IsDate("October 12, 2010")
```

If the date expression includes the day name, as in the following expression, the IsDate() function will return False:

```
IsDate("Sat. October 12, 2010")        ' FALSE
```

> **IsArray()**   Returns True if its argument is an array.

IsDBNull()   Detects whether an object variable has been initialized or is a DBNull value. This function is equivalent to the `IsNull()` function of VB6.

IsReference()   Returns True if its argument is an object. This function is equivalent to the `IsObject()` function of VB6.

Why Declare Variables?

None of the previous versions of Visual Basic enforced variable declaration, which was a good thing for the beginner programmer. When you want to slap together a "quick and dirty" program, the last thing you need is someone telling you to decide which variables you're going to use and to declare them before using them.

Let's examine the side effects of using undeclared variables in your application. To be able to get by without declaring your variables, you must set the Explicit option to Off. Let's assume you're using the following statements to convert German marks to U.S. dollars:

```
DM2USD = 1.562
USDollars = amount * DM2USD
```

The first time your code refers to the *DM2USD* variable name, Visual Basic creates a new variable and then uses it as if it was declared.

Suppose the variable *DM2USD* appears in many places in your application. If in one of these places you type **DM2UDS** instead of **DM2USD** and the program doesn't enforce variable declaration, the compiler will create a new variable, assign it the value zero, and then use it. Any amount converted with the *DM2UDS* variable will be zero! If the application enforces variable declaration, the compiler will complain (the *DM2UDS* variable hasn't been declared), and you will catch the error.

A Variable's Scope

In addition to its type, a variable also has a scope. The *scope* (or *visibility*) of a variable is the section of the application that can see and manipulate the variable. If a variable is declared within a procedure, only the code in the specific procedure has access to that variable. This variable doesn't exist for the rest of the application. When the variable's scope is limited to a procedure, it's called *local*.

Suppose you're coding the Click event of a Button to calculate the sum of all even numbers in the range 0 to 100. One possible implementation is shown in Listing 5.3.

Listing 5.3: Summing Even Numbers

```
Private Sub Button1_Click(ByVal sender As Object, _
                ByVal e As System.EventArguments)
    Dim i As Integer
    Dim Sum As Integer
    For i = 0 to 100 Step 2
        Sum = Sum + i
    Next
    MsgBox "The sum is " & Sum
End Sub
```

The variables *i* and *Sum* are local to the Button1_Click() procedure. If you attempt to set the value of the *Sum* variable from within another procedure, Visual Basic will complain that the variable hasn't been declared. (Or, if you have turned off the Explicit option, it will create another *Sum* variable, initialize it to zero, and then use it. But this won't affect the variable *Sum* in the Button1_Click() subroutine.) The *Sum* variable is said to have *procedure-level* scope. It's visible within the procedure and invisible outside the procedure.

Sometimes, however, you'll need to use a variable with a broader scope, such as one whose value is available to all procedures within the same file. In principle, you could declare all variables outside the procedures that use them, but this would lead to problems. Every procedure in the file would have access to the variable, and you would need to be extremely careful not to change the value of a variable without good reason. Variables that are needed by a single procedure (such as loop counters) should be declared in that procedure.

A new type of scope was introduced with VB .NET: the *block-level* scope. Variables introduced in a block of code, such as an If statement or a loop, are local to the block but invisible outside the block.

Another type of scope is the *module-level* scope. Variables declared outside any procedure in a module are visible from within all procedures in the same module, but they're invisible outside the module. Variables with a module-level scope can be set from within any procedure, so you should try to minimize the number of such variables. Setting many variables from within many procedures can seriously complicate the debugging of the application. You can write procedures that don't accept any arguments—they simply act on module-level variables. Even though they may simplify small projects, too many variables with module-level scope reduce the maintainability and readability of large projects.

Let's say you're writing a text-editing application that provides the usual Save and Save As commands. The Save As command prompts the user for the filename in which the text will be stored. The Save command, however, must remember the name of the file used with the most recent Save As command, so that it can save the text to the same file. It must also remember the name of the file that was read most recently, so that it can save the text back to the same file. The path of the file is needed from within three separate procedures, so it must be saved in a variable with module-level scope: The Open procedure should be able to set this variable, the Save As procedure should be able to either read or set it, and the Save procedure should be able to read it. This is a typical example of a variable with module-level scope.

Finally, in some situations the entire application must access a certain variable. In this case, the variable must be declared as Public. Public variables have a *global* scope; they are visible from any part of the application. To declare a Public variable, use the Public statement in place of the Dim statement. Moreover, you can't declare Public variables in a procedure. If you have multiple forms in your application and you want the code in one form to see a certain variable in another form, you can use the Public modifier. You can also make a control on a form visible outside its own form, by setting its Modifier property to Public. Setting this property causes VB to insert the Public keyword in the declaration of the control.

The Public keyword makes the variable available not only to the entire project, but also to all projects that reference the current project. If you want your variables to be public within a project (in other words, available to all procedures in any module in the project) but invisible to referencing projects, use the Friend keyword in the declaration of the module. Variables that you want to use throughout your project, but not have available to other projects that reference the current one, should be declared as Friend. There is no way to make some of the Public variables available to the referencing projects.

So, why do we need so many different types of scope? You'll develop a better understanding of scope and which type of scope to use for each variable as you get involved in larger projects. In general, you should try to limit the scope of your variables as much as possible. If all variables were declared within procedures, then you could use the same name for storing a temporary value in each procedure and be sure that one procedure's variables don't interfere with those of another procedure, even if you use the same name. Not that you can run out of variable names, but names like *tempString, amount, total,* and so on are quite common. All loop counters should also be local to the procedure that uses them. The variable *counter* in the following loop should never be declared outside the procedure:

```
For counter = 1 To 100
    { statements }
Next
```

Procedure-level variables are necessary, but you should try to minimize their use. If a variable looks like a good candidate for procedure-level scope, see if you can implement the code with two or more local-level scope variables. Many procedure-level variables can be reduced to local-level variables if they're used by a couple of functions only. You can pass their values from one function to the other and avoid the creation of a new procedure-level variable.

The Lifetime of a Variable

In addition to type and scope, variables have a *lifetime*, which is the period for which they retain their value. Variables declared as Public exist for the lifetime of the application. Local variables, declared within procedures with the Dim or Private statement, live as long as the procedure. When the procedure finishes, the local variables cease to exist and the allocated memory is returned to the system. Of course, the same procedure can be called again. In this case, the local variables are recreated and initialized again. If a procedure calls another, its local variables retain their values while the called procedure is running.

You also can force a local variable to preserve its value between procedure calls with the Static keyword. Suppose the user of your application can enter numeric values at any time. One of the tasks performed by the application is to track the average of the numeric values. Instead of adding all the values each time the user adds a new value and dividing by the count, you can keep a running total with the function RunningAvg(), which is shown in Listing 5.4.

Listing 5.4: Calculations with Global Variables

```
Function RunningAvg(ByVal newValue As Double) As Double
    CurrentTotal = CurrentTotal + newValue
    TotalItems = TotalItems + 1
    RunningAvg = CurrentTotal / TotalItems
End Function
```

You must declare the variables *CurrentTotal* and *TotalItems* outside the function so that their values are preserved between calls. Alternatively, you can declare them in the function with the Static keyword, as in Listing 5.5.

Listing 5.5: Calculations with Local Static Variables

```
Function RunningAvg(ByVal newValue As Double) As Double
    Static CurrentTotal As Double
    Static TotalItems As Integer
    CurrentTotal = CurrentTotal + newValue
    TotalItems = TotalItems + 1
    RunningAvg = CurrentTotal / TotalItems
End Function
```

The advantage of using static variables is that they help you minimize the number of total variables in the application. All you need is the running average, which the RunningAvg() function provides without making its variables visible to the rest of the application. Therefore, you don't risk changing the variables' values from within other procedures.

VB6 TO VB .NET

In VB6 you could declare all the variables in a procedure as static by prefixing the procedure definition with the keyword Static. This option is no longer available with VB .NET: The Static modifier does not apply to procedures.

Variables declared in a module outside any procedure take effect when the form is loaded and cease to exist when the form is unloaded. If the form is loaded again, its variables are initialized, as if it's being loaded for the first time.

CONSTANTS

Some variables don't change value during the execution of a program. These are *constants* that appear many times in your code. For instance, if your program does math calculations, the value of pi (3.14159...) may appear many times. Instead of typing the value 3.14159 over and over again, you can define a constant, name it *pi*, and use the name of the constant in your code. The statement

```
circumference = 2 * pi * radius
```

is much easier to understand than the equivalent

```
circumference = 2 * 3.14159 * radius
```

You could declare *pi* as a variable, but constants are preferred for two reasons:

Constants don't change value.   This is a safety feature. Once a constant has been declared, you can't change its value in subsequent statements, so you can be sure that the value specified in the constant's declaration will take effect in the entire program.

Constants are processed faster than variables.   When the program is running, the values of constants don't have to be looked up. The compiler substitutes constant names with their values, and the program executes faster.

The manner in which you declare constants is similar to the manner in which you declare variables, except that in addition to supplying the constant's name, you must also supply a value, as follows:

```
Const constantname As type = value
```

Constants also have a scope and can be Public or Private. The constant *pi*, for instance, is usually declared in a module as Public so that every procedure can access it:

```
Public Const pi As Double = 3.14159265358979
```

The name of the constant follows the same rules as variable names. The constant's value is a literal value or a simple expression composed of numeric or string constants and operators. You can't use functions in declaring constants. The best way to define the value of the *pi* variable is to use the pi member of the Math class:

```
pi = Math.pi
```

However, you can't use this assignment in the *constant declaration.* You must supply the actual value.

Constants can be strings, too, like these:

```
Const ExpDate = #31/12/1997#
Const ValidKey = "A567dfe"
```

Visual Basic uses constants extensively to define method arguments and control properties. The value of a CheckBox control, for instance, can be `CheckState.Checked` or `CheckState.UnChecked`. If the CheckBox control's ThreeState property is True, it can have yet another value, which is `CheckState.Intederminate`. These constants correspond to Integer values, but you don't need to know what these values are. You see only the names of the constants in the Properties window. If you type the expression:

```
CheckBox1.CheckState =
```

a list of all possible values of the CheckState property will appear as soon as you type the equal sign, and you can select one from the list.

VB .NET recognizes numerous constants, which are grouped according to the property they apply to. Each property's possible values form an *enumeration,* and the editor knows which enumeration applies to each property as you type. As a result, you don't have to memorize any of the constant names or look up their names. They're right there as you type, and their names make them self-explanatory. Notice that the name of the constant is prefixed by the name of the enumeration it belongs to.

Constant declarations may include other constants. In math calculations, the value $2 \times$ pi is almost as common as the value pi. You can declare these two values as constants:

```
Public Const pi As Double = 3.14159265358979
Public Const pi2 As Double = 2 * pi
```

ARRAYS

A standard structure for storing data in any programming language is the array. Whereas individual variables can hold single entities, such as one number, one date, or one string, *arrays* can hold sets of data of the same type (a set of numbers, a series of dates, and so on). An array has a name, as does a variable, and the values stored in it can be accessed by an index.

For example, you could use the variable *Salary* to store a person's salary:

```
Salary = 34000
```

But what if you wanted to store the salaries of 16 employees? You could either declare 16 variables—*Salary1, Salary2,* up to *Salary16*—or you could declare an array with 16 elements. An array is similar to a variable: it has a name and multiple values. Each value is identified by an index (an Integer value) that follows the array's name in parentheses. Each different value is an *element* of the array. If the array *Salaries* holds the salaries of 16 employees, the element Salaries(0) holds the salary of the first employee, the element Salaries(1) holds the salary of the second employee, and so on up to the element Salaries(15).

VB6 TO VB .NET

The indexing of arrays in VB .NET starts at zero, and you can't change this behavior, because the Option Base statement, which allowed you to specify whether the indexing of the array would start at 0 or 1, is no longer supported by VB .NET. Whether you like it or not, your arrays must start at index zero. If you don't feel comfortable with the notion of zero being the first element, you can increase the dimensions of your arrays by one and ignore the 0th element.

Declaring Arrays

Unlike simple variables, arrays must be declared with the Dim (or Public, or Private) statement followed by the name of the array and the index of the last element in the array in parentheses—for example,

```
Dim Salaries(15) As Integer
```

As I said before, *Salaries* is the name of an array that holds 16 values (the salaries of the 16 employees), with indices ranging from 0 to 15. Salaries(0) is the first person's salary, Salaries(1) the second person's salary, and so on. All you have to do is remember who corresponds to each salary, but even this data can be handled by another array. To do this, you'd declare another array of 16 elements as follows:

```
Dim Names(15) As String
```

and then assign values to the elements of both arrays:

```
Names(0) = "Joe Doe"
Salaries(0) = 34000
Names(1) = "Beth York"
Salaries(1) = 62000
...
Names(15) = "Peter Smack"
Salaries(15) = 10300
```

This structure is more compact and more convenient than having to hard-code the names of employees and their salaries in variables.

All elements in an array have the same datatype. Of course, when the datatype is Object, the individual elements can contain different kinds of data (objects, strings, numbers, and so on).

Arrays, like variables, are not limited to the basic datatypes. You can declare arrays that hold any type of data, including objects. The following array holds colors, which can be used later in the code as arguments to the various functions that draw shapes:

```
Dim colors(2) As Color
colors(0) = Color.BurlyWood
colors(1) = Color.AliceBlue
colors(2) = Color.Sienna
```

The Color object represents colors, and among the properties it exposes are the names of the colors it recognizes. The Color object recognizes 140 color names (as opposed to the 16 color names of VB6).

As a better technique to store names and salaries together in an array, create a Structure and then declare an array of this type. The following structure holds names and salaries:

```
Structure Employee
    Dim Name As String
    Dim Salary As Single
End Structure
```

Insert this declaration in a form's code file, outside any procedure. Then create an array of the Employee type:

```
Dim Emps(15) As Employee
```

Each elements in the *Emps* array exposes two fields, and you can assign values to them with statements like the following ones:

```
Emps(2).Name = "Beth York"
Emps(2).Salary = 62000
```

The advantage of storing related pieces of information to a structure is that you can access all the items with a single index. The code is more compact, and you need not maintain multiple arrays. You can also use the new ArrayList and HashTable collections to store sets of data.

Initializing Arrays

Just as you can initialize variables in the same line where you declare them, you can initialize arrays, too, with the following constructor:

```
Dim arrayname() As type = {entry0, entry1, … entryN}
```

Here's an example that initializes an array of strings:

```
Dim names() As String = {"Joe Doe", "Peter Smack"}
```

This statement is equivalent to the following statements, which declare an array with two elements and then set their values:

```
Dim names(1) As String
names(0) = "Joe Doe"
names(1) = "Peter Smack"
```

The number of elements in the curly brackets following the array's declaration determines the dimensions of the array, and you can't add new elements to the array without resizing it. If you need to resize the array in your code dynamically, you must use the ReDim statement, as described in the section "Dynamic Arrays," later in this chapter. However, you can change the *value* of the existing elements at will, as you would with any other array. The following declaration initializes an array of Color objects in a single statement:

```
Dim Colors() As Color = {color.BurlyWood, color.AliceBlue, _
                         color.Sienna, color.Azure, _
                         color.Fuchsia, Color.White}
```

Array Limits

The first element of an array has index 0. The number that appears in parentheses in the Dim statement is one less than the array's total capacity and is the array's upper limit (or upper bound).

The index of the last element of an array (its upper bound) is given by the function UBound(), which accepts as argument the array's name. For the array

```
Dim myArray(19) As Integer
```

its upper bound is 19, and its capacity is 20 elements. The function UBound() is also exposed as a method of the Array object, and it's the GetUpperBound method. It returns the same value as the UBound() function. The GetLowerBound method returns the index of the array's first element, which is always zero anyway. As you will see, arrays can have multiple dimensions, so these two methods require that you specify the dimensions whose limits you want to read as arguments. For one-dimensional arrays, like the ones discussed in this section, this argument is zero. Multidimensional arrays are discussed later in this chapter.

Let's say you need an array to store 20 names. Declare it with the following statement:

```
Dim names(19) As String
```

The first element is names(0), and the last is names(19). If you execute the following statements, the values in bold will appear in the Output window:

```
Console.WriteLine(names.GetLowerBound(0))
```
0
```
Console.WriteLine(names.GetUpperBound(0))
```
19

To assign a value to the first and last element of the *names* array, use the following statements:

```
names(0) = "First entry"
names(19) = "Last entry"
```

If you want to iterate through the array's elements, use a loop like the following one:

```
Dim i As Integer, myArray(19) As Integer
For i = 0 To myArray.GetUpperBound(0)
```

```
myArray(i) = i * 1000
Next
```

The actual number of elements in an array is given by the expression `myArray.GetUpperBound(0) + 1`. You can also use the array's Length property to retrieve the count of elements. The following statement will print the number of elements in the array *myArray* on the Output window:

```
Console.WriteLine(myArray.Length)
```

Multidimensional Arrays

One-dimensional arrays, such as those presented so far, are good for storing long sequences of one-dimensional data (such as names or temperatures). But how would you store a list of cities *and* their average temperatures in an array? Or names and scores, years and profits, or data with more than two dimensions, such as products, prices, and units in stock? In some situations you will want to store sequences of multidimensional data. You can store the same data more conveniently in an array of as many dimensions as needed. Figure 5.4 shows two one-dimensional arrays—one of them with city names, the other with temperatures. The name of the third city would be `City(2)`, and its temperature would be `Temperature(2)`.

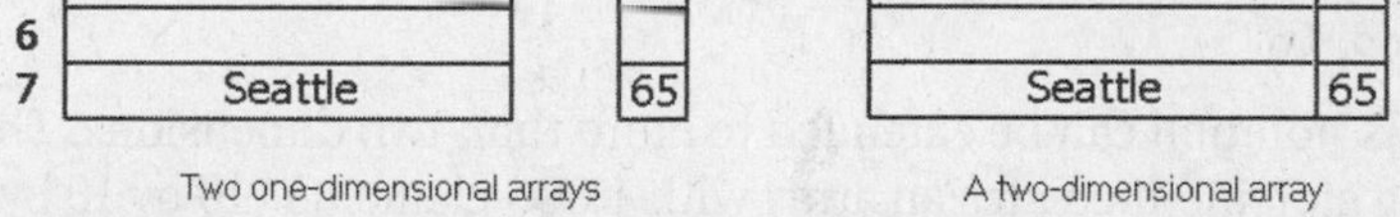

	Cities(7)	Temperatures(7)	Temperatures(7, 1)	
0	San Francisco	78	San Francisco	78
1	Los Angeles	86	Los Angeles	86
2				
3				
4				
5				
6				
7	Seattle	65	Seattle	65

       Two one-dimensional arrays   A two-dimensional array

FIGURE 5.4:   A two-dimensional array and the two equivalent one-dimensional arrays

A two-dimensional array has two indices. The first identifies the row (the order of the city in the array), and the second identifies the column (city or temperature). To access the name and temperature of the third city in the two-dimensional array, use the following indices:

```
Temperatures(2, 0)    ' the third city's name
Temperatures(2, 1)    ' the third city's average temperature
```

The benefit of using multidimensional arrays is that they're conceptually easier to manage. Suppose you're writing a game and want to track the positions of certain pieces on a board. Each square on the board is identified by two numbers (its horizontal and vertical coordinates). The obvious structure for tracking the board's squares is a two-dimensional array, in which the first index corresponds to the row number and the second corresponds to the column number. The array could be declared as follows:

```
Dim Board(9, 9) As Integer
```

When a piece is moved from the square on the first row and first column to the square on the third row and fifth column, you assign the value 0 to the element that corresponds to the initial position:

```
Board(0, 0) = 0
```

and you assign 1 to the square to which it was moved, to indicate the new state of the board:

```
Board(2, 4) = 1
```

To find out if a piece is on the top-left square, you'd use the following statement:

```
If Board(0, 0) = 1 Then
    { piece found }
Else
    { empty square }
End If
```

This notation can be extended to more than two dimensions. The following statement creates an array with 1,000 elements (10 by 10 by 10):

```
Dim Matrix(9, 9, 9)
```

You can think of a three-dimensional array as a cube made up of overlaid two-dimensional arrays, such as the one shown in Figure 5.5.

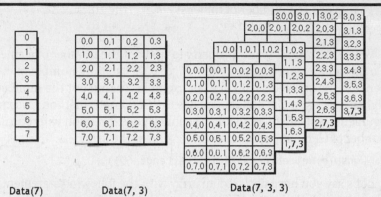

Data(7)   Data(7, 3)   Data(7, 3, 3)

FIGURE 5.5: Pictorial representations of one-, two-, and three-dimensional arrays

It is possible to initialize a multidimensional array with a single statement, just as you do with a one-dimensional array. You must insert enough commas in the parentheses following the array name to indicate the array's rank (the number of commas is one less than the actual dimensions). The following statements initialize a two-dimensional array and then print a couple of its elements:

```
Dim a(,) As Integer = {{10, 20, 30}, _
                        {11, 21, 31}, _
                        {12, 22, 32}}
Console.WriteLine(a(0, 1))        ' will print 20
Console.WriteLine(a(2, 2))        ' will print 32
```

You should break the line that initializes the dimensions of the array into multiple lines to make your code easier to read. Just insert the line-continuation character at the end of each continued line:

```
Dim a(,) As Integer = {{10, 20, 30}, _
                        {11, 21, 31}, _
                        {12, 22, 32}}
```

If the array has more than one dimension, you can find out the number of dimensions with the Array.Rank property. Let's say you have declared an array for storing names as salaries with the following statements:

```
Dim Salaries(1,99) As Object
```

To find out the number of dimensions, use the statement:

```
Salaries.Rank
```

When using the Length property to find out the number of elements in a multidimensional array, you will get back the total number of elements in the array—2 × 100, for our example. To find out the number of elements in a specific dimension, use the GetLength method, passing as argument a specific dimension. The following expression will return the number of elements in the first dimension of the array:

```
Console.WriteLine(Salaries.GetLength(0))
```

Let's say you have declared an array with the following statement to store player statistics for 15 players, and there are five values per player:

```
Dim Statistics(14, 4) As Integer
```

The following statements will return the values shown beneath them, in bold:

```
Console.WriteLine(Statistics.Rank)
2                         ' dimensions in array
Console.WriteLine(Statistics.Length)
75                        ' total elements in array
Console.WriteLine(Statistics.GetLength(0))
15                        ' elements in first dimension
Console.WriteLine(Statistics.GetLength(1))
5                         ' elements in second dimension
Console.WriteLine(Statistics.GetUpperBound(0))
14                        ' last index in the first dimension
Console.WriteLine(Statistics.GetUpperBound(1))
4                         ' last index in the second dimension
```

Dynamic Arrays

Sometimes you may not know how large to make an array. Instead of making it large enough to hold the (anticipated) maximum number of data (which means that, on the average, most of the array may be empty), you can declare a *dynamic array*. The size of a dynamic array can vary during the course of the program. Or you might need an array until the user has entered a bunch of data and the application has processed it and displayed the results. Why keep all the data in memory when it is no longer needed? With a dynamic array, you can discard the data and return the resources it occupied to the system.

To create a dynamic array, declare it as usual with the Dim statement (or Public or Private) but don't specify its dimensions:

```
Dim DynArray() As Integer
```

Later in the program, when you know how many elements you want to store in the array, use the ReDim statement to redimension the array, this time to its actual size. In the following example, *UserCount* is a user-entered value:

```
ReDim DynArray(UserCount)
```

The ReDim statement can appear only in a procedure. Unlike the Dim statement, ReDim is executable—it forces the application to carry out an action at runtime. Dim statements aren't executable, and they can appear outside procedures.

A dynamic array also can be redimensioned to multiple dimensions. Declare it with the Dim statement outside any procedure as follows:

```
Dim Matrix() As Double
```

and then use the ReDim statement in a procedure to declare a three-dimensional array:

```
ReDim Matrix(9, 9, 9)
```

Note that the ReDim statement can't change the type of the array—that's why the As clause is missing from the ReDim statement. Moreover, subsequent ReDim statements can change the bounds of the array *Matrix* but not the number of its dimensions. For example, you can't use the statement ReDim Matrix(99, 99) later in your code. Once an array has been redimensioned once, its number of dimensions can't change. In the preceding example, the *Matrix* array will remain three-dimensional through the course of the application.

NOTE

The ReDim statement can by issued only from within a procedure. In addition, the array to be redimensioned must be visible from within the procedure that calls the ReDim statement.

The *Preserve* Keyword

Each time you execute the ReDim statement, all the values currently stored in the array are lost. Visual Basic resets the values of the elements as if they were just declared. (It resets numeric elements to zero and String elements to empty strings.)

In many situations, when you resize an array, you no longer care about the data in it. You can, however, change the size of the array without losing its data. The ReDim statement recognizes the Preserve keyword, which forces it to resize the array without discarding the existing data. For example, you can enlarge an array by one element without losing the values of the existing elements by using the UBound() function as follows:

```
ReDim Preserve DynamicArray(UBound(DynArray) + 1)
```

If the array *DynamicArray* held 12 elements, this statement would add one element to the array, the element DynamicArray(12). The values of the elements with indices 0 through 11 wouldn't change. The UBound() function returns the largest available index (the number of elements) in a one-dimensional array. Similarly, the LBound() function returns the smallest index. If an array were declared with the statement:

```
Dim Grades(49) As Integer
```

then the functions LBound(Grades) and UBound(Grades) would return the values 0 and 49.

VARIABLES AS OBJECTS

As you have understood by now, variables are objects. This shouldn't come as a surprise, but it's an odd concept for programmers with no experience in object-oriented programming. We haven't covered objects and classes formally yet, but you have a good idea of what an object is. It's an entity that exposes some functionality by means of properties and methods. The TextBox control is an object, and it exposes the Text property, which allows you to read, or set, the text on the control. Any name followed by a period and another name signifies an object. The "other name" is a property or method of the object.

At this point, I'll ask you to take a leap forward. Things will become quite clear when you learn more about objects later in the book, but I couldn't postpone this discussion; you need a good understanding of variables to move on. If you want, you can come back and reread this section. In the meantime, I'll attempt to explain through examples how VB .NET handles variables. It's a simplified view of objects and, at points, I won't even use proper terminology.

So, What's an Object?

An *object* is a collection of data and code. You don't see the code, and you'll never have to change it—unless you've written it, of course. An Integer variable, `intVar`, is an object because it has a value and some properties and methods. Properties and methods are implemented as functions. The method `intVar.ToString` for instance, returns the numeric value held in the variable as a string, so that you can use it in string operations. In other words, an Integer variable is an object that knows about itself. It knows that it holds a whole number; it knows how to convert itself to a string; it knows the minimum and maximum values it can store (properties MinValue and MaxValue); and so on. In the past, a variable was just a named location in the memory. Now, it's a far more complex structure with its own "intelligence." This intelligence consists of code that implements some of the most common actions you're expected to perform on its value. The same is true for strings, even characters. Actually, the Char datatype exposes a lot of very useful properties. In the past, programmers wrote their own functions to determine whether a character is a numeric digit or a letter, whether it's in upper- or lowercase, and so forth. With the Char datatype, all this functionality comes for free. The IsDigit and IsLetter methods return True if the character is a digit or a letter, respectively, False otherwise. The Date datatype even has a property called IsLeapYear.

The main advantage of exposing so much functionality through the datatypes, instead of individual functions, is that you don't have to learn the names of all these functions. Now, you can type the period following a variable's name and see the list of members it exposes. The alternative would be to look up the documentation and try to locate a function that provides the desired functionality.

Another good reason for attaching so much functionality to the datatypes is that the specific functions are meaningless with other datatypes. Because the IsLeapYear method is so specific to dates, we better contain it in the world of the Date datatype.

How about the code that implements all the functionality built into the variable? The code resides in a *class*. A class is the code that implements the properties and methods of a variable. The class that implements the

Date type is the System.Date class, and it exposes the same functionality as a Date variable. A Date variable is nothing more than an instance of the System.Date class. Here's an example. The Date class exposes the IsLeapYear method, which returns True if a specific year is leap. The expression:

```
System.Class.IsLeapYear(2001)
```

will return False, because 2001 is not a leap year.

If you declare a variable of the Date type, it carries with it all the functionality of the System.Date class. The IsLeapYear method can be applied to a Date variable as well:

```
Dim d1 As Date = #3/4/2001#
MsgBox(d1.IsLeapYear(2001))
```

If you execute these statements, a message box will pop up displaying the string "False." But shouldn't the IsLeapYear method be applied to the *d1* variable? The answer is no, because IsLeapYear is a shared method; it requires an argument. You can use the System.Date class to call the IsLeapMethod:

```
Console.WriteLine(System.Date.IsLeapYear(#2001#)
```

It is even possible to use expressions like the following:

```
Console.WriteLine(#3/4/2001#.IsLeapYear(2001))
```

This expression will return False. Change the year to 2004, and it will return True. The date, even though it's a value, is represented by an instance of the System.Date class. The compiler figures out that the expression between the pound signs is a date and loads an instance of the System.Date class automatically to represent the value. As an expression, I think it's rather ridiculous, but it's a valid expression nevertheless. (An even more perplexing expression is #1/1/1901# .IsLeapYear(2020), but it's also valid.)

Formatting Numbers

The ToString method, exposed by all datatypes except the String datatype, converts a value to the equivalent string and formats it at the same time. You can call the ToString method without any arguments, as we have done so far, to convert any value to a string. The ToString method, however, accepts an argument, which determines how the value will be formatted as a string. For example, you can format a number as currency by prefixing it with the appropriate sign (e.g., the dollar symbol).

Notice that ToString is a method, not a property. It returns a value, which you can assign to another variable or pass as argument to a function like MsgBox(), but the original value is not affected. The ToString method can also format a value if called with the Format argument:

```
ToString(formatString)
```

The *formatString* argument is a format specifier (a string that specifies the exact format to be applied to the variable). This argument can be a specific character that corresponds to a predetermined format (*standard numeric format string*, as it's called) or a string of characters that have special meaning in formatting numeric values (a *picture numeric format string*). Use standard format strings for the most common operations and picture strings to specify unusual formatting requirements. To format the value 9959.95 as a dollar amount, you can use the following standard currency format string:

```
Dim int As Single = 9959.95
Dim strInt As String
strInt = int.ToString("C")
```

or the following picture numeric format string:

```
strInt = int.ToString("$###,###.00")
```

Both statements will format the value as "$9,959.95." The "C" argument in the first example means currency and formats the numeric value as currency. The picture format string is made up of literals and characters that have special meaning in formatting. The dollar sign has no special meaning and will appear as is. The # symbol is a digit placeholder. All # symbols will be replaced by numeric digits, starting from the right. If the number has fewer digits than specified in the string, the extra symbols to the left will be ignored. The comma tells the Format function to insert a comma between thousands. The period is the decimal point, which is followed by two more digit placeholders. Unlike the # sign, the 0 is a special placeholder; if there are not enough digits in the number for all the zeros you've specified, a 0 will appear in the place of the missing digits. If the original value had been 9959.9, for example, the last statement would have formatted it as $9,959.90. If you used the # placeholder instead, then the string returned by the Format method would have a single decimal digit.

Standard Numeric Format Strings

VB .NET recognizes the standard numeric format strings shown in
Table 5.6.

TABLE 5.6:   Standard Numeric Format Strings

FORMAT CHARACTER	DESCRIPTION	EXAMPLE
C or c	Currency	12345.67.ToString("C") returns $12,345.67
E or e	Scientific format	12345.67.ToString("E") returns 1.234567E+004
F or f	Fixed-point format	12345.67.ToString("F") returns 12345.67
G or g	General format	Return a value either in fixed-point or scientific format
N or n	Number format	12345.67.ToString("N") returns 12,345.67
X or x	Hexadecimal format	250.ToString("X") returns FA

The format character can be followed by an Integer. If present, the
integer value specifies the number of decimal places that are displayed.
The default accuracy is two decimal digits.

The "C" format string causes the ToString method to return a string
representing the number as a currency value. An integer following the
"C" determines the number of decimal places that are displayed. If no
number is provided, two digits are shown after the decimal separator. The
expression 5596.ToString("c") will return the string "$5,596.00," and
the expression 5596.4499.ToString("c3") will return the string
"$5,596.450."

The fixed-point format returns a number with one or more decimal
digits. The expression (134.5).ToString("f3") will return the value
134.500. I've used the optional parentheses around the value here to
make clear that the number has a decimal point. VB doesn't require that
you supply these parentheses.

NOTE

Notice that not all format strings apply to all datatypes. For example, only Integer values can be converted to hexadecimal format.

Picture Numeric Format Strings

If the format characters listed in Table 5.6 are not adequate for the control you need over the appearance of numeric values, you can provide your own picture format strings. Picture format strings contain special characters that allow you to format your values exactly as you like. Table 5.7 lists the picture formatting characters.

TABLE 5.7: Picture Numeric Format Strings

FORMAT CHARACTER	DESCRIPTION	EFFECT
0	Display zero placeholder	Results in a nonsignificant zero if a number has fewer digits than there are zeros in the format.
#	Display digit placeholder	Replaces the "#" symbol with only significant digits.
.	Decimal point	Displays a "." character.
,	Group separator	Separates number groups; for example, "1,000."
%	Percent notation	Displays a "%" character.
E+0, E-0, e+0, e-0	Exponent notation	Formats the output of exponent notation.
\	Literal character	Used with traditional formatting sequences like "\n" (newline).
" "	Literal string	Displays any string within quotes or apostrophes literally.
;	Section separator	Specifies different output if the numeric value to be formatted is positive, negative, or zero.

Part II

Formatting Dates

To format dates, use the format characters shown in Table 5.8.

TABLE 5.8:   Date Formatting Strings

FORMAT CHARACTER	DESCRIPTION	EFFECT
d	Short date format	MM/dd/yyyy
D	Long date format	dddd, MMMM dd, yyyy
f	Long date followed by short time	dddd, MMMM dd, yyyy HH:mm
F	Long date followed by long time	dddd, MMMM dd, yyyy HH:mm:ss
g	(General) Short date followed by short time	MM/dd/yyyy HH:mm
G	(General) Short date followed by long time	MM/dd/yyyy HH:mm:ss
m or M	Month/day format	MMMM dd
r or R	RFC1123 pattern	ddd, dd MMM yyyy HH:mm:ssGMT
s	Sortable date/time format	yyyy-MM-dd HH:mm:ss
t	Short time format	HH:mm
T	Long time format	HH:mm:ss
u	Universal date/time	yyyy-MM-dd HH:mm:ss
U	Universal sortable date/time format	dddd, MMMM dd, yyyy HH:mm:ss
Y or y	Year month format	MMMM, yyyy

If the variable *birthDate* contains the value #1/1/2000#, the following expressions return the values shown below them, in bold:

```
Console.WriteLine(birthDate.ToString("d"))
```
1/1/2000
```
Console.WriteLine(birthDate.ToString("D"))
```
Saturday, January 01, 2000
```
Console.WriteLine(birthDate.ToString("f"))
```
Saturday, January 01, 2000 12:00 AM

```
Console.WriteLine(birthDate.ToString("s"))
```
2000-01-01T00:00:00
```
Console.WriteLine(birthDate.ToString("U"))
```
Friday, December 31, 1999 10:00:00 PM

FLOW-CONTROL STATEMENTS

What makes programming languages flexible—capable of handling every situation and programming challenge with a relatively small set of commands—is their capability to examine external conditions and act accordingly. Programs aren't monolithic sets of commands that carry out the same calculations every time they are executed. Instead, they adjust their behavior depending on the data supplied; on external conditions, such as a mouse click or the existence of a peripheral; or even abnormal conditions generated by the program itself. For example, a program that calculates averages may work time and again until the user forgets to supply any data. In this case, the program attempts to divide by zero, and it must detect this condition and act accordingly. In effect, the statements discussed in the section are what programs are all about. Without the capability to control the flow of the program, computers would just be bulky calculators. To write programs that react to external events and produce the desired results under all circumstances, you'll have to use the following statements.

Test Structures

An application needs a built-in capability to test conditions and take a different course of action depending on the outcome of the test. Visual Basic provides three such decision structures:

▶ If...Then

▶ If...Then...Else

▶ Select Case

If...Then

The If...Then statement tests the condition specified; if it's True, the program executes the statement(s) that follow. The If structure can have a single-line or a multiple-line syntax. To execute one statement conditionally, use the single-line syntax as follows:

```
If condition Then statement
```

Visual Basic evaluates the *condition*, and if it's True, executes the statement that follows. If the condition is False, the application continues with the statement following the If statement.

You can also execute multiple statements by separating them with colons:

```
If condition Then statement: statement: statement
```

Here's an example of a single-line If statement:

```
If Month(expDate) > 12 Then expYear = expYear + 1: _
                          expMonth = 1
```

You can break this statement into multiple lines by using End If, as shown here:

```
If expDate.Month > 12 Then
    expYear = expYear + 1
    expMonth = 1
End If
```

The Month property of the Date type returns the month of the date to which it's applied as a numeric value. Some programmers prefer the multiple-line syntax of the If...Then statement, even if it contains a single statement, because the code is easier to read.

If...Then...Else

A variation of the If...Then statement is the If...Then...Else statement, which executes one block of statements if the condition is True and another block of statements if the condition is False. The syntax of the If...Then...Else statement is as follows:

```
If condition Then
    statementblock1
Else
    statementblock2
End If
```

Visual Basic evaluates the *condition;* if it's True, VB executes the first block of statements and then jumps to the statement following the End If statement. If the *condition* is False, Visual Basic ignores the first block of statements and executes the block following the Else keyword.

Another variation of the If...Then...Else statement uses several conditions, with the ElseIf keyword:

```
If condition1 Then
    statementblock1
ElseIf condition2 Then
    statementblock2
ElseIf condition3 Then
    statementblock3
Else
    statementblock4
End If
```

You can have any number of ElseIf clauses. The conditions are evaluated from the top, and if one of them is True, the corresponding block of statements is executed. The Else clause will be executed if none of the previous expressions are True. Listing 5.6 is an example of an If statement with ElseIf clauses.

Listing 5.6: Multiple *ElseIf* Statements

```
score = InputBox("Enter score")
If score < 50 Then
    Result = "Failed"
ElseIf score < 75 Then
    Result = "Pass"
ElseIf score < 90 Then
    Result = "Very Good"
Else
    Result = "Excellent"
End If
MsgBox Result
```

Part II

MULTIPLE *IF...THEN* STRUCTURES VERSUS *ELSEIF*

Notice that once a True condition is found, Visual Basic executes the associated statements and skips the remaining clauses. It continues executing the program with the statement immediately after End If. All following ElseIf clauses are skipped, and the code runs a bit faster. That's why you should prefer the complicated structure with ElseIf statements used in Listing 5.6 to this equivalent series of simple If statements:

```
If score < 50 Then
    Result = "Failed"
End If
If score < 75 And score >= 50 Then
    Result = "Pass"
End If
If score < 90 And score > =75 Then
    Result = "Very Good"
End If
If score >= 90 Then
    Result = "Excellent"
End If
```

Visual Basic will evaluate the conditions of all If statements, even if the score is less than 50.

You may have noticed that the order of the comparisons is vital in an If...Then structure that uses ElseIf statements. Had you written the previous code segment with the first two conditions switched, like this:

```
If score < 75 Then
    Result = "Pass"
ElseIf score < 50 Then
    Result = "Failed"
ElseIf score < 90 Then
    Result = "Very Good"
Else
    Result = "Excellent"
End If
```

the results would be quite unexpected. Let's assume that *score* is 49. The code would compare the *score* variable to the value 75. Because 49 is less than 75, it would assign the value "Pass" to the variable *Result,* and then it would skip the remaining clauses. Therefore, a student who made 49 would have passed the test! So be extremely careful and test your code thoroughly if it uses multiple ElseIf clauses.

Select Case

An alternative to the efficient, but difficult-to-read, code of the multiple-ElseIf structure is the Select Case structure, which compares one expression to different values. The advantage of the Select Case statement over multiple If...Then...Else/ElseIf statements is that it makes the code easier to read and maintain.

The Select Case structure tests a single expression, which is evaluated once at the top of the structure. The result of the test is then compared with several values, and if it matches one of them, the corresponding block of statements is executed. Here's the syntax of the Select Case statement:

```
Select Case expression
    Case value1
        statementblock1
    Case value2
        statementblock2

        .

        .

        .

    Case Else
        statementblockN
End Select
```

A practical example based on the Select Case statement is Listing 5.7.

Listing 5.7: Using the *Select Case* Statement

```
Dim Message As String
Select Case Now.DayOfWeek
    Case DayOfWeek.Monday
        message = "Have a nice week"
    Case DayOfWeek.Friday
        message = "Have a nice weekend"
    Case Else
```

```
        message = "Welcome back!"
    End Select
    MsgBox(message)
```

In the listing, the *expression* variable, which is evaluated at the beginning of the statement, is the weekday, as reported by the DayOfWeek property of the Date type. It's a numeric value, but its possible settings are the members of the DayOfWeek enumeration, and you can use the names of these members in your code to make it easier to read. The value of this expression is compared with the values that follow each Case keyword. If they match, the block of statements up to the next Case keyword is executed, and then the program skips to the statement following the End Select statement. The block of the Case Else statement is optional and is executed if none of the previous Case values match the expression. The first two Case statements take care of Fridays and Mondays, and the Case Else statement takes care of the weekdays.

Some Case statements can be followed by multiple values, which are separated by commas. Listing 5.8 is a revised version of the previous example.

Listing 5.8: A *Select Case* Statement with Multiple Cases per Clause

```
    Select Case Now.DayOfWeek
        Case DayOfWeek.Monday
            message = "Have a nice week"
        Case DayOfWeek.Tuesday, DayOfWeek.Wednesday, _
            DayOfWeek.Thursday, DayOfWeek.Friday
            message = "Welcome back!"
        Case DayOfWeek.Friday, _
            DayOfWeek.Saturday, _
            DayOfWeek.Sunday
            message = "Have a nice weekend!"
    End Select
    MsgBox(message)
```

Monday, Friday (and weekends), and the remaining weekdays are handled separately by three Case statements. The second Case statement handles multiple values (all weekdays, except for Monday and Friday). Monday is handled by a separate Case statement. This structure doesn't contain a Case Else statement because all possible values are examined in the Case statements. The DayOfWeek method can't return another value.

TIP

If more than one Case value matches the expression, only the statement block associated with the first matching Case executes.

For comparison, Listing 5.9 contains the equivalent If...Then...Else statements that would implement the example of Listing 5.8.

Listing 5.9: Implemented with *Nested If* Statements

```
If Now.DayOfWeek = DayOfWeek.Monday Then
    message = "Have a nice week"
Else
    If Now.DayOfWeek >= DayOfWeek.Tuesday And _
        Now.DayOfWeek <= DayOfWeek.Friday Then
        message = "Welcome back!"
    Else
        message = "Have a nice weekend!"
    End If
End If
MsgBox(message)
```

To say the least, this coding is verbose. If you attempt to implement a more elaborate Select Case statement with If...Then...Else statements, the code becomes even more difficult to read.

Of course, the Select Case statement can't always substitute for an If...Then structure. The Select Case structure only evaluates the expression at the beginning. By contrast, the If...Then...Else structure can evaluate a different expression for each ElseIf statement, not to mention that you can use more complicated expressions with the If clause.

Loop Structures

Loop structures allow you to execute one or more lines of code repetitively. Many tasks consist of trivial operations that must be repeated over and over again, and looping structures are an important part of any programming language. Visual Basic supports the following loop structures:

▶ For...Next

▶ Do...Loop

▶ While...End While

Part III

For...Next

The For...Next loop is one of the oldest loop structures in programming languages. Unlike the other two loops, the For...Next loop requires that you know how many times the statements in the loop will be executed. The For...Next loop uses a variable (it's called the loop's *counter*) that increases or decreases in value during each repetition of the loop. The For...Next loop has the following syntax:

```
For counter = start To end [Step increment]
    statements
Next [counter]
```

The keywords in the square brackets are optional. The arguments counter, start, end, and increment are all numeric. The loop is executed as many times as required for the counter to reach (or exceed) the end value.

In executing a For...Next loop, Visual Basic completes the following steps:

1. Sets counter equal to *start*.

2. Tests to see if counter is greater than *end*. If so, it exits the loop. If increment is negative, Visual Basic tests to see if counter is less than *end*. If it is, it exits the loop.

3. Executes the statements in the block.

4. Increments counter by the amount specified with the increment argument. If the increment argument isn't specified, counter is incremented by 1.

5. Repeats the statements.

The For...Next loop in Listing 5.10 scans all the elements of the numeric array *data* and calculates their average.

Listing 5.10: Iterating an Array with a *For...Next* Loop

```
Dim i As Integer, total As Double
For i = 0 To data.GetUpperBound(0)
    total = total + data(i)
Next i
Console.WriteLine (total / data.Length)
```

The single most important thing to keep in mind when working with For...Next loops is that the loop's counter is set at the beginning of the loop. Changing the value of the *end* variable in the loop's body won't have any effect. For example, the following loop will be executed 10 times, not 100 times:

```
endValue = 10
For i = 0 To endValue
    endValue = 100
    { more statements }
Next i
```

You can, however, adjust the value of the counter from within the loop. The following is an example of an endless (or infinite) loop:

```
For i = 0 To 10
    Console.WriteLine(i)
    i = i - 1
Next i
```

This loop never ends because the loop's counter, in effect, is never increased. (If you try this, press Ctrl+Break to interrupt the endless loop.)

WARNING

Manipulating the *counter* of a For...Next loop is strongly discouraged. This practice will most likely lead to bugs such as infinite loops, overflows, and so on. If the number of repetitions of a loop isn't known in advance, use a Do...Loop or a While...End While structure (discussed in the following section).

The increment argument can be either positive or negative. If *start* is greater than *end*, the value of increment must be negative. If not, the loop's body won't be executed, not even once.

Finally, the counter variable need not be listed after the Next statement, but it makes the code easier to read, especially when For...Next loops are nested within each other (nested loops are discussed in the section "Nested Control Structures" later in the chapter).

Do...Loop

The Do...Loop executes a block of statements for as long as a condition is True. Visual Basic evaluates an expression, and if it's True, the statements are executed. When the end of the block is reached, the expression is evaluated again and, if it's True, the statements are repeated. If the expression is False, the program continues and the statement following the loop is executed.

There are two variations of the Do...Loop statement; both use the same basic model. A loop can be executed either while the condition is True or until the condition becomes True. These two variations use the keywords While and Until to specify how long the statements are executed. To execute a block of statements while a condition is True, use the following syntax:

```
Do While condition
    statement-block
Loop
```

To execute a block of statements until the condition becomes True, use the following syntax:

```
Do Until condition
    statement-block
Loop
```

When Visual Basic executes these loops, it first evaluates *condition*. If *condition* is False, a Do...While loop is skipped (the statements aren't even executed once) but a Do...Until loop is executed. When the Loop statement is reached, Visual Basic evaluates the expression again and repeats the statement block of the Do...While loop if the expression is True, or repeats the statements of the Do...Until loop if the expression is False.

In short, the Do While loop is executed when the condition is True, and the Do Until loop is executed when the condition is False.

The Do...Loop can execute any number of times as long as *condition* is True or False, as appropriate (zero or nonzero if the condition evaluates to a number). Moreover, the number of iterations need not be known before the loops starts. In fact, the statements may never execute if *condition* is initially False for While or True for Until.

Here's a typical example of using a Do...Loop. Suppose the string MyText holds a piece of text (perhaps the Text property of a TextBox control), and you want to count the words in the text. (We'll assume that there are no multiple spaces in the text and that the space character separates successive words.) To locate an instance of a character in a string, use the InStr() function, which accepts three arguments:

▶ The starting location of the search

▶ The text to be searched

▶ The character being searched

The following loop repeats for as long as there are spaces in the text. Each time the InStr() function finds another space in the text, it returns the location (a positive number) of the space. When there are no more spaces in the text, the InStr() function returns zero, which signals the end of the loop, as shown:

```
Dim MyText As String = "The quick brown fox jumped " & _
                       "over the lazy dog"
Dim position, words As Integer
position = 1
Do While position > 0
    position = InStr(position + 1, MyText, " ")
    words = words + 1
Loop
Console.WriteLine "There are " & _
                  words & " words in the text"
```

The Do...Loop is executed while the InStr() function returns a positive number, which happens for as long as there are more words in the text. The variable *position* holds the location of each successive space character in the text. The search for the next space starts at the location of the current space plus 1 (so that the program won't keep finding the same space). For each space found, the program increments the value of the *words* variable, which holds the total number of words when the loop ends.

NOTE

There are simpler methods of breaking a string into its constituent words, like the Split method of the String class. This is just an example of the Do While loop.

Part II

You may notice a problem with the previous code segment. It assumes that the text contains at least one word and starts by setting the *position* variable to 1. If the *MyText* variable contains an empty string, the program reports that it contains one word. To fix this problem, you must specify the condition, as shown:

```
Do While InStr(position + 1, MyText, " ")
    position = InStr(position + 1, MyText, " ")
    words = words + 1
Loop
Console.WriteLine "There are " & words & _
                " words in the text"
```

This code segment counts the number of words correctly, even if the *MyText* variable contains an empty string. If the *MyText* String variable doesn't contain any spaces, the function InStr(position + 1, MyText, " ") returns 0, which corresponds to False, and the Do loop isn't executed.

You can code the same routine with the Until keyword. In this case, you must continue to search for spaces until *position* becomes zero. Here's the same code with a different loop (the InStr() function returns 0 if the string it searches for doesn't exist in the longer string):

```
position = 1
Do Until position = 0
    position = InStr(position + 1, MyText, " ")
    words = words + 1
Loop
Console.WriteLine "There are " & words & _
                " words in the text"
```

Another variation of the Do loop executes the statements first and evaluates the *condition* after each execution. This Do loop has the following syntax:

```
Do
    statements
Loop While condition
```

or

```
Do
    statements
Loop Until condition
```

The statements in this type of loop execute at least once, since the condition is examined at the end of the loop.

Could we have implemented the previous example with one of the last two types of loops? The fact that we had to do something special about zero-length strings suggests that this problem shouldn't be coded with a loop that tests the condition at the end. Because the loop's body will be executed once, the *words* variable is never going to be zero.

As you can see, you can code loops in several ways with the Do...Loop statement, and the way you use it depends on the problem at hand and your programming style.

While...End While

The While...End While loop executes a block of statements as long as a condition is True. The While loop has the following syntax:

```
While condition
    statement-block
End While
```

FROM VB6 TO VB .NET

The End While statement replaces the Wend statement of VB6.

If *condition* is True, all statements are executed and, when the End While statement is reached, control is returned to the While statement, which evaluates *condition* again. If *condition* is still True, the process is repeated. If *condition* is False, the program resumes with the statement following End While.

The loop in Listing 5.11 prompts the user for numeric data. The user can type a negative value to indicate that all values are entered.

Listing 5.11: Reading an Unknown Number of Values

```
Dim number, total As Double
number = 0
```

```
While number => 0
    total = total + number
    number = InputBox("Please enter another value")
End While
```

You assign the value 0 to the *number* variable before the loop starts because this value can't affect the total. Another technique is to precede the While statement with an InputBox function to get the first number from the user.

Sometimes, the condition that determines when the loop will terminate is so complicated that it can't be expressed with a single statement. In these cases, we declare a Boolean value and set it to True or False from within the loop's body. Here's the outline of such a loop:

```
Dim repeatLoop As Boolean
repeatLoop = True
While repeatLoop
    { statements }
    If condition Then
        repeatLoop = True
    Else
        repeattLoop = False
    End If
End While
```

You may also see an odd Loop statement like the following one:

```
While True
    { statements }
End While
```

This seemingly endless loop must be terminated from within its own body with an Exit statement, which is called when a condition becomes True or False. The following loop terminates when a condition is met in the loop's body:

```
While True
    { statements }
    If condition Then Exit While
    { more statements }
End While
```

Nested Control Structures

You can place, or *nest,* control structures inside other control structures (such as an If...Then block within a For...Next loop). Control structures in Visual Basic can be nested in as many levels as you want. It's common practice to indent the bodies of nested decision and loop structures to make the program easier to read.

When you nest control structures, you must make sure that they open and close within the same structure. In other words, you can't start a For...Next loop in an If statement and close the loop after the corresponding End If. The following pseudocode demonstrates how to nest several flow-control statements:

```
For a = 1 To 100
    { statements }
    If a = 99 Then
        { statements }
    End If
    While b < a
        { statements }
        If total <= 0 Then
            { statements }
        End If
    End While
    For c = 1 to a
        { statements }
    Next
Next
```

I'm not showing the names of the count variables after the Next statement, because it's not necessary. To find the matching closing statement (Next, End If, or End While), move down from the opening statement until you hit a line that starts at the same column. This is the matching closing statement. Notice that you don't have to align the nested structures yourself. The editor reformats the code automatically as you edit. It also inserts the matching closing statement—the End If statement is inserted automatically as soon as you enter an If statement, for example.

Listing 5.12 shows the structure of a nested For...Next loop that scans all the elements of a two-dimensional array.

Listing 5.12: Iterating through a Two-Dimensional Array

```
Dim Array2D(6, 4) As Integer
Dim iRow, iCol As Integer
For iRow = 0 To Array2D.GetUpperBound(0)
    For iCol = 0 To Array2D.GetUpperBound(1)
        Array2D(iRow, iCol) = iRow * 100 + iCol
        Console.Write(iRow & ", " & iCol & " = " & _
                      Array2D(iRow, iCol) & "      ")
    Next iCol
    Console.WriteLine()
Next iRow
```

The outer loop (with the *iRow* counter) scans each row of the array, and the inner loop scans each column in the current row. At each iteration, the inner loop scans all the elements in the row specified by the counter of the outer loop (*iRow*). After the inner loop completes, the counter of the outer loop is increased by one and the inner loop is executed again, this time to scan the elements of the next row. The loop's body consists of two statements that assign a value to the current array element and then print it in the Output window. The current element at each iteration is `Array2D(iRow, iCol)`.

Part of the output produced by this code segment is shown here. The pair of values separated by a comma are the indices of an element, and its value follows the equals sign:

0, 0 = 0	0, 1 = 1	0, 2 = 2	0, 3 = 3	0, 4 = 4
1, 0 = 100	1, 1 = 101	1, 2 = 102	1, 3 = 103	1, 4 = 104
2, 0 = 200	2, 1 = 201	2, 2 = 202	2, 3 = 203	2, 4 = 204
3, 0 = 300	3, 1 = 301	3, 2 = 302	3, 3 = 303	3, 4 = 304
4, 0 = 400	4, 1 = 401	4, 2 = 402	4, 3 = 403	4, 4 = 404
5, 0 = 500	5, 1 = 501	5, 2 = 502	5, 3 = 503	5, 4 = 504
6, 0 = 600	6, 1 = 601	6, 2 = 602	6, 3 = 603	6, 4 = 604

TIP

The presence of the counter names *iCol* and *iRow* aren't really required after the Next statement. Actually, if you supply them in the wrong order, the editor will catch the error and underline the two statements. In practice, few programmers specify Counter values after a Next statement, but you can improve the program's readability by specifying the corresponding *counter* name after each Next statement.

The *Exit* Statement

The Exit statement allows you to exit prematurely from a block of statements in a control structure, from a loop, or even from a procedure. Suppose you have a For...Next loop that calculates the square root of a series of numbers. Because the square root of negative numbers can't be calculated (the Sqrt() function will generate a runtime error), you might want to halt the operation if the array contains an invalid value. To exit the loop prematurely, use the Exit For statement as follows:

```
For i = 0 To UBound(nArray)
    If nArray(i) < 0 Then Exit For
    nArray(i) = Math.Sqrt(nArray(i))
Next
```

If a negative element is found in this loop, the program exits the loop and continues with the statement following the Next statement.

There are similar Exit statements for the Do loop (Exit Do) and the While loop (Exit While), as well as for functions and subroutines (Exit Function and Exit Sub). If the previous loop was part of a function, you might want to display an error and exit not only the loop, but the function itself:

```
For i = 0 To nArray.GetUpperBound()
    If nArray(i) < 0 Then
        MsgBox "Negative value found, " & _
               "terminating calculations"
        Exit Function
    End If
    nArray(i) = Sqr(nArray(i))
Next
```

If this code is part of a subroutine procedure, you use the Exit Sub statement. The Exit statements for loops are Exit For, Exit While, and Exit Do. There is no way (or compelling reason) to exit prematurely from an If or Case statement.

WHAT'S NEXT

It's been a long chapter, but we wouldn't be able to go far without the information presented here. You have learned the base datatypes

Part II

supported by Visual Basic, how to declare variables, and when to use them. Actually, the base datatypes aren't supplied by Visual Basic; they're part of the Common Language Runtime (CLR) and are the same for all languages. At this point, it doesn't really make much difference what part of .NET supplies each feature (the CLR, the Framework, or Visual Basic itself).

You've also learned how to store sets of values to an array, which is a great convenience. Arrays have always been a prime tool for programmers, and they've gotten so much better in .NET.

The base types supported by CLR are just too basic for the needs of a real application. To store more complicated information (like customers, accounts and so on), you can create your own custom structures. After defining the structure of the information, you can declare variables with the same structure. These variables behave like objects (even though they're not technically objects), because they expose the fields of the structure as properties.

Now that you have a good understanding of the Visual Basic .NET language, in the next chapter we will put the language to good use in writing and using procedures.

Chapter 6

WRITING AND USING PROCEDURES

T he one thing you should have learned about programming in Visual Basic so far is that an *application* is made up of small, self-contained segments. The code you write isn't a monolithic listing; it's made up of small segments called *procedures,* and you work on one procedure at a time.

NOTE

You'll find all the code from this chapter on www.sybex.com. Search for the book by its ISBN number, 2887, or its title, *Visual Basic .NET Complete*. You can download the code from the download button.

• •

Adapted from *Mastering Visual Basic .NET* by Evangelos Petroutsos
ISBN 0-7821-2877-7 $49.99

For example, when you write code for a control's Click event, you concentrate on the event at hand—namely, how the program should react to the Click event. What happens when the control is double-clicked, or when another control is clicked, is something you will worry about later, in another control's event handler. This "divide and conquer" approach isn't unique to programming events. It permeates the Visual Basic language, and even the longest applications are written by breaking them into small, well-defined tasks. Each task is performed by a separate procedure that is written and tested separately from the others.

Procedures are also used for implementing repeated tasks, such as frequently used calculations. Suppose you're writing an application that, at some point, must convert temperatures between different scales or calculate the smaller of two numbers. You can always do the calculations inline and repeat them in your code wherever they are needed, or you can write a procedure that performs the calculations and call this procedure. The benefit of the second approach is that code is cleaner and easier to understand and maintain. If you discover a more efficient way to implement the same calculations, you need change the code in only one place. If the same code is repeated in several places throughout the application, you will have to change every instance.

The two types of procedures supported by Visual Basic are the topics we'll explore in this chapter: *subroutines* and *functions*—the building blocks of your applications. We'll discuss them in detail, how to call them with arguments and how to retrieve the results returned by the functions. You may find that some of the topics discussed in this chapter are rather advanced, but I wanted to exhaust the topic in a single chapter, rather than having to interrupt the discussion of other topics to explain an advanced, procedure-related technique. You can skip the sections you find difficult at first reading and come back to these sections later, or look up the technique as needed.

MODULAR CODING

The idea of breaking a large application into smaller, more manageable sections is not new to computing. Few tasks, programming or otherwise, can be managed as a whole. The event handlers are just one example of breaking a large application into smaller tasks. Some event handlers may require a lot of code. A button that calculates the average purchase or sale price of a specific product must scan all the purchase orders or invoices, find the ones that include the specific product, take into consideration all units purchased or sold and the corresponding prices, and then calculate the average price. Each operation could be implemented by a different procedure (function or subroutine), and the application could call them in the proper order.

Functions and subroutines are segments of code that perform well-defined tasks and can be called from various parts of an application to perform the same operation, usually on different data. The difference is that functions return a value, while subroutines don't. This explains why function names are assigned to a variable—we save the value returned by a function and reuse it later.

As you can see, the divide-and-conquer approach in software is nothing less than a requirement in large applications. It's so common in programming, that there's a name for it: *modular programming*. Ideally, every program should be broken down into really simple tasks, and the code should read almost like English. You can write your application at a high level, and then start coding the low-level procedures.

The best thing about modular programming is that it allows programmers with different skills to focus on different parts of the application. A database programmer could write the `RetrieveInvoiceLines()` procedure, while another programmer could use this procedure as a black box to build applications, just like the functions that come with the language.

If you need a procedure to perform certain actions, such as change the background color of a control or display the fields of a record on the form, you can implement it either as a function or subroutine. The choice of the procedure type isn't going to affect the code. The same statements can be used with either type of procedure. However, if your procedure doesn't return a value, then it should be implemented as a subroutine. If it returns a value, then it *must* be implemented as a function. The only difference between subroutines and functions is that functions return a value, while subroutines don't.

Both subroutines and functions can accept *arguments*, which are values you pass to the procedure when you call it. Arguments and the related keywords are discussed in detail in the section "Arguments," later in this chapter.

Subroutines

A *subroutine* is a block of statements that carries out a well-defined task. The block of statements is placed within a set of Sub...End Sub statements and can be invoked by name. The following subroutine displays the current date in a message box and can be called by its name, ShowDate():

```
Sub ShowDate()
    MsgBox(Date())
End Sub
```

Normally, the task a subroutine performs is more complicated than this; nevertheless, even this is a block of code isolated from the rest of the application. All the event handlers in Visual Basic, for example, are coded as subroutines. The actions that must be performed each time a button is clicked are coded in the button's Click procedure.

The statements in a subroutine are executed, and when the End Sub statement is reached, control returns to the calling program. It's possible to exit a subroutine prematurely, with the Exit Sub statement. For example, some condition may stop the subroutine from successfully completing its task.

All variables declared within a subroutine are local to that subroutine. When the subroutine exits, all variables declared in it cease to exist.

Most procedures also accept and act upon *arguments*. The ShowDate() subroutine displays the current date on a message box. If you want to display any other date, you'd have to pass an argument to the subroutine telling it to act on a different value, like this:

```
Sub ShowDate(ByVal birthDate As Date)
    MsgBox(birthDate)
End Sub
```

birthDate is a variable that holds the date to be displayed; its type is Date. (The ByVal keyword means that the subroutine sees a copy of the variable, not the variable itself. What this means practically is that the subroutine can't change the value of the *birthDate* variable.)

To display the current date on a message box, you must call the ShowDate subroutine as follows from within your program:

```
ShowDate()
```

To display another date with the second implementation of the subroutine, use a statement like the following:

```
Dim myBirthDate = #2/9/1960#
ShowDate(myBirthDate)
```

Or, you can pass the value to be displayed directly without the use of an intermediate variable:

```
ShowDate(#2/9/1960#)
```

Subroutines and Event Handlers

An *event handler* is a segment of code that is executed each time an external (or internal to your application) condition triggers the event. When the user clicks a control, the control's Click event handler executes. This handler is nothing more than a subroutine that performs all the actions you want to perform when the control is clicked. It is separate from the rest of the code and doesn't have to know what would happen if another control was clicked, or if the same control was double-clicked. It's a self-contained piece of code that's executed when needed.

Every application is made up of event handlers, which contain code to react to user actions. Event handlers need not return any results, and they're implemented as subroutines. For example, to react to the click of the mouse on the Button1 control, your application must provide a subroutine that handles the `Button1.Click` event. The code in this subroutine is executed independently of any other event handler, and it doesn't return a result because there is no main program to accept it. The code of a Visual Basic application consists of event handlers, which may call other subroutines and functions but aren't called by a main program. They are automatically activated by VB in response to external events.

Functions

A *function* is similar to a subroutine, but a function returns a result. Subroutines perform a task and don't report anything to the calling program; functions commonly carry out calculations and report the result. Because they return values, functions—like variables—have types. The value you pass back to the calling program from a function is called the *return value*, and its type must match the type of the function. Functions accept arguments, just like subroutines. The statements that make up a function are placed in a set of `Function...End Function` statements, as shown here:

```
Function NextDay() As Date
    Dim theNextDay As Date
    theNextDay = DateAdd(DateInterval.Day, 1, Now())
    Return(theNextDay)
End Function
```

DateAdd() is a built-in function that adds a number of intervals to a date. The interval is specified by the first argument (here, it's days), the number of intervals is the second argument (one day), and the third argument is the date to which the number of intervals is added (today). So the NextDay() function returns tomorrow's date by adding one day to the current date. NextDay() is a custom function, which calls the built-in DateAdd() function to complete its calculations. Another custom function might call NextDay() for its own purposes.

The result of a function is returned to the calling program with the Return statement. In our example, the Return statement happens to be the last statement in the function, but it could appear anywhere; it could even appear several times in the function's code. The first time a Return statement is executed, the function terminates and control is returned to the calling program.

You can also return a value to the calling routine by assigning the result to the name of the function. The following is an alternative method of coding the NextDay() function:

```
Function NextDay() As Date
    NextDay = DateAdd(DateInterval.Day, 1, Now())
End Function
```

Notice that this time I've assigned the result of the calculation to the function's name directly and didn't use a variable.

Similar to variables, a custom function has a name, which must be unique in its scope. If you declare a function in a form, the function name must be unique in the form. If you declare a function as Public or Friend, its name must be unique in the project. Functions have the same scope rules as variables and can be prefixed by many of the same keywords. In effect, you can modify the default scope of a function with the keywords Public, Private, Protected, Friend, and Protected Friend.

Built-In Functions

Let's look at a couple of functions, starting with one of the built-in functions, the Abs() function. This function returns the absolute value of its argument. If the argument is positive, the function returns it as is; if it's negative, the function inverts its sign. The Abs() function could be implemented as follows:

```
Function Abs(X As Double) As Double
    If X >= 0 Then
```

```
        Return(X)
    Else
        Return(-X)
    End If
End Function
```

This is a trivial procedure, yet it's built into Visual Basic because it's used frequently in math and science calculations. Developers can call a single function rather than supplying their own Abs() functions. Visual Basic and all other programming languages provide many built-in functions to implement the tasks needed most frequently by developers. But each developer has special needs, and you can't expect to find all the procedures you may ever need in a programming language. Sooner or later, you will have to supply your own.

The .NET Framework provides a large number of functions that implement common or complicated tasks. There are functions for the common math operations, functions to perform calculations with dates (these are complicated operations), financial functions, and many more. When you use the built-in functions, you don't have to know how they work internally.

The Pmt() function, for example, calculates the monthly payments on a loan. All you have to know is the arguments you must pass to the function and retrieve the result. The syntax of the Pmt() function is

```
MPay = Pmt(Rate, NPer, PV, FV, Due)
```

where *MPay* is the monthly payment, *Rate* is the monthly interest rate, *NPer* is the number of payments (the duration of the loan in months), and *PV* is the present value of the loan (the amount you took from the bank). *Due* is an optional argument that specifies when the payments are due (the beginning or the end of the month), and *FV* is another optional argument that specifies the future value of an amount. This isn't needed in the case of a loan, but it can help you calculate how much money you should deposit each month to accumulate a target amount over a given time. (The amount returned by the Pmt() function is negative, because it's a negative cash flow—it's money you owe—so pay attention to the sign of your values.)

To calculate the monthly payment for a $20,000 loan paid off over a period of 6 years at a fixed interest rate of 7.25%, you call the Pmt() function as follows:

```
Dim mPay As Double
Dim Duration As Integer = 6 * 12
```

Part II

```
Dim Rate As Single = (7.25 / 100) / 12
Dim Amount As Single = 20000
mPay = Pmt(Rate, Duration, Amount)
MsgBox("Your monthly payment will be $" & -mPay & vbCrLf & _
        "You will pay back a total of $" & -mPay * duration)
```

Notice that the interest (7.5%) is divided by 12, because the function requires the monthly interest. The value returned by the function is the monthly payment for the loan specified with the *Duration*, *Amount*, and *Rate* variables. If you place the preceding lines in the Click event handler of a Button, run the project, and then click the button, the following message will appear on a message box:

```
Your monthly payment will be $343.3861
You will pay back a total of $24723.8
```

To calculate the monthly deposit amount, you must call the Pmt() function passing 0 as the present value and the target amount as the future value. Replace the statements in the Click event handler with the following and run the project:

```
Dim mPay As Double
Dim Duration As Integer = 15 * 12
Dim Rate As Single = (4 / 100) / 12
Dim Amount As Single = -40000
mPay = Pmt(Rate, Duration, 0, Amount)
MsgBox("A monthly deposit of $" & mPay & vbCrLf & _
        "every month will yield $40,000 in 15 years")
```

It turns out that if you want to accumulate $40,000 over the next 15 years to send your kid to college, assuming a constant interest rate of 4%, you must deposit $162.55 every month.

Pmt() is one of the simpler financial functions provided by the Framework, but most of us would find it really difficult to write the code for this function. Because financial calculations are quite common in business programming, many of the functions you may need already exist, and all you need to know is how to call them. More detailed information about the financial functions can be found in the Visual Studio .NET Help Library.

Custom Functions
The built-in functions, however, aren't nearly enough for all types of applications. Most of the code we write is in the form of custom functions,

which are called from several places in the application. Let's look at an example of a more advanced function that does something really useful.

Every book has a unique International Standard Book Number (ISBN). Every application that manages books—and there are many bookstores on the Internet—needs a function to verify the ISBN, which is made up of nine digits followed by a check digit. To calculate the check digit, you multiply each of the nine digits by a constant; the first digit is multiplied by 10, the second digit is multiplied by 9, and so on. The sum of these multiplications is then divided by 11, and we take the remainder. The check digit is the remainder subtracted from 11. Because the remainder is a digit from 0 to 10, when it turns out to be 10, the check digit is set to "X." This is the only valid character that may appear in an ISBN, and it can only be the check digit. To calculate the check digit for the ISBN 078212283, compute the sum of the following products:

Part II

```
0 * 10 + 7 * 9 + 8 * 8 + 2 * 7 + 1 * 6 + 2 * 5 + 2 * 4 + 8 * _
3 + 3 * 2
```

The sum is 195, and when you divide that by 11, the remainder is 8. The check digit is 11– 8, or 3, and the book's complete ISBN is 0782122833. The ISBNCheckDigit() function, shown in Listing 6.1, accepts the nine digits of the ISBN as argument and returns the appropriate check digit.

Listing 6.1: The *ISBNCheckDigit()* Custom Function

```
Function ISBNCheckDigit(ByVal ISBN As String) As String
Dim i As Integer, chksum, chkDigit As Integer
    For i = 0 To 8
        chkSum = chkSum + (10 - i) * ISBN.Substring(i, 1)
    Next
    chkDigit = 11 - (chkSum Mod 11)
    If chkDigit = 10 Then
        Return ("X")
    Else
        Return (chkDigit.ToString)
    End If
End Function
```

The ISBNCheckDigit() function returns a string value, because the check digit can be either a digit or "X." It also accepts a string, because the complete ISBN (nine digits plus the check digit) is a string, not a number (leading zeros are important in an ISBN but totally meaningless in a numeric value). The Substring method of a String object extracts a number of characters from the string to which it is applied. The first argument is the starting location in the string, and the second is the number of characters to be extracted.

The expression ISBN.Substring(i, 1) extracts one character at a time from the *ISBN* string variable. During the first iteration of the loop, it extracts the first character; during the second iteration, it extracts the second character, and so on.

The character extracted is a numeric digit, which is multiplied by the value $(10 - i)$ and the result is added to the *chkSum* variable. This variable is the checksum of the ISBN. After it has been calculated, we divide it by 11 and take its remainder, which we subtract from 11. This is the ISBN's check digit and the function's return value.

FROM VB6 TO VB .NET

There's something odd about the way the .NET Framework handles strings. The index of the first character in a string is 0, not 1. That's why the loop that scans the first nine digits of the ISBN goes from 0 to 8. Because the variable *i* is one less than the position of the digit in the ISBN, we subtract it from 10 and not from 11. Up to the last version of Visual Basic, the indexing of strings started at 1, but .NET changed all that, and this is something you must get used to.

You can use this function in an application that maintains a book database, to make sure that all books are entered with a valid ISBN. You can also use it with a web application that allows viewers to request books by their ISBN. The same code will work with two different applications, even when passed to other developers. Developers using your function don't have to know how the check digit is calculated, just how to call the function and retrieve its result.

To test the ISBNCheckDigit() function, start a new project, place a button on the form, and enter the following statements in its Click event handler:

```
Private Sub Button1_Click(ByVal sender As System.Object, _
                ByVal e As System.EventArgs) _
            Handles Button1.Click
```

```
Console.WriteLine("The check Digit is " & _
                    ISBNCheckDigit("078212283"))
```

End Sub

After inserting the code of the ISBNCheckDigit() function and the code that calls the function, your code editor should look like Figure 6.1. You can place a TextBox control on the Form and pass the Text property of the control to the ISBNCheckDigit() function to calculate the check digit.

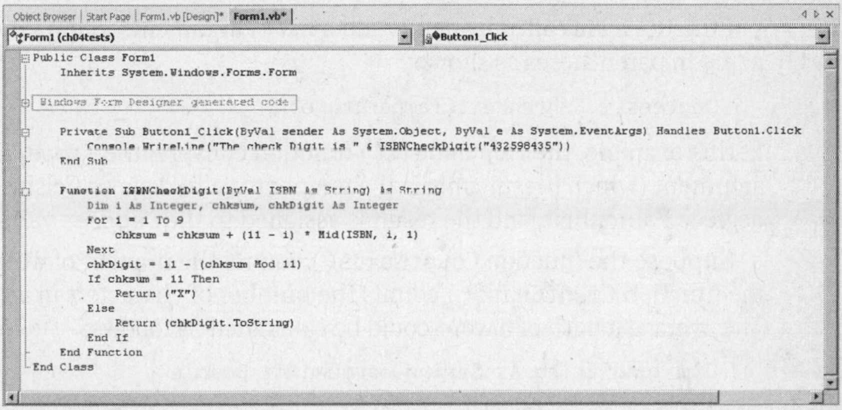

FIGURE 6.1: Calling the ISBNCheckDigit() function

Calling Functions and Subroutines

When you call a procedure, you must supply values for all the arguments specified in the procedure's definition and in the same order. To call a procedure, you simply enter its name, followed by its arguments in parentheses:

```
Dim chDigit As String
ChDigit = ISBNCheckDigit("078212283")
```

The values of the arguments must match their declared type. If a procedure expects an Integer value, you shouldn't supply a Date value or a string. If the procedure is a function, you must assign its return value to a variable so you can use it from within your code. The following statement creates the complete ISBN by calling the ISBNCheckDigit() function:

```
Dim ISBN As String = "078212283"
MsgBox("The complete ISBN is " & ISBN & _
        ISBNCheckDigit(ISBN))
```

The argument of the MsgBox() function needs an explanation. It calls the ISBNCheckDigit() function, passing the ISBN as argument. Then it appends the check digit (which is the value returned by the function) to the ISBN value and prints it. It is equivalent to the following statements, which are simpler to read, but not nearly as common:

```
Dim wholeISBN As String
wholeISBN = ISBN & ISBNCheckDigit(ISBN)
MsgBox("The complete ISBN is " & wholeISBN)
```

Functions are called by name, and a list of arguments follows the name in parentheses as shown:

```
Degrees = Fahrenheit(Temperature)
```

In this example, the Fahrenheit() function converts the *Temperature* argument (which presumably is the temperature in degrees Celsius) to degrees Fahrenheit, and the result is assigned to the *Degrees* variable.

Suppose the function CountWords() counts the number of words and the function CountChars() counts the number of characters in a string. The average length of a word could be calculated as follows:

```
Dim longString As String, avgLen As Double
longString = TextBox1.Text
avgLen = CountChars(longString) / CountWords(longString)
```

The first executable statement gets the text of a TextBox control and assigns it to a variable, which is then used as an argument to the two functions. When the second statement executes, Visual Basic first calls the functions CountChars() and CountWords() with the specified arguments and then divides the results they return.

You can call functions in the same way that you call subroutines, but the result won't be stored anywhere. For example, the function Convert() may convert the text in a textbox to uppercase and return the number of characters it converts. Normally, you'd call this function as follows:

```
nChars = Convert()
```

If you don't care about the return value—you only want to update the text on a TextBox control—you would call the Convert() function with the following statement:

```
Convert()
```

FROM VB6 TO VB .NET

The Call statement of VB6 has disappeared. Also, the parentheses around the argument list are mandatory, even if the subroutine or function doesn't accept any arguments. You can no longer call a subroutine with a statement like:

```
ConvertText myText
```

You must enclose the arguments in a pair of parentheses.

CONVERTTEXT(MYTEXT)
ARGUMENTS

Subroutines and functions aren't entirely isolated from the rest of the application. Most procedures accept arguments from the calling program. Recall that an argument is a value you pass to the procedure and on which the procedure usually acts. This is how subroutines and functions communicate with the rest of the application.

Functions also accept arguments—in many cases, more than one. The function Min(), for instance, accepts two numbers and returns the smaller one:

```
Function Min(ByVal a As Single, ByVal b As Single) As Single
    Min = IIf(a < b, a, b)
End Function
```

IIf() is a built-in function that evaluates the first argument, which is a logical expression. If the expression is True, the IIf() function returns the second argument. If the expression is False, the function returns the third argument.

To call this function, use a few statements like the following:

```
Dim val1 As Single = 33.001
Dim val2 As Single = 33.0011
Dim smallerVal as Single
SmallerVal = Min(val1, val2)
Console.Write("The smaller value is " & smallerVal)
```

If you execute these statements (place them in a button's Click event handler), you will see the following on the Output window:

```
The smaller value is 33.001
```

If you attempt to call the same function with two double values, as in a statement like the following:

```
Console.WriteLine(Min(3.33000000111, 3.33000000222))
```

you will see that the value 3.33 in the Output window. The compiler converted the two values from Double to Single datatype and returned one of them. Which one is it? It doesn't make a difference, because when converted to Single, both values are the same.

Interesting things will happen if you attempt to use the Min() function with the Strict option turned on. Insert the statement Option Strict On at the very beginning of the file. First, the editor will underline the statement that implements the Min() function—the IIf() function. The IIf() function accepts two Object variables as arguments, and you can't call it with Single or Double values. The Strict option prevents the compiler from converting numeric values to objects. To use the IIf() function with the Strict option, you must change its implementation as follows:

```
Function Min(ByVal a As Object, ByVal b As Object) As Object
    Min = IIf(Val(a) < Val(b), a, b)
End Function
```

Argument-Passing Mechanisms

One of the most important issues in writing procedures is the mechanism used to pass arguments. The examples so far have used the default mechanism: passing arguments by value. The other mechanism is passing them by reference. Although most programmers use the default mechanism, it's important to know the difference between the two mechanisms and when to use each.

Passing Arguments

When you pass an argument by value, the procedure sees only a copy of the argument. Even if the procedure changes it, the changes aren't permanent. The benefit of passing arguments by value is that the argument values are isolated from the procedure, and only the code segment in which they are declared can change their values. This is the default argument-passing mechanism in VB .NET.

To specify the arguments that will be passed by value, use the ByVal keyword in front of the argument's name. If you omit the ByVal keyword, the editor will insert it automatically, since it's the default option. To declare that the Degrees() function's arguments are passed by value, use the ByVal keyword in the argument's declaration as follows:

```
Function Degrees(ByVal Celsius as Single) As Single
    Degrees = (9 / 5) * Celsius + 32
End Function
```

To see what the ByVal keyword does, add a line that changes the value of the argument in the function:

```
Function Degrees(ByVal Celsius as Single) As Single
    Degrees = (9 / 5) * Celsius + 32
    Celsius = 0
End Function
```

Now call the function as follows:

```
CTemp = InputBox("Enter temperature in degrees Celsius")
MsgBox(Ctemp.ToString & " degrees Celsius are " & _
        Degrees((CTemp)) & " degrees Fahrenheit")
```

If the value entered in the InputBox is 32, the following message is displayed:

```
32 degrees Celsius are 89.6 degrees Fahrenheit
```

Replace the ByVal keyword with the ByRef keyword in the function's definition, and call the function as follows:

```
Celsius = 32.0
FTemp = Degrees(Celsius)
MsgBox(Celsius.ToString & " degrees Celsius are " & _
        FTemp & " degrees Fahrenheit")
```

This time the program displays the following message:

```
0 degrees Celsius are 89.6 degrees Fahrenheit
```

When the *Celsius* argument was passed to the Degrees() function, its value was 32. But the function changed its value, and upon return it was 0. Because the argument was passed by reference, any changes made by the procedure affected the variable permanently. When the calling program attempted to use it, the variable had a different value than expected.

Part II

NOTE

When you pass arguments to a procedure by reference, you're actually passing the variable itself. Any changes made to the argument by the procedure will be permanent. When you pass arguments by value, the procedure gets a copy of the variable, which is discarded when the procedure ends. Any changes made to the argument by the procedure won't affect the variable of the calling program.

NOTE

When you pass an array as argument to a procedure, the array is *always* passed by reference—even if you specify the ByVal keyword. The reason for this is that it would take the machine some time to create a copy of the array. Because the copy of the array must also live in memory, passing too many arrays back and forth by value would deplete your system's memory.

Passing arguments by reference gives the procedure access to the actual variable. The calling procedure passes the address of the variable in memory so that the procedure can change its value permanently. With VB6, this was the default argument-passing mechanism, but this is no longer the case.

As you type the names of the arguments in the declaration of a subroutine or function, the editor inserts automatically the ByVal keyword if you omit it (unless, of course, you specify the ByRef keyword). In general, you pass arguments by reference only if the procedure has reason to change its value. If the values of the arguments are required later in the program, you run the risk of changing their values in the procedure.

Returning Multiple Values

If you want to write a function that returns more than a single result, you will most likely pass additional arguments by reference and set their values from within the function's code. The following function calculates the basic statistics of a data set. The values of the data set are stored in an array, which is passed to the function by reference.

The Stats() function must return two values, the average and standard deviation of the data set. In a real-world application, a function like Stats() should calculate more statistics than this, but this is just an example to demonstrate how to return multiple values through the function's arguments. Here's the declaration of the Stats() function:

```
Function Stats(ByRef Data() As Double, _
               ByRef Avg As Double, _
               ByRef StDev As Double) As Integer
```

The function returns an integer, which is the number of values in the data set. The two important values calculated by the function are returned in the *Avg* and *StDev* arguments.

```
Function Stats(ByRef Data() As Double, _
               ByRef Avg As Double, _
               ByRef StDev As Double) As Integer
  Dim i As Integer, sum As Double, sumSqr As Double, _
      points As Integer
  points = Data.Length
  For i = 0 To points - 1
      sum = sum + Data(i)
      sumSqr = sumSqr + Data(i) ^ 2
  Next
  Avg = sum / points
  StDev = System.Math.Sqrt(sumSqr / points - Avg ^ 2)
  Return(points)
End Function
```

To call the Stats() function from within your code, set up an array of doubles and declare two variables that will hold the average and standard deviation of the data set:

```
Dim Values(100) As Double
' Statements to populate the data set
Dim average, deviation As Double
Dim points As Integer
points = Stats(Values, average, deviation)
Console.WriteLine points & " values processed."
Console.WriteLine "The average is " & average & " and"
Console.WriteLine "the standard deviation is " & deviation
```

Using ByRef arguments is the simplest method for a function to return multiple values. However, the definition of your functions may become cluttered, especially if you want to return more than a few values. Another problem with this technique is that it's not clear whether an argument must be set before calling the function or not. As you will see shortly, it is possible for a function to return an array, or a custom structure with fields for any number of values.

Passing Objects as Arguments   When you pass objects as arguments, they're passed by reference, even if you have specified the ByVal keyword. The procedure can access and modify the members of the object passed as argument, and the new value will be visible in the procedure that made the call.

The following code segment demonstrates this. The object is an ArrayList, which is an enhanced form of an array. The Add method adds new items to the ArrayList, and you can access individual items with an index value, similar to an array's elements. The Click event handler of a Button control creates a new instance of the ArrayList object and calls the PopulateList() subroutine to populate the list. Even though the ArrayList object is passed to the subroutine by value, the subroutine has access to its items:

```
Private Sub Button1_Click(ByVal sender As System.Object, _
                ByVal e As System.EventArgs) _
                Handles Button1.Click
    Dim aList As New ArrayList()
    PopulateList(aList)
    Console.WriteLine(aList(0).ToString)
    Console.WriteLine(aList(1).ToString)
    Console.WriteLine(aList(2).ToString)
End Sub
Sub PopulateList(ByVal list As ArrayList)
    list.Add("1")
    list.Add("2")
    list.Add("3")
End Sub
```

The same is true for arrays and all other collections. Even if you specify the ByVal keyword, they're passed by reference. A more elegant method of modifying the members of a structure from within a procedure is to implement the procedure as a function returning a structure, as explained in the section "Functions Returning Structures," later in this chapter.

Named Arguments

You've learned how to write procedures with optional arguments and how to pass a variable number of arguments to the procedure. The main limitation of the argument-passing mechanism, though, is the *order* of the arguments. If the first argument is a string and the second is a date, you can't change their order. By default, Visual Basic matches the values passed to a procedure to the declared arguments by their order. That's why the arguments you've seen so far are called *positional arguments*.

This limitation is lifted by Visual Basic's capability to specify *named arguments*. With named arguments, you can supply arguments in any order, because they are recognized by name and not by their order in the list of the procedure's arguments. Suppose you've written a function that expects three arguments: a name, an address, and an e-mail address:

```
Function Contact(Name As String, Address As String, _
                 EMail As String)
```

When calling this function, you must supply three strings that correspond to the arguments *Name*, *Address*, and *EMail*, in that order. However, there's a safer way to call this function: Supply the arguments in any order by their names. Instead of calling the Contact function as follows:

```
Contact("Peter Evans", _
        "2020 Palm Ave., Santa Barbara, CA 90000", _
        "PeterEvans@example.com")
```

you can call it this way:

```
Contact(Address:= _
        "2020 Palm Ave., Santa Barbara, CA 90000", _
        EMail:= _
        "PeterEvans@example.com", Name:="Peter Evans")
```

The := operator assigns values to the named arguments. Because the arguments are passed by name, you can supply them in any order.

To test this technique, enter the following function declaration in a form's code:

```
Function Contact(ByVal Name As String, _
                 ByVal Address As String, _
                 ByVal EMail As String) As String
```

```
        Console.WriteLine(Name)
        Console.WriteLine(Address)
        Console.WriteLine(EMail)
        Return ("OK")
    End Function
```

Then, call the `Contact()` function from within a button's Click event with the following statement:

```
Console.WriteLine Contact(Address:= _
            "2020 Palm Ave., Santa Barbara, CA 90000", _
            Name:="Peter Evans", _
            EMail:="PeterEvans@example.com")
```

You'll see the following in the Immediate window:

```
Peter Evans
2020 Palm Ave., Santa Barbara, CA 90000
PeterEvans@example.com
OK
```

The function knows which value corresponds to which argument and can process them the same way that it processes positional arguments. Notice that the function's definition is the same whether you call it with positional or named arguments. The difference is in how you call the function and how you declare it.

Named arguments make code safer and easier to read, but because they require a lot of typing, most programmers don't use them. Besides, programmers are so used to positional arguments that the notion of naming arguments is like having to declare variables when variants will do. Named arguments are good for situations in which you have optional arguments that require many consecutive commas, which may complicate the code.

More Types of Function Return Values

Functions are not limited to returning simple datatypes like integers or strings. They may return custom datatypes and even arrays. The ability of functions to return all types of data makes them very flexible and can simplify coding, so we'll explore it in detail in the following sections.

Using complex datatypes, such as structures and arrays, allows you to write functions that return multiple values.

Functions Returning Structures

Suppose you need a function that returns a customer's savings and checking balances. So far, you've learned that you can return two or more values from a function by supplying arguments with the ByRef keyword. A more elegant method is to create a custom datatype (a structure) and write a function that returns a variable of this type. The structure for storing balances could be declared as follows:

```
Structure CustBalance
    Dim BalSavings As Decimal
    Dim BalChecking As Decimal
End Structure
```

Then, you can define a function that returns a CustBalance datatype as:

```
Function GetCustBalance(ByVal custID As Integer) _
                        As CustBalance
    { statements }
End Function
```

The GetCustBalance() function must be defined in the same module as the declaration of the custom datatype it returns. If not, you'll get an error message.

When you call this function, you must assign its result to a variable of the same type. First declare a variable of the CustBalance and then use it as shown here:

```
Private Balance As CustBalance
Dim custID As Integer
custID = 13011
Balance = GetCustBalance(custID)
Console.WriteLine Balance.BalSavings
Console.WriteLine Balance.BalChecking
```

Here, *custID* is a customer's ID (a number or string, depending on the application). Of course, the function's body must assign the proper values to the CustBalance variable's fields.

Part II

Here's the simplest example of a function that returns a custom data-type. This example outlines the steps you must repeat every time you want to create functions that return custom datatypes:

1. Create a new project and insert the declarations of a custom datatype in the declarations section of the form:

```
Structure CustBalance
    Dim BalSavings As Decimal
    Dim BalChecking As Decimal
End Structure
```

2. Then implement the function that returns a value of the custom type. You must declare a variable of the type returned by the function and assign the proper values to its fields. The following function assigns random values to the fields *BalChecking* and *BalSavings*. Then, assign the variable to the function's name, as shown next:

```
Function GetCustBalance(ID As Long) As CustBalance
Dim tBalance As CustBalance
    tBalance.BalChecking = CDec(1000 + 4000 * rnd())
    tBalance.BalSavings = CDec(1000 + 15000 * rnd())
    GetCustBalance = tBalance
End Function
```

3. Then place a button on the form from which you want to call the function. Declare a variable of the same type and assign to it the function's return value. The example that follows prints the savings and checking balances on the Output window:

```
Private Sub Button1_Click(ByVal sender As System.Object, _
            ByVal e As System.EventArgs) _
            Handles Button1.Click
    Dim balance As CustBalance
    balance = GetCustBalance(1)
    Console.WriteLine(balance.BalChecking)
    Console.WriteLine(balance.BalSavings)
End Sub
```

For this example, I created a project with a single form. The form contains a single Command button whose Click event handler is shown here. Create this project from scratch, perhaps using your own custom data-type, to explore its structure and experiment with functions that return custom datatypes.

In the following section, I'll describe a more complicated (and practical) example of a custom datatype function.

VB .NET at Work: The Types Project

The Types project demonstrates a function that returns a custom datatype. The Types project consists of a form that displays record fields and is shown in Figure 6.2. Every time you click the Show Next button, the fields of the next record are displayed. When all records are exhausted, the program wraps back to the first record.

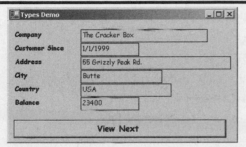

FIGURE 6.2: The Types project demonstrates functions that return custom datatypes.

The project consists of a single form. The following custom datatype appears in the form's code, outside any procedure:

```
Structure Customer
    Dim Company As String
    Dim Manager As String
    Dim Address As String
    Dim City As String
    Dim Country As String
    Dim CustomerSince As Date
    Dim Balance As Decimal
End Structure
Private Customers(8) As Customer
Private cust As Customer
Private currentIndex as Integer
```

The array *Customers* holds the data for 9 customers, and the *cust* variable is used as a temporary variable for storing the current customer's data. The *currentIndex* variable is the index of the current element of the array.

The Click event handler of the Show Next button calls the GetCustomer() function with an index value (which is the order of the current customer), and displays its fields in the Label controls on the form. Then it increases the value of the *currentIndex* variable, so that it points to the next customer.

The GetCustomer() function returns a variable of Customer type (the variable *aCustomer*). The code behind the Show Next button follows:

```
Private Sub Button1_Click(ByVal sender As System.Object, _
                ByVal e As System.EventArgs) _
                Handles Button1.Click
    If currentIndex = CountCustomers() Then currentIndex = 0
    Dim aCustomer As Customer
    aCustomer = GetCustomer(currentIndex)
    ShowCustomer(currentIndex)
    currentIndex = currentIndex + 1
End Sub
```

The CountCustomers() function returns the number of records stored in the *Customers* array. The event handler starts by comparing the value of the current index to the number of elements in the *Customers* array. If they're equal, the *currentIndex* variable is reset to zero. The definitions of the CountCustomers() and GetCustomer() functions are shown next:

```
Function CountCustomers() As Integer
    Return(Customers.Length)
End Function
Function GetCustomer(ByVal idx As Integer) As Customer
    Return(Customers(idx))
End Function
```

Finally, the ShowCustomer() subroutine displays the fields of the current record on the Label controls on the form:

```
Sub ShowCustomer(ByVal idx As Integer)
    Dim aCustomer As Customer
    aCustomer = GetCustomer(idx)
    lblCompany.Text = aCustomer.Company
    lblSince.Text = aCustomer.CustomerSince
```

```
        lblAddress.Text = aCustomer.Address
        lblCity.Text = aCustomer.City
        lblCountry.Text = aCustomer.Country
        lblBalance.Text = aCustomer.Balance
    End Sub
```

The array *Customers* is populated when the program starts with a call to the InitData() subroutine (also in the project's module). The program assigns data to *Customers*, one element at a time, with statements like the following:

```
Dim cust As Customer
cust.Company = "Bottom-Dollar Markets"
cust.Manager = "Elizabeth Lincoln"
cust.Address = "23 Tsawassen Blvd."
cust.City = "Tsawassen"
cust.Country = "Canada"
cust.CustomerSince = #10/20/1996#
cust.Balance = 33500
Customers(1) = cust
```

The code assigns values to the fields of the *cust* variable and then assigns the entire variable to an element of the *Customers* array. The data could originate in a file or even a database. This wouldn't affect the operation of the application, which expects the GetCustomer() function to return a record of Customer type. If you decide to store the records in a file or a collection, the form's code need not change; only the implementation of the GetCustomer() function will change. You should also change the CountCustomers() function, so that it detects when it has reached the last record.

The Types project uses a single button that allows users to view the next record. You can place another button that displays the previous record. This button's code will be identical to the code of the existing button, with the exception that it will decrease the *currentIndex* variable.

Functions Returning Arrays

In addition to returning custom datatypes, VB .NET functions can also return arrays. This is an interesting possibility that allows you to write functions that return not only multiple values, but also an unknown number of values. Earlier in the chapter you saw how to return multiple values from a function as arguments, passed to the function by reference. You can also consider a custom structure as a collection of values. In this section, we'll revise the Stats() function that was described earlier in this chapter, so that it returns the statistics in an array. The new Stats() function will return not only the average and the standard deviation, but the minimum and maximum values in the data set as well. One way to declare a function that calculates all the statistics is the following:

```
Function Stats(ByRef DataArray() As Double) As Double()
```

This function accepts an array with the data values and returns an array of doubles. This notation is more compact and helps you write easier-to-read code.

To implement a function that returns an array, you must do the following:

1. Specify a type for the function's return value, and add a pair of parentheses after the type's name. Don't specify the dimensions of the array to be returned here; the array will be declared formally in the function.

2. In the function's code, declare an array of the same type and specify its dimensions. If the function should return four values, use a declaration like this one:

   ```
   Dim Results(3) As Double
   ```

   The *Results* array will be used to store the results and must be of the same type as the function—its name can be anything.

3. To return the *Results* array, simply use it as argument to the Return statement:

   ```
   Return(Results)
   ```

4. In the calling procedure, you must declare an array of the same type without dimensions:

   ```
   Dim Stats() As Double
   ```

5. Finally, you must call the function and assign its return value to this array:

   ```
   Stats() = Stats(DataSet())
   ```

   Here, *DataSet* is an array with the values whose basic statistics will be calculated by the Stats() function. Your code can then retrieve each element of the array with an index value as usual.

VB .NET at Work: The Statistics Project

The next project, the Statistics project, demonstrates how to design and call functions that return arrays. When you run it, the Statistics application creates a data set of random values and then calls the ArrayStats() function to calculate the data set's basic statistics. The results are returned in an array, and the main program displays them in Label controls, as shown in Figure 6.3. Every time the Show Statistics button is clicked, a new data set is generated and its statistics are displayed.

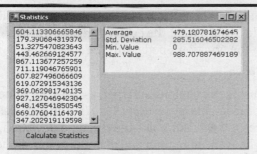

FIGURE 6.3: The Statistics project calculates the basic statistics of a data set and returns them in an array.

Let's start with the ArrayStats() function's code, which is shown in Listing 6.2.

Listing 6.2: The *ArrayStats()* Function

```
Function ArrayStats(ByVal DataArray() As Double) As Double()
    Dim Result(3) As Double
    Dim Sum, SumSquares, DataMin, DataMax As Double
    Dim DCount, i As Integer
    Sum = 0
    SumSquares = 0
    DCount = 0
    DataMin = System.Double.MaxValue
    DataMax = System.Double.MinValue
    For i = 0 To DataArray.GetUpperBound(0)
        Sum = Sum + DataArray(i)
        SumSquares = SumSquares + DataArray(i) ^ 2
```

```
            If DataArray(i) > DataMax Then DataMax = DataArray(i)
            If DataArray(i) < DataMin Then DataMin = DataArray(i)
            DCount = DCount + 1
        Next
        Dim Avg, StdDev As Double
        Avg = Sum / DCount
        StdDev = Math.Sqrt(SumSquares / DCount - Avg ^ 2)
        Result(0) = Avg
        Result(1) = StdDev
        Result(2) = DataMin
        Result(3) = DataMax
        ArrayStats = Result
    End Function
```

The function's return type is Double(), meaning the function will return an array of doubles; that's what the empty parentheses signify. This array is declared in the function's body with the statement:

```
Dim Result(3) As Double
```

The function performs its calculations and then assigns the values of the basic statistics to the elements of the array *Result*. The first element holds the average, the second element holds the standard deviation, and the other two elements hold the minimum and maximum data values. The *Result* array is finally returned to the calling procedure by the statement that assigns the array to the function name, just as you'd assign a variable to the name of the function that returns a single result.

The code behind the Show Statistics button, which calls the ArrayStats() function, is shown in Listing 6.3.

Listing 6.3: Calculating Statistics with the *ArrayStats()* Function

```
Protected Sub Button2_Click(ByVal sender As Object, _
                ByVal e As System.EventArgs)
    Dim SData(99) As Double
    Dim Stats() As Double
    Dim i As Integer
    Dim rnd As New System.Random()
    ListBox1.Items.Clear()
    For i = 0 To 99
        SData(i) = rnd.NextDouble() * 1000
        ListBox1.Items.Add(SData(i))
    Next
    Stats = ArrayStats(SData)
```

```
        TextBox1.Text = "Average" & vbTab & vbTab & Stats(0)
        TextBox1.Text = TextBox1.Text & cvCrLf & _
                        "Std. Deviation" & vbTab & Stats(1)
        TextBox1.Text = TextBox1.Text & vbCrLf & _
                        "Min. Value" & vbTab & Stats(2)
        TextBox1.Text = TextBox1.Text & vbCrLf & _
                        "Max. Value" & vbTab & Stats(3)
    End Sub
```

The code generates 100 random values and displays them on a ListBox control. Then, it calls the ArrayStats() function, passing the data values to it through the *SData* array. The function's return values are stored in the *Stats* array, which is declared as double but without dimensions. Then, the code displays the basic statistics on a TextBox control, one item per line.

Overloading Functions

There are situations where the same function must operate on different datatypes, or a different number of arguments. In the past, you had to write different functions, with different names and different arguments, to accommodate similar requirements. VB .NET introduces the concept of *function overloading*, which means that you can have multiple implementations of the same function, each with a different set of arguments and, possibly, a different return value. Yet, all overloaded functions share the same name. Let me introduce this concept by examining one of the many overloaded functions that come with the .NET Framework.

To generate a random number in the range from 0 to 1 (exclusive), use the NextDouble method of the System.Random class. To use the methods of the Random class, you must first create an instance of the class and then call the methods:

```
    Dim rnd As New System.Random
    Console.WriteLine("Three random numbers")
    Console.Write(rnd.NextDouble() & " - " & _
                  rnd.NextDouble() & " - " & _
                  rnd.NextDouble())
```

The random numbers that will be printed on the Output window will be double precision values in the range 0 to 1:

```
    0.656691639058614 - 0.967485965680092 - 0.993525570721145
```

More often than not, we need Integer random values. The Next method of the System.Random class returns an Integer value from −2,147,483,648 to 2,147,483,647 (this is the range of values that can be represented by the Integer datatype). We also want to generate random numbers in a limited range of Integer values. To emulate the throw of a dice, we want a random value in the range from 1 to 6, while for a roulette game we want an Integer random value in the range from 0 to 36. You can specify an upper limit for the random number with an optional Integer argument. The following statement will return a random integer in the range from 0 to 99:

```
randomInt = rnd.Next(100)
```

Finally, you can specify both the lower and upper limits of the random number's range. The following statement will return a random integer in the range from 1,000 to 1,999:

```
randomInt = rnd.Next(1000, 2000)
```

The same method behaves differently based on the arguments we supply. The behavior of the method depends either on the type of the arguments, the number of the arguments, or both of them. As you will see, there's no single function that alters its behavior based on its arguments. There are as many different implementations of the same function as there are argument combinations. All the functions share the same name, so that they appear to the user as a single, multifaceted function. These functions are overloaded, and you'll see in the following section how they're implemented.

If you haven't turned off the IntelliSense feature of the editor, then as soon as you type the opening parenthesis after a function or method name, you see a yellow box with the syntax of the function or method. You'll know that a function is overloaded when this box contains a number and two arrows. Each number corresponds to a different overloaded form, and you can move to the next or previous overloaded form by clicking the two little arrows or by pressing the arrow keys.

Let's build a custom overloaded function, which makes use of some topics discussed later in this book. The CountFiles() function counts the number of files that meet certain criteria. The criteria could be the size of the files, their type, or the date they were created. You can come up with any combination of these criteria, but here are the most useful combinations. (These are the functions I would use, but you can create even more combinations, or introduce new criteria of your own.) The names of the arguments are self-descriptive, so I need not explain what each form of the CountFiles() function does.

```
CountFiles(ByVal minSize As Integer, _
            ByVal maxSize As Integer) As Integer
CountFiles(ByVal fromDate As Date, _
            ByVal toDate As Date) As Integer
CountFiles(ByVal type As String) As Integer
CountFiles(ByVal minSize As Integer, _
            ByVal maxSize As Integer, _
            ByVal type As String) As Integer
CountFiles(ByVal fromDate As Date, ByVal toDate As Date, _
            ByVal type As String) As Integer
```

Listing 6.4 shows the implementation of these overloaded forms of the CountFiles() function. For the benefit of readers who are totally unfamiliar with file operations, I've included a statement that prints on the Output window the type of files counted by each function. The Console .WriteLine statement prints the values of the arguments passed to the function, along with a description of the type of search it's going to perform. The overloaded form that accepts two Integer values as arguments prints something like:

```
You've requested the files between 1000 and 100000 bytes
```

while the overloaded form that accepts a string as argument prints the following:

```
You've requested the .EXE files
```

Listing 6.4: The Overloaded Implementations of the *CountFiles()* Function

```
Overloads Function CountFiles(ByVal minSize As Integer, _
                            ByVal maxSize As Integer) _
                            As Integer
    Console.WriteLine("You've requested the files between " _
                & minSize & _
                " and " & maxSize & " bytes")
    Dim files() As String
    files = System.IO.Directory.GetFiles("c:\windows")
    Dim i, fileCount As Integer
```

Part II

```
        For i = 0 To files.GetUpperBound(0)
            Dim FI As New System.IO.FileInfo(files(i))
            If FI.Length >= minSize And FI.Length <= maxSize Then
                fileCount = fileCount + 1
            End If
        Next
        Return(fileCount)
    End Function
    Overloads Function CountFiles(ByVal fromDate As Date, _
                                  ByVal toDate As Date) _
                                  As Integer
        Console.WriteLine("You've requested the count of " & _
                          "files created from " & _
                          fromDate & " to " & toDate)
        Dim files() As String
        files = System.IO.Directory.GetFiles("c:\windows")
        Dim i, fileCount As Integer
        For i = 0 To files.GetUpperBound(0)
            Dim FI As New System.IO.FileInfo(files(i))
            If FI.CreationTime.Date >= fromDate And _
                    FI.CreationTime.Date <= toDate Then
                fileCount = fileCount + 1
            End If
        Next
        Return(fileCount)
    End Function
    Overloads Function CountFiles(ByVal type As String) _
                                  As Integer
        Console.WriteLine("You've requested the " & type & _
                          " files")
        Dim files() As String
        files = System.IO.Directory.GetFiles("c:\windows")
        Dim i, fileCount As Integer
        For i = 0 To files.GetUpperBound(0)
            Dim FI As New System.IO.FileInfo(files(i))
            If FI.Extension = type Then
                fileCount = fileCount + 1
            End If
        Next
        Return(fileCount)
    End Function
```

```
Overloads Function CountFiles(ByVal minSize As Integer, _
                    ByVal maxSize As Integer, _
                    ByVal type As String) As Integer
    Console.WriteLine("You've requested the " & type & _
                    " files between " & _
                    minSize & " and " & maxSize & " bytes")
    Dim files() As String
    files = System.IO.Directory.GetFiles("c:\windows")
    Dim i, fileCount As Integer
    For i = 0 To files.GetUpperBound(0)
        Dim FI As New System.IO.FileInfo(files(i))
        If FI.Length >= minSize And _
                FI.Length <= maxSize And _
                FI.Extension = type Then
            fileCount = fileCount + 1
        End If
    Next
    Return(fileCount)
End Function
Overloads Function CountFiles(ByVal fromDate As Date, _
                        ByVal toDate As Date, _
                        ByVal type As String) _
                        As Integer
    Console.WriteLine("You've requested the " & type & _
                    " files created from " & _
                    fromDate & " to " & toDate)
    Dim files() As String
    files = System.IO.Directory.GetFiles("c:\windows")
    Dim i, fileCount As Integer
    For i = 0 To files.GetUpperBound(0)
        Dim FI As New System.IO.FileInfo(files(i))
        If FI.CreationTime.Date >= fromDate And _
                FI.CreationTime.Date <= toDate And _
                FI.Extension = type Then
            fileCount = fileCount + 1
        End If
    Next
    Return(fileCount)
End Function
```

Start a new project and enter the definitions of the overloaded forms of the function on the form's level. Listing 6.4 is lengthy, but all the overloaded functions have the same structure and differ only in how they select the files to count. Then place a TextBox and a button on the form, as shown in Figure 6.4, and enter the statements from Listing 6.5 in the button's Click event handler. The project shown in Figure 6.4 is called OverloadedFunctions, and you'll find it on www.sybex.com.

FIGURE 6.4: The OverloadedFunctions project

Listing 6.5: Testing the Overloaded Forms of the *CountFiles()* Function

```
Private Sub Button1_Click(ByVal sender As System.Object, _
            ByVal e As System.EventArgs) _
            Handles Button1.Click
    TextBox1.AppendText(CountFiles(1000, 100000) & _
                " files with size between 1KB and 100KB" _
                & vbCrLf)
    TextBox1.AppendText(CountFiles(#1/1/2001#, #12/31/2001#) _
                    & " files created in 2001" & vbCrLf)
    TextBox1.AppendText(CountFiles(".BMP") & " BMP files" & _
                    vbCrLf)
    TextBox1.AppendText(CountFiles(1000, 100000, ".EXE") & _
                " EXE files between 1 and 100 KB" & vbCrLf)
    TextBox1.AppendText( _
            CountFiles(#1/1/2000#, #12/31/2001#, ".EXE") & _
            " EXE files created in 2000 and 2001")
End Sub
```

The button calls the various overloaded forms of the CountFiles() function one after the other and prints the results on the TextBox control.

Function overloading is new to VB .NET, but it's used heavily throughout the language. There are relatively few functions (or methods, for that matter) that aren't overloaded. Every time you enter the name of a function followed by an opening parenthesis, a list of its arguments appears in the drop-down list with the arguments of the function. If the function is overloaded, you'll see a number in front of the list of arguments, as shown in Figure 6.5. This number is the order of the overloaded form of the function, and it's followed by the arguments of the specific form of the function. The figure shows all the forms of the CountFiles() function.

▲ 1 of 5 ▼	CountFiles (**minSize As Integer**, maxSize As Integer) As Integer
▲ 2 of 5 ▼	CountFiles (**fromDate As Date**, toDate As Date) As Integer
▲ 3 of 5 ▼	CountFiles (**type As String**) As Integer
▲ 4 of 5 ▼	CountFiles (**minSize As Integer**, maxSize As Integer, type As String) As Integer
▲ 5 of 5 ▼	CountFiles (**fromDate As Date**, toDate As Date, type As String) As Integer

FIGURE 6.5:   The overloaded forms of the CountFiles() function

You will have to overload many of the functions you'll be writing once you start developing real applications, because you'll want your functions to work on a variety of datatypes. This is not the only reason to overload functions. You may also need to write functions that behave differently based on the number and types of their arguments.

NOTE

Notice that you can't overload a function by changing its return type. That's why the Min() function returns a double value, which is the most accurate value. If you don't need more than a couple of decimal digits (or no fractional part at all), you can round the return value in your code accordingly. However, you can't have two Min() functions that accept the exact same arguments and return different datatypes. Overloaded forms of a function are differentiated by the number and/or the type of their arguments, but not by the return value.

WHAT'S NEXT

This chapter concludes the presentation of the core of the language. In the last two chapters, you've learned how to declare and use variables, and how to break your applications into smaller, manageable units of code. These units of code are the subroutines and functions. Subroutines perform actions and don't return any values. Functions, on the other hand, perform calculations and return values. Most of the language's built-in functionality is in the form of functions. The methods of the various controls look and feel like functions, because they're implemented as functions. Functions are indeed a major aspect of the language.

Subroutines aren't as common. Many programmers actually prefer to write only functions and use the return value to indicate the success or failure of the procedure, even if the procedure need not return any value. Event handlers are implemented as subroutines, because they don't return any values. Event handlers aren't called from within your code; they are simply activated by the Common Language Runtime.

Subroutines and functions communicate with the rest of the application through arguments. There are many ways to pass arguments to a procedure, and you've seen them all. You have also seen how to write overloaded functions, which are new to VB .NET; and as you will see in the rest of this book, they're quite common.

In the next chapter, we will look at how to handle errors and bugs in the code. Although the previous code was written with great care, so as not to have any bugs, this is usually not the case when applications are first being written. Therefore, you need a good understanding of how to handle errors.

Chapter 7
Error Handling and Debugging

Writing a piece of software, even a relatively small one, can be an extremely complicated task. Developers usually put careful forethought and planning into the nature of the task and the means they will use to solve the task through the program that they intend to write.

The complex nature of software development invariably leads to errors in programming. This chapter sets out to explain the different types of errors that you might encounter when writing Visual Basic .NET code, some of the tools that you can use to locate these errors, and the coding structures used to prevent these errors when users run your program.

In addition to programming errors, your application should be able to gracefully handle all the abnormal conditions it may encounter—from user errors (when they enter a string where the program expects a date or numeric value) to malfunctioning devices, or simpler situations such as not being able to save data to a file because another application is using it. All these

Adapted from *Mastering Visual Basic .NET*
by Evangelos Petroutsos
ISBN 0-7821-2877-7 $49.99

conditions may be beyond your program's control, but your application should be able to handle them. At the very least, your program shouldn't crash; it's OK to abort an operation and display a warning, but an application shouldn't crash.

TYPES OF ERRORS

The errors caused by a computer program (regardless of the language in which the program is written) can be categorized into three major groups: design-time, runtime, and logic.

The design-time error is the easiest to find and fix. A design-time error occurs when you write a piece of code that does not conform to the rules of the language in which you're writing. They are easy to find because Visual Studio .NET tells you not only where they are, but also what part of the line it doesn't understand.

Runtime errors are harder to locate, because VS doesn't give you any help in finding the error until it occurs in your program. These errors occur when your program attempts something illegal, like accessing data that doesn't exist or a resource to which it doesn't have the proper permissions. These types of errors can cause your program to crash, or hang, unless they are handled properly.

The third type of error, the logic error, is often the most insidious type to locate, because it may not manifest itself as a problem in the program at all. A program with a logic error simply means that the output or operation of your program is not exactly as you intended it. It could be as simple as an incorrect calculation or having a menu option enabled when you wanted it disabled, or something complex like a database that's duplicating order information.

This section will cover and demonstrate all three types of errors, and show you tools and techniques that you can use to hunt them down and squash them.

Design-Time Errors

Also called syntax errors, design-time errors occur when the Visual Basic .NET interpreter cannot recognize one or more lines of code that you have written. Some design-time errors are simply typographical errors, where you have mistyped a keyword. Others are the result of missing items: undeclared or untyped variables, classes not yet imported, incorrect parameter lists in a function or method call, or referencing members on a class that do not exist.

A program with as few as one design-time error cannot be compiled and run—you must locate and correct the error before continuing. Fortunately, design-time errors are the easiest to detect and correct, because VB .NET shows you the exact location of these errors and gives you good information about what part of the code it can't understand. What follows is a brief example showing several design-time errors in just a few lines of code.

The event code shown in Figure 7.1 was typed into the Click event of a button named *Button1*.

```
Private Sub Button1_Click(ByVal sender As System.Object, _
ByVal e As System.EventArgs) _
Handles Button1.Click

    For i = 1 To 100
        lbNumbers.add("item " & i)
    Next

End Sub
```

FIGURE 7.1:   VB .NET identifies the locations of design-time errors.

Note the three blue squiggly lines under various parts of this brief code (under two instances of the letter *i* and under the term *lbNumbers*). Each one of those squiggly lines represents a design-time error. To determine what the errors are, locate the Task List window in the IDE and bring it forward. The Task List displays the errors seen in Figure 7.2 for the code from Figure 7.1.

!	✔	Description	File	Line
		Task List - 3 Build Error tasks shown (filtered)		
		Click here to add a new task		
		The name 'i' is not declared.	C:\vbNet\prjErrors\Form1.vb	61
!		The name 'lbNumbers' is not declared.	C:\vbNet\prjErrors\Form1.vb	62
!		The name 'i' is not declared.	C:\vbNet\prjErrors\Form1.vb	62

FIGURE 7.2:   Corresponding errors in the Task List

Part II

NOTE

You can determine which squiggly blue line corresponds to which design-time error in the Task List by double-clicking the error in the Task List. The corresponding error will become selected in the code window.

Note that two of the errors are the same: they state "The name 'i' is not declared." In this case, these errors are telling you that you've referenced a variable named *i* but you have not declared it. To fix these two errors, you need to modify the code as shown in Figure 7.3.

```
Private Sub Button1_Click(ByVal sender As System.Object, _
ByVal e As System.EventArgs) _
Handles Button1.Click

    Dim i As Integer

    For i = 1 To 100
        lbNumbers.add("item " & i)
    Next

End Sub
```

FIGURE 7.3:   Once declared, the variable doesn't produce an error.

The only error remaining now is "The name 'lbNumbers' is not declared." As the programmer of the application, you would probably have some type of idea what *1bNumbers* is. In this case, I was attempting to add 100 items to a ListBox, and *1bNumbers* is supposed to be the name of the ListBox on the form. This error tells me that I do not have a ListBox on the form named *1bNumbers*. I've either forgotten to put a ListBox on the form entirely, or I did add one but did not name it *1bNumbers*. To correct the problem, I can either make sure a ListBox is on my form with the correct name, or I can change this code so that the name matches whatever I've named the ListBox.

I added a ListBox named *1bNumbers* to my form. After doing so, however, I'm still left with a syntax error on the line, as seen in Figure 7.4.

Note that the text of the error is different. It reads "The name 'add' is not a member of 'System.Windows.Forms.ListBox'." This is telling you that it now recognizes that *1bNumbers* is a ListBox object, but there is no member (property, event, or method) named *add* on a ListBox. So what's the correct way to write a line of code that adds an item to a ListBox? Some brief research in the help menu should yield the correct line of code—the one shown in Figure 7.5.

```
Private Sub Button1_Click(ByVal sender As System.Object, _
ByVal e As System.EventArgs) _
Handles Button1.Click

    Dim i As Integer

    For i = 1 To 100
        lbNumbers.add("item " & i)
    Next

End Sub
d Class
```

- 1 Build Error task shown (filtered)		
Description	File	Line
Click here to add a new task		
The name 'add' is not a member of 'System.Windows.Forms.ListBox'.	C:\vbNet\prjErrors\Form1.vb	73

FIGURE 7.4:   The ListBox statement still produces a design-time error.

```
Private Sub Button1_Click(ByVal sender As System.Object, _
ByVal e As System.EventArgs) _
Handles Button1.Click

    Dim i As Integer

    For i = 1 To 100
        lbNumbers.Items.Add("item " & i)
    Next

End Sub
```

FIGURE 7.5:   This syntax is correct.

Notice all blue squiggly lines are now gone, and the Task List should be empty of errors as well. This means our program is free of syntax errors and is ready to run.

Runtime Errors

Runtime errors are much more insidious to find and fix than design-time errors. Runtime errors are problems encountered by your program while it's running. Runtime errors can take on dozens of different shapes and forms. Here are some examples:

- ▶ Attempting to open a file that doesn't exist
- ▶ Trying to log in to a server with an incorrect username or password

- ▶ Trying to access a folder for which you have insufficient rights

- ▶ Requesting data from a database table that has been renamed

- ▶ Opening a file on a server that is down for maintenance

- ▶ Accessing an Internet URL that no longer exists

- ▶ Allocating a resource without the necessary available RAM

- ▶ Dividing a number by zero

- ▶ Users entering character data where a number is expected (and vice versa)

As you can see, runtime errors can occur due to an unexpected state of the computer or network upon which your program is running, or simply because the user has supplied the wrong information (an invalid password, a bad filename, and so on). Because of this, you can write a program that runs fine on your own machine, and all the machines in your test environment, but fails on a customer site due to the state of that customer's computing resources.

As you might imagine, runtime errors can be many degrees harder to diagnose and fix in comparison to design-time errors. After all, any error you make in design time is right there in front of, on your own development PC. Not only that, but the Visual Studio compiler goes ahead and tells you right where a design-time error is and why it's an error. The runtime error, by comparison, may only manifest itself in strange computing conditions on a PC halfway across the world. We'll see in later sections how runtime errors can be detected and managed.

Logic Errors

Logic errors also occur at runtime, and because of this, they are often difficult to track down. A logic error occurs when a program does not do what the developer intended it to do. For example, you might provide the code to add a customer to a customer list, but when the end user runs the program and adds a new customer, the customer is not there. The error might lie in the code that adds the customer to the database; or perhaps the customer is indeed being added, but the grid that lists all the customers is not being refreshed after the add customer code, so it merely appears that the customer wasn't added.

A second example of a logic error: Suppose you allow the end user to manually type the two-letter state code of every customer address that they enter into your program. One of the functions of your program might be to display a map of the U.S. that shades the states based on the number of customers within each state. How do you suppose your shaded map will display customers with invalid state codes? Most likely, these customers would not be displayed on the map at all. Later, the manager of the department calls you and says, "The Total Customers Entered report for last month tells me that 7,245 customers were entered into our system. However, the Density Map report only shown 6,270 customers on it. Why don't these two reports match?"

In this example, we've made a design decision—the decision to allow the end user to type the two-digit state code—and that decision has led to a major logic error, the fact that two reports from the same system give different results for the number of customers entered into the system for the same time period.

Here are some actual VB .NET code snippets that produce logic errors. Consider the following code snippet.

```
Private Sub Button1_Click(ByVal sender As System.Object, _
            ByVal e As System.EventArgs) _
            Handles Button1.Click
    Dim i As Integer
    i = 1
    Do While i > 0
        i += 1
    Loop
End Sub
```

Here we have an Integer variable set to 1 and incremented by one in a loop. Every time the loop iterates, the number gets bigger. The loop will continue to iterate as long as the variable is greater than 0. See any problem with this? The problem is that the value of the variable will *always* be greater than 0, so the loop will never terminate. This is called an infinite loop, and it's one of my personal favorite types of errors (favorite in the sense that I seem to always find a way to write new and exciting flavors of infinite loop). Of course, this loop isn't exactly infinite—after 2 billion iterations, an overflow will occur, but that's a good indication as to what happened.

Here's another simple example of a logic error:

```
Private Sub ColorTheLabel(ByVal lbl As Label)
    If CInt(lbl.Text) < 0 Then
        lbl.ForeColor = Color.Green
    Else
        lbl.ForeColor = Color.Red
    End If
End Sub
```

This routine was intended to color the text of a label red if the label text contained a negative number, and green if it contained a positive number (or 0). However, I got the logic backward—the label text is green for numbers less than 0, and red otherwise. This code won't produce any design-time errors or runtime crashes. It simply does the opposite of what I intended it to do.

Note finally that logic errors may or may not manifest themselves as program crashes. In the previous logic error examples, the programs wouldn't have crashed or produce any type of error message—they simply did not perform as intended. Some logic errors might indeed produce a program crash, at which point the line between a logic error and a runtime error becomes blurry. The fact that a new customer doesn't appear in a grid might cause a crash if your program tries to highlight that new customer in the grid but the customer row isn't there. In this case, we've made a logic error (not adding the customer to the grid) that's caused a runtime error (program crashes when it tries to highlight a row in a grid that doesn't exist). In this case, fixing the logic error would automatically fix the runtime error.

EXCEPTIONS AND STRUCTURED EXCEPTION HANDLING

A runtime error in VB .NET generates an *exception*. An exception is a response to the error condition that the program just generated. Figure 7.6 is an example of an exception message. This is the dialog that appears when you are running your program in the IDE. If the same error were to be encountered by a user running your program, the dialog would look slightly different, as seen in Figure 7.7.

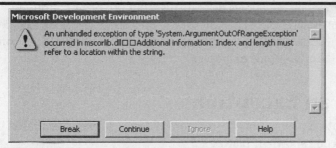

FIGURE 7.6: Design-time error message

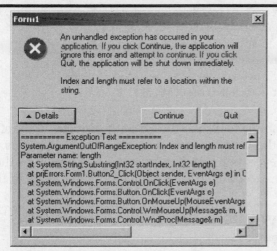

FIGURE 7.7: Runtime error message

Note that this dialog gives the user the opportunity to continue the program. In some rare cases, this might be desirable, but in most cases you probably would not want your users attempting to continue after a program exception has occurred. Think about it—your program has just encountered some form of data that it cannot handle correctly, and now it's asking the user if it should attempt to ignore that bad data and continue. It is difficult to predict what type of further problems might result as the program continues on and attempts to handle the bad data. Most likely, further exceptions will be generated as the subsequent lines of code attempt to deal with the same unexpected data.

If we don't want our users handling an exception that the program generates, then we'll simply have to handle it ourselves. The Visual Basic .NET error-handling model allows us to do just that. An error handler is a section of VB .NET code that allows you to detect exceptions and perform the necessary steps to recover from them. What follows are some exception-handling code examples.

Studying an Exception

The exception dialogs shown in Figures 7.6 and 7.7 were generated by the VB .NET code shown in Listing 7.1.

Listing 7.1: An Unhandled Exception

```
Private Sub Button2_Click(ByVal sender As System.Object, _
                ByVal e As System.EventArgs) _
                Handles Button2.Click
    Dim s As String
    s = "answer"
    Button2.Text = s.Substring(10, 1)
End Sub
```

This code is attempting to display the eleventh character in the string "answer." Seeing as the word "answer" contains only six characters, you can imagine how an exception might be generated. Let's examine the exact phrasing of the exception to learn as much as possible about this particular error.

```
An unhandled exception of type
    'System.ArgumentOutOfRangeException'
    occurred in mscorlib.dll
Additional information:
    Index and length must refer to a location
    within the string.
```

NOTE

This seems almost too trivial to mention, but always thoroughly read the exceptions that your program generates. Their purpose is to give you a brief description of the condition that caused the error, which of course is necessary to know before you can figure out how to handle it.

The first thing to notice is the fact that this message refers to this runtime error as an *unhandled* exception. This means that the line of code that generated this error is not contained within an exception-handling block.

The second interesting piece of information is that this exception is of type System.ArgumentOutOfRangeException, whatever that means. What's important to note is that the different types of errors can be classified into groups. This is important when you realize that the .NET Framework exception-handling mechanism follows the same object-oriented design principles that the rest of the Framework follows. An exception creates an instance of an object, and that object is a descendent of class Exception.

The previous error message is telling us that the exception object instance generated is of class (type) System.ArgumentOutOfRange-Exception, which is a descendent of class Exception.

The "additional information" block gives us some specific notes on the nature of error. It tells us that the index and length parameters of the Substring method must both lie within the boundaries of the string. In our case, we attempted to retrieve the eleventh character of a six-character string, clearly outside the boundary.

Getting a Handle on this Exception

Listing 7.2 is the same defective code statement as 7.1, but with a simple exception handler wrapped around it.

Listing 7.2: Handling an Exception, Version 1

```
Private Sub Button2_Click(ByVal sender As System.Object, _
             ByVal e As System.EventArgs) _
             Handles Button2.Click
    Dim s As String
    s = "answer"
    Try
        Button2.Text = s.Substring(10, 1)
    Catch
        Button2.Text = "error"
    End Try
End Sub
```

This code attempts to do the same thing as the code above, but this time the faulty Substring statement is wrapped around a Try...Catch...End Try block. This block is a basic exception handler. If any of the code after the Try statement generates an exception, then program control automatically jumps to the code after the Catch statement. If no exceptions are generated in the code under the Try statement, then the Catch block is skipped. When this code is run, the System.ArgumentOutOfRangeException is generated, but now the code does not terminate with a message box. Instead, the text property of *Button2* is set to the word "error," and the program continues along.

Listing 7.3 handles the same error in a slightly different way.

Listing 7.3: Handling an Exception, Version 2

```
Private Sub Button2_Click(ByVal sender As System.Object, _
              ByVal e As System.EventArgs) _
              Handles Button2.Click
    Dim s As String
    s = "answer"
    Try
        Button2.Text = s.Substring(10, 1)
    Catch oEX As Exception
        Call MsgBox(oEX.Message)
    End Try
End Sub
```

In this example, the exception generates an instance of the Exception class and places that instance in a variable named *oEX*. Having the exception instance variable is useful because it can give you the text of the exception, which we display in a message box. Of course, displaying the exception message in a message box is pretty much the same thing that your program does when an unhandled exception is generated, so it's doubtful that you would do this in your own program. However, you could log the exception text to the event log or a custom error file.

Note that the previous exception handlers do not differentiate between types of errors. If *any* exception is generated within the Try block, then the Catch block is executed. You can also write exception handlers that handle different classes of errors, as seen in Listing 7.4.

Listing 7.4: Handling an Exception, Version 3

```
Private Sub Button3_Click(ByVal sender As System.Object, _
              ByVal e As System.EventArgs) _
              Handles Button3.Click
    Try
        Button3.Text = lbStates.SelectedItem.ToString
    Catch oEX As System.NullReferenceException
```

```
      Call MsgBox("Please select an item first")
   Catch oEX As Exception
      Call MsgBox("Some other error: " & oEX.Message)
   End Try
 End Sub
```

This code attempts to take the selected item in a ListBox named *lbStates* and display it as the caption of a button. If no item is selected in the ListBox, then a System.NullReferenceException will be generated, and we use that information to tell the user to select an item in the ListBox. If any other type of exception is generated, then this code displays the text of that error message.

Note that, in the list of exceptions in Listing 7.4, the more specific exception handler comes first and the more general exception handler comes last. This is how you'll want to code all of your multiple Catch exception handlers, so that they are handled in the correct order. If you put your more general Catch handlers first, then they will execute first and override the more specific handlers.

Also note that the variable *oEX* is reused in each of the exception blocks. This is possible because the Catch statement actually serves as a declaration of that variable (note that I didn't have to Dim the *oEX* variable anywhere) and that the *oEX* variable has a local scope only within the Catch block.

Note that because the Exception instance is declared in each Catch block, it has scope only within that block. The code in Listing 7.5 is illegal for scoping reasons.

Listing 7.5: Handling an Exception, Version 4 (Illegal)

```
Private Sub Button3_Click(ByVal sender As System.Object, _
            ByVal e As System.EventArgs) _
            Handles Button3.Click
   Try
      Button3.Text = lbStates.SelectedItem.ToString
   Catch oEX As System.NullReferenceException
      Call MsgBox("please select an item first")
   Catch oEX As Exception
      Call MsgBox("some other error")
   End Try
   MsgBox(oEX.message)
End Sub
```

The final MsgBox is not valid because the *oEX* variable that it attempts to display is not in scope at this point of the procedure. The two *oEX* variables have scope only in their Catch blocks.

Finally (!)

You'll recall that when an exception is generated and handled by a Catch statement, the code execution is immediately transferred to the first relevant Catch exception handler block and then continues on out of the Try...Catch...End Try block. Sometimes, it might be necessary to perform some cleanup before moving out of the exception-handling block. Consider the procedure demonstrated in Listing 7.6.

Listing 7.6: A Possible Exception

```
Protected Sub ReadFromATextFile(cFilename as string)
    Dim s As StreamReader
    Dim cLine As String
    Dim bDone As Boolean = False
    lbresults.Items.Clear()
    s = New Streamreader(cFilename)
    Try
        While Not bDone
            cLine = s.ReadLine()
            If cLine Is Nothing Then
                bDone = True
            Else
                Call lbresults.Items.Add(cLine)
            End If
        End While
        s.Close()
    Catch oEX as Exception
        Call MsgBox("some error occurred")
    End Try
End Sub
```

This method attempts to read the contents of a text file and put the results into a ListBox, line by line. Most of the reading code is wrapped within a generic exception handler. If an exception is encountered in the main loop, then the s.Close() line will in all likelihood not be executed. This means that our file stream will never be properly closed, possibly leading to a resource leak.

Fortunately, an additional type of block is available in exception handlers that specifically allows us to avoid this type of problem. This new block is called the Finally block. The code within a Finally block always executes, whether an exception is generated or not. The code in Listing 7.7 is the same as the method in Listing 7.6 but is now modified to wrap the s.Close() method inside a Finally block.

Listing 7.7: Handling an Exception with a *Finally* Block

```
Protected Sub ReadFromATextFile(cFilename as string)
    Dim s As StreamReader
    Dim cLine As String
    Dim bDone As Boolean = False
    lbresults.Items.Clear()
    s = New Streamreader(cFilename)
    Try
        While Not bDone
            cLine = s.ReadLine()
            If cLine Is Nothing Then
                bDone = True
            Else
                Call lbresults.Items.Add(cLine)
            End If
        End While
    Catch oEX as Exception
        Call MsgBox("some error occurred")
    Finally
        s.Close()
    End Try
End Sub
```

Here, you see that any exception within the file-reading loop will be handled with a message box, and then the StreamReader object is closed inside the Finally block. This close statement runs whether the code within the Try...Catch block succeeds or fails. This allows you to guarantee that certain resources or handles are properly disposed of when they are no longer needed.

Customizing Exception Handling

Hundreds of exception classes are built into the .NET Framework, and you may not want to handle all of them the same way. You can customize the way certain exceptions are handled by bringing up the Exceptions dialog (see Figure 7.8) found in the Debug menu.

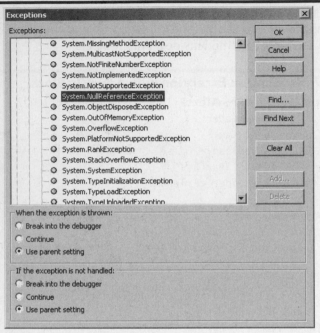

FIGURE 7.8: The Debug ≻ Exceptions dialog

The exception shown in the figure is one we saw in the earlier examples, System.NullReferenceException. When this exception is first encountered, the system is currently set to do whatever the parent setting specifies. Tracing up the tree in this dialog, we eventually find that all .NET Framework exceptions are set to continue when they are first encountered, but to break into the debugger if they are not handled in a Try...Catch...Finally...End Try block. This is consistent with what we saw in the earliest exception examples—a dialog would be displayed when an exception was encountered, but that dialog would disappear once we wrote the proper exception-handling code.

Throwing Your Own Exceptions

As you become more adept at writing VB .NET classes, you will probably encounter the need to throw your own exceptions. Imagine writing the code for an Integer property that has a certain range. If a fellow developer is using your class and attempts to set the property to a value beyond this range, you would probably want to inform the developer that he has entered an invalid value. The best way to inform him of this problem is to send him an exception. That way, the developer using your class can choose to handle this error in his own way by writing an exception handler in his code. Listing 7.8 is an example of "throwing" an exception.

Listing 7.8: Throwing an Exception

```
Private FValue As Integer = 0
Property Value() As Integer
    Get
        Return FValue
    End Get
    Set(ByVal iValue As Integer)
        If iValue <= FMax Then
            FValue = iValue
        Else
            FValue = FMax
            Throw New OverflowException(_
                "Cannot set ProgressBar value to greater " & _
                "than maximum.")
        End If
        Invalidate()
    End Set
```

This code is taken from a ProgressBar control. It is the code that implements the Value property of the ProgressBar control. A check is done to make sure that the value that the property is set to is less than or equal to the value of the Max property, because you can't set the current value to be bigger than the maximum defined value. If the property is trying to be set to a value larger than the max, then an exception is generated via the Throw statement. This statement instantiates an exception of class OverflowException and produces a custom error that the fellow developer can see in his own exception handler.

Part II

DEBUGGING

As you've seen, encountering errors is nearly a certainty when developing a piece of software. Syntax errors, of course, are the easiest to detect, because the IDE tells you right where they are and what the nature of the error is. The runtime errors are harder to locate and correct because of the many forms that these errors can take. You've seen examples of errors that will cause your program to crash, as well as errors that spiral your program off into an infinite loop, and even errors that produce no outward signs at all—they simply cause the program to behave in some unintended way.

Fortunately, Visual Studio .NET provides you with a fine selection of tools to detect and remove the errors in your program. The act of hunting and eliminating errors is called *debugging,* because your goal is to remove the bugs (or de-bug) the program.

Breakpoints

The breakpoint is the first and most important weapon in the war against bugs. When you set a *breakpoint* in your program, you're telling VS .NET to stop execution of the program when it reaches a certain line in the code. Once stopped, you can examine the state of the program, including the values of the variables, the procedure stack, and the contents of memory.

Before we can look at debugging essentials, we need some buggy code. Let's write a program to count all the vowels in a string. To set this program up, start a new WinForms project, and then add a button named *cbCount* and a TextBox named *tbPhrase* to the form. Add the code from Listing 7.9 to the project.

NOTE

You'll find all the code from this chapter on www.sybex.com. Search for the book by its ISBN number, 2887, or its title, *Visual Basic .NET Complete.* You can download the code from the download button.

Listing 7.9: Bug-Filled Code

```
Private Sub cbCount_Click(ByVal sender As System.Object, _
                ByVal e As System.EventArgs) _
                Handles cbCount.Click
```

```
        cbCount.Text = CountTheVowels(cbCount.Text)
    End Sub
    Private Function CountTheVowels _
                (ByVal cSomeString As String) As Integer
        Dim x As Integer = 1
        Dim iTot As Integer = 0
        Dim iPos As Integer
        Do While x <= cSomeString.Length
            iPos = InStr("aeio", _
                        cSomeString.Substring(x, 1).ToLower)
            If iPos > 0 Then
                iTot += 1
            End If
        Loop
        Return iTot
    End Function
```

The Button click event passes the contents of the text box into the function CountTheVowels(), which is where all the dirty work will be performed. When the count is obtained, the caption of the button should be replaced with the vowel count. Once you get the code for the program typed in exactly as seen above, try running the program, entering some text into the text box, and clicking the button. Then wait. And wait. My guess is that the caption of the button will not change until you stop the application by pressing Ctrl+Break (or select Debug ➢ Stop Debugging). If you wait long enough, an overflow exception will occur. This means that the value of the variable *iTot* has exceeded the maximum value you can represent with an Integer.

Obviously, this little function shouldn't take very long to run, so something screwy must be going on, like an infinite loop. Let's set a breakpoint in the function and see if we can spot it.

To set a breakpoint, place the cursor on a line of code in the function where you want the program to stop, and press the F9 key. The line of code should become highlighted in red, as seen in Figure 7.9.

Once a breakpoint is set, you can begin the program, type some text into the text box, and click the button. Like a good soldier, the debugger should come up on that same line of code, this time highlighted in yellow. This means that the program has stopped execution on that exact line of code.

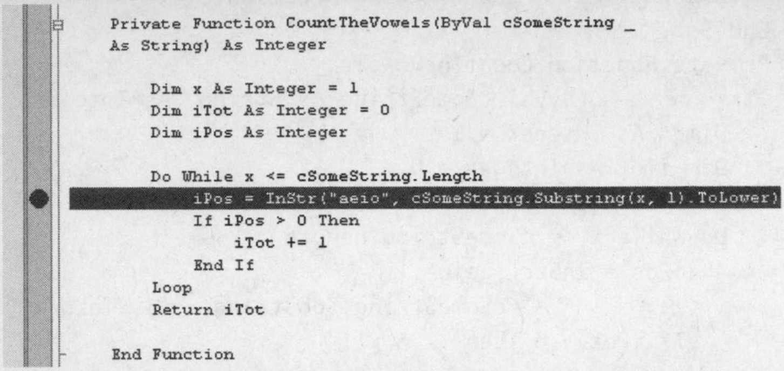

```
Private Function CountTheVowels(ByVal cSomeString _
As String) As Integer

    Dim x As Integer = 1
    Dim iTot As Integer = 0
    Dim iPos As Integer

    Do While x <= cSomeString.Length
        iPos = InStr("aeio", cSomeString.Substring(x, 1).ToLower)
        If iPos > 0 Then
            iTot += 1
        End If
    Loop
    Return iTot

End Function
```

FIGURE 7.9: Setting a breakpoint

Now we can start looking around. First, take the cursor and hover it over some of the areas of code. You should be able to see a tooltip displaying the value of the various variables you rest the mouse over, like the one in Figure 7.10.

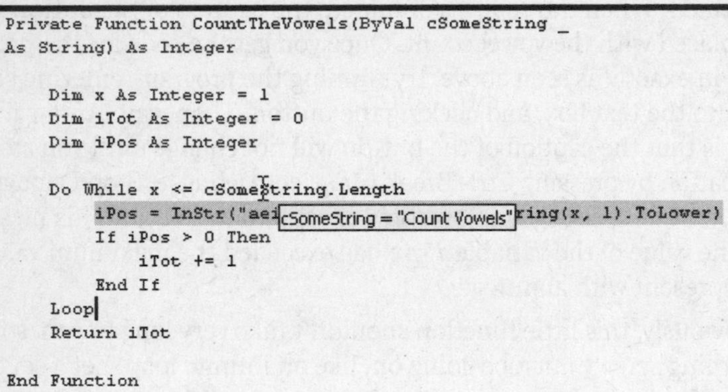

```
Private Function CountTheVowels(ByVal cSomeString _
As String) As Integer

    Dim x As Integer = 1
    Dim iTot As Integer = 0
    Dim iPos As Integer

    Do While x <= cSomeString.Length
        iPos = InStr("aei  cSomeString = "Count Vowels" ring(x, 1).ToLower)
        If iPos > 0 Then
            iTot += 1
        End If
    Loop
    Return iTot

End Function
```

FIGURE 7.10: Tooltips display the value of variables.

The figure displays the first of the errors I've made coding this program. The value of the variable *cSomeString* is "Count Vowels," but this is not the string I typed into my text box. Why is this string being passed into the function? A quick examination of the function call reveals this problem:

```
cbCount.Text = CountTheVowels(cbCount.Text)
```

Note that I inadvertently passed the Text property of the button *cbCount*, when my intention was to pass in the value of tbPhrase.Text. This is a perfect example of a logic error. The code works fine (well, anyway, it will work fine once we find the rest of these bugs), but it won't count the vowels in the string that we intended to count. The fix for this first bug is easy. First, stop the program from running by selecting Stop Debugging from the Debug menu (shortcut key is Shift+F5).

NOTE

Spend some time memorizing the shortcut keys for all the debugging functions. You'll be using these functions quite a bit, and using the shortcut keys will save a ton of time.

Once the program is stopped, change the CountTheVowels() function call as follows (note the change marked in bold font). Now we're passing in the string we intended.

```
cbCount.Text = CountTheVowels(tbPhrase.Text)
```

Stepping Through

As it often happens, we started looking for an infinite loop, but found another, unrelated bug first. Now that we've squashed that bug, we can go back to running the program and looking for the original problem. Start up the program again, type some text into the text box, and click the button. Once again, the program should stop at the breakpoint.

Let's watch a few of the program lines run in sequence and see if that tells us anything. To make the program step through the current line of code, press the F10 key. Each time you press F10, one line of code will execute, and the yellow highlight will move to the next line of code that is about to be executed.

NOTE

The F11 key also steps through the code, but it will step into any procedures that are called. The F10 key steps over the procedure calls, running them all at once and returning back to the original spot. This allows you to skip over the line-by-line tracing of procedures that you are not currently debugging.

You can continue to trace through the loop line by line and examine variable values with the tooltips. Can you figure out the cause of the infinite loop? Perhaps it's time to bring in some more debugging tools.

The Local and Watch Windows

While still stopped in debug mode, select Debug ➤ Windows ➤ Locals from the menu. The Locals window (Figure 7.11) should be displayed in the lower section of the IDE. This window shows you the current value of all of the locally declared variables. Now we can see the value of the variables changing as we step through the program.

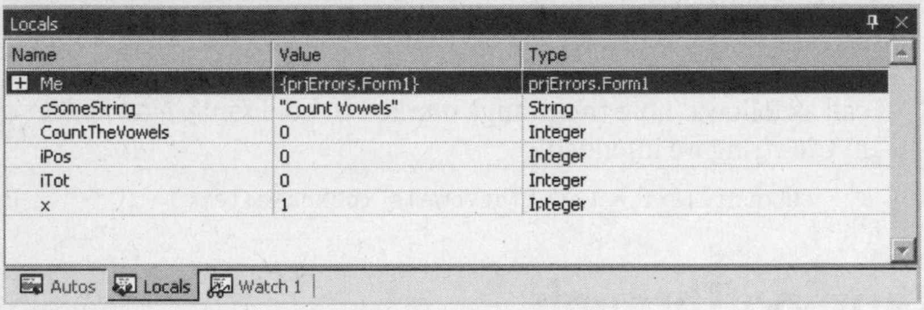

Name	Value	Type
⊞ Me	{prjErrors.Form1}	prjErrors.Form1
cSomeString	"Count Vowels"	String
CountTheVowels	0	Integer
iPos	0	Integer
iTot	0	Integer
x	1	Integer

Autos Locals Watch 1

FIGURE 7.11:   The Locals window

Try stepping through the loop a few more times. You might notice that the values of the variables aren't changing. To get even more information, highlight the entire phrase cSomeString.Substring(x, 1).ToLower, right-click, and select Add Watch from the context menu. This will bring up the Watch window, as seen in Figure 7.12.

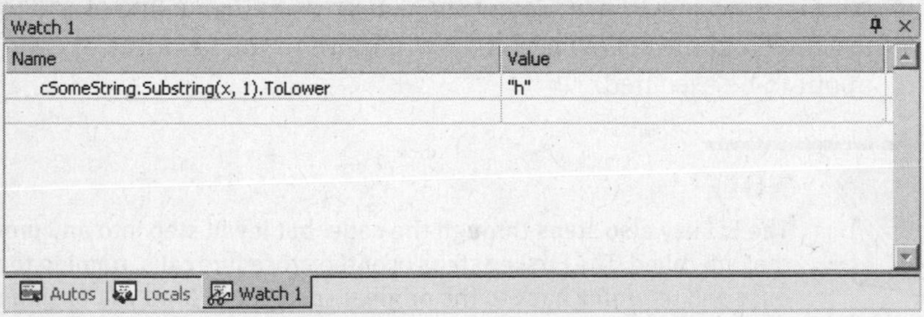

Name	Value
cSomeString.Substring(x, 1).ToLower	"h"

Autos Locals Watch 1

FIGURE 7.12:   The Watch window

The Watch window is similar to the Locals window, but it allows you to look at the value of complex expressions like the one we just placed in it.

Once again, try stepping through the loop a few times. You might expect that the Substring command would be incrementing the letter in the string as the loop iterates, but that isn't happening. The only logical reason for this is that the value of counter variable x isn't changing. Let's look at the loop again.

```
Do While x <= cSomeString.Length
    iPos = InStr("aeio", cSomeString.Substring(x, 1).ToLower)
    If iPos > 0 Then
        iTot += 1
    End If
Loop
```

I've made one of the classic looping blunders here. I set up a counter variable x to loop through the string character by character, but I never added any code to increment the string! That's as sure a recipe for an infinite loop as anything. Fixing that problem is an easy remedy (see the code highlighted in bold).

```
Do While x <= cSomeString.Length
    iPos = InStr("aeio", cSomeString.Substring(x, 1).ToLower)
    If iPos > 0 Then
        iTot += 1
    End If
    x += 1
Loop
```

Okay, that bug is squashed, so it's time to remove the breakpoint and rerun the program to see if it works. This time, however, the program crashes and burns with the following error:

```
An unhandled exception of type
    'System.ArgumentOutOfRangeException'
    occurred in mscorlib.dll. Additional information:
    Index and length must refer to a location within
    the string.
```

We've seen that error before—it means that we tried to look at a character beyond the length of the string. By checking the Locals window, you should be able to eventually track down this problem. The problem here is that the loop counter x starts at character 1 and ends at value cSomeString.Length. Although that range is correct for VB version 6

and below, .NET strings are indexed *starting at 0*. Oops. We need to modify our procedure as shown by the two bold items here, the zero and the
less-than sign:

```
Private Function CountTheVowels _
                (ByVal cSomeString As String) As Integer
    Dim x As Integer = 0
    Dim iTot As Integer = 0
    Dim iPos As Integer
    Do While x < cSomeString.Length
        iPos = InStr("aeio", _
                    cSomeString.Substring(x, 1).ToLower)
        If iPos > 0 Then
            iTot += 1
        End If
        x += 1
    Loop
    Return iTot
End Function
```

This modified loop starts at 0 and ends at `cSomeString.Length - 1`,
which is the correct way to iterate through a .NET string. Once again,
you can try to remove all breakpoints and rerun the application. This
time, it should actually produce a value, like the successful test in
Figure 7.13.

FIGURE 7.13:   We've debugged our program...or have we?

Finally, we got an answer! But is it the correct answer? A manual count gives 11 vowels in the test string "The quick brown fox jumps over the lazy dog." Because this is a fairly long test string, you might want to try a smaller string, like the string "aeiou" shown in Figure 7.14.

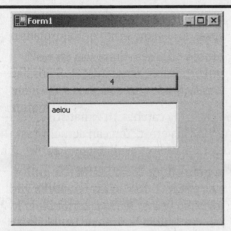

FIGURE 7.14:   It's clear that a mistake occurred.

Now that's definitely wrong—it's counted only four of the five vowels in the string. Looks like there's another logic error. Back to the debugging drawing board.... Actually, this error is pretty easy compared with some of the others we've already squashed. Look at the actual comparison of the character to the vowel list.

```
iPos = InStr("aeio", cSomeString.Substring(x, 1).ToLower)
```

Where's the *u*? It looks like I simply forgot to include the *u* in the vowel list. After adding the *u* back in, the final, working code looks like Listing 7.10.

Listing 7.10: Bug-Free Code

```
Private Sub cbCount_Click(ByVal sender As System.Object, _
            ByVal e As System.EventArgs) _
            Handles cbCount.Click
    cbCount.Text = CountTheVowels(tbPhrase.Text)
End Sub
Private Function CountTheVowels _
            (ByVal cSomeString As String) As Integer
Dim x As Integer = 0
Dim iTot As Integer = 0
```

```
Dim iPos As Integer
Do While x < cSomeString.Length
    iPos = InStr("aeiou", _
                    cSomeString.Substring(x, 1).ToLower)
    If iPos > 0 Then
        iTot += 1
    End If
    x += 1
Loop
Return iTot
End Function
```

This is the type of error you can only catch with exhaustive tests—that is, only a user will likely catch this error. You can actually test the program with a string that doesn't contain the character "u," see that it works nicely, and distribute it. Very soon you will receive messages to the effect that your application doesn't work. Yet this application has been tested and seems to work fine. The tests, however, were not exhaustive.

You should also try to test your applications with extreme situations (a blank string, for example, or a very large one, an invalid numeric value, and so on). The final test, of course, is to pass the applications to users and ask for their comments. Unfortunately, we don't write software for each other. We write software for people knowledgeable enough to crash an application in minutes but not knowledgeable enough to keep it running.

NOTE

There are many more advanced debugging tools available in Visual Studio .NET. A great list of these tools can be found in the Debug menu, under the Window submenu. (Look at the menu when you have a program running). You can get memory dumps, disassembled versions of your program, traces of the procedure call stack, a list of running threads, and other views of your program.

WHAT'S NEXT

Testing and debugging is as critical a step in the complete development process as the design and coding steps. It's obvious that your code won't leave the shop with any syntax errors (because you can't compile if you have any), but tracking down runtime errors and logic errors are just as important. All facets and functions of the program need to be put through a rigorous test procedure to help shake out these problems.

One excellent method of testing software involves asking users who have no preconceived notions about its functionality to test it for you. For example, if you're writing software for the accounting department to use, ask members of the marketing department to test it for you. These users will have much less familiarity with the goals of the software, as well as the expected inputs and outputs. This gives them a larger chance of entering unexpected data, which can lead to unhandled exceptions in your code.

Another hidden benefit of using testers from another department is for some quick usability studies. Again, these users will be unfamiliar with the day-to-day operation of the accounting department, and the task flow of your software won't be intuitively obvious to them. This makes for a good test of how easy your software is to use.

Now that you have a good idea as to how to handle errors, we can put that information to use as we start learning to create windows applications with the new Windows Forms components.

Part II

Chapter 8

WORKING WITH WINDOWS FORMS

Part II

This chapter is an overview of the new features of the Windows Form Designer, introduced with .NET. I'm assuming you know how to design simple interfaces by placing Windows controls on a form. In this chapter, we'll focus on the new features of the Windows Form Designer and the tools for designing more functional forms with less effort.

The first two tools are the Anchor and Dock properties, which allow you to anchor and dock your controls on the form. With the appropriate settings for these two controls, you can design forms that can be easily resized at runtime and maintain the relative locations and sizes of their controls.

Adapted from the forthcoming *Visual Basic .NET Developer's Handbook* by Evangelos Petroutsos and Kevin Hough

ISBN 0-7821-2879-3 $59.99

This chapter focuses on the new features of Visual Basic .NET and the things that are done differently. For example, handling one form from within another form's code isn't as simple as it used to be; you can't use the name of the form followed by the name of a control to access the controls on another form. Multiple Document Interface (MDI) applications are supported in .NET, but the design approach is a little different. The process of designing menus has also been enhanced in Visual Basic .NET. Menus are implemented with two new controls, the MainMenu and ContextMenu controls, and you can easily manipulate your menus from within your code.

The goal of this chapter is to show you how to take advantage of the new features of the IDE, as well as to point out the differences between the VB .NET and previous versions. The changes are not drastic, but many things are done differently now. Many programmers will attempt to apply their previous knowledge to VB .NET and find that some of the techniques they've mastered in the past won't work. Even worse, some techniques may work, even though there are better ones for the job.

THE WINDOWS FORM DESIGNER

One of the major new components of Visual Basic .NET is the Windows Form Designer. For starters, the Designer is used by all .NET languages; it's not a VB-specific environment. Designing forms with the Windows Form Designer has become a very simple process. Many of the tasks that required substantial code in the past are now easily accomplished with point-and-click operations. The basic features of the Designer that relate to form design are discussed in the following sections.

Anchoring and Docking

The Anchor and Dock properties are the basic tools for designing forms that can be easily resized at runtime and that can maintain the relative sizes and locations of their controls. Each control can be anchored to any of the four edges of the form by setting its Anchor property appropriately. (In previous versions of Visual Basic, all controls were anchored to the left and upper sides of the form.) When a control is anchored to a single edge, it's repositioned as the form is resized, so that the distance between the anchored side of the control and the corresponding edge of the form remains the same. If a control is anchored to two opposite sides of the forms, its size changes too. When you anchor a TextBox control to the top and bottom sides of the form, its size will change as the form is resized. The gaps above the control (the distance between the top of the control and the top of the form), as well as the gap below the control, will remain fixed. Finally, if you anchor all four sides of the control, the control will be resized so that it will always be visible in its entirety. Of course, you must make sure that the form isn't resized below a certain threshold, and you'll see shortly how this is done.

The settings of the Anchor property are the members of the AnchorStyles enumeration: Bottom, Left, None, Right, and Top. When you open the Anchor property of a control in the Properties Browser, you will see a small window with a small button and four pegs, one on each side. (See Figure 8.1.) The button is the control you're anchoring, and the four pegs are the control's anchors to the four sides of the form. To anchor the control on one or more sides, click the corresponding peg(s). The pegs on the anchored sides should be gray, and the remaining pegs should be white.

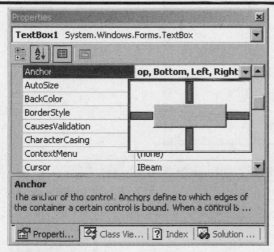

FIGURE 8.1:   Setting a control's Anchor property in the Property Browser

NOTE

You'll find all the code from this chapter on www.sybex.com. Search for the book by its ISBN number, 2887, or its title, *Visual Basic .NET Complete*. You can download the code from the download button.

The Anchor project contains a single form that demonstrates the functionality you can add to your forms by setting the Anchor and Dock properties of its controls. Figure 8.2 shows this form in two totally different sizes. The controls maintain their relative positions, and some of them are resized in the process. The TextBox control is anchored to all four sides of the form. The TextBox control is the main control on the form, and it must be resized along with the form. If not, users will end up with a TextBox control larger than the form itself (in which case, entering text will become awkward) or with a small TextBox on a large form.

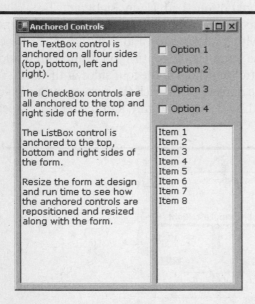

FIGURE 8.2:   Resizing a form with anchored controls

The four check boxes are anchored to the top and right. They will remain at the top-right corner of the form at all times. The last control, the ListBox control, is anchored to the top, bottom, and right. It will remain in the lower-right side of the form, always below the check boxes. Its height will change as the form is resized, to fill the area below the check boxes. Open the project and resize the form to see how its controls will remain visible at all times and that they will not interfere with one another. The check boxes have a fixed size—there's no reason to change the size of these controls. The list has a fixed width, but its height changes to reveal (or hide) some of the items. The text box, finally, takes up all the remaining space on the form because this is the control that should be able to accommodate any amount of information.

Docking is an even more powerful technique that enables controls to take up a section of the form and automatically be resized with the form. You can think of docking as anchoring a control to the edges of all four sides of the form. Docking becomes an incredible tool when used with the Splitter control, which enables certain objects to be resized on their own.

The Dock property allows you to place controls that fill a segment of the form, or the entire form. When you dock a control to the left side of the form, the control maintains its width, but its height changes to fill the form's height. Likewise, the control's width will change if you dock it to the top or the bottom of the form. Finally, you can have a control (most likely a TextBox or a PictureBox control) that fills the entire form. When you fill a form with a control, you can't have other controls on this form (except for a menu, of course).

On its own, the Docking property can't do much for your design. You can place a single TextBox control on a form and set its Dock property to Fill, to fill the form with the text box. A form like this can't have buttons or other controls, short of menus, which don't interfere with the text box.

The settings of the Dock property are the members of the DockStyle enumeration: Bottom, Fill, Left, None, Right, and Top. When you open the Dock property of a control in the Properties Browser, you will see a small window with six buttons, which correspond to the available settings. (See Figure 8.3.)

Part II

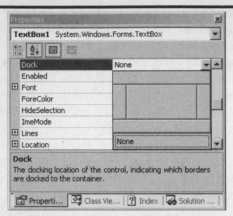

FIGURE 8.3:   Setting a control's Anchor property in the Property Browser

Using the Splitter Control

In addition to anchoring and docking controls on the form, you can use the Splitter control to separate adjacent controls. The splitters are invisible vertical or horizontal separators between forms that make their presence known when the pointer hovers over them. When the pointer hovers over a horizontal splitter, its shape becomes a double vertical arrow, indicating that you can drag it up or down. As you drag the splitter, one of the two controls shrinks and the extra space is taken automatically by the other control. This is a powerful feature that will allow you to build truly elaborate interfaces, as you will see in the following section.

To demonstrate the use of the Splitter control in designing interfaces, we'll build the form shown in Figure 8.4. This is the form of the Explorer-Style project, which you will find at www.sybex.com. The form contains three panes. The left pane is a TreeView control and the other two panes are two ListBox controls. This interface is very similar to the interface of Outlook. If you open the project, you'll see that you can change the relative sizes of the various panes with the mouse. As you will see, all this functionality can be achieved with the Splitter control, without a single line of code. In the following chapter, we'll add code to populate the controls with data, but in this section we'll present the design of the form.

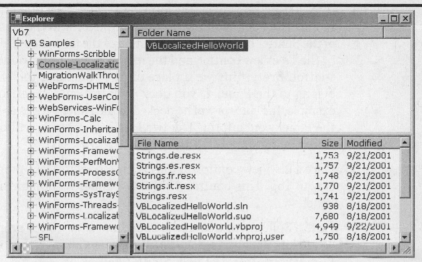

FIGURE 8.4:   This form contains three panes, and you can change the size of any
pane at runtime with the mouse.

To build the form of Figure 8.4, start a new project, name it
ExplorerStyle, and open its form in design mode. Follow these steps:

1. Place a TreeView control on your Form (double-click the
   TreeView control's icon in the Toolbox to create an instance
   of the control on the form, and don't worry about its placement yet).

2. Switch to the control's Properties window, and set the new
   control's Dock property to Left. The control will be attached
   to the left edge of the form. Its width will remain the same,
   but its height will cover the height of the form.

3. Now, place a Splitter control on the form. Double-click
   the control's icon in the Toolbox, and an instance of the
   Splitter control will be placed right next to the TreeView control. To see what you've done so far, run the application and
   place the cursor at the right edge of the TreeView control.
   The mouse pointer will assume the shape of a double horizontal arrow, and you can change the width of the TreeView
   control. Terminate the application, and switch back to the
   Designer.

4. Place a Panel control on the form, and set its Dock property to Fill. The Panel will fill the area of the form to the right of the Splitter control. The left section of the form is covered by the TreeView control, and the rest is covered by the Panel control. Everything we'll place on the Panel control will belong to the Panel. If you dock a control on a Panel, for example, the control will be docked to the Panel's edges as if the Panel were a form. The two ListView controls will be placed on the Panel control.

5. Place a ListView control on the Panel, and set its Dock property to Top. This control will fill the upper section of the Panel.

6. Place a Splitter control on the Panel, and set its Dock property to top. Because the Panel's top section is taken by the top ListView control, the new Splitter will be docked to the bottom of the ListView control, in effect splitting it from the lower half of the Panel.

7. Finally, place another ListView control on the form and set its Dock property to Fill. This control will fill all available area of the Panel control below the Splitter.

You have just designed an Explorer-style interface. Run the application now, and check out the functionality of the interface. You can resize all three controls on the form in any way you like. The TreeView control will remain docked to the left edge of the form, and the two ListView controls will remain docked to the top and bottom of the form, respectively. The Splitter controls on the form are practically invisible, and their function is to allow you to resize the controls on either side of them. If you examine the properties of the Splitter control in the Properties Browser, you'll see that it provides a BorderStyle property and a Cursor property. Set the BorderStyle property to change the appearance of the control (don't expect any dramatic changes, after all it's a narrow strip). The Cursor property determines the shape of the cursor when it hovers over the control.

You must place some data on the controls, but this is something we'll do in the following chapter. You can place data on the various controls at design time, but most practical applications will fill the controls at runtime. To put some sample data on the controls, locate the Nodes property of the TreeView control and the Items property of the ListView controls and add some data. We'll use this form as a navigational interface for folders and files in the following chapter. The same form can be used with many other applications. You can display customers, orders, and order details or accounts, transactions, and transaction details.

Typical Windows Interfaces

Most Windows applications deploy one of the following three styles of user interface:

Single Document Interface   Applications are made up of a main form, which is displayed at startup, and a number of auxiliary forms. Each form is independent of the others, although they can exchange information with one another, and they can be positioned independently on the monitor. This type of interface is suitable for applications that are made up of different forms and need not open multiple documents at once. This is the most common type of interface, and you'll see later how to build applications with multiple forms and how to exchange information between the forms.

Multiple Document Interface   An MDI application consists of a single form, which acts as the host for other forms, which are usually identical, and they host different documents of the same type. Most word processors and image processing applications, for example, use an MDI interface and they can open multiple documents or images. The application's form is the parent for all the forms it can host, and the individual forms with the documents are the child forms. We use the MDI interface to build applications that can manipulate multiple documents through a common menu and/or toolboxes. We'll discuss briefly the MDI interface later in this chapter.

Explorer-Style Interface   This interface consists of two panes arranged horizontally on the form. The left pane displays summary information, while the other pane displays details about the selected item in the left pane. Sometimes, the right pane is split in two panes and you can have two levels of detailed information. The interface of Outlook is a typical example. You can use this interface to display customers, orders, and order details, or accounts, transactions, and transaction details. This type of interface allows the user to start at the highest level of information and drill down to the details. You have already seen how to design this style of interface.

Later in the chapter, we'll discuss interfaces with multiple forms, as well as the MDI interface, but let's continue with the new features of the Windows Form Designer, starting with the properties for sizing and positioning forms.

Form Size and Position

You can use several properties to manipulate the size and position of your forms on the desktop, and they're discussed in this section. Your goal should be the design of a form that can be safely resized at runtime with the Anchor and Dock properties. You will most likely have to impose a minimum size to the form or attach scrollbars to the form if it's resized below a certain size (this is another new feature of the Windows Forms Designer). In general, you should avoid the direct manipulation of the form's appearance from within your code.

The TopMost Property

The TopMost property determines whether a form will be visible at all times or not. The property's default value is False, which means that the form will be covered by another form when another form is activated. If you want to keep the form visible at all times, set its TopMost property to True. Do this when you design Find and Replace forms, which must remain visible even when the user switches to the main form of the application (the form that contains the document being searched). When a form is set to be the application's topmost form, it's not displayed modally. You can switch to any other form of the application, but it will remain visible, even though it doesn't have the focus.

The Opacity Property

This is a rather obscure property that allows you to make semitransparent forms. This property is a numeric value from 0 (complete transparency) to 1 (complete opacity). You can also specify integer values between 0 and 100 (the designer will display the Opacity's property value as a percentage, regardless of how you specify it). We can't think of a good reason to make your forms transparent, especially with business applications, but this is the tool.

The Size Property

Most forms can be rearranged and resized at runtime by the user, which means that you must design forms that remain functional at various sizes. In earlier versions of Visual Basic, designing resizable forms was a major undertaking and developers had to write code to resize and rearrange the controls on the form, so that they would remain visible at various form sizes. Of course, there's a minimum form size beyond which there's not much you can do. Programmers also had to impose a minimum size for the form. Of course, the simplest trick was to set the form to a fixed size, but this isn't the most convenient interface you can design.

The form's size is given by the Size property, which returns a Size object with the same dimensions, and you can use the Width and Height properties of the Size object to read the current dimensions of the form. The form's width can be read with the following expression:

```
Me.Size.Width
```

The following statement, however, won't change the form's width:

```
Me.Size.Width = 2 * Me.Size.Width
```

The Width member is a value, and you can't use it in the left part of an expression. To set the form's dimensions through the Size property, create a new Size object and assign it to the Size property:

```
Me.Size = New Size(Me.Size.Width * 2, Me.Size.Height / 2)
```

Sometimes, we want to prevent the user from resizing certain forms, because the controls on it may not maintain their relative positions and sizes. To force a minimum size, set the form's MinimumSize property to a Size object with the desired dimensions. To specify that the form shouldn't be reduced below a size of 400 by 300, create a size object with these dimensions and assign it to the MinimumSize property with the following statement:

```
Me.MinimiumSize = New Size(400, 300)
```

When the form is resized by the user at runtime, the Resize event is fired. You need not code this event, because you can design forms that resize nicely with the Anchor and Dock properties. Programmers used to place quite a bit of code in this event's handler to resize and reposition the controls on the form. Despite the new Windows Form Designer's features, you may still have to control the resizing process. Let's hope you have a form that must always maintain a certain aspect ratio. To force the desired aspect ratio, you can extract the smaller dimension and adjust

Part II

the other dimension accordingly. The following statements show you how this is done (the aspect ratio of the form's width to its height is 4:3):

```
Private Sub Form1_Resize(ByVal sender As Object, _
                    ByVal e As System.EventArgs) _
                    Handles MyBase.Resize
    If Me.Width < Me.Height Then
        Me.Height = Me.Width * 0.75
    Else
        Me.Width = Me.Height / 0.75
    End If
End Sub
```

The Resize event doesn't take place as you resize the form with the mouse. It's fired once, after you release the mouse. As a result, the form may assume any aspect ration as it's being resized. After the release of the mouse, however, the statements in the Resize event handler will be executed and the form dimensions will change once again—this time to the proper aspect ratio.

The SystemInformation Object

As you write code to arrange controls on a form, you will find the System-Information object very useful. This object exposes a number of properties that provide information about the operating system and they're described in Table 8.1.

TABLE 8.1: Properties of the SystemInformation Object

PROPERTY	DESCRIPTION
Border3Dsize	Returns the dimensions of the 3D border in pixels.
BorderSize	Returns the width and height of the window's border as a Size object expressed in pixels.
CaptionHeight	Returns the height of the window's titles bar in pixels.
ComputerName	Returns the computer name.
CursorSize	Returns the dimensions of the cursor in pixels.
DoubleClickSize	Returns a Size object that determines the area in which the user must click for the operating system to consider the two clicks a double-click.

TABLE 8.1 continued: Properties of the SystemInformation Object

PROPERTY	DESCRIPTION
DoubleClickTime	Returns the number of milliseconds allowed between mouse clicks for the operating system to consider the two clicks a double-click.
FixedFrameBorderSize	Returns the thickness, in pixels, of the border for a window that has a caption and is not resizable.
FrameBorderSize	Returns the thickness, in pixels, of the border for a window that can be resized.
HighContrast	Returns a Boolean value indicating whether the user has selected to run in high-contrast mode.
HorizontalScroll-BarArrowWidth	Returns the width of the arrow in the horizontal scroll bar in pixels.
HorizontalScrollBarHeight	Returns the height of the horizontal scroll bar in pixels.
HorizontalScroll-BarThumbWidth	Returns the width of the button that scrolls the contents of a horizontal scroll bar in pixels.
IconSize	Returns a Size object with the default dimensions of an icon in pixels.
MaxWindowTrackSize	Returns a Size object with the default maximum dimensions of a window with a caption and sizing borders, in pixels.
MenuFont	Returns a Font object the operating system uses for the menus.
MenuHeight	Returns the height of the menu bar.
MinimumWindowSize	Returns a Size object with the minimum allowable dimensions of a window in pixels.
MouseButtons	Returns the number of buttons on the mouse.
MouseButtonsSwapped	Returns a Boolean value indicating whether the functions of the left and right mouse buttons have been swapped.
MousePresent	Returns a Boolean value indicating whether a mouse is installed.
MouseWheelPresent	Returns a Boolean value indicating whether a mouse with a wheel is installed.
Network	Returns True if the computer is connected to a network.
ToolWindowCaption-ButtonSize	Returns a Size object with the dimensions of small caption buttons.
ToolWindowCaptionHeight	Returns the height of a small caption.
UserDomainName	Returns the name of the current user domain.

TABLE 8.1 continued: Properties of the SystemInformation Object

PROPERTY	DESCRIPTION
UserName	Returns the name of the user currently logged on.
VerticalScroll-BarArrowHeight	Returns the height of the arrow on the vertical scroll bar, in pixels.
VerticalScroll-BarThumbHeight	Returns the height of the button that scrolls the contents of a horizontal scroll bar in pixels.
VerticalScrollBarWidth	Gets the width, in pixels, of the vertical scroll bar.
WorkingArea	Returns a Size object with the dimensions of the working area in pixels.

The properties of the SystemInformation object will come in handy when you write code to resize controls from within your code—in situations where the Dock and Anchor properties won't do. Notice that all the SystemInformation properties are read-only, and you can't change any of these settings. These settings are determined by the operating system, and most of them can be modified through the utilities of the Control Panel.

Scrolling Forms

The new Windows Form Designer can design scrolling forms, a feature that was sorely missing from previous versions of the language. Even if you don't want to bother with the Anchor and Dock properties to design elaborate forms, you can set the AutoScroll property to True so that users can always scroll into view the section of the form that interests them. To assist the design of scrolling forms, the following properties are supported (they're properties of the Form object; none of the controls supports them).

AutoScroll

The AutoScroll property is a True/False value that determines whether scroll bars will be automatically attached to the form if it's resized to a point where not all of its controls are visible. The CLR will determine whether one or more of the form's control are invisible, or partially visible, and attach the scroll bars to the form. (See Figure 8.5.)

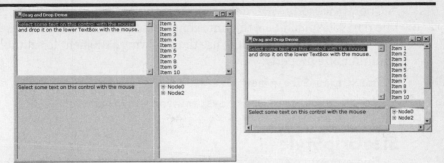

FIGURE 8.5: A typical scrollable form

AutoScrollMargin

This is a margin, expressed in pixels, that is added around all the controls on the form. If the form is smaller than the rectangle that encloses all the controls adjusted by the margin, the appropriate scroll bar(s) will be displayed automatically.

If you expand the AutoScrollMargin property in the Properties window, you will see that it's a Size object and its default value is (0,0). To set this property from within your code, use a statement like the following:

```
Me.AutoScrollMargin = New Size(40, 40)
```

Notice that you can't set the members of the Size object individually:

```
Me.AutoScrollMargin.Width = 40     ' WON'T WORK
Me.AutoScrollMargin.Height = 40    ' WON'T WORK
```

AutoScrollMinSize

Use this property to specify the minimum size of the form, before the scroll bars are attached. Notice that this isn't the form's minimum size; users can make the form even smaller. To specify a minimum size for the form, use the MinimumSize property.

MinimumSize, MaximumSize

These two properties determine the minimum and maximum size of a form. When users resize the form at runtime, the form won't become any smaller than the dimensions specified with the MinimumSize property nor any larger than the dimensions specified by MaximumSize. They're both Size objects, and you can set it with a statement like the following:

```
Me.MinimumSize = New Size(400, 300)
```

The `MinimumSize.Height` property includes the height of the Form's title bar; you should take that into consideration. If the minimum usable size of the Form is 400 by 300, use the following statement to set the MinimumSize property:

```
me.MinimumSize = new Size(400, _
                    300 + SystemInformation.CaptionHeight)
```

SizeGripStyle

This property gets or sets the style of sizing handle to display in the bottom-right corner of the form. Its value is a member of the SizeGrip-Style enumeration, which is shown in Table 8.2. By default, forms are resizable, even if no special mark appears at the bottom-right corner of the form.

TABLE 8.2: The SizeGripStyle Enumeration

MEMBER	DESCRIPTION
Auto	(default) The SizeGrip is displayed as needed.
Show	The SizeGrip is displayed at all times.
Hide	The SizeGrip is not displayed, but the form can still be resized with the mouse (Windows 95/98 style).

THE CONTROLS COLLECTION

The controls you place on a form can be accessed through the Controls property of the form, which is a collection. Each item of the collection corresponds to a different control on the form. If a control acts as a container for other controls, like the Panel control, it has its own Controls collection, which contains the controls sited on this container control.

The items of the Controls collection are of the same type as the controls they represent. When you place an instance of a control on the form, a new item is automatically added to the Controls collection. You can also add a new control to the form by adding an instance of the corresponding type to the Controls collection. The following statements declare a variable that references a new TextBox control, set its properties, and then add it to the Controls collection:

```
Dim txt As New System.WinForms.TextBox
txt.MultiLine = True
txt.Text = "This control was generated in code"
txt.Left = 100
txt.Top = 60
txt.Width = 400
txt.Height = 200
Me.Controls.Add(bttn)
```

You can also remove a control with the Remove method, which accepts as argument either the index of a control in the Controls collection or a reference to the control to be removed. If the variable *txt* of the previous sample were declared outside any procedure in its form, you would be able to remove the control from the Controls collection with the following statement:

```
Me.Controls.Remove(txt)
```

You can also iterate through the Controls collection and retrieve the names and properties of all the controls on a form. This is what the following loop does:

```
Dim i As Integer
For i = 0 To Me.Controls.Count - 1
    Console.WriteLine(Me.Controls(i).Text)
    Console.WriteLine(Me.Controls(i).Width)
    Console.WriteLine(Me.Controls(i).Height)
Next
```

This code segment assumes that all the controls expose a Text property and they have a width and a height. Because you can't be sure that a control provides a specific property, you can find out the type of each control in the collection with a statement like the following:

```
If Me.Controls(i).GetType Is _
              GetType(system.Windows.Forms.Panel) Then
' process an instance of the Panel control
End If
```

Once you know the control's type, you can manipulate it from within your code and request the values of properties that are unique to this control, or call methods that apply to the specific control.

The Controls collection is used in building dynamic forms. A dynamic form contains a variable number of controls, which can be increased or decreased during the course of the application. Not a very common situation, but it's fairly easy to create forms entirely in code from within your code. You can even write code to generate forms by populating the Controls collection.

The dynamically generated controls wouldn't be nearly as useful if you didn't have a method to connect them to events. What good would it do to add a dozen buttons on a form if you couldn't write event handlers to respond to their events?

To create an event handler at runtime, create a subroutine that accepts two arguments—the usual *sender* and *e* arguments—and enter the code you want to execute when a specific control receives a specific event. Let's say you want to add one or more buttons at runtime on your form and these buttons should react to the Click event. Create the ButtonClick() subroutine and enter the appropriate code in it.

Once the subroutine is in place, you must connect it to an event of a specific control. The ButtonClick() subroutine, for example, must be connected to the Click event of a Button control. The statement that connects a control's event to a specific event handler is the AddHandler statement, whose syntax is

```
AddHandler(control.event, New System.EventHandler( _
          AddressOf subName))
```

For example, to connect the ButtonClick() subroutine to the Click event of a button called "Calculate," use the following statement:

```
AddHandler(Calculate.Click, _
          New System.EventHandler(AddressOf ProcessNow))
```

In your delegate, you can use the *sender* argument to find out which control fired the event. The expression sender.Text, for example, returns the value of the Text property of the control that fired the event. Or you can cast the *sender* argument to the proper control type. If the ButtonClick() delegate handles the Click event of the controls Button1 and Button2, the sender.Text property's value will be the name of the button that was clicked.

MULTIPLE FORM APPLICATIONS

A typical Windows application consists of multiple forms and/or dialog boxes. In this section, you'll learn how to display one form from within another form's code and how to access the contents of a form from within another. The process isn't as simple as it used to be with VB6, because you can no longer access the controls on a form by prefixing their names with the name of the form to which they belong. Instead, you must create an instance of the control(s) you want to expose to other forms and make it available to the code of the other forms in the application.

To display a form from within another form's code, you must create an instance of the form to be invoked and then call its Show or ShowDialog method. The Show method displays the form modeless (you can switch to any other form of the application), and the ShowDialog method displays the form modally (you can't switch to any other form while this one has the focus). To return to the application after displaying a modal form, you must close the modal form. Let's say your application has two forms, named *MainForm* and *AuxForm*. As you can guess, the MainForm is the application's startup object. To display the auxiliary form from within the main form, you can use the following statements:

```
Dim aForm As New AuxForm()
aForm.Show()
```

The declaration appears in the same procedure as the following statement—most likely the Click event handler of the button that invokes the form. When this event handler exits, the *aForm* variable ceases to exist.

This approach works well with modal forms, but not as well with modeless forms, and here's why. Let's say you display an instance of the auxiliary form, switch to the main form, and click the same button again. Another instance of AuxForm will be created and it will be displayed. You will have two instances of the auxiliary forms on your screen. Then you can open a third instance, and so on. This is an unusual situation and most users will end up with dozens of auxiliary forms floating around. The *aForm* variable must be declared outside any procedure and be set in the form's Load event handler. This way, your code will be invoking the same instance of the auxiliary form, rather than creating a new instance every time the user requests that form.

Figure 8.6 shows the MultipleForms application, which demonstrates how to invoke a form from within another and how to manipulate the control on a form from within any other form's code. The main form of the application contains a TextBox control and a Find and Replace button. When this button is clicked, a very primitive Find and Replace dialog box is displayed, where you can specify the string to be replaced and the replacement string. When the Replace button is clicked, all instances of the first string on the main form will be replaced by the second string. Not the most functional text editing tool, but it demonstrates how to manipulate the controls on one form from within another form's code.

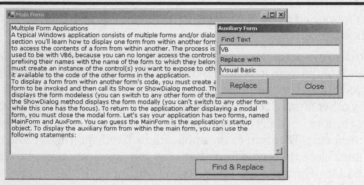

FIGURE 8.6: The MultipleForms application

The project's startup object is the main form. To display the Find and Replace form (it's called *AuxForm* in the project), you must create a reference to this form and then call its Show method.

The auxiliary form needs to access the text on the TextBox control of the main form and perform the necessary replacements. In VB .NET, you can't simply prefix the name of the control by the name of the form it belongs to and access it. The main form must expose a reference of the control, and the auxiliary form will use this reference to access the control.

The following declaration must appear outside any procedure in the main form's file:

```
Public Shared txt As TextBox
```

In the form's Load event handler, we must set the *txt* variable to the instance of the TextBox control on the main Form:

```
Private Sub MainForm_Load(ByVal sender As System.Object, _
                  ByVal e As System.EventArgs) _
                  Handles MyBase.Load
```

```
        txt = TextBox1
End Sub
```

The *txt* variable references the TextBox1 control on the main form and you will see shortly how the auxiliary form uses this variable. When the Find & Replace button is clicked, the following code is executed. This event handler creates a new instance of the auxiliary form, copies the selected text on the main form's TextBox control to the FindBox TextBox control on the auxiliary form, and finally invokes the auxiliary form by calling the Show method:

```
Private Sub Button1_Click(ByVal sender As System.Object, _
                          ByVal e As System.EventArgs) _
                          Handles bttnFind.Click

    Dim aForm As New AuxForm()
    aForm.FindBox.Text = TextBox1.SelectedText
    mForm = Me
    aForm.Show()
End Sub
```

The code in the auxiliary form is located in the event handlers of the two buttons. When the Replace button is clicked, the following statements are executed and they replace all instances of the Find string with the Replace string:

```
Private Sub Button1_Click(ByVal sender As System.Object, _
                          ByVal e As System.EventArgs) _
                          Handles Button1.Click
    MainForm.txt.Text = MainForm.txt.Text.Replace( _
                        FindBox.Text, ReplaceBox.Text)
End Sub
```

When the Close button is clicked, the auxiliary form is closed with a call to the Close method:

```
Private Sub Button2_Click(ByVal sender As System.Object, _
                          ByVal e As System.EventArgs) _
                          Handles Button2.Click
    Me.Close()
End Sub
```

The best method to exchange data between forms is to create properties for each form and set the values of these properties from within the other forms' code. Let's say a form needs to expose a string variable. Create a Public property and every other form will be able to access it. Properties are discussed later in this book in detail, but here's the implementation of a simple form property:

```
Public Property MainText()
    Get
        Return TextBox1.Text
    End Get
    Set(ByVal Value)
        TextBox1.Text = Value
    End Set
End Property
```

This procedure exposes the text on the TextBox1 control as a property. To access this string from within another form's code, create an instance of the form and access the custom property as if it were a built-in property:

```
Dim MForm As MainForm
MForm.MainText = "new string"
```

You can also expose methods as public functions. Let's say that one of the forms contains the Calculate() function, which accepts two numeric values as arguments and return another numeric value. You can implement the Calculate() function as a public function in one of the forms:

```
Public Function Calculate(ByVal a As Double, _
                          ByVal b As Double) As Double
    Return (a / b)
End Function
```

This function can be accessed from within another form of the same project as follows:

```
Dim MForm As MainForm
Dim a, b As Double
a = 1.001
b = 0.999
Console.WriteLine(m.Calculate(a, b))
```

Dialog Boxes

Dialog boxes are special types of forms with rather limited functionality, which we use to prompt the user for data. Windows comes with several built-in dialog boxes for common operations, like the Open File and Save File dialog boxes. These dialog boxes are so common in user interface design that they're known as common dialog boxes. Technically, a dialog box is a Form with its BorderStyle property set to FixedDialog and the ControlBox, MinimizeBox, and MaximizeBox properties set to False. Then add the necessary controls on the form and code the appropriate events, as you would do with a regular Windows form. Like forms, dialog boxes may contain a few simple controls, such as Labels, TextBoxes, and Buttons.

Another difference between forms and dialog boxes is that forms usually interact with each other. If you need to keep two windows open and allow the user to switch from one to the other, you need to implement them as regular forms. If one of them is modal, then you should implement it as a dialog box. A characteristic of dialog boxes is that they provide an OK and a Cancel button (sometimes a Yes and a No, or a Cancel and a Retry button). The OK button tells the application that the user is done using the dialog box, and the application can process the information on it. The Cancel button signals to the application the user's intention to abort the current operation, and the application must act accordingly.

We have the dialog box, but how do we initiate it from within another form's code? The process of displaying a dialog box is no different than displaying another form. To do so, enter the following code in the event handler from which you want to initiate the dialog box (this is the Click event handler of the main form's button):

```
Private Sub Button1_Click(ByVal sender As System.Object, _
                ByVal e As System.EventArgs) _
                Handles Button1.Click
    Dim DLG as new DBoxForm()
    DLG.ShowDialog
End Sub
```

Here, *DBoxForm* is the name of the dialog box. The ShowDialog method displays a dialog box as modal. When you display a modal dialog box, the statement following the one that called the ShowDialog method is not executed. The statements from this point to the end of the event handler will be executed when the user closes the dialog box. Statements following the Show method, however, are executed immediately as soon as the dialog box is displayed.

You already know how to read the values entered on the controls of the dialog box. You also need to know which button was clicked to close the dialog box. To convey this information from the dialog box back to the calling application, the Form object provides the DialogResult property. This property can be set to one of the values shown in Table 8.3, which are the members of the DialogResult enumeration. The DialogResult.OK value indicates that the user has clicked the OK button on the form. There's no need to actually place an OK button on the form; just set the form's DialogResult property to DialogResult.OK.

TABLE 8.3: The DialogResult Enumeration

MEMBER	DESCRIPTION
Abort	The dialog box was closed with the Abort button.
Cancel	The dialog box was closed with the Cancel button.
Ignore	The dialog box was closed with the Ignore button.
No	The dialog box was closed with the No button.
None	The dialog box hasn't been closed yet. Use this option to find out whether a modeless dialog box is still open.
OK	The dialog box was closed with the OK button.
Retry	The dialog box was closed with the Retry button.
Yes	The dialog box was closed with the Yes button.

The dialog box need not contain any of the buttons mentioned here, as long as you set the form's DialogResult property to the appropriate value. This value can be retrieved by the calling application, which will take the appropriate action.

Let's say your dialog box contains a button named *Done*, which signifies that the user is done entering values on the dialog box, and a Cancel button, which aborts the current operation. The Click event handler of the Done button contains a single line:

```
Me.DialogResult = DialogResult.OK
```

Likewise, the Click event handler of the Cancel button contains the following line:

```
Me.DialogResult = DialogResult.Cancel
```

The event handler of the button that displays this dialog box should contain these lines:

```
Dim DLG as Form = new PasswordForm
If DLG.ShowDialog = DialogResult.OK Then
    { process the user selection }
End If
```

The value of the DialogResult property is usually set from within two buttons—one that accepts the data and one that rejects them. Depending on your application, you may allow the user to close the dialog box by clicking more than two buttons. Some of them must set the DialogResult property to DialogResult.OK, others to DialogResult.Abort.

If the dialog box contains an AcceptButton, this button will automatically set the form's DialogResult property to DialogResult.OK. Likewise, the CancelButton will automatically set the form's DialogResult property to DialogResult.Cancel.

MENUS

If there's a feature common to just about any application, it is the menu. The menu is the single element of the visual interface that is as popular with Windows application as it was with DOS applications. Menus are designed with visual tools at design time. Unlike previous versions of Visual Basic, they're designed right on the form and not on a separate dialog box. To add a menu to a form, place an instance of the MainMenu control to the form. Then select the control's icon in the Controls tray at the bottom of the Designer, and start entering the menu's captions right on the form, at the same location where the menu will appear at runtime. You can design multiple menus for a form, and switch them from within your code, but you should use this feature very cautiously. Displaying totally different menus in the course of an application will most likely confuse the users.

To design multiple menus, place additional instances of the Main-Menu control on your form. They'll be named MainMenu1, MainMenu2, and so on. Every time you select a different MainMenu control in the Controls tray at the bottom of the Designer, a different menu structure will appear on the form. Notice that every instance of the MainMenu control is specific to a form.

Designing a menu is quite trivial. You enter the caption, and then press Enter to move to the next item on the same submenu. If you want to spawn a submenu from a specific item, press the right arrow and a submenu will be created next to the current item. To insert items or delete existing items, right-click an item and select the appropriate command from the context menu. Experiment with the new menu designer for a few minutes, and you'll soon realize that it's as convenient as it can get.

To assign names to the menu items, right-click the menu and select Edit Name. You'll be switched to the name-editing mode of the designer, where you can enter the names of the items just as you entered the captions of the various items. When you're done, right-click the menu again and select Edit Names to return to the caption-editing mode. You can select a menu item at any time and set its properties in the Property Browser.

Once the menu has been designed, you can attach it to the form by assigning its name to the Menu property of the form:

```
Me.Menu = MainMenu1
```

You can also set the form's menu from within the Property Browser. The form's Menu property displays the names of all available MainMenu objects, and you can select the appropriate one. The first MainMenu object you place on the form becomes the default menu, so you need not set the form's Menu property. If you have two main menus, you must switch them from within your code. You should avoid displaying totally different menus and try to simply disable/enable commands at different stages of the application and manipulate the commands of the same menu from within your code, rather than switching between totally different menus. These comments don't apply to MDI applications, of course, which are discussed later in this chapter.

In addition to the form's main menu, you can also design context menus. A context menu is identical to a main menu, and it's invoked with the right-click of the mouse on a control or the form. You must add to your form an instance of the ContextMenu control for every context menu you want to design. The context menu is the same, whether it's the context menu of a form or a control. You can even use the same context menu with multiple controls, if it makes sense for the application.

Context menus are designed like main menus, but they're not displayed by default. To attach a context menu to a control, set the control's ContextMenu property to the name of the appropriate context menu. Other than that, context menus are no different than main menus. They may even contain commands that lead to submenus, although this isn't as common.

You can also create menus in your code. The commands of the menu are called items, and they're objects of the MenuItem type. Each command's items are members of the MenuItems collection, and you can manipulate them as members of a collection. The Item property, which is the default property, retrieves a specific item from the collection. To retrieve the third item of the collection, use the following expression:

```
MainMenu1.MenuItems.Item(2)
```

or

```
MainMenu1.MenuItems(2)
```

To add a new item to the MenuItems collection, use the Add method, which accepts as arguments the item's caption and a delegate for the item's Click event handler:

```
MainMenu.MenuItems.Add(caption, _
                    New System.EventHandler( _
                    AddressOf handler_name))
```

The statements of Listing 8.1 create a menu with the following structure:

File

New

Open

Exit

Edit

Copy

Cut

Paste

Part II

Format

Font

Verdana

Tahoma

Georgia

Color

Style

This menu contains three commands, and each command leads to a submenu. The File command leads to a submenu with the commands New, Open, and Exit. The statements that create the menu structure shown earlier must appear in the form's Load event handler:

Listing 8.1: Creating a Menu in Code

```
Private Sub Form1_Load(ByVal sender As System.Object, _
                       ByVal e As System.EventArgs) _
                       Handles MyBase.Load
Dim menu As New MainMenu()
Dim item As MenuItem
    item = New MenuItem("File")
    item.MenuItems.Add("New", _
        New System.EventHandler(AddressOf Me.MenuClick))
    item.MenuItems.Add("Open", _
        New System.EventHandler(AddressOf Me.MenuClick))
    item.MenuItems.Add("Exit", _
        New System.EventHandler(AddressOf Me.MenuClick))
    menu.MenuItems.Add(item)
    item = New MenuItem("Edit")
    item.MenuItems.Add("Copy", _
        New System.EventHandler(AddressOf Me.EditCopy))
    item.MenuItems.Add("Cut", _
        New System.EventHandler(AddressOf Me.EditCut))
    item.MenuItems.Add("Paste", _
        New System.EventHandler(AddressOf Me.EditPaste))
    menu.MenuItems.Add(item)
    item = New MenuItem("Format")
    item.MenuItems.Add("Font")
    item.MenuItems(0).MenuItems.Add("Verdana", _
        New System.EventHandler(AddressOf Me.FormatFont))
```

```
        item.MenuItems(0).MenuItems.Add("Tahoma", _
            New System.EventHandler(AddressOf Me.FormatFont))
        item.MenuItems(0).MenuItems.Add("Georgia", _
            New System.EventHandler(AddressOf Me.FormatFont))
        item.MenuItems.Add("Color", _
            New System.EventHandler(AddressOf Me.FormatColor))
        item.MenuItems.Add("Style", _
            New System.EventHandler(AddressOf Me.FormatStyle))
        menu.MenuItems.Add(item)
        Me.Menu = menu
    End Sub
```

All of the items of the File menu are serviced by the same event handler, the MenuClick subroutine. The same is true for the items of the Font menu of the Format command, which are handled by the FormatFont subroutine. The items of the Edit menu have their own event handlers; they're the Edit-Copy, EditCut, and EditPaste subroutines, which you must provide as well. The signature of a subroutine that will be used as a delegate for the Click event handler of the Click event of a menu item is

```
    Sub MenuClick(ByVal sender As Object, _
                    ByVal e As System.EventArgs)
        MsgBox("You selected the command " & _
                sender.text & " of the File menu")
    End Sub
```

The event handler shown here is quite trivial. You must supply code to perform the necessary operations for each command. Notice how the common event handler figures out which menu item was clicked. The sender argument represents the item that was clicked. You can also cast the sender argument to the MenuItem type, so that you can see the member of the MenuItem object in the Intellisense List Member: CType(sender, MenuItem).

To remove an item from the MenuItems collection, use the Remove and RemoveAt methods. The first method removes the item to which it applies, while the second removes an item by its index:

```
    MainMenu1.MenuItems(3).Remove

    MainMenu1.MenuItems.RemoveAt(3)
```

You can also remove all the items of a specific MenuItem object with the Clear method. If a MenuItem leads to a submenu, its IsParent property returns True. If a MenuItem has its own MenuItems collection, you can iterate through them with the following loop:

```
Dim item As MenuItem
For Each item In MainMenu.MenuItems
    ' process the current item
    ' the item variable exposes the
    ' properties of the MenuItem object
Next
```

Owner-Drawn Menus

Menus are displayed in a font determined by the system. You can find out the menu font, or the height of the menu bar, through the corresponding properties of the SystemInformation object, which was discussed earlier in this chapter. However, you can't change this font from within your code. It is possible, though, to create custom menu items with some additional code. You can actually determine the appearance of each item by drawing the contents of its rectangle and give a custom appearance to your menus. These items are called *owner-drawn*, because their appearance is determined by the code in the form that owns them.

To customize the appearance of a menu item, you must set its Owner-Draw property to True (its default value is False). When the OwnerDraw property of a menu item is True, it raises two events: MeasureItem and DrawItem. These two events are raised in that order when the menu that contains them is opened. In the MeasureItem event you must calculate the dimensions of the rectangle in which the item will be displayed, and in the DrawItem event you must actually draw the menu item. The menu item is displayed in a rectangle, and you have absolute control over the appearance of this rectangle. You can call any of the drawing methods to customize the appearance of the item's rectangle, and each item may even have a different height. You can use a different background color (or bitmap), you can draw the item's caption in any font, or you can fill the rectangle with graphics.

The project OwnerDrawnMenu demonstrates the process of creating owner-drawn menus. It contains a main menu with two items, Color and Alignment, and each item leads to a submenu, as shown in Figure 8.7. The Color menu is made up of differently colored rectangles, and the Alignment menu contains three items with different alignment.

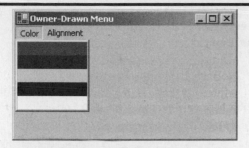

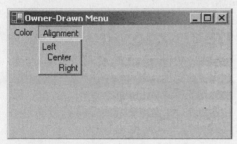

FIGURE 8.7:   An owner-drawn menu

First, you must create a menu with the desired structure, as usual. You need not supply any captions for the items. Even if you do, these captions will be ignored. The Common Language Runtime will ignore them, and it will let the DrawItem event handler draw the item. Obviously, you must provide both a MeasureItem and a DrawItem event handler for each Menu-Item object that has its OwnerDraw method set to True. The code that draws the Red and Green items of the Color menu is shown in Listing 8.2.

Listing 8.2: The MeasureItem and DrawItem Event Handlers of the Color Items

```
Private Sub Red_MeasureItem(ByVal sender As System.Object, _
    ByVal e As System.Windows.Forms.MeasureItemEventArgs) _
    Handles Red.MeasureItem

    Dim itemSize As SizeF
    itemSize = New SizeF(80, 18)
    e.ItemHeight = itemSize.Height
    e.ItemWidth = itemSize.Width
End Sub
```

Part II

```
Private Sub Red_DrawItem(ByVal sender As System.Object, _
    ByVal e As System.Windows.Forms.DrawItemEventArgs) _
    Handles Red.DrawItem

    Dim R As New RectangleF(e.Bounds.X, e.Bounds.Y, _
                    e.Bounds.Width, e.Bounds.Height)
    e.Graphics.FillRectangle(Brushes.Red, R)
End Sub

Private Sub Green_MeasureItem( _
    ByVal sender As System.Object, _
    ByVal e As System.Windows.Forms.MeasureItemEventArgs) _
    Handles Red.MeasureItem

    Dim itemSize As SizeF
    itemSize = New SizeF(80, 18)
    e.ItemHeight = itemSize.Height
    e.ItemWidth = itemSize.Width
End Sub

Private Sub Green_DrawItem(ByVal sender As System.Object, _
    ByVal e As System.Windows.Forms.DrawItemEventArgs) _
    Handles Green.DrawItem

    Dim R As New RectangleF(e.Bounds.X, e.Bounds.Y, _
                    e.Bounds.Width, e.Bounds.Height)
    e.Graphics.FillRectangle(Brushes.Green, R)
End Sub
```

The width of the item is more or less arbitrary. In many cases, the width of each item is determined by its contents. As a consequence, the MeasureItem and DrawItem event handlers contain similar code—just don't draw anything in the MeasureItem event handler. Calculate the proper dimensions, and set the ItemHeight and ItemWidth properties of the second argument. You can retrieve the same values from within the DrawItem event handler through the Bounds property of the second argument. The Bounds property is an object that represents the rectangle in which the drawing will take place. The statement that determines the appearance of the menu item calls the FillRectangle method of the item's Graphics object and draws a rectangle filled with the corresponding color. The rectangle drawn has the exact same dimensions as the item's rectangle. If you make it smaller, then part of the item's box will be empty.

The equivalent code for drawing the items of the Alignment menu is similar. The width of each item is arbitrary, and the corresponding string is printed with a call to the DrawString method. This is a graphics method that has many overloaded forms. We use the one that lets us specify the string to be printed, its font, its color, the rectangle in which it must fit, and a special flag that determines the alignment of the string in the specified rectangle. Listing 8.3 contains the code that displays the item Right:

Listing 8.3: The MeasureItem and DrawItem Event Handlers of the Alignment Items

```
Private Sub AlignRight_MeasureItem( _
    ByVal sender As System.Object, _
    ByVal e As System.Windows.Forms.MeasureItemEventArgs) _
    Handles AlignRight.MeasureItem

    Dim itemSize As SizeF
    itemSize = New SizeF(40, 14)
    e.ItemHeight = itemSize.Height
    e.ItemWidth = itemSize.Width
End Sub

Private Sub AlignRight_DrawItem( _
    ByVal sender As System.Object, _
    ByVal e As System.Windows.Forms.DrawItemEventArgs) _
    Handles AlignRight.DrawItem

    Dim R As New RectangleF(e.Bounds.X, e.Bounds.Y, _
                            e.Bounds.Width, e.Bounds.Height)
    Dim strfmt As New StringFormat()
    strfmt.Alignment = StringAlignment.Far
    e.Graphics.DrawString("Right", Me.Font, Brushes.Black, _
                          R, strfmt)
End Sub
```

I've used the form's font to draw the menus. If you want to use a different font, you can either change the form's Font property at design time (the code will work as is) or create a new Font object in the Draw-Item event handler, set its properties, and then pass it to the DrawString method as argument.

The same techniques apply to the ListBox control. You can customize the appearance of a ListBox control by taking control of the process that draws the control's items. The ListBox control has a DrawMode property, and it exposes the MeasureItem and DrawItem methods. The second argument of these methods, the e argument, supports the Index property (the index of the item being drawn), and the State property, which determines the state of the menu and its value, is one of the members of the DrawItemState enumeration.

Drag-and-Drop Operations

A unique characteristic of the Windows user interface is the ability of the user to grab a control and drop it on another. We don't actually drop the control; we move the contents of the source control to the destination control. This feature is called drag-and-drop and is used extensively on the Windows Desktop. Nearly every item on the Desktop can be dragged and dropped on various other items, such as the Recycle Bin, the printers, folders, and so on. You can use the same techniques in Visual Basic to enhance your applications.

Implementing drag-and-drop operations with Visual Basic .NET is substantially different than earlier versions of the language. For one, the outline of the control is no longer dragged (a feature that many users found annoying anyway). The changes in the shape of the pointer are adequate to indicate that a drag operation is in progress.

To enable a control to accept data when it's dropped, you must set its AllowDrop property to True. You must also insert a statement in its DragEnter event to determine the type of drop operation you will allow the control to perform. The following statement prepares the control to accept a copy of the data on the control being dragged:

```
e.Effect = DragDropEffects.Copy
```

The Effect property determines what type of drop operations the destination control can accept, and its value can be one of the members of the DragDropEffects enumeration, which are shown in Table 8.4.

TABLE 8.4: The DragDropEffects Enumeration

MEMBER	DESCRIPTION
All	The data is copied, removed from the source control, and scrolled in the drop target.
Copy	The data is copied to the destination control.

TABLE 8.4 continued: The DragDropEffects Enumeration

MEMBER	DESCRIPTION
Link	The data from the source control are linked to the destination control.
Move	The data from the source control are moved to the destination control.
None	The control doesn't accept data.
Scroll	Scrolling is about to start or is currently occurring in the destination control.

To initiate the drag operation, you must call the DoDragDrop method of the source control. In other words, you must detect when the user has started a drag-and-drop operation and call the DoDragDrop method of the appropriate control. This takes place in the MouseDown event, because this is the most intuitive method of starting a drag-and-drop operation. You can use any event, as long as you make sure that it doesn't interfere with other operations. The MouseDown event of a TextBox control, for example, doesn't necessarily indicate the start of a drag-and-drop operation. In most cases, it doesn't—and you'll see shortly what you can do about it. The statement in Listing 8.4 will initiate a drag-and-drop operation on a TextBox control (the SourceTextBox control) when the mouse button is clicked.

Listing 8.4: Initiating a Drag-and-Drop Operation

```
Private Sub SourceTextBox_MouseDown( _
    ByVal sender As System.Object, _
    ByVal e As _
    System.Windows.Forms.MouseEventArgs) _
    Handles SourceTextBox.MouseDown

    SourceTextBox.DoDragDrop(SourceTextBox.SelectedText, _
        DragDropEffects.Copy Or DragDropEffects.Move)

End Sub
```

The DoDragDrop method accepts two arguments: the data being dragged and the type of the allowed drop operation(s). This operation allows data to be copied or moved from the source control into the destination control. Once the operation has been initiated, all controls on the form will raise a DragEnter event when the pointer enters them and a DragLeave event when the point leaves them. If a control doesn't allow data to be dropped, the pointer assumes a Stop icon's shape to indicate that the data can't be dropped on the control.

Identify the control that can act as destinations for a drop operation, and enter the statement listed in Listing 8.5 in the DragEnter event.

Listing 8.5: Handling the DragEnter Event

```
Private Sub Destination_DragEnter( _
    ByVal sender As System.Object, _
    ByVal e As System.Windows.Forms.DragEventArgs) _
    Handles DestinationTextBox.DragEnter

    e.Effect = DragDropEffects.Copy
End Sub
```

When a drop operation takes place, the destination control raises the DragDrop event. It's your responsibility to actually copy the data on the destination control. The data has already been placed in a special Clipboard, which you can access through the Data property of the e argument of the event. The following event handler inserts the data being dropped on the control into the current selection. If no text is currently selected, the data is inserted into the location of the pointer in the text, as shown in Listing 8.6.

Listing 8.6: Handling the DragDrop Event

```
Private Sub Destination_DragDrop( _
    ByVal sender As System.Object, _
    ByVal e As System.Windows.Forms.DragEventArgs) _
    Handles DestinationTextBox.DragDrop

    DestinationTextBox.SelectedText = _
                e.Data.GetData(DataFormats.Text).ToString
End Sub
```

If you attempt to start a drag operation on a TextBox control when the left mouse button is clicked, you will give up the editing operations of the mouse. Every time you attempt to select some text with the mouse, a drag operation starts and the editing features of the mouse are taken over by the dragging operations. Clearly, this isn't what users expect and you must handle it carefully. My suggestion is to initiate drag-and-drop operations only if the Alt key is pressed while the left button is clicked, or with the right mouse button—as long as the control doesn't have its own context menu.

The following event handler initiates a drag-and-drop operation if the MouseDown event was fired with the right mouse button:

```
Private Sub SourceTextBox_MouseDown( _
    ByVal sender As System.Object, _
    ByVal e As System.Windows.Forms.MouseEventArgs) _
    Handles SourceTextBox.MouseDown

    If e.Button = MouseButtons.Right Then
        SourceTextBox.DoDragDrop( _
            SourceTextBox.SelectedText, _
            DragDropEffects.Copy Or DragDropEffects.Move)
    End If
End Sub
```

To demonstrate simple drag-and-drop operations, we've included the DragDrop project on the Sybex website at www.sybex.com. This project demonstrates how to drag text from a TextBox control and drop it onto another TextBox control, as well as how to drag one or more items from a ListBox and a TreeView control and drop it onto the same TextBox control. The form of the DragDrop operation is shown in Figure 8.8. The destination for all drop operations is the lower TextBox, while the other three controls can initiate a drag-and-drop operation. The ListBox control allows the selection of multiple items, and you can drag all selected items with a single operation to the TextBox control.

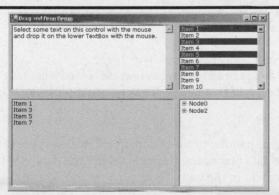

FIGURE 8.8: The DragDrop project's main form

All drag-and-drop operations are initiated with the right mouse button. When we call the DoDragDrop method of the ListBox control, the event handler creates a string with all the selected items (each item on a separate line) and uses this string as the drag operation's data, as shown in Listing 8.7.

Listing 8.7: Starting a Drag-and-Drop Operation in a ListBox Control

```
Private Sub ListBox1_MouseDown(ByVal sender As Object, _
    ByVal e As System.Windows.Forms.MouseEventArgs) _
    Handles ListBox1.MouseDown

    If e.Button = MouseButtons.Right Then
        Dim i As Integer, selItems As String
        For i = 0 To ListBox1.SelectedItems.Count - 1
            selItems = selItems & _
                ListBox1.SelectedItems.Item(i) & vbCrLf
        Next
        SourceTextBox.DoDragDrop(selItems, _
            DragDropEffects.Copy Or DragDropEffects.Move)
    End If
End Sub
```

In the TreeView control's MouseDown event, we extract the selected node and use its caption as the operation's data, as shown in Listing 8.8.

Listing 8.8: Starting a Drag-and-Drop Operation in a TreeView Control

```
Private Sub TreeView1_MouseDown(ByVal sender As Object, _
    ByVal e As System.Windows.Forms.MouseEventArgs) _
    Handles TreeView1.MouseDown

    If e.Button = MouseButtons.Right Then
        TreeView1.DoDragDrop(TreeView1.SelectedNode.Text, _
            DragDropEffects.Copy Or DragDropEffects.Move)
    End If
End Sub
```

The DragDrop event handler of the destination TextBox is the same, no matter where the data originates. It simply inserts the data into the current pointer's location in the text:

```
Private Sub Destination_DragDrop( _
```

```
    ByVal sender As System.Object, _
    ByVal e As System.Windows.Forms.DragEventArgs) _
    Handles DestinationTextBox.DragDrop

    DestinationTextBox.Text = _
        e.Data.GetData(DataFormats.Text).ToString
End Sub
```

MDI APPLICATIONS

To demonstrate the design of an MDI application, we'll build a simple project for viewing images. Each image will be loaded on a new child window, and you'll be able to have multiple images open at once. We'll also add a couple of primitive processing commands to our project. Figure 8.9 shows the MDIProject application's main form with several images open in their respective windows. Notice that the images can be scrolled on their forms. Images are displayed on PictureBox controls, and these controls have their SizeMode property set to AutoSize. They're resized according to the dimensions of the image you load onto them. The child forms have their AutoScroll property set to True, so that when the PictureBox doesn't fit in the window, the appropriate scrollbars appear automatically. In effect, the child windows look like scrolling PictureBox controls.

FIGURE 8.9: The MDIProject application demonstrates the design of an MDI application.

Now let's build the application. Start a new project, and name it **MDIProject**. Select the project's form in the Solution window, and rename it from Form1.vb to **MDIParent.vb**. To make this form the parent window that will host the child forms at runtime, set its IsMDI-Container property to True. The child form is a regular form. Add a new form to the project, and name it **MDIChild**. This form will serve as a template for all child windows. By the way, not all child forms in an MDI application need be identical. It is possible for the parent form to host several types of child forms, but this is rather unusual.

When an MDI application starts, it displays an empty parent form with a minimal menu. This menu contains commands to load child forms and the usual Window menu, which we'll explore shortly. The File menu of the parent form contains a New or an Open item, which brings up a new child and, optionally, loads a document. In our case, we'll prompt the user with the FileOpen dialog box to select an image and we'll display it on a new child form. Let's start with the menu of the parent form. This menu contains two submenus with the following items:

File

    Open

    Exit

Window

    Tile Vertical

    Tile Horizontal

    Cascade

    Arrange Icons

Don't worry about the Window menu; we'll get to it shortly. Notice the lack of the Save and Save As items from the parent form's File menu? The reason we haven't added these commands to the File menu is because the corresponding operations are meaningless without a child form. All other operations that require a child window, like the Save command of the File menu and the Process menu, belong to the menu of the child form. Technically, it's possibly to access any child form from within the parent form's code, but this will complicate the code. Operations that apply to child forms are best implemented in the child form's code.

But child forms don't have their own menus, or do they? Child forms have menus, but they're merged with the parent form's menu. As you already know, the menu of an MDI application is sketchy with no child documents open. Some MDI menus contain a full menu, but most of the items are disabled. As you will see in this section, it is possible to merge the menus of the parent and child forms (you'll actually specify how the two menus will be merged). When you design an MDI application, you build a child form with the full menu of the application. This menu will appear as soon as the first child window is opened. Open the child form, and add the following menu to it:

File

    Close

    Save

    Save As

Process

    Rotate Left

    Rotate Right

    Flip Vertical

    Flip Horizontal

We have the two menus; now we must specify how they'll be merged. Both the parent and child forms have a File menu, but the application shouldn't have two File menus. The corresponding items will be merged under a single File menu.

First, let's see how they're merged by default. Switch to the parent form, place an instance of the FileOpenDialog control on the form, and insert the following statements in the Click event handler of the Open menu item. This event handler will create an instance of the child form and load an image on its PictureBox control, as shown in Listing 8.9.

Listing 8.9: Displaying a Child Form in an MDI Application

```
Private Sub FileOpen_Click(ByVal sender As System.Object, _
                    ByVal e As System.EventArgs) _
                    Handles FileOpen.Click
    OpenFileDialog1.Filter = "Images|*.jpg;*.tif"
    OpenFileDialog1.ShowDialog()
    If OpenFileDialog1.FileName = "" Then Exit Sub
    Dim child As New MDIChild()
```

```
        child.MdiParent = Me
        child.Text = System.IO.Path.GetFileName( _
                   OpenFileDialog1.FileName)
        child.PictureBox1.Image = Image.FromFile( _
                   OpenFileDialog1.FileName)
        child.ImageFileName.Text = OpenFileDialog1.FileName
        child.Show()
    End Sub
```

To open a child window on the main form of the application, we create an instance of the child form, set its MDIParent property to the parent form, and then we call its Show method. It's no different than displaying another form on the desktop, except for setting its parent form. There's another statement you may find odd in this listing. The ImageFileName control is a TextBox control that resides on the child form. It's a hidden control that stores the name of the file with the image that we loaded onto the PictureBox control of the child form. We need a simple method to access the paths of the images from within the Save command, and this a very simple approach. You can't create a form variable with the name of the open document, as you would do with an SDI application, because there can be many open documents. You could create a collection with pathnames for each of the open documents, but this requires substantial overhead. The method suggested here is as simple as it gets. You can store any piece of information you may need later in your code to a hidden control and retrieve it at will.

If you run the application now, you will see the parent window with its minimal menu. Open a child form with the File ➤ Open command. As soon as the first child window will open, the menus of the parent and child forms will merge and the combined menu will appear on the parent form's menu bar (a characteristic of MDI applications). There will be two File menus on the form, the first one with the items of the parent form's File menu and the second one with the items of the child form's File menu. The two menus were merged, but not as you'd expect. We must set a few properties to specify how the menus will merge. These are the MergeType and MergeOrder properties.

The MergeType property determines how the items of two menus are merged, and its value can be one of the members of the MenuMerge enumeration, which are shown in Table 8.5.

TABLE 8.5: The MenuMerge Enumeration

MEMBER NAME	DESCRIPTION
Add	(default) The menu items of the child form are added to the menu items of the parent form.
MergeItems	The menu items of the child form are merged with the items of the parent form. The items are merged according to their order in the respective menus, not by their captions.
Remove	The menu item is ignored when two menus are merged.
Replace	The menu item replaces another item at the same position in the merged menu. The Replace option allows you to design the complete menu on the child form and have it replace the MDI form's menu as soon as the first child form is opened.

When menu items are merged, the parent form's menu items appear first, followed by the items of the child form's menu items. You can change the order in which the items are merged by setting their MergeOrder property, which is an Integer value specifying the order in which the items will be merged. Items with a smaller value will appear in front of others with larger MergeOrder values. The Window item, for example, is always the last menu in an MDI application, with the exception of the Help menu. To make sure it is the last item in the merged menu structure, set its MergeType property to Add and its MergeOrder property to 100.

The File menu of the MDI form must be merged with the File menu of the child form, so you must set the MergeType property of both items to MergeItems. Their MergeOrder property must be 0. Menus are merged based on their MergeOrder value, not by their caption or their name.

Then you must set the MergeOrder property of the items in each menu. The settings for the File menu's item on the parent form are as follows:

Menu Item	MergeType	MergeOrder
File	Merge	0
Open	Add	0
Exit	Add	4

The settings for the File menu's items on the child form are as follows:

Menu Item	MergeType	MergeOrder
File	Merge	0
Save	Add	1
Save As	Add	2
Close	Add	3

The Process menu will be displayed next to the File menu, so its MergeType should be Add and its MergeOrder 1. If you run the project now, you'll see that the menus are displayed correctly when a child form is opened.

Let's switch back to the application's code. The Save and SaveAs commands call the Save method of the Image object to save the image of the current child form to a file. The Save command finds the filename in the hidden TextBox control we placed on the child form. The Save As command prompts the user for a new filename and saves the image to this file. It also stores the user-supplied filename to the hidden TextBox, so that the Save command will find it there. Listing 8.10 shows the code behind the two Save commands.

Listing 8.10: The Save and Save As Commands

```
Private Sub FileSave_Click(ByVal sender As System.Object, _
                           ByVal e As System.EventArgs) _
                           Handles FileSave.Click
    PictureBox1.Image.Save(ImageFileName.Text)
End Sub

Private Sub FileSaveAs_Click( _
      ByVal sender As System.Object, _
      ByVal e As System.EventArgs) _
      Handles FileSaveAs.Click

    SaveFileDialog1.Filter = "Images|*.jpg;*.tif"
    SaveFileDialog1.ShowDialog()
    If SaveFileDialog1.FileName = "" Then Exit Sub
    PictureBox1.Image.Save(SaveFileDialog1.FileName)
```

```
     ImageFileName.Text
  End Sub
```

The Close command calls the Close method of the child form. Normally, you should prompt the user to save any changes before closing the child window. You can add another hidden control to the child form, like a CheckBox control, and set it (or reset it), every time the user applies a transformation to the image (or saves the image to a file).

Now we can implement the processing commands. All the commands call the RotateFlip method of the Image object with the appropriate argument. The code behind the Flip Vertical command contains the following statements:

```
PictureBox1.Image.RotateFlip(RotateFlipType.Rotate180FlipX)

PictureBox1.Invalidate()
```

Run the MDIProject application and check it out. It doesn't perform any advanced tasks, but it works as expected. You can open any number of child forms, switch to any child form through the Window menu, or by clicking the desired child form, you can apply transformations to any image. As you have noticed, we carefully divided the operations that must be performed from within the parent form and the operations that must be performed on the child forms, and we've added the appropriate code in different forms. Handling the document on a child form is no different than handling a document on a regular form from within its own code. There are situations, however, when we want to access a child form outside its own form. Consider an MDI text editor, for example, with a Find and Replace dialog box. This form's code should be able to access the controls of the currently active child form and manipulate their contents.

Accessing the Active Child Form

To access the active child form, use the ActiveMdiChild property of the parent form, which returns a reference to the active child form. To demonstrate how this works, we'll add a new form to our application. The new form will be invoked from within the parent form, and it will display the properties of the image on the active child form. Figure 8.10 shows this form in action.

Part II

FIGURE 8.10:   Accessing the properties of the image in the active child form

Edit the File menu of the parent form, and insert the command Properties below the Open command in its File menu. Then add a new form to the project, and name it PropForm (this is where we'll display the properties of the active child form). The PropForm is not an MDI child form. There won't be multiple instances of this form. It's a regular form we're going to display modally. The user must close it to return to the application. This form should have a Close button, but the default Close icon at the top of the form will do for this example. The properties are displayed on a TextBox control that fills the form (Dock = Fill).

To invoke this form from within the parent form's code, we must create an instance of the PropForm and then call its ShowDialog method. Before showing the form, however, we must populate the TextBox control with the properties of the image on the currently active child form. To access the Image object with the properties of the image on the child form's PictureBox control, we access the active child form with the expression:

```
Me.ActiveMdiChild
```

Then we cast this object to the MDIChild type:

```
CType(Me.ActiveChild, MDIChild)
```

This expression is a reference to the active child form. Then we obtain a reference to the image on the PictureBox1 control of the child form:

```
Dim img As Image

img = CType(Me.ActiveMdiChild, MDIChild).PictureBox1.Image()
```

Now, we can use the *img* object to retrieve the properties of the image and display them on the TextBox control of the PropForm. The code behind the Properties command in the parent form's File menu is shown in Listing 8.11.

Listing 8.11: Displaying the Properties of the Active Image

```
Private Sub FileProperties_Click( _
        ByVal sender As System.Object, _
        ByVal e As System.EventArgs) _
        Handles FileProperties.Click


    Dim img As Image
    img = CType( _
            Me.ActiveMdiChild, MDIChild).PictureBox1.Image()
    Dim props As New PropForm()
    props.TextBox1.Text = "WIDTH: " & vbTab & img.Width & _
            vbCrLf
    props.TextBox1.Text = props.TextBox1.Text & _
            "HEIGHT: " & vbTab & img.Height & vbCrLf
    props.TextBox1.Text = props.TextBox1.Text & "HRES: " & _
            vbTab & img.HorizontalResolution & vbCrLf
    props.TextBox1.Text = props.TextBox1.Text & "VRES: " & _
            vbTab & img.VerticalResolution & vbCrLf
    props.ShowDialog()
End Sub
```

When you code MDI applications, you should try to contain the operations in the child form to which they apply. You can manipulate the child forms through the parent form's code, but this will complicate your program. If you need to access the active child form from within the parent form's code, use the ActiveMdiChild property and cast this property to the appropriate type, as we did in the example. You can also activate a child form from within the parent form's code with the ActivateMdiChild method. This method requires as argument a reference to the child form to be activated.

The Window Menu

A common feature among MDI applications is the Window menu, which contains two groups of commands. The first group of commands arranges the child windows on the MDI form, and the second group contains the captions of all open child windows. To create a Window menu, add a new item to the parent form's menu, name it Window, and insert the following items under it:

Tile Horizontally

Tile Vertically

Cascade

Arrange Icons

Then, locate the MDIList property of the Window menu in the Property Browser and set it to True. This property causes the menu to keep track of all open child forms and display their names at the bottom of the Window submenu.

The other four items of the Window menu are implemented with a call to the LayoutMdi method of the parent form. This method can be called only if the IsMdiContainer property has already been set to True. This method accepts as argument one of the members of the MdiDILayout enumeration: TileHorizontal, TileVertical, Cascade, and ArrangeIcons. The following event handler will tile all child forms horizontally on the parent window:

```
Private Sub WindowTileH_Click( _
    ByVal sender As System.Object, _
    ByVal e As System.EventArgs) Handles WindowTileH.Click


    Me.LayoutMdi(MdiLayout.TileHorizontal)
End Sub
```

The MDILayoutMdi method of the parent form automatically rearranges the child forms; all you have to do is supply the proper argument.

At the bottom of the Window menu, you will see a list with all the child windows currently open on the parent form. This list is maintained automatically, and its purpose is to allow you to select one of the child windows.

WHAT'S NEXT

This chapter was a quick introduction to the new features of the .NET Windows Form Designer. There are several important new features, and many of the basic operations, like the design of a menu or the display of a form, are now done differently. We didn't describe minor new properties of the Form object or other trivial issues. Once you get started with the new designer, you'll figure them out easily.

Designing the visual interface of an application requires that you have a good understanding of the capabilities of the various Windows controls and how to manipulate them from within your code.

This chapter concludes the new Visual Basic .NET language features. In the next chapter, you will have the opportunity to learn about the enhancements made to Visual Basic .NET in creating web applications. This is one of the areas where Visual Basic .NET has been greatly enhanced, making it very easy to create and distribute web applications.

Part III
ASP.NET ESSENTIALS

Chapter 9
INTRODUCTION TO ASP.NET

A SP.NET is the .NET framework layer that handles web requests for specific types of files, namely those with .aspx and .acsx extensions. The ASP.NET engine provides a robust object model for creating dynamic content and is loosely integrated into the .NET framework. This integration makes it easy to change the implementation when the .NET framework migrates to platforms other than Windows.

Adapted from *Mastering ASP.NET with VB.NET*
by A. Russell Jones
ISBN 0-7821-2875-0 $49.99

Part III

WHAT IS ASP.NET?

What is ASP.NET? This may seem like a relatively simple question, but I assure you that it's not. Because ASP.NET is part of the .NET Framework, it is available on any server with the framework installed. In other words, it's not an add-on anymore; ASP has become legitimate. ASP.NET is implemented in an assembly that exposes classes and objects that perform predetermined specific tasks. If you are familiar with "classic" ASP (the versions of ASP that preceded .NET), you'll find that your approach to programming in ASP.NET is somewhat different, but the concepts behind building a web application are much the same. If you're not familiar with classic ASP, so much the better—you won't have as much information to forget!

ASP.NET programs are centralized applications hosted on one or more web servers that respond dynamically to client requests. The responses are dynamic because ASP.NET intercepts requests for pages with a specific extension (.aspx or .ascx) and hands off the responsibility for answering those requests to just-in-time (JIT) compiled code files that can build a response "on-the-fly." Figure 9.1 shows how ASP.NET integrates with the rest of the .NET Framework.

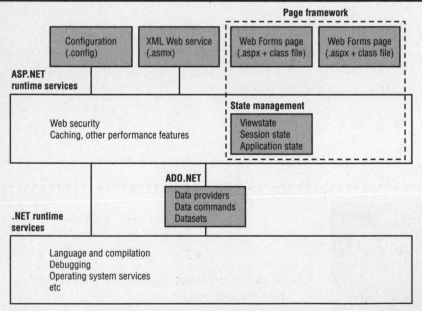

FIGURE 9.1: ASP.NET integration with the .NET Framework

From looking at Figure 9.1, you can see that ASP.NET deals specifically with configuration (`web.config` and `machine.config`) files, Web Services (ASMX) files, and Web Forms (ASPX) files. The server doesn't "serve" any of these file types—it returns the appropriate content type to the client. The configuration file types contain initialization and settings for a specific application or portion of an application. Another configuration file, called `machine.web`, contains machine-level initialization and settings. The server ignores requests for web files, because serving them might constitute a security breach.

This book concentrates on Web Forms and Web Services. Client requests for these file types cause the server to load, parse, and execute code to return a dynamic response. For Web Forms, the response usually consists of HTML or WML. For Web Services, the server typically creates a Simple Object Access Protocol (SOAP) response. While SOAP requests are inherently stateless and can thus execute immediately, Web Forms are stateful by default. Web Forms maintain state by round-tripping user interface and other persistent values between the client and the server automatically for each request. In Figure 9.1, the dashed rectangle titled Page Framework shows the difference—a request for a Web Form can use ViewState, Session State, or Application State to maintain values between requests. It is possible (but not by default) to take advantage of ASP.NET's state maintenance architecture from a Web Service, but for performance reasons, you should generally avoid doing so.

Both Web Forms and Web Services requests can take advantage of ASP.NET's integrated security and data access through ADO.NET, and they can run code that uses system services to construct the response.

So the major difference between a static request and a dynamic request is that a typical web request references a static file. The server reads the file and responds with the contents of the requested file. With ASP.NET, there's no such limitation. You don't have to respond with an existing file—you can respond to a request with anything you like, including dynamically created HTML, XML, graphics, raw text, or binary data—anything. Capability, by itself, is nothing new—you've been able to create CGI programs, JavaServer pages, classic ASP pages, ColdFusion, and NetObjects Fusion pages for quite some time. All these technologies give you the ability to respond to an HTTP request dynamically. So, what are the differences? They include the following:

► Unlike classic ASP, ASP.NET uses .NET languages. Therefore, you have access to the full power of any .NET assembly or class in

Part III

exactly the same way as you do from VB .NET. In this sense, ASP.NET is similar to early compiled CGI programs, but with CGI, a separate copy of the program had to be loaded and executed for each request. ASP.NET code exists in multithreaded JIT-compiled DLL assemblies, which can be loaded on demand. Once loaded, the ASP.NET DLLs can service multiple requests from a single in-memory copy.

▶ ASP.NET supports all the .NET languages (currently C#, C++, VB .NET, and JScript, but there are well over 20 different languages in development for .NET), so you will eventually be able to write web applications in your choice of almost any modern programming language. JavaServer pages support only Java, but because Java now has a wide support base, that's not much of a limitation. Classic ASP supports several scripting language versions (although in practice, VBScript and JScript are by far the most prevalent). The scripting languages let you extend ASP's basic functionality by writing DLLs in any COM-compliant language. ColdFusion uses ColdFusion Markup Language (CFML) tags, which have a powerful but limited set of capabilities; however, you can extend CFML with custom programming.

▶ Microsoft was able to draw on millions of hours of developer experience with classic ASP—so in addition to huge increases in speed and power, ASP.NET provides substantial development improvements, like seamless server-to-client debugging, automatic validation of form data, and a programming model very similar to that of a Windows application.

Framework for Processing HTTP Requests

Microsoft's web server, Internet Information Server (IIS), handles HTTP requests by handing the request off to the appropriate module based on the type of file requested. Note that the IIS responds with one of only a few possible actions when it receives a request:

Respond with the file's contents   The server locates and reads the requested file's contents and then streams the contents back to the requester. The server responds in this manner to .htm and .html file requests, as well as to all requests that have no associated application type—for example, EXE files.

Respond by handing off the request   The server hands off
requests for files that end in .asp to the classic ASP processor,
and files that end in .aspx, .ascx, or .asmx to the ASP.NET
processor.

Respond with an error   IIS responds with a customizable
error message when a requested file does not exist or when
an error occurs during processing.

Classic ASP versus ASP.NET

In classic ASP, the server handed off file requests that ended in .asp to
the ASP engine, an Internet Server Application Programming Interface
(ISAPI) ASP DLL. Because there's a difference in the file extension (.asp
versus .aspx, .ascx, and .asmx) for classic ASP and ASP.NET files,
respectively, you can have both running on the same server simultaneously. Fortunately for ASP programmers, ASP.NET supports all the functionality available in classic ASP and a great deal more besides. Table 9.1
shows the major differences between the two technologies.

TABLE 9.1:   Comparison of Classic ASP and ASP.NET

CLASSIC ASP	ASP.NET	DESCRIPTION
Intercept client requests for files with an .asp extension.	Intercept client requests for files with the .aspx extension.	Provides the ability to create content "on-the-fly"—dynamic content.
Write server-side script in one of a small number of languages. Script languages are interpreted at runtime.	Write server-side code in any .NET language. The .NET languages are compiled, not interpreted.	Compiled code is faster. The development environments and debug facilities are more powerful.
Extend ASP scripting functionality with COM objects.	Use any of the .NET System classes or call existing COM objects.	Provides the ability to extend ASP capabilities by writing custom code.
All processing happens *after* the server passes control to the ASP engine. Cannot take advantage of ISAPI services.	You can write code to intercept requests *before* the ASP engine takes control. You can write ISAPI services within the .NET framework.	Sometimes, you want to respond to a request *before* the ASP engine parses the request. You can do that in .NET, but not with classic ASP.

Part III

TABLE 9.1 continued: Comparison of Classic ASP and ASP.NET

CLASSIC ASP	ASP.NET	DESCRIPTION
Code and HTML are usually mixed inline within a page.	Code may be placed inline in ASP.NET pages, but is usually separated from the HTML in "code-behind" files.	The .NET code-behind pages provide a cleaner separation of display and logic code and also simplify code reuse.
Developer responsible for implementing ways to maintain state data between pages.	Web Forms and Web Form controls act much like classic VB forms and controls, with properties and methods for retrieving and setting values.	While both classic ASP and ASP.NET render output in HTML, ASP.NET introduces ViewState, a scheme that automatically maintains the state of controls on a page across round trips to the server. Web Forms, Web Form controls, and ViewState simplify development and eliminate much of the gap between programming web applications and stand-alone Windows applications.
Process submitted HTML form fields.	Process and validate submitted form fields.	Provides the ability to gather user input. Automatic validation takes much of the grunt work out of programming pages that require user input.
Settings stored in special ASP page that executes code for special events (such as Application startup and shutdown).	Settings stored in XML-formatted files. Settings for subdirectories may override settings for their parent directories.	ASP.NET uses XML files to store settings, giving you programmatic access to configuration settings.
ADO	ADO.NET	ADO.NET is faster, more powerful, and much better integrated with XML for passing data between tiers.
MTS/COM+	Same, through COM interoperability.	VB .NET components can support object pooling, whereas VB6-generated components do not. Eventually, COM+ will be completely integrated into .NET.

WHY DO YOU NEED ASP.NET?

The first computer languages were little more than mnemonics substituting for raw machine code instructions, but as computers became more complex, each new language generation has supported an increasing level of abstraction. Visual Basic, for example, abstracted user interface design and construction into simple drag-and-drop operations. For the first time, you could create a working Windows application with very little effort.

Similarly, when web programming first became widespread, there were few tools to help programmers write web applications. To create a web application, you started by writing low-level socket communications code. Over the years, the abstraction level has increased for web programming as well. ASP.NET is the latest (and arguably the best) of these abstractions, because it lets you work almost exclusively with rich high-level classes and objects rather than directly with raw data. Without ASP.NET, building a web application is a chore. With ASP.NET, building a web application is similar to building a Win32 application.

Client Changes

ASP.NET lets you build web-based applications that interact with pages displayed remotely. Originally, classic ASP was designed to work with browsers, which at that time were capable of little more than displaying data and images wrapped in HTML markup. While the integration hasn't changed, the clients have changed dramatically. For example, modern browsers are much more capable. Not only can they display HTML and images, they also support Dynamic HTML (DHTML), animations, complex image effects, vector graphics, sound, and video—and they can run code, letting you offload appropriate portions of your application's processing requirements from your server to the client.

Centralized Web-Based Applications

But it's not only browsers that have changed. Centralized web-based applications have garnered a huge investment from companies that increasingly need to support mobile and remote clients. The cost of supplying private network connectivity to such clients is prohibitive, yet the business advantages of supporting such clients continue to rise. The only cost-effective way to supply and maintain corporate applications to these mobile and remote workers is to uncouple them from the network and build the applications to work over HTTP through the Internet, WAP, and other advanced protocols. Therefore, web-based applications are no longer the exclusive purview of webmasters and specialist developers; they've become an integral part of the corporate IT operations.

Distributed Web-Based Applications

For all the advantages of centralized web applications, they mostly ignore a huge reservoir of processing power that exists on the client machines. Recently, a new breed of application has begun to attract attention—the *point-to-point* program (often abbreviated as "P-to-P" or "P2P"). These programs typically use XML to pass messages and content directly from one machine to another. Most current implementations, such as Groove and Napster, use a centralized server as a directory service that helps individuals or machines contact one another. Peer-to-peer applications are often called *distributed* because the application runs at many points on the network simultaneously. In addition, the data used by distributed applications is usually (but not necessarily) stored in multiple locations.

Functional Interoperability

As the client transition from stand-alone applications to browser-based interfaces occurred, another factor came into play: interoperability. IT departments have struggled with interoperability ever since programming escaped the confines of the mainframe. As the number of computers and computing devices within the business and entertainment worlds expanded, the problem grew. Today, computing is no longer limited to full-size desktop machines or even laptops. Handheld and notepad computers, telephones, and even pagers communicate with the web servers and need to display data—sometimes even display the same data or run the same application as a desktop box. Similarly, IT departments now run critical applications on mainframes, minicomputers, and several different types of servers, from small departmental servers to server farms that supply computing power to the entire enterprise and beyond. These servers are made by different vendors and often run differing and incompatible operating systems, yet companies often need to transport and consume data between the various machines, databases, application tiers, and clients.

Companies have attacked the interoperability problem in several ways. They've tried limiting the hardware and software—creating tight corporate standards for desktop, laptop, and handheld computers. That approach hasn't worked very well—the industry changes too fast. They've tried and discarded the thin-client network computer approach. Too little benefit, too late. They've tried implementing Java as both the platform and the language—but performance issues, a lack of cooperation between the major software suppliers, and lack of commercial-quality software have—at least temporarily—quelled that approach as well. Fortunately, a new interoperability standard has recently presented itself—XML.

Standardization, Verifiability, and HTTP Affinity

XML provides a possible solution to some of these interoperability problems. XML is not a panacea, but it does provide a standardized and *verifiable* text-based file format that can help ease the problems involved in moving data from one server to another, as well as accommodate displaying identical data on disparate clients. XML's standardization helps, because the file format is universally recognized. XML simplifies programming because it can verify, by using a *document type definition (DTD)* or *schema*, that a file does indeed contain a specific type of content. Finally, XML's text-based format transfers very well over a plain HTTP connection, which helps avoid problems with firewalls and malicious code.

Web Services

These attributes, standardization, verifiability, and HTTP affinity, led to a new use for ASP—creating server-based code that delivers data without necessarily delivering HTML. In .NET, such pages are called Web Services. You can think of a Web Service as a function call or as an object instantiation and method call across the Web. Just as web browsers and web servers use a common protocol, HTTP, to communicate across the network, a Web Service uses a common XML structure, called Simple Object Access Protocol (SOAP) to communicate with the calling application.

WHAT DOES ASP.NET DO?

What does ASP.NET do? Again, this is not a simple question. Classic ASP was limited to simple script languages that could respond to requests, but provided no intrinsic direct access to system services other than those few required to read and respond to a request, such as writing output text. While you could extend classic ASP through commercial or custom-built COM components, the relatively high overhead required to create COM objects, and classic ASP's reliance on untyped interpreted scripting languages, limited system performance. In contrast, creating .NET Framework objects requires very little overhead, and ASP.NET lets you use fully object-oriented languages with seamless access to system services. Therefore, I'll describe just the primary tasks that ASP.NET accomplishes now, and then I'll fill in the practical details in the remainder of this book.

Accepts Requests

All ASP.NET pages work essentially the same way. A client application makes an HTTP request to a web server using a URL. The web server hands off the request to the ASP.NET processor, which parses the URL and all data sent by the client into collections of named values. ASP.NET exposes these values as properties of an object called the HttpRequest object, which is a member of the System.Net assembly. An assembly is a collection of classes. Although an assembly *can* be a DLL, it may consist of more than one DLL. Conversely, a single DLL may contain more than one assembly. For now, think of an assembly as a group of related classes.

When a browser, or more properly a *user agent*, makes a request, it sends a string containing type and version information along with the request. You can retrieve the HTTP_USER_AGENT string via the HttpRequest object. For example, the following code fragment retrieves several items from the user agent and writes them back to the client. An ASP.NET Web Form Page object exposes the HttpRequest with the shorter (and familiar to ASP).

```
Response.Write("UserAgent=" & Request.UserAgent & "<br>")
Response.Write("UserHostAddress=" & _
        Request.UserHostAddress & "<br>")
Response.Write("UserHostName=" & Request.UserHostName & _
        "<br>")
```

Builds Responses

Just as ASP.NET abstracts incoming data in the HttpRequest object, it provides a way to respond to the request via the HttpResponse object. Abstracting responses in this manner has been so successful that you'll find you need to know almost nothing about HTTP itself to use the HttpRequest and HttpResponse objects.

Assists with State Maintenance

Unlike stand-alone or standard client-server applications, web applications are "stateless," which means that neither the client nor the server "remembers" each other after a complete request/response cycle for a single page completes. Each page requested is a complete and isolated transaction, which works fine for browsing static HTML pages but is the single largest problem in constructing web applications.

Classic ASP introduced the idea of a *session*, which begins the first time a client requests any page in your application. At that point, the ASP engine created a unique cookie, which the browser then accepted and returned to the server for each subsequent page request. ASP used the cookie value as a pointer into data saved for that particular client in an object called the Session object. Unfortunately, because the client data was stored in memory on a single server, this scheme did not scale well, nor was it fault-tolerant. If the web server went down, the users lost the in-memory data.

ASP.NET uses much the same cookie scheme to identify specific clients, but the equivalent of the Session object is now called the HttpSessionState object. ASP.NET addresses the session-scalability and data-vulnerability problems in classic ASP by separating state maintenance from the ASP.NET engine. ASP.NET has a second server application, called the Session server, to manage Session data. You can run the Session server in or out of the IIS process on the same machine as your web server or out of process on a separate computer. Running it on a separate computer lets you maintain a single Session store across multiple web servers. ASP.NET also adds the option to maintain state in SQL Server, which increases fault tolerance in case the Session server fails.

Part III

Why Is ASP.NET in a VB .NET Book?

VB6 had a project type called an IIS Application—a technology more commonly known as WebClasses. I wrote a book about using WebClasses, called the *Visual Basic Developer's Guide to ASP and IIS* (Sybex, 1999). Using WebClasses, a VB programmer had access to the ASP intrinsic objects—Request, Response, Server, Application, and Session—and could use the compiled code within WebClasses to respond to client web requests. But IIS Applications required ASP to be installed on the server and, in fact, were called as COM components from an automatically generated ASP page. Therefore, a WebClass-based application in VB6 was really an ASP application that followed a specific track to instantiate and use VB COM components. Although the entire underlying technology has changed, that aspect has not.

TIP

A VB .NET web application project *is* an ASP.NET application!

ASP.NET, although advertised as if it were a separate technology, is not. It is part of, and completely dependent on, the .NET Framework (see Figure 9.1). In fact, an ASP.NET project is *exactly the same thing* as a VB .NET web application project. You'll hear that you can write an ASP.NET application using Notepad—and you can! You can also write a VB .NET application using Notepad. But the big advantage of writing a VB .NET application within the Visual Studio .NET (VS .NET) IDE is that you have access to a number of productivity tools, including syntax highlighting, IntelliSense, macros and add-ins, the ToolBox, HTML, XML, code editors, the Server Explorer, etc., etc., etc. Remember that when you create a VB .NET web application project, you're really creating an ASP.NET project—you're just approaching the technology through a specific language and IDE.

VB .NET Provides Code-Behind

In an ASP.NET application, you can either write code inline, as with classic ASP, or you can place the HTML code in a file with the .aspx extension and the code in a separate file with the .aspx.vb extension,

called a *code-behind module* or *code-behind class*. There's little or no
difference in performance between the two methods, but there's a fairly
large difference in maintenance costs and reusability between the two
approaches. For example, Listing 9.1 shows that you can still write code
embedded in HTML in a manner very similar to the classic ASP style.

Listing 9.1: Classic ASP Embedded Code (*ch9-1.aspx*)

```
<%@ Page Language="vb" AutoEventWireup="false"%>
<html>
  <head>
    <meta name="CODE_LANGUAGE" content="Visual Basic 7.0">
  </head>
  <body>
    <%Response.write("Hello world")%>
    <form id="ch9-1" method="post" runat="server">
    </form>
  </body>
</html>
```

Alternatively, you can create exactly the same output using a code-
behind class by placing the line Response.Write("Hello World") in
the Load event for a Web Form (see Listing 9.2). Don't worry if that
doesn't exactly make sense at the moment—it will at the end of this
chapter.

Listing 9.2: Code behind a Web Form Example (*ch9-2.aspx.vb*)

```
' VS.NET autogenerated code omitted
Protected Sub Page_Load(ByVal Sender As System.Object, _
   ByVal e As System.EventArgs) Handles MyBase.Load
   If Not IsPostBack Then
      ' Evaluates to true the first time
      ' client requests the page
      Response.Write("Hello World")
   End If
End Sub
```

.NET's Unified Platform for Designing, Coding, and Debugging

You may already be familiar with the event model for Windows Form
controls. One of the goals of .NET was to create that same sense of

programmatic unity in working with web applications. Therefore, even though there's usually a physical separation between the control in a browser and the application on a server, you can often develop pages as if that distance were not present. In .NET, HTML pages containing code are called Web Forms. Don't be misled by the name—both of the preceding code examples are "Web Forms" even though one looks exactly like an HTML page with two lines of code inserted, and the other looks exactly like a VB .NET subroutine.

For those of you who might have used WebClasses (the class type from IIS web application projects in VB6), a Web Form (with code-behind) is similar to the combination of an HTML template and a WebClass. The Web Form contains the HTML layout, while the code-behind class contains the program logic and exposes page-level events. But don't be confused—a Web Form is much more powerful than a WebClass.

In the VS .NET IDE, you design a Web Form in much the same way you design a Windows Form—by dragging and dropping controls from the Toolbox onto the Web Form drawing surface. When you add a new Web Form to your project in VB, you can elect to use the drag-and-drop metaphor, or if you're more comfortable editing HTML directly, you can click a tab and move into the HTML text-mode editor.

Because Web Forms aren't Windows Forms, you need to select a target client type. The first VS .NET release lets you target HTML 3.2 –compliant clients (Internet Explorer (IE) version 3.x and earlier browsers, Netscape version 4.x and earlier) or HTML 4 ones (IE 4.x and 5.x, Netscape 6). Unless you have good reason to support the earlier browsers, you should make sure you target the HTML 4 clients. You can lay out a Web Form in either FlowLayout mode or in GridLayout mode. These two settings control how and where the browser places controls on the page.

When you select the FlowLayout option, the browser uses its standard internal HTML layout rules to place the controls. In other words, it places the controls linearly, from left to right, top to bottom, wrapping to the next line where necessary and exceeding the viewable width and height of the browser where wrapping is not possible, adding scroll bars as needed.

In contrast, GridLayout mode lets you place controls at fixed positions on the page. GridLayout mode is equivalent to writing an HTML `input` control where the `style` attribute specifies the `position:absolute` cascading style sheet (CSS) style. In fact, that's exactly what it does—for example:

```
<input
type="text"
style="position: absolute;
left: 10;
top: 10">
```

After placing controls and content on the Web Form, double-click any control (if necessary, click OK in response to the prompt regarding conversion to a server-based control). VS .NET will open the code-behind module. If you insist on writing embedded code, click the HTML tab at the bottom of the Web Form window and VS .NET will switch to the HTML text editor. You can insert code by enclosing it between <% and %> tags or between `<script language="VB" runat="server"></script>` tags.

NOTE

Use the <% %> syntax only for *inline* code—code that you want to execute when the page is rendered. Code written in this manner is a *code render block*. To display a variable or the result of an expression, you can use the shorthand <%=*var or expression*%>. For all other embedded code, use the `<script></script>` syntax. You must declare page-level variables, subroutines, and functions within `<script></script>` blocks. You can reference external code using the src attribute of the `<script>` tag. You must include the `runat="server"` attribute for all server-side code.

The ASP.NET engine treats all content on the page that is *not* between those tags as HTML content and streams it directly to the browser. You'll see a few examples of inline code and code within `<script runat="server">` blocks in this book, but not many, because this book discusses VB .NET–generated code-behind modules almost exclusively.

CREATING YOUR FIRST WEB FORM

In this section, you'll create a Web Form that lets you enter some text into a text box—nothing fancy here. You click a Submit button to send the text you enter to the server. But then I'll show you just a tantalizing glimpse of how VB .NET exceeds both VB6 and classic ASP in terms of power. The server will respond with a GIF image, created on-the-fly, containing the text you type into the text box.

Step 1: Creating a Project

Launch VS .NET. Choose File ➤ New ➤ Project and select the item Visual Basic Projects in the left pane of the New Project dialog (see Figure 9.2). In the right pane, select the Web Application icon (you may need to scroll to see the icon).

By default, VB .NET names your Web Application projects "WebApplication" with an appended number, for example, WebApplication1, but you should always enter a specific name. Click in the Name field and enter **VBNetWeb**. Check the Location field; it should contain the name of the web server you want to host this application. Typically, this will read `http://localhost`. However, you may create a project on any web server for which you have sufficient permissions to create a virtual directory and write files.

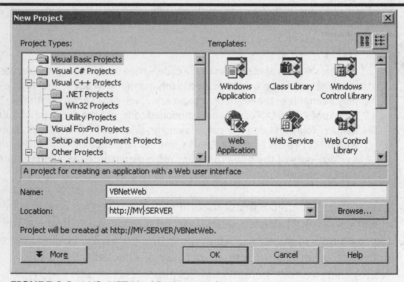

FIGURE 9.2: VS .NET New Project window

Make sure the information you entered is correct, and then click OK. VS .NET will create the new project.

You should see the Solution Explorer pane (see Figure 9.3). If the Solution Explorer is not visible, select View ➤ Solution Explorer from the menu bar.

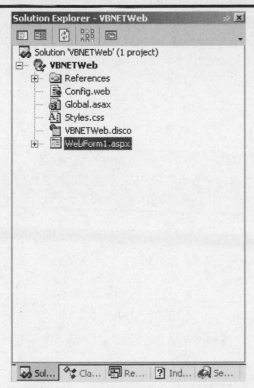

FIGURE 9.3:   Solution Explorer pane containing a new project

You'll use the VBNetWeb project throughout this book. When VB .NET creates a web application project, it adds several items to the Solution Explorer pane. I'll explain all these in a minute, but first, create a new folder named ch9. Creating subfolders works exactly like creating subfolders in a website: You simply add the name of the folder to the root URL to view a page in that folder. To create the subfolder, right-click the VBNetWeb virtual root in the Solution Explorer, click Add, and then click New Folder. Finally, type **ch9** for the folder name.

Select the Web Form1.aspx file, and drop it on top of your new ch9 folder. When you drop the file, VS .NET will move the ASPX file (and any associated files) into the ch9 folder. If the file is already open, close it first, and then move it. Your Solution Explorer pane should look similar to Figure 9.4.

Part III

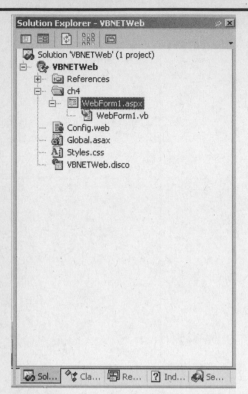

FIGURE 9.4: Solution Explorer pane after creating the ch9 folder

Step 2: Laying Out the Page

Select the Web Form1.aspx file, and then right-click it to bring up the context menu. Select Rename from the menu, and rename the file to DynamicImage.aspx (don't forget or mistype the extension—it's required).

TIP

You can press F2 to rename a file, just as you can in Windows Explorer.

Double-click the DynamicImage.aspx file to open it in the editing pane. By default, ASPX pages open in Design mode. If you're not in Design mode, click the Design tab at the bottom of the editing window to complete this example.

TIP

If you usually prefer to edit the HTML directly, you can change the default by choosing Tools ➢ Options, and then selecting the HTML Designer item from the list of options. Change the Start Active Server Pages In option to Design View and then click OK.

Right-click somewhere on the surface of the Web Form in the editing window, and select Properties from the context menu. You'll see the DOCUMENT Property Pages dialog (see Figure 9.5).

DOCUMENT Property Pages ✕

| General | Color and Margins | Keywords |

Page title: Dynamic Image Example

Background image: [   ] Browse...
☐ Nonscrolling background

Target Schema: HTML 4.0 ▾

Character Set: [   ] ▾

Page Layout: GridLayout ▾   ☑ Show Grid

Default scripting language

Server: VBScript ▾

Client: VBScript ▾

[OK] [Cancel] [Apply] [Help]

FIGURE 9.5:   DOCUMENT Property Pages dialog

Enter **Dynamic Image Example** in the Page Title field. Set the targetSchema property to Internet Explorer 5.0, and change the Page Layout setting to GridLayout. Hit OK when you are finished.

On the left side of your screen, you'll see a Toolbox tab. Move your mouse cursor over the tab; Visual Studio displays the Toolbox. Click the Web Forms bar, then click the Label Control item. Move your cursor back into the editing window and draw the Label control. You've just placed a Web Form label on the page. You should remember that Web Form controls are *not* the same as HTML controls, although they look identical; they have a different namespace from the equivalent HTML controls. Web Form Label controls and HTML Label controls (and most other controls that contain text) have a Text property like a VB .NET Windows Form Text control rather than a Caption property like a classic VB .NET Form Label control.

Next, drop a TextBox control next to the label. Your Web Form should look similar to Figure 9.6. That's it for page design—not elaborate, but functional. Next, you need to write a little code.

Step 3: Writing the Code behind the Page

Right-click the surface of the Web Form and select View Code from the context menu. If you're not very familiar with VB .NET, the code is somewhat intimidating, but don't worry, most of it is template code. The method you want to modify is the code for the Page_Load event.

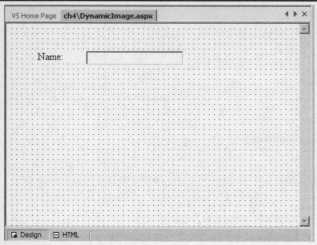

FIGURE 9.6:   The DynamicImage.aspx Web Form after placing controls

A Web Form executes the Page_Load event each time it's requested; however, the event contains code to differentiate between an HTTP GET request and a POST request. The correct .NET terminology is IsPostBack, meaning that the Web Form has been submitted back to the server. In other words, when IsPostBack is True, the user has already seen the Web Form page at least once.

In this sample page, you want to capture the text that the user enters into the text box, so your code will go into the bottom section of the If structure. For example, Listing 9.3 shows the code you need to add to the Page_Load event.

Listing 9.3: The *DynamicImage Page_Load* Event Code (*DynamicImage.vb*)

```
' Generic VB.NET code omitted
Imports System.Drawing.Text
Private Sub Page_Load(ByVal Sender As System.Object, _
    ByVal e As System.EventArgs) Handles MyBase.Load
    If Not IsPostBack Then
        Response.Write("Page before posting<br>")
    Else
        Response.ContentType = "image/gif"
        getImage(TextBox1.Text).Save(Response.OutputStream, _
            System.Drawing.Imaging.ImageFormat.Gif)
        Response.End()
    End If
End Sub
```

I won't walk you through the entire code to create the image. But I want to point out just a couple of things. First, the ability to dynamically create an image—any image—in memory simply wasn't available in classic ASP, or intrinsically in VB6 or earlier versions without extensive use of the Windows API. What you're seeing here is brand-new functionality. Second, while this function returns a Windows bitmap-formatted image, the DynamicImage.aspx Web Form returns a GIF-formatted image. In other words, VB .NET has the power to transform an image from a BMP to a GIF image. Again, this wasn't possible in earlier versions. Here's a function that creates a BMP file (yellow text on a black background) from the text entered by the user in the DynamicImage.aspx Web Form (see Listing 9.4).

Listing 9.4: The *getImage* Function (*DynamicImage.vb*)

```
Public Function getImage(ByVal s As String) As Bitmap
    Dim b As Bitmap = New Bitmap(1, 1)

    'Create a Font object
    Dim aFont As Font = New Font("Times New Roman", 24, _
        System.Drawing.GraphicsUnit.Point)

    'Create a Graphics Class to measure the text width
    Dim aGraphic As Graphics = Graphics.FromImage(b)

    'Resize the bitmap
    b = New Bitmap( _
```

Part III

```
            CInt(aGraphic.MeasureString(s, aFont).Width), _
            CInt(aGraphic.MeasureString(s, aFont).Height))
        aGraphic = Graphics.FromImage(b)
        aGraphic.Clear(Color.Black)
        aGraphic.TextRenderingHint = TextRenderingHint.AntiAlias
        aGraphic.DrawString(s, aFont, _
            New SolidBrush(Color.Yellow), 0, 0)
        aGraphic.Flush()
        Return b
    End Function
```

In the Page_Load method (see Listing 9.3), the page sets the Response.ContentType to image/gif, because the browser needs to know how to interpret the response. Next, it calls the getImage method and transforms the resulting BMP to a GIF file. Finally, it writes the binary stream of bytes containing the GIF file to the browser, which displays the image.

Web applications don't have a defined beginning and end—users can request any page in the application at any time. To test a specific page, you need to tell VS .NET which page it should run at startup. In this case, you want the DynamicImage.aspx page to appear when you start the program. Right-click the DynamicImage.aspx file in the Solution Explorer, and select the Set As Start Page item from the pop-up menu.

You can build the project first, or you can simply tell VS .NET to launch the program and it will build the project automatically. To build the project, use one of the Build options on the Build menu. To begin running, you can click the Run icon on the toolbar, or press F5, or select Start from the Debug menu.

The first time you view the page, the Page_Load event fires, and you'll see the text "Page before posting" in your browser. In IE, HTML forms with a single <asp:TextBox> or HTML <input> control submit automatically when you press the Enter key.

When you submit the form, the browser requests the DynamicImage .aspx page again, this time with the POST request. The Page_Load routine fires again, but this time, IsPostback will have the value True (because it's a POST request), so the page performs the process to create an image.

Step 4: Viewing the Results in a Browser

Try it. Save the project, and then press F5 to compile and run the project. The IDE opens up a new browser instance (see Figure 9.7).

FIGURE 9.7:   The DynamicImage.aspx Web Form before posting

Enter some text into the TextBox control, and press Enter to submit the form. The server will respond with the text you entered in a GIF image sized appropriately to contain the text (see Figure 9.8).

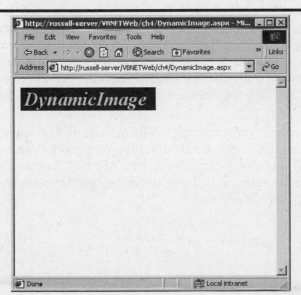

FIGURE 9.8:   The DynamicImage.aspx Web Form after posting

Now, I don't know your level of experience with either VB6 or VB .NET, or with ASP.NET, but I can tell you—the first time I made this code run, I was seriously impressed. Not only is the code to create the bitmap only 10 (unwrapped) lines long, but there are no API calls, no handles, no special Declare statements, no memory management, no worries about memory leaks, and no DLLs to call or register. It just works. Now think of the hundreds of thousands of hours that people have spent doing exactly this kind of task for web applications—drawing text in rectangles. I think this is a better way.

WHAT'S NEXT

You've created a project and a Web Form, retrieved data from the client browser, and responded with custom code. At this point, you should begin to see how VS .NET has made the process of creating a VB .NET web application very similar to the process of creating a standard Windows application. You create a project, create forms, drag and drop controls onto the forms, and write code to activate the form in a code window associated with, but not tightly bound to, that form. This loose binding is an improvement on ASP, because it facilitates code reuse. Just as you can create a generic Windows Form and use it repeatedly in multiple applications, you can do the same with Web Forms. You can reuse the user interface code of a Web Form by changing the code-behind class. Similarly, you can alter the look and layout of the user interface without recoding by changing the Web Form. Finally, you should realize that what you're really doing is using inheritance to customize generic classes to the needs of a specific application. The result is that you can now build a VB .NET web application with a familiar set of tools and operations.

Whether you've been programming in VB6 or building ASP applications, the examples in this chapter should show you the greatly increased power of VB .NET and its tight integration with ASP.NET; but you've only begun to see the changes. In the next chapter, you'll explore Web Forms in much greater detail.

Chapter 10

INTRODUCTION TO WEB FORMS

I n VB6, Microsoft introduced a technology that used HTML
templates in conjunction with an ASP page and a special
type of VB6 dynamic link library (DLL) called a WebClass.
Although the implementation had some serious problems,
WebClasses clearly foreshadowed the direction that Microsoft
has taken with .NET. WebClasses let you cleanly separate your
code from the visual interface. Microsoft obviously learned a lot
from the WebClass experiment. Web Forms are like WebClasses
on steroids.

Part III

Adapted from *Mastering ASP.NET with VB.NET*
by A. Russell Jones
ISBN 0-7821-2875-0 $49.99

WEB FORMS ARE SERVER-SIDE OBJECTS

To create a VB .NET web application, click the New Project button from the Visual Studio (VS) Start page to display the New Project dialog. Next, select Visual Basic Projects from the Project Types list, and then click the ASP.NET Web Application icon in the Templates pane of the dialog (see Figure 10.1). The fact that you must select the ASP.NET project type to create a VB .NET web application should reinforce the idea that VB .NET web applications and ASP.NET web applications are the same thing.

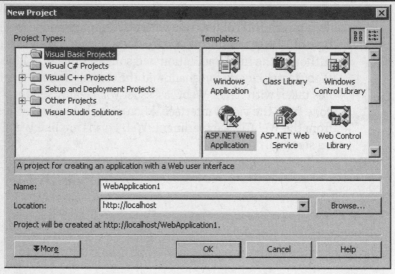

FIGURE 10.1: Visual Studio New Project dialog: Create a VB .NET web application

When you first create an ASP.NET web application project, VB .NET adds a file called (by default) WebForm1.aspx to your workspace. This file is marked as the *startup page* and is the web equivalent of a VB6 standard project's Form1.vb. You can compile and run the program, and VB .NET will open a browser instance and call the WebForm1.aspx file. However, you won't see anything, because the page has no content and no controls. By default, it's a blank page.

The key to working efficiently with Web Forms is to think of them as templates for content—and that content usually comes from the server, from the *code-behind* code. Therefore, while you *can* create and use Web Forms just as you may have built ASP pages in the past, it's not the most efficient way to use them. Instead, try to think of Web Forms in exactly the same way you think of WinForms—as templates to hold information. For example, consider the MessageBox class in VB .NET (MsgBox function in VB6). You can control the *content* of the message display, the title, text, and buttons, but you don't need to alter the window display to make efficient use of message boxes. Web Forms are similar. Try to build Web Forms that you can reuse for many different purposes.

Creating Web Forms with Notepad

Despite the name and some very clever coding, there's nothing really new about Web Forms themselves. You can easily create a Web Form in Notepad as long as you include the required header information at the top of the page and name the file with the .aspx extension. Because .NET will compile changed or added Web Forms on-the-fly, you can simply place a file in a web virtual directory and immediately request it from a browser; you're not required to perform an explicit compile step. In contrast, when you create the application from within VS, you need to compile the application before you can run it.

In the rest of this chapter, you'll work with the VBNetWeb application you created in Chapter 9, "Introduction to ASP.NET," but within a new folder. Launch VS .NET, open the VBNetWeb solution, and then right-click the VBNetWeb entry in the Solution Explorer window. Choose Add ➢ New Folder, and then name the new folder **ch10**. Press Enter to save the folder.

Next, open Notepad and type or copy Listing 10.1 into the editing window.

Listing 10.1: Create a Web Form with Notepad (*notepadForm.aspx*)

```
<%@ Page Language="vb"%>
<html>
  <head>
  </head>
  <body>
    <%Response.write("This form was created in Notepad")%>
  </body>
</html>
```

Choose File ➤ Save and navigate to the folder referenced by the VBNetWeb project. (Unless you specified a special location when you created the VBNetWeb project, in most cases, the folder will be `C:\Inetpub\wwwroot\VBNetWeb`.) Expand the subfolder list for the VBNetWeb folder, and save the file as `NotePadForm.aspx` in the `ch10` folder. To force Notepad to save the file without a `.txt` extension, put double-quotes around the filename in the File Save dialog, or change the file type to All Files.

Finally, open your browser, and type the URL of your new file. Again, in most cases, you'll be able to reach the file using the URL `http://localhost/VBNetWeb/ch10/NotePadForm.aspx`. You will see the line "This form was created in Notepad."

You may never need to create pages like this, but it's extremely useful to know that you don't need to have VS .NET installed to make minor changes to a file. I won't take you through the exercise, but you should know that you can change the code-behind VB .NET class files using a text editor in exactly the same way—and .NET will also recompile those dynamically.

Code Render Blocks—Mix Code and HTML

You've seen how you can insert code directly into an ASP.NET page in the classic ASP manner. Now that you know it's possible, try your best to forget it for the rest of this section. There are times when it's convenient to place code directly into a page, but normally you should avoid the temptation. As soon as you place code into a page, it becomes isolated code. You can't inherit from classes defined inline in ASPX pages, so the practice is considerably less reusable than placing the same code in VB .NET class files.

Web Forms' Compatibility with Existing ASP Pages

Despite being driven by a completely different technology than classic ASP, Web Forms have better backward compatibility with classic ASP pages than does VB .NET with VB. For example, the only differences between the code in Listing 10.1 and the equivalent code in classic ASP are the language directive at the top of the page and the fact that the `Response.Write` method requires parentheses around the string argument in VB .NET, whereas no parentheses are required in VBScript.

For classic ASP pages that use only the intrinsic ASP objects (like the Response object), all you need to do is change a little of the syntax. However, Web Forms aren't directly compatible with COM-based DLLs. Many classic ASP pages use calls to external DLLs to add functionality. If you need to use an existing COM DLL in your VB .NET application, you can add a special page-level attribute called AspCompat. You must add the AspCompat attribute to pages that call COM DLLs, or to call any code that requires access to any of the classic ASP intrinsic objects (Request, Response, Session, Application, or Server). Unfortunately, when you include the attribute AspCompat=True on a page, ASP.NET forces the Web Form to run in a single-threaded mode, which has a tremendous adverse performance impact. The AspCompat feature is intended to ease upgrades and to let you begin to integrate ASP.NET pages into an existing site easily, without having to change the entire site at once, but is not suitable for a long-term migration strategy.

Examples of ASP.NET Pages

The best way to understand an ASP.NET page is to walk through it in detail, examining what happens at each step.

Web Forms Are HTML/XHTML/XML Pages

As you just saw when you created a Web Form with Notepad, no magic is happening here. Web Forms really *are* just HTML pages—or more properly, they're XHTML pages by default.

NOTE

XHTML is a specific form of HTML that meets the XML 1.0 specification by requiring stricter syntax than does HTML. For example, all tags must be closed, case is relevant, and all attribute values must be enclosed in quotes.

When the ASP.NET engine reads the page content, it looks for tags with a specific namespace prefix, called asp:. Take a minute to go back and look at the DynamicImage.aspx file from Chapter 9. Load the file into the VS editor, and then click the HTML tab at the bottom of the editing window. The Web Form has two controls: a label and a text box. Here's the code that the VS Web Forms design engine inserted when you placed the controls on the Web Form (note, the details may differ, depending on your settings, the order you placed the controls on the form, and their position):

```
<form id="Web Form1" method="post" runat="server">
<asp:Label id=lblName style="Z-INDEX: 101; LEFT: 48px;
    POSITION: absolute; TOP: 43px" runat="server" Width="78"
    Height="19">Name:</asp:Label>
<asp:TextBox id=TextBox1 style="Z-INDEX: 102; LEFT: 125px;
    POSITION: absolute; TOP: 43px" runat="server">
</asp:TextBox>
</form>
```

This code contains several interesting features. First, whenever you place controls on a Web Form, VS wraps them in a form tag. That by itself is a major departure from simple HTML, where you could use input controls that were not part of a form. Note that the form tag uses the POST method rather than the GET method, that the form posts data back to the current page (it has no action attribute), and that it has a runat=server attribute.

Now run the page (use the context menu and select Set As Start Page) for the DynamicImage.aspx file. Don't enter any text into the text box; instead, right-click a blank space in the browser window, and select View Source from the context menu. Here's the portion of the HTML code on the client that corresponds to the form tag on the server.

```
<form name="Web Form1" method="post"
    action="DynamicImage.aspx" id="Web Form1">
<input type="hidden" name="__VIEWSTATE"
    value="YTB6LTM3MDk3ODU5M19fX3g=ce6a788f" />
<span id="lblName" style="height:19px;width:78px;
    Z-INDEX: 101; LEFT: 48px; POSITION: absolute;
    TOP: 43px">Name:</span>
<input name="TextBox1" type="text" id="TextBox1"
    style="Z-INDEX: 102; LEFT: 125px; POSITION: absolute;
    TOP: 43px" />
</form>
```

Viewstate—Automatic Control State Maintenance

Look at the code now! At first glance it looks the same, but there are several differences. First, the form now has an `action` attribute (it points back to the generating page, meaning the page posts data to itself). Second, there's a hidden input named `__VIEWSTATE` that contains a string of what looks like gibberish. Web Forms generate this hidden `viewstate` control as part of the VB-like event model on the server; when a user changes the content of a control, the server must have the original value so it can compare the original contents with the changed contents and thus raise some sort of `changed` event. The string value is encrypted not so much to hide its contents from the user (after all, the user can see the "real" values in the controls on the page) as to minimize the size of the container. You can imagine how the `viewstate` control's contents can get fairly large when pages contain multiple-line text fields (`<input type="textarea">` controls in HTML) filled with text or entire tables containing data from a database.

Finally, you don't see the `<asp:Label>` and `<asp:TextBox>` tags that were present in the server-side code. That's because those tags are not HTML input controls—they're ASP.NET-specific server controls. If you've been building web applications with classic ASP, working with HTML input controls, and managing *view state* yourself, you'll appreciate the time savings that automatic view state management provides.

Introducing Server Controls

A *server control* is a class that specifies output and event behavior for the ASP.NET engine. The built-in ASP.NET Web Controls render as XML-formatted elements. Remember that when the ASP.NET engine reads the page content, it looks for tags with the `asp:` namespace prefix. The `<asp:>` tags provide a layer of indirection. The tags "stand for" HTML but are not part of the HTML specification. Instead, you can think of the tags as a combination of standard HTML and script. The exact HTML/script output generated by the ASP.NET engine depends on several page properties. For example, the page property named targetSchema controls which version/type of HTML the ASP.NET engine generates in response to a page request. The default target is Internet

Explorer 5.0, but you can target downlevel browsers by setting the targetSchema property value to a less capable browser version. When you do that, the output may change (depending on the controls you have placed on the Web Form). Similarly, you can control the client script language using the defaultClientScript property. At present, VS lets you select either JScript (the default) or VBScript. The number of client languages will likely expand to include VB and C# in the future, as the .NET framework becomes more widely distributed.

Until the advent of server controls, it was the developer's responsibility to write HTML and script that would display and function properly on the range of clients using the site. Despite Internet Explorer's market dominance, several different types and versions of browsers are still used. Server controls let you bypass the difficulties involved in writing and testing different page versions on different browsers.

Browsers aren't the only clients, though. In the past couple years, new types of HTTP clients have proliferated. Palm, palmtop, notepad, and telephone devices can all browse the Web (and your sites) to varying degrees, and all have special display requirements due to their small form factors and display area. Fortunately, as ASP.NET matures, it will support more devices. You can target any specific type of client by setting the targetSchema to an appropriate value for that client type. Out of the box, the available targetSchema types are as follows:

- ▶ Internet Explorer 3.02/Navigator 3

- ▶ Internet Explorer 5

- ▶ Navigator 4

The first two correspond roughly to HTML 3.2 and HTML 4 with CSS and DHTML support, respectively. The Navigator 4 option reflects the requirement to output Netscape-specific DHTML. However, if you need to target clients that have special output requirements (like wireless devices), you can customize the ASP.NET engine through class inheritance. The salient point is that the mechanism is in place to target multiple device types from a single code base.

So, one reason for the development of server controls is to let you concentrate more on the program and less on cross-browser or client-device issues.

HTML Display, VB Event-Driven Model

Server controls have another purpose in addition to solving disparate client-device display requirements. They give you a VB-like, server-side, event-handling mechanism. For example, when a user clicks a button, you can "catch" and handle the click event on the server! That's a nice feature because it lets you develop, debug, and deploy centrally located and compiled code running in a known environment in response to user events, rather than distributed, interpreted client script running in unknown environments.

Because they run on remote machines, many server controls have *delayed* events: the client doesn't send a message to the server for *every* client action. For example, a text input control has an onchange event that fires when the control loses the focus. In classic ASP, to respond to the onchange event, you would have had to handle the event on the client. Now, you can wait until the user submits the form. At that point, the server can compare the stored ViewState values with the current values. If the contents of the text input control changed after the page was sent (in other words, the user changed the text), the values will differ, and the ASP.NET engine will raise the onchange event.

Of course, you're still completely free to trap and respond to events in client-side code as well. For example, you probably want to respond to invalid input as soon as possible—when the user enters the value—rather than waiting until the user submits the form. Checking input values is called *form validation*. ASP.NET can simplify validation as well, as you'll see later in this chapter.

ASP.NET Ships with 45 Web Controls

Windows users are spoiled. They're used to rich controls, like TreeViews, ListViews, Coolbars, Toolbars, splitters, and spinners. So far, browser-based HTML controls have been rather like poor relations—they often have the same names but bear few of the trappings. While ASP.NET doesn't exactly revolutionize client controls, it does give you a much wider assortment than you had with HTML, and if that's not enough, it also gives you the ability to create your own. Table 10.1 contains the 20 most commonly used server input controls that ship with ASP.NET.

Part III

TABLE 10.1:   ASP.NET Server Input Controls

Control Name	Description
<asp:Button>	A pushbutton. Similar to a VB CommandButton. The Text attribute is the equivalent of the VB Caption property. When clicked, the Button control submits the form to the server.
<asp:Calendar>	Provides a Calendar control in HTML. The level of functionality of this control (as of all Server controls) depends on the client's level of support for script and compliance with HTML specifications.
<asp:CheckBox>	Check box control. Unlike tristate VB check boxes, these have only two values: True (checked) or False (unchecked).
<asp:CheckBoxList>	A grouped series of check boxes. Similar in function to placing a series of check boxes on a VB Frame control.
<asp:DataGrid>	Probably the first of *many* grid controls. You can specify edit and sort options.
<asp:DataList>	Complex List control that lets you easily format data from a data set, and even has options for letting the user edit the data.
<asp:DropDownList>	Single selection from an expandable drop-down list. Similar to a VB ComboBox with its Locked property set to True.
<asp:HyperLink>	The equivalent of a standard HTML anchor tag.
<asp:ImageButton>	The same effect as wrapping an <img> tag in an anchor (<a>) tag and giving it an href attribute. When clicked, the ImageButton control submits the form to the server.
<asp:Image>	Image display (GIF, JPG, etc.). The equivalent of a VB Image control.
<asp:Label>	Text-only, read-only display. The equivalent of a VB Label control.
<asp:LinkButton>	Acts like a button—looks like a hyperlink. When clicked, the LinkButton control submits the form to the server.
<asp:Panel>	Just like a VB Frame, the Panel control serves to group or contain other controls, except that, by default, a Panel control has no border and no label.
<asp:RadioButton>	A radio button control.
<asp:RadioButtonList>	A grouped series of radio buttons. Similar in function to placing a series of radio buttons on a VB Frame control.
<asp:Repeater>	Used to format rows from a data set. The Repeater control applies a custom format to the data in each row of the data set.
<asp:Table>	Creates an HTML table tag.
<asp:TableRow>	Lets you control events, content, and display characteristics for any row in a table.

TABLE 10.1 continued: ASP.NET Server Input Controls

CONTROL NAME	DESCRIPTION
<asp:TableCell>	Lets you control events, content, and display characteristics for any cell in a table.
<asp:TextBox>	Single-line or multiline text input control. This control replaces both the <input type="text"> and <textarea> HTML controls.

You can bind all—yes, all—the server controls to data sources. Those sources, of course, can consist of data retrieved from a database, but may also be XML documents, XML that you generate dynamically, or array data.

Your familiarity with some of these controls depends largely on your background. If you've been programming ASP pages, you should almost immediately feel comfortable with the controls that substitute for standard HTML input controls and tags, like the Table or HyperLink controls. In contrast, if you've been programming VB Windows applications, you'll probably recognize that Microsoft has extended some of the most popular VB controls to the Web, by including the DataGrid, DataList, and Calendar controls. There are a few controls that have no direct single predecessor, like the CheckBoxList control and the Repeater control.

runat="server"

Despite their similarity to common Windows controls and HTML input controls, server controls are considerably different. They run on the server, not on the client. To be more specific, by default, the events and data generated by the user on the client are posted back to the server, and you handle them there, not on the client as you would in a Windows application. The model is robust enough to let you perform many common operations with little or no code. For example, one of the most common operations on websites is to create a login/password security page to force users to authenticate before viewing the contents of a site. Typically, these pages have two text fields, one for the username that displays the user's entry in plain text, and one for the password, which typically displays asterisks rather than the characters that the user types. They usually have one or more buttons as well (see Figure 10.2 and Listing 10.2).

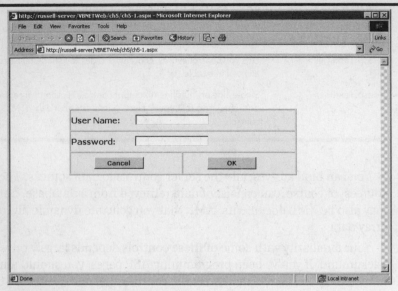

FIGURE 10.2:   A simple login page

Listing 10.2: HTML Code for Login Form (*ch10-1.aspx*)

```
<%@ Page Language="vb" AutoEventWireup="false"
    Codebehind="ch10-1.vb" Inherits="VBNETWeb.ch10_1"%>
<html><head>
<META http-equiv=Content-Type content="text/html;
    charset=windows-1252">
<meta content="HTML 4.0" name=vs_targetSchema>
<meta content="Microsoft Visual Studio.NET 7.0"
    name=GENERATOR>
<meta content="Visual Basic 7.0" name=CODE_LANGUAGE>
</head>
<body ms_positioning="GridLayout">
<form id=FORM1 method=post runat="server">
<table style="LEFT: 122px; POSITION: absolute;
   TOP: 106px" height=137
   cellSpacing=1 cellPadding=1 width=474
   bgColor=#ffffcc border=1>
  <tr>
    <td colSpan=2><asp:label id=Label1 runat="server"
      Width="127" Height="18" font-size="Small"
      font-bold="True" font-names="Verdana"
```

```
            bordercolor="Transparent" borderstyle="None"
            backcolor="#FFFFC0">User Name:</asp:label>
            <asp:textbox id=txtUserName runat="server">
                </asp:textbox></td></tr>
    <tr>
      <td colSpan=2>
        <asp:label id=Label2 runat="server" Width="127"
         Height="18"
        font-size="Small" font-bold="True"
        font-names="Verdana"
        bordercolor="Transparent" borderstyle="None"
        backcolor="#FFFFC0">
        Password:
        </asp:label>

        <asp:textbox id=txtPassword runat="server"
             textmode="Password">
        </asp:textbox>
      </td>
    </tr>
    <tr>
      <td align=middle width=200>
        <asp:button id=cmdCancel runat="server" Text="Cancel"
        font-bold="True" font-names="Verdana"
        commandname="cmdCancel"
        height="24" width="104"></asp:button>
      </td>
      <td align=middle width=200>
        <asp:button id=cmdOK runat="server" Text="OK"
        font-bold="True"
        font-names="Verdana" commandname="cmdOK" height="25"
        width="101"></asp:button>
      </td>
    </tr>
  </table>
</form>
</body>
</html>
```

When you run this example, you can enter text into the fields, just
like a standard HTML page. When you click one of the buttons, the
browser submits the form data. But unlike a standard HTML form, *you
get the entered data back*! By default, the server uses the ViewState

hidden control to rebuild the state of the page and send it right back to the browser.

OK, you may not think that's exciting, but here's the pseudocode to perform the same operation by coding it manually in a classic ASP page:

1. Check to see if the page was reached via a GET (first display) or POST request.

2. If POST, then retrieve the form data from the request.

3. Using embedded code, rebuild the page. For each control, insert the value you just obtained from the POST operation to redisplay the values on the client side, e.g., `<input type= "text" value= "<%=Request.Form("txtUserName")%>" id="txtUserName">`.

4. For each control, create hidden form variables to hold the current field values, e.g., `<input type="hidden" value="<%= Request.Form("txtUserName")%>" id="txtUserName">`.

Using ASP.NET, you didn't have to do anything but lay out some controls. But that's not all: You can perform complex input validation without writing any code.

FORM VALIDATION

It's been said that the only way to write a perfect data input program is to eliminate the users. While you probably don't want to go that far, you should recognize that the single greatest source of bad data is bad programs. The best data-entry programs don't let users enter invalid data. Less elegant but still acceptable programs let users know when they *do* enter invalid data. Bad programs not only let users enter invalid data, but also skip the check stage, invariably resulting in data integrity problems, expensive fixes, angry clients, and a lot of trouble all around.

To solve the problem, you *must* perform data validity checks. The general rule to follow is that the closer you perform these checks to the point of input, the more likely you are to get consistently good data and provide a good user experience. Unfortunately, I've seen programs that go far overboard by displaying annoying messages whenever a user types an invalid key. Similarly, many programs check field validity only after the user completes the entire form. In certain cases, that's acceptable, but more often, a better method is to check the fields when the user completes a defined part of the input task.

For example, on the login Web Form, you know that both the Username and Password fields *must* contain a value, because you will be unable to authenticate the user without both values. Therefore, you must ensure that both values have been entered. Beyond that, you should have rules for the contents of each field. For example, you might force passwords to be at least six characters, and you might not allow the username to contain any characters except letters and numbers.

Whenever a user submits the form without meeting the validation requirements, you want to redisplay the form and show a message stating what the problem is and how to fix it. In ASP.NET, you can perform many common data validation tasks without writing any code, using a set of server controls called validators.

Client-Side Validation

Here's an example that performs client-side validation using the Validator controls. Create a copy of the Web Form ch10-1.aspx. You can copy files within the Solution Explorer just as you do in the Windows Explorer. Right-click the ch10-1.aspx file in the Solution Explorer pane, then select Copy from the context menu. Next, right-click the ch10 folder, and then select Paste from the context menu. That will paste a copy of the ch10-1.aspx file named Copy of ch10-1.aspx into the ch10 folder. Rename the file to ch10-2.aspx by selecting the new file and pressing F2 or right-clicking and selecting Rename from the context menu, and then typing the new name.

Copying and pasting a Web Form also pastes a copy of the code-behind file, ch10-1.aspx.vb. That can be a problem when you rename the ASPX file, because while renaming the file also renames the code-behind file, it does *not* rename the class created in the code-behind file. You must rename that manually. Double-click the ch10-2.aspx.vb file and rename the class to **ch10_2** (note the underscore rather than the dash).

Double-click the new Web Form to load it into the editing window. Click the Toolbox, and drag two RequiredFieldValidator controls onto the design surface. Place them just to the right of the two TextBox controls. Next, set the ID property of the new controls to UsernameValidator and

PasswordValidator, respectively. Set other properties for the controls as follows:

Property	UsernameValidator	PasswordValidator
ControlToValidate	txtUserName	txtPassword
ErrorMessage	Username Required	Password Required

When you finish, the Web Form should look like Figure 10.3.

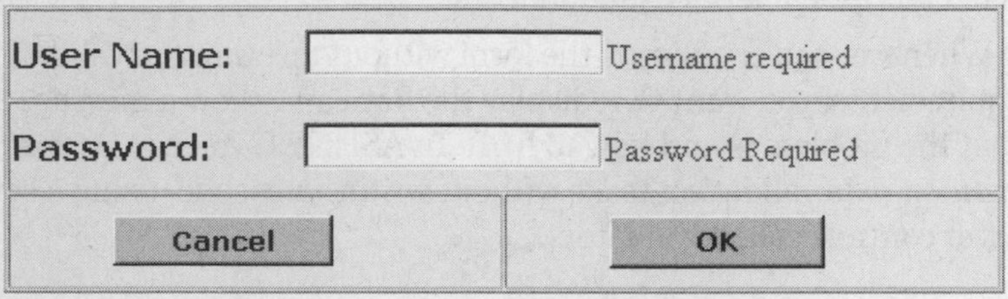

User Name:	[ ]Username required
Password:	[ ]Password Required
Cancel	OK

FIGURE 10.3:   Simple login page with RequiredFieldValidators

Run the Web Form again. This time, submit the form without entering text into either the Username or Password fields. The submission triggers the validation check. The validation check fails for both controls, because the RequiredFieldValidator control performs only one check—it tests whether the control referred to by its ControlToValidate property contains a value different from the control's initial value. Stop the program and run it again. Enter some text into one of the two fields, but not the other. You should see the error message appear for the empty field only.

Validators are "smart" controls. They follow the rule mentioned in the beginning of this section and perform the validation as closely as possible to the point of input. In this case, that point is heavily dependent on the browser. Using IE5 or higher, the controls generate client-side JavaScript or VBScript (depending on the setting of the defaultClientScript page property). Using downlevel browsers, the controls generate no client script and validation fires on the server when the user submits the form.

How does this all work? It's worth exploring a bit so you'll understand the model. Using IE5, for example, with the defaultClientScript property set to JavaScript, the page generates the script in Listing 10.3. You can see the full HTML generated by the page yourself by running the program and then selecting View Source from the browser context menu. The highlighted sections show how ASP.NET translates the validation controls into HTML.

Listing 10.3: HTML Code for Login Form with RequiredFieldValidator (ch10-2.aspx)

```html
<html>
<head>
<META http-equiv="Content-Type" content="text/html;
    charset=windows-1252">
<meta content="HTML 4.0" name="vs_targetSchema">
<meta content="Microsoft Visual Studio.NET 7.0"
        name="GENERATOR">
<meta content="Visual Basic 7.0" name="CODE_LANGUAGE">
</head>
<body ms_positioning="GridLayout">
<form name="FORM1" method="post" action="ch10-2.aspx"
    language="javascript" onsubmit="ValidatorOnSubmit();"
    id="FORM1">
<input type="hidden" name="__VIEWSTATE"
    value="dDwtMTYzMDIzNDQwMjs7Pg==" />

<script language="javascript"
  src="/aspnet_client/system_web/1_4000_2914_16/
  WebUIValidation.js">
</script>

<table style="Z-INDEX: 101; LEFT: 122px;
    POSITION: absolute; TOP: 106px"
    height="137" cellSpacing="1" cellPadding="1" width="474"
    bgColor="#ffffcc" border="1">
<tr>
<td colSpan="2">
<span id="Label1" style="background-color:#FFFFC0;border-
    color:Transparent;border-style:None;font-family:Verdana;
    font-size:Small;font-weight:bold;height:18px;
    width:135px;">User Name:</span>
<input name="txtUserName" type="text" id="txtUserName" />
<span id="UsernameValidator" controltovalidate="txtUserName"
    errormessage="Username required"
    evaluationfunction=
      "RequiredFieldValidatorEvaluateIsValid"
    initialvalue="" style="color:Red;visibility:hidden;">
    Username required</span>
```

```
    </td>
    </tr>
    <tr>
    <td colSpan="2">
    <span id="Label2" style="background-color:#FFFFC0;
        border-color:Transparent;border-style:None;
        font-family:Verdana;
        font-size:Small;font-weight:bold;height:18px;
        width:136px;"> Password:</span>
    <input name="txtPassword" type="password"
        id="txtPassword" />
    <span id="PasswordValidator" controltovalidate="txtPassword"
        errormessage="Password Required"
        evaluationfunction=
            "RequiredFieldValidatorEvaluateIsValid"
        initialvalue="" style="color:Red;visibility:hidden;">
            Password Required</span>
    </td>
    </tr>
    <tr>
    <td align="middle" width="200">
    <input type="submit" name="cmdCancel" value="Cancel"
        onclick="if (typeof(Page_ClientValidate) == 'function')
        Page_ClientValidate(); " language="javascript"
        id="cmdCancel"
        style="font-family:Verdana;font-weight:bold;height:24px;
        width:104px;" />
    </td>
    <td align="middle" width="200">
    <input type="submit" name="cmdOK" value="OK"
        onclick="if (typeof(Page_ClientValidate) == 'function')
        Page_ClientValidate(); " language="javascript" id="cmdOK"
        style="font-family:Verdana;font-weight:bold;height:25px;
        width:101px;" />
    </td>
    </tr>
    </table>

    <script language="javascript">
    <!--
        var Page_Validators =  new
```

```
        Array(document.all["UsernameValidator"],
        document.all["PasswordValidator"]);
        // -->
</script>


<script language="javascript">
<!--
var Page_ValidationActive = false;
if (typeof(clientInformation) != "undefined" &&
    clientInformation.appName.indexOf("Explorer") != -1)
        {
        if (typeof(Page_ValidationVer) == "undefined")
            alert("Unable to find script library
'/aspnet_client/system_web/1_4000_2914_16/WebUIValidation.js'.
    Try placing this file manually, or reinstall by running
            'aspnet_regiis -c'.");
          else if (Page_ValidationVer != "121")
           alert("This page uses an incorrect version of
           WebUIValidation.js. The page expects version 121.
           The script library is " + Page_ValidationVer + ".");
           else
              ValidatorOnLoad();
        }

function ValidatorOnSubmit() {
    if (Page_ValidationActive) {
        ValidatorCommonOnSubmit();
    }
}
// -->
</script>


</form>
</body>
</html>
```

The interesting and functional part here is the client-side script. First, note that the page includes a script file:

```
<script language="javascript"
  src=
"/aspnet_client/system_web/1_4000_2914_16/
```

Part III

```
        WebUIValidation.js">
    </script>
```

That script file contains several utility functions for validating input. You should be able to find the file by following the path from your root web directory. On my computer, the full path is as follows:

```
<script language="javascript"
    src="/aspnet_client/system_web/1_4000_2914_16/
        WebUIValidation.js">
</script>
```

The path may vary on your computer, because it's version dependent, but you should be able to match the value of the script's src attribute to a physical path on your server. Farther down in the file, you'll see a script that defines several variables and then checks whether the script was found and loaded by checking the *Page_ValidationVer* variable defined in the included script. The page displays message boxes (using the alert function in JScript) if either condition fails.

```
if (typeof(clientInformation) != "undefined" &&
    clientInformation.appName.indexOf("Explorer") != -1) {
        if (typeof(Page_ValidationVer) == "undefined")
            alert("Unable to find script library
            '/aspnet_client/system_web/1_4000_2914_16/
                WebUIValidation.js'.
            Try placing this file manually, or reinstall by
              running
            'aspnet_regiis -c'.");
        else if (Page_ValidationVer != "121")
          alert("This page uses an incorrect version of
          WebUIValidation.js. The page expects version 121.
          The script library is " + Page_ValidationVer + ".");
        else
            ValidatorOnLoad();
}
```

The real work occurs when the user clicks a button. Each submit button calls a function to check the data entered into the form. For example, here's the OK button definition. The onClick event checks to see whether a function called `Page_ClientValidate` exists. If so, it calls the function.

```
<input type="submit" name="cmdOK" value="OK"
    onclick="if (typeof(Page_ClientValidate) == 'function')
    Page_ClientValidate(); " language="javascript" id="cmdOK"
    style="font-family:Verdana;font-weight:bold;height:25px;
    width:101px;" />
</td>
```

The `Page_ClientValidate` function iterates through the Validator controls in the document, calling the ValidatorValidate function for each one.

```
function Page_ClientValidate() {
    var i;
    for (i = 0; i < Page_Validators.length; i++) {
        ValidatorValidate(Page_Validators[i]);
    }
    ValidatorUpdateIsValid();
    ValidationSummaryOnSubmit();
    Page_BlockSubmit = !Page_IsValid;
    return Page_IsValid;
}
```

The ValidatorValidate function fires the evaluation function bound to each validator, which in turn performs the appropriate test on the value of the control to which the validator is bound through its `ControlToValidate` property.

```
function ValidatorValidate(val) {
    val.isvalid = true;
    if (val.enabled != false) {
        if (typeof(val.evaluationfunction) == "function") {
            val.isvalid = val.evaluationfunction(val);
        }
    }
    ValidatorUpdateDisplay(val);
}
```

After iterating through all the validators, the Page_ClientValidate function calls a ValidatorUpdateIsValid() function, which iterates through the page validators again, checking the isvalid property for each. If any of the isvalid properties returns false, the script sets a page-level variable called Page_IsValid to false and exits the loop.

So far, nothing's prevented the form from submitting, though. The <form> tag's onsubmit property calls another function called ValidatorOnSubmit(). That script checks to see if the validators are loaded and working properly by checking the value of a variable named *Page_Validationactive* that is set to true only when the ValidatorOnLoad() function executes properly. Finally, it calls the ValidatorCommonOnSubmit() function.

```
function ValidatorOnSubmit() {
    if (Page_ValidationActive) {
        ValidatorCommonOnSubmit();
    }
}
```

The common validation routine ValidatorCommonOnSubmit sets the event object's returnValue property to the inverse value of the *Page_BlockSubmit* variable that was set in the Page_ClientValidate() function. That's a little difficult to read; but if you translate it to English, it sounds better. "If the page should block submission, then return False, otherwise return True." If the event.returnValue is true, the form will submit the data to the server; otherwise, it won't do anything.

```
function ValidatorCommonOnSubmit() {
    event.returnValue = !Page_BlockSubmit;
    Page_BlockSubmit = false;
}
```

Finally, the function sets the *Page_BlockSubmit* variable to false to get ready for the next validation round (in other words, clear the variable so the form will submit the next time if the user fixes the invalid input values). While all this client script is anything but simple, you won't usually need to think about it at all.

NOTE

There have been several versions of the client-side validation script file. I've used version 121 in this example. Your version may be later, but the differences in later versions are minor.

Now that you've seen a simple validation control, you can extend the validation a little. As I stated earlier, in addition to checking that the user has entered a value, you will want to perform a couple of other checks. The next example enforces a complex rule that usernames may contain only letters and numbers, that they must be between three and 10 characters long, and that passwords may contain any characters but must be between six and 10 characters long. You can perform these types of tests with a RegularExpressionValidator control. Make a copy of the ch10-2.aspx Web Form and rename it to **ch10-3.aspx** (see the procedure listed earlier in this chapter to copy a Web Form). Drag two Regular-ExpressionValidator controls onto the Web Form. Place them under the table. Make them as wide as the table, and two or three lines high. Set the ID property of the new controls to UsernameRegExpValidator and PasswordRegExpValidator, respectively. Set other properties for the controls as follows:

Property	Username-RegExpValidator	Password-RegExpValidator
ControlToValidate	TxtUserName	txtPassword
ErrorMessage	Invalid Username: Usernames must be between 3 and 10 characters, and may contain only letters and numbers.	Invalid Password
ValidationExpression	[a-zA-Z_0-9]{3,10}	.{6,10}
Display	Dynamic (or Static)	Dynamic (or Static)
EnableClientScript	True	True

The ValidationExpression property contains the regular expression that the validator uses to test the value of the control specified by the ControlToValidate property. The expression [a-zA-Z_0-9]{3, 10} means that when you run the program, the same actions occur as before; the page generates client-side JavaScript to validate the control. Try it. Enter two characters into the Username field and then press the Tab key. The validation fires immediately. Your browser should look similar to Figure 10.4.

Part III

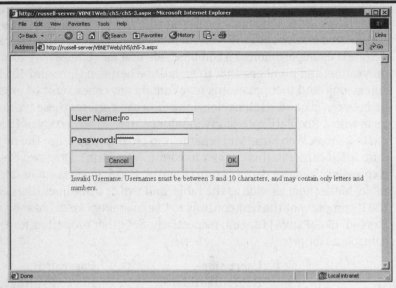

FIGURE 10.4:   RegularExpressionValidator control example

Server-Side Validation

Validation always fires on the server—even when validation has *already* fired on the client. This may seem odd, considering that you may have spent a lot of time making sure the client is unable to submit invalid values, but don't let that bother you. You may want to reuse the server-side code at some point—for example, you might inherit from your Web Form. In any case, you don't have to let the controls validate on the client—you can force them to validate only on the server by setting the Web Form's clientTarget property to DownLevel. That prevents the page from generating any client validation script; instead, the Web Form submits all the values to the server just as with a standard HTML form, and the controls perform their validation tasks there.

In some cases where you know the clients may consist of downlevel browsers, you may have to perform validation on the server. Another reason to validate on the server is if you want to closely control the position and content of the messages that appear. You can't easily alter the client-side validation code (although I'll show you how to work around that problem), but by writing a small amount of code in the code-behind class, you can change the messages that appear very easily.

Change the validation location to the server by entering **DownLevel** in the document clientTarget property field. You need to click the design surface to see the document properties. Next, double-click any control to open up the code-behind form. Find the ch10-3.aspx Page_Load subroutine; this is the event that fires each time the page loads. The IsPostback property is False when the user first loads the page but True whenever the user submits the page. You need to check the values after the user submits the page, so extend the If statement to check when the value is True. Change the method so it reads as follows:

```
Private Sub Page_Load(ByVal sender As System.Object, _
    ByVal e As System.EventArgs) Handles MyBase.Load
    Dim val As BaseValidator
    If IsPostBack Then
        Page.Validate()
        If Not Page.IsValid Then
            For Each val In Page.Validators
                If Not val.IsValid Then
                    Response.Write(val.ErrorMessage & "<br>")
                End If
            Next
        End If
    End If
End Sub
```

Congratulations! Although the result isn't pretty, you've just coded a server-side loop that validates values entered on the client—and you didn't have to find the values, assign them to variables, or write any special validation code. By setting the clientTarget property to Down-Level, you turned off VS .NET's automatic client-side validation script generation. Therefore, when the user submits the form, the values return to the server—but you use the same validation controls to check the values. As I mentioned earlier, the server-side validation always occurs—even if you don't use it.

So when or why would you want to turn off client-side validation? First, you should need to turn it off when the target browser is not Internet Explorer. Ideally, in some utopian future state, all browsers would be equally capable of performing dynamic HTML operations and running the same version of client script code. Unfortunately, we haven't

Part III

reached that state yet. Second, you may have noticed that VS .NET translates Validator controls into an HTML <span> tag. The <span> tag defines a specified area of the browser window where the Validator controls can display their error messages. But the tags are transparent; therefore, you can't stack them on top of one another unless you're sure that only one Validator control can fire at a time—and as you've seen, you can easily create a form that fires multiple validation errors when submitted. So, a third reason to validate on the server is to control the way the Validator controls display error messages.

NOTE

Microsoft chose to use a <span> rather than a <div> tag for the error messages because <div> tags always begin on a new line in downlevel browsers, whereas <span> tags do not necessarily begin on a new line. This lets you put the error messages on the same line as the control that contains the invalid input.

The simple example you just created writes the error messages at the top of the screen, but you can easily change that. Drag a Label control onto the Web Form and place it underneath the table. Edit the ID property so it reads lblErrors, and set the Color property to Red, leaving the Text property blank. Next, change the code in the method so you concatenate all the error messages during the Load event, and set the lblErrors.Text property to the concatenated string. Listing 10.4 shows the code. Finally, change the Display property for the two RegularExpressionValidator controls to None, and change their EnableClientScript property to False.

Listing 10.4: Web Form *Load* Event with Server-Side Validation (*ch10-3.aspx*)

```
Private Sub Page_Load(ByVal sender As System.Object, _
    ByVal e As System.EventArgs) Handles MyBase.Load
Dim val As BaseValidator
Dim s As New System.Text.StringBuilder()
If IsPostBack Then
    Page.Validate()
    If Not Page.IsValid Then
        For Each val In Page.Validators
            If Not val.IsValid Then
                s.Append(val.ErrorMessage)
```

```
                    s.Append("<br>")
                End If
            Next
            lblErrors.Visible = True
            lblErrors.Text = s.ToString()
        End If
    End If
End Sub
```

I dimensioned the variable *val* as a BaseValidator object. As the name implies, all Validator objects inherit from BaseValidator; therefore, you can assign any Validator object to a variable with the BaseValidator type. Of course, you could use Object just as well, or iterate through the Page.Validators collection using an index variable, like the client-side code you saw earlier in this chapter. In this example, the code uses a StringBuilder object to create a string of error messages, so it needs to check the IsValid property for each Validator object separately. When your only interest is whether all values entered on the page are valid, you can test the Page.IsValid property, which will return False unless *all* the Validator controls validate successfully.

At this point, you've built a reasonably complicated form that does the following:

▶ Maintains user view state between pages

▶ Performs two different types of validation

▶ Displays customizable error messages when validation fails

And here's the interesting part—you've had to write only a few lines of code—and then only when you wanted to customize the validation error message display. After this short introduction to code, I'm sure you're eager for more, so let's move on.

CODE-BEHIND PROGRAMMING

VS .NET uses the code-behind model to separate user-interface components of web applications from the logic components. In classic ASP, several *intrinsic objects* simplified the grunt work of parsing HTTP requests and delivering responses. VS .NET extends that model by encapsulating almost all the parts of a web application. Of course, extending the model also meant that the number of objects you used had to increase as well. The .NET framework groups most of these objects in the System.Web namespace.

Page Object   The Page object is the base object for a Web Form. The Page object provides events, methods, and properties for a single page. You can think of a Page object and a Web Form interchangeably—although that's not entirely accurate. Web Forms inherit from the System.Web.UI.Page class. In object-oriented terms, you can say that a Web Form is a Page object. The Page object is your primary means of accessing the rest of the objects in this list, as it exposes them all as properties. The Page object fires events you can hook to perform initialization and cleanup, as well as providing properties that help you determine the client type, the list of controls on a Web Form, the type and source of data bound to those controls, and (as you've already seen) the set of Validator controls.

HttpRequest Object   The HttpRequest object encapsulates the data sent by the client with each request. This object is similar to the classic ASP Request object. Each Page object exposes an HttpRequest object as a property called Page.Request. This book usually refers to the HttpRequest object as the Request object. For example, when a user submits a form, you can access the individual data values as items in the Page.Request.Form collection object.

HttpResponse Object   The HttpResponse object encapsulates the data returned by the server in response to each client request. This object is similar to the classic ASP Response object. Each Page object exposes an HttpResponse object as a property called Page.Response. You use the Response object each time you want to send data to the client. This book usually refers to the HttpResponse object as the Response object. For example, you've already seen the Response.Write method, which returns text data, and the Response.BinaryWrite method, which returns binary data.

HttpApplicationState Object   Container class for all objects in an ASP.NET application running on a single server. Values stored at Application scope are shared between pages in a single application, but not between applications, nor between servers or processes. Each Page object exposes an instance of this class as a property called Page.Application. This book usually refers to the HttpApplicationState object as the Application object. You'll use it in web applications to store values common to the entire application—in other words, to store global variables.

HttpServerUtility Object   Provides a set of methods and properties through which you can obtain information about the local server on which your web application is running. These are similar to but more extensive than the set of methods available through the classic ASP Server object. Each Page object exposes an instance of this class as a property called Page.Server. This book usually refers to the HttpServerUtility object as the Server object. For example, you can obtain the local machine name with the MachineName property, or encode/decode data via the HtmlEncode/HtmlDecode and UrlEncode/UrlDecode/UrlPathEncode methods.

HttpSession Object   Provides a container associated with a specific IP address. This object is similar to (but much more robust and scalable than) the classic ASP Session object. Each client has a unique IP address. Whenever the server receives a request from an unrecognized (meaning new) IP address, it creates a Session object and provides an in-memory cookie to the requesting client. If the client accepts the cookie, then the client will send the cookie with each subsequent request to that server. The server can use the cookie value, called a SessionID, to associate data with that specific client. Sessions are not required. In classic ASP, the Session object worked on only one server at a time; you couldn't use Sessions for multiprocess or multiserver web applications. Because classic ASP stored Session data entirely in RAM, you could easily lose the data if the web server crashed. Classic ASP Sessions were also slow. For these reasons, web developers rarely used the Session object in classic ASP for large-scale web applications, although Sessions were widely used for smaller sites. ASP.NET has made many changes to the Session object that make it much more robust and scalable, so it's easier to write applications that must store state data for each client. Each Page object exposes an instance of this class as a property called Page.Session. This book usually refers to the HttpSessionState object as the Session object.

Cache Object   Unlike earlier versions of ASP, where if you wanted caching, you had to implement it yourself, ASP.NET gives you fine-grained control over what to cache, how long to maintain the cache, and how often to refresh it. For example, you can cache a page, the results of a database query, the contents of a file, or an object or collection of objects. The Page object exposes an instance of this class as the `Page.Cache` property.

Use of Any .NET Language

In classic ASP, you could write in any scripting language supported by the Microsoft Scripting Runtime model. The two most common scripting languages were VBScript and JScript, both of which shipped with ASP. In ASP.NET, you can write in any language that supports the Common Language Runtime (CLR) model. Initially, that means you can write in VB .NET, C#, or JScript (which has been upgraded to a more full-featured, compiled language in its VS .NET implementation).

Scripting languages are interpreted, not compiled. While using interpreted languages has some advantages, it also means that operations written with script are slower than equivalent operations written in a compiled language. Although scripting languages have grown more powerful over the past couple years, they have a limited ability to interoperate with the operating system itself, they have limited debugging facilities, and they don't use type-safe variables.

These limitations led to a complex model for creating web applications where web developers used ASP pages primarily as collection points for Request and Response data. They encapsulated most of the important operations in Common Object Model (COM) or ActiveX objects so they could get the benefits of compiled execution speed and deliver code encapsulated in ActiveX DLLs (hidden from clients).

Well, you don't have to do that anymore. Although you still must learn a scripting language to write good web applications, you only need to use it on the client.

Only One Language Per Page

As I mentioned in the previous section, the use of scripting languages in classic ASP did have some advantages. One advantage was that you could mix routines written in more than one scripting language on a single page. You can't do that in VS .NET. You must choose and stick with a single language for each page—although you're perfectly free to use as many different .NET-compliant languages within an application as you want. To be frank, mixing languages on a single ASP page was not a common practice anyway; most developers used VBScript for server-side code and JScript for client-side code. In larger groups, programming in multiple languages is somewhat more common, so I suspect that many applications in the future will contain code written in more than one language.

Display Separated from Data Processing

Another disadvantage of the classic ASP model was that the HTML code used to create the display and the logic code used to power the application were often mixed into a single page. There's nothing wrong with doing this if you don't ever plan to use the code again, but it promotes single-use coding, which is *not* the way to think if you're planning to make a career out of programming. The more you program, the more you find that with a little work, you can abstract most operations into classes with methods, properties, and events that you can reuse in many different situations.

PAGE/FORM LAYOUT

If you were familiar with the Forms layout engine in VB6, you'll be instantly at home with the page layout capabilities of Web Forms. Using the Web Form designer, you can drag and drop controls on a form using the familiar VB forms design model.

Designing HTML Pages

HTML pages have several advantages over Windows forms. First, they scroll automatically—and people are used to scrolling in web pages—so you can take advantage of that feature in your own applications to give yourself a little extra vertical space when required. Also, you don't have to give HTML elements a predetermined size. By using percentages rather than fixed pixel widths, you can design pages that adapt to clients with different screen resolutions.

HTML pages also have built-in links, which makes it relatively easy to tie pages together visually, and avoids some of the problems with using list boxes, drop-down lists, and rows of buttons (I'm sure you've all seen some of those VB applications where buttons are highly overused).

By default, HTML pages refresh completely whenever the user browses to the page for the first time in a given browser session. That means you can change the page on the server, and most clients will see the updated version right away. In contrast, installed Windows applications must be uninstalled and then reinstalled for you to make updates or alter the program.

Inline versus GridLayout

Web Form layout is a little strange and awkward when you work in FlowLayout mode, because the HTML rendering engine has final control over the placement and appearance of controls. When you drop a control on a Web Form, it doesn't stay where you put it; it moves into the next available standard layout position! However, if you ever worked with a WYSIWYG HTML editor, such as Macromedia's Dreamweaver or FrontPage, you're familiar with the problems involved in laying out page elements in HTML.

When you work in GridLayout mode, though, things immediately feel much more familiar—especially if you're targeting an "uplevel" browser like IE5. Controls stay where you put them; you can resize them, move them around the screen, and even overlay them on top of one another much as you can in the VB6 form designer.

However, being able to work in a familiar model can be misleading, because the clients—typically browsers—don't work like Windows forms.

Generated HTML Code

As presented earlier in this chapter, you can access the HTML that the Web Form designer generates by clicking the HTML tab at the bottom of the Web Form designer window, but by default, you don't have access to the HTML that ASP.NET generates automatically and sends to the browser. In most cases, that's a good thing, because ASP.NET can generate fairly complicated code, and it's not always pretty. However, if you need to gain control over the generated HTML, you need to move up the object hierarchy and investigate the WebControl object. All WebControls inherit from this object. While I won't go into much detail at this point, it's worth pointing out several members that render the HTML for a control, so you'll know where to start when you want to create a customized control.

WebControls have most of the properties that you would expect from working with VB6 and WinForm controls. Properties such as Height, Width, Font, ForeColor, BackColor, BorderStyle, BorderColor, BorderWidth, AccessKey, Enabled, and Visible are fairly self-explanatory. But several properties and methods are specific to Web applications:

Style Property   Most WebControls have a Style property that returns the CSSStyleCollection object. The Style property corresponds to the `style` attribute for HTML elements; in other words, it gives you programmatic server-side access to the cascading style sheets (CSS) attributes for the control. For example, you can get the Style object for a WebControl, set its properties, and then merge the Style with another Style object using the MergeStyle method. This is essentially what happens when you set the `class` attribute to a CSS class. The element inherits the CSS style attributes *unless* those attributes are already defined locally within the element. In other words, merging styles adds attributes and values from the source Style object to the target Style object, but it does not overwrite any attributes or values that already exist in the target. You can also overwrite existing style attributes using the ApplyStyle method.

CSSClass Property   This property returns or sets the CSS class name with which the control is associated. Using this property, you can change the CSS class of a control programmatically on the server.

MaintainState Property   This property controls whether a control uses ViewState to maintain its properties across client page requests. By default, all WebControls use ViewState, but you will definitely want to disable it for specific controls. When you set the value of the MaintainState property to `False`, the control still appears and functions normally on the client, but values entered by the client during one page request will not reappear automatically after the user posts the form. For example, you may wish to disable this property for a password field, forcing the field to appear empty whenever the login information submitted by a user is incorrect.

Page Property   Returns a reference to the Page containing this WebControl.

Site Property   Returns a reference to the Site containing this WebControl.

RenderBeginTag Method   Renders the HTML starting tag (e.g., <div>) that represents this WebControl.

RenderControl Method   Renders the HTML tag attributes and values for this WebControl.

RenderEndTag Method   Renders the HTML tag attributes and values for this WebControl.

DesignTimeRender Method   This method takes an HTML-TextWriter object as a parameter. It uses the HTMLTextWriter object to render the HTML string representing the control during design time—this is what happens when you drop a control on a Web Form. If you create your own controls, you would use this method to create the HTML for those controls. Note that you would *not* need to use this method if you create custom WebControls that are an amalgam of existing controls, only if you were to create a brand-new WebControl.

What's Next

As you've seen, the ideas behind Web Forms, WebControls, and ASP.NET aren't new, but the implementation *is*. Specifically, the ability to treat a web page as a single entity is revolutionary. By creating the .NET and ASP.NET objects, Microsoft has raised the level of abstraction in programming. For example, the web programming model has become extremely similar to the Windows programming model. Similarly, by creating the CLR, Microsoft has raised the level of programming-language abstraction. Now, one language differs from another in syntax and degree of nonconformance with the CLR.

Still, to be an effective web developer, you need some special knowledge about how the Web works. In the next chapter, we will begin to explore how to build more in-depth websites by using the WebServices built by Visual Basic .NET.

Chapter 11
WORKING WITH XML WEB SERVICES

W eb Services are the single most advertised, and most promising, feature of the .NET platform. A Web Service is a class that resides on a web server, and its methods can be called over the Internet. Unlike a web application, however, the methods of this class don't return an HTML page. Instead, they return one or more values, packaged as XML documents. As a result, any application that can handle XML can call these methods and use their results. The idea is that every application, no matter its language or the operating system, can access Web Services; conversely, any web server can expose functionality in the form of Web Services. What makes it all possible is that everything is based on a (soon to become) universal standard, the XML standard.

Part III

Adapted from *Mastering Visual Basic .NET Database Programming* by Evangelos Petroutsos and Asli Bilgin

ISBN 0-7821-2878-5 $49.99

You don't have to develop Web Services for a typical application, and there are hardly any Web Services around to use from within your code. Companies that provide stock quote services will most likely expose their services as Web Services, but the Web isn't going to flood with Web Services. However, many corporations will expose Web Services to share information with other corporations. Later in this chapter, you'll see how to create and set up a Web Service to accept orders. This Web Service can be accessed from within a web application, or a Windows application.

When would you use a Web Service? Web Services are another step, probably the most important one so far, toward providing software services. Consider for a moment why you're spending so much time on the Internet today. You locate information, which arrives to your computer in the form of static pages (text and images). You can either read the information, or save it to a local file and read it later. The form of information that arrives to the client computer is suitable for consumption by humans, but you can't reuse it from within your applications. With some code you can parse HTML documents and extract the information you're interested in, but if the structure of the page changes, you'll have to modify your application accordingly.

With a Web Service you can provide information in a form that can be easily reused by another application. You can also charge for this information, if there are people willing to pay for it—or if the information you provide is worth any money. Different applications can access your Web Service and use the same information in different ways. Initially, Web Services will be used almost exclusively in business-to-business (B2B) scenarios. You will see later in this chapter how to write a Web Service to accept orders over the Web. This Web Service consists of a method that provides product information (product IDs, names, and prices) and a method that accepts an order made up of product IDs and quantities. The consumers of this Web Service are free to set up their own interface, which can be incorporated into their applications. The client applications don't access your database directly. They can only retrieve the information you provide or submit information to the server. They don't have to know how you store your data or maintain a local list of the product. They can retrieve your products at any time and submit an order. Some client applications may be Windows applications; some others may be web applications. Their interfaces will be totally different, but they all provide the same data and place orders with your company.

BUILDING A WEB SERVICE

Building a Web Service with Visual Studio is as simple as writing a class. The class inherits from `System.Web.Services`, and this base class includes all the plumbing necessary to make the functions (methods) of the class available on the Web. Basically, if you can write a function, you can write a Web method; it's that simple. The difference between a class and a Web Service is that the members of the Web Service can be called remotely, over the Internet.

Building a web application is almost trivial with Visual Studio .NET. You start a new project of the Web Service type and enter the definition of one or more functions. Then, you prefix the names of the functions with the following keyword to turn them into Web methods:

```
<WebMethod()>
```

The following is a Web method that translates a sentence from German into English (provided you have the appropriate software installed on your computer):

```
<WebMethod()> Public Function TranslateGE _
    (ByVal strGerman As String) As String
    ' call the appropriate methods to translate
    ' the argument into English
    ' and store the translated text into the string strenglish
    Return(strenglish)
End Function
```

Any client application that has access to the Internet can call this method, passing a string in German and retrieve the same text in English. Instead of translating the text, we'll simply change the order of the words in the `strGerman` argument. Let's build the Web Service that exposes the TranslateGE method and then test it.

The SimpleWebService Project

Create a new Web Service project and name it **SimpleWebService**. Web Services don't have a visible interface, so the designer's surface is empty. You can place components on it, like DataAdapters and DataSets, and use them in your code. However, you can't use any components with a visual interface. The Service1 item will automatically be added to the project,

Part III

and this is a class that contains all the code that implements the Web methods. This is actually the name of the Web Service; it's named after the class and not after the project. Notice that a project may contain multiple Web Services, each one implemented by a different class.

Double-click the designer's surface to open the code window. Then enter the code of the TranslateGE Web method. The Web Service template contains a sample Web method, which is commented out; you can delete or ignore it. Then enter the code shown earlier; the code of the new Web Service is shown in Listing 11.1. (I have omitted the code generated automatically by the Web Services Designer that you do not need to view.)

Listing 11.1: Your First Web Service

```
Imports System.Web.Services

Public Class Service1
    Inherits System.Web.Services.WebService
    <WebMethod()> Public Function _
      TranslateGE(ByVal strGerman As String) As String
        ' call the appropriate methods to translate the
        ' argument into English
        ' and store the translated text into the string
        ' strenglish
        Dim strEnglish As String
        strEnglish = StrReverse(strGerman)
        Return (strenglish)
    End Function
End Class
```

NOTE

The class's name is Service1. If you want to change its name, you must rename the Service1 item in the Solution Explorer's window, as well as the name of the class in the code.

Testing the Web Service

Now press F5 to run the Web Service. The Web Service doesn't have a visible interface; how do we test it? The CLR will create a small site that allows you to test each method. If you press F5 to run the project, Internet Explorer will display the page shown in Figure 11.1. This page displays all the methods of the Web Service you're testing and warns you that it uses the default namespace. Once you decide to make the Web Service available to others on the Internet, you should change the namespace to something like **http://yourServer.com/** (where *yourServer* is the name of the web server where the code resides).

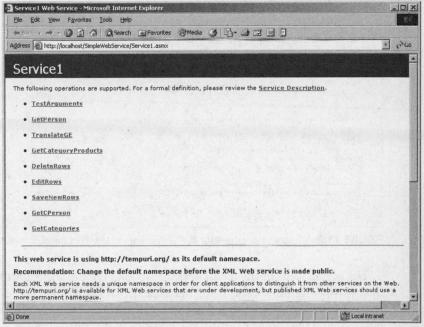

FIGURE 11.1: Viewing the methods of a Web Service in Internet Explorer

The page shown in Figure 11.1 contains additional methods, which you will add to the Web Service shortly. On your screen you will see only the TranslateGE method. Click this hyperlink, and you will see the page shown in Figure 11.2, which prompts you to enter the **strGerman** argument (the string to be processed). Enter a string in the text box, and click the Invoke button to call the method. If the method accepts more arguments, they will all be listed here.

The result will be returned in XML format, and it's shown here:

```
<?xml version="1.0" encoding="utf-8" ?>
<string xmlns="http://tempuri.org/"> _
    zyxwvutsrqponmlkjihgfedcba</string>
```

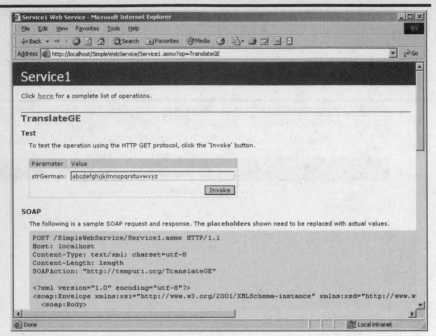

FIGURE 11.2:   Supplying values for the arguments of the TranslateGE method

The actual value of the result appears in bold. It's the string surrounded by the two delimiters. Everything between the two delimiters is the string returned by the Web method. You can try throwing off Internet Explorer by supplying the value "</string>" backward (without the quotes, of course). If you pass the value >gnirts< to the method, you'll get back the following response:

```
<?xml version="1.0" encoding="utf-8" ?>
  <string xmlns="http://tempuri.org/"></string></string>
```

Internet Explorer isn't thrown off by the two identical delimiters. To understand why, open the View menu and select Source to see the HTML document sent to the client:

```
<?xml version="1.0" encoding="utf-8"?>
  <string xmlns="http://tempuri.org/">&lt;string&gt;</string>
```

The string was HTML encoded, and the browser had no problem figuring out the text from the tags. Even though the result is transmitted to the client in XML format, there's nothing special you have to do in order to extract it.

Using the Web Service in Your Apps

Let's write a Windows application that uses the Web Service. Start a Windows Application project, and design a form with a single button on it. First, we must include in our new project a reference to the SimpleWebService Web Service. Open the Project menu, and select Add Web Reference. You will see the Add Web Reference dialog box, as shown in Figure 11.3. On the left pane there are three hyperlinks: one to the UDDI (Universal Description Discovery Integration) Directory, another one to the Microsoft's UDDI, and a third one to the Web References on the local machine. The first two links lead to directories of Web Services on Microsoft sites. The first one is intended for real, practical Web Services and the second one for testing purposes. You can post your own Web Services either to the test directory or to the UDDI directory with the "real" services, if you think it's of interest to other developers.

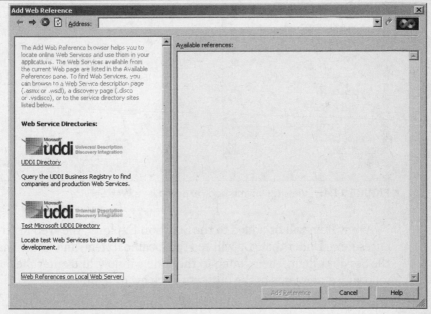

FIGURE 11.3:   The Add Web Reference dialog box

Our task is to test the newly created Web Service. Click the last hyperlink, and you will see a list of all Web Services installed on the local machine (you will most likely see a single service name in the right pane of the dialog box). Select the SimpleWebService item in the right pane, and you will see two new hyperlinks on the right pane, as shown in Figure 11.4. Click the View Documentation hyperlink to view a list with the names of the Web methods provided by the SimpleWebService. Figure 11.4 also shows a number of Web methods, which we'll explore in the following section. At this point, click the Add Reference button on the dialog box to add a reference to the specific Web Service to the current project.

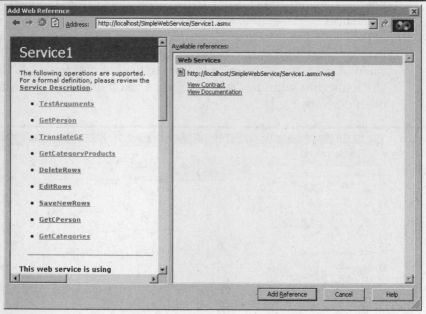

FIGURE 11.4: Viewing the methods exposed by a Web Service

A new item will be added to the Solution Explorer, the Web References item. Under that you will see the localhost item, and under that the Service1 item. Then switch to the code window, and enter the following statements in the button's Click event handler:

```
Private Sub Button1_Click(ByVal sender As System.Object, _
    ByVal e As System.EventArgs) Handles Button1.Click
    Dim WS As localhost.Service1
    MsgBox(WS.TranslateGE("Enter your German text here"))
End Sub
```

This code creates an instance of the Web Service and then calls its TranslateGE method. Run the project, and a few seconds later a message box with the "translated" (reversed) string will pop up. The Windows application contacts the Web Server, requests the URL of the TranslateGE method, and retrieves the result. The result is returned to the client in XML format, and it's presented to the application as a string. You don't have to deal with decoding the value; you don't even have to know what goes on behind the scenes. As far as your code goes, it's like calling a method of any class on the local machine. The same will happen regardless of the location of the web server on which the Web Service is running. It could be the same machine (as in your tests), another server on your LAN, or any web server on the Internet.

Writing a fictitious Web Service that does nothing really useful was fairly easy. As I mentioned earlier, writing a Web method is as simple as writing a function. Before we move on to a practical Web method that interacts with a database, let's experiment a little with passing arguments to and retrieving values from a Web method. As with regular VB.NET functions, there are two methods to pass an argument to a Web method: by value, which is the default mechanism, and by reference. If you want to pass multiple values from your Web method to the caller, you can write a Web method that accepts one or more arguments by reference, sets their values, and then retrieves these values in the client application's code. Web methods accept base data types as arguments, as well as arrays.

The Web method shown in Listing 11.2 accepts three arguments: an integer, a string, and an array of integers. All three arguments are passed by reference and the Web method sets their values in its code: It doubles the integer, adds three days to the Date argument, and negates all the elements of the array. The return value is a string.

Part III

Listing 11.2: Experimenting with a Web Method's Arguments and Return Values

```
<WebMethod()> Public Function TestArguments _
        (ByRef arg1 As Integer, _
        ByRef arg2 As Date, _
        ByRef arg3() As Integer) As String

    arg1 = 2 * arg1
    arg2 = arg2.AddDays(3)
    Dim i As Integer
```

```
        For i = 0 To arg3.GetUpperBound(0)
            arg3(i) = -arg3(i)
        Next
        Return "Done!"

    End Function
```

On the client, you can call this method and display the values of the arguments after the return of the Web method with the statements shown in Listing 11.3.

Listing 11.3: Using the TestArguments Web Method in a Windows Application

```
    Private Sub Button2_Click(ByVal sender As System.Object, _
        ByVal e As System.EventArgs) Handles Button2.Click

        Dim WS As New localhost.Service1()
        Dim ints(9) As Integer
        Dim i As Integer

        For i = 0 To 9
            ints(i) = i
        Next

        Dim D As Date = Now()
        Dim Int As Integer = 999
        Dim Str As String
        Str = WS.TestArguments(Int, D, ints)
        Console.WriteLine("Return value = " & Str)
        Console.WriteLine("Integer argument = " & Int)
        Console.WriteLine("Date argument = " & D)
        For i = 0 To 9
            Console.Write(ints(i) & vbTab)
        Next

    End Sub
```

If you run the test application again and click the Call TestArguments Web Method button, these lines will appear in the Output window:

```
    Return value = Done!
    Integer argument = 1998
```

```
Date argument = 11/29/2001 6:38:46 PM
0    -1    -2    -3    -4    -5    -6    -7    -8    -9
```

Reference and Value Arguments

If you want to retrieve multiple values from the Web method, you can pass arguments by reference. The Web method will marshal back the arguments passed by reference, which are presumably set in the method's code. Notice that the ByRef and ByVal keywords work a little differently with Web methods than they do with regular VB .NET functions. All arguments are passed by value; the Web Service's code can't access the memory of the client computer and directly alter the values of the arguments. Instead, it marshals back the values of the arguments passed by reference. In other words, the ByRef and ByVal keywords are used as tags, telling the Web Service whether it should pass the arguments' values back to the caller.

Arrays, for example, are passed to regular functions by reference even if you specify the ByVal keyword in front of their names. When a function changes the elements of an array passed as argument, the caller sees the modified values of these elements. If you pass an array to a Web method by value, the Web Service won't marshal back to the caller of the array. Change the keyword ByRef in front of the arg3 argument of the Test-Arguments method to ByVal, and run the client application. The values you will see in the Output window will be the same as the ones you passed to the method (this wouldn't happen with a VB .NET function).

Using Structures with Web Methods

Beyond simple data types, Web methods also support custom structures. Of course, the fields of the structure used by the Web method must be known to the client application. Let's say the Web Service contains the following structure:

```
Public Structure Person
    Dim Name As String
    Dim Age As Integer
    Dim SSN As String
    Dim BDate As Date
End Structure
```

This declaration must appear in the Web Service's file, outside any method. Using this structure in a Web method is straightforward. You assign values to its fields and return an object of this type. The following Web method does exactly that:

```
<WebMethod()> Public Function GetPerson() As Person
    Dim p As Person
    p.Name = "My Name"
    p.Age = 35
    p.SSN = "555-66-0009"
    p.BDate = #9/9/1999#
    Return (p)
End Function
```

The structure is exposed by the Web Service because it's public, which means that you can declare a variable of the localhost.Person type to represent a Person object. Then, you can call the GetPerson method and assign its return value to the proper variable and access the values of the structure's fields as properties. The following statements call the GetPerson method and display the fields it returns on the Output window:

```
Dim WS As New localhost.Service1()
Dim p As localhost.Person

p = WS.GetPerson
Console.WriteLine("NAME = " & p.Name)
Console.WriteLine("AGE  = " & p.Age)
Console.WriteLine("SSN  = " & p.SSN)
Console.WriteLine("BDATE= " & p.BDate)
```

If you test the Web Service by pressing F5 and invoke the GetPerson method from the test page, you will see the following XML description of the result:

```
<?xml version="1.0" encoding="utf-8" ?>
- <Person _
    xmlns:xsi="http://www.w3.org/2001/XMLSchema-instance" _
      xmlns:xsd="http://www.w3.org/2001/XMLSchema" _
      xmlns="http://tempuri.org/">
  <Name>My Name</Name>
```

```
<Age>35</Age>
<SSN>555-66-0009</SSN>
<BDate>1999-09-09T00:00:00.0000000-04:00</BDate>
</Person>
```

This is a simple schema description. An object variable set to this schema exposes the four attributes as properties. Notice that you don't have to parse the XML document in your client application's code to extract the names of the attributes and their values. The CLR uses XML behind the scenes, and you do not need to be aware of this.

If you're wondering how the client application knows about the Person structure, the answer is in the Service1.swdl file. If you open this file (you must first activate the button Show All Files at the top of the Project Explorer), you will find the following lines:

```
<s:complexType name="Person">
  <s:sequence>
    <s:element minOccurs="0" maxOccurs="1" name="Name" _
      type="s:string" />
    <s:element minOccurs="1" maxOccurs="1" name="Age" _
      type="s:int" />
    <s:element minOccurs="0" maxOccurs="1" name="SSN" _
      type="s:string" />
    <s:element minOccurs="1" maxOccurs="1" name="BDate" _
      type="s:dateTime" />
  </s:sequence>
</s:complexType>
```

The WSDL file is read into the client application when you add a reference to the Web Service. Then the CLR creates a class for you, which resides in the file Reference.vb. To view this file's contents expand the localhost branch under Web References in the Solution Explorer and then expand the Reference.map branch. The class generated by the CLR is shown next:

```
'<remarks/>
Public Name As String


'<remarks/>
Public Age As Integer
```

```
'<remarks/>
Public SSN As String


'<remarks/>
Public BDate As Date
End Class
```

Even a trivial structure like the one used in this example can be implemented as a class. To complete the demonstration, I've included the CPerson class to the SimpleWebService. The implementation of the CPerson class is just as trivial:

```
Public Class CPerson
    Public Name As String
    Public Age As Integer
    Public SSN As String
    Public BDate As Date
End Class
```

The current implementation of Web Services doesn't support properties. In other words, there's no WebProperty attribute and you can't add Property procedures in your Web Service.

The Properties of the *<WebMethod>* Attribute

The <WebMethod> attribute supports a few properties, which must appear in the angle brackets of the WebMethod qualifier as a name/value pair. Multiple attributes are separated with commas:

```
<WebMethod() Description = "This is a test Web Service", _
    BufferResponse = False>
```

These properties are described in the following text.

BufferResponse   This is a Boolean value that determines whether or not to buffer the method's response.

CacheDuration   This is the duration (in seconds) to keep the method's response in the cache. The default value is 0 (the result isn't buffered).

Description   This is a string with additional information about the Web method. The method's description appears in the test pages created by the CLR when you test the Web Service.

EnableSession   This is a Boolean value that enables or disables the session state, and it's True by default. Turn it off if you don't need to maintain state for a marginal performance improvement. When this attribute is True, the Web method maintains session IDs for each client accessing the method.

MessageName   Web methods can't be overloaded like regular functions and classes. If you have a class with overloaded functions that you want to convert to a web class, you can still use the same name for multiple functions. However, you must provide alternative names, which will be different for each function. The alternative names are specified with the MessageName property. The clients see the method's Message-Name and, in effect, each method in the Web Service has a different name.

TransactionOption   The TransactionOption attribute can be one of following values, which determine whether the Web method participates in a transaction: Disabled, NotSupported, Supported, Required, and RequiresNew. Web methods can only be the root objects in a transaction, so both the Required and RequiresNew options create a new transaction. The other three settings do not create a transaction.

The TransactionOption is used with distributed transactions—such as updating two different databases or updating a single database and placing a message into a transactional message queue. The database's built-in transactional capabilities (T-SQL transactions for SQL Server, for example) or ADO .NET transactions should be adequate for all but rare occasions, and you shouldn't have to use the TransactionOption attribute on a Web method.

So far you've seen the basics of building a Web Service and how to use it in your applications. In the following section, we'll build a couple of data-bound Web Services to move data in and out of a database. These services can be used with remote clients running Windows and web applications.

BUILDING A DATA-BOUND WEB SERVICE

In this section, we'll create a Web Service that returns DataSets, and later we'll revise it so that it can accept DataSets from the client and update

Part III

the database. It's actually quite simple to retrieve data from a database and pass it to the client as a DataSet. Updating the database is a bit more complicated, because there's no wizard to generate any code for you. You must select the modified rows (or the deleted, or the new ones), store them to a new DataSet, and pass it to the Web Service as an argument. In the Web Service's code, you must perform the updates and then pass the DataSet with the error information to the client. If a row fails to update the database, you can't display a message from within the Web Service. You must reject the changes and send back the DataSet to the client. The client application will handle these rows (most likely, with the user's interaction).

The DataSet is among the data types that a Web method recognizes. You can write a function that returns a DataSet and turn it into a Web method. The DataSet will be encoded in XML format, which means that it's usable by any client (Windows or otherwise). Using the DataSet with Windows applications, however, is no different from what you've learned so far.

To retrieve data from a database, the Web Service must execute an SQL statement against the database. Any parameters must be passed to the service as arguments, and it will return a DataSet object to the calling application. The DataSet may contain multiple tables, and even relations between them. The Web Service you'll build in this section exposes two methods, the GetCategories and GetProductCategories methods. As you have guessed, the first method returns the categories of the Northwind database, and the second method returns the products in a specific category, whose ID is passed to the Web Service as an argument.

The two methods of the Web Service are simple functions that return a DataSet object. You can implement the two methods entirely in code, or you can use the visual database tools to set up the appropriate Connection and DataAdapter objects. Let's add on to the SimpleWebService project; you can also create a new Web Service project from scratch.

Return to the SimpleWebService project, open the Server Explorer, locate the tables of the Northwind database, and drop the Categories and Products tables on the design surface of the Web Service. Rename the DataAdapter objects to **DACategories** and **DAProducts**, and configure them. The DACategories adapter uses the following SQL statement to retrieve the category IDs and names:

```
SELECT CategoryID, CategoryName
FROM    Categories
```

Likewise, the DAProducts adapter uses the following SQL statement to retrieve the products of a category, which is specified with the @category parameter:

```
SELECT ProductID, ProductName, UnitPrice
FROM   Products WHERE (CategoryID = @category)
```

You should let the wizard generate the Insert, Delete, and Update statements for the Products table. In the following section, we'll build a client that allows the user to edit the rows of the table and we'll pass the edited DataSet to another method of the Web Service, which will update the underlying table in the database.

Then create two DataSets, one for each DataAdapter, and add them to the project. The first DataSet, **DSCategories**, should contain the Categories table. The second one, **DSProducts**, should contain the Products table (even though it contains a small section of the table). With the DataAdapters and the DataSets in place, you can easily implement the GetCategories and GetCategoryProducts methods, as shown in Listing 11.4.

Listing 11.4: The GetCategories and GetCategoryProducts Methods

```
<WebMethod()> Public Function GetCategories() As DataSet
    DACategories.Fill(DsCategories1)
    Return (DsCategories1)
End Function


<WebMethod()> Public Function GetCategoryProducts(ByVal _
        categoryID As Integer) _
            As DataSet
    DAProducts.SelectCommand.Parameters("@category").Value _
        = categoryID
    DAProducts.Fill(DsProducts1)
    Return (DsProducts1)
End Function
```

To test the new Web Service, just press F5 and run the application. Visual Studio .NET will start Internet Explorer, and it will display the usual test page with the names of all the Web Service methods. This page isn't part of the project, it was generated on the fly by Visual Studio .NET for testing purposes. If you select the GetCategories hyperlink on the first page, you will see the XML description of the DataSet with the categories. If you select the GetProductCategories hyperlink, you will see another page that prompts you to enter the ID of a category. Enter a category's ID (a value from 1 to 7) and then click the Invoke button. A new Internet Explorer window will open, and you will see on it the XML description of the DataSet. This description consists of two sections, the schema section and the diffgram section. The schema section contains information about the structure of each row in the Products table.

The *diffgram* is the XML representation of the data. The data section is called a "diffgram" because it contains the initial data. However, after the DataSet is edited, it will store the modified data as well. The following lines are two product descriptions:

```
- <Products diffgr:id="Products5" msdata:rowOrder="4">
  <ProductID>59</ProductID>
  <ProductName>Raclette Courdavault</ProductName>
  <UnitPrice>55</UnitPrice>
  </Products>
- <Products diffgr:id="Products6" msdata:rowOrder="5">
  <ProductID>60</ProductID>
  <ProductName>Camembert Pierrot</ProductName>
  <UnitPrice>34</UnitPrice>
  </Products>
```

We have tested the methods of our new Web Service, and they behave as expected. In the following section, we'll consume them in a Windows application.

How about updating the DataSet on the client? As you will see in the following section, it's possible to edit the data on the client and then submit the changes to the server. Because the DataSet retains the original values of its fields, we can write a method that accepts the modified DataSet and call its Update method to update the underlying table. Chances are that a small percentage of the DataSet's rows will be modified, so we should write a separate Web method for the edited, deleted, and added rows. This way, we will not move the unchanged rows to the server.

We must construct three new methods—the SaveNewRows, DeleteRows, and EditRows Web methods. Their code is quite simple. Each method accepts a DataSet with the appropriate rows (the new, deleted, and edited rows) of the original DataSet and calls the Update method of the corresponding Data Adapter. See Listing 11.5.

Listing 11.5: The SaveNewRows, DeleteRows, and EditRows Web Methods

```
<WebMethod()> Public Function SaveNewRows (
    (ByVal DS As DataSet) As Integer
    Dim newRows As Integer
    newRows = DAProducts.Update(DS)
    Dim row As DataRow
    For Each row In DS.Tables("Products").Rows
        If row.HasErrors Then
            row.RejectChanges()
        Else
            row.AcceptChanges()
        End If
    Next
    Return newRows
End Function

<WebMethod()> Public Function DeleteRows _
    (ByVal DS As DataSet) As Integer
    Dim newRows As Integer
    newRows = DAProducts.Update(DS)
    Dim row As DataRow
    For Each row In DS.Tables("Products").Rows
        If row.HasErrors Then
            row.RejectChanges()
        Else
            row.AcceptChanges()
        End If
    Next
    Return newRows
End Function

<WebMethod()> Public Function EditRows _
    (ByVal DS As DataSet) As Integer
    Dim newRows As Integer
    newRows = DAProducts.Update(DS)
```

```
    Dim row As DataRow
    For Each row In DS.Tables("Products").Rows
        If row.HasErrors Then
            row.RejectChanges()
        Else
            row.AcceptChanges()
        End If
    Next
    Return newRows
End Function
```

Consuming the Web Service

The pages generated by Visual Studio for testing a new Web Service's methods are quite convenient, but this isn't how we use Web Services, obviously. A Web Service can be used in a Windows application to exchange information with a web server, or it can be used in a web application to interact with a web server. To consume a Web Service from within either type of application, you follow the same steps:

1. Add a reference to the Web Service. This means that the server on which the Web Service is running must be accessible, so that your project can retrieve information about the Web Service's members.

2. Create an instance of the Web Service in your code by declaring a variable of the appropriate type. To the application, the Web Service is like another class that exposes methods. It just happens that the class's code is executed on another machine and your application contacts it through the Internet.

To test the data-bound methods of the SimpleWebService project, we'll add another form to the TestSimpleWebService project. The new form is called TestForm2. You must change the properties of the test project to make the new form the Startup object for the project. The new test form is shown in Figure 11.5.

First, declare the following variables. *WS* represents the Web Service—we need it to access the Web Service's methods—and *DS* represents a DataSet. We'll use this variable to store the data we want to send to the server.

```
    Dim WS As New localhost.Service1()
    Dim DS As DataSet
```

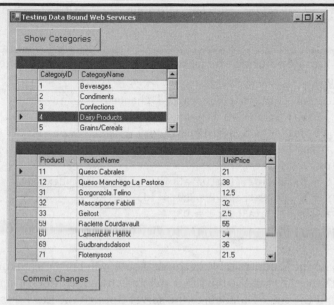

FIGURE 11.5:   Testing the data-bound methods of the
SimpleWebService project

Then enter the following code behind the Show Categories button.
This button calls the GetCategories Web method, and it uses the DataSet
returned by the method to populate the top DataGrid control.

```
Private Sub Button1_Click(ByVal sender As System.Object, _
        ByVal e As System.EventArgs) Handles Button1.Click
    DataGrid1.DataSource = WS.GetCategories
    DataGrid1.DataMember = "Categories"
End Sub
```

To view the products in a specific category, click the category's row in
the upper DataGrid and the lower one will be populated. The action of
selecting a category is signaled to the application through the Current-
CellChanged event, whose handler is shown in Listing 11.6. The code in
this handler retrieves the value of the first cell in the selected row, which
is the ID of the corresponding category. Then it passes it as an argument
to the GetCategoryProducts Web method, which in turn returns a

Part III

DataSet. This DataSet becomes the data source for the lower DataGrid control:

Listing 11.6: Populating the Grid with the Products of a Selected Category

```
Private Sub DataGrid1_CurrentCellChanged _
    (ByVal sender As Object, _
    ByVal e As System.EventArgs) _
    Handles DataGrid1.CurrentCellChanged
    Dim id As Integer
    id = DataGrid1.Item(DataGrid1.CurrentRowIndex, 0)
    DS = WS.GetCategoryProducts(id)
    DataGrid2.DataSource = DS
    DataGrid2.DataMember = "Products"
End Sub
```

To update the Products table in the database, you must create three different DataSets, with the modified, deleted and added rows. Then, you must submit the three DataSets to the server through the EditRows, SaveNewRows, and DeleteRows methods. See Listing 11.7.

Listing 11.7: Submitting the Modified Rows to the Server

```
Private Sub Button2_Click(ByVal sender As System.Object, _
    ByVal e As System.EventArgs) Handles Button2.Click
    Dim DSEdit As DataSet
    ' Uncomment the following two statements to
    ' save the DataSet's rows
    ' to a local XML file:
    'DS.WriteXml("c:\ProductDiffgram.xml", _
    ' XmlWriteMode.DiffGram)
    'Exit Sub
    ' EDITED ROWS
    DSEdit = DS.GetChanges(DataRowState.Modified)
    Dim returnedDS As DataSet
    If Not DSEdit Is Nothing Then
        returnedDS = WS.EditRows(DSEdit)
    End If
    AcceptRejectRows(returnedDS)
    '    NEW ROWS
    Dim DSNew As DataSet
    DSNew = DS.GetChanges(DataRowState.Added)
    If Not DSNew Is Nothing Then
```

```
            returnedDS = WS.SaveNewRows(DSEdit)
        End If
        AcceptRejectRows(returnedDS)
        '   DELETED ROWS
        Dim DSDel As DataSet
        DSDel = DS.GetChanges(DataRowState.Deleted)
        If Not DSDel Is Nothing Then
            returnedDS = WS.DeleteRows(DSEdit)
        End If
        AcceptRejectRows(returnedDS)
    End Sub
```

The few commented lines at the beginning of the code save the DataSet to an XML file. You can uncomment these lines to see what the DataSets you submit to the server look like. I've used these statements to prepare the diffgrams shown earlier.

The code creates three smaller DataSets with the edited, deleted, and added rows. Each time it calls the GetChanges method of the DataSet object, passing the appropriate constant as an argument. If the corresponding DataSet contains one or more rows, it's submitted to the Web Service through the appropriate Web method. After sending each DataSet to the client, the AcceptRejectRows subroutine is called to reject the changes that couldn't be committed to the database.

The AcceptRejectRows() subroutine goes through each row of the DataSet returned by the server and examines its HasErrors property. If true, it rejects the changes (restores the row's fields to the values that were originally read from the database) and displays a message in the Output window. The rows that fail to update are also marked on the DataGrid control. If the row has no errors, the changes are accepted. See Listing 11.8.

Part III

Listing 11.8: Rejecting Changes that Couldn't Be Committed to the Database

```
Sub AcceptRejectRows(ByVal newDS As DataSet)
    Dim row As DataRow
    For Each row In newDS.Tables(0).Rows
        If Not row.HasErrors Then
            Console.WriteLine("Product " & _
                row.Item("ProductID").ToString & _
                " accepted")
            row.AcceptChanges()
```

```
        Else
            Console.WriteLine("Product " & _
                row.Item("ProductID").ToString & _
                " has errors")
            Dim col As DataColumn
            For Each col In row.GetColumnsInError
                Console.WriteLine("   " & _
                    row.GetColumnError(col))
            Next
            row.RejectChanges()
        End If
    Next
    DS.Merge(newDS)
End Sub
```

Placing an Order

OK, we can bind a DataGrid control to a DataSet to display data to the
client. Let's build a new Web Service that will accept orders over the Web.
We aren't going to build a web application, just a Web Service that other
developers can use to build their own front-ends, either as web applications or as Windows applications. The client that uses this Web Service
must provide an interface that will allow users to add quantities to the
list of products and then submit the modified DataSet to the server,
where a new order will be placed. We'll build a new Web Service with
two methods: the GetAllProducts method that returns all the products
in the Products table as a DataSet and the NewOrder method that
accepts the same DataSet with quantities and records a new order.

The GetAllProducts method will return a DataSet with all the products
in the Products table. We don't need to send all the columns to the client,
just the product's ID, name, and price. We also need a new column to
store the quantities and allow the client application to edit this column's
cells. We'll get to this soon, but let's start by adding a method to our Web
Service to accept the modified DataSet and insert a new order to the
Northwind database.

As you know by now, a new order involves a new row in the Orders
table and a number of new rows (one for each product ordered) in the
Order Details table. The row added to the Orders table will be automatically assigned an order ID. This numeric value is the foreign key in the
Order Details table, and the ID of the new order must be repeated in
every line of the order that will be placed in the Order Details table. We
also need the ID of the customer that placed the order, which will be

passed as an argument to the new method. You can add even more arguments, like the shipping address, the ID of the salesperson, and so on. We'll only use the customer's ID in our example.

The signature of the new method is

```
<WebMethod()> Public Function _
     NewOrder(ByVal custID As String, _
     ByVal details As DataSet) As Integer
```

The *custID* argument is a string argument with the customer's ID and the *details* argument is a DataSet with the product IDs, names, prices, and quantities. The NewOrder method inserts the proper rows to the Orders and Order Details tables. You already know how to add a new order to the Northwind database, but let me repeat the two stored procedures that add a new order and the order's details. Listing 11.9 shows the code for adding a new order into the Orders table and Listing 11.10 shows the code for adding all the new rows into the Order Details table.

Listing 11.9: The NewOrder Stored Procedure

```
CREATE PROCEDURE NewOrder
@custID nchar(5)
AS
INSERT INTO Orders (CustomerID, OrderDate) _
   VALUES(@custID, GetDate())
RETURN (@@IDENTITY)
GO
```

Listing 11.10: The NewOrderLine Stored Procedure

```
CREATE PROCEDURE NewOrderLine
@OrderID integer, @ProductID integer, @quantity integer
AS
DECLARE @ProductPrice money
SET @ProductPrice=(SELECT UnitPrice FROM Products WHERE _
   ProductID=@ProductID)
INSERT INTO [Order Details]
    (OrderID, ProductID, Quantity, UnitPrice)
VALUES (@OrderID, @ProductID, @Quantity, @ProductPrice)
GO
```

The Web method that adds a new order to the Northwind database is shown in Listing 11.11. It adds all the necessary rows as a transaction, so that even if one of the insertions fails, the entire order will be rolled back. If the transaction is rolled back, an exception is also raised. This exception

Part III

can be handled at the client with a structured exception handler. Alternatively, you can comment out the line in the NewOrder web method that throws the exception and uncomment the following line that returns the value −1 for the web method. Then, modify the client application so that it examines the value returned by the Web method and displays the appropriate message. Listing 11.11 shows the code of the NewOrder web method.

NOTE   The connection string should be changed to match your individual environment.

WARNING   A username of sa and a blank password is not advisable in a production system.

Listing 11.11: The NewOrder Web Method

```
<WebMethod()> Public Function NewOrder _
            (ByVal custID As String, _
             ByVal details As DataSet) As Integer
    Dim CMD As New SqlClient.SqlCommand()
    CMD.CommandText = "NewOrder"
    CMD.CommandType = CommandType.StoredProcedure
    Dim sqlParam As New SqlClient.SqlParameter()
    sqlParam.SqlDbType = SqlDbType.Char
    sqlParam.Size = 5
    sqlParam.ParameterName = "@CustID"
    sqlParam.Direction = ParameterDirection.Input
    CMD.Parameters.Add(sqlParam)

    sqlParam = New SqlClient.SqlParameter()
    sqlParam.ParameterName = "RETURN"
    sqlParam.SqlDbType = SqlDbType.Int
    sqlParam.Direction = ParameterDirection.ReturnValue
    CMD.Parameters.Add(sqlParam)
    CMD.Parameters("@custID").Value = custID

    Dim CNstr As String
    Dim CN As New SqlClient.SqlConnection()
```

```
CNstr = _
    "server=localhost;database=northwind;uid=sa;pwd=;"
CN.ConnectionString = CNstr
CN.Open()
Dim DetailTrans As SqlClient.SqlTransaction
DetailTrans = CN.BeginTransaction()
CMD.Connection = CN
CMD.Transaction = DetailTrans
Dim orderID As Integer
Dim totalItems As Integer
Dim retValue As Integer
Try
    CMD.ExecuteNonQuery()
    orderID = CMD.Parameters("RETURN").Value
    CMD.CommandText = "NewOrderLine"
    CMD.CommandType = CommandType.StoredProcedure
    CMD.Parameters.Clear()
    sqlParam = New SqlClient.SqlParameter()
    sqlParam.SqlDbType = SqlDbType.Int
    sqlParam.ParameterName = "@OrderID"
    sqlParam.Direction = ParameterDirection.Input
    CMD.Parameters.Add(sqlParam)

    sqlParam = New SqlClient.SqlParameter()
    sqlParam.SqlDbType = SqlDbType.Int
    sqlParam.ParameterName = "@ProductID"
    sqlParam.Direction = ParameterDirection.Input
    CMD.Parameters.Add(sqlParam)

    sqlParam = New SqlClient.SqlParameter()
    sqlParam.SqlDbType = SqlDbType.Int
    sqlParam.ParameterName = "@quantity"
    sqlParam.Direction = ParameterDirection.Input
    CMD.Parameters.Add(sqlParam)

    sqlParam = New SqlClient.SqlParameter()
    sqlParam.ParameterName = "RETURN"
    sqlParam.SqlDbType = SqlDbType.Int
    sqlParam.Direction = ParameterDirection.ReturnValue
    CMD.Parameters.Add(sqlParam)

    Dim row As DataRow
    For Each row In details.Tables(0).Rows
```

Part III

```
              CMD.Parameters("@OrderID").Value = orderID
              CMD.Parameters("@ProductID").Value = row.Item(0)
              CMD.Parameters("@quantity").Value = row.Item(3)
              ' this variable isn't used in the code,
              ' but you can return the number
              ' of the items ordered if the order is
              ' registered successfully
              totalItems = totalItems + row.Item(3)
              CMD.ExecuteNonQuery()
         Next
         DetailTrans.Commit()
         retValue = orderID
    Catch exc As Exception
         DetailTrans.Rollback()
         Throw exc
         ' retValue = -1
    Finally
         CN.Close()
    End Try
    Return retValue
End Function
```

The code starts by setting up a Command object for the NewOrder stored procedure. This stored procedure accepts a single argument, the customer's ID, and returns the ID of the new row it adds to the Orders table. This ID is an integer value generated by the database, and we'll need it when we add the details to the Order Details table. Notice that the stored procedure isn't executed immediately. Instead, the code creates a Transaction object and executes the NewOrder stored procedure in the context of this transaction (in the Try...Catch statement, later in the code).

Listing 11.12 shows the GetAllProducts method. Instead of using the visual tools of the Designer, I've implemented everything in code. It creates a SqlDataAdapter object and uses it to execute a SELECT command against the Northwind database. The resulting DataSet is passed back to the client, but not before setting the DataSet's rows to read-only. This way the user won't be allowed to edit product names or prices.

Listing 11.12: The GetAllProducts Web Method

```
<WebMethod()> Public Function GetAllProducts() As DataSet
    Dim CNstr As String
    Dim CMDstr As String
```

```
CNstr = _
    "server=localhost;database=northwind;uid=sa;pwd=;"
CMDstr = _
"SELECT ProductID, ProductName, UnitPrice FROM Products"
Dim DA As New SqlClient.SqlDataAdapter(CMDstr, CNstr)
Dim Orders As New DataSet()
DA.Fill(Orders, "Products")
Orders.Tables(0).Columns(0).ReadOnly = True
Orders.Tables(0).Columns(1).ReadOnly = True
Orders.Tables(0).Columns(2).ReadOnly = True
Return Orders
End Function
```

Let's switch our attention to the client application now. We'll first build a Windows application that uses the GetAllProducts and NewOrder methods, and later we'll do the same with a web application. The Windows application is called TestOrder, and it calls the GetAllProducts method to retrieve all the products from the database. The DataSet will be displayed on a DataGrid control, as shown in Figure 11.6. The Northwind happens to be a small database with fewer than 100 products, so you can afford to download the entire product list to the client. In a real database, you'd have to limit the number of rows transferred to the client. One way to do this would be to download the products in a specific category, or the products from a specific supplier.

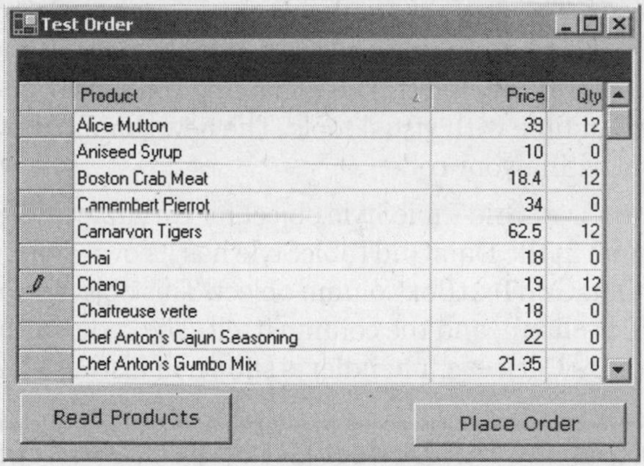

FIGURE 11.6: The TestOrder Windows application uses the Orders Web Service's methods to place an order.

The information will be sent to the client in the form of a DataSet, and we'll display it on a DataGrid control. You can build all kinds of different interfaces for the application, but the DataGrid is the most convenient method of displaying a table. In order to allow the users to place orders, we must provide a new column, where they can type the quantity of each item they wish to order. This will be a numeric column (its cells must be aligned to the right) and editable (its ReadOnly property set to False). The remaining columns must be read-only; there's no reason to allow users to edit the product IDs or names.

First, we must retrieve the DataSet with the products by calling the GetAllProducts method:

```
NewOrder = WS.GetAllProducts
```

Then we can add the extra column with the following statements:

```
Dim qtyCol As New DataColumn()
qtyCol.DataType = GetType(Integer)
qtyCol.DefaultValue = 0
qtyCol.Caption = "Qty"
qtyCol.ColumnName = "Quantity"

NewOrder.Tables(0).Columns.Add(qtyCol)
```

qtyCol is the name of a new DataColumn object, which is added to the Columns collection of one of the tables in the DataSet. Our DataSet just happens to contain a single table, and you can access it as NewOrder.Tables(0). The new column holds the quantity ordered for each product, and it must be editable and aligned to the right. We must also specify a header for this column. The remaining columns of the table can be set up at design time with visual tools. The new column, however, must be set up from within your code.

Finally, we create a DataGridTableStyle object for the table in the DataSet. Each column in the DataGridTableStyle has its own style, which is specified with a DataGridTextBoxColumn object. This object represents the style of a specific column, and the column itself. The code for the Read Products button's Click event handler is shown in Listing 11.13.

Listing 11.13: Displaying the Product List on a DataGrid control

```
Private Sub Button1_Click(ByVal sender As System.Object, _
    ByVal e As System.EventArgs) Handles Button1.Click
  NewOrder = WS.GetAllProducts
```

```
            Dim qtyCol As New DataColumn()
            qtyCol.DataType = GetType(Integer)
            qtyCol.DefaultValue = 0
            qtyCol.Caption = "Qty"
            qtyCol.ColumnName = "Quantity"

            NewOrder.Tables(0).Columns.Add(qtyCol)

            Dim tbl As New DataGridTableStyle()
            tbl.MappingName = "Products"
            Dim col As New DataGridTextBoxColumn()
            col.MappingName = "ProductID"
            col.ReadOnly = True
            col.Width = 0
            tbl.GridColumnStyles.Add(col)

            col = New DataGridTextBoxColumn()
            col.MappingName = "ProductName"
            col.HeaderText = "Product"
            col.ReadOnly = True
            col.Width = 150
            col.Alignment = HorizontalAlignment.Left
            tbl.GridColumnStyles.Add(col)

            col = New DataGridTextBoxColumn()
            col.MappingName = "UnitPrice"
            col.HeaderText = "Price"
            col.Width = 60
            col.ReadOnly = True
            col.Alignment = HorizontalAlignment.Right
            tbl.GridColumnStyles.Add(col)

            col = New DataGridTextBoxColumn()
            col.MappingName = "Quantity"
            col.HeaderText = "Qty"
            col.Width = 30
            col.Alignment = HorizontalAlignment.Right
            tbl.GridColumnStyles.Add(col)
            DataGrid1.TableStyles.Add(tbl)
            DataGrid1.SetDataBinding(NewOrder, "Products")
        End Sub
```

Part III

As you realize, this code does what we'd normally do in the DataGridTableStyle Collection Editor of the DataGrid control. Because we can't bind the data to the control before the actual execution of the project, we can't use the visual tools of the IDE.

The last step is to submit the new order to the server. We need not transmit the entire DataSet, only the rows that were edited. We can isolate these columns with the DataSet's GetChanges method. Because all of the rows are not editable, users can't add or delete rows, and we need not care about deleted or inserted rows. The code in Listing 11.14 is executed when the Place Order button is clicked and submits the edited rows of the original DataSet to the NewOrder Web method.

Listing 11.14: Submitting an Order through a Web Method

```
Private Sub Button2_Click(ByVal sender As System.Object, _
    ByVal e As System.EventArgs) Handles Button2.Click
Try
    NewOrder = _
      NewOrder.GetChanges(DataRowState.Modified)
    Dim newOrderID As Integer
    newOrderID = WS.NewOrder("ALFKI", NewOrder)
    ' Thw NewOrder method will never return a
    ' negative value for the order ID
    ' Change the Web Method so that is
    ' doesn't throw an exception and returns
    ' a negative value if it can't successfully
    ' complete the transaction
    ' See the code of the SimpleWebService for
    ' more details
    If newOrderID > 0 Then
        MsgBox("Your order's number is " & newOrderID)
    Else
        MsgBox("There was an error in processing " & _
                "your order, please try again")
    End If
Catch exc As Exception
    MsgBox(exc.Message)
End Try
End Sub
```

Run the TestOrder project, load the products, and enter some quantities in the last column of the grid. The other columns are locked and you can't change product IDs or names.

The TestOrder Web Application

Now we'll build a web application that uses the same Web Service to place orders through the browser. The web version of the application shouldn't be much different from the equivalent Windows application, right? In our case, it's a totally new application. You will find some interesting techniques in this example, which will also help you understand and use the DataGrid web control a little better. Let me start by discussing how this application differs from the previous one.

The web version of the DataGrid control doesn't have nearly as much functionality as the Windows DataGrid control. As you recall from the previous chapter, the DataGrid is rendered on the client as an HTML table and it doesn't provide editing features. To edit a row, you must notify the DataGrid that it should prepare a row for editing and then end the operation by clicking another button. Moreover, the web DataGrid control can't be scrolled. You must either settle for a very long table, which is out of the question for all but real trivial applications, or use the paging feature of the control. Users should be able to edit any row of any page on the control, and you'll see how this is done. But what do you think will happen when the user switches to another page of the DataSet? The current page will be posted back to the server, and the application will request another page of the DataSet without storing the quantities ordered to the database. The application will request another page, but in reality it will retrieve the entire DataSet from the database and ignore the rows it doesn't need.

Once the new DataSet arrives to the application, you must find out whether any of the items contained on the current page have been ordered already and display the appropriate quantity. This means that the orders must be stored somewhere. Obviously, we can't store them in the Order Details table before the entire order has been finalized. Another approach is to set up a new table and store there all partial orders (the current user's shopping basket). Since our application is running in a Business-to-Business environment, we can safely assume that there won't be hundreds or thousands of concurrent users. As a result, we can use the application's Session object to store the items ordered and their quantities. This is what we'll do in our example, because it will allow us to reuse the existing Web Service. You can also develop an application for storing the basket's contents to another table in the database. This means that you will have to change the Web Service as well, so that it will accept a DataSet with quantities and store it in this intermediate table.

To summarize, our application will create a paged DataSet for each request by calling the GetProducts method of the Web Service. Then it will place the DataSet's rows (the products) on a DataGrid and send the page to the client. The DataGrid should have an extra column with the quantities and a column with buttons that users can click to signify their intention to edit the quantity of the current row, as shown in Figure 11.7. When a button is clicked, the product name of the corresponding row is displayed on a Label control at the top of the form and the row's current quantity is displayed on a TextBox control. The user can enter the desired quantity and then click the Add to Basket button to confirm the new quantity, or click another row's Buy button. You can use the techniques described in the previous chapter to edit the grid in place, but I found this approach a little simpler. The selected product appears near the top of the form in blue, and users can confirm the new quantity with the Add to Basket button.

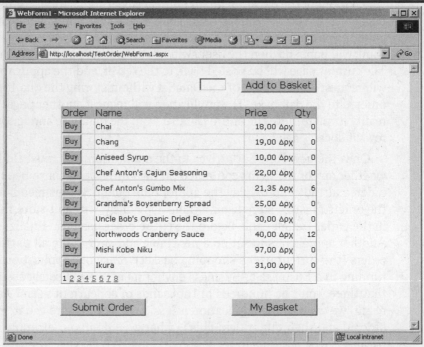

FIGURE 11.7:   The TestOrder web application demonstrates how to receive an order through the browser using the methods of the Orders Web Service.

The code of the TestOrder web application is fairly similar to the code of the equivalent Windows application. We call the same Web method to retrieve the DataSet with the products, and we add a new column for the quantities to the DataSet, as well as a column with the Buy buttons. However, the column with the quantities must be populated from within our code. With every postback, the code extracts the quantities and updates the corresponding Session variables. Each item is stored in a Session variable, whose name is the ID of the product prefixed with the "P" character. The product IDs are numeric values, and the variable names must be strings—that's why the prefix is necessary. When a new page of the DataSet is prepared to be submitted to the client, the code goes through the DataSet's rows and tries to find out whether the current product has been ordered or not. If a quantity for the current product is stored in the Session object, this quantity is copied to the last column of the same row in the DataSet—the column with the quantities. The modified DataSet is then submitted to the client.

Let's start with the simpler parts of the application. The DataGrid control has been set up to accommodate paged DataSets with the following statements, which appear in the subroutine that sets up and loads the control:

```
DataGrid1.AllowPaging = True

DataGrid1.PageSize = 10

DataGrid1.PagerStyle.Mode = PagerMode.NumericPages
```

In addition to specifying some properties, you must also provide some code to handle the selection of another page. This is signaled to your application with the PageIndexChanged event, whose handler is shown next:

```
Private Sub DataGrid1_PageIndexChanged _
        (ByVal source As Object, _
         ByVal e As _ System.Web.UI.WebControls _
         .DataGridPageChangedEventArgs) _
        Handles DataGrid1.PageIndexChanged
    DataGrid1.CurrentPageIndex = e.NewPageIndex
    LoadDataSet()
End Sub
```

Part III

When the page is loaded, the following statement calls the LoadDataSet() subroutine from within the page's Load event handler:

```
Private Sub Page_Load(ByVal sender As System.Object, _
        ByVal e As System.EventArgs) Handles MyBase.Load
    'Put user code to initialize the page here
    LoadDataSet()
End Sub
```

The LoadDataSet() subroutine is the heart of the application. First, it retrieves a DataSet with all the products in the database. Then it adds two columns: the Order column, which contains the Buy buttons, and the Quantity column, which contains the quantity of each item. Notice that the first column is of the ButtonColumn type and the second is of the DataColumn type. All other columns are of the BoundColumn type, and they'll be bound to a column of the DataSet.

After adding the Quantity column, the code populates it with the corresponding quantities. The DataSet with the products is created new with every postback, so we must add the quantities from within our code. When an item is ordered, a new Session variable is created to hold the product's ID and quantity. The For...Next loop in the code goes through all the products in the DataSet and finds out if there's a Session variable for the current product. If so, it sets the value of the last cell in the row. If not, this cell's value is set to zero.

In the last section, the code adds to the DataGrid a BoundColumn for each column in the DataSet, binds it to the appropriate column of the DataSet, and then sets some properties. The column that's bound to the ProductID field, for example, has its Visible property set to False. The numeric columns are right-aligned with the HorizontalAlign property. Listing 11.15 shows the LoadDataSet() subroutine.

Listing 11.15: Creating the DataSet with Products and Quantities

```
Sub LoadDataSet()
    Dim WS As New localhost.Service1()
    Dim neworder As DataSet
    neworder = WS.GetAllProducts
```

```
' CLEAR THE STRUCTURE OF THE DATAGRID TO AVOID
' ADDING MULTIPLE COLUMNS WITH BUTTONS
DataGrid1.Columns.Clear()

Dim editcol As New ButtonColumn()
editcol.ButtonType = ButtonColumnType.PushButton
editcol.CommandName = "SelectItem"
editcol.HeaderText = "Order"
editcol.Text = "Buy"
DataGrid1.Columns.Add(editcol)

Dim qtyCol As New DataColumn()
qtyCol.Caption = "QTY"
qtyCol.DataType = GetType(System.Int16)
qtyCol.DefaultValue = 0
neworder.Tables(0).Columns.Add(qtyCol)
neworder.Tables(0).Columns(3).ColumnName = "Quantity"
neworder.Tables(0).Columns(3).Caption = "QTY"

Dim iRow As Integer
Dim itm As Integer
Dim qty As Integer
For iRow = 0 To neworder.Tables(0).Rows.Count - 1
    itm = Val(neworder.Tables(0).Rows(iRow).Item(0))
    If Session("P" & itm.ToString) Is Nothing Then
        qty = 0
    Else
        qty = Val(Session("P" & itm.ToString))
    End If
    neworder.Tables(0).Rows(iRow).Item(3) = qty
Next
DataGrid1.AllowPaging = True
DataGrid1.PageSize = 10
DataGrid1.PagerStyle.Mode = PagerMode.NumericPages

Dim col As New BoundColumn()
col.HeaderText = "ID"
col.DataField = "ProductID"
col.Visible = False
DataGrid1.Columns.Add(col)
```

Part III

```
col = New BoundColumn()
col.HeaderText = "Name"
col.DataField = "ProductName"
DataGrid1.Columns.Add(col)

col = New BoundColumn()
col.HeaderText = "Price"
col.DataField = "UnitPrice"
col.ItemStyle.HorizontalAlign = HorizontalAlign.Right
DataGrid1.Columns.Add(col)

col = New BoundColumn()
col.HeaderText = "Qty"
col.DataField = "Quantity"
col.ItemStyle.HorizontalAlign = HorizontalAlign.Right
DataGrid1.Columns.Add(col)

DataGrid1.DataSource = neworder
DataGrid1.DataMember = "Products"
DataGrid1.DataBind()

End Sub
```

When the user clicks one of the Buy buttons, the ItemCommand event is raised at the server and the code in Listing 11.16 is executed. This code prepares the controls at the top of the form to accept the new quantity for the selected product.

Listing 11.16: The Buy Button's Click Event Handler

```
Private Sub DataGrid1_ItemCommand(ByVal source As Object, _
    ByVal e As _
        System.Web.UI.WebControls.DataGridCommandEventArgs) _
        Handles DataGrid1.ItemCommand
    If e.Item.ItemType = ListItemType.Item Or _
        e.Item.ItemType = ListItemType.AlternatingItem Then
        Label1.Text = e.Item.Cells(2).Text
        Label2.Text = e.Item.Cells(1).Text
        TextBox1.Text = e.Item.Cells(4).Text
    End If
End Sub
```

The action of clicking one of the buttons on the DataGrid control is signaled to the application through the control's ItemCommand event. This event takes place when clicking just about any part of the control, including the paging buttons; that's why the code examines the Item.ItemType property and reacts only if an item (or an alternative item) was clicked.

The Add to Basket button updates the appropriate Session variable, or creates a new one with the specified quantity. Then it also clears the controls at the top of the form to indicate the completion of the edit operation. The handler of the Add to Basket button is shown in Listing 11.17. Notice that after collecting and saving the data (the quantity of a product), it calls the LoadDataSet() subroutine to populate the DataGrid control. If you let the CLR handle the postbacks on its own, you won't see the new quantity on the grid after clicking the Add button. Instead, you will see the new quantity the next time the control is populated, which will happen the next time you click a Buy button. Comment out the last statement in the following listing, and observe how the application behaves.

Listing 11.17: Handling the Add to Basket Button

```
Private Sub Button1_Click(ByVal sender As System.Object, _
        ByVal e As System.EventArgs) Handles Button1.Click
    If Label2.Text = "" Then Exit Sub
    If Session("P" & Label2.Text) Is Nothing Then
        Session("P" & Label2.Text) = Val(TextBox1.Text)
    Else
        Session("P" & Label2.Text) = _
              Session("P" & Label2.Text) + Val(TextBox1.Text)
    End If
    Label1.Text = ""
    Label2.Text = ""
    TextBox1.Text = ""
    LoadDataSet()
End Sub
```

The application behaves as expected. The quantities are maintained through the Session variables, and the proper quantities are displayed on each page of the DataSet. You can add the necessary logic to the application to maintain a running total, and display it on another Label control on the same form.

When the user is done entering quantities, he can click the Submit Order button to post the DataSet with the quantities to the server. The NewOrder Web method accepts the ID of a customer and the DataSet with the order. The sample code uses the same customer ID for all orders,

Part III

but you can prompt the user for an ID through a new Web Form. Listing 11.18 is the handler of the Submit Order button.

Listing 11.18: Submitting an Order through the NewOrder Web Method

```
Private Sub Button3_Click(ByVal sender As System.Object, _
    ByVal e As System.EventArgs) Handles Button3.Click
    Dim DS As DataSet
    DS = DataGrid1.DataSource
    DS.AcceptChanges()
    Dim iRow As Integer
    For iRow = 0 To DS.Tables(0).Rows.Count - 1
        If Val(DS.Tables(0).Rows(iRow).Item(3)) = 0 Then
            DS.Tables(0).Rows(iRow).Delete()
        End If
    Next
    DS.AcceptChanges()
    Dim WS As New localhost.Service1()
    Response.Write(WS.NewOrder("BLAUS", DS))
End Sub
```

The code goes through the rows of the DataSet and deletes all the rows that have a zero quantity. These rows are deleted and then the AcceptChanges method is called to actually remove the deleted lines from the DataSet. The new DataSet is submitted to the server by calling the New Order Web method as shown previously in Listing 11.18.

Calling Web Methods Asynchronously

When you contact a Web Service from within an application, unexpected delays may occur. A slow connection, a busy server, even an overloaded database may introduce substantial delays between the moment you call a Web method and the moment the result arrives at the application. The application can't complete before the Web method returns, but there may be other tasks that you can perform before the response arrives. When the Web method is called synchronously, your application can't react to any previous event, so it's a good idea to call the Web method asynchronously. An asynchronous call initiates an action, but doesn't wait for the action to complete. It relinquishes control to your application and an event is raised when the specific action completes. If your application calls multiple Web methods, you can initiate them at once and then continue with other tasks, while you're waiting for the results to arrive from the web server.

At the very least, your application won't appear frozen to the user. Even trivial Web methods should be called asynchronously to enhance the responsiveness of your application. As you will see in this section, it is possible to call a Web method asynchronously with very little extra code. The infrastructure is there, and all you have to do is to provide the event handler that will be invoked when the method returns.

To demonstrate how to call Web methods asynchronously, we'll build a Web Service that exposes a single method, the PrimeNumber method. The PrimeNumber method calculates prime numbers with a brute force method. The only reason I've chosen to use a prime number calculator is because the algorithm is simple, yet it involves many calculations. The PrimeNumber method accepts an integer as an argument and returns the prime number that corresponds to the specified order. If you pass the value 1,000 as an argument, it will return the 1,000th prime number (it took several seconds to do so on my system). The PrimeNumber method starts with the number 1 and increases it by one. Each number is divided repeatedly by 1, 2, 3, and so on, until we find a number that can't be divided evenly by any numbers other than itself and 1. This is a prime number. You don't really need to understand anything about prime numbers or how they're calculated. The PrimeNumber method we'll build in this section takes an Integer argument and returns a value, which is also an integer. The method takes a while to calculate the result, and you'll see how you can call the method asynchronously, perform other tasks, and retrieve the result when it becomes available.

The form of the test application is shown in Figure 11.8. The two buttons call the PrimeNumber method synchronously and asynchronously, respectively. The Label control below the two buttons displays the current time, and it's updated every 500 milliseconds, with the help of a Timer control. When the method is called synchronously, the Label isn't updated for a while. As soon as you call the method synchronously, the interface will freeze and the time will be updated several seconds later, when the Web method returns its result. When the method is called asynchronously, the Label is being updated every second and you will not notice anything unusual, except that you will have to wait a while before you see the result on a message box.

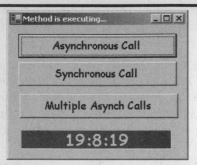

FIGURE 11.8:   The TestPrimeNumbers application calls the same method synchronously and asynchronously.

The PrimeNumbers Web Service exposes a single method, and its implementation is shown in Listing 11.19. The code is quite trivial, and there's nothing of interest here. Just notice that it's a very simple function you could have used in any other project. The method's code is the same, regardless of how you call it.

Listing 11.19: The PrimeNumber Web Method

```
Imports System.Web.Services

Public Class Service1
    Inherits System.Web.Services.WebService

    <WebMethod()> Public Function PrimeNumber _
        (ByVal upper As Integer) As Integer
        If upper = 1 Then Return 1
        Dim iNum As Integer = 1
        Dim IsPrime As Boolean
        Dim i As Decimal = 1
        Dim N As Decimal = 2
        While True
            IsPrime = True
            For i = 2 To N - 1
                If N Mod i = 0 Then
                    IsPrime = False
                    Exit For
                End If
```

```
                Next
                If IsPrime Then
                    iNum = iNum + 1
                    If iNum = upper Then Return N
                End If
                N = N + 1
            End While
        End Function
    End Class
```

Now we'll build the client application for the PrimeNumbers Web method. Create a new Windows application project, design the form shown in Figure 11.8, and add a reference to the PrimeNumbers Web Service. In the Solution Explorer, click the Show All Files button to see all the files of the project. Under Web References ➢ localhost, there's a node called Reference.map. Expand this node and you will see the file Reference.vb. Double-click this file and you will see the code of a class with a method for each of the methods of the web service. The method for the PrimeNumber Web method is shown next:

```
Public Function PrimeNumber _
        (ByVal upper As Integer) As Integer
    Dim results() As Object = _
        Me.Invoke("PrimeNumber", New Object() {upper})
    Return CType(results(0),Integer)
End Function
```

In addition, there are two more methods for each Web method, the Begin*XXX* and End*XXX* methods (where *XXX* is the name of the corresponding Web method). The two methods for the PrimeNumber Web method are the BeginPrimeNumber and the EndPrimeNumber methods:

```
Public Function BeginPrimeNumber(ByVal upper As Integer, _
            ByVal callback As System.AsyncCallback, _
            ByVal asyncState As Object) _
            As System.IAsyncResult
    Return Me.BeginInvoke("PrimeNumber", _
            New Object() {upper}, callback, asyncState)
End Function
```

Part III

```
Public Function EndPrimeNumber _
    (ByVal asyncResult As System.IAsyncResult) As Integer
  Dim results() As Object = Me.EndInvoke(asyncResult)
  Return CType(results(0),Integer)
End Function
```

To call the PrimeNumber method asynchronously, call the Begin-PrimeNumber method of the variable that references the Web Service in your code, passing the arguments you would normally pass to the PrimeNumber method (plus two additional arguments that are discussed next). Notice that the BeginInvoke method doesn't report the return value of the Web method it's calling—it couldn't possibly return any values created by the Web method, because it doesn't wait for the Web method to complete its execution.

In addition to the arguments needed by the Web method, the Begin-PrimeNumber method also expects an event delegate and a variable that represents the Web Service whose method you're calling. When the Web method completes, the event handler you specified is invoked automatically. To retrieve the Web method's return value, you must assign the return value of the EndPrimeNumber method to a variable.

First, you must create a variable to reference the Web Service in your code, so that you can call its methods, as usual. Insert the following statement at the beginning of the code (outside any procedure):

```
Dim WSprime As New localhost.Service1()
```

To initiate the PrimeNumber procedure, you will call the BeginPrimeNumber method passing the *upper* argument of the PrimeNumber method, followed by an AsyncCallback object, which represents the handler that will be automatically invoked when the Web method completes its execution. An object of the System.AsyncCallback type is a delegate: a reference to a method that resides in the client application and is invoked when the asynchronous call to the Web method is finished. The last argument is an instance of the Web Service. Assuming there's a subroutine called primeCallback in your project (which we'll write shortly), the following lines initiate the Web method:

```
Dim cback As New AsyncCallback(AddressOf primeCallback)
WSprime.BeginPrimeNumber(500, cback, WSprime)
```

The last argument of the BeginPrimeNumber method associates a local variable with the asynchronous call. The EndPrimeNumber method is used to retrieve the Web method's return value, and we call it when we know that the method has completed its execution. In other words, the EndPrimeNumber method must be called from within the primeCallback delegate's code. Listing 11.20 shows how to call the PrimeNumbers Web method asynchronously.

Listing 11.20: Calling the PrimeNumber Method Asynchronously

```
Private Sub Button1_Click(ByVal sender As System.Object, _
        ByVal e As System.EventArgs) Handles Button1.Click
    Dim cback As New AsyncCallback(AddressOf primeCallback)
    Console.WriteLine("Will call Web Service asynchronously")
    Me.Text = "Method is executing..."
    Dim ord As Integer
    ord = InputBox("Enter the order of " & _
        "the prime number you wish to calculate")
    WSprime.BeginPrimeNumber(ord, cback, WSprime)
End Sub
```

We need to implement an event handler to handle the completion of the Web method. The primeCallback delegate will be invoked automatically when the Web method completes its execution. We'll use this event to retrieve the return value. Enter the subroutine in Listing 11.21 in the code window.

Listing 11.21: Retrieving the Results of an Asynchronous Call

```
Sub primeCallback(ByVal ar As IAsyncResult)
    Console.WriteLine("Service completed at " & _
        Now.TimeOfDay.ToString)
    Dim prm As localhost.Service1
    prm = CType(ar.AsyncState, localhost.Service1)
    Dim primeNum As Integer
    primeNum = WSprime.EndPrimeNumber(ar)
    Console.WriteLine("Web Service returned " & primeNum)
    Me.Text = "Calling Web Methods"
    MsgBox("The prime number is " & primeNum.ToString)
End Sub
```

This method receives an IasyncResult object as argument, creates a reference to the Web Service (variable *prm*), and uses this reference to call the EndPrimeNumber method. The EndPrimeNumber method returns the same result as the original Web method that was called asynchronously. All other statements simply display the time of the completion of the asynchronous call and the result returned by the PrimeNumber method.

To demonstrate the nature of the asynchronous call, the form of the client application displays the current time on a Label control and updates it every half second. If you request the prime number of an unusual order (the 1,000th prime number, for instance), the PrimeNumber method will take a while to calculate and return the result. If the call was made synchronously, the application will freeze and the time won't be updated. When the result becomes available, everything will return to normal, the client application will react to the usual events, and the Label will display the correct time again. If the call was made synchronously, the client application will continue reacting to the events and the time will continue being updated every half second. The Web method is running in the background, and it steals CPU cycles (quite a few of them). Keep in mind that this is a test environment. If the method is executing on a remote computer (which will be the case in a production environment), there will be no process running in the background. Between the time you call the method and the time it returns the result, you computer is free to carry on other tasks.

The top two buttons on the client application demonstrate how to call the PrimeNumber method synchronously and asynchronously. The last button calls the PrimeNumber method three times, one after the other. All the calls are asynchronous, and as each method completes its calculations and returns a value to the client application, a message box with the corresponding prime number will appear. The code behind this button is shown in Listing 11.22.

Listing 11.22: Calling Multiple Instances of the Same Web Method Asynchronously

```
Private Sub Button3_Click(ByVal sender As System.Object, _
        ByVal e As System.EventArgs) Handles Button3.Click
    Dim WSprime1 As New localhost.Service1()
    Dim WSprime2 As New localhost.Service1()
    Dim WSprime3 As New localhost.Service1()
    Dim cback As New AsyncCallback(AddressOf primeCallback)
    Console.WriteLine("Will call Web " & _
            "Service asynchronously")
    Me.Text = "Method is executing..."
    WSprime1.BeginPrimeNumber(1200, cback, WSprime1)
    Console.WriteLine("Will call Web " & _
            "Service asynchronously")
```

```
WSprime2.BeginPrimeNumber(600, cback, WSprime2)
Console.WriteLine("Will call Web " & _
        "Service asynchronously")
WSprime3.BeginPrimeNumber(300, cback, WSprime3)
    End Sub
```

Notice that I've used three different instances of the Service1 Web Service? The three instances will execute in parallel, and you will get back the results of the methods that take the least time to execute first. If you use the same instance of the Web Service to call all three methods, then the results will arrive in an unpredictable order. The three methods are executing on the same CPU, which doesn't reduce the total time. If you called three methods on three different servers, however, the three processes would be running in parallel and you'd get the results much sooner.

WHAT'S NEXT

In this chapter, you learned a great deal about Web Services. You learned how to create a simple service and how to include a service inside an application. Then you were presented with the information necessary to tie all that together with database data, and you learned how to bind data to a Web Service. As you can see, Web Services are now easier than ever, and they are a very powerful tool for extending a website.

In the next chapter, we will conclude this section on ASP.NET by presenting more detailed information on how to use Visual Basic .NET and ASP.NET to create full web applications.

Part III

Chapter 12

DEVELOPING WEB APPLICATIONS WITH ASP.NET

ASP.NET is more than just the next version of Active Server Pages (ASP). It is a unified web development platform that provides the services necessary for developers to build enterprise-class web applications. While ASP.NET is largely syntax compatible with ASP, it also provides a new programming model and infrastructure that enables a powerful new class of applications. You can feel free to augment your existing ASP applications by incrementally adding ASP.NET functionality to them.

In this chapter, we will take a look at ASP.NET development.

Part III

Adapted from the forthcoming *Visual Basic .NET Developer's Handbook* by Evangelos Petroutsos and Kevin Hough

ISBN 0-7821-2879-3 $59.99

NOTE

Although Visual Studio .NET provides an amazing environment for designing, coding, and debugging, you do not have to use it to build ASP.NET applications. Because ASP.NET follows the same design principle as ASP, you can use any text-based editor to create ASP.NET applications. When an ASP.NET page is first accessed, it is compiled automatically, and future requests will access the compiled resource.

CODING ASP.NET PAGES

The two basic ways to code ASP pages in .NET are Inline Coding, in which the code and controls share the same page; and Code Behind, in which the code and HTML are separated into different pages.

In this section, we will examine both of these approaches and see how they fit into the ASP.NET development environment.

Inline Coding

Inline Coding is the approach that is more closely related to the old style of writing ASP pages, where the code and HTML is in the same page. With this approach, you can write your ASP.NET pages with almost any type of text editor, including Notepad, WordPad, or Visual Studio .NET.

The following example code employs Inline Coding methodology to create a simple web page that allows the user to enter their name into a Text box control and display it in a Label control when a button is clicked:

```
<%@ Page Language="VB" %>
<HTML>

    <script runat="server">
    'This is the code section


    Sub ButtonClick(Sender As Object, E As EventArgs)
        Label1.Text = Textbox1.Text
    end sub
    </script>
    <!-- This is the HTML section -->
```

```
<body>
    <FORM id="Form1" runat="server">
        <P align="left">Name:  
            <asp:TextBox id="TextBox1"
            runat="server"></asp:TextBox>
        </P>
        <P align="left">
            <asp:Button id="Button1"
            runat="server" OnClick="ButtonClick"
            Text="Button"></asp:Button></P>
        <P align="left">
            <asp:Label id="Label1"
            runat="server" Width="134px"
            >Label</asp:Label></P>
    </FORM>
</body>
</HTML>
```

As the previous code section demonstrates, the Inline Coding approach is similar to the ASP page approach. In the next section, we will take another look at the same web page; but this time, we will use the Code Behind approach and see how it fits with ASP.NET Web Forms.

Code Behind

There are often times when it is extremely difficult for a developer to come up with a world-class form layout or that special graphic that sets a site apart and makes it memorable. Most of us can develop the site, but "the look" somehow eludes us. Well, ASP.NET to the rescue! ASP.NET provides an approach called Code Behind that allows you to separate the code from the HTML. This approach is called *Web Forms*.

Let's take another look at the example that was presented in the previous section; however, this time we will use the Code Behind approach and separate the code section from the HTML section.

Listing 12.1 presents the HTML, and Listing 12.2 presents the Code Behind.

Listing 12.1: The HTML Code Section

```
<%@ Page Language="vb" AutoEventWireup="false"
 Codebehind="WebForm2.aspx.vb"
  Inherits="WebApplication20.WebForm2"%>
<!DOCTYPE HTML PUBLIC
 "-//W3C//DTD HTML 4.0 Transitional//EN">
<HTML>
    <HEAD>
        <title>WebForm2</title>
        <meta name="GENERATOR"
         content="Microsoft Visual Studio.NET 7.0">
        <meta name="CODE_LANGUAGE"
         content="Visual Basic 7.0">
        <meta name="vs_defaultClientScript"
         content="JavaScript">
    </HEAD>
    <body>
     <form id="Form1" method="post" runat="server">
        <P>Name:
            <asp:TextBox id="TextBox1"
             runat="server"></asp:TextBox></P>
        <P>
            <asp:Button id="Button1"
             runat="server" Text="Button"></asp:Button></P>
        <P>
          <asp:Label id="Label1"
          runat="server" Width="140px">Label</asp:Label></P>
     </form>
    </body>
</HTML>
```

Listing 12.2: The Code Behind Page

```
Public Class WebForm2
     Inherits System.Web.UI.Page
     Protected WithEvents TextBox1 _
     As System.Web.UI.WebControls.TextBox
     Protected WithEvents Button1 _
     As System.Web.UI.WebControls.Button
     Protected WithEvents Label1 _
     As System.Web.UI.WebControls.Label

   + Form Web Designer Generated Code
```

```
    Private Sub Button1_Click _
    (ByVal sender As System.Object, _
    ByVal e As System.EventArgs) Handles Button1.Click
        Label1.Text = TextBox1.Text
    End Sub
End Class
```

The previous code demonstrates the Code Behind approach to development in ASP.NET. Notice the + Form Web Designer Generated Code section in Listing 12.2. This is hidden code that the designer created based on the web page on the Design tab. In the next section, we will create a sample Login project using the Inline Coding approach to see how this approach works in building an ASP.NET website.

INLINE LOGIN PROJECT

The Inline Login project, shown in Figure 12.1, is a simple ASP.NET site that allows the user to enter a username and password to gain access to a secure page. The Login page is comprised of server controls that are created in the ASPX page.

NOTE

You can download the Login project from the www.sybex.com website. Search for the book by its ISBN number, 2887, or its title, *Visual Basic .NET Complete*.

Part III

![The Login project screenshot]

FIGURE 12.1: The Login project

Creating the Login Controls

The first step in the process is to create the controls that will be used by the Login page. For this project, we will use the Label, Text box, and Button controls in a table to create the GUI, as shown in Figure 12.1.

There are two ways to accomplish the task of creating the user controls in the ASP page. The first option is to code each one by hand, as shown below:

```
<P align="left">
    <asp:Label id="lblMessage" runat="server"
    ForeColor="Blue" Font-Bold="True">
    Please Login to the Site!</asp:Label></P>
```

The second method is to use the Design tab of Visual Studio .NET, shown in Figure 12.2, and drag the controls from the Toolbox, as you would in a client application. This is the approach that is used in this chapter.

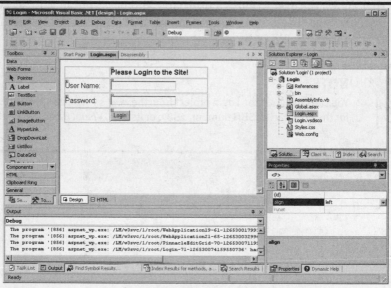

FIGURE 12.2: The Visual Studio .NET Design tab

Adding Controls to the ASPX Page

If you have had any prior experience using Visual Studio 6, Visual Basic, or VB .NET, you should feel fairly comfortable adding controls to ASPX pages in Visual Studio .NET. The process is just about the same. First, you find the control on the toolbar, and then you drag it to the page. The controls that we will use are listed in Table 12.1.

TABLE 12.1: The Login Project's Controls

CONTROL	NAME	PROPERTIES
Table	Table1	None
Label	Label1	Font=Arial, Font Bold=True, ForeColor=Black, Text=Please Login to the Site!
Label	Label2	Font=Arial, Font Bold=False, Text=User Name:
Text box	txtUserName	None
Label	Label3	Font=Arial, Font Bold=False, Text=Password:
Text box	txtPassword	None
Button	cmdLogin	Text=Login

Follow these steps to add the controls to the ASPX page:

1. Choose Table ➢ Insert ➢ Table to display the Insert Table dialog box.

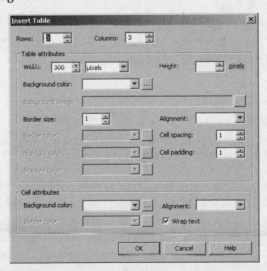

2. Set Rows to 4, Columns to 2, Border Size to 0, and click the OK button to insert the blank table on the page.

3. Drag a Label Server control from the toolbar to the right column in the first row of the table.

4. Drag a Label Server control from the toolbar to the left column in the second row of the table.

5. Drag a Text box Server control from the toolbar to the right column in the second row of the table.

6. Drag a Label Server control from the toolbar to the left column in the third row of the table

7. Drag a Text box Server control from the toolbar to the right column in the third row of the table.

8. Drag a Button Server control from the toolbar to the right column of the fourth row of the table.

9. Set the properties of the controls according to the Properties column in Table 12.1.

Your finished table should look like the one in Figure 12.3.

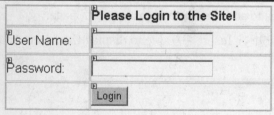

FIGURE 12.3: The completed table

NOTE

As I mentioned earlier in this chapter, you can always code the controls by hand if you are more comfortable using that approach.

Listing 12.3 creates the Login page for our project by defining the controls in the HTML section and coding the VerifyLogin subroutine to process the OnClick event of the Login button. If the user enters "demo" as the username and "test" as the password, then the login is successful and the Login button changes the text to read "Successful Login!" If the user does not enter the proper username and password, then the Login button text changes to "Incorrect Login."

Listing 12.3: The Login Page

```
<%@ Page Language="VB" %>
<HTML>
  <script runat="server">
   sub Page_Load(obj as object, e as eventargs)

   end sub

   Sub VerifyLogin(Sender As Object, E As EventArgs)
     if txtUserName.Text = "demo" and _
       txtPassword.Text = "test" then
       cmdLogin.Text = "Successful Login!"
     else
       cmdLogin.Text = "Incorrect Login!"
     End if
   end sub
  </script>
  <body>
  <FORM id="Form1" runat="server">
    <P align="left">
    <TABLE id="Table1" height="133"
     cellSpacing="1" cellPadding="1"
     width="338" border="0">
    <TR>
      <TD width="104"></TD>
      <TD><asp:label id="Label1" runat="server"
      ForeColor="Blue" Font-Bold="True"
      Font-Names="Arial">Please Login to the Site!
      </asp:label></TD>
    </TR>
    <TR>
      <TD width="104"><asp:label id="Label2"
        runat="server" Font-Names="Arial"
        >User Name:</asp:label></TD>
      <TD><asp:textbox id="txtUserName"
        runat="server"></asp:textbox></TD>
    </TR>
    <TR>
        <TD width="104"><asp:label id="Label3"
          runat="server" Font-Names="Arial">Password:
```

```
          </asp:label></TD>
          <TD><asp:textbox id="txtPassword"
          runat="server"></asp:textbox></TD>
        </TR>
        <TR>
          <TD width="104"></TD>
          <TD><asp:button id="cmdLogin"
          onclick="VerifyLogin" runat="server"
          Text="Login"></asp:button></TD>
        </TR>
      </TABLE>
      </P>
    </FORM>
    </body>
</HTML>
```

TESTING THE LOGIN PROJECT

As you can see from Listing 12.3, ASP.NET makes it very easy to define server controls and react to events that are raised. All of the ASPX pages that you create will follow a similar model.

Let's take a look at the Login Project form as a website. To start the build process, press F5. The project will build, and the Login page will open in your browser. Try entering a username and a password. Click the Verify button. If you entered the correct information, **demo** and **test**, you will see a message that the login was successful, as shown in Figure 12.4. If you entered incorrect information, a message will inform you of this.

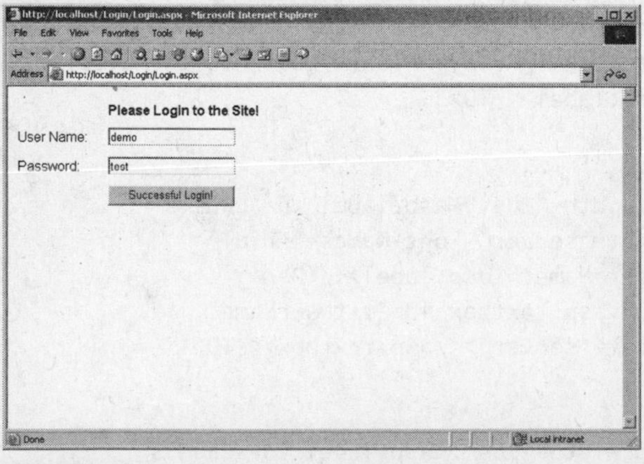

FIGURE 12.4:   The Login project in action

You can use the Login project as a starting place for your Login page.

In the next section, we will explore the Code Behind approach, discussed in a previous section of this chapter, in greater detail.

CODE BEHIND WEB FORMS

In this section, we will examine Web Forms that are based on the Code Behind approach.

Overview of ASP.NET and Web Forms

Web Forms are the heart and soul of ASP.NET. Web Forms, which are similar to Windows Forms, are the user interface (UI) elements that give your Web applications their look and feel.

Web Forms provide properties, methods, and events for the controls that are placed onto them in a separate page from the code, which is in a Code Behind form, as shown in Figure 12.5.

FIGURE 12.5: Web Form architecture

Using Web Form Controls

Web Form controls differ from normal HTML controls in that they are created and run on the server, render the appropriate HTML, and send that HTML into the output stream. The Web Form controls perform all types of actions and solve all kinds of application problems. Table 12.2 outlines the categories of controls that are available for use on Web Forms.

TABLE 12.2: Web Form Controls Categories

CONTROLS CATEGORY	DESCRIPTION
Display	Display static information, such as Labels
Data Entry	Accept data entry, such as Text box and Option Box
Buttons	Allow the user to signal the form to process a request, such as Button and Hyperlink
Images	Display images, such as Image Control
Validation Controls	Monitor and report on data entry rules, such as the RequiredFieldValidator and the RangeValidator
List Controls	Display lists of data, such as the DataGrid and the DataRepeater
Specialty Controls	Perform special actions, such as AdRotator and the Calendar controls

ASP.NET Web Forms includes controls for just about every application that you can imagine. In the next section, we will create a sample Web Form project that relies on validation controls and the Code Behind architecture.

VALIDATING DATA INPUT WITH ASP.NET

If you are used to writing ASP pages, or even Visual Basic applications, you are no doubt familiar with the problems associated with validating data from your users. We have all written applications that either ask the user to enter specific types of data, such as Social Security numbers or phone numbers, or that ask the user to enter more generalized types of data. Well, the days of struggling with the drudgery of writing custom validation routines can be a thing of the past with ASP.NET's validation controls. In this section, we will look at these controls and see just how they can fit into your websites.

Using ASP.NET Validation Controls

In ASP.NET websites, you can enable validation of user input by adding validation controls to your forms, just as you would other server controls. Each validation control is set to "watch" an input control, such as a text box or check box elsewhere on the page. When the user's input is being processed, the ASP.NET page passes the user's entry to the appropriate validation control, and the validation controls test the user's input. After all validation controls have been tested, a property on the page is set. If any of the controls show that a validation check failed, the entire page is set to invalid. In the next section, we will create and test the Validation project, which tests for the proper input of a user's name, address, and phone number.

Anatomy of a Validation Control

Validation controls work by "watching" another control and ensuring that a value is entered. They ensure that the value that is entered matches a set of requirements. You can specify that a user must provide information in a specific control by adding a RequiredFieldValidator control to the page and linking it to the required control. Your web page can specify that the users must fill in a First Name field, for example, before they can submit a registration form. This is accomplished by setting the ControlToValidate property of the RequiredFieldValidator control to the text box that will hold the First Name entry, as shown in the following code:

```
<asp:Textbox id="txtFirstName" runat="server"></asp:Textbox>
<asp:RequiredFieldValidator id="RequiredFieldValidator1" _
    runat="server"
    ControlToValidate="txtFirstName"
    ErrorMessage="First Name is a required field."
    ForeColor="Red">
</asp:RequiredFieldValidator>
```

The validation process may be fired by calling the Page.IsValid method. This method will be covered in the next section.

Validating a Web Page

When you call the Page.IsValid method to validate a web page, a value is returned indicating whether the page validations succeeded or failed. The following example demonstrates the IsValid property and sets up a conditional statement to notify the user of the status of the page validation. If the IsValid property returns True, the Text property of the lblError control is set to "The page is valid." If the IsValid property returns False, it is set to "Some of the required fields are empty."

```
Sub cmdValidate_Click(sender As Object, e As EventArgs)
    If (Page.IsValid) Then
        lblError.Text = "The page is Valid"
    Else
        lblError.Text = "Some of the required fields are empty"
    End If
End Sub
[C#]
void ValidateBtn_Click(Object Sender, EventArgs E) {

    if (Page.IsValid == true) {
        lblOutput.Text = "Page is Valid!";
    }
    else {
        lblOutput.Text = "Some of the required fields are empty";
    }
        }
[JScript]
function ValidateBtn_Click(Sender, e : EventArgs) {

    if (Page.IsValid == true) {
        lblOutput.Text = "Page is Valid!";
    }
    else {
        lblOutput.Text = "Some of the required fields are empty";
    }
        }
```

No example is available for C++. To view a Visual Basic, C#, or JScript example, click the Language Filter button in the upper-left corner of the page.

The sample project presented in the next section utilizes the IsValid method and several RequiredFieldValidator controls to monitor and ensure that all fields in a web page are entered.

Validation Project

The Validation project, shown in Figure 12.6, validates the user's first name, last name, and address entries. To accomplish this, we will rely on the Validation controls that are included in Visual Studio .NET.

NOTE

You can download the Validation project from www.sybex.com. Search for the book by its ISBN number, 2887, or its title, *Visual Basic .NET Complete*.

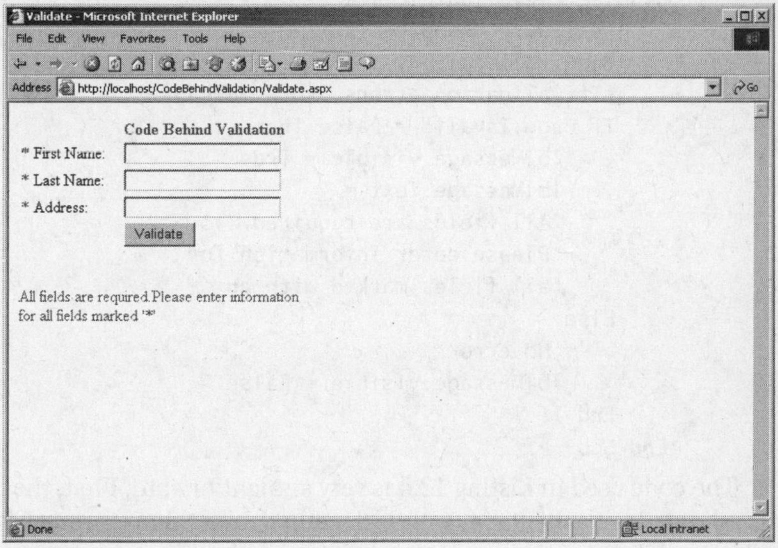

FIGURE 12.6:   The Validation project

The Validation project consists of three fields that must be entered and RequiredFieldValidator controls that are set to watch these fields. A button is supplied that calls the Page.IsValid method when it is clicked to validate the controls. If there is an error, one or more of the text boxes does not have data, then the RequiredFieldValidator control displays its ErrorMessage, in this case an asterisk (*), and sets the Text property of the Error Label control.

Validating the Project Page

The Validation project includes a button that the user can click to validate the page. This button calls the Page.IsValid method, which causes the controls to be verified for the existence of data and verifies the user of the status. The code in Listing 12.4 is used to perform these checks.

Listing 12.4: Validating the Controls

```
Private Sub cmdValidate_Click _
    (ByVal sender As System.Object, _
    ByVal e As System.EventArgs) _
    Handles cmdValidate.Click
        'Validate the page
        Page.Validate()
        'If validation errors, show message
        If Page.IsValid = False Then
            lblMessage.Visible = True
            lblMessage.Text = _
            "All fields are required." & _
            "Please enter information for " & _
            "all fields marked with an '*'"
        Else
            'No errors
            lblMessage.Visible = False
        End If
End Sub
```

The code used in Listing 12.4 is very straightforward. First, the page is validated with the Page.IsValid method, and then a message is displayed if any of the text boxes do not have data.

ASP.NET Testing the Validation Project

To test the Validation project, press F5 to build and run the project. Enter your first name in the First Name text box and press the Validate button. The code will execute, and you will see an asterisk appear to the left of the Last Name and Address text boxes. You will receive a message stating that the fields marked with an asterisk are required. If you enter your last name and address in the appropriate text boxes and click the Validate button again, you will see that the asterisks and error message are not displayed, indicating that the data has passed the required field validation check.

In the next section, we will look at the process of accessing data in ASP.NET.

ACCESSING DATA WITH ASP.NET

Accessing data has become a mainstay in almost all enterprises today, and the need to add, edit, and maintain data from our websites is becoming very important. To fulfill this need, ASP.NET provides a wealth of tools. In fact, most of the tools that are available to the client/server programmer that were discussed earlier in this book are indeed available to the ASP developer, and we will take a quick look at them in this chapter.

NOTE

For an in-depth look at data access (ADO) in .NET, please see Part IV, "Database Programming."

CONNECTING TO A DATABASE

All of the connections, manipulations, and management of database objects in ASP.NET are controlled by ADO.NET.

To achieve data access in ASP.NET, the first task you must accomplish is to make a connection to the database, as shown in Listing 12.5.

Listing 12.5: The Connection String

```
Dim myConnection As SqlConnection
myConnection = New SqlConnection("server=localhost; _
  database=Pubs; uid=sa; pwd=sql;")
myConnection.Open()
```

First, a variable is declared to hold the connection string, and then the SQLConnection is made to the database. Once the connection is made, the database and all of its tables, views, stored procedures, and items are available to your web application.

Part III

Let's take a look at a complete page that uses the SQLConnection to make a database connection and then report on the state of the connection, as shown in Listing 12.6. In this ASPX page, a connection is made to the Pubs sample database, and the status of the connection is reported as the text of a Label control that is defined on the page.

Listing 12.6: The Connection State

```vb
<%@ Page Language="VB" %>
<%@ Import Namespace="System.Data.SqlClient" %>
<script runat="server">
 Sub Page_Load(Sender As Object, E As EventArgs)
  Dim myConnection As SqlConnection
  myConnection = New SqlConnection _
  ("server=localhost;database=Pubs;uid=sa;pwd=sql;")
  myConnection.Open()
  ConnectionState.Text = myConnection.State.ToString()
  myConnection.Close()
 End Sub
</script>
<html>
  <head>
  <title>VB. Net Developer's Handbook Chapter 15:
         Developing Web Applications with ASP. NET</title>
  </head>
  <body>
  <form runat="server" method="post" ID="Form1">
   Connection State:
   <asp:Label runat="server" id="ConnectionState" />
  </form>
  </body>
</html>
```

The code in Listing 12.6 is very straightforward. First, a connection is made to the database in the script section at the top, and then, a Label control is defined in the HTML section to display the results of the connection state, as shown in Figure 12.7.

Now that we have a good sense of the process of connecting to a database, we will look at the code necessary to return records from a database table.

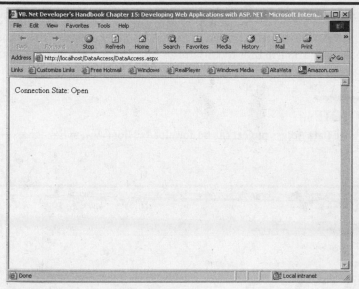

FIGURE 12.7: The connection state

RETURNING DATA IN ASP.NET

Connecting to a database, as we did in the previous section, is just the beginning when it comes to the power and flexibility provided in ASP.NET. In this section, we will look at the process and code necessary to display a record on an ASPX page. To accomplish this task, we will call on the help of the SqlDataAdapter and the DataSet object. The SqlDataAdapter serves as a bridge between a DataSet and SQL Server for retrieving and saving data.

The process of selecting and retrieving records from SQL Server is very straightforward, as outlined in the following list:

1. Define a connection object and a DataSet.

2. Open a connection to the database, as we did in the previous section.

3. Define the DataSet, and set the DataRow and DataTable.

4. Fill the DataSet with the table.

5. Populate a label, or some other control, with the data from the DataSet.

Part III

The Data Access Project

The Data Access project, shown in Figure 12.8, connects to the Pubs database, returns the first record in the Authors table, and displays the fields in labels on a web page.

NOTE

The Data Access project can be downloaded from www.sybex.com.

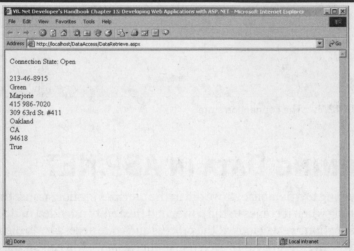

FIGURE 12.8: The Data Access project

Returning Database Records

The code to connect to the database and return the record is performed in the Page_Load subroutine as shown in Listing 12.7. In this subroutine, a connection is made to the database and a series of Label controls are populated with the first record from the Authors table.

Listing 12.7: Returning Data Replace with Web Form

```
<%@ Import Namespace="System.Data" %>
<%@ Import Namespace="System.Data.SqlClient" %>
<%@ Page Language="VB" %>
<HTML>
```

```
    <HEAD>
        <title>VB. Net Developer's Handbook Chapter 15:
        Developing Web Applications with
            ASP. NET</title>
        <script runat="server">

Sub Page_Load(Sender As Object, E As EventArgs)
Dim SqlCon As New SqlConnection _
("server=localhost;uid=sa;pwd=sql;database=pubs")
SqlCon.Open()
ConnectionState.Text = SqlCon.State.ToString()
Dim SqlDA As New SqlDataAdapter _
("SELECT * FROM authors", SqlCon)
Dim ds As New DataSet()

SqlDA.Fill(ds, "authors")

Dim DR() As DataRow = ds.Tables("authors").Select()

    'View the data
Label1.Text = (DR(1)("au_id").ToString())
Label2.Text = (DR(1)("au_lname").ToString())
Label3.Text = (DR(1)("au_fname").ToString())
Label4.Text = (DR(1)("phone").ToString())
Label5.Text = (DR(1)("address").ToString())
Label6.Text = (DR(1)("city").ToString())
Label7.Text = (DR(1)("state").ToString())
Label15.Text = (DR(1)("zip").ToString())
Label9.Text = (DR(1)("contract").ToString())
'Close the connection
SqlCon.Close()

End Sub
    </script>
  </HEAD>
  <body>
    <form runat="server" method="post" ID="Form1">
    <P>
        Connection State:
        <asp:Label runat="server"
        id="ConnectionState"/></P>
    <P>
        <asp:Label id="Label1" runat="server"
```

Part III

```
            Width="161px">Label</asp:Label><BR>
            <asp:Label id="Label2" runat="server"
            Width="172px">Label</asp:Label><BR>
            <asp:Label id="Label3" runat="server"
            Width="164px">Label</asp:Label><BR>
            <asp:Label id="Label4" runat="server"
            Width="164px">Label</asp:Label><BR>
            <asp:Label id="Label5" runat="server"
            Width="154px">Label</asp:Label><BR>
            <asp:Label id="Label6" runat="server"
            Width="179px">Label</asp:Label><BR>
            <asp:Label id="Label7" runat="server"
            Width="151px">Label</asp:Label><BR>
            <asp:Label id="Label8" runat="server"
            Width="174px">Label</asp:Label><BR>
            <asp:Label id="Label9" runat="server"
            Width="203px">Label</asp:Label></P>
        <P> </P>
        </form>
    </body>
</HTML>
```

The code in Listing 12.7 creates an ASPX page that fetches the Authors table from the Pubs database and displays the data from the first row in a series of Label controls, as shown previously in Figure 12.8.

Testing the Data Access Project

Testing the Data Access project is simply a matter of downloading the project, opening it in Visual Studio .NET, and pressing F5 to build and display the web page. A database connection is established in the Page_Load event, and the first record from the Authors table populates a series of Labels, as shown previously in Figure 12.8.

WHAT'S NEXT

This concludes Part III on the coverage of ASP.NET. Now that you have a good understanding of the new ASP.NET, we will begin to cover data access in the next section.

In Part IV, you will learn all about Database Programming with Visual Basic .NET. We will start with a basic overview of databases and work through the retrieving and editing of data with ADO.NET.

Part IV

DATABASE
PROGRAMMING

Chapter 13

BASIC CONCEPTS OF RELATIONAL DATABASES

Have you ever heard of Nancy Davolio and Alfreds Futterkiste? If you have or if you have designed simple databases with Microsoft SQL Server, then you can safely skip this chapter. If you haven't done any database programming, take the time to review this chapter. Before looking at any tools, you should learn the basic principles of database design and familiarize yourself with the basic terms you'll see in the rest of the book: tables and indexes, relationships, primary and foreign keys, referential integrity, and a bunch of other goodies.

This chapter covers the principles of databases and the nature of relational databases, why you use a specific methodology to design them, and other related topics, including the normalization of databases. An important part of this chapter is the discussion of the structure of the Northwind and Pubs sample databases. These databases ship with SQL Server 2000, and we use them for our examples throughout the book.

Adapted from *Mastering Visual Basic .NET Database Programming* by Evangelos Petroutsos and Asli Bilgin
ISBN 0-7821-2878-5 $49.99

Part IV

TIP

You can also install the Northwind and Pubs databases from a typical Visual Studio .NET installation by running the installation programs for the .NET QuickStart tutorials: Select Programs ➢ Microsoft .NET Framework SDK ➢ Samples and QuickStart Tutorials from the Windows Start menu. Keep in mind that this doesn't install SQL Server, but the lightweight MSDE database server. Be warned that this version doesn't include the SQL Server IDE that we discuss throughout the book. Even if you already have SQL Server installed, you will still find these QuickStart tutorials useful because they contain many data access samples for using the .NET Framework.

Why examine the structure of existing databases instead of creating a new one from scratch? Because it's simpler to understand the structure of an existing database, especially a database designed by the people who designed the data engine itself. Besides, because we use these databases in the examples in the following chapters, you should make sure you understand their structures. Finally, the basic concepts of relational databases covered in this chapter provide stepping stones to the more advanced topics discussed later in this book.

FUNDAMENTALS OF DATABASE DESIGN

In principle, designing databases is simple. More than anything else, it requires common sense and organization. The strength of any business lies in its ability to retrieve and store information efficiently. As a database designer, you should consider certain principles before creating the actual database:

▶ Organization

▶ Integrity

▶ Optimization

First, a well-designed database system should always have well-organized data that is quick and easy to retrieve. In addition, the system should accurately record and store the data without corruption. Last, you must optimize the data and data manipulation code that you write. This way, your database management system (DBMS) can find and return the data in the least amount of time. Don't skip these steps, because any errors in the design of a database will surface later, when you try to extract its data. Let's consider these points in more detail:

Organization   If your data isn't well organized in the database, you won't be able to extract the data you want (or you'll have to extract a lot of unwanted information along with the useful data). Before you even begin working with any tools, you should first consider how you want to store your data. The easiest way to do this is to write down (or think about) what you want the system to do. Use no more than four or five sentences. Then, pick out all the nouns in those sentences. Generally, these nouns will correspond to the tables of your system. The next step is to get a paper and pen and to draw a pictorial representation of your data. Write down the nouns and draw boxes around them. Hang on to this sketch. You'll use it in just a bit, as you learn how to build relationships between these data items and create entity-relationship diagrams.

Integrity   Another important aspect of databases is integrity, which keeps your data accurate and consistent. Even the best-designed database can be incapacitated if it's populated with invalid data. The impact of corruption isn't a technical one. Rather, it's an impact on the business that relies on the database. Imagine the cost to a business if orders were lost and shipments delayed due to missing or invalid data. If you don't do something to maintain the integrity and consistency of your database, you might never be able to locate data. For instance, if you allow the users of a database to change the name of a company, how will you retrieve the invoices issued to the same company before its name was changed? For this reason, you can't rely on the users to maintain the integrity of the database. A modern DBMS provides built-in mechanisms to help you with this task. SQL Server, for example, can enforce the integrity of the relationships between data items. Say a customer places some orders. The DBMS should not allow you to remove the customer from the database, without first removing their associated orders. If a customer is deleted from the database, the corresponding orders will no longer refer to a valid customer. *Orphaning* describes the concept of broken relationships between associated sets of data. Later in this chapter, in the "Normalization Rules" section, you will see how to

Part IV

incorporate rules for maintaining the integrity. You can build these rules right into the database itself, in order to prevent orphaned records or other data corruption.

Optimization   After you incorporate organization and integrity into your database, you should think about tuning and optimization. Performance tuning isn't something you do after you have your database up and running. On the contrary, you should performance-tune your database throughout database design. Although SQL Server 2000 has made some serious advances in self-tuning, you still have to make sure you write solid data manipulation code to take advantage of these optimizations. Throughout this book, we provide you with tips and tricks to keep your database running like a well-oiled engine.

As you will see, the design of a database shouldn't be taken lightly. You can trace most problems in database applications back to the design of the database. You will find it difficult, if not impossible, to optimize a poorly designed database. The queries will be unnecessarily slow and, in many cases, unnecessarily complicated.

What Is a Database?

A database is one of those objects that is hard to define, yet everyone knows what it is. Here's a simple definition, which even people with no prior programming experience will understand: A *database* is a system for storing complex, structured information. The same is true for a file, or even for the filesystem on your hard disk. What makes a database unique is that databases are designed for responsiveness. The purpose of a database is not so much the storage of information as its quick retrieval. In other words, you must structure your database so that it can be queried quickly and efficiently.

Relational Databases

The databases that we focus on in this book are *relational*, because they are based on relationships between the data they contain. The data is stored in tables, and tables contain related data, or *entities*, such as customers, products, orders, and so on. The idea is to keep the tables small and manageable; thus, separate entities are kept in their own tables. For example, if you start mixing customers and invoices, products and their suppliers in the same table, you'll end up repeating information—a highly undesirable situation. If there's one rule to live by as a database designer and programmer, this is it: Unless you are building a data warehouse, do not unnecessarily duplicate information. As we mentioned before, if you can name your table by using a single noun, then you are on the right track. So when we mention that duplicate data is not desirable, we do so in the context of OLTP systems.

OLAP VERSUS OLTP

How you design your database depends on the type of system you need. Database systems come in two distinct flavors: online analytical processing (OLAP) and online transaction processing (OLTP) systems. Each uses completely different design models, and you should never have a database that uses both models.

OLAP systems are often referred to as *data warehouses*, or *data mines*. These databases are generally read-only representations of volumes of data often used for reporting purposes. Thus, you'll often hear these systems called *decision support systems*, because they are often used to help high-level managers make business decisions. Their retrieval mechanism is quite different from that of OLTP systems. OLAP systems use the concept of cubes. *Cubes* are multidimensional representations of data, which you can think of like pivot tables in Excel. The storage also vastly differs from OLTP. In data warehouses, speed is the highest priority, so databases tend to be de-normalized, with lots of redundant data. We define *normalization* later in this chapter.

OLTP systems consist of users retrieving subsets of data based on specific criteria and manipulating single sets of data in an atomic process referred to as a *transaction*. Because OLTP systems update data, considerations such as concurrency, locking, and archival have a higher priority than with data warehouses. OLTP systems attempt to reduce the amount of data that is stored so that SQL Server can process the data faster.

The systems that we are referring to in this book center around OLTP systems, rather than OLAP.

Of course, entities are not independent of each other. Pull out the diagram you drew earlier with the boxes containing your nouns. Draw lines connecting the boxes that are related. For example, customers place

Part IV

orders, so the rows of a Customers table would link to the rows of an Orders table. Figure 13.1 shows a segment of a table with customers (top left) and the rows of a table with orders that correspond to one of the customers (bottom right). The lines that connect the rows of the two tables represent *relationships*. These databases are called *relational*, because they're based on relationships.

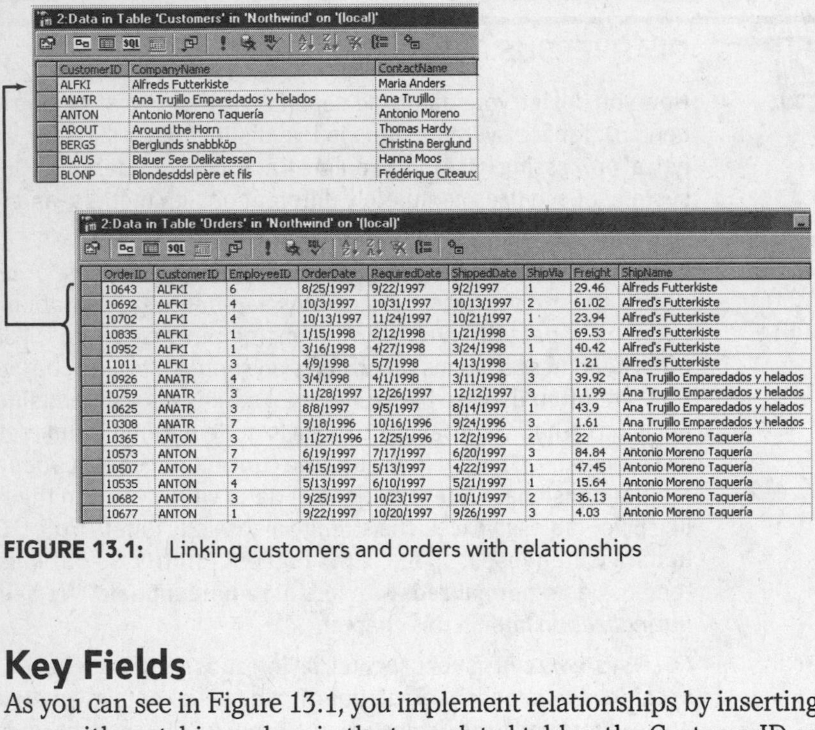
2:Data in Table 'Customers' in 'Northwind' on '(local)'

CustomerID	CompanyName	ContactName
ALFKI	Alfreds Futterkiste	Maria Anders
ANATR	Ana Trujillo Emparedados y helados	Ana Trujillo
ANTON	Antonio Moreno Taquería	Antonio Moreno
AROUT	Around the Horn	Thomas Hardy
BERGS	Berglunds snabbköp	Christina Berglund
BLAUS	Blauer See Delikatessen	Hanna Moos
BLONP	Blondesddsl père et fils	Frédérique Citeaux

2:Data in Table 'Orders' in 'Northwind' on '(local)'

OrderID	CustomerID	EmployeeID	OrderDate	RequiredDate	ShippedDate	ShipVia	Freight	ShipName
10643	ALFKI	6	8/25/1997	9/22/1997	9/2/1997	1	29.46	Alfreds Futterkiste
10692	ALFKI	4	10/3/1997	10/31/1997	10/13/1997	2	61.02	Alfred's Futterkiste
10702	ALFKI	4	10/13/1997	11/24/1997	10/21/1997	1	23.94	Alfred's Futterkiste
10835	ALFKI	1	1/15/1998	2/12/1998	1/21/1998	3	69.53	Alfred's Futterkiste
10952	ALFKI	1	3/16/1998	4/27/1998	3/24/1998	1	40.42	Alfred's Futterkiste
11011	ALFKI	3	4/9/1998	5/7/1998	4/13/1998	1	1.21	Alfred's Futterkiste
10926	ANATR	4	3/4/1998	4/1/1998	3/11/1998	3	39.92	Ana Trujillo Emparedados y helados
10759	ANATR	3	11/28/1997	12/26/1997	12/12/1997	3	11.99	Ana Trujillo Emparedados y helados
10625	ANATR	3	8/8/1997	9/5/1997	8/14/1997	1	43.9	Ana Trujillo Emparedados y helados
10308	ANATR	7	9/18/1996	10/16/1996	9/24/1996	3	1.61	Ana Trujillo Emparedados y helados
10365	ANTON	3	11/27/1996	12/25/1996	12/2/1996	2	22	Antonio Moreno Taquería
10573	ANTON	7	6/19/1997	7/17/1997	6/20/1997	3	84.84	Antonio Moreno Taquería
10507	ANTON	7	4/15/1997	5/13/1997	4/22/1997	1	47.45	Antonio Moreno Taquería
10535	ANTON	4	5/13/1997	6/10/1997	5/21/1997	1	15.64	Antonio Moreno Taquería
10682	ANTON	3	9/25/1997	10/23/1997	10/1/1997	2	36.13	Antonio Moreno Taquería
10677	ANTON	1	9/22/1997	10/20/1997	9/26/1997	3	4.03	Antonio Moreno Taquería

FIGURE 13.1: Linking customers and orders with relationships

Key Fields

As you can see in Figure 13.1, you implement relationships by inserting rows with matching values in the two related tables; the CustomerID column is repeated in both tables. The rows with a common value in their `CustomerID` field are related. In other words, the lines that connect the two tables simply indicate that there are two fields, one on each side of the relationship, with a common value. These two fields are called *key fields*. The `CustomerID` field of the Customers table is the *primary key*, because it identifies a single customer. The primary key must be unique and appear only in a single row of a table. The `CustomerID` field in the Orders table is the *foreign key* of the relationship, because it references another primary key. A foreign key can appear in multiple rows of a table. In this example, it will appear in as many rows of the Orders table as there are orders for the specific customer. (You'll read more about keys a bit later in this chapter.)

NOTE
This simple idea of linking tables based on the values of two columns that are common to both tables is at the heart of relational databases. It enables you to break your data into smaller units, the tables, yet be able to combine rows in multiple tables to retrieve and present the desired information.

Exploring the Northwind Database

So let's go back to the question we asked earlier: "Who are Nancy Davolio and Alfreds Futterkiste?" This is a great DBA interview question, and the answer lies in the Northwind database, which is a sample data database that ships with SQL Server. Nancy is the first record of the Employees table in Northwind. Alfreds is the first name that comes up in the Customers table. After you spend a lot of time working with Northwind, these names will inevitably come up over and over again. You'll get quite familiar with them by the time you finish this book. Before you examine the objects of databases in detail, let's look at the structure of the Northwind database. In the process, you'll develop a good feel for how relational databases are structured, and you'll find the discussion of the objects of a database easier to follow.

The Northwind database stores sales information: the customers and products of the Northwind Corporation and which products each customer has ordered, along with their prices, discounts, shipping information, and so on. Let's begin by examining the Northwind tables and their attributes. As you go through the tables, you'll learn the rationale that's used to help determine the Northwind database design. That way, you will have greater insight on both design and implementation.

The first step in database design is to break the information you want to store into smaller units, the tables, and establish relationships between them. To do so, you must identify the entities you want to store (products, customers, and so on) and create a table for each entity. As we've said, the best way to identify the entities is to find the nouns that represent your business case. More often than not, they will equate to the tables of your system.

For example, in the Northwind system, you need to track **orders** for your **customers** based on the **products** they choose. We've made the nouns bold for you, and as you can see, they correspond to the tables in the Northwind database.

You can picture a table as a grid: Each row corresponds to a different item, but all items have the same structure. *Columns* (also known as *domains*) define the structure of the table, and each column represents an *attribute* of the entity stored in the table. You can think of attributes as terms that describe your nouns (tables). A table that stores products has a column for the product's name, another column for the product's price, and so on. As you can see, all these columns use terms that describe the product. Each product is stored in a different row. As you add or remove products from the table, the number of rows changes, but the number of columns remains the same; they determine the information you store about each product. This representation of columns in a table is also referred to as the table's *schema*. We provide more details about schemas throughout this book. Although it is possible to add and remove columns after you've added data to them, you should do your best to anticipate database use beforehand.

Products Table

The Products table stores information about the products sold by the Northwind Corporation. This information includes the product's name, packaging information, price, and other relevant fields. Additionally, a unique, numeric ID number identifies each product in the table, as you can see in Figure 13.2.

Why not use the product name as the ID? Product names might be easier to remember, but you shouldn't use them because the product might not be unique and can change. Although SQL Server 2000 has new features (such as cascading updates) that can handle changes to the product name, each product name update would task the database with additional activity. Because the rows of the Products table are referenced by invoices, each product name change would entail a number of changes in the Order Details table (which is discussed later), as well. The product ID that identifies each product need not change; it's a numeric value used to reference a product. Therefore, by using a unique numeric value to identify each product, you can change the product's name without affecting any other tables.

ProductID	ProductName	SupplierID	CategoryID	QuantityPerUnit	UnitPrice	UnitsInStock	UnitsOnOrder
1	Chai	1	1	10 boxes x 20 bags	18	39	0
2	Chang	1	1	24 - 12 oz bottles	19	17	40
3	Aniseed Syrup	1	2	12 - 550 ml bottles	10	13	70
4	Chef Anton's Cajun Seasoning	2	2	48 - 6 oz jars	22	53	0
5	Chef Anton's Gumbo Mix	2	2	36 boxes	21.35	0	0
6	Grandma's Boysenberry Spread	3	2	12 - 8 oz jars	25	120	0
7	Uncle Bob's Organic Dried Pears	3	7	12 - 1 lb pkgs.	30	15	0
8	Northwoods Cranberry Sauce	3	2	12 - 12 oz jars	40	6	0
9	Mishi Kobe Niku	4	6	18 - 500 g pkgs.	97	29	0
10	Ikura	4	8	12 - 200 ml jars	31	31	0
11	Queso Cabrales	5	4	1 kg pkg.	21	22	30
12	Queso Manchego La Pastora	5	4	10 - 500 g pkgs.	30	86	0
13	Konbu	6	8	2 kg box	6	24	0
14	Tofu	6	7	40 - 100 g pkgs.	23.25	35	0
15	Genen Shouyu	6	2	24 - 250 ml bottles	15.5	39	0

FIGURE 13.2:   Each line in the Products table holds information about a specific product.

The SupplierID and CategoryID columns contain integer values that point to rows of two other tables, the Suppliers and Categories tables, respectively. These two tables contain information about the Northwind Corporation's suppliers and various product categories.

NOTE

Supplier information can't be stored in the Products table, because the same supplier's name and address would be repeated for multiple products. The category name isn't stored in the Products table because storing a number takes up less space than the category name itself.

Suppliers Table

Each product in the Northwind database has a supplier. Because the same supplier might offer more than one product, the supplier information is stored in a different table, and a common field, the `SupplierID` field, is used to link each product to its supplier. For example, the products Mishi Kobe Niku and Ikura are purchased from the same supplier, Tokyo Traders. Their `SupplierID` fields point to the same row in the Suppliers table, as shown in Figure 13.3.

Part IV

ProductID	ProductName	SupplierID	CategoryID	QuantityPerUnit	UnitPrice	UnitsInStock	UnitsOnOrder	ReorderLevel
1	Chai	1	1	10 boxes x 20 bags	18	39	0	10
2	Chang	1	1	24 - 12 oz bottles	19	17	40	25
3	Aniseed Syrup	1	2	12 - 550 ml bottles	10	13	70	25
4	Chef Anton's Cajun Seasoning	2	2	48 - 6 oz jars	22	53	0	0
5	Chef Anton's Gumbo Mix	2	2	36 boxes	21.35	0	0	0
6	Grandma's Boysenberry Spread	3	2	12 - 8 oz jars	25	120	0	25
7	Uncle Bob's Organic Dried Pears	3	7	12 - 1 lb pkgs.	30	15	0	10
8	Northwoods Cranberry Sauce	3	2	12 - 12 oz jars	40	6	0	0
9	Mishi Kobe Niku	4	6	18 - 500 g pkgs.	97	29	0	0
10	Ikura	4	8	12 - 200 ml jars	31	31	0	0
11	Queso Cabrales	5	4	1 kg pkg.	21	22	30	30
12	Queso Manchego La Pastora	5	4	10 - 500 g pkgs.	38	86	0	0
13	Konbu	6	8	2 kg box	6	24	0	5

SupplierID	CompanyName	ContactName
1	Exotic Liquids	Charlotte Cooper
2	New Orleans Cajun Delights	Shelley Burke
3	Grandma Kelly's Homestead	Regina Murphy
4	Tokyo Traders	Yoshi Nagase
5	Cooperativa de Quesos 'Las Cabras'	Antonio del Valle Saavedra
6	Mayumi's	Mayumi Ohno
7	Pavlova, Ltd.	Ian Devling
8	Specialty Biscuits, Ltd.	Peter Wilson
9	PB Knäckebröd AB	Lars Peterson

FIGURE 13.3: Linking products to their suppliers

Categories Table

In addition to having a supplier, each product belongs to a category. Categories are not stored with product names, but in a separate table, the Categories table, whose structure is shown in Figure 13.4. Again, each category is identified by a numeric value and has a name (the CategoryID and CategoryName fields, respectively). In addition, the Categories table has two more columns: Description, which contains text, and Picture, which stores a bitmap in the form of an image datatype.

The Products table (back in Figure 13.2) has a CategoryID column as well, which links each product to its category. By storing the categories in a separate table, you don't have to enter the actual name of the category (or its bitmap) along with each product. The CategoryID field of the Products table points to the product's category, and you can locate each product's category very quickly in the Categories table. You will learn how to do that in the "Database Objects" section later in this chapter.

Customers Table

The Customers table stores information about the company's customers. Before you can accept an order, you must create a new row in the Customers table with the customer's data (name, phone number, address, and so on), if one doesn't exist already. Each row in the Customers table represents a different customer and is identified by the CustomerID field. This field has a unique value for each row, similar to the ProductID field of the Products table. However, the CustomerID field is a five-character-long string, and not an integer (refer to Figure 13.1). As you can see, a primary key does not have to be a numeric value.

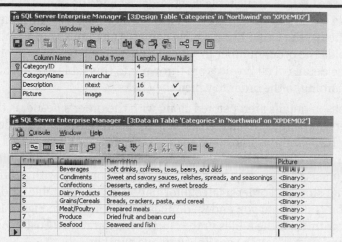

FIGURE 13.4: The structure of the Categories table (top) and the rows of the table (bottom)

Orders Table

The Orders table stores information (customer, shipping address, date of order, and so on) about the orders placed by Northwind's customers. The OrderID field, which is an integer value, identifies each order. Orders are numbered sequentially, so this field is also the order's number. As you will see in the "Database Objects" section later in this chapter, each time you append a new row to the Orders table, the value of the new OrderID field is generated automatically by the database. Moreover, you can set this feature on only one column set in the table. A *column set* can consist of one or more columns. When you define multiple columns as a primary key, you create a *composite key*. If you have already declared a primary key, you won't get any warning if you try to declare another primary key column set; SQL Server automatically reverts the previous primary key to a non-key column.

The Orders table is linked to the Customers table through the CustomerID field. By matching rows with identical values in their CustomerID fields in the two tables, you can combine a customer with their orders as shown previously in Figure 13.1.

Order Details Table

You probably have noticed that the Northwind database's Orders table doesn't store any details about the items ordered. This information is stored in the Order Details table. Each order is made up of one or more items, and each item has a price, a quantity, and a discount. In addition to these fields, the Order Details table contains an OrderID column, which holds the order number to which the detail line belongs. In other words, the details of all invoices are thrown into this table and are organized according to the order to which they belong.

The reason details aren't stored along with the order's header is that the Orders and Order Details tables store different entities. The order's header, which contains information about the customer who placed the order, the date of the order, and so on, is quite different from the information you must store for each item ordered. Try to come up with a different design that stores all order-related information in a single table, and you'll soon realize that you end up duplicating information. Figure 13.5 shows how three of the tables in the Northwind database (Customers, Orders, and Order Details) are linked to one another.

We should probably explain why the order's total doesn't appear in any table. To calculate an order's total, you must multiply the quantity by the price, taking into consideration the discount. If the order's total were stored in the Orders table, you'd be duplicating information. The order's total is already available for you. Because you can derive the total from existing columns, and those column values may change, there's no guarantee that the total values will always be correct. A good rule of thumb is to avoid storing calculated information in your database, because you can dynamically generate it.

Employees Table

This table holds employee information. The employees of the Northwind Corporation work on commission. When a sale is made, the ID of the employee who made the sale is recorded in the Orders table.

Shippers Table

Northwind Corporation uses three shippers. The Shippers table holds information about the shippers, and each shipper's ID appears in the Orders table, along with the order date, shipment date, address, and so on.

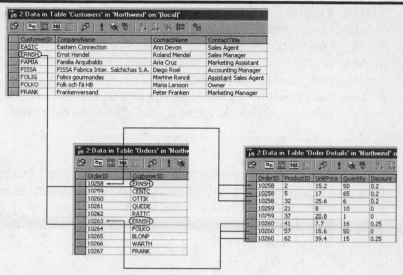

FIGURE 13.5: Linking customers to orders and orders to their details

Territories Table

Northwind uses the Territories table to capture the regions and cities that are associated with sales people. A separate *association table* called EmployeeTerritories enforces this relationship. We explain association tables in the "Database Objects" section later in this chapter.

Exploring the Pubs Database

The Pubs database is a sample database that comes with SQL Server, and it is used almost exclusively in the examples of SQL Server's online help. The tables of the Pubs database contain very few rows, but they were designed to demonstrate many of the operations you perform on databases. We use this database in many of the examples in this book.

As you did with the Northwind database, in this section you'll examine the tables of the Pubs database and the relationships between them. This will give you a prelude to the next section, where you'll examine relationships in more detail.

Titles Table

This table holds book information. Each book is identified by the title_id field, which is neither its ISBN nor an Identity field, but a made-up key. This table also contains a column named ytd_sales (year-to-date sales), which is the number of copies sold in the current year. Because there's no information about the total sales, you can assume that this column contains the running total of sales for each title.

Authors Table

This table contains author information. Each author is identified by the au_id field (which is the author's social security number), as well as contact information (phone number, address). The last column in the Authors table is the contract column, which indicates whether the author has a contract.

Titleauthor Table

This table connects titles to authors. Its rows contain pairs of title IDs and author IDs. In addition, it contains each author's order in a title, along with the author's royalty split per title. The title ID BU1032 appears twice in this table, which means that this title has two authors. The first one is the author with ID 409-56-7008, and his share of the royalties is 60 percent. The second author has the ID 213-46-8915, and his share of the royalties is 40 percent. The same person is the single author of another title (ID BU2075) and gets 100 percent of the royalties generated by this title.

Roysched Table

This table stores the information needed to calculate the royalties generated by each title. Books earn royalties according to a royalty schedule; the royalty escalates as sales increase. The title with ID BU1032 has a breakpoint at 5,000 copies. For the first 5,000 copies, it will make a royalty of 10 percent. After that, this percentage increases to 12 percent. The title with ID BU2075 has many breakpoints (10 percent for the first 1,000 copies, 12 percent for the next 2,000 copies, 14 percent for the next 2,000 copies, 16 percent for the next 3,000 copies, and so on). Figure 13.6 shows the relationships between the tables of the Pubs database that are used in calculating royalties. The royalty breakpoints are shown in Figure 13.7.

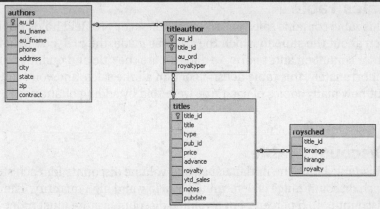

FIGURE 13.6:   Linking titles, authors, and royalties in the Pubs database

title_id	title	price	ytd_sales
BU1032	The Busy Executive's Database Guide	19.99	4095
BU1111	Cooking with Computers: Surreptitious Balance Sheets	11.95	3876
BU2075	You Can Combat Computer Stress!	2.99	18722
BU7832	Straight Talk About Computers	19.99	4095
MC2222	Silicon Valley Gastronomic Treats	19.99	2032
MC3021	The Gourmet Microwave	2.99	22246
MC3026	The Psychology of Computer Cooking	<NULL>	<NULL>
PC1035	But Is It User Friendly?	22.95	8780
PC8888	Secrets of Silicon Valley	20	4095
PC9999	Net Etiquette	<NULL>	<NULL>
PS1372	Computer Phobic AND Non-Phobic Individuals: Behavior Variations	21.59	375

au_id	title_id	au_ord	royaltyper
172-32-1176	PS3000	1	100
213-46-8915	BU1032	2	40
213-46-8915	BU2075	1	100
238-95-7766	PC1035	1	100
267-41-2394	BU1111	2	40
267-41-2394	TC7777	2	30
274-80-9391	BU7832	1	100
409-56-7008	BU1032	1	60

title_id	lorange	hirange	royalty
BU1032	0	5000	10
BU1032	5001	50000	12
PC1035	0	2000	10
PC1035	2001	3000	12
PC1035	3001	4000	14
PC1035	4001	10000	16
PC1035	10001	50000	18
BU2075	0	1000	10
BU2075	1001	3000	12
BU2075	3001	5000	14
BU2075	5001	7000	16
BU2075	7001	10000	18
BU2075	10001	12000	20
BU2075	12001	14000	22
BU2075	14001	50000	24
PS2091	0	1000	10
PS2091	1001	5000	12
PS2091	5001	10000	14

au_id	au_lname	au_fname	phone
172-32-1176	White	Johnson	408 496-7223
213-46-8915	Green	Marjorie	415 986-7020
238-95-7766	Carson	Cheryl	415 548-7723
267-41-2394	O'Leary	Michael	408 286-2428
274-80-9391	Straight	Dean	415 834-2919
341-22-1782	Smith	Meander	913 843-0462
409-56-7008	Bennet	Abraham	415 658-9932
427-17-2319	Dull	Ann	415 836-7128

FIGURE 13.7:   Applying the relationships of Figure 13.6 to some actual data

pub_info Table

This table holds information about the publishers. Each publisher is identified in the pub_id field, and the same value is repeated in the Titles table.

Stores Table

This table stores the names and addresses of a number of bookstores to which sales are made. Each store is identified by a store ID (stor_id field). This table is linked to the Sales table.

Sales Table

This table contains sales information. The `stor_id` field holds information about the store to which the sale was made, the `ord_num` field is the order's number, and `title_id` and `qty` are the title and quantity sold. Unfortunately, this table doesn't contain all the sales, and you can't find out how many copies of each title were sold by adding quantities in this table.

Discounts Table

This table holds the initial, usual, and volume discounts for each store. Each discount range is determined by a low and high quantity. The initial discount is 10.5 percent. For a volume discount, a store must order 100 or more copies. In addition, you can store specific discounts for each store in this table.

The remaining tables of the Pubs database have to do with employees and jobs and are not used in this book's examples. The Employees table holds personnel information, and the Jobs table holds job descriptions.

Understanding Relations

In a database, each table has a field with a unique value for every row. This field is marked with a key icon in front of its name, as you can see back in Figure 13.4, and it is the table's *primary key*.

The primary key does not have to be a meaningful entity, because in most cases there's no single field that's unique for each row. The primary key need not resemble the entity it identifies. The only requirement is that primary keys are unique in the entire table. You can even have more than one column serving as a primary key, which is referred to as a *composite key*. Keep in mind that the combined values of a composite key must be unique.

In most designs, you use an integer as the primary key. To make sure they're unique, you can even let the DBMS generate a new integer for each row added to the table. Each table can have one primary key only, and this field can't be Null.

The references to primary keys in other tables are called *foreign keys*. Foreign keys need not be unique (in fact, they aren't), and any field can serve as a foreign key. What makes a field a foreign key is that it matches the primary key of another table. The `CategoryID` field is the primary key of the Categories table, because it identifies each category. The

CategoryID field in the Products table is the foreign key, because it references the primary key in the Categories table. The same CategoryID might appear in many rows in the Products table, because many products can belong to the same category. When you relate the Products and Categories tables, for example, you must also make sure of the following:

► Every product added to the foreign table must point to a valid entry in the primary table. If you are not sure which category the product belongs to, you can leave the CategoryID field of the Products table empty. The primary keys, however, can't be Null.

► No rows in the Categories table should be removed if there are rows in the Products table pointing to the specific category. This will make the corresponding rows of the Products table point to an invalid category.

These two restrictions would be quite a burden on the programmer if the DBMS didn't protect the database against actions that could impair its integrity. The integrity of your database depends on the validity of the relations. Fortunately, all DBMSs can enforce rules to maintain their integrity. You'll learn how to enforce rules that guarantee the integrity of your database in the "Database Integrity" section later in this chapter.

Querying Relational Databases

Now let's consider the most common operations you'd like to be able to perform on the Northwind database's tables. The process of retrieving data from tables is known as *querying,* and the statements you execute against a database to retrieve selected rows are called *queries.* These statements are written in Structured Query Language (SQL), which is the development language used to program in SQL Server. In this section, you'll look at a few simple queries and how the DBMS combines rows from multiple tables to return the data you're interested in.

Retrieving a Customer's Orders

This is probably the most common operation you would perform on a database such as Northwind. To retrieve a customer's orders, start with the customer's ID and locate all the lines in the Orders table whose CustomerID field matches the CustomerID field of the selected row in the Customers table. To retrieve the customer's orders, the DBMS must search the Orders table with its foreign key. To help the DBMS with this operation, you should index the Orders table by using the CustomerID field. Both versions of the Northwind database define an index on this field. We discuss indexes in the "Database Objects" section later in this chapter.

Retrieving the Products for a Category

This example is a great way to understand how relationships work. The CategoryID field in the Categories table is the primary key, because it identifies each row in the table. Each category has a unique CategoryID, which can be repeated many times in the Products table. The CategoryID field in the Products table is the foreign key.

When you look up products, you want to be able to quickly locate the category to which they belong. You read the value of the CategoryID field in the Products table, locate the row in the Categories table with the same value in the CategoryID column, and voila!—you have matched the two tables. You can also search the Products table for products that belong to a specific category. You start with the ID of a category and then locate all the rows in the Products table with a CategoryID field that matches the selected ID. The relationship between the two tables links each row of the first table to one or more rows of the second table.

Here is a simple T-SQL statement that retrieves a list of products for the "Seafood" category:

```
SELECT Products.ProductName from Products, Categories
   WHERE Categories.CategoryName = 'Seafood' AND
   Products.CategoryID = Categories.CategoryID
```

NOTE

The operation of matching rows in two (or more) tables based on their primary and foreign keys is called a *join*. Joins are basic operations in manipulating tables. You may also see the word JOIN used in some queries, although this more generic version of a JOIN will work with Oracle, as well as SQL Server.

Calculating the Total for Each Order

The Orders table doesn't contain the total for each order—and it shouldn't. The totals must be calculated directly from the details. As mentioned earlier, databases shouldn't duplicate information, and storing the totals in the Orders table would be a form of duplication; you'd duplicate the information that's already present in another table. Had you stored the totals along with each order, then every time you changed a detail line, you'd have to change a row in the Orders table as well.

To calculate an order's total, the DBMS must search the Order Details table with its foreign key (OrderID), multiply quantities by prices, and add the results for all rows that belong to the specific order (it must also take into consideration the discount). To help the DBMS with this operation, you should index the Order Details table on its OrderID field. The Northwind database defines an index on the OrderID field to allow fast retrieval of orders based on the OrderID.

Calculating the Total for Each Customer

This operation is similar to totaling an order, but it uses three tables. Start with the customer's ID and select all the rows in the Orders table whose CustomerID field matches the ID of the specific customer. This is a list with the IDs of the orders placed by the selected customer. Then scan all the rows of the Order Details table whose OrderID field is in this list, multiply quantities by prices, and then add those results.

DATABASE OBJECTS

Now that you've been introduced to the basic concepts (and objects) of a relational database by means of examples, you should have a good idea of what a relational database is. You understand how data is stored in separate tables in the database and how the tables are linked to one another through relationships. You also know how relationships are used to execute complicated queries that retrieve data from multiple tables. You might have questions about specific attributes and techniques, which are addressed in the following sections of this chapter. Let's begin our detailed discussion of the objects of a relational database with the most basic objects, tables.

Tables

A *table* is a collection of rows with the same structure that stores information about an entity such as a person, an invoice, a product, and so on. Each row contains the same number of columns, and each column can store data of the same datatype. You can think of a table as a grid that stores records, much like a spreadsheet.

A DBMS such as SQL Server doesn't store tables in separate files. All the data resides in a single file, along with auxiliary information required by the DBMS to access the data quickly. In reality, the DBMS uses more space to store the auxiliary information than for the data itself. The tables in a database are an abstraction; they form a conceptual model of the data. This is how we, humans, view the database. Tables don't reflect the actual structure of the data in the database. Instead, they reflect the logical entities in the database, and the relations between tables reflect actions (products are *purchased,* customers *place* orders, and so on).

Internally, every DBMS stores information in a proprietary format, and you need not know anything about this format. In effect, this is one of the requirements of the relational database model: *The physical structure might change, but these changes shouldn't affect how you see the database.* For example, SQL Server databases are physically stored with a Master Data File extension (.mdf). Microsoft might change the physical structure of the data in an MDF file, but SQL Server will still see tables and indexes, it will still be able to relate tables to each other by using common field values (the primary and foreign keys), and your applications will keep working. You will see the same tables, the same SQL statements will retrieve the same data, and you won't even notice the difference (there will be new features, of course, but existing applications will continue to work without any modifications).

CUSTOMERS AND SUPPLIERS: SAME ENTITIES, DIFFERENT FUNCTION

You will notice that the Northwind database's Customers and Suppliers tables have the same structure. As far as the operations of an application are concerned, customers and suppliers are two separate entities, and there's no overlap between the two. This is a rather unusual situation, where two different entities have the same (or nearly the same) structure.

Keep in mind that Northwind is a sample database. In a real-world situation, the two tables might not be totally isolated, because the same company might act both as a supplier and as a customer. In other words, it might not only sell to your company, but buy from it as well. In some instances, using a single table for customers and suppliers might make sense. This approach can complicate the programming a little, but it simplifies operations from a user's point of view. If you don't know that a supplier is also a customer, you might end up paying for the items you purchase regularly and never know

CONTINUED ➡

that the other party is not keeping up with their obligations. There are other practical reasons for treating both customers and suppliers as a single entity, such as preferring a supplier who is also a good customer of yours.

Although this approach makes logical sense and might improve the performance of ad hoc reporting, you should always keep scalability in mind. If you expect to have another entity, such as Distributors, it might make sense to keep the tables separate. Keeping the tables separate will allow for looser coupling of your entities, thereby increasing your scalability. Many articles on the Web can give you data design patterns that can help you map your object relationships back to your database.

Creating Tables

To create a table, you must specify its structure by declaring its columns: specify how many columns the table has, their names, and their types. Generally, no matter what DBMS you're using, here's how tables are created:

1. Make up a name for the table. Table names can be quite long (128 characters, maximum), so you should name them after the entity they represent. Table names, as well as column names, can include spaces as long as you enclose them in a pair of square brackets ([Order Details], [Sales in Europe], and so on) in your code. SQL Server Enterprise Manager will automatically add the brackets for you behind the scenes.

SHOULD YOU USE NAMING CONVENTIONS?

Naming standards make it easier for other developers to work with your database. Many corporations will provide development guidelines to follow. Although Northwind doesn't follow a strict naming convention, you should stick with a consistent naming convention when designing your database. Here are some sample naming conventions that you might find effective when you create your table structure.

CONTINUED ➡

Part IV

Naming Tables   You should name your table as a singular, lower-case noun. Although Northwind doesn't follow this convention, it is a generally accepted practice. Keep in mind that a SQL Server database can be case sensitive, depending on installation settings. So two tables called ORDERS and Orders can exist in the same database.

Intersection tables (also known as *crossover*, *linking*, or *association tables*) are used to store many-to-many relationships. You should name an intersection table after the two tables that they connect. For example, if you have an intersection table for Order and Item, your table should be named OrderItem. You will learn more about many-to-many relationships later, in the "Establishing Relationships" subsection.

Naming Columns   Although SQL Server supports the use of spaces in a name (enclosed in square brackets), try to avoid them. If your column is a primary or foreign key, distinguish it with an *ID* suffix for easier readability. If possible, use the same name for the foreign key as the primary key. If you are pointing to more than one table that has the same primary key name, then use the referenced table name as a prefix for the foreign key.

Casing   The .NET Framework embraces the support of *camel casing* to separate words. Camel casing keeps the first word as lowercase, uppercasing the rest (for example, orderItem). However, in database structures, *Pascal casing* is the generally accepted practice. This involves title casing your entities (for example, OrderItem). If you need to increase readability due to long names or duplication, underscores can be used. For example, if you have an intersection table for Order and OrderItem, you would name your table Order_OrderItem. It really doesn't matter which standard you choose, as long as your development team is using the same standard consistently.

2. Make up a name for each column of the table. Columns are the attributes of the entity represented by the table. Think of the items that uniquely describe your table when you

determine your columns. For example, the columns of a table that stores customers should probably contain a customer's name, address, phone numbers, electronic address, and so on. Each column must have a name with a maximum length of 128 characters (for SQL Server databases). You can have up to 1,024 columns in a table.

TIP

If you can, limit your column names to 30 characters or fewer. Some SQL Server utilities, such as the isql utility, will truncate the name of a column to 30 characters. The same thing will happen if you are using ODBC drivers from SQL Server 6.5 or earlier.

3. Decide the datatype for each column. Because different columns store different types of information, the value should match the column type. A column that stores quantities should be defined as Integer, whereas a column that stores prices should be defined as Currency. Likewise, a column that stores dates should be defined accordingly. By default, SQL Server 2000 will use the datatype char. You will learn more about datatypes later in this section.

That's all it takes to design a simple table. If later you decide that you need an additional column, you can always add one without affecting the structure, or the content, of the existing ones.

TIP

Deleting a column is also referred to as dropping a column. Be careful when dropping columns from a database that's already in production. Although SQL Server 2000 now supports robust features for replicated data, such as maintaining data schema in the subscriber databases, you have to do it in a very specific way. Moreover, you can't drop columns if there is full-text indexing enabled on that column.

When you create a new table, a grid with the names and the attributes of the fields is displayed. Figure 13.8 shows the table design grid for SQL Server 2000. Each row in the grid corresponds to a table column.

Part IV

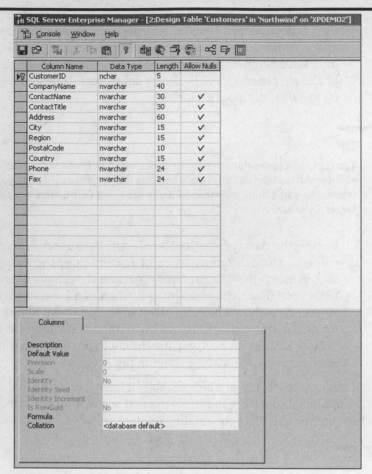

FIGURE 13.8:   Designing a table in SQL Server's Enterprise Manager

Determining Column Datatypes

Different DBMSs use different names for the datatypes they support, yet they support all the basic datatypes according to standards published by the American National Standards Institute (ANSI) and the International Organization for Standardization (ISO). In SQL Server, you select the column's datatype—one of the values shown in the first column of Table 13.1—from a drop-down list. When you program against your database by using ADO.NET, the SQL Server datatypes equate to .NET Framework types, rather than the constants you once used with ADO 2.*x*.

The .NET Framework types don't apply only to SQL Server; they are independent of their data source. For those of you who have worked with ADO 2.x, we have included the list of ADO constants for comparison. This table will help you understand the conversion between ADO 2.x, and ADO.NET and will help you understand how they relate back to OLE DB provider types, such as SQL Server.

TABLE 13.1: SQL Server Datatypes, .NET Framework Types, and ADO Constants

SQL SERVER	.NET FRAMEWORK TYPES	ADO 2.x CONSTANT
bigint	Int64	adBigInt
binary	Byte[]	adBinary
bit	Boolean	adBoolean
char	String Char[]	adChar
datetime	DateTime	adDBTimeStamp
decimal	Decimal	adNumeric
float	Double	adDouble
image	Byte[]	adVarbinary
int	Int32	adInteger
money, smallmoney	Decimal	adCurrency
nchar, nvarchar, ntext	String Char[]	adWChar
numeric	Decimal	adNumeric
real	Single	adSingle
smalldatetime	DateTime	adTimeStamp
smallint	Int16	adSmallInt
sql_variant	Object	adVariant
text	String Char[]	adChar
timestamp	Byte[]	adBinary
tinyint	Byte[]	adVarbinary

Part IV

TABLE 13.1 continued: SQL Server Datatypes, .NET Framework Types, and ADO Constants

SQL SERVER	.NET FRAMEWORK TYPES	ADO 2.x CONSTANT
uniqueidentifier	Guid	adGUID
varbinary	Byte[]	adVarBinary
varchar	String	adChar
	Char[]	

NEW SQL SERVER 2000 DATATYPES

SQL Server 2000 has introduced several new datatypes, most of which have serious advantages if you are considering making the move from SQL Server 7 code to SQL Server 2000. Here are a few pointers:

▶ The bigint datatype is a 64-bit integer that you can use when your integers exceed the traditional maximum integer size. Note an important caveat: SQL Server will not convert the other Integer types to bigint, so if you want to get a row count, you'll have to use the new SQL function ROWCOUNT_BIG, which returns a datatype of bigint. Use bigint judiciously, because it takes up 8 bytes of storage capacity, versus the 4 bytes used by the int datatype.

▶ You should use the nchar, nvarchar, and ntext datatypes only when your application needs to support Unicode. (Unicode format is often used for non-English data storage.) Using Unicode support increases the size of your traditional char, varchar, and ntext values, so use these datatypes sparingly.

▶ The sql_variant datatype converts to an Object type in the .NET Framework. It works almost like the Variant datatype in VB6, except that it doesn't support all the SQL datatypes, such as text or image. It is useful with the new SQL Server 2000

CONTINUED ➡

feature, user-defined functions. As with `bigint`, be careful when using the `sql_variant` datatype because it adversely affects performance. Another caveat is that `sql_variant` cannot be part of any keys or computed columns.

Another new feature of SQL Server 2000 is the `table` datatype. The `table` datatype works as a local variable for storing rows and can be used in lieu of temporary tables. It cannot be used for column datatypes. Unlike temporary tables, the `table` datatype is not written to the `tempdb` database and is instead stored in memory. Temporary tables cause performance degradation, which can be avoided by judicious use of the `table` datatype.

You can also define *user-defined datatypes*. You can use the SQL Server 2000 datatypes as the base type for your own user-defined datatypes. For example, you could create a special zip code datatype based on the `char` datatype and name it accordingly. In the Pubs database, a user-defined datatype is used to represent the employee ID as a `char` datatype with a length of nine characters. You can see this user-defined datatype, `empid`, from the SQL Server Enterprise Manager in the User Defined Datatypes folder.

As you can see, there are many types from which to choose. Here are some tips that can help you decide the best datatype to use:

▶ Always choose the smallest datatype to hold your data. For example, choose the `tinyint` instead of the `int` if you are storing only numbers 0 through 255. This not only reduces the amount of data you pass across the network, but also gives you more room in your data pages to store data rows and indexes. *Data pages* are 8KB units of storage in SQL Server.

▶ If you have a large string that has fewer than 8,000 characters, use the `varchar` datatype instead of the `text` datatype because you will have better performance, with less overhead.

▶ Only use the *n*-prefixed datatypes (for example, `nvarchar`, `nchar`, `ntext`) if you need to support Unicode, because they take up more space and will slow down your server performance.

► Use varchar instead of char if you expect considerable changes in the length of your values. Although the varchar datatype has more overhead, it can ultimately save more space, which will increase your performance. However, if you don't have much variation in the length, use the char datatype because it will speed up processing.

NOTE

Prior to SQL Server 2000, larger datatypes were stored outside the row, on a separate data page. SQL Server would store a pointer in the row, rather than the actual data. Now, you can specify the new "text in row" property so that your image, ntext, and text datatypes are stored with the data row. If you expect your data to be small for these datatypes, definitely choose this option, because you will get faster performance and use less storage space.

Datatypes are much richer in ADO.NET, providing greater interoperability, because they inherently support XML text streams rather than proprietary and binary COM datatypes. ADO.NET datatypes also improve performance because they eliminate the overhead of COM marshalling when transmitting data across the network. We discuss what goes on "under the covers" in detail in Chapter 14, "A First Look at ADO.NET."

Entering Data into Tables

There are many ways to enter data into a database's tables. You can use SQL statements; the INSERT statement appends a new row to a table and sets its fields to the value specified with the command. You can also open the actual table and edit it. Just right-click the name of a SQL server and choose Open Table ➤ Return All Rows from the shortcut menu. Of course, you can write applications that enable users to edit tables through a custom interface, such as Windows Forms or Web Forms. Obviously, this is the recommended method, because it enables you to validate the data and protect the database against user mistakes. You'll find a lot of information in this book on building practical, functional user interfaces with Visual Basic .NET and ASP.NET.

Null Values

If you're not familiar with database programming, you probably haven't used Null values yet, and you'll be surprised how important Null values are to databases. A *Null value* means that the actual field value is unknown. A numeric field with a zero value is not Null. Likewise, a blank string is not a Null value either. Nulls were introduced to deal with incomplete or exceptional data, and they should be handled in a special manner. A field that has not been assigned a value is considered incomplete. If this field is involved in an operation, the result of the operation is considered exceptional, because it's neither zero nor a blank string. When a new row is created, all of its nullable columns are set to Null, and unless you specify a value, they remain Null. You can modify this default behavior by requesting that certain columns can't be Null. If you attempt to add a new row with a Null value in a column that's not allowed to accept Nulls, the database will reject the insertion. The same will happen if you edit a row and set to Null the value of a column that's not allowed to accept Nulls. Another option is to set a *default definition* on that column. Default definitions enable you to pre-populate the column value for a new row.

Primary key fields (the fields that link tables to one another), for example, can never be Null. To specify that any other field cannot accept the Null value, you must set the Allow Nulls property in SQL Server to False.

If your tables contain Null values, you should be aware of how the DBMS handles them. When you total the values of a column with the SUM() function, Null values are ignored. If you count the rows with the COUNT() function, the Null fields are also ignored. The same is true for the AVG() function, which calculates the average value. If it treated the Null values as zeros, then the average would be wrong. The AVG() function returns the average of the fields that are not Null. If you want to include the Null values in the average, you must first replace them with the zero numeric value.

TIP

Where it is possible, limit the use of Nulls. Nulls can increase the complexity of your queries and adversely affect the performance of your database. The use of Nulls forces you to check for Nulls in your SQL statements so you don't perform operations on invalid data. In addition, comparison of Null values can result in an UNKNOWN return, which adds a third element of logic to a TRUE/FALSE evaluation. Moreover, SQL Server 2000 will use more processing power and storage to store and process Nulls. This is because Nulls are treated as fixed-length datatypes. For example, if you would like to have a nullable char datatype, opt to use the varchar datatype instead, especially if you have large variations in the length of your data.

Null values are so important in working with databases that SQL recognizes the keywords IS NULL and IS NOT NULL. (SQL statements are not case sensitive, but this book uses uppercase so that you can quickly spot the SQL keywords in the examples.) To exclude the Null values in an SQL statement, use the following clause:

```
WHERE column_name IS NOT NULL
```

Here's a simple example of an SQL statement that retrieves the customers who have a postal code, ignoring those who don't:

```
SELECT CompanyName, Phone
FROM Customers
WHERE PostalCode IS NOT NULL
```

To retrieve the customers without a postal code, use a statement similar to this:

```
SELECT CompanyName, Phone
FROM Customers
WHERE PostalCode IS NULL
```

Indexes

OK, so you've created a few tables and have entered some data into them. Now the most important thing you can do with a database is extract data from it (or else, why store the information in the first place?). And we don't mean view all the customers or all the products. You'll rarely browse the rows of a single table. Instead, you should be interested in summary information that will help you make business decisions. You'll need answers to questions like "What's the most popular product in California?" or "What's the month with the largest sales for a specific product?" and so on. To retrieve this type of information, you must combine multiple tables. To answer the first question, you must locate all the customers in California, retrieve their orders, total the quantities of the items they have purchased, and then select the product with the largest sum of quantities. As you can guess, a DBMS must be able to scan the tables and locate the desired rows quickly. An index is nothing more than a mechanism for speeding up searches.

SQL Server uses a special technique, called *indexing*, to locate information very quickly. This technique requires that the data or data references be maintained in some order. This works just like the index at the back of this book, which uses page numbers as references. As you will see, the indexed rows in a database need not be in a specific physical order, as long as you can retrieve the references in a specific order. If you want to retrieve the name of the category of a specific product, the references to the rows of the Categories table must be ordered according to the CategoryID field. CategoryID links each row in the Products table to the corresponding row in the Categories table.

To search for a value in an ordered list, the DBMS compares the middle element of the list with the value you're looking for. If the value is larger than the middle element, you know that you need not search in the first (upper) half of the list. The same process is repeated with the bottom half of the list. Again, it compares the value with the middle element in the remaining list, and rejects one half of the list again. This process repeats until you're left with a single element. This element must be the one you're looking for.

This searching scheme is called a *binary search*, and it's the basic idea behind indexing. To get an idea of the efficiency of this method, consider a list with 1,024 elements. After the first comparison, the list is reduced to 512 elements. After the second search, the list is reduced to 256 elements. After the 10th comparison, the list is reduced to a single element. It takes only 10 comparisons to locate an element in a list with 1,024 elements. If the list had a million elements, it would take just 20 comparisons.

Fortunately, you don't have to maintain the rows of the tables in any order yourself. The DBMS does it for you. You simply specify that a table maintains the rows in a specific order according to a column's value, and the DBMS will take over. SQL Server supports two types of indexing schemas: *clustered index* and *non-clustered indexes.* A clustered index maintains the actual data in order, whereas a non-clustered index does not maintain a specific order on the data. The DBMS can maintain multiple indexes for the same table. You might wish to search the products by name and supplier. It's customary to search for a customer by name, city, zip code, country, and so on. To speed up the searches, you maintain an index for each field you want to search.

TIP

The best way to come up with an index is to examine the WHERE clause of your SQL statement. Generally, the items that appear in a WHERE clause are good candidates for indexing because they are used as search criteria. Foreign keys are often a good candidate for indexes, because they are often referenced to extract related data. In addition, the SQL Profiler and Index Tuning Wizard can help you identify areas that need indexing. SQL Server 2000 Query Analyzer introduces a new tool that uses a graphical interface to manage indexes.

Part IV

The binary search algorithm just described is a simplified description of how a DBMS locates items in an ordered list. As you have probably guessed, searching an ordered list is the easy part. The difficult part is to make sure that each time a new row is added (or edited), it's inserted in the proper place so that the table's rows are always ordered. The details of maintaining ordered lists are far more complicated. SQL Server uses a data structure known as *Balanced Trees (B-Trees)* to maintain the rows of a table in order at all times and search them. You need not understand what B-Trees are, because this is exactly what a DBMS does for you: it frees you from low-level details and enables you to focus on data, rather than the actual organization of the data on the disk.

The DBMS doesn't actually sort the rows of a table. It keeps a list of numbers, which reflects the order of the elements sorted according to a field. This list is the *index.* After a table has been indexed, every time you add a new row to the table, the table's indexes are updated accordingly. If you need to search a table in many ways, you can maintain multiple indexes on the same table. Keep in mind, you can have only one clustered index and up to 249 non-clustered indexes on a table. Indexes take additional storage room, so use them judiciously.

Indexes are manipulated by the DBMS, and all you have to do is define them. Every time a new row is added, or an existing row is deleted or edited, the table's indexes are automatically updated. You can use the index at any time to locate rows very quickly. Practically, indexes enable you to instantly select a row based on an indexed field. When searching for specific rows, the DBMS will automatically take into consideration any index that can speed the search.

EFFICIENCY ISSUES

Tables are not static objects. Most tables in a database change constantly: New rows are added, and existing rows are deleted or edited. This also means that the DBMS must constantly update the table indexes. This process can become quite a burden, so you shouldn't create too many indexes. On the other hand, indexes speed up lookup operations enormously. So, where do you draw the line?

One of the many tools that comes with SQL Server 7 and SQL Server 2000 is the Index Tuning Wizard, which helps you decide

CONTINUED ➡

which indexes to keep and which ones to drop. The Index Tuning Wizard monitors the performance of the database, logs the necessary statistics, and tells you which indexes are responsible for most of the performance. These are the indexes you need in your database; the rest can be dropped at the price of slowing down some queries that are not used as frequently. The wizard can also create a script with the changes it suggests and implement them immediately. Keep in mind that indexes that worked well for previous versions of SQL Server might not be efficient for SQL Server 2000. Use the wizard to help resolve such issues.

Views

In addition to tables, SQL Server 2000 supports views. A *view* is a virtual table: It looks and behaves just like a table (and in some cases, it can be updated too), but standard views do not exist as an object in the database. Views derive from *base tables*. Views come to life when you request them, and they're released when they're no longer needed. Any operations you perform on a view automatically translate into operations on the base table(s) from which the view is derived.

NOTE

SQL Server 2000 (Developer and Enterprise editions) enhances views by now allowing you to create *indexed* views. Indexed views work similarly to the table indexing we talked about in the previous section. Unlike standard views, which store only the source code, indexed views are stored as objects in the database. SQL Server treats these indexed views the same way it treats the base tables. A good time to use indexed views is when you are working with large DataSets or multiple tables. You can improve performance by creating an index on the view to speed up processing, because now the view doesn't have to generate on the fly. Indexed views offer a fantastic benefit that you might not have considered. Even if you don't explicitly reference a view, when you pull data from a base table, SQL Server 2000 will determine and choose the fastest index—whether it comes from the base table or any derived views. To really take advantage of this new feature, try to select indexed views that can be used by many of your queries.

Views enhance the security of the database. Consider a personnel table, which stores information about employees, including their salaries and other sensitive information. Although most of the information is public (names, telephone extensions, departments, the projects each employee is involved with, and so on), some fields should be restricted to authorized users only. While you could split the table into smaller ones, SQL Server enables you to create unique views and assign access rights to those views to selected user groups.

You can also use views to hide the complexity introduced by the normalization process and the relationships between tables. Users don't really care about normalization rules or relationships. They would rather see a list of customer names, their orders, and the actual product names. This information exists in the database, but it could be scattered in four tables: Customers, Orders, Order Details, and Products. By defining a view on the database, you can maintain a structure that eases your development, yet gives the users the "table" they would rather see.

Updating Tables and Views

Changes in the data of a view are reflected immediately to the underlying table(s). When the underlying tables change, however, these changes are not reflected immediately in the views based on them. Views are based on the data in the tables the moment the query was executed. You can think of them as a snapshot of time. A view that hides a few of its base table rows (or columns) can be updated, as long as it contains the primary key of the base table. (As we mentioned already, the primary key uniquely identifies a table's row. Without this piece of information, SQL Server wouldn't know which row to update.)

Some views cannot be updated. Views based on SQL statements that combine multiple tables and views that contain aggregate functions can't be updated. *Aggregate functions* such as AVG(), COUNT(), and MAX() are based on many rows, and SQL Server doesn't know which specific data row it must change.

Figure 13.9 shows a section of the Invoices view. (We hid many of the columns by setting their width to zero.) Start SQL Server's Enterprise Manager, open the Northwind database folder in the left pane, and click Views under the Northwind database name. The names of all the views defined for the database will be displayed in the right pane. To open a view, right-click on its name and select Open View ➢ Return All Rows from the shortcut menu.

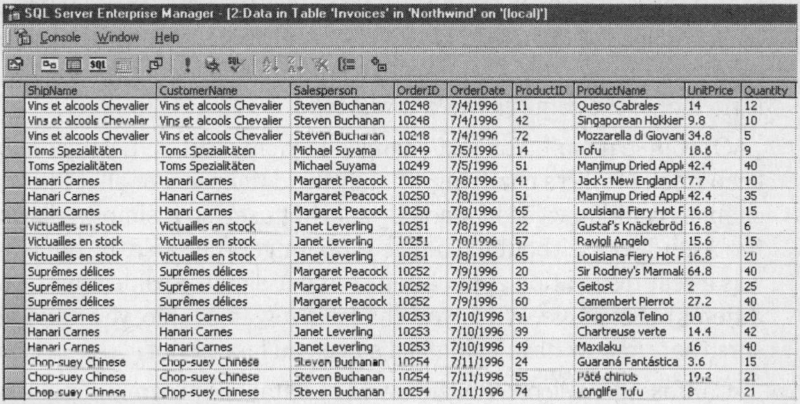

ShipName	CustomerName	Salesperson	OrderID	OrderDate	ProductID	ProductName	UnitPrice	Quantity
Vins et alcools Chevalier	Vins et alcools Chevalier	Steven Buchanan	10248	7/4/1996	11	Queso Cabrales	14	12
Vins et alcools Chevalier	Vins et alcools Chevalier	Steven Buchanan	10248	7/4/1996	42	Singaporean Hokkier	9.8	10
Vins et alcools Chevalier	Vins et alcools Chevalier	Steven Buchanan	10248	7/4/1996	72	Mozzarella di Giovani	34.8	5
Toms Spezialitäten	Toms Spezialitäten	Michael Suyama	10249	7/5/1996	14	Tofu	18.6	9
Toms Spezialitäten	Toms Spezialitäten	Michael Suyama	10249	7/5/1996	51	Manjimup Dried Appl	42.4	40
Hanari Carnes	Hanari Carnes	Margaret Peacock	10250	7/8/1996	41	Jack's New England (	7.7	10
Hanari Carnes	Hanari Carnes	Margaret Peacock	10250	7/8/1996	51	Manjimup Dried Appl	42.4	35
Hanari Carnes	Hanari Carnes	Margaret Peacock	10250	7/8/1996	65	Louisiana Fiery Hot F	16.8	15
Victuailles en stock	Victuailles en stock	Janet Leverling	10251	7/8/1996	22	Gustaf's Knäckebröd	16.8	6
Victuailles en stock	Victuailles en stock	Janet Leverling	10251	7/8/1996	57	Ravioli Angelo	15.6	15
Victuailles en stock	Victuailles en stock	Janet Leverling	10251	7/8/1996	65	Louisiana Fiery Hot F	16.8	20
Suprêmes délices	Suprêmes délices	Margaret Peacock	10252	7/9/1996	20	Sir Rodney's Marmale	64.8	40
Suprêmes délices	Suprêmes délices	Margaret Peacock	10252	7/9/1996	33	Geitost	2	25
Suprêmes délices	Suprêmes délices	Margaret Peacock	10252	7/9/1996	60	Camembert Pierrot	27.2	40
Hanari Carnes	Hanari Carnes	Janet Leverling	10253	7/10/1996	31	Gorgonzola Telino	10	20
Hanari Carnes	Hanari Carnes	Janet Leverling	10253	7/10/1996	39	Chartreuse verte	14.4	42
Hanari Carnes	Hanari Carnes	Janet Leverling	10253	7/10/1996	49	Maxilaku	16	40
Chop-suey Chinese	Chop-suey Chinese	Steven Buchanan	10254	7/11/1996	24	Guaraná Fantástica	3.6	15
Chop-suey Chinese	Chop-suey Chinese	Steven Buchanan	10254	7/11/1996	55	Pâté chinois	19.2	21
Chop-suey Chinese	Chop-suey Chinese	Steven Buchanan	10254	7/11/1996	74	Longlife Tofu	8	21

FIGURE 13.9:   The Invoices view displays the order details along with customer names and product names.

Try editing the data in the Invoices view to see how it behaves. Bring the CustomerName column into view, change the name *Hanari Carnes* into uppercase, and then move to another cell. The customer's name changes, not only in the open view, but in the base table as well. If you opened the Customers table, you would see that the changes have already been committed to the database. Yet, the remaining instances of the same name on the view didn't change. That's because the view isn't refreshed constantly. Because SQL Server doesn't maintain a "live" link to the database, it can't update the view every time.

Things can get even worse. Locate another instance of the same customer in the view and change the name to *Hanny Carnes*. As soon as you move to another cell, the following message will pop up:

```
Data has changed since the Results pane was last updated.
Do you want to save your changes now?
Click Yes to save your changes and update the database
Click No to discard your changes and refresh the
 Results pane
Click Cancel to continue editing
```

What's happened here? The name of the customer you read from the database was Hanari Carnes, and you changed it to uppercase. This change was committed to the Customers table. Then you attempted to change the name Hanari Carnes into something else again, and SQL Server attempted to update the Customers table for a second time. This time, SQL Server didn't find the name Hanari Carnes there; it had already been changed (to HANARI CARNES). And that's exactly what the message tells you. You have attempted to change a field, but its original value is no longer the same as when it was read.

Of course it isn't. You just changed it, right? But SQL Server doesn't keep track of who's changing what in the database. For all it knows, the changes could have been made by another user, so it simply tells you that the record you're about to change is no longer the same. Imagine if this was a seat reservation application. You'd assign the same seat to two different customers. When you change a row in a table, you must be sure that the row hasn't changed since you last read it.

Confusing? Welcome to the world of database programming! As you can understand, this behavior is not unique to views. It's a major issue in database programming known as *concurrency control.* In a multiuser environment, there's always a risk of two or more people attempting to update the same information at once. The behavior you just witnessed is actually a feature of the database: It lets you know that someone else has already changed the row you read. Otherwise, you'd have to implement the same logic from within your application. We've introduced you to one of the most troublesome aspects of database programming.

Establishing Relationships

After the information has been broken up logically into separate tables, you must establish relationships between the tables, which is the essence of the relational database model. To relate tables to each other, you use fields with common values.

Primary and Foreign Keys

Primary and foreign keys are one way of ensuring data integrity. The Categories table has a `CategoryID` field, which holds a value that identifies each category. This value must be unique for each row of the Categories table, and it's the table's primary key. The Products table also has a `CategoryID` field, which is set to the ID of the product's category. The two fields have the same name, but this is not a requirement. It's just a convenience. The mere existence of the two fields doesn't mean that the two tables are related to each other. You must specify how the tables will be related, as well as which field is the primary key and which field is the foreign key. As we already discussed, the primary key is unique to each row, while the foreign key may appear in more than one row. This relationship is called one-to-many, because a single row of the Categories table is usually pointed to by multiple rows of the Products table.

BE CAREFUL WHEN APPLYING FOREIGN KEYS

Be judicious in your use of foreign keys. Too many foreign keys can cause *deadlocking* because they not only lock the table that they reference, but they also make it hard for data to resolve itself. Deadlocking occurs when units of processing, or *threads*, hold onto resources, causing bottlenecks for the other threads waiting to use those same resources. SQL Server 2000 can identify and terminate deadlocks. Even so, you might not accomplish what you originally wanted to do. For example, if your DELETE query has to go through more than 16 foreign key validations, it will end up timing out, and you won't be able to delete the desired entry. You would end up with a deadlock on not only the table containing the foreign key, but also the table containing the primary key referenced by the foreign key. You might think that you could get around this by disabling the foreign key constraints, but unfortunately, you can do this only on INSERT and UPDATE statements.

Consider another caveat. If you would like to track who created your customer records, you could create a column in your Customers table called CreateUserID. This column stores the foreign key reference to UserID in the Users table. However, what if you also wanted to track who updates your customer data? It would be nice to add another foreign key column, UpdateUserID, that points to the UserID in the Users table. Unfortunately, SQL Server doesn't allow you to have more than one foreign key relationship between two tables. You could add some validation code to your INSERT statement, but that would really hinder performance. The other alternative is to make sure your application logic outside the database ensures that invalid IDs are not added.

Figure 13.10 shows how SQL Server depicts relationships between tables. To view the relationships between the tables of a database, start the Enterprise Manager and open the Northwind database in the left pane. Right-click the Diagrams icon under the database's name and select New Diagram. The Database Diagram Wizard pops up. Select the Orders and Customers tables from the available table list and finish the wizard. The Relationships diagram will appear in a new window. Each table is represented by a list box with the table's field names, and the relationships between tables are represented by arrows. On one end of the arrow is the key icon, which indicates the primary key. On the other end of the arrow is the infinity symbol, which indicates the table with the foreign key. The infinity symbol means that there can be many rows pointing to the row with the primary key.

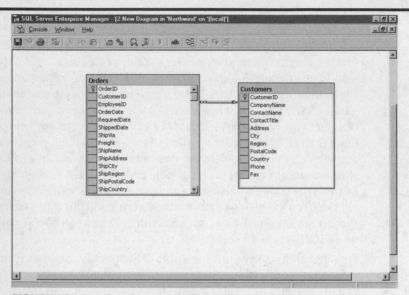

FIGURE 13.10: The `CustomerID` field in the Orders table is the foreign key, which points to the primary key in the Customers table.

Here's a simple SQL statement that retrieves the orders placed by the customer Alfreds Futterkiste:

```
SELECT * FROM Orders, Customers
WHERE Customers.CompanyName = 'Alfreds Futterkiste' AND
    Orders.CustomerID = Customers.CustomerID
```

This statement tells the DBMS to retrieve the rows of the Orders and Customers tables that match the following criteria:

▶ The customer's `CompanyName` field is the customer's name.

and

▶ The foreign key in the Orders table matches the primary key in the Customers table.

This query will return all the rows of the Orders and Customers tables whose `CustomerID` field is the same as the `CustomerID` field of the specified customer's row. Primary and foreign keys are used to match rows in two tables. (The asterisk is a special character that means "all the fields." You could have specified a comma-separated list of the desired fields in the place of the asterisk.)

You can use foreign keys to prevent deletions if there are related records, as already explained. Foreign keys are also useful to prevent inserts or updates to records if there is no parent record. For example, if you tried to insert an order detail to an order that didn't exist, foreign key constraints would prevent this from happening.

Viewing and Editing Relationships

You can modify the relationship from this same Relationships diagram. To delete a relationship, right-click the line that joins the two tables and select Delete Relationship From Database. To view or edit the properties of the relationship, again, right-click the line that joins the tables and select the Properties option. The Properties window specifies the primary and foreign keys, the relationship name, and some other options.

Identity and Identity Increment

SQL Server can automatically increment the value of the primary key every time you add a new row. SQL Server uses the term *Identity* for this datatype. You can specify the initial value of an Identity field and its increment amount by using the *Identity Seed* and the *Identity Increment* properties respectively. To use the Identity datatype, your column needs to be a numeric value such as `bigint`, `decimal`, `int`, `numeric`, `smallint`, or `tinyint`. Refer to the earlier section, "Database Objects," for an explanation of these datatypes.

To create the new value for an Identity field, the DBMS adds a value (usually 1, which is the default value) to the last value of this field in the same table. This operation is simple in principle, but it would be quite a task if you had to implement it on your own. With many users adding rows to the same table, you'd have to lock the table, read the last row's Identity value, add the proper increment, and then commit the newly added row.

GUIDs

As you can see in the Northwind example, the `CustomerID` is a string, created from the company name. Keep in mind that it is much easier to have an integer represent a primary key, because keeping an integer unique by incrementing the number is easier than ensuring that your algorithm for generating keys stays unique. Numeric IDs provide a unique identifier for a single record, making it much easier to merge disparate sources of data with minimal conflicts. However, they are certainly not globally unique.

Integers as primary keys are easy to use and very useful; however, they have limits, especially if you are dealing with heterogeneous data sources. An integer primary key is unique only to the table from which it was generated. Globally Unique Identifiers (GUIDs) should be used when you need an identifier across a database or multiple databases. A good example for using GUIDs is when you need to combine data from multiple databases into a single reporting system.

Lately, GUIDs have become popular as primary key datatypes. Microsoft has embraced the concept of GUIDs as primary keys in its release of Active Directory. This triggered an evolution from using numeric identity columns to using GUIDs.

In SQL Server, the `uniqueidentifier` datatype designates GUIDs. Keep in mind that SQL Server doesn't automatically generate these values for you. An easy way to program this is to designate a *default* on the column that uses the `NEWID()` function to generate a value for you.

More Complicated Relations

Not all relations can be resolved with a pair of primary and foreign keys. Let's say you're designing a database for storing book titles. The structure of the table with the titles is rather obvious. The relationship between titles and publishers is also obvious: Each title has a single publisher, and the same publisher might appear in multiple titles. The relationship between publishers and titles is called one-to-many. Conversely, the relationship between titles and publishers is called many-to-one, because multiple titles might point to the same publisher. One-to-many and many-to-one relationships interpret relationships in a similar fashion— both follow the order of the related tables when asserting the type of relationship.

But how about the relationship between titles and authors? Each book has a varying number of authors: Some books have no author, and others might have six authors. Likewise, the same author might have written more than one title. The relationship between titles and authors is called many-to-many. To establish a direct relationship between the Titles and Authors tables, some rows in the Titles table should point to many rows in the Authors table. Likewise, some rows in the Authors table should point to many rows in the Titles Table. To avoid this type of relationship in your design, introduce a new table, which is linked with a one-to-many relationship to the Titles table and a many-to-one relationship to the Authors table.

This example introduces an intermediate table between the Titles and Authors tables: the Titleauthor table, which contains one row per title-author pair, as shown in Figure 13.11. This table has a simple structure (you could say that it doesn't even contain any original information). It simply maps books to authors. If a book has three authors, you add three rows to the Titleauthor table. All rows have the same ISBN (the title's key) and the authors' ID keys.

Intermediate tables such as the Titleauthor table are common in database design. Practically, there's no other method of implementing many-to-many relations between tables.

TITLES

Title	ISBN
Mastering Foxpro 2.6 Special Edition	0-7821157-6-4
Mastering Alpha Four : Version 4	0-7821158-7-X
Mastering Paradox 5 for Windows	0-7821159-2-6
Programming Paradox 5 for Windows	0-7821159-3-4
Mastering Visual Basic 3/Book and Disk	0-7821160-5-1
Mastering Microsoft Visual C++ X Programming/Book and Disk	0-7821160-6-X
Understanding Sql	0-7821160-7-8
Programmer's Guide to Foxpro 2.6/Book and Disk	0-7821160-9-4
Novell's Guide to Network Security/Book and Disk	0-7821161-7-5
Mastering Windows Nt Server 3.5	0-7821162-2-1
Novell's Quickpath to Netware 4.1 Networks/Book and Disk	0-7021163-4-5
Mastering Visual Foxpro 3 Special	0-7821164-7-7
The Visual Foxpro 3 Codebook	0-7821164-8-5
Mosaic Access to the Internet/Book and Disk	0-7821165-6-6

TITLEAUTHOR

ISBN	Au_ID
0-7821160-5-1	2331
0-7821160-5-1	2532
0-7821160-6-X	456
0-7821160-6-X	580
0-7821160-7-8	3934
0-7821160-7-8	7920
0-7821160-9-4	3495
0-7821160-9-4	4504
0-7821161-7-5	9383
0-7821161-7-5	11625
0-7821162-2-1	9266
0-7821162-2-1	9314
0-7821162-2-1	9315
0-7821162-2-1	9316
0-7821163-4-5	12431

AUTHORS

Au_ID	Author
9289	Melenhorst, Glenn
9290	Bousquet, Michele
9303	Spuler, David A.
9308	Gehani, Narain
9310	Jones, R. S.
9314	Creegan, Elizabeth
9315	Anderson, Christa
9316	Minasi, Mark
9320	Motet, Gilles
9324	Dawe, C.M.

FIGURE 13.11: Connecting the Titles table to the Authors table with an intermediate table, the Titleauthor table

NORMALIZATION RULES

By now you have a good idea as to how relational databases are designed, and you could easily design a simple relational database yourself by using the information discussed earlier and your common sense. Most important, you should be able to understand how information is stored in a database by looking at its relational diagram.

However, there are a few rules in relational database design, known as the *normalization rules*. These rules will help you design a normalized database, or at least verify your design. A database is *normalized* if it doesn't repeat information and doesn't exhibit update and delete anomalies. Although the number of these rules varies, the basic normalization rules are just three: the first, second, and third normalization rules. Don't be surprised, however, if you find as many as half a dozen normalization rules listed within a particular database standard.

A table normalized according to the first rule is said to be in *first normal form (1NF)*. A table normalized according to the second rule is said to be in *second normal form (2NF)*. Notice that a table must be in 1NF before you can apply the second normalization rule. Finally, a table that's in 2NF can be normalized according to the third rule, in which case it's said to be in *third normal form (3NF)*. Higher normal forms are often used with very specific and rare situations, which most programmers handle on an individual basis.

TIP

Normalization applies to OLTP rather than OLAP systems. However, even in an OLTP system, there is a trade-off between normalization and performance. You might sometimes want to de-normalize some of your tables if you find that the tables are accessed for read-only purposes and the performance isn't satisfactory.

Database Design Errors

To help you understand the need for database normalization, this section illustrates a few common mistakes in database design. These mistakes are so obvious that it doesn't take a degree in computer science to understand why and how to avoid them. Yet the same mistakes are repeated over and over. You'll find it easy to spot the mistakes in the example designs, which are small in size. In larger databases, even ones with a few dozen tables, it's not as simple to spot the same mistakes.

Let's start with the following simple table for storing information about books:

Table Title

```
ISBN    Title    Pages    Topic
```

This table seems perfectly good, until you decide to add a second topic to a title. A book about HTML could be classified under the category "programming," but also under the category "Internet." To add multiple topics, you'd have to repeat each title's data for each category:

```
0144489890    Total .NET    850    programming
0144489890    Total .NET    850    Internet
```

The problem with this table is that certain information is repeated (actually, most of the information is repeated). The primary objective in designing OLTP databases is to avoid duplication of information. To avoid this unnecessary duplication, you must move the topics to another table. Some of you might consider adding columns for multiple topics, but then you must make an (arbitrary) assumption as to the maximum number of topics per title and come up with a table like the following one:

Table Title

```
ISBN    Title    Pages    Topic1    Topic2    Topic3
```

This table is even worse. In trying to avoid duplicating the table's data, you've introduced duplication of information in the structure of the table itself. As you will see, the first rule in database design is to avoid groups of columns with information of the same type. If you decide to change the name of the "programming" category to something else, for example, "computer languages," you'd have to change too many rows, in too many places. Some titles might have "programming" under Topic1, others under Topic2, and so on.

Another common mistake people make is to create a Boolean flag. Often, as a database matures, more types are added. A lazy approach is to create a bunch of columns rather than a whole new table, as seen in the next example.

Table Title

```
ISBN Title Pages ProgrammingTopic InternetTopic
```

You end up with data that looks like the following:

```
0144489890    Total .NET    850    0 1
0144489890    Total .NET    850    1 0
```

But as you can already deduce, this isn't a very scalable design. As more topics are added, the actual design of the database will have to change.

To solve the problem of multiple columns of the same type, you introduce two new tables, as shown here:

Table Title

ISBN   Title   Pages

Table TitleTopic

ISBN   TopicID

Table Topic

TopicID   TopicName

This design uses a table that stores topics only. To change the description of a topic, you must change a single row in the Topic table. Topics are related to titles through the TitleTopic table, the link table. If a title must be classified under multiple topics, you insert multiple lines in the Title-Topic table. To find out the topics of a specific title, use its ISBN to search the TitleTopic table and extract the rows whose ISBN matches the ISBN of the book. You'll end up with none, one, or a few rows of the TitleTopic table. Use the TopicID of these lines to locate the topic(s) of the title. Sounds complicated? It's simpler than it sounds, because all tables are appropriately indexed, and the DBMS will perform the necessary searches for you.

Update and Delete Anomalies

Now drop the Topic column from your original table design and add some publication information. Here's the structure of another table that holds information about books:

Table Title

ISBN   Title   Pages   PubYear   Publisher   PubAddress

Notice that the publisher's address doesn't belong to the Title table. This structure can lead to two highly undesirable situations:

▶ If a publisher relocates, then you must change the address in not one, but hundreds, perhaps thousands, of records. This is known as an *update anomaly*. If you forget to change the publisher's address in a few records, the database will contain bad information. This situation can be avoided by moving the publishers to a different table.

▶ Even worse, if you delete the last book of a publisher, you will lose all the information about the specific publisher. This situation is known as a *delete anomaly*, and it can also be avoided by moving the publishers to a different table.

Here's a better structure for storing the same information:

```
Table Title
ISBN    Title    Pages    PubYear    PublisherID
```

```
Table Publisher
PublisherID    Publisher    PubAddress
```

The PublisherID field is a unique number that identifies a publisher, and it must have the same value in both tables. To find out a title's publisher, you retrieve the PublisherID field from the Title table and then locate the row in the Publisher table that has the same value in its PublisherID field. In effect, the PublisherID field in the Publisher table is the primary key (it cannot appear in more than one row), and the PublisherID fields in the Title table are the foreign keys (they can appear in many rows).

OK, this is pretty obvious, but why did you have to introduce a new field? Couldn't you use the publisher's name to relate the two tables? Had you used the publisher's name as a key, then you wouldn't be able to change the publisher's name in a single place. If Drennan Press is incorporated and changes its name to Drennan Press Inc., you should be able to change the publisher's name in a single place to avoid update anomalies.

Using a number to identify each row in a table is a common practice. Numeric IDs need not be changed, so they will not cause any update anomalies. Assuming names do not change is dangerous in database design. Companies merge, they incorporate, and you can't assume their names won't change. Even when such an assumption might appear reasonable, you shouldn't base the design of a database on an assumption.

Part IV

First Normal Form

This rule is simple. It says that a table shouldn't contain repeating groups. Here's a table that contains all the mistakes of the previous (unacceptable) designs. Let's start with the repeating groups (the book's topics):

```
ISBN  Title  Pages  Publisher  PubAddress  Topic1  Topic2
```

To remove a group from a table, keep the first column of the group and repeat the additional topics in multiple rows of the table. A title with two topics will be stored in this table as follows:

```
ISBN         Title       Pages  Publisher  Topic
01254889391  SQL Server  850    Sybex      Programming
01254889391  SQL Server  850    Sybex      Databases
```

NOTE

The first row in the preceding code contains field names, and the following rows are data. We have omitted the PubAddress column to shorten the lines.

The first normal form doesn't require that a table be broken into multiple tables. It turns some of the table's columns into additional rows. This structure has the following advantages:

No Empty Fields   If a title belongs to a single topic, then the fields Topic2 and Topic3 in the example would be empty.

No Artificial Limitations   If a specific title should be located under half a dozen categories, you can add as many lines as necessary to the table.

We've discussed the shortcomings of this design already. The table design is in first normalized form, and you must now apply the second normalization rule.

Second Normal Form

The second normalization rule says that any fields that do not depend fully on the primary key should be moved to another table. The Topic field in the last table structure is not functionally dependent on the ISBN (the primary key). *Functionally dependent* means that a field is fully determined by the key. A book's page count is functionally dependent on the book's ISBN. If you know the book's ISBN, you can determine the book's page count uniquely. The same is true for the book's publication year. But the topic is not dependent on the ISBN, because the same ISBN can lead to multiple topics.

The second normalization rule requires that the topics be moved to a different table:

Table Title

ISBN   Title   Pages   Publisher   PubAddress

Table TitleTopic

ISBN   Topic

Now, why is this better than the previous table structure? The same ISBN can lead to multiple topics. The TitleTopic table doesn't repeat information. Only the primary key is repeated, and you can't avoid it. A single title might have multiple topics. This is a one-to-many relationship, and you can't avoid the duplication of the primary key.

However, there's a problem with this table, too. Because a book's topic is described with a string, you haven't avoided the update anomaly. If you change the description of a category, you'd have to change many rows in the TitleTopic table. To avoid the update anomaly, you must create a separate table with the topics and assign a unique ID to each topic:

Table Topic

TopicID   Topic

To connect each title to one or more topics, you must change the TitleTopic table that connects the Title and Topic tables. The TitleTopic table must contain pairs of ISBNs and topic IDs:

Table TitleTopic

ISBN   TopicID

Third Normal Form

The third normalization rule says that there should be no dependency between non-key fields. In the preceding table design, you have such a dependency. The publisher's address depends on the publisher, not the book's ISBN. To remove this type of dependency, you must move the publisher information to another table. Because each book must have a publisher, you add the `PubID` field to the Title table and to the new table with the publishers. The `PubID` field of the Title table must have the same value as the `PubID` field in the Publisher table. Here's the original table in the third normal form:

Table Title

ISBN   Title   Pages   PubID

Table Publisher

PubID   PubAddress

Table Topic

TopicID   Topic

Table TitleTopic

ISBN   TopicID

Figure 13.12 shows the final tables and the relationships between them. As you can see, the normalization rules are simple and resemble the practical rules we derived earlier based on our intuition and common sense. The second and third rules are almost identical—some people combine them into a single rule. The difference is that the second rule removes the dependencies between the fields and the primary key: You test the dependency of each field against the key field. The third rule removes the dependencies between fields other than the key field.

To summarize, you must use your common sense to split your data into separate tables. Use a separate table for each entity. Then establish relationships between tables (if they can be related, of course). In the process, you might need to introduce additional tables to connect the basic tables of your design. Some tables can't be linked directly. At each stage, apply the three normalization rules to your tables to make sure your database is normalized.

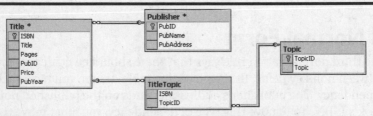

FIGURE 13.12:   A normalized database's relational diagram

NORMALIZATION AND JOINS

Let's return to the Northwind database for a moment and see how the DBMS uses relations. Each time you connect two tables with a common key, the DBMS must perform an operation known as *join*. It logically joins the two tables by using the primary and foreign keys. Joins are quite expensive operations, and you should try to minimize them. You must also see that the foreign keys used in the join operations are indexed, to help the DBMS with the lookup operations. Some databases might use as many as a few dozen joins to get the desired results out of the database—very slow operations.

As you might notice, a conflict exists between normalization and the performance of joins. In a very large database, you might end up with too many related tables, which also means a large number of joins. Many database administrators and programmers will de-normalize their databases a little to reduce the number of joins in the queries. Although this is a rather common practice, don't base the design of your databases on this premise. If you ever design a database with many tables, you might have to trade off some normalization for fewer joins.

When you do use joins, make sure that they are efficient. Here are a couple of tips on making sure your joins work well:

▶ Try to join only numeric columns.

▶ It's better to join columns that are the same datatype. This way, SQL Server can do the comparison more quickly.

▶ Try to limit your joins on columns that have unique values. SQL Server can ignore the index if most of your data is not unique.

▶ Keep your join column length as small as you can.

▶ Don't put indexes on data with a small number of rows, because it would be faster for SQL Server to scan the table rather than use the index.

Previous versions of SQL Server had a limit of 16 joins in a single SQL statement. SQL Server 2000 supports a larger number of joins, but even 16 joins are too many. If an operation requires too many joins, you could replace them with subqueries. *Subqueries* are queries that are nested within a query and in some cases might yield faster performance than a join. If some of your queries require excessive joins, you should probably revise the design of the database.

DATABASE INTEGRITY

The major challenge in database design is maintaining the integrity of the database. Designing a database is only the beginning; you must also make sure that you keep the database in good shape at all times. The burden of keeping a database in good shape is shared by the database administrator (DBA) and the programmers. As a programmer, you must make sure that all the data your code places into the database is valid. This is quite a task and would require an enormous amount of validation, but, as you'll learn in this section, the database itself can help.

Modern databases include tools that enable you to protect the integrity of the database from within. SQL Server, for example, lets you incorporate rules that enforce database integrity. By specifying each column's type, you're actually telling the database not to accept any data that doesn't conform. If a user or an application attempts to assign a numeric value to a field that stores dates, the database will reject the value to protect data integrity.

The rules for enforcing the integrity of a database can be classified into three categories, which are described next.

Domain Integrity

The first, and simplest, type of integrity is *domain integrity*, a fancy term that means each column must have a specific datatype. If a column holds dates, then users shouldn't be allowed to store integers or Boolean values in this column. As you already know, when you create a table, you must declare the datatype for each column. If you attempt to assign a value of the wrong type to a column, the database will reject the operation and raise a trappable runtime error. As far as your application is concerned, you can either test the datatype of a user-supplied value against the column's datatype, or intercept the runtime error that will be raised and act accordingly.

Entity Integrity

The second type of integrity is *entity integrity*. This means that an entity (a customer, product, invoice, and so on) must have a unique column, such as a primary key, identifying the entity with a valid value. If a table's primary key is Null, then no rows in other tables can connect to this row. All DBMSs can enforce this type of integrity by not allowing the insertion of rows with Null keys, or by preventing changes that would result in a Null value for a primary key. All you have to do to enforce this type of integrity is to choose a column type (such as primary key or identity properties) that does not allow Nulls.

Referential Integrity

Referential integrity (RI) is one of the most important topics in database design. Designing the database is a rather straightforward process, once you understand the information that will be stored in the database, how you will retrieve it, and the relations among the various tables. Just as important, if not more important, is ensuring that the various relationships remain valid at all times.

Relationships are based on primary and foreign keys. What will happen if the primary key in a relationship is deleted? If you delete a row in the Customers table, for instance, then some orders will become orphaned; they will refer to a customer who doesn't exist. Your applications will keep working, but every now and then you'll get incorrect results. Nothing will go wrong in calculating the total for an existing customer, for example.

If you calculate the grand total for all customers, you'll get one value. If you calculate the grand total for all the detail lines, you'll get a different value. This inconsistency shouldn't exist in a database. After you realize that your database is in an inconsistent state, you must start examining every table to find out why and when it happened and what other reports are unusable. This is a major headache that you want to avoid. And it's simple to avoid such problems by enforcing the database's referential integrity.

Problems related to the referential integrity of the database can be intermittent, too. If the deleted customer hasn't placed an order in the last 12 months, all the totals you calculate for the last 12 months will be correct. If you receive a (very) late payment from this customer, however, you won't be able to enter it into the database. There's no customer to link the payment to!

Enforcing Referential Integrity

Primary and foreign keys are a form of *declarative referential integrity (DRI)*. This means that you can create this integrity by adding constraints to the table design. *Constraints* are exactly what you think they are—a way of preventing an action from occurring.

If you enforce the integrity of the relationship between Customers and Orders, for example, when an application attempts to delete a customer, the database will raise a runtime error and not allow the deletion of the record. If the customer has no orders in the Orders table, then the application will be allowed to delete the customer. This action will not impair the integrity of the database, because there are no related rows.

TIP

Enforcing referential integrity is expensive. High performance database systems often remove referential integrity on their production machines in order to increase speed. Of course, this is done only after the database has been fully tested to ensure that there is no chance for data corruption.

The good news is that you don't need to write any code to enforce referential integrity. When you specify a relationship, you can also specify that the integrity of the relationship be enforced.

SQL Server enforces referential integrity by rejecting any changes in the primary key if this key is referenced by another table. Open the Properties window of a relationship by right-clicking the arrow that represents the relationship between two tables in the Relationships diagram and then selecting Properties from the shortcut menu. Click the Relationships tab, which is shown in Figure 13.13, and check Enforce Relationship For INSERTs And UPDATEs. The Check Existing Data On Creation option is valid when you create a new relationship between two tables that contain data already. It tells SQL Server to make sure that existing data does not violate the new relationship.

You can also use triggers to enforce referential integrity. Generally, using DRI is much more efficient than using triggers for RI. You would use triggers when you are trying to enforce cross-database referential integrity because DRI does not support it.

With SQL Server 2000, you now have the ability to create expanded programmatic referential integrity with cascading updates and deletes. This is a new feature of SQL Server 2000. You will explore both of these options next.

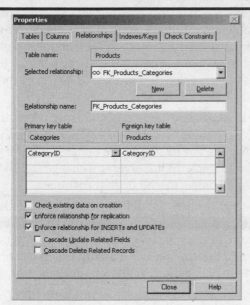

FIGURE 13.13: Specifying the properties of a relationship in a SQL Server database

Cascading Referential Integrity

Imagine you try to delete an order that has order details associated to it. The foreign keys in Northwind would prevent you from doing this. You would have to first delete the associated order details, then delete the order itself. With cascading deletes, you can opt to programmatically delete the order details with the order. Now you have a choice to *cascade updates* and *cascade deletes* from the referred table (for example, Order Details) to the table it refers to (for example, Orders).

NOTE

As you can see from Figure 13.13, SQL Server 2000 supports cascading referential integrity constraints for updates and deletes, based on ANSI specifications. If you have worked with Access, this feature might be familiar to you; but until now, it was not supported in SQL Server.

Part IV

When the Cascade Delete option is in effect and you delete an order, all related rows in every table in the database will also be deleted. If you use cascade deletes to enforce referential integrity, then all the orders placed by the specific customer in the Orders table will also be deleted. As each row in the Orders table is deleted, it must take with it all the related rows in the Order Details table as well.

Cascading updates are a less drastic method of enforcing referential integrity. When you change the value of a primary key, SQL Server 2000 changes the foreign keys in all tables related to the updated table. If you change a customer's ID, for example, SQL Server will change the OrderID field in the Orders table for all orders placed by that customer.

Cascading referential integrity offers greater performance value than using triggers. If you are upgrading a pre–SQL Server 2000 database, then you should consider migrating your referential integrity triggers to utilize cascading updates and deletes instead. Actually, this is one of the top reasons to migrate over to SQL Server 2000 from previous versions.

You will learn more about the syntax of how you would do this in Chapter 14 with an example using cascading updates.

Triggers

A *trigger* is a special stored procedure that's invoked automatically, like an event. For example, you can write a trigger that runs every time a row is updated and takes the appropriate action. Triggers are commonly used to store information about the changes made to a table's rows, such as the name of the user and the time of the action. In the case of deletions, the trigger could save the original row into an auditing table.

Triggers are implemented in T-SQL, an extension of SQL. T-SQL is a mix of SQL statements and more traditional programming statements such as control flow statements, loop structures, and so on.

NOTE

SQL Server 2000 greatly enhances the power of triggers with the INSTEAD OF and AFTER triggers. INSTEAD OF triggers give you a new ability to update views, which never existed in SQL Server before.

WHAT'S NEXT

This concludes the introduction to database design. You've learned about important database concepts such as normalization, database integrity, and datatypes. We discussed how these concepts can be implemented with the use of relationships, primary and foreign keys, and column datatypes.

In the next chapter, you will expand on your knowledge of database programming by taking an introductory look at ADO.NET. ADO.NET is the technology used to work with data from a variety of data sources, although the content covered throughout this section will deal primarily with data in relational databases.

In particular, you will learn about the .NET managed data providers, the different ADO.NET classes and how XML fits into the ADO.NET picture. Chapter 14 will focus on both the DataReader, which is designed for quick, forward-only access of data and the DataSet, which is designed as a disconnected collection of data that acts as a mini-relational database.

Chapter 14

A FIRST LOOK AT ADO.NET

It's time now to get into some real database programming with the .NET Framework components. In this chapter, you'll explore the Active Data Objects (ADO).NET base classes. ADO.NET, along with the XML namespace, is a core part of Microsoft's standard for data access and storage. ADO.NET components can access a variety of data sources, including Access and SQL Server databases, as well as non-Microsoft databases such as Oracle. Although ADO.NET is a lot different from classic ADO, you should be able to readily transfer your knowledge to the new .NET platform. Throughout this chapter, we make comparisons to ADO 2.x objects to help you make the distinction between the two technologies.

Adapted from *Mastering Visual Basic .NET Database Programming* by Evangelos Petroutsos and Asli Bilgin
ISBN 0-7821-2878-5 $49.99

For those of you who have programmed with ADO 2.*x*, the ADO.NET interfaces will not seem all that unfamiliar. Granted, a few mechanisms, such as navigation and storage, have changed, but you will quickly learn how to take advantage of these new elements. ADO.NET opens up a whole new world of data access, giving you the power to control the changes you make to your data. Although native OLE DB/ADO provides a common interface for universal storage, a lot of the data activity is hidden from you. With client-side disconnected RecordSets, you can't control how your updates occur. They just happen "magically." ADO.NET opens that black box, giving you more granularity with your data manipulations. ADO 2.*x* is about common data access. ADO.NET extends this model and factors out data storage from common data access. Factoring out functionality makes it easier for you to understand how ADO.NET components work. Each ADO.NET component has its own specialty, unlike the RecordSet, which is a jack-of-all-trades. The RecordSet could be disconnected or stateful; it could be read-only or updateable; it could be stored on the client or on the server—it is multifaceted. Not only do all these mechanisms bloat the RecordSet with functionality you might never use, it also forces you to write code to anticipate every possible chameleon-like metamorphosis of the RecordSet. In ADO.NET, you always know what to expect from your data access objects, and this lets you streamline your code with specific functionality and greater control.

Although other chapters are dedicated to XML (Chapter 18, "Using XML and VB .NET," and Chapter 19, "Using XML in Web Applications"), we must touch upon XML in our discussion of ADO.NET. In the .NET Framework, there is a strong synergy between ADO.NET and XML. Although the XML stack doesn't technically fall under ADO.NET, XML and ADO.NET belong to the same architecture. ADO.NET persists data as XML. There is no other native persistence mechanism for data and schema. ADO.NET stores data as XML files. Schema is stored as XSD files.

There are many advantages to using XML. XML is optimized for disconnected data access. ADO.NET leverages these optimizations and provides more scalability. To scale well, you can't maintain state and hold resources on your database server. The disconnected nature of ADO.NET and XML provide for high scalability.

In addition, because XML is a text-based standard, it's simple to pass it over HTTP and through firewalls. Classic ADO uses a binary format to pass data. Because ADO.NET uses XML, a ubiquitous standard, more platforms and applications will be able to consume your data. By using the XML model, ADO.NET provides a complete separation between the data and the data presentation. ADO.NET takes advantage of the way XML splits the data into an XML document, and the schema into an XSD file.

By the end of this chapter, you should be able to answer the following questions:

- ► What are .NET data providers?

- ► What are the ADO.NET classes?

- ► What are the appropriate conditions for using a DataReader versus a DataSet?

- ► How does OLE DB fit into the picture?

- ► What are the advantages of using ADO.NET over classic ADO?

- ► How do you retrieve and update databases from ADO.NET?

- ► How does XML integration go beyond the simple representation of data as XML?

Let's begin by looking "under the hood" and examining the components of the ADO.NET stack.

How Does ADO.NET Work?

ADO.NET base classes enable you to manipulate data from many data sources, such as SQL Server, Exchange, and Active Directory. ADO.NET leverages .NET data providers to connect to a database, execute commands, and retrieve results.

The ADO.NET object model exposes very flexible components, which in turn expose their own properties and methods, and recognize events. In this chapter, you'll explore the objects of the ADO.NET object model and the role of each object in establishing a connection to a database and manipulating its tables.

Part IV

IS OLE DB DEAD?

Not quite. Although you can still use OLE DB data providers with ADO.NET, you should try to use the managed .NET data providers whenever possible. If you use native OLE DB, your .NET code will suffer because it's forced to go through the COM interoperability layer in order to get to OLE DB. This leads to performance degradation. Native .NET providers, such as the `System.Data.SqlClient` library, skip the OLE DB layer entirely, making their calls directly to the native API of the database server.

However, this doesn't mean that you should avoid the OLE DB .NET data providers completely. If you are using anything other than SQL Server 7 or 2000, you might not have another choice. Although you will experience performance gains with the SQL Server .NET data provider, the OLE DB .NET data provider compares favorably against the traditional ADO/OLE DB providers that you used with ADO 2.*x*. So don't hold back from migrating your non-managed applications to the .NET Framework for performance concerns. In addition, there are other compelling reasons for using the OLE DB .NET providers. Many OLE DB providers are very mature and support a great deal more functionality than you would get from the newer SQL Server .NET data provider, which exposes only a subset of this full functionality. In addition, OLE DB is still the way to go for universal data access across disparate data sources. In fact, the SQL Server distributed process relies on OLE DB to manage joins across heterogeneous data sources.

Another caveat to the SQL Server .NET data provider is that it is tightly coupled to its data source. Although this enhances performance, it is somewhat limiting in terms of portability to other data sources. When you use the OLE DB providers, you can change the connection string on the fly, using declarative code such as COM+ constructor strings. This loose coupling enables you to easily port your application from an SQL Server back-end to an Oracle back-end without recompiling any of your code, just by swapping out the connection string in your COM+ catalog.

Keep in mind, the only native OLE DB provider types that are supported with ADO.NET are SQLOLEDB for SQL Server, MSDAORA for Oracle, and `Microsoft.Jet.OLEDB.4` for the Microsoft Jet engine. If you are so inclined, you can write your own .NET data providers for any data source by inheriting from the `System.Data` namespace.

CONTINUED ➡

At this time, the .NET Framework ships with only the SQL Server .NET data provider for data access within the .NET runtime. Microsoft expects the support for .NET data providers and the number of .NET data providers to increase significantly. (In fact, the ODBC.NET data provider is available for download on Microsoft's website.) A major design goal of ADO.NET is to synergize the native and managed interfaces, advancing both models in tandem.

You can find the ADO.NET objects within the System.Data namespace. When you create a new VB .NET project, a reference to the System.Data namespace will be automatically added for you, as you can see in Figure 14.1.

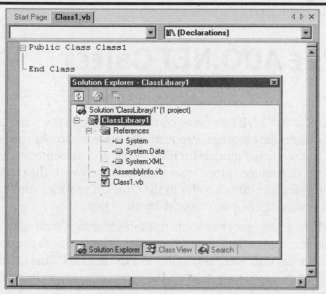

FIGURE 14.1:   To use ADO.NET, reference the System.Data namespace.

To comfortably use the ADO.NET objects in an application, you should use the Imports statement. By doing so, you can declare ADO.NET variables without having to fully qualify them. You could type the following Imports statement at the top of your solution:

```
Imports System.Data.SqlClient
```

After this, you can work with the SqlClient ADO.NET objects without having to fully qualify the class names. If you want to dimension the SqlClientDataAdapter, you would type the following short declaration:

```
Dim dsMyAdapter as New SqlDataAdapter
```

Otherwise, you would have to type the full namespace, as in:

```
Dim dsMyAdapter as New System.Data.SqlClient.SqlDataAdapter
```

Alternatively, you can use the visual database tools to automatically generate your ADO.NET code for you. The various wizards that come with VS .NET provide the easiest way to work with the ADO.NET objects. Nevertheless, before you use these tools to build production systems, you should understand how ADO.NET works programmatically. In this chapter, we don't focus too much on the visual database tools, but instead concentrate on the code behind the tools. By understanding how to program against the ADO.NET object model, you will have more power and flexibility with your data access code.

USING THE ADO.NET OBJECT MODEL

You can think of ADO.NET as being composed of two major parts: .NET data providers and data storage. Respectively, these fall under the connected and disconnected models for data access and presentation. *.NET data providers*, or *managed providers*, interact natively with the database. Managed providers are quite similar to the OLE DB providers or ODBC drivers that you most likely have worked with in the past.

The .NET data provider classes are optimized for fast, read-only, and forward-only retrieval of data. The managed providers talk to the database by using a fast data stream (similar to a file stream). This is the quickest way to pull read-only data off the wire, because you minimize buffering and memory overhead.

If you need to work with connections, transactions, or locks, you would use the managed providers, not the DataSet. The DataSet is completely disconnected from the database and has no knowledge of transactions, locks, or anything else that interacts with the database.

Five core objects form the foundation of the ADO.NET object model, as you see listed in Table 14.1. Microsoft moves as much of the provider model as possible into the managed space. The Connection, Command,

DataReader, and DataAdapter belong to the .NET data provider, whereas the DataSet is part of the disconnected data storage mechanism.

TABLE 14.1:   ADO.NET Core Components

OBJECT	DESCRIPTION
Connection	Creates a connection to your data source.
Command	Provides access to commands to execute against your data source.
DataReader	Provides a read-only, forward-only stream containing your data.
DataSet	Provides an in-memory representation of your data source(s).
DataAdapter	Serves as an ambassador between your DataSet and data source, proving the mapping instructions between the two.

Figure 14.2 summarizes the ADO.NET object model. If you're familiar with classic ADO, you'll see that ADO.NET completely factors out the data source from the actual data. Each object exposes a large number of properties and methods, which are discussed in this and following chapters.

The ADO.NET Framework

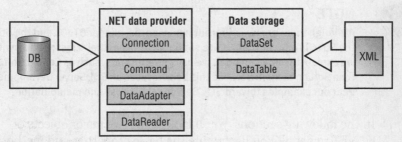

FIGURE 14.2:   The ADO Framework

NOTE

If you have worked with collection objects, this experience will be a bonus to programming with ADO.NET. ADO.NET contains a collection-centric object model, which makes programming easy if you already know how to work with collections.

Four core objects belong to .NET data providers, within the ADO.NET managed provider architecture: the Connection, Command, DataReader, and DataAdapter objects. The *Connection object* is the simplest one, because its role is to establish a connection to the database. The *Command object* exposes a Parameters collection, which contains information about the parameters of the command to be executed. If you've worked with ADO 2.*x*, the Connection and Command objects should seem familiar to you. The *DataReader object* provides fast access to read-only, forward-only data, which is reminiscent of a read-only, forward-only ADO RecordSet. The *DataAdapter object* contains Command objects that enable you to map specific actions to your data source. The DataAdapter is a mechanism for bridging the managed providers with the disconnected DataSets.

The *DataSet object* is not part of the ADO.NET managed provider architecture. The DataSet exposes a collection of DataTables, which in turn contain both DataColumn and DataRow collections. The DataTables collection can be used in conjunction with the DataRelation collection to create relational data structures.

First, you will learn about the connected layer by using the .NET data provider objects and touching briefly on the DataSet object. Next, you will explore the disconnected layer and examine the DataSet object in detail.

NOTE

Although there are two different namespaces, one for OleDb and the other for the SqlClient, they are quite similar in terms of their classes and syntax. As we explain the object model, we use generic terms, such as Connection, rather than SqlConnection. Because this book focuses on SQL Server development, we gear our examples toward SQL Server data access and manipulation.

In the following sections, you'll look at the five major objects of ADO.NET in detail. You'll examine the basic properties and methods you'll need to manipulate databases, and you'll find examples of how to use each object. ADO.NET objects also recognize events.

THE CONNECTION OBJECT

Both the SqlConnection and OleDbConnection namespaces inherit from the IDbConnection object. The Connection object establishes a connection to a database, which is then used to execute commands against the database or retrieve a DataReader. You use the SqlConnection object when you are working with SQL Server, and the OleDbConnection for all other data sources. The ConnectionString property is the most important property of the Connection object. This string uses name-value pairs to specify the database you want to connect to. To establish a connection through a Connection object, call its Open() method. When you no longer need the connection, call the Close() method to close it. To find out whether a Connection object is open, use its State property.

WHAT HAPPENED TO YOUR ADO CURSORS?

One big difference between classic ADO and ADO.NET is the way they handle cursors. In ADO 2.x, you have the option to create client- or server-side cursors, which you can set by using the CursorLocation property of the Connection object. ADO.NET no longer explicitly assigns cursors. This is a good thing.

Under classic ADO, many times programmers accidentally specify expensive server-side cursors, when they really mean to use the client-side cursors. These mistakes occur because the cursors, which sit in the COM+ server, are also considered client-side cursors. Using server-side cursors is something you should never do under the disconnected, *n*-tier design. You see, ADO 2.x wasn't originally designed for disconnected and remote data access. The CursorLocation property is used to handle disconnected and connected access within the same architecture. ADO.NET advances this concept by completely separating the connected and disconnected mechanisms into managed providers and DataSets, respectively.

In classic ADO, after you specify your cursor location, you have several choices in the type of cursor to create. You could create a static cursor, which is a disconnected, in-memory representation of your database. In addition, you could extend this static cursor into a forward-only, read-only cursor for quick database retrieval.

Under the ADO.NET architecture, there are no updateable server-side cursors. This prevents you from maintaining state for too long on your database server. Even though the DataReader does maintain state on the server, it retrieves the data rapidly as a stream. The ADO.NET DataReader works much like an ADO read-only, server-side cursor. You can think of an ADO.NET DataSet as analogous to an ADO client-side, static cursor. As you can see, you don't lose any of the ADO disconnected cursor functionality with ADO.NET; it's just architected differently.

Connecting to a Database

The first step to using ADO.NET is to connect to a data source, such as a database. Using the Connection object, you tell ADO.NET which database you want to contact, supply your username and password (so that the DBMS can grant you access to the database and set the appropriate privileges), and, possibly, set more options. The Connection object is your gateway to the database, and all the operations you perform against the database must go through this gateway. The Connection object encapsulates all the functionality of a data link and has the same properties. Unlike data links, however, Connection objects can be accessed from within your VB .NET code. They expose a number of properties and methods that enable you to manipulate your connection from within your code.

NOTE

You don't have to type this code by hand. The code for all the examples in this chapter is located on the Sybex website. You can find many of this chapter's code examples in the solution file Working with ADO.NET.sln. Code related to the ADO.NET Connection object is listed behind the Connect To Northwind button on the startup form.

Let's experiment with creating a connection to the Northwind database. Create a new Windows Application solution and place a command button on the Form; name it **Connect to Northwind**. Add the **Imports** statement for the System.Data.SqlClient name at the top of the form module. Now you can declare a Connection object with the following statement:

```
Dim connNorthwind As New SqlClient.SqlConnection()
```

As soon as you type the period after SqlClient, you will see a list with all the objects exposed by the SqlClient component, and you can select the one you want with the arrow keys. Declare the connNorthwind object in the button's Click event.

NOTE

All projects available on the Sybex website use the setting (local) for the data source. In other words, we're assuming you have SQL Server installed on the local machine. Alternatively, you could use localhost for the data source value.

The ConnectionString Property

The ConnectionString property is a long string with several attributes separated by semicolons. Add the following line to your button's Click event to set the connection:

```
connNorthwind.ConnectionString="data source=(local);"& _
    "initial catalog=Northwind;integrated security=SSPI;"
```

Replace the data source value with the name of your SQL Server, or keep the local setting if you are running SQL Server on the same machine. If you aren't using Windows NT integrated security, then set your user ID and password like so:

```
connNorthwind.ConnectionString="data source=(local);"& _
    "initial catalog=Northwind; user ID=sa;password=xxx"
```

TIP

Some of the names in the connection string also go by aliases. You can use `Server` instead of `data source` to specify your SQL Server. Instead of `initial catalog`, you can specify `database`.

Those of you who have worked with ADO 2.x might notice something missing from the connection string: the provider value. Because you are using the `SqlClient` namespace and the .NET Framework, you do not need to specify an OLE DB provider. If you were using the `OleDb` namespace, then you would specify your provider name-value pair, such as `Provider=SQLOLEDB.1`.

OVERLOADING THE CONNECTION OBJECT CONSTRUCTOR

One of the nice things about the .NET Framework is that it supports constructor arguments by using overloaded constructors. You might find this useful for creating your ADO.NET objects, such as your database Connection. As a shortcut, instead of using the ConnectionString property, you can pass the string right into the constructor, as such:

```
Dim connNorthwind as New SqlConnection _
("data source=localhost; initial catalog=Northwind; _
  user ID=sa;password=xxx")
```

CONTINUED ➡

Part IV

Or you could overload the constructor of the connection string by using the following:

```
Dim myConnectString As String = "data source= _
    localhost; initial
      catalog=Northwind; user ID=sa;password=xxx"
```

You have just established a connection to the SQL Server Northwind database. You can also do this visually from the Server Explorer in Visual Studio .NET. The ConnectionString property of the Connection object contains all the information required by the provider to establish a connection to the database. As you can see, it contains all the information that you see in the Connection properties tab when you use the visual tools.

Keep in mind that you can also create connections implicitly by using the DataAdapter object. You will learn how to do this when we discuss the DataAdapter later in this section.

In practice, you'll never have to build connection strings from scratch. You can use the Server Explorer to add a new connection, or use the appropriate ADO.NET data component wizards. These visual tools will automatically build this string for you, which you can see in the Properties window of your Connection component.

TIP

The connection pertains more to the database server rather than the actual database itself. You can change the database for an open SqlConnection, by passing the name of the new database to the ChangeDatabase() method.

The *Open ( )* Method

After you have specified the ConnectionString property of the Connection object, you must call the Open() method to establish a connection to the database. You must first specify the ConnectionString property and then call the Open() method without any arguments, as shown here (connNorthwind is the name of a Connection object):

```
connNorthwind.Open()
```

NOTE
Unlike ADO 2.x, the Open() method doesn't take any optional parameters. You can't change this feature because the Open() method is not overridable.

The *Close ( )* Method

Use the Connection object's Close() method to close an open connection. Connection pooling provides the ability to improve your performance by reusing a connection from the pool if an appropriate one is available. The OleDbConnection object will automatically pool your connections for you. If you have connection pooling enabled, the connection is not actually released, but remains alive in memory and can be used again later. Any pending transactions are rolled back.

NOTE
Alternatively, you could call the Dispose() method, which also closes the connection: connNorthwind.Dispose().

You must call the Close() or Dispose() method, or else the connection will not be released back to the connection pool. The .NET garbage collector will periodically remove memory references for expired or invalid connections within a pool. This type of lifetime management improves the performance of your applications because you don't have to incur expensive shutdown costs. However, this mentality is dangerous with objects that tie down server resources. Generational garbage collection polls for objects that have been recently created, only periodically checking for those objects that have been around longer. Connections hold resources on your server, and because you don't get deterministic cleanup by the garbage collector, you must make sure you explicitly close the connections that you open. The same goes for the DataReader, which also holds resources on the database server.

THE COMMAND OBJECT

After you instantiate your connection, you can use the Command object to execute commands that retrieve data from your data source. The Command object carries information about the command to be executed. This command is specified with the control's CommandText property. The

CommandText property can specify a table name, an SQL statement, or the name of an SQL Server stored procedure. To specify how ADO will interpret the command specified with the CommandText property, you must assign the proper constant to the CommandType property. The CommandType property recognizes the enumerated values in the CommandType structure, as shown in Table 14.2.

TABLE 14.2:   Settings of the CommandType Property

CONSTANT	DESCRIPTION
Text	The command is an SQL statement. This is the default CommandType.
StoredProcedure	The command is the name of a stored procedure.
TableDirect	The command is a table's name. The Command object passes the name of the table to the server.

When you choose StoredProcedure as the CommandType, you can use the Parameters property to specify parameter values if the stored procedure requires one or more input parameters, or it returns one or more output parameters. The Parameters property works as a collection, storing the various attributes of your input and output parameters.

Executing a Command

After you have connected to the database, you must specify one or more commands to execute against the database. A command could be as simple as a table's name, an SQL statement, or the name of a stored procedure. You can think of a Command object as a way of returning streams of data results to a DataReader object or caching them into a DataSet object.

Command execution has been seriously refined since ADO 2.x., now supporting optimized execution based on the data you return. You can get many different results from executing a command:

▶ If you specify the name of a table, the DBMS will return all the rows of the table.

▶ If you specify an SQL statement, the DBMS will execute the statement and return a set of rows from one or more tables.

▶ If the SQL statement is an action query, some rows will be updated, and the DBMS will report the number of rows that were updated but will not return any data rows. The same is true for stored procedures:

> ▶ If the stored procedure selects rows, these rows will be returned to the application.
>
> ▶ If the stored procedure updates the database, it might not return any values.

TIP

As we have mentioned, you should prepare the commands you want to execute against the database ahead of time and, if possible, in the form of stored procedures. With all the commands in place, you can focus on your VB .NET code. In addition, if you are performing action queries and do not want results being returned, specify the NOCOUNT ON option in your stored procedure to turn off the "rows affected" result count.

You specify the command to execute against the database with the Command object. The Command objects have several methods for execution: the ExecuteReader() method returns a forward-only, read-only DataReader, the ExecuteScalar() method retrieves a single result value, and the ExecuteNonQuery() method doesn't return any results. There is also an ExecuteXmlReader() method, which returns the XML version of a DataReader.

NOTE

ADO.NET simplifies and streamlines the data access object model. You no longer have to choose whether to execute a query through a Connection, Command, or RecordSet object. In ADO.NET, you will always use the Command object to perform action queries.

You can also use the Command object to specify any parameter values that must be passed to the DBMS (as in the case of a stored procedure), as well as specify the transaction in which the command executes. One of the basic properties of the Command object is the Connection property, which specifies the Connection object through which the command will be submitted to the DBMS for execution. It is possible to have multiple connections to different databases and issue different commands to each one. You can even swap connections on the fly at runtime, using the same Command object with different connections. Depending on the database to which you want to submit a command, you must use the appropriate Connection object. Connection objects are a significant load on the server, so try to avoid using multiple connections to the same database in your code.

WHY ARE THERE SO MANY METHODS TO EXECUTE A COMMAND?

Executing commands can return different types of data, or even no data at all. The reason why there are separate methods for executing commands is to optimize them for different types of return values. This way, you can get better performance if you can anticipate what your return data will look like. If you have an AddNewCustomer stored procedure that returns the primary key of the newly added record, you would use the ExecuteScalar() method. If you don't care about returning a primary key or an error code, you would use ExecuteNonQuery(). In fact, now that error raising, rather than return codes, has become the de facto standard for error handling, you should find yourself using the ExecuteNonQuery() method quite often.

Why not use a single overloaded Execute() method for all these different flavors of command execution? Initially, Microsoft wanted to overload the Execute() method with all the different versions, by using the DataReader as an optional output parameter. If you passed the DataReader in, then you would get data populated into your DataReader output parameter. If you didn't pass a DataReader in, you would get no results, just as the ExecuteNonQuery() works now. However, the overloaded Execute() method with the DataReader output parameter was a bit complicated to understand. In the end, Microsoft resorted to using completely separate methods and using the method names for clarification.

Selection queries return a set of rows from the database. The following SQL statement will return the company names for all customers in the Northwind database:

```
SELECT CompanyName FROM Customers
```

SQL is a universal language for manipulating databases. The same statement will work on any database (as long as the database contains a table called Customers and this table has a CompanyName column).

Therefore, it is possible to execute this command against the SQL Server Northwind database to retrieve the company names.

NOTE

For more information on the various versions of the sample databases used throughout this book, see the sections "Exploring the Northwind Database," and "Exploring the Pubs Database" in Chapter 13, "Basic Concepts of Relational Databases."

Let's execute a command against the database by using the conn-Northwind object you've just created to retrieve all rows of the Customers table. The first step is to declare a Command object variable and set its properties accordingly. Use the following statement to declare the variable:

```
Dim cmdCustomers As New SqlCommand
```

NOTE

If you do not want to type these code samples from scratch as you follow along, you can take a shortcut and download the code from the Sybex website. The code in this walkthrough is listed in the Click event of the Create DataReader button located on the startup form for the Working with ADO.NET solution.

Alternatively, you can use the CreateCommand() method of the Connection object.

```
cmdCustomers = connNorthwind.CreateCommand()
```

OVERLOADING THE COMMAND OBJECT CONSTRUCTOR

Like the Connection object, the constructor for the Command object can also be overloaded. By overloading the constructor, you can pass in the SQL statement and connection, while instantiating the Command object—all at the same time. To retrieve data from the Customers table, you could type the following:

```
Dim cmdCustomers As OleDbCommand = New OleDbCommand _
("Customers", connNorthwind)
```

CONTINUED ➡

Then set its CommandText property to the name of the Customers table:

```
cmdCustomers.CommandType = CommandType.TableDirect
```

The TableDirect property is supported only by the OLE DB .NET data provider. The TableDirect is equivalent to using a SELECT * FROM *tablename* SQL statement. Why doesn't the SqlCommand object support this? Microsoft feels that when using specific .NET data providers, programmers should have better knowledge and control of what their Command objects are doing. You can cater to your Command objects more efficiently when you explicitly return all the records in a table by using an SQL statement or stored procedure, rather than depending on the TableDirect property to do so for you. When you explicitly specify SQL, you have tighter reign on how the data is returned, especially considering that the TableDirect property might not choose the most efficient execution plan.

The CommandText property tells ADO.NET how to interpret the command. In this example, the command is the name of a table. You could have used an SQL statement to retrieve selected rows from the Customers table, such as the customers from Germany:

```
strCmdText = "SELECT ALL FROM Customers"
strCmdText = strCmdText & "WHERE Country = 'Germany'"
cmdCustomers.CommandText = strCmdText
cmdCustomers.CommandType = CommandType.Text
```

By setting the CommandType property to a different value, you can execute different types of commands against the database.

NOTE

In previous versions of ADO, you are able to set the command to execute asynchronously and use the State property to poll for the current fetch status. In VB .NET, you now have full support of the threading model and can execute your commands on a separate thread with full control, by using the Threading namespace.

Regardless of what type of data you are retuning with your specific Execute() method, the Command object exposes a ParameterCollection that you can use to access input and output parameters for a stored procedure or SQL statement. If you are using the ExecuteReader() method, you must first close your DataReader object before you are able to query the parameters collection.

WARNING

For those of you who have experience working with parameters with OLE DB, keep in mind that you must use named parameters with the SqlClient namespace. You can no longer use the question mark character (?) as an indicator for dynamic parameters, as you had to do with OLE DB.

THE DATAADAPTER OBJECT

The DataAdapter represents a completely new concept within Microsoft's data access architecture. The DataAdapter gives you the full reign to coordinate between your in-memory data representation and your permanent data storage source. In the OLE DB/ADO architecture, all this happened behind the scenes, preventing you from specifying how you wanted your synchronization to occur.

The DataAdapter object works as the ambassador between your data and data-access mechanism. Its methods give you a way to retrieve and store data from the data source and the DataSet object. This way, the DataSet object can be completely agnostic of its data source.

The DataAdapter also understands how to translate *deltagrams*, which are the DataSet changes made by a user, back to the data source. It does this by using different Command objects to reconcile the changes, as shown in Figure 14.3. We show how to work with these Command objects shortly.

The DataAdapter implicitly works with Connection objects as well, via the Command object's interface. Besides explicitly working with a Connection object, this is the only other way you can work with the Connection object.

The DataAdapter object is very "polite," always cleaning up after itself. When you create the Connection object implicitly through the DataAdapter, the DataAdapter will check the status of the connection. If it's already open, it will go ahead and use the existing open connection. However, if it's closed, it will quickly open and close the connection when it's done with it, courteously restoring the connection back to the way the DataAdapter found it.

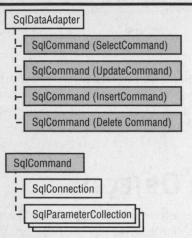

FIGURE 14.3:   The ADO.NET SqlClient DataAdapter object model

The DataAdapter works with ADO.NET Command objects, mapping them to specific database update logic that you provide. Because all this logic is stored outside of the DataSet, your DataSet becomes much more liberated. The DataSet is free to collect data from many different data sources, relying on the DataAdapter to propagate any changes back to its appropriate source.

Populating a DataSet

Although we discuss the DataSet object in more detail later in this chapter, it is difficult to express the power of the DataAdapter without referring to the DataSet object.

The DataAdapter contains one of the most important methods in ADO.NET: the Fill() method. The Fill() method populates a DataSet and is the only time that the DataSet touches a live database connection. Functionally, the Fill() method's mechanism for populating a DataSet works much like creating a static, client-side cursor in classic ADO. In the end, you end up with a disconnected representation of your data.

The Fill() method comes with many overloaded implementations. A notable version is the one that enables you to populate an ADO.NET DataSet from a classic ADO RecordSet. This makes interoperability between your existing native ADO/OLE DB code and ADO.NET a breeze. If you wanted to populate a DataSet from an existing ADO 2.*x* RecordSet called adoRS, the relevant segment of your code would read:

```
Dim daFromRS As OleDbDataAdapter = New OleDbDataAdapter
Dim dsFromRS As DataSet = New DataSet
daFromRS.Fill(dsFromRS, adoRS)
```

WARNING

You must use the OleDb implementation of the DataAdapter to populate your DataSet from a classic ADO RecordSet. Accordingly, you would need to import the System.Data.OleDb namespace.

Updating a Data Source from a DataSet by Using the DataAdapter

The DataAdapter uses the Update() method to perform the relevant SQL action commands against the data source from the deltagram in the DataSet.

TIP

The DataAdapter maps commands to the DataSet via the DataTable. Although the DataAdapter maps only one DataTable at a time, you can use multiple DataAdapters to fill your DataSet by using multiple DataTables.

Using SqlCommand and SqlParameter Objects to Update the Northwind Database

NOTE

The code for the walkthrough in this section can be found in the Updating Data Using ADO.NET.sln solution file. Listing 14.1 is contained within the Click event of the Inserting Data Using DataAdapters With Mapped Insert Commands button.

The DataAdapter gives you a simple way to map the commands by using its SelectCommand, UpdateCommand, DeleteCommand, and InsertCommand properties. When you call the Update() method, the

DataAdapter maps the appropriate update, add, and delete SQL statements or stored procedures to their appropriate Command object. (Alternatively, if you use the SelectCommand property, this command would execute with the Fill() method.) If you want to perform an insert into the Customers table of the Northwind database, you could type the code in Listing 14.1.

Listing 14.1: Insert Commands by Using the DataAdapter Object with Parameters

```
Dim strSelectCustomers As String = "SELECT * FROM " & _
 "Customers ORDER BY CustomerID"
Dim strConnString As String = "data source=(local);" & _
  "initial catalog=Northwind;integrated security=SSPI;"
' We can't use the implicit connection created by the
' DataSet since our update command requires a
' connection object in its constructor, rather than a
' connection string
Dim connNorthwind As New SqlConnection(strConnString)
' String to update the customer record - it helps to
' specify this in advance so the CommandBuilder doesn't
' affect our performance at runtime
Dim strInsertCommand As String = _
  "INSERT INTO Customers(CustomerID,CompanyName) " & _
  "VALUES (@CustomerID, @CompanyName)"
Dim daCustomers As New SqlDataAdapter()
Dim dsCustomers As New DataSet()
Dim cmdSelectCustomer As SqlCommand = New SqlCommand _
                (strSelectCustomers, connNorthwind)
Dim cmdInsertCustomer As New SqlCommand(strInsertCommand, _
  connNorthwind)
daCustomers.SelectCommand = cmdSelectCustomer
daCustomers.InsertCommand = cmdInsertCustomer
connNorthwind.Open()
daCustomers.Fill(dsCustomers, "dtCustomerTable")
cmdInsertCustomer.Parameters.Add _
 (New SqlParameter _
 ("@CustomerID", SqlDbType.NChar, 5)).Value = "ARHAN"
cmdInsertCustomer.Parameters.Add _
 (New SqlParameter _
 ("@CompanyName", SqlDbType.VarChar, 40)).Value = _
   "Amanda Aman Apak Merkez Inc."
```

```
cmdInsertCustomer.ExecuteNonQuery()
connNorthwind.Close()
```

This code sets up both the SelectCommand and InsertCommand for the DataAdapter and executes the Insert query with no results. To map the Insert command with the values you are inserting, you use the Parameters property of the appropriate SqlCommand objects. This example adds parameters to the InsertCommand of the DataAdapter. As you can see from the DataAdapter object model in Figure 14.3, each of the SqlCommand objects supports a ParameterCollection.

As you can see, the Insert statement need not contain all the fields in the parameters—and it usually doesn't. However, you must specify all the fields that can't accept Null values. If you don't, the DBMS will reject the operation with a trappable runtime error. In this example, only two of the new row's fields are set: the CustomerID and the CompanyName fields, because neither can be Null.

WARNING

In this code, notice that you can't use the implicit connection created by the DataSet. This is because the InsertCommand object requires a Connection object in its constructor rather than a connection string. If you don't have an explicitly created Connection object, you won't have any variable to pass to the constructor.

TIP

Because you create the connection explicitly, you must make sure to close your connection when you are finished with it. Although implicitly creating your connection takes care of cleanup for you, it's not a bad idea to explicitly open the connection, because you might want to leave it open so you can execute multiple fills and updates.

Each of the DataSet's Command objects have their own Command-Type and Connection properties, which make them very powerful. Consider how you can use them to combine different types of command types, such as stored procedures and SQL statements. In addition, you can combine commands from multiple data sources, by using one database for retrievals and another for updates.

As you can see, the DataAdapter with its Command objects is an extremely powerful feature of ADO.NET. In classic ADO, you don't have any control of how your selects, inserts, updates, and deletes are handled.

What if you wanted to add some specific business logic to these actions? You would have to write custom stored procedures or SQL statements, which you would call separately from your VB code. You couldn't take advantage of the native ADO RecordSet updates, because ADO hides the logic from you.

In summary, you work with a DataAdapter by using the following steps:

1. Instantiate your DataAdapter object.

2. Specify the SQL statement or stored procedure for the SelectCommand object. This is the only Command object that the DataAdapter requires.

3. Specify the appropriate connection string for the Select-Command's Connection object.

4. Specify the SQL statements or stored procedures for the InsertCommand, UpdateCommand, and DeleteCommand objects. Alternatively, you could use the CommandBuilder to dynamically map your actions at runtime. This step is not required.

5. Call the Fill() method to populate the DataSet with the results from the SelectCommand object.

6. If you used Step 4, call the appropriate Execute() method to execute your command objects against your data source.

 WARNING

Use the CommandBuilder sparingly, because it imposes a heavy performance overhead at runtime.

THE DATAREADER OBJECT

The DataReader object is a fast mechanism for retrieving forward-only, read-only streams of data. The SQL Server .NET provider have completely optimized this mechanism, so use it as often as you can for fast performance of read-only data. Unlike ADO RecordSets, which force you to load more in memory than you actually need, the DataReader is a toned-down, slender data stream, using only the necessary parts of the ADO.NET

Framework. You can think of it as analogous to the server-side, read-only, forward-only cursor that you used in native OLE DB/ADO. Because of this server-side connection, you should use the DataReader cautiously, closing it as soon as you are finished with it. Otherwise, you will tie up your Connection object, allowing no other operations to execute against it (except for the Close() method, of course).

As we mentioned earlier, you can create a DataReader object by using the ExecuteReader() method of the Command object. You would use DataReader objects when you need fast retrieval of read-only data, such as populating ComboBox lists.

Listing 14.2 depicts an example of how you create the DataReader object, assuming you've already created the Connection object connNorthwind.

Listing 14.2: Creating the DataReader Object

```
Dim strCustomerSelect as String = "SELECT * from Customers"
Dim cmdCustomers as New SqlCommand(strCustomerSelect, _
  connNorthwind)
Dim drCustomers as SqlDataReader
connNorthwind.Open()
drCustomers = cmdCustomers.ExecuteReader()
```

NOTE   The code in Listing 14.2 can be found in the Click event of the Create DataReader button on the startup form for the Working with ADO.NET solution, which you can download from the Sybex website.

Notice that you can't directly instantiate the DataReader object, but must go through the Command object interface.

WARNING   You cannot update data by using the DataReader object.

The DataReader absolves you from writing tedious MoveFirst() and MoveNext() navigation. The Read() method of the DataReader simplifies your coding tasks by automatically navigating to a position prior to the first record of your stream and moving forward without any calls to navigation methods, such as the MoveNext() method. To continue our

Part IV

example from Listing 14.2, you could retrieve the first column from all the rows in your DataReader by typing in the following code:

```
While(drCustomers.Read())

    Console.WriteLine(drCustomers.GetString(0))

End While
```

NOTE

The Console.WriteLine statement is similar to the Debug.Print() method you used in VB6.

Because the DataReader stores only one record at a time in memory, your memory resource load is considerably lighter. Now if you wanted to scroll backward or make updates to this data, you would have to use the DataSet object, which we discuss in the next section. Alternatively, you can move the data out of the DataReader and into a structure that is updateable, such as the DataTable or DataRow objects.

WARNING

By default, the DataReader navigates to a point prior to the first record. Therefore, you must always call the Read() method before you can retrieve any data from the DataReader object.

THE DATASET OBJECT

There will come a time when the DataReader is not sufficient for your data manipulation needs. If you ever need to update your data, or store relational or hierarchical data, look no further than the DataSet object. Because the DataReader navigation mechanism is linear, you have no way of traversing between relational or hierarchical data structures. The DataSet provides a liberated way of navigating through both relational and hierarchical data, by using array-like indexing and tree walking, respectively.

Unlike the managed provider objects, the DataSet object and friends do not diverge between the OleDb and SqlClient .NET namespaces. You declare a DataSet object the same way regardless of which .NET data provider you are using:

```
Dim dsCustomer as DataSet
```

Realize that DataSets stand alone. A DataSet is not a part of the managed data providers and knows nothing of its data source. The DataSet has no clue about transactions, connections, or even a database. Because the DataSet is data source agnostic, it needs something to get the data to it. This is where the DataAdapter comes into play. Although the DataAdapter is not a part of the DataSet, it understands how to communicate with the DataSet in order to populate the DataSet with data.

DataSets and XML

The DataSet object is the nexus where ADO.NET and XML meet. The DataSet is persisted as XML, and only XML. You have several ways of populating a DataSet: You can traditionally load from a database or reverse engineer your XML files back into DataSets. You can even create your own customized application data without using XML or a database, by creating custom DataTables and DataRows. We show you how to create DataSets on the fly in this chapter in the section "Creating Custom DataSets."

DataSets are perfect for working with data transfer across Internet applications, especially when working with WebServices. Unlike native OLE DB/ADO, which uses a proprietary COM protocol, DataSets transfer data by using native XML serialization, which is a ubiquitous data format. This makes it easy to move data through firewalls over HTTP. Remoting becomes much simpler with XML over the wire, rather than the heavier binary formats you have with ADO RecordSets. We demonstrated how you do this in Chapter 12, "Developing Web Applications with ASP.NET."

As we mentioned earlier, DataSet objects take advantage of the XML model by separating the data storage from the data presentation. In addition, DataSet objects separate navigational data access from the traditional set-based data access. We show you how DataSet navigation differs from RecordSet navigation later in this chapter in Table 14.4.

DataSets versus RecordSets

As you can see in Figure 14.4, DataSets are much different from tabular RecordSets. You can see that they contain many types of nested collections, such as relations and tables, which you will explore throughout the examples in this chapter.

Part IV

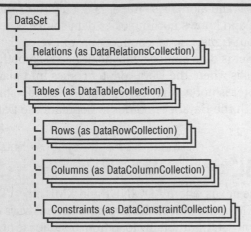

FIGURE 14.4:   The ADO.NET DataSet object model

What's so great about DataSets? You're happy with the ADO 2.*x* RecordSets. You want to know why you should migrate over to using ADO.NET DataSets. There are many compelling reasons. First, DataSet objects separate all the disconnected logic from the connected logic. This makes them easier to work with. For example, you could use a DataSet to store a web user's order information for their online shopping cart, sending deltagrams to the server as they update their order information. In fact, almost any scenario where you collect application data based on user interaction is a good candidate for using DataSets. Using DataSets to manage your application data is much easier than working with arrays, and safer than working with connection-aware RecordSets.

Another motivation for using DataSets lies in their capability to be safely cached with web applications. Caching on the web server helps alleviate the processing burden on your database servers. ASP caching is something you really can't do safely with a RecordSet, because of the chance that the RecordSet might hold a connection and state. Because DataSets independently maintain their own state, you never have to worry about tying up resources on your servers. You can even safely store the DataSet object in your ASP.NET Session object, which you are warned never to do with RecordSets. RecordSets are dangerous in a Session object; they can crash in some versions of ADO because of issues with marshalling, especially when you use open client-side cursors that aren't streamed. In addition, you can run into threading issues with ADO RecordSets, because they are apartment threaded, which causes your web server to run in the same thread.

DataSets are great for remoting because they are easily understandable by both .NET and non-.NET applications. DataSets use XML as their storage and transfer mechanism. .NET applications don't even have to deserialize the XML data, because you can pass the DataSet much like you would a RecordSet object. Non-.NET applications can also interpret the DataSet as XML, make modifications using XML, and return the final XML back to the .NET application. The .NET application takes the XML and automatically interprets it as a DataSet, once again.

Last, DataSets work well with systems that require tight user interaction. DataSets integrate tightly with bound controls. You can easily display the data with DataViews, which enable scrolling, searching, editing, and filtering with nominal effort.

Now that we've explained how the DataSet gives you more flexibility and power than using the ADO RecordSet, examine Table 14.3, which summarizes the differences between ADO and ADO.NET.

TABLE 14.3:   Why ADO.NET Is a Better Data Transfer Mechanism than ADO

Feature Set	ADO	ADO.NET	ADO.NET's Advantage
Data persistence format	RecordSet	Uses XML	With ADO.NET, you don't have datatype restrictions.
Data transfer format	COM marshalling	Uses XML	ADO.NET uses a ubiquitous format that is easily transferable and that multiple platforms and sites can readily translate. In addition, XML strings are much more manageable than binary COM objects.
Web transfer protocol	You would need to use DCOM to tunnel through Port 80 and pass proprietary COM data, which firewalls could filter out.	Uses HTTP	ADO.NET data is more readily transferable though firewalls.

Let's explore how to work with the various members of the DataSet object to retrieve and manipulate data from your data source. Although the DataSet is designed for data access with any data source, in this chapter we focus on SQL Server as our data source.

Working with DataSets

Often you will work with the DataReader object when retrieving data, because it offers you the best performance. As we have explained, in some cases the DataSet's powerful interface for data manipulation will be more practical for your needs. In this section, we discuss techniques you can use for working with data in your DataSet.

The DataSet is an efficient storage mechanism. The DataSet object hosts multiple result sets stored in one or more DataTables. These DataTables are returned by the DBMS in response to the execution of a command. The DataTable object uses rows and columns to contain the structure of a result set. You use the properties and methods of the DataTable object to access the records of a table. Table 14.4 demonstrates the power and flexibility you get with ADO.NET when retrieving data versus classic ADO.

TABLE 14.4: Why ADO.NET Is a Better Data Storage Mechanism than ADO

Feature Set	ADO	ADO.NET	ADO.NET's Advantage
Disconnected data cache	Uses disconnected RecordSets, which store data into a single table.	Uses DataSets that store one or many DataTables.	Storing multiple result sets is simple in ADO.NET. The result sets can come from a variety of data sources. Navigating between these result sets is intuitive, using the standard collection navigation. DataSets never maintain state, unlike RecordSets, making them safer to use with *n*-tier, disconnected designs.

TABLE 14.4 continued: Why ADO.NET Is a Better Data Storage Mechanism than ADO

Feature Set	ADO	ADO.NET	ADO.NET's Advantage
Relationship management	Uses JOINs, which pull data into a single result table. Alternatively, you can use the SHAPE syntax with the shaping OLE DB service provider.	Uses the Data-Relation object to associate multiple DataTables to one another.	ADO.NET's DataTable collection sets the stage for more robust relationship management. With ADO, JOINs bring back only a single result table from multiple tables. You end up with redundant data. The SHAPE syntax is cumbersome and awkward. With ADO.NET, DataRelations provide an object-oriented, relational way to manage relations such as constraints and cascading referential integrity, all within the constructs of ADO.NET. The ADO shaping commands are in an SQL-like format, rather than being native to ADO objects.
Navigation mechanism	RecordSets give you the option to only view data sequentially.	DataSets have a nonlinear navigation model.	DataSets enable you to traverse the data among multiple DataTables, using the relevant DataRelations to skip from one table to another. In addition, you can view your relational data in a hierarchical fashion by using the tree-like structure of XML.

There are three main ways to populate a DataSet:

▶ After establishing a connection to the database, you prepare the DataAdapter object, which will retrieve your results from your database as XML. You can use the DataAdapter to fill your DataSet.

▶ You can read an XML document into your DataSet. The .NET Framework provides an XMLDataDocument namespace, which is modeled parallel to the ADO.NET Framework.

Part IV

▶ You can use DataTables to build your DataSet in memory without the use of XML files or a data source of any kind. You will explore this option in the section "Updating Your Database by Using DataSets" later in this chapter.

Let's work with retrieving data from the Northwind database. First, you must prepare the DataSet object, which can be instantiated with the following statement:

```
Dim dsCustomers As New DataSet()
```

Assuming you've prepared your DataAdapter object, all you would have to call is the Fill() method. Listing 14.3 shows you the code to populate your DataSet object with customer information.

Listing 14.3: Creating the DataSet Object

```
Dim strSelectCustomers As String = "SELECT * FROM " & _
   "Customers ORDER BY CustomerID"
Dim strConnString As String = "data source=(local);" & _
   "initial catalog=Northwind;integrated security=SSPI;"
Dim daCustomers As New SqlDataAdapter(strSelectCustomers, _
   strConnString)
Dim dsCustomers As New DataSet()
Dim connNorthwind As New SqlConnection(strConnString)

daCustomers.Fill(dsCustomers, "dtCustomerTable")
MsgBox(dsCustomers.GetXml, , _
   "Results of Customer DataSet in XML")
```

NOTE

The code in Listing 14.3 can be found in the Click event of the Create Single Table DataSet button on the startup form for the Working with ADO.NET solution, which you can download from the Sybex website.

This code uses the GetXml() method to return the results of your DataSet as XML. The rows of the Customers table are retrieved through the *dsCustomers* object variable. The DataTable object within the DataSet exposes a number of properties and methods for manipulating the data by using the DataRow and DataColumn collections. You will explore how to navigate through the DataSet in the upcoming section, "Navigating Through DataSets." However, first you must understand the main collections that comprise a DataSet, the DataTable, and DataRelation collections.

The DataTableCollection

Unlike the ADO RecordSet, which contained only a single table object, the ADO.NET DataSet contains one or more tables, stored as a DataTableCollection. The DataTableCollection is what makes DataSets stand out from disconnected ADO RecordSets. You never could do something like this in classic ADO. The only choice you have with ADO is to nest RecordSets within RecordSets and use cumbersome navigation logic to move between parent and child RecordSets. The ADO.NET navigation model provides a user-friendly navigation model for moving between DataTables.

In ADO.NET, DataTables factor out different result sets that can come from different data sources. You can even dynamically relate these DataTables to one another by using DataRelations, which we discuss in the next section.

NOTE

If you want, you can think of a DataTable as analogous to a disconnected RecordSet, and the DataSet as a collection of those disconnected RecordSets.

Let's go ahead and add another table to the DataSet created earlier in Listing 14.3. Adding tables is easy with ADO.NET, and navigating between the multiple DataTables in your DataSet is simple and straight-forward. In the section "Creating Custom DataSets," we show you how to build DataSets on the fly by using multiple DataTables. The code in Listing 14.4 shows how to add another DataTable to the DataSet that you created in Listing 14.3.

NOTE

The code in Listing 14.4 can be found in the Click event of the Create DataSet With Two Tables button on the startup form for the Working with ADO.NET solution, which you can download from the Sybex website.

Listing 14.4: Adding Another DataTable to a DataSet

```
Dim strSelectCustomers As String = "SELECT * FROM "& _
  "Customers ORDER BY CustomerID"
Dim strSelectOrders As String = "SELECT * FROM Orders"
Dim strConnString As String = "data source=(local);" & _
  "initial catalog=Northwind;integrated security=SSPI;"
```

```
Dim daCustomers As New SqlDataAdapter(strSelectCustomers, _
    strConnString)
Dim dsCustomers As New DataSet()
Dim daOrders As New SqlDataAdapter(strSelectOrders, _
    strConnString)
daCustomers.Fill(dsCustomers, "dtCustomerTable")
daOrders.Fill(dsCustomers, "dtOrderTable")
Console.WriteLine(dsCustomers.GetXml)
```

WARNING

DataTables are conditionally case sensitive. In Listing 14.4, the DataTable is called dtCustomerTable. This would cause no conflicts when used alone, whether you referred to it as dtCustomerTable or dtCUSTOMERTABLE. However, if you had another DataTable called dtCUSTOMERTABLE, it would be treated as an object separate from dtCustomerTable.

As you can see, all you had to do was create a new DataAdapter to map to your Orders table, which you then filled into the DataSet object you had created earlier. This creates a collection of two DataTable objects within your DataSet. Now let's explore how to relate these DataTables together.

The DataRelation Collection

The DataSet object eliminates the cumbersome shaping syntax you had to use with ADO RecordSets, replacing it with a more robust relationship engine in the form of DataRelation objects. The DataSet contains a collection of DataRelation objects within its Relations property. Each DataRelation object links disparate DataTables by using referential integrity such as primary keys, foreign keys, and constraints. The DataRelation doesn't have to use any joins or nested DataTables to do this, as you had to do with ADO RecordSets.

In classic ADO, you create relationships by nesting your RecordSets into a single tabular RecordSet. Aside from being clumsy to use, this mechanism also made it awkward to dynamically link disparate sets of data.

With ADO.NET, you can take advantage of new features such as cascading referential integrity. You can do this by adding a ForeignKeyConstraint object to the ConstraintCollection within a DataTable. The ForeignKeyConstraint object enforces referential integrity between a set of columns in multiple DataTables. As we explained in Chapter 13, in the "Database Integrity" section, this will prevent orphaned records. In addition, you can cascade your updates and deletes from the parent table down to the child table.

Listing 14.5 shows you how to link the CustomerID column of your Customer and Orders DataTables. Using the code from Listing 14.3, all you have to do is add a new declaration for your DataRelation.

Listing 14.5: Using a Simple DataRelation

```
Dim drCustomerOrders As DataRelation = New _
  DataRelation("CustomerOrderRelation",
    dsCustomers.Tables("Customers").Columns("CustomerID"),
    dsCustomers.Tables("Orders").Columns("CustomerID"))
    dsCustomers.Relations.Add(drCustomerOrders)
```

NOTE

The code in Listing 14.5 can be found in the Click event of the Using Simple DataRelations button on the startup form for the Working with ADO.NET solution, which you can download from the Sybex website.

As you can with other ADO.NET objects, you can overload the DataRelation constructor. In this example, you pass in three parameters. The first parameter indicates the name of the relation. This is similar to how you would name a relationship within SQL Server. The next two parameters indicate the two columns that you wish to relate. After creating the DataRelation object, you add it to the Relations collection of the DataSet object. The datatype of the two columns you wish to relate must be identical.

Listing 14.6 shows you how to use DataRelations between the Customers and Orders tables of the Northwind database to ensure that when a customer ID is deleted or updated, it is reflected within the Orders table.

Listing 14.6: Using Cascading Updates

```
Dim fkCustomerID As ForeignKeyConstraint
fkCustomerID = New ForeignKeyConstraint
  ("CustomerOrderConstraint", dsCustomers.Tables
  ("Customers").Columns("CustomerID"),
dsCustomers.Tables("Orders").Columns("CustomerID"))
```

```
fkCustomerID.UpdateRule = Rule.Cascade
fkCustomerID.AcceptRejectRule = AcceptRejectRule.Cascade
dsCustomers.Tables("CustomerOrder").Constraints.Add
(fkCustomerID)
dsCustomers.EnforceConstraints = True
```

NOTE

The code in Listing 14.6 can be found in the Click event of the Using Cascading Updates button on the startup form for the Working with ADO.NET solution, which you can download from the Sybex website.

In this example, you create a foreign key constraint with cascading updates and add it to the ConstraintCollection of your DataSet. First, you declare and instantiate a ForeignKeyConstraint object, as you did earlier when creating the DataRelation object. Afterward, you set the properties of the ForeignKeyConstraint, such as the UpdateRule and AcceptRejectRule, finally adding it to your ConstraintCollection. You have to ensure that your constraints activate by setting the EnforceConstraints property to True.

Navigating through DataSets

We already discussed navigation through a DataReader. To sum it up, as long as the DataReader's Read() method returns True, then you have successfully positioned yourself in the DataReader. Now let's discuss how you would navigate through a DataSet.

In classic ADO, to navigate through the rows of an ADO RecordSet, you use the Move() method and its variations. The MoveFirst(), MovePrevious(), MoveLast(), and MoveNext() methods take you to the first, previous, last, and next rows in the RecordSet, respectively. This forces you to deal with cursoring and absolute positioning. This makes navigation cumbersome because you have to first position yourself within a RecordSet and then read the data that you need.

In ADO 2.x, a fundamental concept in programming for RecordSets is that of the *current row*: To read the fields of a row, you must first move to the desired row. The RecordSet object supports a number of navigational methods, which enable you to locate the desired row, and the Fields property, which enables you to access (read or modify) the current row's fields. With ADO.NET, you no longer have to use fixed positioning to locate your records; instead, you can use array-like navigation.

Unlike ADO RecordSets, the concept of the current row no longer matters with DataSets. DataSets work like other in-memory data representations, such as arrays and collections, and use familiar navigational behaviors. DataSets provide an explicit in-memory representation of data in the form of a collection-based model. This enables you to get rid of the infamous Do While Not rs.EOF() And Not rs.BOF() loop. With ADO.NET, you can use the friendly For Each loop to iterate through the DataTables of your DataSet. If you want to iterate through the rows and columns within an existing DataTable named tblCustomers, stored in a dsCustomers DataSet, you could use the following loop in Listing 14.7.

Listing 14.7: Navigating through a DataSet

```
For Each tblCustomer In dsCustomers.Tables
        Dim rowCustomer As DataRow
        For Each rowCustomer In  tblCustomer.Rows
            Dim colCustomer As DataColumn
            For Each colCustomer In  thisTable.Columns
                Console.WriteLine(rowCustomer (colCustomer))
            Next colCustomer
        Next rowCustomer
    Next tblCustomer
```

This will print out the values in each column of the customers DataSet created in Listing 14.3. As you can see, the For Each logic saves you from having to monitor antiquated properties such as EOF and BOF of the ADO RecordSet.

DataTables contain collections of DataRows and DataColumns, which also simplify your navigation mechanism. Instead of worrying about the RecordCount property of RecordSets, you can use the traditional UBound() property to collect the number of rows within a DataTable. For the example in Listing 14.7, you can calculate the row count for the customer records by using the following statement:

```
UBound(rowCustomer)
```

DataTable Capacities

In classic ADO, you could specify *paged RecordSets*—the type of Record-Sets displayed on web pages when the results of a query are too many to be displayed on a single page. The web server displays 20 or so records and a number of buttons at the bottom of the page that enable you to move quickly to another group of 20 records. This technique is common in web applications, and ADO supports a few properties that simplify the creation of paged RecordSets, such as the AbsolutePage, PageSize, and PageCount properties.

With ADO.NET, you can use the MinimumCapacity property to specify the number of rows you wish to bring back for a DataTable. The default setting is 25 rows. This setting is especially useful if you want to improve performance on your web pages in ASP.NET. If you want to ensure that only 50 customer records display for the Customers DataTable, you would specify the following:

```
dtCustomers.MinimumCapacity = 50
```

If you have worked with paged RecordSets, you will realize that this performance technique is much less involved than the convoluted paging logic you had to use in ADO 2.*x*.

Navigating a Relationship between Tables

ADO.NET provides a navigation model for navigating through Data-Tables by using the relationships that connect them. Keep in mind that relations work as separate objects. When you create the relationship between the Customers and Orders tables, you can't directly jump from a customer DataRow to the related order DataRows. You must open the DataRelation separately and then pull the related rows. This is fine with one-to-many relationships; however, if you are using one-to-one relationships, you should stick with SQL JOIN statements.

You will explore the many techniques you can do with your retrieved data later in this chapter. First, let's review basic ways of updating your data sources by using DataSets.

UPDATING YOUR DATABASE BY USING DATASETS

The two connected and disconnected models of ADO.NET work very differently when updating the database. Connected, or managed, providers communicate with the database by using command-based updates. As we showed you in "The DataSet Object" section earlier, disconnected DataSets update the database by using a cached, batch-optimistic method. DataSets work independently from a connection, working with the deltagram of data on the disconnected DataSet and committing the changes only after you call the Update() method from the DataAdapter. The separation between the command-based model used with managed providers and the optimistic model carried out by the DataSet objects enables the programmer to make a distinction between server-side execution and cached execution.

WARNING

In ADO 2.x, there was a good amount of confusion regarding client-side cursors. Some implementations mistakenly used server-side cursors when they meant to use client-cursors on the application server. Don't confuse disconnected, cached DataSets as user-side data. The DataSets can also be stored on your middle tier, which you should consider as a client-side cache, even though it is stored on your application server. You'll explore how to use DataSets within your ASP.NET code in Part IV, "Database Programming."

To update data, you make changes to your DataSet and pass them up to the server. Obviously, you can't use the DataReader, because its forward-only, read-only nature can't be updated. There are many ways that you can make updates to a DataSet:

▶ Make changes to an existing DataSet which was retrieved from a query executed on your database server(s). Pass the changes to the data source via the Data Adapter.

▶ Load data from an XML file by using the ReadXml() method. Map the resulting DataSet to your data source by using the DataAdaptcr.

▶ Merge multiple DataSets by using the Merge() method, passing the results to the data source via the DataAdapter.

▶ Create a new DataSet with new schema and data on the fly, mapping it to a data source by using the DataAdapter.

As you can see, all these options have one thing in common: Your changes are not committed back to the server until the DataAdapter intervenes. DataSets are completely unaware of where their data comes from and how their changes relate back to the appropriate data source. The DataAdapter takes care of all this.

Realize that updating a record is not always a straightforward process. What happens if a user changes the record after you have read it? And what will happen if the record you're about to update has already been deleted by another user? In this chapter, you will learn the basics of updating databases through the ADO.NET DataSet, assuming no concurrency is involved. However, we discuss the implications of concurrency at the end of this chapter. In the meantime, let's set up your ADO.NET objects to insert a customer row into the Northwind database.

Updating Your DataSet by Using the DataTable and DataRow Objects

Earlier in this chapter, we showed you how to update your database by using parameterized stored procedures. Although this is efficient for making single row changes, it isn't quite useful when you have a significant number of changes to pass to the server. What happens when you want to apply changes in bulk? Consider an e-commerce application that uses an online shopping cart. The shopping cart could have multiple rows of data that would be inserted and updated as the user browsed through the site. When it comes time to push these changes to the server, it would be much easier to pass them in one single batch, rather than call the stored procedure multiple times for each row that's modified.

In ADO 2.x, you use disconnected RecordSets along with the `UpdateBatch()` method to pass your changes on to the server. In ADO.NET, you pass the disconnected deltagram from the DataSet object to the DataAdapter `Update()` method. Once again, ADO.NET clearly draws the line between your data and your data source. The DataSet object doesn't directly contact the data source.

First, let's see how you can manage changes within a DataSet. As the user edits the in-memory cache, the changes are stored into a buffer and not yet committed to the DataSet. You can commit modifications to a DataSet by using the `AcceptChanges()` method of the DataSet, DataTable, or DataRow objects. If you execute this method on the parent object, it will propagate down onto the children. For example, if you call `AcceptChanges()` on the DataSet object, it will cascade down onto the DataTables within the DataSet's Table collection (likewise for a DataTable to its relevant DataRow collection).

When you insert a row into a DataTable, you can monitor the "dirtiness" of a row by examining the RowState property. Let's go ahead and add a new row to your dsCustomers DataSet. In Figure 14.5, we continue the logic that we used in Listing 14.3 to populate your dsCustomers DataSet.

NOTE

Until you call the Update() method, your DataSet changes will not be committed to your data source.

First, let's look at the code that pulls down the data that you want to work with from your database into a DataSet. Using the existing DataSet, you will add a new row directly to the DataSet by using the DataTable and DataRow collections of the DataSet.

NOTE

The code depicted in Figure 14.5 can be found in the Updating Data using ADO.NET.sln solution file, within the Click event of the Inserting Data With DataSets And DataTables button.

As you see in Figure 14.5, DataSet updates are very straightforward. All you have to do is fill your DataSet, as we've shown you earlier in the chapter. Then you set up a new DataRow object with the DataTable's NewRow() method. The Add() collection of the Rows collection will add your new row to the collection. Finally, you call the AcceptChanges() method of the DataSet, which will automatically cascade all changes down to its inner DataTables and DataRows. Alternatively, you could call the AcceptChanges() method specifically on the inner object you wish to update because the DataTable and DataRow also support the AcceptChanges() method.

As the note indicates, the source code for this example is available for download on the companion website. Go ahead and load the code into Visual Studio .NET and place a breakpoint on the Add() method. Execute the code by pressing F5. When you get to your breakpoint, type the following in the Command window:

```
?dtcustomer.rows.count
```

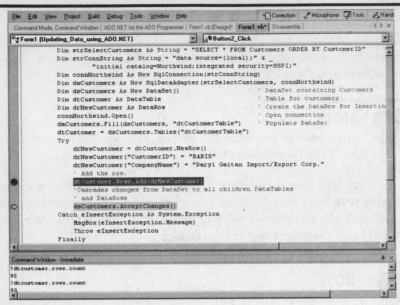

```
File  Edit  View  Project  Build  Debug  Tools  Window  Help          Correction    Microphone    Tools    Hand

Command Mode, Command Window | ADO.NET for the ADO Programmer | Form1.vb [Design]* | Form1.vb* | Disassembly |

Form1 (Updating_Data_using_ADO.NET)                    Button2_Click

        Dim strSelectCustomers As String = "SELECT * FROM Customers ORDER BY CustomerID"
        Dim strConnString As String = "data source=(local);" & _
                "initial catalog=Northwind;integrated security=SSPI;"
        Dim connNorthwind As New SqlConnection(strConnString)
        Dim daCustomers As New SqlDataAdapter(strSelectCustomers, connNorthwind)
        Dim dsCustomers As New DataSet()                    ' DataSet containing Customers
        Dim dtCustomer As DataTable                         ' Table for customers
        Dim drNewCustomer As DataRow                        ' Create the DataRow for Insertin
        connNorthwind.Open()                                ' Open connection
        daCustomers.Fill(dsCustomers, "dtCustomerTable")    ' Populate DataSet
        dtCustomer = dsCustomers.Tables("dtCustomerTable")
        Try
            drNewCustomer = dtCustomer.NewRow()
            drNewCustomer("CustomerID") = "BABIS"
            drNewCustomer("CompanyName") = "Daryl Gaitan Import/Export Corp."
            ' Add the row.
            dtCustomer.Rows.Add(drNewCustomer)
            'Cascades changes from DataSet to all children DataTables
            ' and DataRows
            dsCustomers.AcceptChanges()
        Catch eInsertException As System.Exception
            MsgBox(eInsertException.Message)
            Throw eInsertException
        Finally
```

```
Command Window - Immediate                                                              ? ×
?dtcustomer.rows.count
92
?dtcustomer.rows.count
93
```

FIGURE 14.5: Updating your DataSet object

WARNING

If you have difficulty working with the Command window, it might be because you are not in Immediate mode. If you see a > prompt, then this is most likely the case. Toggle the mode from Command mode to Immediate mode by typing immed at the prompt and pressing Enter. Now you should be able to debug your code.

You will see the number of rows in your Customers table, within your DataSet, prior to making changes. Hit F11 to step into the Add() method. This will update your DataSet with the newly added row. Go back to the Command window and hit the Up arrow key and Enter to re-execute the row count statement. The results will show that the Add() method increments your row count in your DataRow by one record. However, if you compare the result to the data in the database, you will see that your data still has the same number of original rows. This is an important point. None of your changes will be committed to the data source until you call the Update() method of the DataAdapter object. Finish the execution of the code to commit the changes in your DataSet.

In summary, all you have to do is execute the following steps to commit updates to your DataSet:

1. Instantiate your DataSet and DataAdapter objects.

2. Fill your DataSet object from the DataAdapter object.

3. Manipulate your DataSet by using the DataRow objects.

4. Call the `AcceptChanges()` method of the DataSet, Data-Table, or DataRow object to commit your changes to your DataSet.

Updating Your Data Source by Using the DataSet and DataAdapter

In this section, we show you how to insert a new row into your DataSet with the DataRow and DataTable objects. After you've updated your DataSet, we show you how you can commit those changes to the DataSet. Committing changes to a DataSet doesn't mean that they are committed to the database. To commit your changes to the database, you use the `Update()` method, which is similar to the `Fill()` method, only it works in reverse, updating your data source with the deltagram from the DataSet. Listing 14.8 contains the code that enables you to update a database with changes from a DataSet object.

NOTE

The code in Listing 14.8 can be found in the `Updating Data Using ADO.NET` solution, within the Click event of the Committing Changes From Your DataSet To Your Database button. You can download this solution from the companion website.

Although the `Update()` method is the only method you need to call to commit your changes back to the database, you must do some preparation work in advance. You must set up the appropriate action-based Command objects before you call the DataAdapter's `Update()` method. These Command objects map to the relevant insert, update, and delete stored procedures or SQL statements. Alternatively, you can use the CommandBuilder object to dynamically generate the appropriate SQL statements for you.

Part IV

Listing 14.8: Committing DataSet Changes to a Database

```
Dim strSelectCustomers As String = "SELECT * FROM " & _
  "Customers ORDER BY CustomerID"
Dim strConnString As String = "data source=(local);" & _
  "initial catalog=Northwind;integrated security=SSPI;"
Dim connNorthwind As New SqlConnection(strConnString)
Dim daCustomers As New SqlDataAdapter(strSelectCustomers, _
  connNorthwind)
Dim dsCustomers As New DataSet()
Dim dtCustomer As DataTable
Dim drNewCustomer As DataRow
Dim custCB As SqlCommandBuilder = +
  New SqlCommandBuilder(daCustomers)
connNorthwind.Open()
daCustomers.Fill(dsCustomers, "dtCustomerTable")
connNorthwind.Close()
dtCustomer = dsCustomers.Tables("dtCustomerTable")
Try
   drNewCustomer = dtCustomer.NewRow()
   drNewCustomer(0) = "OTISP"
   drNewCustomer(1) = "Otis P. Wilson Spaghetti House."
   dtCustomer.Rows.Add(drNewCustomer)

   Dim drModified As DataRow() = _
     dsCustomers.Tables("dtCustomerTable").Select(Nothing, _
       Nothing, DataViewRowState.Added)
     connNorthwind.Open()
     daCustomers.Update(drModified)
Catch eInsertException As Exception
     MsgBox(eInsertException.Message)
   Throw eInsertException
Finally
   connNorthwind.Close()
End Try
```

In summary, all you have to do is execute the following steps to update your data source from your DataSet, after you've made your changes to the DataSet:

1. Create a new row object that contains all the modified rows. You can use the DataViewRowState property to extract the appropriate rows. In our case, we used the DataViewRowState .Added value.

2. Call the Update() method of the DataAdapter object to send your changes back to the appropriate data source(s). Pass a copy of the DataRow containing your changes.

That's it. As you see, it's quite simple to add new rows to your database. Updates and deletes work the same way.

Managing DataSet Changes

Because the DataSet is inherently disconnected from the data source, it must manage its changes by itself. The DataSet supports several "dirty" flags that indicate whether changes have occurred. These flags come in the form of the GetChanges() and HasChanges() methods, which enable it to reconcile changes back to its data source via the DataAdapter object. These methods are used in conjunction with the RowState property, which we discuss next.

The RowState Property

The RowState property enables you to track the condition of your rows. It works hand in hand with the AcceptChanges() method, which we discuss next. Until the AcceptChanges() method is called, the row state will be dirty. After AcceptChanges() has been called on the row, the row state will reflect a committed record that is no longer in flux. The RowState depends on what type of modification was made on the row, such as an insert, update, or delete. Table 14.5 shows you the possible values that the RowState might contain and why.

TABLE 14.5:   Values of the RowState Property

CONSTANT	DESCRIPTION
Added	Occurs when a new row is first added to the DataRowCollection
Deleted	Indicates that the row was marked for deletion
Detached	Indicates that the row is "floating" and not yet attached to a DataRowCollection
Modified	Indicates that the row is "dirty"
Unchanged	Indicates that either the row was never touched in the first place, or the AcceptChanges() method was called, committing the changes to the row

Part IV

The *AcceptChanges ( )* Method

Until you call this method, all the modified rows in your DataSet will remain in edit mode. The `AcceptChanges()` commits your modifications to a DataSet. The DataTable and DataRow objects also support this method. Keep in mind that this will not update your database, just your DataSet and friends. `AcceptChanges()` works incrementally, updating the DataSet with the modifications since the last time you called it. As we noted earlier, you can cascade your changes down to children objects. If you wanted to automatically accept changes for all the DataRows within a DataTable, you would need to call only the `AcceptChanges()` method on the DataTable, which automatically commits the changes for all its member DataRows.

The *RejectChanges ( )* Method

If you decide not to commit the new row to the DataSet, call the `RejectChanges()` method. This method doesn't require any arguments. It simply deletes the newly added row or reverses the changes you made to an existing row.

The *HasChanges ( )* Method

The `HasChanges()` method queries whether a DataSet contains "dirty" rows. Generally, you would call this method before you called the `GetChanges()` method, so you don't unnecessarily retrieve changes that might not exist. This method can be overloaded by passing in the RowState as a parameter. By doing this, you can filter out specific change types. If you only wanted to query if the DataSet had any deletions, you would type:

```
If dsCustomers.HasChanges(DataRowState.Deleted)Then
    ' Do some logic to get the changes
End If
```

The *GetChanges ( )* Method

The `GetChanges()` method creates a DataSet containing the changes made to it since the last time you called the `AcceptChanges()` method. If you haven't called `AcceptChanges()`, then it will retrieve a copy of the DataSet with all your changes. You can optionally use the overloaded version of this method, which accepts the DataRowState as a parameter. This way, you can get only the changes based on a certain state. If you wanted to get only the deletions for a DataSet, you would first call the HasChanges() method to see if any deletions occurred and then retrieve the changes:

```
dsCustomers = dsCustomers.GetChanges(DataRowState.Deleted)
```

Merging

Another technique for working with DataSets uses the ability to merge results from multiple DataTables or DataSets. The merge operation can also combine multiple schemas together. The Merge() method enables you to extend one schema to support additional columns from the other, and vice versa. In the end, you end up with a union of both schemas and data. This is useful when you want to bring together data from heterogeneous data sources, or to add a subset of data to an existing DataSet. The merge operation is quite simple:

```
dsCustomers.Merge (dsIncomingCustomers)
```

Typed DataSets

There are many data typing differences between ADO and ADO.NET. In classic ADO, you have more memory overhead than ADO because the fields in a RecordSet are late-bound, returning data as the Variant datatype. ADO.NET supports stricter data typing. ADO.NET uses the Object, rather than the Variant datatype for your data. Although Objects are more lightweight than Variants, your code will be even more efficient if you know the type ahead of time. You could use the GetString() method to convert your column values to strings. This way, you avoid boxing your variables to the generic Object type. You can use similar syntax for the other datatypes, such as GetBoolean() or GetGuid(). Try to convert your values to the native format to reduce your memory overhead.

When you work with classic ADO, you experience performance degradation when you refer to your fields by name. You would type the following:

```
strName = rsCustomers.Fields("CustomerName").Value
```

Now, with ADO.NET, you can use strong typing to reference the fields of a DataSet directly by name, like so:

```
strName = dsCustomers.CustomerName
```

Because the values are strictly typed in ADO.NET, you don't have to write type-checking code. ADO.NET will generate a compile-time error if your have a type mismatch, unlike the ADO runtime errors you get much too late. With ADO.NET, if you try to pass a string to an integer field, you will raise an error when you compile the code.

Creating Custom DataSets

You don't need a database to create a DataSet. In fact, you can create your own DataSet without any data at all. The ADO.NET DataSet enables you to create new tables, rows, and columns from scratch. You can use these objects to build relationships and constraints, ending up with a mini-database into which you can load your data.

Listing 14.9 contains code that enables you to build a simple three-column online shopping cart DataSet on the fly. First, let's create a BuildShoppingCart() method that will create your table schema.

Listing 14.9: Creating a DataSet on the Fly

```
Public Function BuildShoppingCart() As DataTable
  Dim tblCart As DataTable = New DataTable("tblOrders")
  Dim dcOrderID As DataColumn = New
   DataColumn("OrderID", Type.GetType("System.Int32"))
  Dim dcQty As DataColumn = New
   DataColumn("Quantity",Type.GetType("System.Int32"))
  Dim dcCustomerName As DataColumn = New _
   DataColumn("CustomerName",
   Type.GetType("System.String"))
  tblCart.Columns.Add(dcOrderID)
  tblCart.Columns.Add(dcQty)
  tblCart.Columns.Add(dcCustomerName)
  Return tblCart
End Function
```

Now, all you have to do is set a DataTable variable to the results of your method and populate it. Place a breakpoint on the Add() method of the DataRow collection, as shown in Figure 14.6. This way, you can use the Immediate mode of the Command window to see if your custom DataSet was successfully updated. With ADO.NET, it's easy to use array-like navigation to return the exact value you are looking for. In this example, you query the value of the customer name in the first row by using the tblCart.Rows(0).Item(2)statement. Figure 14.6 shows you the results.

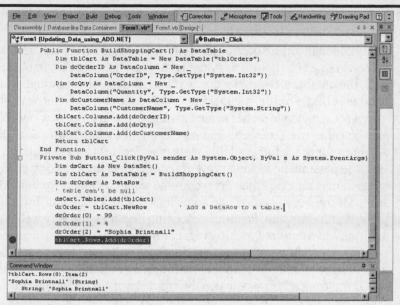

```
Public Function BuildShoppingCart() As DataTable
    Dim tblCart As DataTable = New DataTable("tblOrders")
    Dim dcOrderID As DataColumn = New _
        DataColumn("OrderID", Type.GetType("System.Int32"))
    Dim dcQty As DataColumn = New _
        DataColumn("Quantity", Type.GetType("System.Int32"))
    Dim dcCustomerName As DataColumn = New _
        DataColumn("CustomerName", Type.GetType("System.String"))
    tblCart.Columns.Add(dcOrderID)
    tblCart.Columns.Add(dcQty)
    tblCart.Columns.Add(dcCustomerName)
    Return tblCart
End Function
Private Sub Button1_Click(ByVal sender As System.Object, ByVal e As System.EventArgs)
    Dim dsCart As New DataSet()
    Dim tblCart As DataTable = BuildShoppingCart()
    Dim drOrder As DataRow
    ' table can't be null
    dsCart.Tables.Add(tblCart)
    drOrder = tblCart.NewRow        ' Add a DataRow to a table.
    drOrder(0) = 99
    drOrder(1) = 4
    drOrder(2) = "Sophia Brintnall"
    tblCart.Rows.Add(drOrder)
```

```
Command Window
?tblCart.Rows(0).Item(2)
"Sophia Brintnall" (String)
    String: "Sophia Brintnall"
```

FIGURE 14.6:   Populating your custom DataSet object

TIP

Again, you can see the power of constructors. In this sample, you see how you can set your constructor to a method result.

Being able to create your own DataSet from within your code enables you to apply many of the techniques discussed in this book. You can use these custom DataSets to store application data, without incurring the cost of crossing your network until you need to commit your changes.

MANAGING CONCURRENCY

When you set up your DataSet, you should consider the type of locking, or concurrency control, that you will use. Concurrency control determines what will happen when two users attempt to update the same row.

ADO.NET uses an optimistic architecture, rather than a pessimistic model. *Pessimistic locking* locks the database when a record is retrieved for editing. Be careful when you consider pessimistic locking. Pessimistic locking extremely limits your scalability. You really can't use pessimistic locking in a system with a large number of users. Only certain types of designs can support this type of locking.

Consider an airline booking system. A passenger (let's call her Sam) makes a request to book a seat and retrieves a list of the available seats from the database. Sam selects a seat and updates the information in the database. Under optimistic locking, if someone else took her seat, she would see a message on her screen asking her to select a new one. Now let's consider what happens under pessimistic locking. After Sam makes a request for the list of available seats, she decides to go to lunch. Because pessimistic locking prevents other users from making changes when Sam is making edits, everyone else would be unable to book their seats. Of course, you could add some logic for lock timeouts, but the point is still the same. Pessimistic locking doesn't scale very well. In addition, disconnected architecture cannot support pessimistic locking because connections attach to the database only long enough to read or update a row, not long enough to maintain an indefinite lock. In classic ADO, you could choose between different flavors of optimistic and pessimistic locks. This is no longer the case. The .NET Framework supports only an optimistic lock type.

An *optimistic lock* type assumes that the data source is locked only at the time the data update commitment occurs. This means changes could have occurred while you were updating the disconnected data cache. A user could have updated the same *CompanyName* while you were making changes to the disconnected DataSet. Under optimistic locking, when you try to commit your *CompanyName* changes to the data source, you will override the changes made by the last user. The changes made by the last user could have been made after you had retrieved your disconnected DataSet. You could have updated the *CompanyName* for a customer, after someone else had updated the *Address*. When you push your update to the server, the updated address information would be lost. If you expect concurrency conflicts of this nature, you must make sure that your logic detects and rejects conflicting updates.

If you have worked with ADO 2.x, you can think of the Update() method of the DataAdapter object as analogous to the UpdateBatch() method you used with the RecordSet object. Both models follow the concept of committing your deltagram to the data source by using an optimistic lock type.

Understanding how locking works in ADO.NET is an essential part of building a solid architecture. ADO.NET makes great strides by advancing the locking mechanism. Let's take a look at how it changes from classic ADO in order to get an idea of how much power ADO.NET gives you.

In ADO 2.x, when you make changes to a disconnected RecordSet, you call the UpdateBatch() method to push your updates to the server. You really don't know what goes on under the covers and you hope that your inserts, updates, and deletes will take. You can't control the SQL statements that modify the database.

When you use optimistic concurrency, you still need some way to determine whether your server data has been changed since the last read. You have three choices with managing concurrency: time-date stamps, version numbers, and storing the original values.

Time-date stamps are a commonly used approach to tracking updates. The comparison logic checks to see if the time-date of the updated data matches the time-date stamp of original data in the database. It's a simple yet effective technique. Your logic would sit in your SQL statements or stored procedures, such as:

```
UPDATE Customers SET CustomerID = "SHAMSI",
  CustomerName = "Irish Twinkle SuperMart"
WHERE DateTimeStamp = olddatetimestamp
```

The second approach is to use version numbers, which is similar to using the time-date stamp, but this approach labels the row with version numbers, which you can then compare.

The last approach is to store the original values so that when you go back to the database with your updates, you can compare the stored values with what's in the database. If they match, you can safely update your data because no one else has touched it since your last retrieval. ADO.NET does data reconciliation natively by using the HasVersion() method of your DataRow object. The HasVersion() method indicates the condition of the updated DataRow object. Possible values for this property are *Current*, *Default*, *Original*, or *Proposed*. These values fall under the DataRowVersion enumeration. If you wanted to see whether the DataRow changes still contained original values, you could check to see if the DataRow has changed by using the HasVersion() method:

```
If r.HasVersion(datarowversion.Proposed) Then
' Add logic
End if
```

Part IV

What's Next

This concludes our discussion of the basic properties of the ADO.NET objects. After reading this chapter, you should be able to answer the questions that we asked you in the beginning:

- ▶ What are .NET data providers?

- ▶ What are the ADO.NET classes?

- ▶ What are the appropriate conditions for using a DataReader versus a DataSet?

- ▶ How does OLE DB fit into the picture?

- ▶ What are the advantages of using ADO.NET over classic ADO?

- ▶ How do you retrieve and update databases from ADO.NET?

- ▶ How does XML integration go beyond the simple representation of data as XML?

Although you covered a lot of ground in this chapter, there is still a good amount of ADO.NET functionality we haven't discussed. We use this chapter as a building block for the next few chapters.

In the next chapter, you will learn more about retrieving data using ADO.NET. Chapter 15 will deal primarily with retrieving data from a data source. This chapter is a good introduction to how you will use data in most of your ASP.NET applications. ASP.NET was covered in Part II.

Part IV rounds out with a couple of chapters on editing data and using this data in your Windows Forms applications.

Chapter 15

USING THE ADO.NET OBJECTS TO RETRIEVE DATA

Now that you understand the basics of .NET and have seen how to use your legacy ADO code in the .NET environment, it's time to tackle the new world of data access provided by ADO.NET. In this chapter, I'll introduce you to the ADO.NET objects and the available data providers. Then you'll see how to use the DataSet object to work with data, and the Command object to interface directly with a database.

THE ADO.NET OBJECT MODEL

The ADO.NET object model is broken up into two distinct sets of objects: data provider objects and DataSet objects. There are two sets of objects because the .NET Framework separates the task of using data from the task of storing data. The DataSet objects provide a memory-resident, disconnected set of objects that you can load with data. The provider objects handle the task of working directly with data sources. One of the provider

Adapted from *ADO and ADO.NET Programming*
by Mike Gunderloy
ISBN 0-7821-2994-3 $59.99

Part IV

objects, the DataAdapter object, serves as a conduit between the two sets of objects. By using a DataAdapter, you can load data into a DataSet and later save changes back to the original data source.

Figure 15.1 provides an overview of the ADO.NET object model.

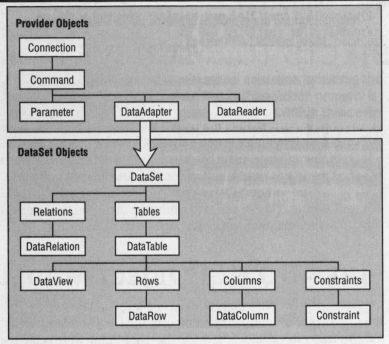

FIGURE 15.1:   ADO.NET objects

In this section, I'll describe the various ADO.NET objects so that you can get the overall picture before digging into the actual mechanics of using these objects.

The Data Provider Objects

Depending on how you look at it, there are either four or twelve main data provider objects. How can this be? The answer is that there are four important types of data provider objects, but each of these is implemented within several .NET namespaces. These four objects are as follows:

► Connection

► Command

▶ DataReader

▶ DataAdapter

The .NET data provider namespaces are as follows:

▶ `System.Data.OleDb`

▶ `System.Data.SqlClient`

▶ `System.Data.Odbc`

Thus, there are twelve objects to learn about, as shown in Table 15.1. But the only difference between the objects is the data sources with which they work. For example, the OleDbConnection, SqlConnection, and OdbcConnection all implement the same methods and properties. The difference is that they are used with OLE DB data sources, SQL Server data sources, and ODBC data sources, respectively.

TABLE 15.1:   Core Data Provider Objects

OBJECT	IMPLEMENTATIONS
Connection	OleDbConnection, SqlConnection, OdbcConnection
Command	OleDbCommand, SqlCommand, OdbcCommand
DataReader	OleDbDataReader, SqlDataReader, OdbcDataReader
DataAdapter	OleDbDataAdapter, SqlDataAdapter, OdbcDataAdapter

In the discussion that follows, I'll refer mostly to the generic object names. In actual code, you'll see the particular class names. I'll continue the discussion of the .NET data providers after you've seen the objects in the ADO.NET object model.

There are sometimes minor differences between the implementations of these objects. For example, both the OdbcConnection and the OleDbConnection implement a ReleaseObjectPool method, which is not shared by the SqlConnection object.

NOTE

Data providers also implement some helper objects, such as the Parameter object, which can be used to supply parameters to a Command object. Like the objects discussed above, these helper objects come in multiple versions.

Part IV

Connection

The Connection object in ADO.NET, just like its namesake in ADO, represents a single persistent connection to a data source. ADO.NET automatically handles connection pooling, which contributes to better application performance. When you close a Connection, it is returned to a connection pool. Connections in a pool are not immediately destroyed by ADO.NET. Instead, they're available for reuse if another part of your application requests a connection that matches in details a previously closed connection.

Table 15.2 lists the important members of the Connection object.

TABLE 15.2: Connection Members

NAME	TYPE	DESCRIPTION
BeginTransaction	Method	Start a new transaction on this Connection.
ChangeDatabase	Method	Switch current databases.
Close	Method	Close the Connection and return it to the connection pool.
ConnectionString	Property	Connection string that determines the data source to be used for this Connection.
ConnectionTimeout	Property	Number of seconds to wait before timing out when connecting.
CreateCommand	Method	Returns a new Command object.
Database	Property	Name of the current database open on this Connection.
DataSource	Property	Name of the current server for this Connection.
Driver	Property	ODBC driver in use by this Connection. Applies to OdbcConnection only.
GetOleDbSchemaTable	Method	Returns schema information from the data source. Applies to OleDbConnection only.
InfoMessage	Event	Fired when the server sends an informational message.
Open	Method	Opens the Connection.
PacketSize	Property	Size of network packets (in bytes) used by this Connection. Applies to SqlConnection only.

TABLE 15.2 continued: Connection Members

NAME	TYPE	DESCRIPTION
Provider	Property	OLE DB provider in use by this Connection. Applies to OleDbConnection only.
ReleaseObjectPool	Method	Releases Connections held in the connection pool. Applies to OdbcConnection and OleDbConnection.
ServerVersion	Property	String containing the version number of the server.
State	Property	State of the Connection.
StateChange	Event	Fired when the state of the Connection changes.
WorkstationID	Property	String that identifies the connection client. Applies to SqlConnection only.

Here's some code to open a connection to a SQL Server data source, from the frmObjects form in the ADOChapter15 sample project. You'll see that it's very similar to ADO code that performs the same task.

```
Private Sub btnConnection_Click(ByVal sender _
As System.Object, ByVal e As System.EventArgs) _
Handles btnConnection.Click


    Dim cnn As New SqlClient.SqlConnection()


    Try
        lboResults.Items.Clear()
        cnn.ConnectionString = "Data Source=SKYROCKET;" & _
          "Initial Catalog=Northwind;" & _
          "Integrated Security=SSPI"
        cnn.Open()
        With lboResults.Items
            .Add("Connection succeeded:")
            .Add("Database = " & cnn.Database)
            .Add("DataSource = " & cnn.DataSource)
```

```
                        .Add("ServerVersion = " & cnn.ServerVersion)
            End With
            cnn.Close()
        Catch ex As Exception
            MsgBox("Error: " & ex.Source & ": " & ex.Message, _
              MsgBoxStyle.OKOnly, "btnConnection")
        End Try


    End Sub
```

WARNING

The examples in this chapter use a SQL Server named SKYROCKET as their data source. You'll need to change this to the name of your server in the source code.

Command

The ADO.NET Command object is also very close in meaning to its ADO counterpart. The Command object represents a string (such as a SQL statement or a stored procedure name) that can be executed through a Connection. Table 15.3 lists the important members of the Command object.

TABLE 15.3:   Command Members

NAME	TYPE	DESCRIPTION
Cancel	Method	Cancels execution of the Command.
CommandText	Property	Statement to be executed at the data source.
CommandTimeout	Property	Number of seconds to wait for a Command to execute.
CommandType	Property	An enumeration indicating the type of Command. Possible values are StoredProcedure, TableDirect, and Text. You can omit this property, in which case the data provider will determine the appropriate Command type.
Connection	Property	Connection through which this Command will be executed.

TABLE 15.3 continued: Command Members

NAME	TYPE	DESCRIPTION
CreateParameter	Method	Creates a new Parameter object for the Command.
ExecuteNonQuery	Method	Executes a Command that does not return results.
ExecuteReader	Method	Executes a Command and puts the results in a DataReader object.
ExecuteScalar	Method	Executes a Command and returns the value of the first column of the first row of results. Any other results are discarded.
ExecuteXmlReader	Method	Executes a Command and puts the results in an XmlReader object. Applies to SqlCommand only.
Parameters	Property	Collection of Parameter objects (if any) for this Command.
Prepare	Method	Prepares the Command for faster execution.
ResetCommandTimeout	Method	Resets the CommandTimeout property to its default value.

As an example of the use of the Command object, here's some code from the frmObjects form in this chapter's sample project; it uses the ExecuteScalar method to return the results of a SELECT COUNT statement:

```
Private Sub btnCommand_Click(ByVal sender _
As System.Object, ByVal e As System.EventArgs) _
Handles btnCommand.Click

    Dim cnn As New SqlClient.SqlConnection()
    Dim cmd As New SqlClient.SqlCommand()

    Try
        lboResults.Items.Clear()

        cnn.ConnectionString = "Data Source=SKYROCKET;" & _
```

```
            "Initial Catalog=Northwind;" & _
            "Integrated Security=SSPI"

        cnn.Open()
        cmd = cnn.CreateCommand
        cmd.CommandText = "SELECT COUNT(*) FROM Customers"
        lboResults.Items.Add("Customer count:")
        lboResults.Items.Add(cmd.ExecuteScalar)
        cnn.Close()
    Catch ex As Exception
        MsgBox("Error: " & ex.Source & ": " & ex.Message, _
        MsgBoxStyle.OKOnly, "btnCommand")
    End Try


    End Sub
```

Like the ADO Command object, the ADO.NET Command object includes a collection of Parameter objects. I'll discuss the use of Parameters later in the chapter, in the "Running Stored Procedures" section.

DataReader

The DataReader object has no direct analog in the old ADO way of doing things. The closest ADO concept is that of a forward-only, read-only Recordset. The DataReader gives you a "firehose" set of results based on a Command. You can create a DataReader only from a Command (not by declaring it using the New keyword), and you can only move forward in the data. The DataReader represents the fastest, but least flexible, way to retrieve data in ADO.NET.

Table 15.4 lists the important members of the DataReader object.

TABLE 15.4: DataReader Members

NAME	TYPE	DESCRIPTION
Close	Method	Closes the DataReader.
Depth	Property	Depth of nesting for the current row of the DataReader.
FieldCount	Property	Number of columns in the current row of the DataReader.

TABLE 15.4 continued: DataReader Members

NAME	TYPE	DESCRIPTION
GetBoolean	Method	Gets a Boolean value from the specified column.
GetByte	Method	Gets a byte value from the specified column.
GetBytes	Method	Gets a stream of bytes from the specified column.
GetChar	Method	Gets a character from the specified column.
GetChars	Method	Gets a stream of characters from the specified column.
GetDataTypeName	Method	Gets the name of the source datatype for a column.
GetDateTime	Method	Gets a date/time value from the specified column.
GetDecimal	Method	Gets a decimal value from the specified column.
GetDouble	Method	Gets a double value from the specified column.
GetFieldType	Method	Gets the ADO.NET field type for a column.
GetFloat	Method	Gets a floating-point value from the specified column.
GetGuid	Method	Gets a GUID from the specified column.
GetInt16	Method	Gets a 16-bit integer from the specified column.
GetInt32	Method	Gets a 32-bit integer from the specified column.
GetInt64	Method	Gets a 64-bit integer from the specified column.
GetName	Method	Gets the name of the specified column.
GetOrdinal	Method	Gets the column ordinal, given the column name.
GetSchemaTable	Method	Returns schema information for the DataReader object.
GetString	Method	Gets a string value from the specified column.
GetTimeSpan	Method	Gets a time value from the specified column.
GetValue	Method	Gets a value from the specified column in its native format.

Part IV

TABLE 15.4 continued: DataReader Members

Name	Type	Description
GetValues	Method	Gets an entire row of data into an array of objects.
IsClosed	Property	A Boolean value that indicates whether the DataReader is closed.
IsDbNull	Method	Indicates whether the specified column contains a Null.
Item	Property	Gets a value from the specified column in its native format.
NextResult	Method	Retrieves the next result set from the Command object.
Read	Method	Loads the next row of data into the DataReader object.
RecordsAffected	Property	Number of rows changed by the DataReader's SQL statement.

NOTE

The SqlDataReader also has methods such as GetSqlBinary and GetSqlBoolean that retrieve data into native objects from the `System.Data.SqlClient` namespace. Refer to the .NET Framework help for details on these methods.

Here's an example of using the DataReader class, once again with the SQL Server versions of the ADO.NET objects; it's from the frmObjects form in this chapter's sample project:

```
Private Sub btnDataReader_Click(ByVal sender _
As System.Object, ByVal e As System.EventArgs) _
Handles btnDataReader.Click

    Dim cnn As New SqlClient.SqlConnection()
    Dim cmd As New SqlClient.SqlCommand()
    Dim dr As SqlClient.SqlDataReader

    Try
        lboResults.Items.Clear()
```

```
        cnn.ConnectionString = "Data Source=SKYROCKET;" & _
          "Initial Catalog=Northwind;" & _
          "Integrated Security=SSPI"
        cnn.Open()
        cmd = cnn.CreateCommand
        cmd.CommandText = "SELECT CustomerID, " & _
          "CompanyName FROM Customers"
        dr = cmd.ExecuteReader
        While dr.Read
            lboResults.Items.Add(dr.GetString(0) & " " &
dr.GetString(1))
        End While
        dr.Close()
        cnn.Close()
    Catch ex As Exception
        MsgBox("Error: " & ex.Source & ": " & ex.Message, _
          MsgBoxStyle.OKOnly, "btnDataReader")
    End Try

    End Sub
```

Figure 15.2 shows the results of running this procedure in the sample database.

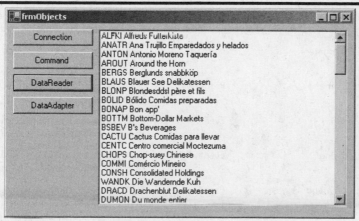

FIGURE 15.2:   Retrieving data with a DataReader object

DataAdapter

The DataAdapter object has no direct equivalent in old-style ADO. This object provides the essential link between the data provider objects and the DataSet (which I'll discuss in the next section). The DataAdapter is a two-way pipeline between the data as it's stored and the data in a more abstract form that's designed for manipulation. Methods of the DataAdapter can be used to move the data back and forth between the two representations.

Table 15.5 lists the important members of the DataAdapter object.

TABLE 15.5:   DataAdapter Members

NAME	TYPE	DESCRIPTION
AcceptChangesDuringFill	Property	If True, all rows in the DataSet are marked as committed when they're added with the Fill method. Not available for OdbcDataAdapter.
ContinueUpdateOnError	Property	If True, updates continue even after updating a single row fails. Not available for OdbcDataAdapter.
DeleteCommand	Property	SQL statement used to delete records from the data source.
Fill	Method	Transfers data from the data source to the DataSet.
FillError	Event	Fires when an error occurs during the Fill method.
FillSchema	Method	Adjusts the schema of the DataSet to match the schema of the data source.
GetFillParameters	Method	Gets any parameters supplied to the SelectCommand.
InsertCommand	Property	SQL statement used to insert records into the data source.
RowUpdated	Event	Fired during the Update method just after a row is updated.
RowUpdating	Event	Fired during the Update method just before a row is updated.
SelectCommand	Property	SQL statement used to select records from the data source.
TableMappings	Property	Specifies the mapping between tables in the data source and DataTables in the DataSet.

TABLE 15.5 continued: DataAdapter Members

NAME	TYPE	DESCRIPTION
Update	Method	Transfers data from the DataSet to the data source.
UpdateCommand	Property	SQL statement used to update records in the data source.

The following code for the DataAdapter, from the frmObjects form in this chapter's sample project, uses several objects that you won't meet until later in the chapter. Note that filling the DataSet from the DataAdapter requires that the SelectCommand property of the DataAdapter be set, but not the other Command properties (DeleteCommand, InsertCommand, and UpdateCommand). Those properties are needed only to move information back from the DataSet to the data source.

```
Private Sub btnDataAdapter_Click(ByVal sender _
 As System.Object, ByVal e As System.EventArgs) _
 Handles btnDataAdapter.Click
    Dim cnn As New SqlClient.SqlConnection()
    Dim cmd As New SqlClient.SqlCommand()
    Dim da As New SqlClient.SqlDataAdapter()
    Dim ds As New DataSet()
    Dim drw As DataRow

    Try
        lboResults.Items.Clear()
        cnn.ConnectionString = "Data Source=SKYROCKET;" & _
         "Initial Catalog=Northwind;" & _
         "Integrated Security=SSPI"
        cnn.Open()
        cmd = cnn.CreateCommand
        cmd.CommandText = "SELECT CustomerID, " & _
         "CompanyName FROM  Customers"
        da.SelectCommand = cmd
        da.Fill(ds, "Customers")
        For Each drw In ds.Tables("Customers").Rows
```

```
                    lboResults.Items.Add(drw.Item(0) & " " & _
                drw.Item(1))
            Next
            cnn.Close()
        Catch ex As Exception
            MsgBox("Error: " & ex.Source & ": " & ex.Message, _
            MsgBoxStyle.OKOnly, "btnDataAdapter")
        End Try


    End Sub
```

Minor Data Provider Objects

There are a number of other objects supplied by the data provider name-spaces that are used less often than the four I've already covered. Table 15.6 summarizes these objects.

TABLE 15.6: Other Data Provider Objects

OBJECT	DESCRIPTION
CommandBuilder	Automatically generates the DeleteCommand, Insert-Command, and UpdateCommand properties for a DataAdapter object.
Error	Provides information on an error returned by the data source.
ErrorCollection	A collection of Error objects.
Parameter	A single Parameter to a Command object.
ParameterCollection	A collection of Parameter objects.
Transaction	A database transaction in progress.

The DataSet Objects

Unlike the ADO.NET data provider objects, there is only one set of DataSet objects, implemented in the System.Data namespace. These objects provide an abstract, disconnected way to manipulate almost any sort of data. You can use a DataSet to represent a table or set of tables from a relational data source, an XML document, or any other data that you can access via an OLE DB provider. You can also create completely synthetic DataSets and load them with data directly from your application. In this section, I'll introduce the DataSet and the major objects that it contains:

- ▶ DataSet
- ▶ DataTable
- ▶ DataRelation
- ▶ DataRow
- ▶ DataColumn
- ▶ Constraint
- ▶ DataView

DataSet

The DataSet object itself is a memory-resident representation of data. It's designed to be self-contained and easy to move around between the various components of a .NET application. Table 15.7 lists some of the important members of the DataSet object.

TABLE 15.7:   DataSet Members

Name	Type	Description
AcceptChanges	Method	Commits all changes made to the DataSet since it was loaded or since the previous call to AcceptChanges.
Clear	Method	Removes all data in the DataSet.
DataSetName	Property	Name of the DataSet.
EnforceConstraints	Property	If True, constraints are enforced during updates.
GetChanges	Method	Gets a DataSet containing only the changed rows from the DataSet.
GetXml	Method	Returns an XML representation of the DataSet.
GetXmlSchema	Method	Returns an XSD schema of the DataSet.
HasChanges	Method	Returns True if the DataSet has changes that have not yet been committed.
Merge	Method	Merges two DataSets.

Part IV

TABLE 15.7 continued: DataSet Members

NAME	TYPE	DESCRIPTION
ReadXml	Method	Loads the DataSet from an XML file.
ReadXmlSchema	Method	Loads the DataSet schema from an XSD file.
RejectChanges	Method	Discards all changes made to the DataSet since it was loaded or since the previous call to AcceptChanges.
Relations	Property	The collection of DataRelation objects within the DataSet.
Tables	Property	The collection of DataTable objects within the DataSet.
WriteXml	Method	Writes the DataSet out as XML.
WriteXmlSchema	Method	Writes the DataSet schema out as an XML schema (XSD) file.

DataTable

As you might guess from the name, the DataTable object represents a single table within a DataSet. A DataSet can contain multiple DataTables. Table 15.8 lists some of the important members of the DataTable object.

TABLE 15.8:   DataTable Members

NAME	TYPE	DESCRIPTION
AcceptChanges	Method	Commits all changes to this DataTable since it was loaded or since the last call to AcceptChanges.
CaseSensitive	Property	Read-write property that returns True if string comparisons within this DataTable are case-sensitive.
ChildRelations	Property	The collection of DataRelation objects that refer to children of this DataTable.
Clear	Method	Clears all data from the DataTable.
ColumnChanged	Event	Fires when the data in any row of a specified column has been changed.
ColumnChanging	Event	Fires when the data in any row of a specified column is about to change.

TABLE 15.8 continued: DataTable Members

NAME	TYPE	DESCRIPTION
Columns	Property	The collection of DataColumn objects in this DataTable.
Constraints	Property	The collection of Constraint objects for this table.
GetChanges	Method	Gets a DataTable containing only the changed rows from this DataTable.
ImportRow	Method	Imports a DataRow into this DataTable.
LoadDataRow	Method	Finds and updates a row in this DataTable.
NewRow	Method	Creates a new, blank row in the DataTable.
ParentRelations	Property	The collection of DataRelation objects that refer to parents of this DataTable.
PrimaryKey	Property	Array of columns that provide the primary key for this DataTable.
RejectChanges	Method	Discards all changes to this DataTable since it was loaded or since the last call to AcceptChanges.
RowChanged	Event	Fires when any data in a DataRow is changed.
RowChanging	Event	Fires when any data in a DataRow is about to change.
RowDeleted	Event	Fires when a row is deleted.
RowDeleting	Event	Fires when a row is about to be deleted.
Rows	Property	The collection of DataRow objects in this DataTable.
Select	Method	Selects an array of DataRow objects that meet specified criteria.
TableName	Property	The name of this DataTable.

WARNING

Unlike other object models with which you may be familiar, the ADO.NET object model doesn't necessarily use the same name for a property and the object that it returns. For example, the Rows property of a DataTable returns a DataRowCollection object, which contains a collection of DataRows. In practice, this seldom causes confusion because you're less likely to operate directly on the collection objects.

DataRelation

The DataRelation object represents a relation between two DataTables. The DataSet has a Relations collection that contains all of the DataRelation objects defined within the DataSet. In addition, each DataTable has Child-Relations and ParentRelations collections containing the DataRelation objects that refer to that DataTable. Each DataRelation is made up of Data-Column objects that specify the relationship between the DataTables involved. You can optionally use a Constraint object (discussed later in this section) to add cascading deletes or updates to a DataRelation. Table 15.9 lists some of the important members of the DataRelation object.

TABLE 15.9: DataRelation Members

Name	Type	Description
ChildColumns	Property	Collection of DataColumn objects that define the child side of the DataRelation.
ChildKeyConstraint	Property	Returns the foreign key constraint for the DataRelation.
ChildTable	Property	Returns the child DataTable for the DataRelation.
ParentColumns	Property	Collection of DataColumn objects that define the parent side of the DataRelation.
ParentKeyConstraint	Property	Returns the primary key constraint for the DataRelation.
ParentTable	Property	Returns the parent DataTable for the DataRelation.
RelationName	Property	Name of the DataRelation.

DataRow

The DataRow object provides row-by-row access to the data contained in a DataTable. When you're selecting, inserting, updating, or deleting data, you'll usually work with DataRow objects. I'll discuss data selection later in this chapter and data manipulation in the next chapter. Table 15.10 lists some of the important members of the DataRow object.

TABLE 15.10: DataRow Members

NAME	TYPE	DESCRIPTION
AcceptChanges	Property	Commits changes made to this row since the last time AcceptChanges was called.
BeginEdit	Method	Starts editing the DataRow.
CancelEdit	Method	Discards an edit in progress.
Delete	Method	Deletes the DataRow from its parent DataTable.
EndEdit	Method	Ends an editing session on the DataRow.
GetChildRows	Method	Gets the child rows related to this DataRow.
GetParentRow	Method	Gets the parent row related to this DataRow.
Item	Property	Returns the data from a particular column of the DataRow.
ItemArray	Property	Returns the data from the entire DataRow as an array.
IsNull	Method	Returns True if a specified column is Null.
RejectChanges	Method	Discards changes made to this row since the last time AcceptChanges was called.
RowState	Property	Returns information on the current state of the DataRow (for example, whether the row has been modified).

DataColumn

The DataColumn object represents a single column in a DataTable. By manipulating the DataColumns in a DataTable, you can investigate and even change the DataTable's schema. Table 15.11 lists some of the important members of the DataColumn object.

TABLE 15.11: DataColumn Members

NAME	TYPE	DESCRIPTION
AllowDbNull	Property	True if the DataColumn can contain Nulls.
AutoIncrement	Property	True if the DataColumn automatically assigns new values to new rows.

TABLE 15.11 continued: DataColumn Members

NAME	TYPE	DESCRIPTION
AutoIncrementSeed	Property	Starting value for an AutoIncrement DataColumn.
AutoIncrementStep	Property	Increment value for an AutoIncrement DataColumn.
Caption	Property	Caption for the DataColumn.
ColumnName	Property	Name of the DataColumn.
DataType	Property	Datatype for the DataColumn.
DefaultValue	Property	Default value for this DataColumn in new rows of the DataTable.
MaxLength	Property	Maximum length of a text DataColumn.
Ordinal	Property	Position of the DataColumn in the Columns collection of the parent DataTable.
ReadOnly	Property	True if the value in the DataColumn cannot be changed after it has been set.
Unique	Property	True if values in the DataColumn must be unique.

Constraint

The Constraint object comes in two varieties: The ForeignKeyConstraint object represents a foreign key, while the UniqueConstraint object represents a unique constraint. DataTable objects have a Constraints collection that contains both types of Constraint objects. Table 15.12 lists some of the important members of the Constraint objects.

TABLE 15.12:   Constraint Members

NAME	TYPE	DESCRIPTION
AcceptRejectRule	Property	Constant that specifies cascading commit behavior. Applies to ForeignKeyConstraint only.
Columns	Property	Array of DataColumns that are affected by this Constraint.
DeleteRule	Property	Constant that specifies cascading delete behavior. Applies to ForeignKeyConstraint only.

TABLE 15.12 continued: Constraint Members

NAME	TYPE	DESCRIPTION
ConstraintName	Property	Name of the Constraint.
RelatedColumns	Property	Collection of DataColumns that are the parent of this Constraint. Applies to ForeignKey-Constraint only.
RelatedTable	Property	DataTable that is the parent table of this Constraint. Applies to ForeignKeyConstraint only.
IsPrimaryKey	Property	True if this Constraint represents a primary key. Applies to UniqueConstraint only.
UpdateRule	Property	Constant that specifies cascading update behavior. Applies to ForeignKeyConstraint only.

DataView

The DataView object represents a view of the data contained in a DataTable. This view can contain all of the data from the DataTable, or it can be filtered to return only specific rows. You can filter either with SQL expressions or by looking for rows in a particular state. For example, a DataView could show only selected columns from a DataTable, or it could show only rows that have been modified since the last call to the AcceptChanges method. Table 15.13 lists some of the important members of the DataView object.

TABLE 15.13:   DataView Members

NAME	TYPE	DESCRIPTION
AddNew	Method	Adds a new row to the DataView.
AllowDelete	Property	True if deletions can be performed via this DataView.
AllowEdit	Property	True if updates can be performed via this DataView.
AllowNew	Property	True if new rows can be added via this DataView.
Count	Property	Number of records contained in this DataView.
Delete	Method	Deletes a row from the DataView.

TABLE 15.13 continued:　DataView Members

Name	Type	Description
Find	Method	Searches for a specified row in the DataView.
FindRows	Method	Returns an array of rows matching a filter expression.
Item	Property	Returns the data from a particular row of the DataView in a DataRowView object.
ListChanged	Event	Fired when the data in this DataView changes.
RowFilter	Property	Filter expression to limit the data returned in the DataView.
RowStateFilter	Property	Filter to limit the data returned in the DataView by the state of the rows.
Sort	Property	Sorts columns and order for the DataView.

.NET Data Providers

Just as ODBC data access uses ODBC drivers, and ADO data access uses OLE DB providers, ADO.NET uses .NET data providers. In all three cases, the purpose is the same: to provide a layer of software that can hide the differences between various data sources by presenting a uniform interface to the more abstract objects (in ADO.NET, these more abstract objects are the DataSet and its child objects).

As of this writing, the .NET Framework includes two data providers: the SQL Server .NET Data Provider and the OLE DB .NET Data Provider. In addition, there is an ODBC .NET Data Provider available as a separate download; it's not clear whether this provider will remain as a download or will ship as part of the final product.

NOTE

During the beta period, the ODBC .NET Data Provider was available from `http://msdn.microsoft.com/downloads/sample.asp?url=/MSDN-FILES/027/001/668/msdncompositedoc.xml&frame=true`. This may change in the final release.

The SQL Server .NET Data Provider

The SQL Server .NET Data Provider can be used with SQL Server data sources that use SQL Server 7 or later. This data provider uses the native SQL Server protocols to talk directly to the database server, without any intervening OLE DB or ODBC layers. This allows it to deliver the fastest possible performance with SQL Server data, at the expense of not working with any other data source.

The SQL Server .NET Data Provider is implemented in the System .Data.SqlClient namespace. As with ADO, you control the data that will be returned by setting the ConnectionString property of the SqlConnection object. The ConnectionString property syntax is similar (but not identical) to that of the SQLOLEDB provider used by traditional ADO. The ConnectionString property must contain a semicolon-delimited set of property-value pairs:

```
Property1=Value1;Property2=Value2...
```

Table 15.14 lists the properties that are recognized in the SqlConnection .ConnectionString property. Note that some of these properties have alternative names, separated by *or* in the table.

TABLE 15.14:   Arguments for the SqlConnection.ConnectionString Property

PROPERTY	DESCRIPTION
Application Name	Name of the connecting application. Defaults to ".NET SqlClient Data Provider."
AttachDbFilename or Initial File Name	Name of a database file to attach.
Connect Timeout or Connection Timeout	Number of seconds to wait for the Connection to contact the server. Defaults to 15 seconds.
Connection Lifetime	Maximum age (in seconds) for a Connection returned to the connection pool before it is automatically destroyed.
Connection Reset	True if Connections are reset when they are returned to the connection pool.
Current Language	The SQL Server language used by this Connection.
Data Source or Server or Address or Addr or Network Address	The server to connect to. This can be a machine name, the special name (local), or a network address.

Part IV

TABLE 15.14 continued: Arguments for the SqlConnection .ConnectionString Property

PROPERTY	DESCRIPTION
Enlist	Specifies whether to enlist the Connection in the calling thread's transaction context. Defaults to True.
Initial Catalog or Database	Database to connect to.
Integrated Security or Trusted_Connection	Set to True or SSPI to use Windows integrated security. Otherwise, uses SQL Server security, which is the default.
Max Pool Size	Maximum number of Connections to pool. Defaults to 100.
Min Pool Size	Minimum number of Connections to pool. Defaults to 0.
Network Library or Net	Name of the SQL Server network DLL used by this Connection.
Packet Size	Packet Size to use when communicating with the server. Defaults to 8,192.
Password or Pwd	SQL Server password.
Persist Security Info	Set to True to save passwords in the connection string. Defaults to False.
Pooling	Set to True (the default) to enable Connection pooling.
User ID	SQL Server username.
Workstation ID	Name of the computer that's connecting to SQL Server. Defaults to the local computer name.

The OLE DB .NET Data Provider

The OLE DB .NET Data Provider is used for connecting to data sources from .NET via existing OLE DB providers. Microsoft has implemented a special OLE DB service component to handle connection pooling and transactions on such providers. This sounds like it should be a universal solution, but, unfortunately, the only supported OLE DB data providers are these:

- ▶ Microsoft OLE DB Provider for SQL Server
- ▶ Microsoft OLE DB Provider for Oracle
- ▶ OLE DB Provider for Microsoft Jet (4.0 version only)

Some OLE DB providers are known definitely not to work with this .NET data provider. These include the OLE DB Provider for ODBC, the Microsoft OLE DB Provider for Exchange, and the Microsoft OLE DB Provider for Internet Publishing. You may have success with other OLE DB providers, but you should thoroughly test your solution before depending on an unsupported provider.

Although the OLE DB .NET Data Provider works with the Microsoft OLE DB Provider for SQL Server, you should reserve this solution for SQL Server 6.5 and earlier versions. For SQL Server 7 or later, you'll get better performance by using the SQL Server .NET Data Provider instead.

The OLE DB .NET Data Provider is implemented in the `System.Data` `.OleDb` namespace. The ConnectionString syntax for this provider is the same as for the underlying OLE DB providers.

TIP

Connection strings for the SQL Server provider are discussed in Chapter 14, "A First Look at ADO.NET," under the section "The Connection String Property."

The ODBC .NET Data Provider

The ODBC .NET Data Provider supplies data access through ODBC drivers, similar to the way in which the OLE DB .NET Data Provider supplies data access through OLE DB providers. There is a short list of ODBC drivers that are supported with this data provider:

- ▶ Microsoft SQL ODBC Driver
- ▶ Microsoft ODBC Driver for Oracle
- ▶ Microsoft Jet ODBC Driver

Other ODBC drivers may work with this data provider, but once again, you'll need to thoroughly test such solutions before depending on them in a production setting.

The `OdbcConnection.ConnectionString` property is passed through unchanged to the ODBC Manager and ODBC driver that are being used. Thus, the syntax for the connection string precisely matches that of the underlying drivers.

Part IV

USING DATASETS

In this section, you'll learn the basic syntax for working with DataSets. This chapter concentrates on populating a DataSet and retrieving the data that it contains. Chapter 16, "Editing Data with ADO.NET," discusses the use of the DataSet to change data and to persist the changes back to the original data source.

Populating a DataSet from a Database

If you want to display data from a database without writing changes back to the database, you can do so by using the data provider objects to move data from the database to a DataSet, and then using the DataGrid control on a Windows Form to display the data. To do so, follow these steps:

1. Open a Connection to the database containing the data.

2. Create a Command that retrieves the data that you want to display.

3. Create a DataAdapter, and set its SelectCommand property to point to the Command object.

4. Create a DataSet by calling the Fill method of the DataAdapter.

5. Set the DataSource property of a DataGrid control to refer to the DataSet.

6. Set the DataMember property of a DataGrid control to refer to the table that you want to display.

Here's some code from frmDataSet in this chapter's sample project that carries out these steps:

```
Private Sub btnPopulateDatabase_Click(ByVal sender _
As System.Object, ByVal e As System.EventArgs) _
Handles btnPopulateDatabase.Click
    Dim cnn As New SqlClient.SqlConnection()
    Dim cmd As New SqlClient.SqlCommand()
    Dim da As New SqlClient.SqlDataAdapter()
    Dim ds As New DataSet()
```

```
Try
    cnn.ConnectionString = "Data Source=SKYROCKET;" & _
        "Initial Catalog=Northwind;" & _
        "Integrated Security=SSPI"
    cnn.Open()

    cmd = cnn.CreateCommand
    cmd.CommandText = "SELECT * FROM Customers"
    da.SelectCommand = cmd
    da.Fill(ds, "Customers")
    cnn.Close()

    dgMain.DataSource = ds
    dgMain.DataMember = "Customers"

Catch ex As Exception
    MsgBox("Error: " & ex.Source & ": " & ex.Message, _
        MsgBoxStyle.OKOnly, "btnPopulateDatabase")

End Try

End Sub
```

Figure 15.3 shows the result of running this code.

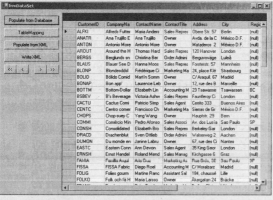

FIGURE 15.3:   Data on a DataGrid control

Note that this code actually closes the connection to the database before displaying the data. Once the DataSet has been filled, it doesn't need the connection to the data source any longer; the data is entirely contained in memory. Of course, you need to reconnect to the data source to save any changes in the data. You'll see that technique in the next chapter.

The name supplied to the Fill method of the DataAdapter object is not the name of the table in the original data source, but rather the name of the DataTable to be created within the DataSet. The Fill method creates this DataTable and then fills it with whatever data is returned by the SelectCommand. The DataMember property of the DataGrid also holds a DataTable name, not an original table name. Thus, you could replace the fill and display portions of the preceding code snippet with this code, and it would work as well:

```
da.Fill(ds, "Peanuts")
cnn.Close()


dgMain.DataSource = ds
dgMain.DataMember = "Peanuts"
```

TIP

Of course, for code readability and maintainability, you'll probably want to use the same names for DataTable objects as for the tables that they are filled from!

Although the preceding code does produce the desired result, it's not the best way to solve the problem in a distributed environment such as .NET. In practice, you should strive to minimize the amount of time that you hold an open Connection. You can do this by letting the DataAdapter implicitly open the Connection when it needs it. Here's the actual code that's used in the sample project:

```
Private Sub btnPopulateDatabase_Click(ByVal sender _
  As System.Object, e As System.EventArgs) _
  Handles btnPopulateDatabase.Click
    Dim cnn As SqlClient.SqlConnection = New _
      SqlClient.SqlConnection("Data Source=SKYROCKET;" & _
```

```
      "Initial Catalog=Northwind;Integrated Security=SSPI")
   Dim cmd As New SqlClient.SqlCommand()
   Dim da As New SqlClient.SqlDataAdapter()
   Dim ds As New DataSet()

   Try
        cmd = cnn.CreateCommand
        cmd.CommandText = "SELECT * FROM Customers"
        da.SelectCommand = cmd
        da.Fill(ds, "Customers")

        dgMain.DataSource = ds
        dgMain.DataMember = "Customers"

   Catch ex As Exception
        MsgBox("Error: " & ex.Source & ": " & ex.Message, _
        MsgBoxStyle.OKOnly, "btnPopulateDatabase")
   End Try

   End Sub
```

This version of the code places the connection string directly into the constructor for the Connection object. In this case, the DataAdapter will open the Connection when its own Fill method is invoked, and close it immediately after it has retrieved the necessary data.

NOTE

If you perform multiple operations requiring an open Connection in a single procedure, it will be more efficient to call the Open and Close methods of the Connection object explicitly than to allow other objects to manage the Connection implicitly.

You've already seen that you can specify the name of the DataTable object in the call to the DataAdapter's Fill method. More generally, you can specify both the DataTable name and the names of the DataColumn

Part IV

objects within the DataTable by using the System.Data.Common .DataTableMapping object. This object lets you set up a series of associations between source table and column names and the destination DataTable and DataColumn names. Here's an example:

```
Private Sub btnTableMapping_Click(ByVal sender _
As System.Object, ByVal e As System.EventArgs) _
Handles btnTableMapping.Click
  Dim cnn As SqlClient.SqlConnection = New _
  SqlClient.SqlConnection("Data Source=SKYROCKET;" & _
  "Initial Catalog=Northwind;Integrated Security=SSPI")
  Dim cmd As New SqlClient.SqlCommand()
  Dim da As New SqlClient.SqlDataAdapter()
  Dim ds As New DataSet()

  Try
      cmd = cnn.CreateCommand
      cmd.CommandText = "SELECT * FROM Customers"
      da.SelectCommand = cmd

      Dim dtm As System.Data.Common.DataTableMapping = _
      da.TableMappings.Add("Table", "CurrentCustomers")
      With dtm.ColumnMappings
          .Add("CustomerID", "Identifier")
          .Add("CompanyName", "Company")
          .Add("ContactName", "Contact")
      End With

      da.Fill(ds)

      dgMain.DataSource = ds
      dgMain.DataMember = "CurrentCustomers"
```

```
Catch ex As Exception
    MsgBox("Error: " & ex.Source & ": " & ex.Message, _
    MsgBoxStyle.OKOnly, "btnPopulateDatabase")
End Try
```

```
End Sub
```

The new DataTableMapping object is created by calling the Add method of the DataAdapter's TableMappings collection. This method takes the name of the table as seen by the DataAdapter (which defaults to "Table" in the case of a result set that returns a single table) and the name of the DataTable to deliver. In turn, the DataTableMapping object has a collection of DataColumnMapping objects that associate source columns with destination DataColumns. Figure 15.4 shows the result of running this code.

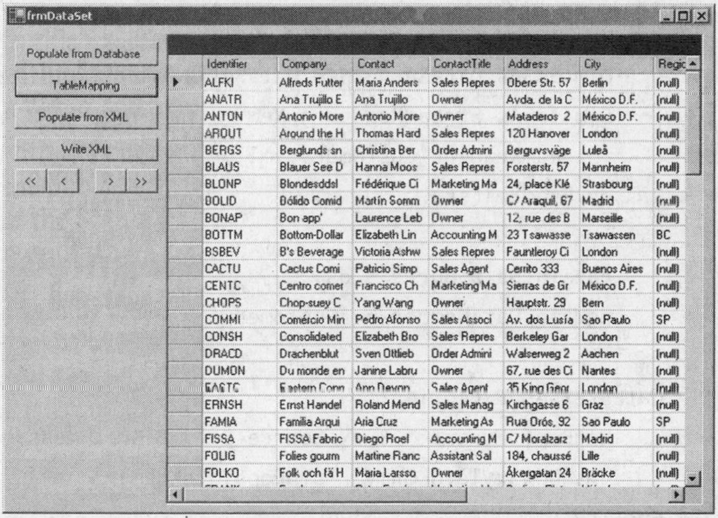

FIGURE 15.4:   Table displayed with column names specified by mapping

As you can see in Figure 15.4, the DataAdapter object uses the source column name as the destination DataColumn name for any column that doesn't appear in the ColumnMappings collection.

Part IV

Using XML with the DataSet Object

The .NET Framework supplies close connections between the DataSet object and XML. DataSets can be loaded from XML or persisted to XML files. One way to think about the connection is that XML can be used to provide a transmission format for the DataSet. By converting a DataSet to XML, you end up with a representation of the DataSet in a format that can be easily moved around without your worrying about the problems of transmitting binary data past firewalls.

Populating a DataSet from an XML file is simple. For example, this code from the frmDataSet form in this chapter's sample project will do just that:

```
Private Sub btnPopulateXML_Click(ByVal sender _
As System.Object, ByVal e As System.EventArgs) _
Handles btnPopulateXML.Click


    Try
        Dim ds As DataSet = New DataSet()
        Dim sr As StreamReader = New _
         StreamReader("Customers.xml")
        ds.ReadXml(sr)

        dgMain.DataSource = ds
        dgMain.DataMember = "Customers"

    Catch ex As Exception
        MsgBox("Error: " & ex.Source & ": " & ex.Message, _
        MsgBoxStyle.OKOnly, "btnPopulateXML")
    End Try

End Sub
```

As you can see, the DataSet object's ReadXml method can be used to directly read an XML file into the DataSet. The StreamReader object (part of the System.IO namespace) simply provides a way to read a disk file. In this particular case, the XML file was created by exporting the Customers table from the Access 2002 version of the Northwind sample database. Here's a portion of that file:

```xml
<?xml version="1.0" encoding="UTF-8"?>
<dataroot xmlns:od="urn:schemas-microsoft-com:officedata">
<Customers>
<CustomerID>ALFKI</CustomerID>
<CompanyName>Alfreds Futterkiste</CompanyName>
<ContactName>Maria Anders</ContactName>
<ContactTitle>Sales Representative</ContactTitle>
<Address>Obere Str. 57</Address>
<City>Berlin</City>
<PostalCode>12209</PostalCode>
<Country>Germany</Country>
<Phone>030-0074321</Phone>
<Fax>030-0076545</Fax>
</Customers>
<Customers>
<CustomerID>ANATR</CustomerID>
<CompanyName>Ana Trujillo Emparedados y helados
</CompanyName>
<ContactName>Ana Trujillo</ContactName>
<ContactTitle>Owner</ContactTitle>
...
```

This file contains all the data from the original Customers table, but none of the schema information. So, how does .NET know what to do with it? It infers a schema by looking at the data and making the best choices that it can about datatypes. The ReadXml method actually takes two parameters:

```
DataSet.ReadXml(Stream, XmlReadMode)
```

The XmlReadMode parameter can be any one of the constants listed in Table 15.15.

TABLE 15.15:   XmlReadMode Constants

Constant	Meaning
Auto	If the XML file is recognized as a DiffGram, read it as a DiffGram. If it's not a Diffgram but there is schema information in the XML file or in an associated XSD file, use that schema to build the DataSet. Otherwise, infer the schema from the data. This is the default.
DiffGram	Treats the XML file as a DiffGram. A DiffGram is a special format that specifies changes to a DataSet by supplying original rows and change information.
Fragment	Reads XML files containing inline XDR schema information.
IgnoreSchema	Ignores any schema information contained in the XML file and attempts to fit the data into the current schema of the DataSet.
InferSchema	Infers the schema of the XML file by examining the data.
ReadSchema	Uses XSD information to define the schema of the DataSet.

WARNING

Although Access 2002 can save XSD information when exporting an XML file, the XSD file from Access uses an XML namespace that .NET doesn't recognize.

The DataSet object also provides several ways to convert its contents to XML. First, there's the GetXml method, which returns an XML representation of the DataSet as a string:

```
Dim strXML As String = ds.GetXml()
```

The GetXml method is useful when you want to make a DataSet available as XML through an object property or when you want to display the XML on the user interface.

There's also the WriteXml method, which can persist the XML representation of the DataSet directly to a file:

```
ds.WriteXml("SavedCustomers.xml")
```

The WriteXml method takes an optional second parameter to specify schema behavior. This parameter can be one of three constants from the XmlWriteMode enumeration, as shown in Table 15.16.

TABLE 15.16: XmlWriteMode Constants

Constant	Meaning
IgnoreSchema	Writes the XML file without any schema information. This is the default.
WriteSchema	Writes XSD information directly to the XML file.
Diffgram	Writes the DataSet out in DiffGram format.

The Write XML button on frmDataSet in the sample application calls code to write a DataSet out as XML:

```
Private Sub btnWriteXml_Click(ByVal sender _
  As System.Object, ByVal e As System.EventArgs) _
  Handles btnWriteXml.Click
    Dim cnn As SqlClient.SqlConnection = New _
     SqlClient.SqlConnection("Data Source=SKYROCKET;" & _
     "Initial Catalog=Northwind;Integrated Security=SSPI")

    Dim cmd As New SqlClient.SqlCommand()
    Dim da As New SqlClient.SqlDataAdapter()
    Dim ds As New DataSet()

    Try
        cmd = cnn.CreateCommand
        cmd.CommandText = "SELECT * FROM Customers"
        da.SelectCommand = cmd
        da.Fill(ds, "Customers")
        ds.WriteXml("SQLCustomers.xml", _
         XmlWriteMode.WriteSchema)
```

```
        Catch ex As Exception
            MsgBox("Error: " & ex.Source & ": " & _
                ex.Message, MsgBoxStyle.OKOnly, "btnWriteXml")
        End Try


    End Sub
```

Listing 15.1 shows the beginning of the resulting file.

Listing 15.1: A DataSet Saved as XML with Schema Information

```xml
<?xml version="1.0" standalone="yes"?>
<NewDataSet>
  <xs:schema id="NewDataSet" xmlns=""
    xmlns:xs="http://www.w3.org/2001/XMLSchema"
    xmlns:msdata="urn:schemas-microsoft-com:xml-msdata">
    <xs:element name="NewDataSet" msdata:IsDataSet="true">
      <xs:complexType>
        <xs:choice maxOccurs="unbounded">
          <xs:element name="Customers">
            <xs:complexType>
              <xs:sequence>
                <xs:element name="CustomerID"
                  type="xs:string" minOccurs="0" />
                <xs:element name="CompanyName"
                  type="xs:string" minOccurs="0" />
                <xs:element name="ContactName"
                  type="xs:string" minOccurs="0" />
                <xs:element name="ContactTitle"
                  type="xs:string" minOccurs="0" />
                <xs:element name="Address"
                  type="xs:string" minOccurs="0" />
                <xs:element name="City"
                  type="xs:string" minOccurs="0" />
                <xs:element name="Region"
                  type="xs:string" minOccurs="0" />
                <xs:element name="PostalCode"
                  type="xs:string" minOccurs="0" />
                <xs:element name="Country"
                  type="xs:string" minOccurs="0" />
                <xs:element name="Phone"
                  type="xs:string" minOccurs="0" />
                <xs:element name="Fax"
```

```
                          type="xs:string" minOccurs="0" />
                </xs:sequence>
            </xs:complexType>
          </xs:element>
        </xs:choice>
      </xs:complexType>
    </xs:element>
  </xs:schema>
  <Customers>
    <CustomerID>ALFKI</CustomerID>
    <CompanyName>Alfreds Futterkiste</CompanyName>
    <ContactName>Maria Anders</ContactName>
    <ContactTitle>Sales Representative</ContactTitle>
    <Address>Obere Str. 57</Address>
    <City>Berlin</City>
    <PostalCode>12209</PostalCode>
    <Country>Germany</Country>
    <Phone>030-0074321</Phone>
    <Fax>030-0076545</Fax>
  </Customers>
  <Customers>
    <CustomerID>ANATR</CustomerID>
    <CompanyName>Ana Trujillo Emparedados y helados
      </CompanyName>
    <ContactName>Ana Trujillo</ContactName>
    <ContactTitle>Owner</ContactTitle>
    <Address>Avda. de la Constitución 2222</Address>
    <City>México D.F.</City>
    <PostalCode>05021</PostalCode>
    <Country>Mexico</Country>
    <Phone>(5) 555-4729</Phone>
    <Fax>(5) 555-3745</Fax>
  </Customers>
```

The information at the top of the file, in the xs: namespace, is the XSD schema information created by the WriteXml method. This information includes the field names and datatypes for the columns within the DataSet.

TIP

For more information on XSD and other XML topics, refer to *XML Schemas* by Chelsea Valentine, Lucinda Dykes, and Ed Tittel (Sybex, 2002).

TIP

For more general information on the DataSet and XML, including why ADO.NET's use of XML is superior to ADO's use of a disconnected Recordset, look at Chapter 14.

Moving Around in DataSets and Retrieving Data

In some ways, the DataSet requires completely different thinking than the ADO Recordset. Moving around in the data is a case in point. A Recordset, of course, consists of a set of rows plus a current-row pointer (a cursor). A DataSet doesn't have a concept of a current row. In this respect, it's much closer to a traditional SQL View, which is a set of records of no particular order that is processed as a group.

So forget about the EOF and BOF properties and the various Move methods when you migrate from Recordsets to DataSets. You can still move around in the data, but the code is a bit different. At first, you might feel a bit lost without your trusty MoveNext method, but after a while, it will seem simple. Instead of having their own particular methods, DataSets work like any other collection.

In particular, the DataSet contains a Tables collection made of DataTable objects. The DataTable, in turn, contains a Rows collection of DataRow objects, and a Columns collection of DataColumn objects. A DataRow has an Item collection (its default) that is indexed by column number and returns data. You can move through all these collections with a zero-based index or by name, or by using a For Each loop. So, to dump all the data in a DataSet, you could use code like this:

```
Dim dt As DataTable
Dim dr As DataRow
Dim dc As DataColumn
For Each dt In ds.Tables
    For Each dr In dt.Rows
        For each dc In dt.Columns
            Console.WriteLine(dr(dc))
        Next dc
    Next dr
Next dt
```

If you want to do some sort of row-based navigation, you'll need to maintain your own current-record pointer. The navigation buttons on the DataSet form in this chapter's sample application take this approach. The form's New event is used to instantiate a DataSet:

```
Dim mds As DataSet = New DataSet()
Dim mlngCurRow As Long

Public Sub New()

    MyBase.New()

    'This call is required by the Windows Form Designer.
    InitializeComponent()

    'Add any initialization after the
    'InitializeComponent() call
    Dim cnn As SqlClient.SqlConnection = New _
     SqlClient.SqlConnection("Data Source=SKYROCKET;" & _
      "Initial Catalog=Northwind;Integrated Security=SSPI")
    Dim cmd As New SqlClient.SqlCommand()
    Dim da As New SqlClient.SqlDataAdapter()

    Try
        cmd = cnn.CreateCommand
        cmd.CommandText = "SELECT * FROM Customers"
        da.SelectCommand = cmd
        da.Fill(mds, "Customers")
        mlngCurRow = 0

    Catch ex As Exception
        MsgBox("Error: " & ex.Source & ": " & _
            ex.Message, MsgBoxStyle.OKOnly, "New")
    End Try

End Sub
```

Part IV

The individual navigation buttons then manipulate the current row number and call a common subroutine to display the first couple of columns from that row:

```
Private Sub DisplayCurrentRow()
  MsgBox(mds.Tables("Customers").Rows(mlngCurRow).Item(0) _
  & ": " & _
  mds.Tables("Customers").Rows(mlngCurRow).Item(1))
End Sub


Private Sub btnFirst_Click(ByVal sender As System.Object, _
 ByVal e As System.EventArgs) Handles btnFirst.Click
  mlngCurRow = 0
  DisplayCurrentRow()
End Sub


Private Sub btnPrevious_Click(ByVal sender _
 As System.Object, ByVal e As System.EventArgs) _
 Handles btnPrevious.Click
  mlngCurRow = Math.Max(mlngCurRow - 1, 0)
  DisplayCurrentRow()
End Sub


Private Sub btnNext_Click(ByVal sender _
 As System.Object, ByVal e As System.EventArgs) _
 Handles btnNext.Click
  mlngCurRow = Math.Min(mlngCurRow + 1, _
   mds.Tables("Customers").Rows.Count - 1)
  DisplayCurrentRow()
End Sub


Private Sub btnLast_Click(ByVal sender As System.Object, _
 ByVal e As System.EventArgs) Handles btnLast.Click
  mlngCurRow = mds.Tables("Customers").Rows.Count - 1
  DisplayCurrentRow()
End Sub
```

Note the use of the Math.Min and Math.Max methods to make sure that the current-row pointer always stays between zero and one less than the number of rows in the DataTable. This is necessary because DataTables have no EOF or BOF property to trap.

Using Strongly Typed DataSets

The DisplayCurrentRow method in the preceding code uses the Item method of the Rows collection to return data. There are several equivalent ways to return information with this method. Assuming *dt* is a DataTable variable, all of these statements are equivalent:

```
dt.Rows(0).Item(0)
dt.Rows(0)(0)
dt.Rows(0).Item("CustomerID")
dt.Rows(0)("CustomerID")
dt.Rows(0)!CustomerID
```

All of these syntaxes have one thing in common: They're all late-bound. That is, .NET doesn't know until runtime that "CustomerID" is a valid column name in the DataTable. One of the innovations of the .NET Framework is the concept of a strongly typed DataSet, in which the columns actually become properties of the row. With such a DataSet, an early-bound version of the data-retrieval code becomes available:

```
dt.Rows(0).CustomerID
```

In addition to being faster than the late-bound syntax, this syntax also has the benefit that the column names show up in the IntelliSense list that Visual Studio .NET displays when you type the dot after Rows(0).

There are several ways to create a strongly typed DataSet. One is to craft an XSD schema file representing the DataSet and then use the command-line xsd.exe tool to generate source code that you can then compile into your application. In practice, though, you're more likely to use the visual tools built into Visual Studio .NET to hide the command-line tool. Here's how to add a strongly typed DataSet to an existing project through the Visual Basic .NET interface:

1. Select Project ➢ Add New Item from the Visual Basic .NET menu. Select the DataSet object, give it a name (I'll use Customers.xsd for this example), and click Open. Visual Basic .NET will add the new schema file to the Solution Explorer and open the blank object in the designer. At the

bottom of the designer, you'll see tabs for DataSet and XML; these let you toggle between a data-oriented view of the schema and the XML view.

2. In the Server Explorer window, right-click the Data Connections node and select Add Connection. The Data Link Properties dialog box will open. Fill in appropriate connection information and then click OK.

3. Expand the Data Connections tree to find the table, stored procedure, or view that you'd like to use in the DataSet. Drag the object (the Customers table in my example) from the Server Explorer to the design surface. You can drag selected columns if you don't need all the columns in a source table. You can also drag multiple source objects to create a DataSet that contains multiple DataTables.

4. Save the XSD file or the entire project. This step is important, because Visual Basic .NET doesn't generate the class file corresponding to the XSD file until the XSD file is saved.

Figure 15.5 shows the visual representation of the Customers table as an XSD file on the DataSet tab of the XSD designer. The "E" icons indicate that each row of the table has been rendered as an XML element.

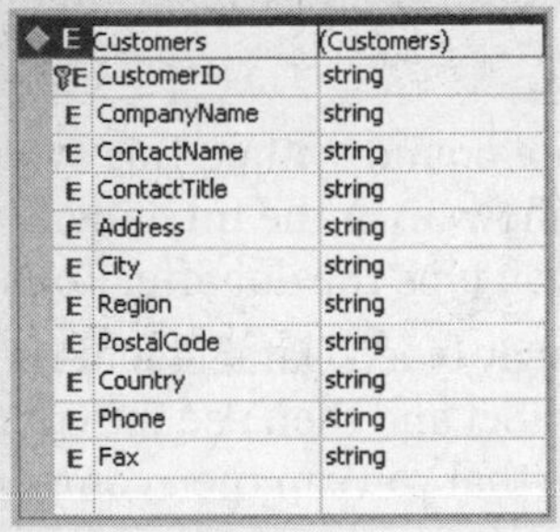

FIGURE 15.5:   XSD schema in the designer

At this point, your project contains a new class named Customers. This class consists of a DataSet that implements strong typing based on the Customers table. With this class, you can write code such as this:

```
Private Sub btnOpen_Click(ByVal sender As System.Object, _
    ByVal e As System.EventArgs) Handles btnOpen.Click
```

```
Dim cnn As SqlClient.SqlConnection = New _
 SqlClient.SqlConnection("Data Source=SKYROCKET;" & _
 "Initial Catalog=Northwind;Integrated Security=SSPI")
Dim cmd As New SqlClient.SqlCommand()
Dim da As New SqlClient.SqlDataAdapter()
Dim cust As New Customers()
Dim custRow As Customers.CustomersRow

Try

    cmd = cnn.CreateCommand
    cmd.CommandText = "SELECT * FROM Customers"
    da.SelectCommand = cmd
    da.Fill(cust, "Customers")

    For Each custRow In cust.Customers
        lboData.Items.Add(custRow.CustomerID & _
        " " & custRow.CompanyName)
    Next custRow

Catch ex As Exception

    MsgBox("Error: " & ex.Source & ": " & _
        ex.Message, MsgBoxStyle.OKOnly, "btnOpen")
End Try


    End Sub
```

As you can see, using the Customers class to define a DataSet lets you treat the Customers DataTable as a property of the DataSet. The class also defines a Customers.CustomersRow class to represent a single DataRow in the DataTable, and it creates properties of this class to represent each column in the DataRow.

To see the code that Visual Basic .NET generated for the class, select the project in Solution Explorer and click the Show All Files button. This will let you expand the Customers.xsd file in the tree and display the Customers.vb file beneath it. You may also see a Customers.xsx file that holds layout information for the XSD design surface. You can load the Customers.vb file into the design window to view the auto-generated code that makes the strong typing possible.

WARNING

Any changes that you make to the auto-generated code will be lost the next time that you save the XSD file that was used to create it.

DataSets with Multiple Tables

So far, each of the DataSets that you've seen in this chapter contains only one DataTable. But DataSets are much more flexible than that; they may contain as many DataTables as you need to represent your data. In this section, I'll show you four different ways to load multiple tables from a data source into a DataSet:

▶ Using a join

▶ Using the Shape provider

▶ Using multiple result sets

▶ Using multiple DataAdapters

Using a Join

The easiest way to bring data from multiple tables together into a single DataSet is to join the tables in the Command that initializes the DataAdapter:

```
Private Sub btnJoin_Click(ByVal sender _
As System.Object, ByVal e As System.EventArgs) _
Handles btnJoin.Click
    Dim cnn As SqlClient.SqlConnection = New _
     SqlClient.SqlConnection("Data Source=SKYROCKET;" & _
     "Initial Catalog=Northwind;Integrated Security=SSPI")
    Dim cmd As New SqlClient.SqlCommand()
    Dim da As New SqlClient.SqlDataAdapter()
    Dim ds As New DataSet()

    Try
        cmd = cnn.CreateCommand
```

```
cmd.CommandText = "SELECT * FROM Customers " & _
  "INNER JOIN Orders " & _
  "ON Customers.CustomerID = Orders.CustomerID"
da.SelectCommand = cmd
da.Fill(ds, "Customers")

dgMain.DataSource = ds
dgMain.DataMember = "Customers"

Catch ex As Exception
    MsgBox("Error: " & ex.Source & ": " & _
      ex.Message, MsgBoxStyle.OKOnly, "btnJoin")
End Try


End Sub
```

As I mentioned, even though the DataTable in the DataSet is assigned the name *Customers*, the content of this table is determined by the SQL statement that's used to fill it. Figure 15.6 shows the result of running this code: a single virtual table that includes columns from both Customers and Orders, with the customer information repeated multiple times.

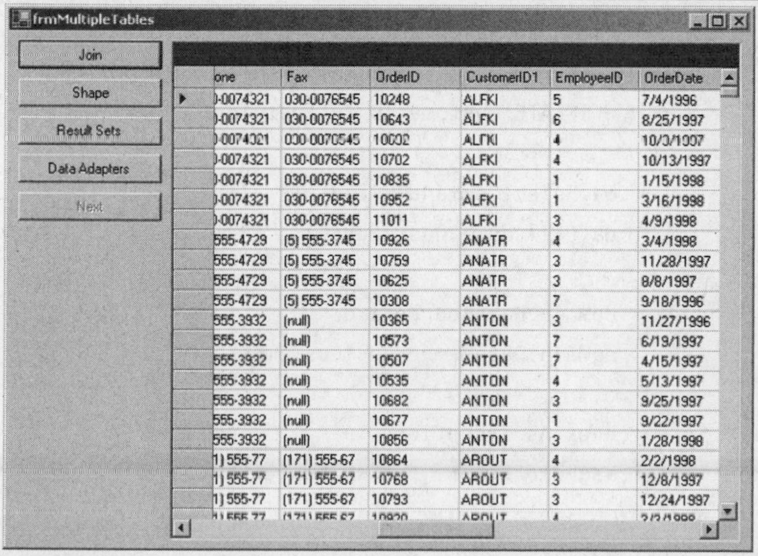

FIGURE 15.6:   DataTable based on a join

Using the Shape Provider

Another way to bring multiple tables into a DataSet is to use the Shape provider along with a SQL statement that creates a hierarchical view of a data source. This method actually produces multiple DataTables within the DataSet (one for each result set within the hierarchy).

Here's an example of this technique from the sample project for this chapter:

```
Private Sub btnShape_Click(ByVal sender _
As System.Object, ByVal e As System.EventArgs) _
Handles btnShape.Click
    Dim cnn As OleDbConnection = New _
    OleDbConnection("Provider=MSDataShape;" & _
    "Data Provider=SQLOLEDB;Data Source=SKYROCKET;" & _
    "Initial Catalog=Northwind;Integrated Security=SSPI")
    Dim cmd As New OleDbCommand()
    Dim da As New OleDbDataAdapter()
    Dim ds As New DataSet()

    Try
        cmd = cnn.CreateCommand
        cmd.CommandText = "SHAPE {SELECT CustomerID, " & _
        "CompanyName FROM Customers} " & _
        "APPEND ({SELECT * FROM Orders} " & _
        "RELATE CustomerID to CustomerID)"

        da.SelectCommand = cmd
        da.Fill(ds, "Customers")

        dgMain.DataSource = ds
        dgMain.DataMember = "Customers"

    Catch ex As Exception
        MsgBox("Error: " & ex.Source & ": " & _
```

```
                  ex.Message, MsgBoxStyle.OKOnly, "btnShape")
      End Try

  End Sub
```

NOTE

This example uses the OLE DB data provider classes instead of the SQL Server data provider classes. That's because the SQL Server data provider classes don't allow you to use any OLE DB provider other than the SQL Server provider, and the SHAPE syntax requires the use of the MSDataShape provider.

Figure 15.7 shows two views of the resulting DataSet on a DataGrid control. The initial view, shown in the background on the figure, displays the parent result set. You can click the plus sign next to the parent to see the name of the child result set, and click the hyperlinked name to view the child result set, as shown in the foreground.

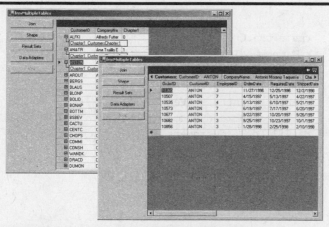

FIGURE 15.7:   Hierarchical result sets on a DataGrid

Although the DataGrid uses this rather complex user interface to show the entire contents of the DataSet, there are two distinct Data-Tables within the DataSet: Customers and CustomersChapter1. When the DataAdapter's Fill method hits a chapter column, it automatically creates a new DataTable to hold the child rows. All child rows from the same position in the result set hierarchy are stored in a single DataTable. The Fill method adds a column to the parent and child result sets that serves to link the parent and child DataTables together.

Part IV

Using Multiple Result Sets

A third option for populating a DataSet with multiple DataTables is to use a stored procedure or SQL statement that returns multiple result sets as the Command for the DataAdapter. Listing 15.2 shows an example.

Listing 15.2: Using a SQL Statement to Display Data from Multiple Tables

```
Private Sub btnResultSets_Click(ByVal sender _
  As System.Object, ByVal e As System.EventArgs) _
  Handles btnResultSets.Click
    Dim cnn As SqlClient.SqlConnection = New _
     SqlClient.SqlConnection("Data Source=SKYROCKET;" & _
     "Initial Catalog=Northwind;Integrated Security=SSPI")

    Dim cmd As New SqlClient.SqlCommand()
    Dim da As New SqlClient.SqlDataAdapter()
    Dim ds As New DataSet()

    Try
        cmd = cnn.CreateCommand
        cmd.CommandText = "SELECT * FROM Customers " & _
         "WHERE Country = 'Germany' " & _
         "SELECT * FROM Customers " & _
         "WHERE Country = 'Venezuela'"
        da.SelectCommand = cmd
        da.Fill(ds, "Customers")

        dgMain.DataSource = ds
        dgMain.DataMember = "Customers"

        btnNext.Enabled = True

    Catch ex As Exception
        MsgBox("Error: " & ex.Source & ": " & _
          ex.Message, MsgBoxStyle.OKOnly, "btnResultSets")
    End Try

End Sub

Private Sub btnNext_Click(ByVal sender As System.Object, _
  ByVal e As System.EventArgs) Handles btnNext.Click
```

```
      Try
          dgMain.DataMember = "Customers1"
          btnNext.Enabled = False
      Catch ex As Exception
          MsgBox("Error: " & ex.Source & ": " & _
              ex.Message, MsgBoxStyle.OKOnly, "btnNext")
      End Try
  End Sub
```

In this case, no connection between the two result sets is specified, so the DataGrid control doesn't know how to display both of them at the same time. The code assigns the contents of the Customers DataTable to the DataGrid and then enables the Next button on the form's user interface. When you click the Next button, the code assigns the other DataTable, Customers1, to the DataGrid. The Fill method of the Data-Adapter automatically serializes DataTable naming in this way if it encounters multiple result sets.

Using Multiple DataAdapters

Finally, you can use more than one DataAdapter object to fill a single DataSet. This allows you complete control of the DataTables that the DataSet contains. You can also use DataRelation objects to specify how these DataTables are related.

TIP

The DataAdapters don't all need to use the same data source for their data. The DataSet, remember, is a completely virtual view of the data. As such, it has no problem combining results from multiple heterogeneous data sources.

Listing 15.3 shows the code for a sample procedure that uses three different DataAdapter objects, all of which draw from the same data source to create a DataSet containing Customers, Orders, and Order Details.

Listing 15.3: Using Multiple DataAdapters to Display Data from Multiple Tables

```
  Private Sub btnDataAdapters_Click(ByVal sender _
    As System.Object, ByVal e As System.EventArgs) _
    Handles btnDataAdapters.Click
      Dim cnn As SqlClient.SqlConnection = New _
```

```
SqlClient.SqlConnection("Data Source=SKYROCKET;" & _
"Initial Catalog=Northwind;Integrated Security=SSPI")
Dim cmdCustomers As New SqlClient.SqlCommand()
Dim daCustomers As New SqlClient.SqlDataAdapter()
Dim cmdOrders As New SqlClient.SqlCommand()
Dim daOrders As New SqlClient.SqlDataAdapter()
Dim cmdOrderDetails As New SqlClient.SqlCommand()
Dim daOrderDetails As New SqlClient.SqlDataAdapter()
Dim ds As New DataSet()

Try
    cmdCustomers = cnn.CreateCommand
    cmdCustomers.CommandText = "SELECT * " & _
      "FROM Customers"
    daCustomers.SelectCommand = cmdCustomers
    daCustomers.Fill(ds, "Customers")

    cmdOrders = cnn.CreateCommand
    cmdOrders.CommandText = "SELECT * FROM Orders"
    daOrders.SelectCommand = cmdOrders
    daOrders.Fill(ds, "Orders")

    cmdOrderDetails = cnn.CreateCommand
    cmdOrderDetails.CommandText = "SELECT * " & _
      "FROM [Order Details]"
    daOrderDetails.SelectCommand = cmdOrderDetails
    daOrderDetails.Fill(ds, "Order Details")

    Dim relCustOrder As DataRelation = _
      ds.Relations.Add("CustOrder", _
      ds.Tables("Customers").Columns("CustomerID"), _
      ds.Tables("Orders").Columns("CustomerID"))

    Dim relOrderOrderDetail As DataRelation = _
      ds.Relations.Add("OrderOrderDetail", _
      ds.Tables("Orders").Columns("OrderID"), _
      ds.Tables("Order Details").Columns("OrderID"))

    dgMain.DataSource = ds
    dgMain.DataMember = "Customers"
```

```
Catch ex As Exception
    MsgBox("Error: " & ex.Source & ": " & _
    ex.Message, MsgBoxStyle.OKOnly, "btnJoin")
End Try

End Sub
```

Creating the DataRelation objects sets up primary key–foreign key relationships between the DataTable objects. The Add method of the Relations collection of the DataSet takes three arguments:

- ▶ A name for the DataRelation object to be created
- ▶ The column from the primary key side of the relationship
- ▶ The column from the foreign key side of the relationship

The DataGrid control contains built-in logic to help navigate between related DataTables in a DataSet. Figure 15.8 shows three successive stages of drilling into the information from this example. Note the rows of information above the grid area that provide context for the currently displayed information.

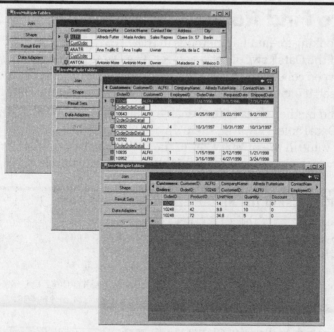

FIGURE 15.8:   Drilling into hierarchical information on a DataGrid

FINDING AND SORTING DATA IN DATASETS

The DataSet objects offer a variety of ways to find and sort data. Some of these are similar to methods you already know from ADO Recordsets, but others are new to the ADO.NET world. In this section, I'll explain the basics:

- ▶ Using the `DataRowCollection.Find` method to find rows
- ▶ Using the `DataTable.Select` method to filter and sort rows
- ▶ Using a DataView to filter and sort rows

The DataSet object has no equivalent of the `Recordset.Supports` method. Because all DataSets are completely present in memory, they all have the same capabilities. The old distinction between client-side and server-side cursors no longer applies.

Using the *DataRowCollection.Find* Method to Find Rows

If you go looking for familiar methods in ADO.NET, you'll find the Find method of the DataRowCollection object. The DataRowCollection is the strongly typed collection that's returned by the Rows property of the Data-Table object; it contains all of the DataRow objects within the DataTable.

The Find method does indeed enable you to find a particular DataRow within a DataTable. However, there's a catch: It searches only for a matching value in the primary key of the table. See Listing 15.4, for example, which shows code from this chapter's sample project.

Listing 15.4: Using the Find Method to Locate Data

```
Private Sub btnFind_Click(ByVal sender _
As System.Object, ByVal e As System.EventArgs) _
Handles btnFind.Click
  Dim cnn As SqlClient.SqlConnection = New _
  SqlClient.SqlConnection("Data Source=SKYROCKET;" & _
  "Initial Catalog=Northwind;Integrated Security=SSPI")

  Dim cmd As New SqlClient.SqlCommand()
  Dim da As New SqlClient.SqlDataAdapter()
```

```
Dim ds As New DataSet()
Dim dr As DataRow
Dim dc As DataColumn
Dim pk(1) As DataColumn

Try
    lboResults.Items.Clear()

    cmd = cnn.CreateCommand
    cmd.CommandText = "SELECT * FROM Customers"
    da.SelectCommand = cmd
    da.Fill(ds, "Customers")
    pk(0) = _
      ds.Tables("Customers").Columns("CustomerID")
    ds.Tables("Customers").PrimaryKey = pk

    dr = ds.Tables("Customers").Rows.Find("BONAP")
    If Not dr Is Nothing Then
        For Each dc In ds.Tables("Customers").Columns
            lboResults.Items.Add(dr(dc))
        Next
    Else
        lboResults.Items.Add("Not Found")
    End If

Catch ex As Exception
    MsgBox("Error: " & ex.Source & ": " & _
      ex.Message, MsgBoxStyle.OKOnly, "btnFind")
End Try

End Sub
```

You might be surprised to see the two lines of code in this snippet that set the primary key for this table by assigning an array of columns (that happens to have only a single member) to the PrimaryKey property of the DataTable. That's necessary because the DataAdapter.Fill method doesn't move any schema information other than column names to the DataTable. An alternative would be to use an XSD schema to define a strongly typed DataSet that includes primary key information.

You can also use the Find method to find DataRows that have a multiple-part primary key. In that case, you supply an array of objects as the argument to the Find method. Each object is the value to be found in one column of the primary key.

Part IV

Using the *DataTable.Select* Method to Filter and Sort Rows

The Find method is quick and useful, but inflexible: It can find only a single row, and it searches only the primary key field of the DataTable. For a more flexible way to filter and sort DataTables, take a look at the DataTable.Select method. This method allows you to extract an array of DataRow objects from a DataTable. When building the array, you can specify a filter expression to select DataRows, a sort expression to sort the DataRows in the array, and a state constant to select only DataRows in a particular state.

If you call the Select method with no arguments, it selects all the DataRows in the DataTable. This is a quick way to get an array that holds the content of a DataTable:

```
Dim adrAll() As DataRow = dt.Select()
```

To select a subset of the DataRows in the DataTable, you can supply a filter expression. Filter expressions are essentially SQL WHERE clauses constructed according to these rules:

- ▶ Column names containing special characters should be enclosed in square brackets.

- ▶ String constants should be enclosed in single quotes.

- ▶ Date constants should be enclosed in pound signs.

- ▶ Numeric expressions can be specified in decimal or scientific notation.

- ▶ Expressions can be created using AND, OR, NOT, parentheses, IN, LIKE, comparison operators, and arithmetic operators.

- ▶ The + operator is used to concatenate strings.

- ▶ Either * or % can be used as a wildcard to match any number of characters. Wildcards may be used only at the start or end of strings.

- ▶ Columns in a child table can be referenced with the expression Child.Column. If the table has more than one child table, use the expression Child(RelationName).Column to choose a particular child table.

▶ The Sum, Avg, Min, Max, Count, StDev, and Var aggregates can be used with child tables.

▶ Supported functions include CONVERT, LEN, ISNULL, IIF, and SUBSTRING.

TIP

For more details on the syntax of filter expressions, see the .NET Framework help for the DataColumn.Expression property.

If you don't specify a sort order in the Select method, the rows are returned in primary key order, or in the order of addition if the table doesn't have a primary key. You can also specify a sort expression consisting of one or more column names and the keywords ASC or DESC to specify ascending or descending sorts. For example, this is a valid sort expression:

```
Country ASC, CompanyName DESC
```

That expression will sort first by country in ascending order, and then by company name within each country in descending order.

Finally, you can also select DataRows according to their current state by supplying one of the DataViewRowState constants. Table 15.17 shows these constants.

TABLE 15.17:   DataViewRowState Constants

CONSTANT	MEANING
Added	A new row that has not yet been committed.
CurrentRows	All current rows, including unchanged, modified, and new rows.
Deleted	A row that has been deleted.
ModifiedCurrent	A row that has been modified.
ModifiedOriginal	The original data from a row that has been modified.
None	Does not match any rows in the DataTable.
OriginalRows	Original rows, including rows that have since been modified or deleted.
Unchanged	Rows that have not been changed.

Part IV

Listing 15.5 contains a snippet from this chapter's sample project that demonstrates the use of the Select method with a filter and a sort. This code extracts all the DataRows for customers in Venezuela to an array and sorts them by the ContactName field. Figure 15.9 shows the results of running this code.

Listing 15.5: Using the Select Method to Locate Data

```
Private Sub btnSelect_Click(ByVal sender _
As System.Object, ByVal e As System.EventArgs) _
Handles btnSelect.Click
    Dim cnn As SqlClient.SqlConnection = New _
     SqlClient.SqlConnection("Data Source=SKYROCKET;" & _
     "Initial Catalog=Northwind;Integrated Security=SSPI")
    Dim cmd As New SqlClient.SqlCommand()
    Dim da As New SqlClient.SqlDataAdapter()
    Dim ds As New DataSet()
    Dim dr As DataRow
    Dim dc As DataColumn
    Dim pk(1) As DataColumn

    Try
        lboResults.Items.Clear()

        cmd = cnn.CreateCommand
        cmd.CommandText = "SELECT * FROM Customers"
        da.SelectCommand = cmd
        da.Fill(ds, "Customers")
        pk(0) = _
         ds.Tables("Customers").Columns("CustomerID")
        ds.Tables("Customers").PrimaryKey = pk

        Dim adr() As DataRow = _
         ds.Tables("Customers").Select( _
         "Country = 'Venezuela'", "ContactName ASC")

        For Each dr In adr
            lboResults.Items.Add(dr(0) & " " & dr(1) & _
            " " & dr(2))
        Next

    Catch ex As Exception
        MsgBox("Error: " & ex.Source & ": " & _
```

```
                    ex.Message, MsgBoxStyle.OKOnly, "btnSelect")
            End Try

        End Sub
```

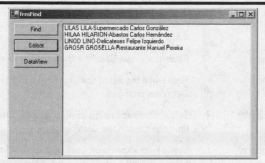

FIGURE 15.9:   Array of rows produced by the `DataTable.Select` method

Using a DataView to Filter and Sort Rows

Another alternative for presenting a filtered or sorted subset of the data in a DataTable is to use one or more DataView objects. The DataView is derived from a DataTable and has the same rows-and-columns structure, but it allows you to specify sorting and filtering options. One great advantage of using the DataView object in a user interface application is that it can be bound to controls.

Table 15.18 lists some of the important members of the DataView object.

TABLE 15.18:   DataView Members

NAME	TYPE	DESCRIPTION
AddNew	Method	Adds a new row to the DataView.
AllowDelete	Property	True if deletions through this DataView are allowed.
AllowEdit	Property	True if edits through this DataView are allowed.
AllowNew	Property	True if new rows can be added through this DataView.
Count	Property	Number of records in the DataView.
Delete	Method	Deletes a row from the DataView.

Part IV

TABLE 15.18 continued: DataView Members

NAME	TYPE	DESCRIPTION
Find	Method	Finds a row in the DataView by matching the primary key.
FindRows	Method	Finds a row in the DataView with columns matching a specified set of values.
Item	Property	Returns a single DataRow from the DataView.
ListChanged	Event	Fires when the list of rows managed by the DataView changes.
RowFilter	Property	Sets a filter expression using a WHERE clause to limit the rows in the DataView.
RowStateFilter	Property	Sets a filter expression using a DataViewRow-State constant to limit the rows in the DataView.
Sort	Property	Sets the sort order for the DataView.

Figure 15.10 shows a form with two DataGrid controls bound to different DataViews based on the same underlying DataTable object. Here's the code that was used to instantiate this form:

```
Private Sub frmDataView_Load(ByVal sender _
  As System.Object, ByVal e As System.EventArgs) _
  Handles MyBase.Load
    Dim cnn As SqlClient.SqlConnection = New _
     SqlClient.SqlConnection("Data Source=SKYROCKET;" & _
     "Initial Catalog=Northwind;Integrated Security=SSPI")
    Dim cmd As New SqlClient.SqlCommand()
    Dim da As New SqlClient.SqlDataAdapter()
    Dim ds As New DataSet()

    Try
        cmd = cnn.CreateCommand
        cmd.CommandText = "SELECT * FROM Customers"
        da.SelectCommand = cmd
        da.Fill(ds, "Customers")
```

```
                Dim dv1 As DataView = +
                    New DataView(ds.Tables("Customers"))
                dv1.RowFilter = "Country = 'Germany'"
                dv1.Sort = "CompanyName DESC"
                dg1.DataSource = dv1

                Dim dv2 As DataView = +
                    New DataView(ds.Tables("Customers"))
                dv2.RowFilter = "Country = 'Brazil'"
                dv2.Sort = "CompanyName ASC"
                dg2.DataSource = dv2

        Catch ex As Exception
            MsgBox("Error: " & ex.Source & ": " & _
              ex.Message, MsgBoxStyle.OKOnly, _
              "btnPopulateDatabase")
        End Try

    End Sub
```

FIGURE 15.10:   Multiple DataViews based on a single table

RUNNING STORED PROCEDURES

Like classic ADO, ADO.NET also allows you to retrieve data by using a stored procedure. A stored procedure is a SQL statement or collection of SQL statements saved as a persistent object on the database server. By supplying values for the input parameters of the stored procedure, you can determine which records it will retrieve. By moving this piece of logic from the client to the server, you can both increase performance and make sure that particular business rules are enforced. Some databases precompile statements saved as stored procedures so that they will execute more quickly. In addition, you may find it easier to maintain the logic of your application by using stored procedures, which provide a central point for modification.

In this section, I'll demonstrate the use of an ADO.NET Command object to return a DataSet based on a stored procedure.

Using the Command Object

I'll start the discussion with a look at the "Ten Most Expensive Products" stored procedure from the Northwind database. The stored procedure to retrieve the most expensive products is defined with this SQL statement:

```
CREATE PROCEDURE "Ten Most Expensive Products" AS

SET ROWCOUNT ten

SELECT Products.ProductName AS TenMostExpensiveProducts,
 Products.UnitPrice

FROM Products

ORDER BY Products.UnitPrice DESC
```

This stored procedure returns a result set consisting of the 10 most expensive products stored in the Products table.

To open a DataSet based on the results of a stored procedure such as this one, you can use a Command object in conjunction with a DataAdapter object:

```
Private Sub btnWithoutParameters_Click(ByVal sender _
  As System.Object, ByVal e As System.EventArgs) _
  Handles btnWithoutParameters.Click
    Dim cnn As SqlClient.SqlConnection = New _
      SqlClient.SqlConnection("Data Source=SKYROCKET;" & _
```

```
                "Initial Catalog=Northwind;Integrated Security=SSPI")
        Dim cmd As New SqlClient.SqlCommand()
        Dim da As New SqlClient.SqlDataAdapter()
        Dim ds As New DataSet()

        Try
            cmd = cnn.CreateCommand
            cmd.CommandText = "[Ten Most Expensive Products]"
            cmd.CommandType = CommandType.StoredProcedure
            da.SelectCommand = cmd
            da.Fill(ds, "Products")

            dgMain.DataSource = ds
            dgMain.DataMember = "Products"

        Catch ex As Exception
            MsgBox("Error: " & ex.Source & ": " & _
              ex.Message, MsgBoxStyle.OKOnly, _
              "btnWithoutParameters")
        End Try

    End Sub
```

The connection to the database is made via the Command object.
Because this object was created with the CreateCommand method of
the Connection object, it uses that Connection to retrieve data. The
CommandText property holds the name of the stored procedure to be
executed by the command. Calling the DataAdapter's Fill method tells
the database to execute the stored procedure and returns the results
to the specified DataSet.

TIP

Explicitly setting the Command object's CommandType property to CommandType
.StoredProcedure is not a requirement. The code will run without this setting,
but it will run faster if you use this property to tell ADO.NET what type of object it's
dealing with.

Part IV

In this particular case, using a stored procedure with the Command object offers no advantage over filling the DataSet directly from the text of the SQL statement. In general, though, you'll find that stored procedures are useful and necessary. That's because you can use parameters to customize a stored procedure to return only the desired rows, as shown in the next section.

Using Parameters

Stored procedures can take input parameters and return output parameters. For example, in the Northwind SQL Server database, there's a stored procedure named SalesByCategory. Here's the SQL that creates that stored procedure:

```
CREATE PROCEDURE SalesByCategory
    @CategoryName nvarchar(15),
    @OrdYear nvarchar(4) = '1998'
AS
IF @OrdYear != '1996'
 AND @OrdYear != '1997'
 AND @OrdYear != '1998'
BEGIN
    SELECT @OrdYear = '1998'
END
SELECT ProductName,
    TotalPurchase=ROUND(SUM(CONVERT(decimal(14,2),
    OD.Quantity * (1-OD.Discount) * OD.UnitPrice)), 0)
FROM [Order Details] OD, Orders O, Products P, Categories C
WHERE OD.OrderID = O.OrderID
    AND OD.ProductID = P.ProductID
    AND P.CategoryID = C.CategoryID
    AND C.CategoryName = @CategoryName
    AND SUBSTRING(CONVERT(
    nvarchar(22), O.OrderDate, 111), 1, 4) = @OrdYear
GROUP BY ProductName
ORDER BY ProductName
```

Here, @CategoryName and @OrdYear are a pair of input parameters to the stored procedure, both defined as being of the nvarchar datatype. The stored procedure uses these parameters to filter a Recordset of order information. The Recordset becomes the return value of the stored procedure.

Retrieving a DataSet from a stored procedure with input parameters is a four-step process:

1. Create a Command object and connect it to a data source.

2. Supply values for the input parameters.

3. Use the Command object as the SelectCommand for a DataAdapter.

4. Use the DataAdapter's Fill method to retrieve the data to a DataSet object.

As an example, consider the code in Listing 15.6, which is from this chapter's sample project.

Listing 15.6: Retrieving a DataSet from a Stored Procedure

```
Private Sub btnWithParameters1_Click(ByVal sender _
As System.Object, ByVal e As System.EventArgs) _
Handles btnWithParameters1.Click
    Dim cnn As SqlClient.SqlConnection = New _
    SqlClient.SqlConnection("Data Source=SKYROCKET;" & _
    "Initial Catalog=Northwind;Integrated Security=SSPI")

    Dim cmd As New SqlClient.SqlCommand()
    Dim da As New SqlClient.SqlDataAdapter()
    Dim ds As New DataSet()
    Dim cb As SqlClient.SqlCommandBuilder
    Dim prm As SqlClient.SqlParameter

    Try
        cmd = cnn.CreateCommand
        cmd.CommandText = "SalesByCategory"
        cmd.CommandType = CommandType.StoredProcedure

        cnn.Open()
        cb.DeriveParameters(cmd)
        cnn.Close()
        For Each prm In cmd.Parameters
```

```
            If (prm.Direction = ParameterDirection.Input) _
            Or (prm.Direction = _
         ParameterDirection.InputOutput) Then
               prm.Value = InputBox(prm.ParameterName, _
                 "Enter parameter value")
             End If
        Next

        da.SelectCommand = cmd
        da.Fill(ds, "Products")

        dgMain.DataSource = ds
        dgMain.DataMember = "Products"

    Catch ex As Exception
        MsgBox("Error: " & ex.Source & ": " & _
          ex.Message, MsgBoxStyle.OKOnly, _
          "btnWithParameters1")
    End Try

End Sub
```

TIP

To test the code in Listing 15.6, try "Beverages" for the category name and "1996" for the order year.

WARNING

This procedure requires a build of .NET later than beta 2 to execute.

This code starts by defining a Connection to the Northwind database on a SQL Server named SKYROCKET, using Windows NT security. (As always, if your environment is different, you may have to modify the connection string.) Then it creates a Command object and loads it with the SalesByCategory stored procedure.

The code then opens the Connection and calls the DeriveParameters method of a SqlCommandBuilder object. This call tells ADO to query the data source and find out what parameters are required by this stored procedure. Once the Parameters collection is populated, the code walks through it one parameter at a time and prompts the user for values for all input parameters.

Finally, the DataAdapter is used to fill the DataSet, just as in the previous example, and the results are displayed on the form.

Although this method works, it's not the most efficient way to execute a stored procedure. The bottleneck is the `DeriveParameters` call. This method requires you to open a Connection to the server and transmits information both ways to do its job. If you already know the details of the stored procedure, you can avoid using this method by creating your own parameters. This method is also demonstrated in the sample project for this chapter; you'll find the subroutine in Listing 15.7.

Listing 15.7: Creating Parameters for a Stored Procedure

```
Private Sub btnWithParameters2_Click(ByVal sender _
  As System.Object, ByVal e As System.EventArgs) _
  Handles btnWithParameters2.Click
    Dim cnn As SqlClient.SqlConnection = New _
      SqlClient.SqlConnection("Data Source=SKYROCKET;" & _
      "Initial Catalog=Northwind;Integrated Security=SSPI")
    Dim cmd As New SqlClient.SqlCommand()
    Dim da As New SqlClient.SqlDataAdapter()
    Dim ds As New DataSet()
    Dim prm As SqlClient.SqlParameter
    Dim strCategoryName As String
    Dim strOrderYear As String

    Try
        cmd = cnn.CreateCommand
        cmd.CommandText = "SalesByCategory"
        cmd.CommandType = CommandType.StoredProcedure

        strCategoryName = InputBox("Enter category name:")
        strOrderYear = InputBox("Enter order year:")

        prm = cmd.Parameters.Add("@CategoryName", _
          SqlDbType.NVarChar, 15)
        prm.Value = strCategoryName
        prm = cmd.Parameters.Add("@OrdYear", _
          SqlDbType.NVarChar, 4)
        prm.Value = strOrderYear
```

```
            da.SelectCommand = cmd
            da.Fill(ds, "Products")

            dgMain.DataSource = ds
            dgMain.DataMember = "Products"

        Catch ex As Exception
            MsgBox("Error: " & ex.Source & ": " & _
            ex.Message, MsgBoxStyle.OKOnly, _
            "btnWithParameters2")
        End Try

    End Sub
```

The difference between this procedure and the previous one is in the method used to populate the Parameters collection of the Command object. This procedure uses the Add method of the Command object's Parameters collection:

```
Cmd.Parameters.Add(Name, Type, Size)
```

The Add method takes three arguments:

▶ The *Name* argument must match exactly the name that the underlying data source is expecting for the parameter.

▶ The *Type* argument specifies a datatype for the parameter. These datatypes are expressed by constants supplied by the data provider—in this case, the SQL Server .NET Data Provider. If you have trouble determining the required type, you can first use the `CommandBuilder.DeriveParameters` method to get the parameter from the server and then examine the Type property of the returned parameter. Once you know what this type is, you can create your own matching parameter in the future.

▶ The *Size* argument specifies the size of the parameter. You don't need to specify a size for fixed-length datatypes such as Integer or Datetime.

All these arguments are optional when you're calling the Add method. You can create parameters and then set the properties afterwards if you prefer not to do the entire operation in one line of code.

In general, if you're writing code that will always call the same stored procedure, it's worth your while to explicitly code the parameters using the Add method of the Parameters collection. You should save the `CommandBuilder.DeriveParameters` method for situations in which you don't know in advance what the Parameters collection should contain.

WHAT'S NEXT

In this chapter, you've seen the basics of using ADO.NET to retrieve data from a data source. You learned about the two broad groups of ADO.NET objects: data provider objects and DataSet objects. You saw that multiple versions of the data provider objects exist to facilitate connections to different data sources, but that a single group of DataSet objects provides a uniform representation in code of diverse data.

You also learned a variety of methods for retrieving data in ADO.NET applications. These include the use of the DataAdapter object to fill a DataSet, the construction of strongly typed DataSets through the user interface, and the use of multiple tables or stored procedures to provide the data for a DataSet. You also saw several methods for sorting and filtering the data in a DataTable.

As you can tell by now, ADO.NET offers a great deal of flexibility (and complexity!) in its operations. And that's without even having edited any of the data that the samples have retrieved. Editing data is the subject of the next chapter.

In the next chapter, you will build on your knowledge of ADO.NET by learning to edit data from your data source. The primary object you will use is the DataSet, and you will learn how to set up your SELECT, INSERT, UPDATE, and DELETE commands using a DataAdapter.

You will also be exposed to concurrency issues and transactions using ADO.NET, along with the many events you can use to gain greater control of editing data using ADO.NET.

Chapter 16

EDITING DATA WITH ADO.NET

When you're working with a data source, retrieving the data for display is normally only one of the requirements. Often, making changes to data is even more important. As you'd expect, ADO.NET provides support for the full suite of editing operations, including updating existing data, adding new data, and deleting existing data. In this chapter, I'll explore the syntax for these fundamental data operations in ADO.NET. I'll also introduce you to the events supported by the DataSet and DataTable objects, and discuss concurrency and transactions in ADO.NET.

ADO *and* ADO.NET
Programming

Adapted from *ADO and ADO.NET Programming*
by Mike Gunderloy
ISBN 0-7821-2994-3 $59.99

Part IV

UPDATING DATA

At the highest level, you can think of updating data with ADO.NET as a three-part task. That's because updates have to take into account the fact that the DataSet is designed to be kept in a disconnected state.

1. Use the Fill method of the DataAdapter object to retrieve the data into a DataSet.

2. Edit the data in the DataSet.

3. Use the Update method of the DataAdapter to reconcile changes with the original data source.

In this section, I'll go into each of those topics in more depth.

Filling the DataSet

You've already seen many examples of filling a DataSet from a DataAdapter in Chapter 15, "Using the ADO.NET Objects to Retrieve Data." But there's a problem with those examples. The code in Chapter 15 sets the SelectCommand property of the DataAdapter but sets none of its other Command-related properties. As a result, although those examples are useful for filling DataSets, they lack the ability to persist any changes back to the original data source.

The key to enabling two-way communication between the DataSet and the original data source is to supply Command objects for all four of the Command-related properties of the DataAdapter. To recap, these Commands and their functions are as follows:

SelectCommand   Called by the `DataAdapter.Fill` method to load the initial data into the DataSet.

UpdateCommand   Called by the `DataAdapter.Update` method to save changes to existing rows of the DataSet.

InsertCommand   Called by the `DataAdapter.Update` method to save new rows of the DataSet.

DeleteCommand   Called by the `DataAdapter.Update` method to delete existing rows from the DataSet.

Listing 16.1 shows an example of setting up a DataAdapter with all four Commands. This code is from the frmUpdate form in the ADOChapter16 sample project.

Listing 16.1: Setting Up a DataAdapter to Persist Changes

```
Dim mda As New SqlClient.SqlDataAdapter()
Dim mds As New DataSet()

Private Sub frmUpdate_Load(ByVal sender _
 As System.Object, ByVal e As System.EventArgs) _
 Handles MyBase.Load
    Dim cnn As SqlClient.SqlConnection = _
     New SqlClient.SqlConnection("Data Source=SKYROCKET;" & _
     "Initial Catalog=Northwind;Integrated Security=SSPI")
    Dim cmdSelect As New SqlClient.SqlCommand()
    Dim cmdUpdate As New SqlClient.SqlCommand()
    Dim cmdInsert As New SqlClient.SqlCommand()
    Dim cmdDelete As New SqlClient.SqlCommand()
    Dim prm As SqlClient.SqlParameter

    Try

        ' Create the Select command to grab the initial data
        cmdSelect = cnn.CreateCommand
        cmdSelect.CommandText = "SELECT CustomerID, " & _
            "CompanyName, ContactName FROM Customers"
        mda.SelectCommand = cmdSelect

        ' The Update command handles updates
        ' to existing rows
        cmdUpdate = cnn.CreateCommand
        cmdUpdate.CommandText = "UPDATE Customers " & _
         "SET CompanyName = @CompanyName, " & _
         "ContactName = @ContactName " & _
         "WHERE CustomerID = @CustomerID"
        ' Now create the parameters that will be
        ' passed to this command
        prm = cmdUpdate.Parameters.Add("@CompanyName", _
            SqlDbType.NVarChar, 40, "CompanyName")
        prm = cmdUpdate.Parameters.Add("@ContactName", _
            SqlDbType.NVarChar, 30, "ContactName")
        prm = cmdUpdate.Parameters.Add("@CustomerID", _
            SqlDbType.NChar, 5, "CustomerID")
        prm.SourceVersion = DataRowVersion.Original
        mda.UpdateCommand = cmdUpdate
```

```
                    ' The Delete command handles deletions
                    ' of existing rows
                    cmdDelete = cnn.CreateCommand
                    cmdDelete.CommandText = "DELETE FROM Customers " & _
                      "WHERE CustomerID = @CustomerID"
                    ' Now create the parameter that will be
                    ' passed to this command
                    prm = cmdDelete.Parameters.Add("@CustomerID", _
                      SqlDbType.NChar, 5, "CustomerID")
                    prm.SourceVersion = DataRowVersion.Original
                    mda.DeleteCommand = cmdDelete

                    ' And the Insert command adds new rows
                    cmdInsert = cnn.CreateCommand
                    cmdInsert.CommandText = "INSERT INTO Customers " & _
                      "(CustomerID, CompanyName, ContactName) " & _
                      "VALUES(@CustomerID, @CompanyName, @ContactName)"
                    ' Now create the parameters that will be
                    ' passed to this command
                    prm = cmdInsert.Parameters.Add("@CompanyName", _
                      SqlDbType.NVarChar, 40, "CompanyName")
                    prm = cmdInsert.Parameters.Add("@ContactName", _
                      SqlDbType.NVarChar, 30, "ContactName")
                    prm = cmdInsert.Parameters.Add("@CustomerID", _
                      SqlDbType.NChar, 5, "CustomerID")
                    mda.InsertCommand = cmdInsert

                    ' Fill the DataSet and display it on the UI
                    mda.Fill(mds, "Customers")
                    dgMain.DataSource = mds
                    dgMain.DataMember = "Customers"

            Catch ex As Exception
                MsgBox("Error: " & ex.Source & ": " & ex.Message, _
                    MsgBoxStyle.OKOnly, "btnPopulateDatabase")
            End Try

    End Sub

    Private Sub btnSaveUpdates_Click(ByVal sender As _
        System.Object, ByVal e As System.EventArgs)_
```

```
Handles btnSaveUpdates.Click

    Try
        mda.Update(mds, "Customers")
    Catch ex As Exception
        MsgBox("Error: " & ex.Source & ": " & ex.Message, _
        MsgBoxStyle.OKOnly, "frmUpdate_Load")
    End Try

  End Sub
```

Of particular interest for the task of editing data is the block that creates the Command object that is assigned to the DataAdapter.Update-Command property. This Command is based on a SQL statement with three parameters:

```
UPDATE Customers
    SET CompanyName = @CompanyName,
    ContactName = @ContactName
    WHERE CustomerID = @CustomerID
```

After the code creates the Command with this CommandText, it calls the `Parameters.Add` method of the Command once for each of the three parameters. In this case, the format of the Add method used takes four arguments:

- ▶ The name of the parameter to create
- ▶ The datatype of the parameter
- ▶ The size of the parameter
- ▶ The source column to which this parameter will be bound

Supplying the source column is essential to transferring updates seamlessly from the DataSet back to the original data source.

Editing Data

Editing data in a DataSet is easy. You don't need to worry about entering some special editing mode, as was the case with some of the older data access libraries. Instead, you can simply assign a new value to the appropriate item in the DataRow of interest. For example, here's some code that finds a particular row and then prompts the user for a new value of the ContactName column in that row:

```
Private Sub btnPromptedEdit_Click(ByVal sender As _
    System.Object, ByVal e As System.EventArgs) _
    Handles btnPromptedEdit.Click


    Dim strCustomerID As String
    Dim strContactName As String
    Dim dr As DataRow

    Try
        strCustomerID = InputBox("Customer ID to edit:")
        Dim adrEdit() = mds.Tables("Customers").Select( _
         "CustomerID = '" & strCustomerID & "'")
        If UBound(adrEdit, 1) > -1 Then
            dr = adrEdit(0)
            strContactName = InputBox("New contact name:", _
             , dr("ContactName"))
            dr("ContactName") = strContactName
        Else
            MsgBox(strCustomerID & " not found!")
        End If

    Catch ex As Exception
        MsgBox("Error: " & ex.Source & ": " & ex.Message, _
        MsgBoxStyle.OKOnly, "btnPromptedEdit")
    End Try
End Sub
```

Note the check of the upper bound of the array after the call to the Select method, to make sure that a matching row was found. Generally, you'd need to write code to loop through the entire array. In this case, though, because the filtering is on the primary key of the underlying table, you know that there can be, at most, one matching row.

The edit is performed by this line:

```
dr("ContactName") = strContactName
```

This line of code simply assigns a new value to the ContactName column in the selected DataRow.

Although this sort of editing is convenient when you're performing some operation entirely in code, in many cases it will be easier to allow the Windows Forms user interface to handle the editing chore. Figure 16.1 shows the frmUpdate form open, with a row being edited via the user interface. The DataGrid is displaying the Customers member from the DataSet. As you can see, the DataGrid allows editing in place.

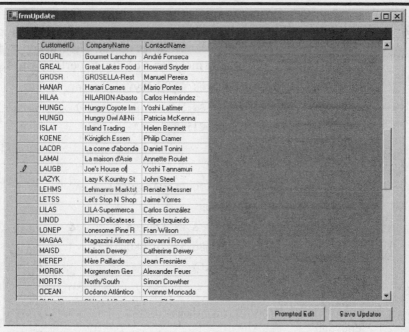

FIGURE 16.1: Editing a row via the DataGrid control

In fact, the DataGrid allows all three of the fundamental editing operations:

- ▶ To update the data in a row, click in the column to be updated and type a new value.

- ▶ To add a new row, scroll to the end of the list and type the values for the row into the last row of the grid.

- ▶ To delete an existing row, click on the record selector to the left of the row and then press the Delete key on the keyboard.

Part IV

TIP

To selectively disable any of these features, build a DataView based on the DataTable that you want to edit, and set the AllowEdit, AllowNew, or AllowDelete property of the DataView to False. Then bind the DataView rather than the DataTable to the DataGrid.

Reconciling Changes

Changes in the DataSet affect only the in-memory copy of the data. To actually write the changes back to the original data source, you need to call the Update method of the DataAdapter object. The frmUpdate form in this chapter's sample project includes a button to perform this task:

```
Private Sub btnSaveUpdates_Click(ByVal sender As _
System.Object, ByVal e As System.EventArgs) _
Handles btnSaveUpdates.Click


    Try
        mda.Update(mds, "Customers")
    Catch ex As Exception
        MsgBox("Error: " & ex.Source & ": " & _
        ex.Message, MsgBoxStyle.OKOnly, _
        "btnSaveUpdates")
    End Try


End Sub
```

The Update method is syntactically similar to the Fill method. It takes as its parameters the DataSet to be reconciled with the data source and the name of the DataTable whose changes should be saved back to the data source.

You don't need to worry about how many changes were made to the data in the DataSet, or which columns were changed. The DataAdapter automatically locates the changed rows and executes the Update-Command for each of them, filling in the parameters of the Command from the data in the DataSet.

If you need finer control over the updates, you can pass a subset of the rows in the DataSet to the DataAdapter to be updated. There's no requirement to make the entire DataTable available. For example, you could save new rows to the data source, without committing any edits or deletions, by calling the Update method this way:

```
Mda.Update(mds.Tables("Customers").Select( _
    Nothing, Nothing, DataViewRowState.Added))
```

In most cases, editing conflicts between different users will be resolved with a simple optimistic-locking rule of "last edit wins." For example, suppose both Cindy and Chuck are editing the Customers table. Cindy changes the record whose key is ALFKI so that the company name is Alfreds Place, and Chuck changes the same record so that the contact name is Maria Anderson. In this case, when Cindy's change is reconciled with the database, the Update method will run this SQL statement:

```
UPDATE Customers
SET CompanyName = 'Alfreds Place',
ContactName = 'Maria Anders'
WHERE CustomerID = 'ALFKI'
```

When Chuck calls the Update method, it will run this SQL statement:

```
UPDATE Customers
SET CompanyName = 'Alfreds Futterkiste',
ContactName = 'Maria Anderson'
WHERE CustomerID = 'ALFKI'
```

The net effect will be to overwrite Cindy's change. Of course, some changes can't be reconciled that way. For example, if Cindy deletes the ALFKI record and then Chuck tries to update the same record, Chuck will receive a concurrency violation error. I'll discuss concurrency issues in more detail later in the chapter.

ADDING DATA

The DataAdapter can also recognize new rows added to the DataSet and save them back to the database. It does this by invoking the Command referred to by the InsertCommand property. In the example you saw earlier, this Command uses an INSERT INTO SQL statement:

```
INSERT INTO Customers
  (CustomerID, CompanyName, ContactName)
  VALUES(@CustomerID, @CompanyName, @ContactName)
```

Part IV

The parameters for this statement are defined just as they are for the UpdateCommand.

In this particular case, that statement is sufficient because all the data to be inserted comes from the user. Tables that use autonumber or identity keys require a bit more effort to keep the DataSet and the underlying data source synchronized in the case of added rows. The problem, of course, is that the autonumber column is generated at the data source at the time the new row is added. To make this column available to the user interface, the DataAdapter must actually return data as part of its InsertCommand.

The solution is to use a stored procedure with an output parameter on the server to perform the insert and then return the autonumber. Listing 16.2 shows an example, from frmProducts in this chapter's sample project.

Listing 16.2: Using a Stored Procedure to Update an Identity Column

```
Dim mda As New SqlClient.SqlDataAdapter()
Dim mds As New DataSet()

Private Sub frmProducts_Load(ByVal sender _
 As System.Object, ByVal e As System.EventArgs) _
 Handles MyBase.Load
   Dim cnn As SqlClient.SqlConnection = _
   New SqlClient.SqlConnection("Data Source=SKYROCKET;" & _
   "Initial Catalog=Northwind;Integrated Security=SSPI")
   Dim cmdCreate As New SqlClient.SqlCommand()
   Dim cmdSelect As New SqlClient.SqlCommand()
   Dim cmdUpdate As New SqlClient.SqlCommand()
   Dim cmdInsert As New SqlClient.SqlCommand()
   Dim cmdDelete As New SqlClient.SqlCommand()
   Dim prm As SqlClient.SqlParameter
   Dim strCreate As String

   Try
       ' Make sure the stored proc we need
       ' for inserts exists in the database
       strCreate = "CREATE PROC spInsertProduct " & _
       "@ProductName nvarchar(40), " & _
       "@ProductID int OUT " & _
```

```
                "AS " & _
                " INSERT INTO Products(ProductName)" & _
                "   VALUES(@ProductName) " & _
                "SET @ProductID = @@Identity"
            cmdCreate = cnn.CreateCommand
            cmdCreate.CommandText = strCreate
            cnn.Open()
            cmdCreate.ExecuteNonQuery()
            cnn.Close()
        Catch
            ' We don't care if it fails because
            ' the stored proc already exists
        End Try

        Try
            ' Create the Select command to grab the initial data
            cmdSelect = cnn.CreateCommand
            cmdSelect.CommandText = "SELECT ProductID, " & _
            "ProductName FROM Products"
            mda.SelectCommand = cmdSelect

            ' The Update command handles updates
            'to existing rows
            cmdUpdate = cnn.CreateCommand
            cmdUpdate.CommandText = "UPDATE Products " & _
            "SET ProductName = @ProductName " & _
            "WHERE ProductID = @CustomerID"
            ' Now create the parameters that will be
            ' passed to this command
            prm = cmdUpdate.Parameters.Add("@ProductName", _
            SqlDbType.NVarChar, 40, "ProductName")
            prm = cmdUpdate.Parameters.Add("@ProductID", _
            SqlDbType.Int)
            prm.SourceColumn = "ProductID"
            prm.SourceVersion = DataRowVersion.Original
            mda.UpdateCommand = cmdUpdate
            ' The Delete command handles deletions _
            ' of existing rows
            cmdDelete = cnn.CreateCommand
            cmdDelete.CommandText = "DELETE FROM Products " & _
            "WHERE ProductID = @ProductID"
            ' Now create the parameter that will be
```

Part IV

```
                    ' passed to this command
                    prm = cmdDelete.Parameters.Add("@ProductID", _
                      SqlDbType.Int)
                    prm.SourceColumn = "ProductID"
                    prm.SourceVersion = DataRowVersion.Original
                    mda.DeleteCommand = cmdDelete

                    ' And the Insert command adds new rows
                    cmdInsert = cnn.CreateCommand
                    cmdInsert.CommandText = "spInsertProduct"
                    cmdInsert.CommandType = CommandType.StoredProcedure
                    ' Now create the parameters that will be
                    ' passed to this command
                    prm = cmdInsert.Parameters.Add("@ProductName", _
                      SqlDbType.NVarChar, 40, "ProductName")
                    prm = cmdInsert.Parameters.Add("@ProductID", _
                      SqlDbType.Int)
                    prm.SourceColumn = "ProductID"
                    prm.Direction = ParameterDirection.Output
                    mda.InsertCommand = cmdInsert

                    ' Fill the DataSet and display it on the UI
                    mda.Fill(mds, "Products")
                    dgMain.DataSource = mds
                    dgMain.DataMember = "Products"

            Catch ex As Exception
                MsgBox("Error: " & ex.Source & ": " & ex.Message, _
                  MsgBoxStyle.OKOnly, "frmProducts_Load")
            End Try

        End Sub

        Private Sub btnMain_Click(ByVal sender As System.Object, _
          ByVal e As System.EventArgs) Handles btnMain.Click

            Try

                mda.Update(mds, "Products")
```

```
      Catch ex As Exception
          MsgBox("Error: " & ex.Source & ": " & ex.Message, _
          MsgBoxStyle.OKOnly, "btnMain")
      End Try

  End Sub
```

Most of this is very similar to the code you already saw for the frmUpdate form. The difference is in the InsertCommand. The frmProducts_Load procedure starts by creating a stored procedure on the target SQL Server:

```
CREATE PROC spInsertProduct
@ProductName nvarchar(40),
@ProductID int OUT
AS
INSERT INTO Products(ProductName)
VALUES(@ProductName)
SET @ProductID = @@Identity
```

This stored procedure inserts a new row into the table and then uses the *@@Identity* system variable to retrieve the most recent identity value used by the connection (this, of course, will be the new ProductID value in this case). There are some minor differences in setting up the Insert-Command for the DataAdapter:

```
          ' And the Insert command adds new rows
          cmdInsert = cnn.CreateCommand
          cmdInsert.CommandText = "spInsertProduct"
          cmdInsert.CommandType = CommandType.StoredProcedure
          ' Now create the parameters that will be
          ' passed to this command
          prm = cmdInsert.Parameters.Add("@ProductName", _
           SqlDbType.NVarChar, 40, "ProductName")
          prm = cmdInsert.Parameters.Add("@ProductID", _
           SqlDbType.Int)
          prm.SourceColumn = "ProductID"
          prm.Direction = ParameterDirection.Output
          mda.InsertCommand = cmdInsert
```

Part IV

Note that the CommandType is explicitly set to `CommandType` `.StoredProcedure`; without this, you'll get a syntax error when trying to execute the update. Also, the Direction property of the Parameter object representing the `@ProductID` parameter must be set to `ParameterDirection.Output` to tell the DataAdapter that this is information that should be sent back to the DataSet.

To try this code out, follow these steps:

1. Run the sample project.

2. Open the Products form.

3. Scroll to the end of the DataGrid, and enter a new name in the ProductName column.

4. Click the Update button.

You'll see the newly assigned ProductID automatically appear on the DataGrid when the DataAdapter finishes the update process.

DELETING DATA

As you've no doubt guessed by now, deleting data is a matter of supplying an appropriate DeleteCommand to the DataAdapter. Here's the version from the code you saw in Listing 16.1:

```
' The Delete command handles deletions +
' of existing rows
cmdDelete = cnn.CreateCommand
cmdDelete.CommandText = "DELETE FROM Customers" & _
    " WHERE CustomerID = @CustomerID"
' Now create the parameter that will be
' passed to this command
prm = cmdDelete.Parameters.Add("@CustomerID", _
    SqlDbType.NChar, 5, "CustomerID")
prm.SourceVersion = DataRowVersion.Original
mda.DeleteCommand = cmdDelete
```

The DeleteCommand can be simpler than the InsertCommand or UpdateCommand in most cases. All it needs to do is locate the appropriate row in the original source table by using a WHERE clause that includes all the columns of the primary key, and then delete that row.

USING AUTO-GENERATED COMMANDS

In some cases, you can avoid the tedium of writing your own SQL strings to manage updates, insertions, and deletions. The .NET data providers include an object called the CommandBuilder (depending on the provider, this will be the OleDbCommandBuilder, SqlCommandBuilder, or OdbcCommandBuilder object). You saw this object briefly in Chapter 15, where I used its DeriveParameters method to automatically retrieve the parameters for a stored procedure. But there's a lot more to the CommandBuilder object than that: It also knows how to build the Command objects required by the DataAdapter object in simple cases.

In particular, there are three constraints in using the Command-Builder object to automatically configure a DataAdapter:

▶ The SelectCommand property of the DataAdapter must be set first.

▶ The SelectCommand can draw columns from only a single database table.

▶ The columns loaded by the SelectCommand must include at least one primary key or unique constraint.

The frmUpdate2 form in this chapter's sample project demonstrates the syntax. Listing 16.3 presents the code.

Listing 16.3: Generating Commands with the SqlCommand-Builder Object

```
Private Sub frmUpdate2_Load(ByVal sender As System.Object, _
ByVal e As System.EventArgs) Handles MyBase.Load
  Dim cnn As SqlClient.SqlConnection = _
  New SqlClient.SqlConnection("Data Source=SKYROCKET;" & _
  "Initial Catalog=Northwind;Integrated Security=SSPI")
  Dim cmdSelect As New SqlClient.SqlCommand()

  Try
      ' Create the Select command to grab the initial data
      cmdSelect = cnn.CreateCommand
      cmdSelect.CommandText = "SELECT CustomerID, " & _
      "CompanyName, ContactName FROM Customers"
```

```
mda.SelectCommand = cmdSelect

' Automatically generate the Update, Insert,
' and Delete commands
Dim cb As SqlClient.SqlCommandBuilder = _
New SqlClient.SqlCommandBuilder(mda)

' Fill the DataSet and display it on the UI
mda.Fill(mds, "Customers")
dgMain.DataSource = mds
dgMain.DataMember = "Customers"

Catch ex As Exception
    MsgBox("Error: " & ex.Source & ": " & ex.Message, _
    MsgBoxStyle.OKOnly, "frmUpdate_Load")
End Try

End Sub

Private Sub btnSaveUpdates_Click(ByVal sender As _
System.Object, ByVal e As System.EventArgs) _
Handles btnSaveUpdates.Click

Try
    mda.Update(mds, "Customers")
Catch ex As Exception
    MsgBox("Error: " & ex.Source & ": " & ex.Message, _
    MsgBoxStyle.OKOnly, "btnSaveUpdates")
End Try

End Sub
```

If you compare this with the code for frmUpdate, you'll see that the CommandBuilder object can considerably simplify the task of setting up a DataAdapter for two-way communication between a DataSet and a data source. But remember, if your data source is complex, you'll probably have to write the Commands that modify the data by hand, because the CommandBuilder won't work for SelectCommands based on multiple tables. Also, because the CommandBuilder has to retrieve schema information from the data source to do its job, you'll have one more round-trip to the database server in your code, which may slow things down a bit (especially if you're working over a slow link).

The CommandBuilder object won't overwrite properties that are set manually. So it's possible to craft a custom Command for, say, the UpdateCommand property and still let the CommandBuilder do the work of building the InsertCommand and the DeleteCommand.

When it's building the UpdateCommand and DeleteCommand, the CommandBuilder object creates WHERE clauses that check the values of all the columns in the DataTable. This ensures that updates will be made only if no other user has changed the row since it was loaded.

ADDING PRIMARY KEYS TO A DATASET

One of the problems with the Fill method of the DataAdapter is that it transfers only data to the DataSet; it doesn't transfer any of the constraints from the data source to the DataSet. This means that you can, for example, add rows with a duplicate primary key to a DataTable in that DataSet. Although these rows cannot be saved back to the data source (the problem will cause an error to be raised when you call the DataAdapter.Update method), it's much better practice to prevent the user from entering these rows in the first place. That's the purpose of adding constraints to a DataSet.

The most important constraints to add to the DataSet are primary keys. There are three ways to take care of adding primary keys when filling a DataSet:

- ▶ Call the DataAdapter.FillSchema method.
- ▶ Set the DataAdapter.MissingSchemaAction property.
- ▶ Create the primary key in code.

The DataAdapter.FillSchema method copies primary key constraint information from a specified data source table to the DataSet. You can see an example in frmConstraints in this chapter's sample project. That form's code is shown in Listing 16.4.

Listing 16.4: Copying Constraint Information to a DataSet

```
Private Sub btnFillSchema_Click(ByVal sender As _
    System.Object, ByVal e As System.EventArgs) _
    Handles btnFillSchema.Click
```

```
Dim cnn As SqlClient.SqlConnection = _
New SqlClient.SqlConnection("Data Source=SKYROCKET;" & _
"Initial Catalog=Northwind;Integrated Security=SSPI")
Dim cmdSelect As New SqlClient.SqlCommand()

Try
    ' Create the Select command to grab the initial data
    cmdSelect = cnn.CreateCommand
    cmdSelect.CommandText = "SELECT CustomerID, " & _
      "CompanyName, ContactName FROM Customers"
    mda.SelectCommand = cmdSelect

    ' Automatically generate the Update, Insert,
    ' and Delete commands
    Dim cb As SqlClient.SqlCommandBuilder = _
      New SqlClient.SqlCommandBuilder(mda)

    ' Fill the DataSet and display it on the UI
    mds.Clear()
    mda.FillSchema(mds, SchemaType.Source, "Customers")
    mda.Fill(mds, "Customers")
    dgMain.DataSource = mds
    dgMain.DataMember = "Customers"

Catch ex As Exception
    MsgBox("Error: " & ex.Source & ": " & ex.Message, _
      MsgBoxStyle.OKOnly, "btnFillSchema")
End Try

End Sub
```

When you call the FillSchema method in this case, it will add the primary key constraint to the Customers DataTable within the specified DataSet. This has the effect of bringing primary key validation to the user interface, before any call to the DataAdapter.Fill method. If you try to enter a row whose primary key duplicates that of an existing row, you'll get the warning message shown in Figure 16.2.

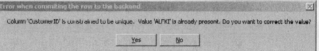

FIGURE 16.2: Trapping a duplicate primary key with a DataTable constraint

If you answer Yes to this prompt, you'll be returned to the row on the DataGrid to continue editing. If you answer No, the row with the duplicate primary key will be erased from the DataGrid and discarded.

NOTE

Remember, any edits you make through the DataGrid are reflected in the DataSet, but not saved to the original data source. To save the changes permanently, you'll need to click the Save Updates button.

You can also copy schema information to the DataTable at the time the Fill method is called by setting the MissingSchemaAction property of the DataAdapter to AddWithKey. Listing 16.5 shows this technique in action.

Listing 16.5: Adding Schema Information to a DataTable Automatically

```
Private Sub btnMissingSchemaAction_Click(ByVal sender _
As System.Object, ByVal e As System.EventArgs) _
Handles btnMissingSchemaAction.Click
  Dim cnn As SqlClient.SqlConnection = _
  New SqlClient.SqlConnection("Data Source=SKYROCKET;" & _
```

```
        "Initial Catalog=Northwind;Integrated Security=SSPI")
    Dim cmdSelect As New SqlClient.SqlCommand()

    Try
        ' Create the Select command to grab the initial data
        cmdSelect = cnn.CreateCommand
        cmdSelect.CommandText = "SELECT CustomerID, " & _
        "CompanyName, ContactName FROM Customers"
        mda.SelectCommand = cmdSelect

        ' Automatically generate the Update, Insert,
        ' and Delete commands
        Dim cb As SqlClient.SqlCommandBuilder = _
        New SqlClient.SqlCommandBuilder(mda)

        ' Fill the DataSet and display it on the UI
        mds.Clear()
        mda.MissingSchemaAction = _
        MissingSchemaAction.AddWithKey
        mda.Fill(mds, "Customers")
        dgMain.DataSource = mds
        dgMain.DataMember = "Customers"
    Catch ex As Exception
        MsgBox("Error: " & ex.Source & ": " & ex.Message, _
        MsgBoxStyle.OKOnly, "btnFillSchema")
    End Try

  End Sub
```

This code is nearly identical to that of Listing 16.4, and it has the same effect on the user interface. The MissingSchemaAction property does allow some additional flexibility. This property is checked whenever you're adding a new column to the DataSet, and the DataSet doesn't contain a matching DataColumn. The property can take any of these values:

▶ MissingSchemaAction.Add to just add the column

▶ MissingSchemaAction.AddWithKey to add the column and any primary key constraint that includes the column

▶ MissingSchemaAction.Error to throw a runtime error

▶ MissingSchemaAction.Ignore to ignore the column

Using the FillWithSchema method or the MissingSchemaAction property has the same drawback as using the CommandBuilder object: It requires additional trips to the data source to retrieve the schema information, with the consequent performance penalty. If you know the structure of the data in advance, you may want to create the primary key constraint directly in code instead. To do this, you actually need to build the entire DataTable in code. Listing 16.6 provides an example.

Listing 16.6: Creating a DataTable from Scratch

```
Private Sub btnCreatePK_Click(ByVal sender _
As System.Object, As System.EventArgs) _
Handles btnCreatePK.Click
  Dim cnn As SqlClient.SqlConnection = _
  New SqlClient.SqlConnection("Data Source=SKYROCKET;" & _
  "Initial Catalog=Northwind;Integrated Security=SSPI")
  Dim cmdSelect As New SqlClient.SqlCommand()

  Try
      ' Create the Select command to grab the initial data
      cmdSelect = cnn.CreateCommand
      cmdSelect.CommandText = "SELECT CustomerID, " & _
      "CompanyName, ContactName FROM Customers"
      mda.SelectCommand = cmdSelect
      ' Automatically generate the Update, Insert,
      ' and Delete commands
      Dim cb As SqlClient.SqlCommandBuilder = _
      New SqlClient.SqlCommandBuilder(mda)
      ' Create the DataTable with a PK
      Dim dtCustomers As DataTable = _
      mds.Tables.Add("Customers")
      Dim dcPK As DataColumn = dtCustomers.Columns.Add( _
      "CustomerID", Type.GetType("System.String"))
      dtCustomers.Columns.Add("CompanyName", _
      Type.GetType("System.String"))
      dtCustomers.Columns.Add("ContactName", _
      Type.GetType("System.String"))
      dtCustomers.PrimaryKey = New DataColumn() {dcPK}

      ' Fill the DataSet and display it on the UI
      mds.Clear()
      mda.Fill(mds, "Customers")
      dgMain.DataSource = mds
```

```
            dgMain.DataMember = "Customers"

        Catch ex As Exception
            MsgBox("Error: " & ex.Source & ": " & ex.Message, _
            MsgBoxStyle.OKOnly, "btnFillSchema")
        End Try

    End Sub
```

As you can see, building a DataTable is a relatively straightforward process:

1. Create the DataTable by calling the Add method of the `DataSet.Tables` collection.

2. Create the individual DataColumn objects in the DataTable by calling the Add method of the `DataTable.Columns` method. Note that this method takes system datatypes rather than data source datatypes.

3. Set the PrimaryKey property of the DataTable to point to one of the just-created columns. The code shows how to do this by creating a new DataColumn object from an existing DataColumn.

Although this method is the most tedious of the three demonstrated in this section, it's also the fastest (because it doesn't have to query the data source for schema information). At runtime, this code has the same effect as the FillSchema or MissingSchemaAction method; you'll get the same warning prompt if you try to enter a duplicate primary key.

WORKING WITH ADO.NET EVENTS

Working with data always presents challenges. The user may enter data that makes no sense in the context of the application, you might need to do special processing for certain values, or you might be faced with the necessity to keep a record of changes for audit trail purposes. Fortunately, ADO.NET provides a reasonably rich set of events to allow you to intervene in the data editing process with your own code. In this section, I'll discuss the two main objects in the ADO.NET model that support data-related events:

▶ DataTable events

▶ DataAdapter events

Figure 16.3 shows the frmEvents form in this chapter's sample project. This form dumps information on events to the listbox as they happen. You can use it to see how user interaction with a DataSet triggers the various events. Listing 16.7 shows the code from frmEvents.

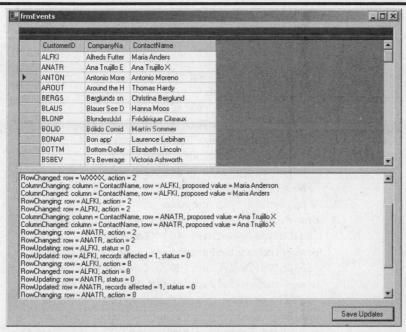

FIGURE 16.3:   Events during an editing session

Listing 16.7: frmEvents Source Code

```
Dim mda As New SqlClient.SqlDataAdapter()
Dim mds As New DataSet()

Private Sub frmEvents_Load(ByVal sender As System.Object, _
ByVal e As System.EventArgs) Handles MyBase.Load
  Dim cnn As SqlClient.SqlConnection = _
    New SqlClient.SqlConnection("Data Source=SKYROCKET;" & _
    "Initial Catalog=Northwind;Integrated Security=SSPI")
  Dim cmdSelect As New SqlClient.SqlCommand()
  Dim cmdUpdate As New SqlClient.SqlCommand()
  Dim cmdInsert As New SqlClient.SqlCommand()
  Dim cmdDelete As New SqlClient.SqlCommand()
```

```
Dim prm As SqlClient.SqlParameter

Try
    ' Create the Select command to grab the initial data
    cmdSelect = cnn.CreateCommand
    cmdSelect.CommandText = "SELECT CustomerID, " & _
    "CompanyName, ContactName FROM Customers"
    mda.SelectCommand = cmdSelect

    ' The Update command handles updates
    ' to existing rows
    cmdUpdate = cnn.CreateCommand
    cmdUpdate.CommandText = "UPDATE Customers " & _
    "SET CompanyName = @CompanyName, " & _
    "ContactName = @ContactName " & _
    "WHERE CustomerID = @CustomerID"
    ' Now create the parameters that will be
    ' passed to this command
    prm = cmdUpdate.Parameters.Add("@CompanyName", _
    SqlDbType.NVarChar, 40, "CompanyName")
    prm = cmdUpdate.Parameters.Add("@ContactName", _
    SqlDbType.NVarChar, 30, "ContactName")
    prm = cmdUpdate.Parameters.Add("@CustomerID", _
    SqlDbType.NChar, 5, "CustomerID")
    prm.SourceVersion = DataRowVersion.Original
    mda.UpdateCommand = cmdUpdate

    ' The Delete command handles deletions
    ' of existing rows
    cmdDelete = cnn.CreateCommand
    cmdDelete.CommandText = "DELETE FROM " & _
    "Customers WHERE CustomerID = @CustomerID"
    ' Now create the parameter that will be
    ' passed to this command
    prm = cmdDelete.Parameters.Add("@CustomerID", _
    SqlDbType.NChar, 5, "CustomerID")
    prm.SourceVersion = DataRowVersion.Original
    mda.DeleteCommand = cmdDelete

    ' And the Insert command adds new rows
    cmdInsert = cnn.CreateCommand
    cmdInsert.CommandText = "INSERT INTO Customers" & _
```

```
        " (CustomerID, CompanyName, ContactName) " & _
        "VALUES(@CustomerID, @CompanyName, @ContactName)"
      ' Now create the parameters that will be
      ' passed to this command
      prm = cmdInsert.Parameters.Add("@CompanyName", _
        SqlDbType.NVarChar, 40, "CompanyName")
      prm = cmdInsert.Parameters.Add("@ContactName", _
        SqlDbType.NVarChar, 30, "ContactName")
      prm = cmdInsert.Parameters.Add("@CustomerID", _
        SqlDbType.NChar, 5, "CustomerID")
      mda.InsertCommand = cmdInsert
      ' Fill the DataSet and display it on the UI
      mda.Fill(mds, "Customers")
      dgMain.DataSource = mds
      dgMain.DataMember = "Customers"

      ' Set up event handlers
      AddHandler mds.Tables("Customers").ColumnChanging, _
        New DataColumnChangeEventHandler(AddressOf _
        Column_Changing)
      AddHandler mds.Tables("Customers").ColumnChanged, _
        New DataColumnChangeEventHandler(AddressOf _
        Column_Changed)
      AddHandler mds.Tables("Customers").RowChanging, _
        New DataRowChangeEventHandler(AddressOf _
        Row_Changing)
      AddHandler mds.Tables("Customers").RowChanged, _
        New DataRowChangeEventHandler(AddressOf _
        Row_Changed)
      AddHandler mds.Tables("Customers").RowDeleting, _
        New DataRowChangeEventHandler(AddressOf _
        Row_Deleting)
      AddHandler mds.Tables("Customers").RowDeleted, _
        New DataRowChangeEventHandler(AddressOf _
        Row_Deleted)
      AddHandler mda.RowUpdated, _
        New SqlClient.SqlRowUpdatedEventHandler(AddressOf _
        Row_Updated)
      AddHandler mda.RowUpdating, _
        New SqlClient.SqlRowUpdatingEventHandler(AddressOf _
        Row_Updating)

    Catch ex As Exception
```

```
            MsgBox("Error: " & ex.Source & ": " & ex.Message, _
            MsgBoxStyle.OKOnly, "frmUpdate_Load")
        End Try

    End Sub

    Private Sub btnSaveUpdates_Click(ByVal sender As _
    System.Object, ByVal e As System.EventArgs) _
    Handles btnSaveUpdates.Click

        Try
            mda.Update(mds, "Customers")
        Catch ex As Exception
            MsgBox("Error: " & ex.Source & ": " & ex.Message, _
            MsgBoxStyle.OKOnly, "btnSaveUpdates")
        End Try

    End Sub

    Private Sub Column_Changing(ByVal sender As Object, _
     ByVal e As DataColumnChangeEventArgs)
        lboEvents.Items.Add("ColumnChanging: column = " & _
        e.Column.ColumnName & ", row = " & _
        e.Row("CustomerID") & ", proposed value = " & _
        e.ProposedValue)
        If MsgBox("Cancel column change?", MsgBoxStyle.YesNo) = _
        MsgBoxResult.Yes Then
            e.ProposedValue = e.Row(e.Column.ColumnName)
        End If
    End Sub

    Private Sub Column_Changed(ByVal sender As Object, _
     ByVal e As DataColumnChangeEventArgs)
        lboEvents.Items.Add("ColumnChanged: column = " & _
        e.Column.ColumnName & ", row = " & _
        e.Row("CustomerID") & ", proposed value = " & _
        e.ProposedValue)
    End Sub

    Private Sub Row_Changing(ByVal sender As Object, _
```

```
      ByVal e As DataRowChangeEventArgs)
        lboEvents.Items.Add("RowChanging: row = " & _
        e.Row("CustomerID") & _
        ", action = " & e.Action)
    End Sub

    Private Sub Row_Changed(ByVal sender As Object, _
     ByVal e As DataRowChangeEventArgs)
        lboEvents.Items.Add("RowChanged: row = " & _
        e.Row("CustomerID") & _
        ", action = " & e.Action)
    End Sub

    Private Sub Row_Deleting(ByVal sender As Object, _
     ByVal e As DataRowChangeEventArgs)
        lboEvents.Items.Add("RowDeleting: row = " & _
        e.Row("CustomerID") & _
        ", action = " & e.Action)
    End Sub

    Private Sub Row_Deleted(ByVal sender As Object, _
     ByVal e As DataRowChangeEventArgs)
        lboEvents.Items.Add("RowDeleted: " & _
        "action = " & e.Action)
    End Sub

    Private Sub Row_Updated(ByVal sender As Object, _
     ByVal e As SqlClient.SqlRowUpdatedEventArgs)
        lboEvents.Items.Add("RowUpdated: row = " & _
        e.Row("CustomerID") & _
        ", records affected = " & e.RecordsAffected & _
        ", status = " & e.Status)
    End Sub

    Private Sub Row_Updating(ByVal sender As Object, _
     ByVal e As SqlClient.SqlRowUpdatingEventArgs)
        lboEvents.Items.Add("RowUpdating: row = " & _
        e.Row("CustomerID") & _
        ", status = " & e.Status)
    End Sub
```

DataTable Events

When you're editing data in a DataTable, you can monitor events on either a row-by-row or column-by-column basis. The six events supported by the DataTable come in three pairs, whose before-and-after structure will be familiar to you if you've looked at ADO Recordset events:

- ColumnChanging and ColumnChanged
- RowChanging and RowChanged
- RowDeleting and RowDeleted

The ColumnChanging and ColumnChanged Events

The ColumnChanging and ColumnChanged events fire whenever the data in a column of a DataSet is changed. The ColumnChanging event fires just before the change is committed to the DataSet; the ColumnChanged event fires just after the change is made.

ADO.NET passes to each of these events an argument whose type is DataColumnChangeEventArgs. This argument has three properties containing information about the event:

Column   The DataColumn object whose contents are being changed

ProposedValue   The new value being assigned to the data

Row   The DataRow object whose contents are being changed

Although the ColumnChanging event doesn't have an explicit Cancel argument, you can achieve the effect of cancelling the change by reassigning the original data to the ProposedValue property within the event procedure. The code for frmEvents prompts the user with a message box asking whether to discard the change:

```
If MsgBox("Cancel column change?", MsgBoxStyle.YesNo) = _
MsgBoxResult.Yes Then
    e.ProposedValue = e.Row(e.Column.ColumnName)
End If
```

The ColumnChanging and ColumnChanged events fire as soon as you leave the affected column. If you're editing multiple columns in the same row of data, these events will fire once per column. They fire when you're adding a new row of data to a DataSet, as well as when you're editing an existing row.

The RowChanging and RowChanged Events

The RowChanging and RowChanged events fire whenever the data in a row of a DataSet is changed. The RowChanging event fires just before the change is committed to the DataSet; the RowChanged event fires just after the change is made. These events fire once per row, regardless of how many columns are edited in the row. The RowChanging and RowChanged events fire after all of the ColumnChanging and Column-Changed events for the row.

ADO.NET passes to each of these events an argument whose type is DataRowChangeEventArgs. This argument has two properties containing information about the event:

Action   Specifies the action that fired the event. Table 16.1 lists the values for this property.

Row   The DataRow whose contents are being changed.

TABLE 16.1:   Action Values

VALUE	MEANING
Add	The row has been added to the table.
Change	The row has been edited.
Commit	The changes in the row have been committed.
Delete	The row has been deleted from the table.
Nothing	The row has not changed.
Rollback	A change has been rolled back.

The RowDeleting and RowDeleted Events

The RowDeleting and RowDeleted events fire whenever a row is deleted from the DataSet. The RowDeleting event fires just before the row is deleted; the RowDeleted event fires just after the deletion is final. These events fire once per row. Deletions do not trigger any column-level events.

Part IV

ADO.NET passes to each of these events an argument whose type is DataRowChangeEventArgs. This argument has two properties containing information about the event:

Action   Specifies the action that fired the event. Table 16.1 lists the values for this property.

Row   The DataRow whose contents are being changed.

The Row property isn't valid in the RowDeleted event, because by then the row has already been deleted.

You might think that you could cancel a deletion by setting the Action property to DataRowAction.Nothing, but the Action property is read-only in these events. You can't cancel a deletion within these events. Remember, though, that you have full control over whether the deletion is committed back to the underlying data source through your calls to the DataAdapter.Update method, as you saw earlier in the chapter. Alternatively, you could carry out the deletion in the context of a transaction and commit or roll back the transaction as you see fit. I'll discuss transactions later in the chapter.

DataAdapter Events

The DataAdapter, too, has a pair of data-related events: RowUpdated and RowUpdating. These events fire when data is being written back to the data source in the course of the DataAdapter.Update method.

The RowUpdating and RowUpdated Events

When you call the DataAdapter.Update method, the following sequence of actions and events occurs:

1. The values in the DataRow are moved to the parameters of the appropriate Command (InsertCommand, Update-Command, or DeleteCommand).

2. The RowUpdating event fires.

3. The appropriate Command is executed.

4. Any output parameters are copied back to the DataRow.

5. The RowUpdated event fires.

6. The DataRow.AcceptChanges method is called.

These actions happen once for each row that's being altered by the Update method.

ADO.NET passes an argument of type SqlRowUpdatingEventArgs to the RowUpdating event. This argument has these properties:

Command   The Command about to be executed.

Errors   Any errors generated by the Command.

Row   The DataRow being updated.

StatementType   The type of SQL statement being executed (Select, Insert, Update, or Delete).

Status   The UpdateStatus of the change. See Table 16.2 for the possible values of this argument.

TableMapping   The TableMapping object being changed by this update.

TABLE 16.2:   UpdateStatus Values

VALUE	MEANING
Continue	Continue processing rows.
ErrorsOccurred	Errors occurred during this update.
SkipAllRemainingRows	Stop updating entirely.
SkipCurrentRow	Skip this row and continue updating.

ADO.NET passes an argument of type SqlRowUpdatedEventArgs to the RowUpdated event. This argument has these properties:

Command   The Command that was executed.

Errors   Any errors generated by the Command.

RecordsAffected   The number of rows in the data source affected by the Command.

Row   The DataRow being updated.

StatementType   The type of SQL statement being executed (Select, Insert, Update, or Delete).

Status   The UpdateStatus of the change. See Table 16.2 for the possible values of this argument.

Part IV

TableMapping   The TableMapping object being changed by this update.

Order of Updating Events

If you're monitoring all the events for the DataTable and DataAdapter, you'll discover that the events of both objects fire when you call the `DataAdapter.Update` method. Here's the order of update events:

1. The RowUpdating event fires for the appropriate row.

2. The RowUpdated event fires for the appropriate row.

3. The RowChanging event fires for the appropriate row with an Action value of `DataRowAction.Commit`. This is the result of the call to AcceptChanges in the update sequence.

4. The RowChanged event fires for the appropriate row with an Action value of `DataRowAction.Commit`.

MANAGING CONCURRENCY AND TRANSACTIONS

Just about any data access library offers facilities for dealing with multi-user issues, and ADO.NET is no exception. Broadly speaking, these facilities break down into two areas:

▶ *Concurrency* deals with the problems that come about when multiple users work with the same data at the same time.

▶ *Transactions* deal with the problems that arise when multiple tables need to be updated in a single operation.

In this section, I'll demonstrate the concurrency and transaction support in ADO.NET.

Concurrency

You're probably familiar with the distinction between optimistic locking and pessimistic locking from libraries such as ADO:

With *optimistic locking*, users are prevented from updating a record while another user is updating that record.

With *pessimistic locking*, users are prevented from editing a record while another user is editing that record.

In ADO.NET, the choices change somewhat. That's because disconnected DataScts (thc core data-editing tool in ADO.NET) are fundamentally inconsistent with pessimistic locking. In almost all applications, it doesn't make sense to lock records for the entire time that someone has them loaded into a DataSet, which is what you'd need to do to implement pessimistic locking.

Instead, ADO.NET lets you choose between two strategies when you're creating the Command objects that will be used with a DataAdapter to update data:

▶ With optimistic concurrency control, you can update a row only if no one else has updated that row since you loaded it into your DataSet.

▶ With "last one wins" concurrency control, you can always update a row, whether another user has changed it or not.

The frmConcurrency form in this chapter's sample project lets you experiment with these two strategies. It does this by switching the Commands for the DataAdapter between two versions. To illustrate, Listing 16.8 shows the bit of code that sets the UpdateCommand property.

Listing 16.8: Switching Versions of the UpdateCommand

```
If rbOptimistic.Checked Then
    ' Optimistic concurrency


    ' The Update command handles updates to existing rows
    cmdUpdate = cnn.CreateCommand
    cmdUpdate.CommandText = "UPDATE Customers " & _
     "SET CompanyName = @CompanyName, " & _
     "ContactName = @ContactName " & _
     "WHERE CustomerID = @CustomerID AND " & _
     "CompanyName = @CompanyNameOrig AND " & _
     "ContactName = @ContactNameOrig"
    ' Now create the parameters that will be
    ' passed to this command
    prm = cmdUpdate.Parameters.Add("@CompanyName", _
     SqlDbType.NVarChar, 40, "CompanyName")
    prm = cmdUpdate.Parameters.Add("@ContactName", _
```

```
              SqlDbType.NVarChar, 30, "ContactName")
          prm = cmdUpdate.Parameters.Add("@CustomerID", _
          SqlDbType.NChar, 5, "CustomerID")
          prm.SourceVersion = DataRowVersion.Original
          prm = cmdUpdate.Parameters.Add("@CompanyNameOrig", _
          SqlDbType.NVarChar, 40, "CompanyName")
          prm.SourceVersion = DataRowVersion.Original
          prm = cmdUpdate.Parameters.Add("@ContactNameOrig", _
          SqlDbType.NVarChar, 30, "ContactName")
          prm.SourceVersion = DataRowVersion.Original
          mda.UpdateCommand = cmdUpdate
    ' other code omitted
    Else
          ' "Last one wins" concurrency

          ' The Update command handles updates to existing rows
          cmdUpdate = cnn.CreateCommand
          cmdUpdate.CommandText = "UPDATE Customers " & _
            "SET CompanyName = @CompanyName, " & _
            "ContactName = @ContactName " & _
            "WHERE CustomerID = @CustomerID"
          ' Now create the parameters that will be
          ' passed to this command
          prm = cmdUpdate.Parameters.Add("@CompanyName", _
            SqlDbType.NVarChar, 40, "CompanyName")
          prm = cmdUpdate.Parameters.Add("@ContactName", _
            SqlDbType.NVarChar, 30, "ContactName")
          prm = cmdUpdate.Parameters.Add("@CustomerID", _
            SqlDbType.NChar, 5, "CustomerID")
          prm.SourceVersion = DataRowVersion.Original
          mda.UpdateCommand = cmdUpdate
    ' other code omitted
    End If
```

To implement optimistic concurrency, the code uses a SQL WHERE clause that checks to see that every column in the data source exactly matches the original value of that column in the DataSet. This ensures that the record will be found (and therefore updated) only if no other user has changed the record. To implement last-one-wins concurrency, the code locates the record by primary key only and then updates it regardless of what values are in the other columns. Figure 16.4 shows this form in action.

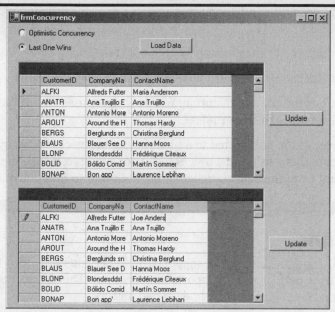

FIGURE 16.4:   Experimenting with concurrency

To see the effects of these two choices, follow these steps:

1. Run the sample project, and open the Concurrency form.

2. Select the Optimistic Concurrency radio button, and click the Load Data button.

3. Make a change to the first row of the first DataGrid.

4. Make a different change to the first row of the second DataGrid.

5. Click the Update button for the first DataGrid.

6. Click the Update button for the second DataGrid.

7. Click the Load Data button. You'll see that only the first update was made to the data. That's because when you clicked the second Update button, the WHERE clause didn't match any records; thus, the update was silently discarded.

8. Select the Last One Wins radio button, and click the Load Data button.

9. Make a change to the first row of the first DataGrid.

10. Make a different change to the first row of the second Data-Grid.

11. Click the Update button for the first DataGrid.

12. Click the Update button for the second DataGrid.

13. Click the Load Data button. You'll see that the second update overwrote the first update.

Of course, you're not limited to a silent failure in the case of an optimistic update that can't find a row. You can, for example, return the record count from the SQL statement and check that to find out whether an update was rejected.

Transactions

ADO.NET also provides built-in support for transactions (provided that the underlying data provider supports transactions). This support is implemented through three methods of two objects:

```
Connection.BeginTransaction
Transaction.Commit
Transaction.Rollback
```

When you call the BeginTransaction method of the Connection object, the Connection's underlying data provider will return a Transaction object. It then starts grouping all subsequent data changes associated with this object into a transaction. This includes updates, additions, and deletions. None of these changes will be immediately written to the database.

When you call the Commit method of the Transaction object, all data changes associated with that Transaction object are committed to the database.

When you call the Rollback method of the Transaction object, all data changes associated with that Transaction object are discarded.

By associating transactions with a particular object, ADO.NET allows you to execute both transacted and non-transacted operations on the same Connection at the same time. This is an improvement over ADO, in which all operations on the Connection are part of a single transaction.

The btnTransactions_Click procedure in the frmMenu form in this chapter's sample project demonstrates the use of the transaction methods. Listing 16.9 shows the code behind this form.

Listing 16.9: Using Transactions with ADO.NET

```
Private Sub btnTransactions_Click(ByVal sender As _
System.Object, ByVal e As System.EventArgs) _
Handles btnTransactions.Click
  Dim cnn As SqlClient.SqlConnection = New _
   SqlClient.SqlConnection("Data Source=SKYROCKET;" & _
   "Initial Catalog=Northwind;Integrated Security=SSPI")
  ' Start a transaction
  cnn.Open()
  Dim trn As SqlTransaction = cnn.BeginTransaction()
  Try
      ' Create a command and associate it
      ' with the transaction
      Dim cmd As SqlCommand = New SqlCommand()
      cmd.Transaction = trn
      ' Now execute a couple of SQL statements
      ' on the transaction
      cmd.CommandText = "INSERT INTO Customers " & _
       "CustomerID, CompanyName " & _
       "VALUES ('ZZZZZ', 'Z Industries')"
      cmd.ExecuteNonQuery()
      cmd.CommandText = "INSERT INTO Customers " & _
       "CustomerID, CompanyName " & _
       "VALUES ('ZZZZZ', 'Zebra Riders Inc.')"
      cmd.ExecuteNonQuery()
      ' And try to commit the transaction
      trn.Commit()
      MsgBox("Transaction succeeded")
  Catch ex As Exception
      ' In case of any problem, roll back
      ' the whole transaction
      trn.Rollback()
      MsgBox("Transaction failed")
  Finally
      cnn.Close()
  End Try
End Sub
```

In this particular case, you'll see the "Transaction failed" message. That's because the second Command tries to insert a record in the table that would duplicate the key of the record that the first Command loaded. This causes an error, which forces the code into the `Catch` block, where it executes the Rollback method.

WHAT'S NEXT

In this chapter, you saw how to use ADO.NET to perform the basic data-editing operations of updating an existing record, adding a new record, and deleting an existing record. The key to all these operations lies in the proper configuration of the DataAdapter object. You also learned how to use the CommandBuilder object to eliminate some code, how to use primary key constraints, and how to monitor ADO.NET data events. Finally, you saw how to use particular Command objects to give you some control over concurrency and how to work with transactions in ADO.NET.

In the next chapter, I'll dig into the notion of data binding, which lies at the heart of using ADO.NET in your applications. In specific, I will focus on binding data to DataGrid controls in ASP.NET.

Chapter 17

USING WINDOWS FORMS WITH ADO.NET

Windows Forms provide the user interface for Windows applications built with the .NET development languages. Over the course of the past several chapters, you've seen many examples of Windows Forms. But the code in those chapters has concentrated on the data, not on its connection with the user interface. In this chapter, I'll look at some of the finer points of using Windows Forms with ADO.NET data.

ADO and ADO.NET Programming

Adapted from *ADO and ADO.NET Programming* by Mike Gunderloy
ISBN 0-7821-2994-3 $59.99

Part IV

Data Binding with Windows Forms

Data binding refers to the action of making a persistent connection between some element of the Windows Forms user interface and a source of data such as a DataSet. Data binding can be broken down into two main classes:

- ▶ *Simple data binding* means connecting a single value from a data source to a single property of a control.

- ▶ *Complex data binding* means connecting a collection of values from a data source to a control.

Most of the examples you've seen so far in this book have used complex data binding to display an entire DataSet on a DataGrid control. In this section, I'll demonstrate the flexibility that both simple and complex data binding offer beyond that model of user interface for data.

Simple Data Binding

Simple data binding can be performed from either the Visual Studio .NET design interface or entirely in code. First, I'll discuss the user interface actions that you can use to bind data; then I'll show you how to achieve the same effect entirely in code.

Data Binding in the IDE

In this example, I'll bind the Text property of a control to a field from a query contained in the Access database ADOChapter17.mdb, which you can download from the Sybex website. To create this example of simple data binding, follow these steps:

1. Launch Visual Studio .NET, and create a new Visual Basic .NET Windows application.

2. Open the Server Explorer window. Right-click the Data Connections node, and select Add Connection.

3. In the Data Link Properties dialog box, select the Provider tab and then choose the Microsoft Jet 4.0 OLE DB provider.

4. In the Data Link Properties dialog box, select the Connection tab and use the Browse button to locate the ADOChapter17 .mdb database in the /bin directory of the sample project. Click Open. Click OK to create the new Data Connection.

5. Expand the new Data Connection in Server Explorer and then expand the Views node. Drag qryOrderTotals from the Views node, and drop it on your form. You'll get a Data Adapter configuration error, because this query is a Totals query and thus isn't an appropriate target for updating. That's not a problem; click OK to continue, and Visual Basic .NET will automatically create an OleDbConnection object and an OleDbDataAdapter object for this query.

6. Select the OleDbDataAdapter object. In the Properties window, click the Generate DataSet hyperlink.

7. In the Generate DataSet dialog box, click the New radio button and name the new DataSet **dsTotals**. Select the Add This DataSet to the Designer check box. Click OK.

8. Add a TextBox control to the form. Name the text box **txtCompanyName**.

9. Expand the DataBindings section at the top of the Properties window. Select the drop-down arrow for the Text property. Expand the tree that drops down, and then click the CompanyName field.

10. Double-click the form to open the code editor with the form's Load event procedure selected. Enter this code to fill the DataSet when you open the form:

```
OleDbDataAdapter1.Fill(DsTotals1)
```

11. Run the project. You should see the name of the first customer from the database on your form.

Data Binding from Code

It's also possible to bind fields to properties in code without using the user interface. Here's how to add a second binding to the same form by using code:

1. Add a second TextBox control to the form. Name the text box **txtTotalBusiness**.

2. Add this code to the form's Load event procedure:

```
txtTotalBusiness.DataBindings.Add( _
  "Text", DsTotals1.Tables("qryOrderTotals"), _
  "TotalBusiness")
```

3. Run the project. You should see the TotalOrders value from the first row of the DataSet on your form, along with the customer name.

This sort of runtime data binding uses the DataBindings property of the control to associate properties of the control with properties of an object. The DataBindings property returns a ControlBindingsCollection object, which, in turn, returns individual Binding objects.

TIP

The object that supplies the properties that are bound to a control need not be a data object. The .NET Framework generalizes the notion of bindings to include many binding sources. For example, you can bind an array to a property. In this chapter, I'll discuss bindings only as they relate to objects from the System.Data namespace.

The ControlBindingsCollection object supports a standard set of collection methods and properties. In particular, you can use the methods and properties shown in Table 17.1 to manage this collection in code.

TABLE 17.1: ControlBindingsCollection Interfaces

NAME	TYPE	DESCRIPTION
Add	Method	Adds a Binding object to the collection.
Clear	Method	Removes all Binding objects from the collection.
Control	Property	Returns the control that owns this collection.
Count	Property	Total number of active Bindings.
Item	Property	Returns a specific Binding object.
Remove	Method	Removes a particular Binding object from the collection.

The most common form of the Add method of the Control-
BindingsCollection takes three parameters:

propertyName   The name of the property of the control to
which this binding is attached

dataSource   The object that provides the data for the binding

dataMember   The property of the object that should be
bound to the control

NOTE

Unlike data binding in earlier versions of Visual Basic, .NET data binding allows
you to choose which property of a control should be bound. I'll discuss this
more in the next section.

The `ControlBindingsCollection.Add` method returns a Binding
object. You can use properties of the Binding object to retrieve all the
information originally passed to the Add method, or a pointer back to the
control to which the Binding object is attached. The Binding object also
supports a Parse event, which is fired whenever the value of the control
changes. In some circumstances, you may want to trap this event to react
to the data with custom code, rather than write it back to the original
data source.

Data Binding to Other Properties

As I mentioned in the preceding section, you can bind to properties other
than the Text property. In fact, you can do so from either the user interface or code. To see this capability in action, follow these steps:

1. Add a Panel control to the form. Name this control
   pnlTotalOrders.

2. Expand the DataBindings section at the top of the Properties window. You'll see that the default property for data
   binding on a Panel control is the Tag property. Click in the
   (Advanced) section of the DataBindings section, and then
   click the Build button. This will open the Advanced Data
   Binding dialog box shown in Figure 17.1.

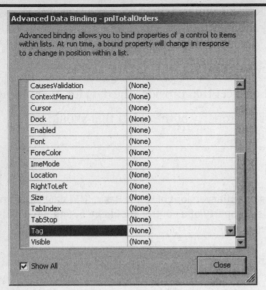

FIGURE 17.1:   Advanced Data Binding dialog box

3. Select the right column of the dialog box for any property, and you'll find that you can browse to almost any member of the DsTotals1 DataSet for binding.

4. To bind to a member that doesn't appear in the Advanced Data Binding dialog box, close the dialog box and enter this line of code in the form's Load procedure:

```
pnlTotalOrders.DataBindings.Add( _
  "Width", DsTotals1.Tables("qryOrderTotals"), _
    "TotalOrders")
```

5. Run the project. The result will be a Panel whose Width property is set at runtime to a value drawn from the TotalOrders field in the data source.

TIP

The user interface method doesn't let you bind to all the properties of the control, even if you select the Show All check box on the dialog box. In particular, the Advanced Data Binding dialog box doesn't let you bind to properties such as X or Width that are grouped into more complex properties within the Properties window. Fortunately, you can bind any of these properties in code, as this example shows.

You can even bind multiple properties of the same control to fields at the same time. To see this in action, first look at the actual data returned by qryOrderTotals, shown in Figure 17.2.

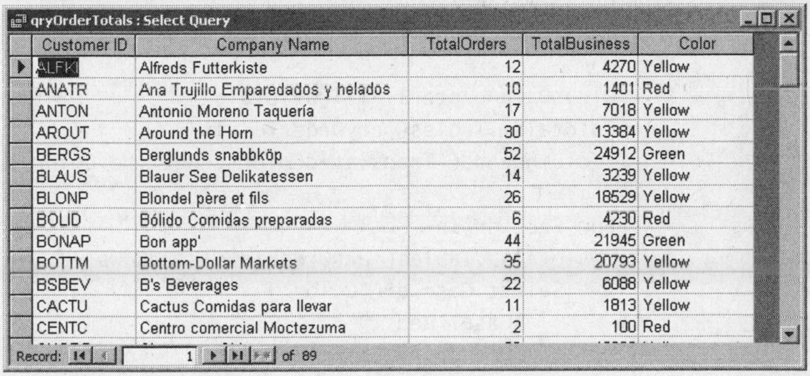

Customer ID	Company Name	TotalOrders	TotalBusiness	Color
ALFKI	Alfreds Futterkiste	12	4270	Yellow
ANATR	Ana Trujillo Emparedados y helados	10	1401	Red
ANTON	Antonio Moreno Taquería	17	7018	Yellow
AROUT	Around the Horn	30	13384	Yellow
BERGS	Berglunds snabbköp	52	24912	Green
BLAUS	Blauer See Delikatessen	14	3239	Yellow
BLONP	Blondel père et fils	26	18529	Yellow
BOLID	Bólido Comidas preparadas	6	4230	Red
BONAP	Bon app'	44	21945	Green
BOTTM	Bottom-Dollar Markets	35	20793	Yellow
BSBEV	B's Beverages	22	6088	Yellow
CACTU	Cactus Comidas para llevar	11	1813	Yellow
CENTC	Centro comercial Moctezuma	2	100	Red

FIGURE 17.2: Source data for simple data binding

In addition to the columns that I've already added to the form, this query returns a column named Color that specifies a color associated with the record. This column is calculated by the query at runtime using this expression:

```
Color:
IIf(Count([Orders.OrderID])>10,
IIf(Count([Orders.OrderID])>35,"Green","Yellow"),"Red")
```

In Microsoft Access syntax, this expression instructs the query to return the value *Red* if the count of orders is 10 or less, *Yellow* if the count is between 11 and 35, and *Green* for a count greater than 35.

If you inspect the Properties window for the Panel control, you might think that you could simply bind this column to the BackColor property. After all, Red, Yellow, and Green are valid values for that property in the IDE. Unfortunately for this idea, the BackColor property takes values from the `System.Drawing.Color` class, and there's a difference between `Green` and `System.Drawing.Color.Green`. Worse yet, .NET provides no automatic conversion between strings and system color values.

Fortunately, you can get around this problem in code. The frmSimple form in the ADOChapter17 sample project demonstrates a technique for doing so. Listing 17.1 shows the code from the form's Load event.

Listing 17.1: Binding an Enumerated Property

```
Private Sub frmSimple_Load(ByVal sender As System.Object, _
ByVal e As System.EventArgs) Handles MyBase.Load
    Dim dr As DataRow

    Try
        OleDbDataAdapter1.Fill(DsTotals1)
        DsTotals1.Tables("qryOrderTotals"). _
         Columns.Add("TranslatedColor", GetType(Color))

        For Each dr In _
         DsTotals1.Tables("qryOrderTotals").Rows
            Select Case dr("Color")
                Case "Red"
                    dr("TranslatedColor") = Color.Red
                Case "Yellow"
                    dr("TranslatedColor") = Color.Yellow
                Case "Green"
                    dr("TranslatedColor") = Color.Green
            End Select
        Next

        txtCompanyName.DataBindings.Add( _
         "Text", DsTotals1.Tables("qryOrderTotals"), _
         "CompanyName")
        txtTotalBusiness.DataBindings.Add( _
         "Text", DsTotals1.Tables("qryOrderTotals"), _
         "TotalBusiness")
        pnlTotalOrders.DataBindings.Add( _
         "Width", DsTotals1.Tables("qryOrderTotals"), _
         "TotalOrders")
        pnlTotalOrders.DataBindings.Add( _
         "BackColor", DsTotals1.Tables("qryOrderTotals"), _
         "TranslatedColor")

    Catch ex As Exception
        MsgBox("Error: " & ex.Source & ": " & ex.Message, _
```

```
                    MsgBoxStyle.OKOnly, "frmSimple_Load")
        End Try

    End Sub
```

The approach that this code takes to the problem is to add an extra column to the DataSet after it has been filled by the DataAdapter. DataSet columns added in this manner are not limited to datatypes that can be stored in a database; the columns can use any available datatype. The GetType function returns the datatype of the specified class. After the code adds the column, it runs through all the rows in the DataSet with a For Each loop, and uses a Select statement to insert appropriate values in the new column. This new column can then be bound to the BackColor property of the Panel control.

Navigating in the Data

So far, all the samples in this chapter have had one failing: They retrieve the first record from the DataTable and sit there. In the real world, you need a way to navigate between the rows that are bound to the user interface. Fortunately, .NET provides a robust way to do this. Figure 17.3 shows the finished frmSimple, with its navigation buttons.

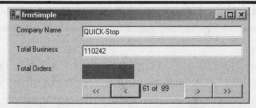

FIGURE 17.3:   Navigating through simple-bound data

You may recall that a DataTable doesn't map well to a traditional database cursor. In particular, the DataTable doesn't have any concept of a current row; it's just a collection of rows. But to navigate between rows, the concept of a cursor is necessary. Bound forms solve this problem by introducing a new object, the CurrencyManager object. This object adds a current row to a data source (whether that data source is a DataTable or some other bindable data source).

Table 17.2 lists some of the important members of the CurrencyManager. I'll be using some of the editing methods later in the chapter.

TABLE 17.2: CurrencyManager Interface

Name	Type	Description
AddNew	Method	Add a new row to the underlying data source.
Bindings	Property	The collection of Binding objects managed by this CurrencyManager.
CancelCurrentEdit	Method	Cancel any editing operation in progress.
EndCurrentEdit	Method	Commit any editing operation in progress.
Count	Property	Number of rows in the data source being managed.
Current	Property	Current row for this CurrencyManager.
Position	Property	Number of the current row within the data source. The Position property is zero-based, with valid values running from zero to Count minus one.
Refresh	Method	Repopulate all controls managed by this CurrencyManager.
RemoveAt	Method	Remove a row from the underlying data source.

You can retrieve a CurrencyManager object using the BindingContext property of a form or a control. The navigation code for frmSimple, shown in Listing 17.2, makes extensive use of the CurrencyManager object for this form.

Listing 17.2: Navigation Code for frmSimple

```
Private Sub btnNext_Click(ByVal sender As System.Object, _
    ByVal e As System.EventArgs) Handles btnNext.Click

    Try
        Me.BindingContext( _
        DsTotals1.Tables("qryOrderTotals")).Position += 1
        Me.lblPosition.Text = ((Me.BindingContext( _
        DsTotals1.Tables("qryOrderTotals")).Position _
```

```
               + 1).ToString + " of   " + Me.BindingContext( _
               DsTotals1.Tables("qryOrderTotals")).Count.ToString)

       Catch ex As Exception
           MsgBox("Error: " & ex.Source & ": " & ex.Message, _
           MsgBoxStyle.OKOnly, "btnNext_Click")
       End Try

   End Sub

   Private Sub btnFirst_Click(ByVal sender As System.Object, _
   ByVal e As System.EventArgs) Handles btnFirst.Click

       Try
           Me.BindingContext( _
           DsTotals1.Tables("qryOrderTotals")).Position = 0
           Me.lblPosition.Text = ((Me.BindingContext( _
           DsTotals1.Tables("qryOrderTotals")).Position _
           + 1).ToString + " of   " + Me.BindingContext( _
           DsTotals1.Tables("qryOrderTotals")).Count.ToString)

       Catch ex As Exception
           MsgBox("Error: " & ex.Source & ": " & ex.Message, _
           MsgBoxStyle.OKOnly, "btnFirst_Click")
       End Try

   End Sub

   Private Sub btnPrevious_Click(ByVal sender As _
   System.Object, ByVal e As System.EventArgs) _
   Handles btnPrevious.Click

       Try
           Me.BindingContext( _
           DsTotals1.Tables("qryOrderTotals")).Position -= 1
           Me.lblPosition.Text = ((Me.BindingContext( _
           DsTotals1.Tables("qryOrderTotals")).Position _
           + 1).ToString + " of   " + Me.BindingContext( _
           DsTotals1.Tables("qryOrderTotals")).Count.ToString)

       Catch ex As Exception
           MsgBox("Error: " & ex.Source & ": " & ex.Message, _
```

```
                    MsgBoxStyle.OKOnly, "btnNext_Click")
        End Try

    End Sub

    Private Sub btnLast_Click(ByVal sender As System.Object, _
    ByVal e As System.EventArgs) Handles btnLast.Click

      Try
          Me.BindingContext( _
          DsTotals1.Tables("qryOrderTotals")).Position = _
          Me.BindingContext( _
          DsTotals1.Tables("qryOrderTotals")).Count - 1
          Me.lblPosition.Text = ((Me.BindingContext( _
          DsTotals1.Tables("qryOrderTotals")).Position _
          + 1).ToString + " of  " + Me.BindingContext( _
          DsTotals1.Tables("qryOrderTotals")).Count.ToString)

      Catch ex As Exception
          MsgBox("Error: " & ex.Source & ": " & ex.Message, _
          MsgBoxStyle.OKOnly, "btnLast_Click")
      End Try
```

As you can probably guess from looking at Listing 17.2, the BindingContext property of the form actually returns a collection of CurrencyManager objects. That makes sense, because a form can have many different controls bound to many different data sources. Each data source that is used for data binding is represented by a separate CurrencyManager object. All the CurrencyManager objects are accessible through the BindingContext property.

Complex Data Binding

If that was simple data binding, you may be wondering how tough the code might be for complex data binding! Fortunately, complex data binding isn't really any more complicated than simple data binding; it's just a different way to hook up a control to data. With complex data binding, instead of connecting a property to a single value from a data source, you connect a property to a collection of values from a data source. That collection might be one-dimensional (such as all the values in a particular column), two-dimensional (such as all the values in a particular table), or even more complex (such as all the values in an entire DataSet).

Binding Data to a ListBox, CheckedListBox, or ComboBox

The ListBox, CheckedListBox, and ComboBox controls can each be bound to a DataColumn. To do so, you need to set two properties of the control:

▶ The *DataSource* property specifies a DataTable or DataView that contains the DataColumn to be bound.

▶ The *DisplayMember* property specifies the DataColumn to be bound.

The frmComplex sample form includes one of each of these controls. They're all bound to SQL Server data in the form's Load event, as shown in the following code.

NOTE

The Load procedure for this form connects to data on a server named SKYROCKET. To run the project, you'll need to change this to match the name of your own server.

```
cmdEmployees = cnn.CreateCommand
cmdEmployees.CommandText = _
  "SELECT FirstName + ' ' + LastName AS FullName " & _
  "FROM Employees"
daEmployees.SelectCommand = cmdEmployees
daEmployees.Fill(dsMain, "Employees")

lboEmployees.DataSource = dsMain.Tables("Employees")
lboEmployees.DisplayMember = "FullName"


cmdProducts = cnn.CreateCommand
cmdProducts.CommandText = _
  "SELECT ProductName FROM Products"
daProducts.SelectCommand = cmdProducts
daProducts.Fill(dsMain, "Products")


clbProducts.DataSource = dsMain.Tables("Products")
clbProducts.DisplayMember = "ProductName"
```

```
cmdShippers = cnn.CreateCommand
cmdShippers.CommandText = _
  "SELECT ShipperID, CompanyName FROM Shippers"
dashippers.SelectCommand = cmdShippers
dashippers.Fill(dsMain, "Shippers")

cboShippers.DataSource = dsMain.Tables("Shippers")
cboShippers.DisplayMember = "CompanyName"
cboShippers.ValueMember = "ShipperID"
```

NOTE

This code stores three DataTables in a single DataSet without creating any relationships between the DataTables. The DataSet is just used as a container to hold all the DataTables.

The code to initialize the cboShippers ComboBox control demonstrates that you can use these controls to perform database lookups by utilizing their ValueMember property as well as their DisplayMember property. (Although it's not shown in this sample, the ListBox and CheckedListBox controls share these properties.) The DisplayMember property provides the data to be displayed in the control, but the ValueMember property provides the data for the SelectedValue property of the control. The sample form includes a small bit of code to display the SelectedValue in a TextBox control whenever the user selects a row in the ComboBox:

```
Private Sub cboShippers_SelectedIndexChanged( _
  ByVal sender As System.Object, _
  ByVal e As System.EventArgs) _
  Handles cboShippers.SelectedIndexChanged

    Try
        txtShipperID.Text = cboShippers.SelectedValue
    Catch
    End Try

End Sub
```

Binding Data to a DataGrid

The next step up in complexity is to bind a DataTable to a DataGrid. The DataGrid, of course, can display data in both rows and columns—the perfect visual metaphor for a table of data. To display a DataTable on a DataGrid, simply supply the DataSet object as the DataSource property for the DataGrid and supply the name of the DataTable as the DataMember property of the DataGrid:

```
dgShippers.DataSource = dsMain
dgShippers.DataMember = "Shippers"
```

You can also bind an entire DataSet to a DataGrid. The frmComplex form includes code to build a DataSet containing two different DataTables. The code then binds this to a pair of DataGrids in two ways:

```
Dim cmdCustomers As New SqlCommand()
Dim daCustomers As New SqlDataAdapter()
Dim cmdOrders As New SqlCommand()
Dim daOrders As New SqlDataAdapter()

cmdCustomers = cnn.CreateCommand
cmdCustomers.CommandText = _
 "SELECT * FROM Customers"
daCustomers.SelectCommand = cmdCustomers
daCustomers.Fill(dsCustomerOrders, "Customers")

cmdOrders = cnn.CreateCommand
cmdOrders.CommandText = _
 "SELECT * FROM Orders"
daOrders.SelectCommand = cmdOrders
daOrders.Fill(dsCustomerOrders, "Orders")

Dim relCustOrder As DataRelation = _
 dsCustomerOrders.Relations.Add("CustOrder", _
 dsCustomerOrders.Tables( _
   "Customers").Columns("CustomerID"), _
 dsCustomerOrders.Tables("Orders").Columns("CustomerID"))
```

Part IV

```
dgCustomerOrders1.DataSource = dsCustomerOrders
dgCustomerOrders2.DataSource = dsCustomerOrders
dgCustomerOrders2.DataMember = "Customers"
```

Figure 17.4 shows the completed frmComplex with its variety of complex data-bound controls.

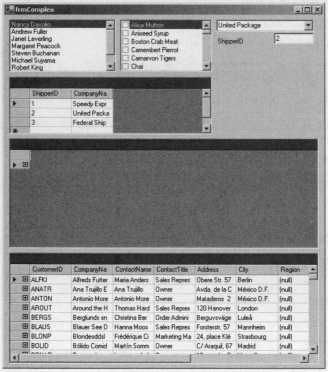

FIGURE 17.4:   Complex data binding

The differences in appearance of the three DataGrid controls result from the differences in the ways that they were bound:

▸ A DataGrid bound to a single DataTable that isn't related to any other DataTables, or to a DataTable that doesn't have any child DataTables, loads and displays all the rows of the DataTable when it is instantiated.

▸ A DataGrid bound to an entire DataSet shows only a single record selector with the + expander button when it is instantiated.

Clicking the expander button will show hyperlinks to all the DataTables within the DataSet. Clicking one of those hyperlinks will load and display all the rows of the selected DataTable. You can click the Back button in the upper-right corner of the DataGrid to return to the hyperlinks after loading a DataTable.

▶ A DataGrid bound to a DataTable that does have child Data-Tables loads and displays all the rows of the parent DataTable and displays a + expander button with each row when it is instantiated. Clicking the expander button will show hyperlinks to all the DataRelations in which this DataTable is the parent. Clicking a hyperlink from the list will load and display the related child rows, and compress the parent row to a header row in the Data-Grid. You can click the Back button in the upper-right corner of the DataGrid to return to the parent DataTable after loading a child DataTable.

MANIPULATING DATA THROUGH WINDOWS FORMS

In addition to displaying data on a Windows Form in bound controls, you can save changes in that data back to the original data source. With complex-bound controls such as the DataGrid, manipulating the data is just a matter of making changes to the user interface. If the DataSet that provides the data was instantiated with enough information (via the Command properties of the DataAdapter), changes will automatically be passed back to the data source when you call the Update method of the DataAdapter. This technique is covered in Chapter 16, "Editing Data with ADO.NET."

If you're using simple-bound controls, there's a bit more to learn. As I hinted earlier in the chapter, you can use methods of the Currency-Manager class to edit data shown in simple-bound controls. In this section, I'll show how you can use these methods to perform the fundamental data manipulation tasks:

▶ Editing existing data

▶ Adding new data

▶ Deleting existing data

Part IV

In this chapter's sample project, the frmCustomers form demonstrates all of these tasks, as well as navigation and saving the changes back to the original data source. Listing 17.3 shows the code that runs this form. The form itself is shown in Figure 17.5.

TIP

Although this chapter will teach you to write the code for manipulating data in bound forms, you may find that you never actually have to write that code yourself. Visual Studio .NET comes with a tool, called the Data Form Wizard, that allows you to build a data form without writing any code. It's important, though, that you understand the code before you start using the wizard, so that you can tune it for your own use.

TIP

In Listing 17.3, you'll see that the data is loaded from a database in `AppDomain .CurrentDomain.BaseDirectory`. That's the closest equivalent that Visual Basic .NET offers for the App.Path property of Visual Basic 6. It gives you the directory from which the current assembly was loaded. This is not guaranteed to be the source code directory—the assembly, for example, could have been placed in the Global Assembly Cache—but in the case of simple applications like this, it's likely to be correct.

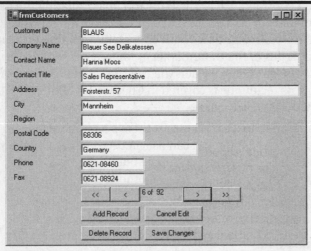

FIGURE 17.5:   The frmCustomers form

Listing 17.3: Code for frmCustomers

```
Dim daCustomers As New OleDbDataAdapter()
Dim dsCustomers As New DataSet()

Private Sub frmCustomers_Load(ByVal sender As _
 System.Object, ByVal e As System.EventArgs) _
 Handles MyBase.Load

   Dim cnn As OleDbConnection = New OleDbConnection( _
    "Provider=Microsoft.Jet.OLEDB.4.0;" & _
    "Data Source=" & AppDomain.CurrentDomain.BaseDirectory & _
    "ADOChapter17.mdb")
   Dim cmdCustomers As New OleDbCommand()

   Try
       cmdCustomers = cnn.CreateCommand
       cmdCustomers.CommandText = _
        "SELECT * FROM Customers"
       daCustomers.SelectCommand = cmdCustomers
       ' Automatically generate the Update, Insert,
       ' and Delete commands
       Dim cb As OleDbCommandBuilder = _
        New OleDbCommandBuilder(daCustomers)
       daCustomers.Fill(dsCustomers, "Customers")
       txtCustomerID.DataBindings.Add( _
        "Text", dsCustomers.Tables("Customers"), _
        "CustomerID")
       txtCompanyName.DataBindings.Add( _
        "Text", dsCustomers.Tables("Customers"), _
        "CompanyName")
       txtContactName.DataBindings.Add( _
        "Text", dsCustomers.Tables("Customers"), _
        "ContactName")
       txtContactTitle.DataBindings.Add( _
        "Text", dsCustomers.Tables("Customers"), _
        "ContactTitle")
       txtAddress.DataBindings.Add( _
        "Text", dsCustomers.Tables("Customers"), _
        "Address")
```

```
                txtCity.DataBindings.Add( _
                 "Text", dsCustomers.Tables("Customers"), _
                 "City")
                txtRegion.DataBindings.Add( _
                 "Text", dsCustomers.Tables("Customers"), _
                 "Region")
                txtPostalCode.DataBindings.Add( _
                 "Text", dsCustomers.Tables("Customers"), _
                 "PostalCode")
                txtCountry.DataBindings.Add( _
                 "Text", dsCustomers.Tables("Customers"), _
                 "Country")
                txtPhone.DataBindings.Add( _
                 "Text", dsCustomers.Tables("Customers"), _
                 "Phone")
                txtFax.DataBindings.Add( _
                 "Text", dsCustomers.Tables("Customers"), _
                 "Fax")

                UpdatePosition()

        Catch ex As Exception
            MsgBox("Error: " & ex.Source & ": " & ex.Message, _
                MsgBoxStyle.OKOnly, "frmCustomers_Load")
        End Try

    End Sub

    Private Sub UpdatePosition()
        Me.lblPosition.Text = ((Me.BindingContext( _
            dsCustomers.Tables("Customers")).Position _
            + 1).ToString + " of " + Me.BindingContext( _
            dsCustomers.Tables("Customers")).Count.ToString)
    End Sub

    Private Sub btnNext_Click(ByVal sender As System.Object, _
      ByVal e As System.EventArgs) Handles btnNext.Click

        Try
            Me.BindingContext( _
              dsCustomers.Tables("Customers")).Position += 1
            UpdatePosition()
```

```
        Catch ex As Exception
            MsgBox("Error: " & ex.Source & ": " & ex.Message, _
            MsgBoxStyle.OKOnly, "btnNext_Click")
        End Try

    End Sub

    Private Sub btnFirst_Click(ByVal sender As System.Object, _
     ByVal e As System.EventArgs) Handles btnFirst.Click

        Try
            Me.BindingContext( _
            dsCustomers.Tables("Customers")).Position = 0
            UpdatePosition()

        Catch ex As Exception
            MsgBox("Error: " & ex.Source & ": " & ex.Message, _
            MsgBoxStyle.OKOnly, "btnFirst_Click")
        End Try

    End Sub

    Private Sub btnPrevious_Click(ByVal sender As _
     System.Object, ByVal e As System.EventArgs) _
     Handles btnPrevious.Click

        Try
            Me.BindingContext( _
            dsCustomers.Tables("Customers")).Position -= 1
            UpdatePosition()

        Catch ex As Exception
            MsgBox("Error: " & ex.Source & ": " & ex.Message, _
            MsgBoxStyle.OKOnly, "btnNext_Click")
        End Try

    End Sub

    Private Sub btnLast_Click(ByVal sender As System.Object, _
     ByVal e As System.EventArgs) Handles btnLast.Click
```

```
        Try
            Me.BindingContext( _
             dsCustomers.Tables("Customers")).Position = _
             Me.BindingContext( _
             dsCustomers.Tables("Customers")).Count - 1
             UpdatePosition()

        Catch ex As Exception
            MsgBox("Error: " & ex.Source & ": " & ex.Message, _
             MsgBoxStyle.OKOnly, "btnLast_Click")
        End Try

    End Sub

    Private Sub btnSaveChanges_Click(ByVal sender As _
     System.Object, ByVal e As System.EventArgs) _
     Handles btnSaveChanges.Click

        Try
            Me.BindingContext( _
             dsCustomers.Tables("Customers")).EndCurrentEdit()
             daCustomers.Update(dsCustomers.Tables("Customers"))

        Catch ex As Exception
            MsgBox("Error: " & ex.Source & ": " & _
             ex.Message, MsgBoxStyle.OKOnly, _
             "btnSaveChanges_Click")
        End Try

    End Sub

    Private Sub btnCancelEdit_Click(ByVal sender As _
     System.Object, ByVal e As System.EventArgs) _
     Handles btnCancelEdit.Click

        Try
            Me.BindingContext( _
             dsCustomers.Tables( _
             "Customers")).CancelCurrentEdit()
             UpdatePosition()

        Catch ex As Exception
            MsgBox("Error: " & ex.Source & ": " & _
```

```vb
            ex.Message, MsgBoxStyle.OKOnly, _
            "btnCancelEdit_Click")
    End Try

End Sub

Private Sub btnAddRecord_Click(ByVal sender As _
  System.Object, ByVal e As System.EventArgs) _
  Handles btnAddRecord.Click

    Try
        Me.BindingContext( _
          dsCustomers.Tables("Customers")).EndCurrentEdit()
        Me.BindingContext( _
          dsCustomers.Tables("Customers")).AddNew()
        UpdatePosition()

    Catch ex As Exception
        MsgBox("Error: " & ex.Source & ": " & _
          ex.Message, MsgBoxStyle.OKOnly, _
          "btnAddRecord_Click")
    End Try

End Sub

Private Sub btnDeleteRecord_Click(ByVal sender As _
  System.Object, ByVal e As System.EventArgs) _
  Handles btnDeleteRecord.Click

    Try
        Me.BindingContext( _
          dsCustomers.Tables("Customers")).RemoveAt( _
          Me.BindingContext( _
          dsCustomers.Tables("Customers")).Position)
        UpdatePosition()

    Catch ex As Exception
        MsgBox("Error: " & ex.Source & ": " & _
          ex.Message, MsgBoxStyle.OKOnly, _
          "btnAddRecord_Click")
    End Try

End Sub
```

Editing a Row of Data

You don't have to do anything special to edit data in bound controls (you may have noticed that there's no BeginEdit method in Listing 17.3). Once the control is bound, changes to the data are automatically reflected in the underlying DataSet. But there are two methods of the CurrencyManager object that you may need to use in the course of editing data:

▶ The CancelCurrentEdit method throws away any changes that have been made to the current row of data before they can be saved to the DataSet.

▶ The EndCurrentEdit method takes all the changes to the current row of data and saves them to the DataSet. Changes are also saved whenever you navigate to another row by changing the Position property of the CurrencyManager object.

Remember, though, that any changes you make by editing data in a bound control are made only to the DataSet and not to the underlying data source. You still need to call the Update method of the appropriate DataAdapter (which must have the appropriate Command properties filled in) to finally save the changes. That's the purpose of the code that gets called from the Save Changes button:

```
Private Sub btnSaveChanges_Click(ByVal sender As _
System.Object, ByVal e As System.EventArgs) _
Handles btnSaveChanges.Click

    Try
        Me.BindingContext( _
        dsCustomers.Tables("Customers")).EndCurrentEdit()
        daCustomers.Update(dsCustomers.Tables("Customers"))

    Catch ex As Exception
        MsgBox("Error: " & ex.Source & ": " & ex.Message, _
        MsgBoxStyle.OKOnly, "btnSaveChanges_Click")
    End Try

End Sub
```

The call to EndCurrentEdit makes sure that any changes to the current record are saved to the DataSet before the DataSet, in turn, is saved to the data source.

Adding a Row of Data

To add a fresh row of data to the DataSet, call the AddNew method of the CurrencyManager object:

```
Private Sub btnAddRecord_Click(ByVal sender As _
    System.Object, ByVal e As System.EventArgs) _
    Handles btnAddRecord.Click


    Try
        Me.BindingContext( _
            dsCustomers.Tables("Customers")).EndCurrentEdit()
        Me.BindingContext( _
            dsCustomers.Tables("Customers")).AddNew()
        UpdatePosition()

    Catch ex As Exception
        MsgBox("Error: " & ex.Source & ": " & ex.Message, _
            MsgBoxStyle.OKOnly, "btnAddRecord_Click")
    End Try

End Sub
```

This procedure calls the EndCurrentEdit method before it calls the AddNew method. This avoids losing any changes that might have been pending on the current record when the user clicks the Add Record button.

If you call the AddNew method, and then call the CancelCurrentEdit method without either moving off the record or calling the EndCurrent-Edit method, the new row will not be added to the DataSet.

Deleting a Row of Data

Deleting a row of data via simple-bound controls requires a call to the RemoveAt method of the CurrencyManager object. There isn't any DeleteRow method to operate on the current row. Instead, the RemoveAt method removes a row at a particular index in the data source. Fortunately, you can use the Position property of the CurrencyManager to get the index of the current row:

```
Private Sub btnDeleteRecord_Click(ByVal sender As _
System.Object, ByVal e As System.EventArgs) _
Handles btnDeleteRecord.Click


    Try
        Me.BindingContext( _
        dsCustomers.Tables("Customers")).RemoveAt( _
          Me.BindingContext( _
        dsCustomers.Tables("Customers")).Position)
        UpdatePosition()

    Catch ex As Exception
        MsgBox("Error: " & ex.Source & ": " & ex.Message, _
        MsgBoxStyle.OKOnly, "btnAddRecord_Click")
    End Try


    End Sub
```

Note that there isn't any "undo" for a deletion. If you call RemoveAt and then call CancelCurrentEdit, the deletion won't be cancelled. Of course, if you don't call the Update method of the DataAdapter, the deletions won't be made in the original data source.

TIP

You can prevent any deletions from being made by removing the DataAdapter's DeleteCommand before calling its Update method.

Part I

A MORE COMPLEX SAMPLE

As a final example, I'll look at the order entry form shown in Figure 17.6. This form lets you browse and alter the data in three related tables (Customers, Orders, and Order Details). Listing 17.4 contains the code for this form.

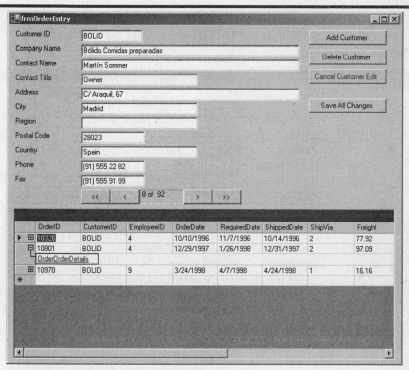

FIGURE 17.6:   The frmOrderEntry form

Listing 17.4: Code for frmOrderEntry

```
Dim daCustomers As New OleDbDataAdapter()
Dim daOrders As New OleDbDataAdapter()
Dim daOrderDetails As New OleDbDataAdapter()
Dim dsMain As New DataSet()
```

```
Private Sub frmOrderEntry_Load(ByVal sender As _
System.Object, ByVal e As System.EventArgs) _
Handles MyBase.Load

  Dim cnn As OleDbConnection = New OleDbConnection( _
   "Provider=Microsoft.Jet.OLEDB.4.0;" & _
   "Data Source=" & _
   AppDomain.CurrentDomain.BaseDirectory & _
   "ADOChapter17.mdb")
  Dim cmdCustomers As New OleDbCommand()
  Dim cmdOrders As New OleDbCommand()
  Dim cmdOrderDetails As New OleDbCommand()

  Try
      cmdCustomers = cnn.CreateCommand
      cmdCustomers.CommandText = _
       "SELECT * FROM Customers"
      daCustomers.SelectCommand = cmdCustomers
      Dim cbCustomers As OleDbCommandBuilder = _
       New OleDbCommandBuilder(daCustomers)
      daCustomers.Fill(dsMain, "Customers")

      cmdOrders = cnn.CreateCommand
      cmdOrders.CommandText = _
       "SELECT * FROM Orders"
      daOrders.SelectCommand = cmdOrders
      Dim cbOrders As OleDbCommandBuilder = _
       New OleDbCommandBuilder(daOrders)
      daOrders.Fill(dsMain, "Orders")

      cmdOrderDetails = cnn.CreateCommand
      cmdOrderDetails.CommandText = _
       "SELECT * FROM [Order Details]"
      daOrderDetails.SelectCommand = cmdOrderDetails
      Dim cbOrderDetails As OleDbCommandBuilder = _
       New OleDbCommandBuilder(daOrderDetails)
      daOrderDetails.Fill(dsMain, "OrderDetails")

      Dim relCustOrder As DataRelation = _
       dsMain.Relations.Add("CustOrder", _
       dsMain.Tables("Customers").Columns("CustomerID"), _
       dsMain.Tables("Orders").Columns("CustomerID"))
```

```
            Dim relOrderOrderDetails As DataRelation = _
             dsMain.Relations.Add("OrderOrderDetails", _
             dsMain.Tables("Orders").Columns("OrderID"), _
             dsMain.Tables("OrderDetails").Columns("OrderID"))
            txtCustomerID.DataBindings.Add( _
             "Text", dsMain, "Customers.CustomerID")
            txtCompanyName.DataBindings.Add( _
             "Text", dsMain, "Customers.CompanyName")
            txtContactName.DataBindings.Add( _
             "Text", dsMain, "Customers.ContactName")
            txtContactTitle.DataBindings.Add( _
             "Text", dsMain, "Customers.ContactTitle")
            txtAddress.DataBindings.Add( _
             "Text", dsMain, "Customers.Address")
            txtCity.DataBindings.Add( _
             "Text", dsMain, "Customers.City")
            txtRegion.DataBindings.Add( _
             "Text", dsMain, "Customers.Region")
            txtPostalCode.DataBindings.Add( _
             "Text", dsMain, "Customers.PostalCode")
            txtCountry.DataBindings.Add( _
             "Text", dsMain, "Customers.Country")
            txtPhone.DataBindings.Add( _
             "Text", dsMain, "Customers.Phone")
            txtFax.DataBindings.Add( _
             "Text", dsMain, "Customers.Fax")

            dgOrders.DataSource = dsMain
            dgOrders.DataMember = "Customers.CustOrder"

            UpdatePosition()

        Catch ex As Exception
            MsgBox("Error: " & ex.Source & ": " & ex.Message, _
             MsgBoxStyle.OKOnly, "frmOrderEntry_Load")
        End Try

    End Sub

    Private Sub UpdatePosition()
        Me.lblPosition.Text = ((Me.BindingContext( _
         dsMain, "Customers").Position + 1).ToString _
```

Part IV

```vb
            + " of  " + Me.BindingContext( _
        dsMain, "Customers").Count.ToString)
    End Sub

    Private Sub btnNext_Click(ByVal sender As System.Object, _
     ByVal e As System.EventArgs) Handles btnNext.Click

        Try
            Me.BindingContext( _
             dsMain, "Customers").Position += 1
            UpdatePosition()

        Catch ex As Exception
            MsgBox("Error: " & ex.Source & ": " & ex.Message, _
             MsgBoxStyle.OKOnly, "btnNext_Click")
        End Try

    End Sub

    Private Sub btnFirst_Click(ByVal sender _
     As System.Object, ByVal e As System.EventArgs) _
     Handles btnFirst.Click

        Try
            Me.BindingContext( _
             dsMain, "Customers").Position = 0
            UpdatePosition()

        Catch ex As Exception
            MsgBox("Error: " & ex.Source & ": " & ex.Message, _
             MsgBoxStyle.OKOnly, "btnFirst_Click")
        End Try

    End Sub

    Private Sub btnPrevious_Click(ByVal sender As _
     System.Object, ByVal e As System.EventArgs) _
     Handles btnPrevious.Click

        Try
            Me.BindingContext( _
             dsMain, "Customers").Position -= 1
            UpdatePosition()
```

```vb
        Catch ex As Exception
            MsgBox("Error: " & ex.Source & ": " & ex.Message, _
            MsgBoxStyle.OKOnly, "btnNext_Click")
        End Try

End Sub

Private Sub btnLast_Click(ByVal sender As System.Object, _
 ByVal e As System.EventArgs) Handles btnLast.Click

    Try
        Me.BindingContext( _
        dsMain, "Customers").Position = _
        Me.BindingContext( _
        dsMain, "Customers").Count - 1
        UpdatePosition()

    Catch ex As Exception
        MsgBox("Error: " & ex.Source & ": " & ex.Message, _
        MsgBoxStyle.OKOnly, "btnLast_Click")
    End Try

End Sub

Private Sub btnSaveChanges_Click(ByVal sender As _
 System.Object, ByVal e As System.EventArgs) _
 Handles btnSaveChanges.Click

    Try
        Me.BindingContext( _
        dsMain, "Customers").EndCurrentEdit()
        daCustomers.Update(dsMain.Tables("Customers"))

    Catch ex As Exception
        MsgBox("Error: " & ex.Source & ": " & ex.Message, _
        MsgBoxStyle.OKOnly, "btnSaveChanges_Click")
    End Try

End Sub

Private Sub btnCancelEdit_Click(ByVal sender As _
 System.Object, ByVal e As System.EventArgs) _
 Handles btnCancelEdit.Click
```

```
    Try
        Me.BindingContext( _
        dsMain, "Customers").CancelCurrentEdit()
        UpdatePosition()

    Catch ex As Exception
        MsgBox("Error: " & ex.Source & ": " & ex.Message, _
        MsgBoxStyle.OKOnly, "btnCancelEdit_Click")
    End Try

End Sub

Private Sub btnAddRecord_Click(ByVal sender As _
System.Object, ByVal e As System.EventArgs) _
Handles btnAddRecord.Click

    Try
        Me.BindingContext( _
        dsMain, "Customers").EndCurrentEdit()
        Me.BindingContext( _
        dsMain, "Customers").AddNew()
        UpdatePosition()

    Catch ex As Exception
        MsgBox("Error: " & ex.Source & ": " & ex.Message, _
        MsgBoxStyle.OKOnly, "btnAddRecord_Click")
    End Try

End Sub

Private Sub btnDeleteRecord_Click(ByVal sender As _
System.Object, ByVal e As System.EventArgs) _
Handles btnDeleteRecord.Click

    Try
        Me.BindingContext( _
        dsMain, "Customers").RemoveAt(Me.BindingContext( _
        dsMain, "Customers").Position)
        UpdatePosition()

    Catch ex As Exception
        MsgBox("Error: " & ex.Source & ": " & ex.Message, _
```

```
        MsgBoxStyle.OKOnly, "btnAddRecord_Click")
    End Try

  End Sub
```

Most of this code should be familiar to you from earlier in the chapter, but it's worthwhile to take a close look at the data-binding code. If you try the form, you'll discover that the Customer data and the DataGrid that shows Orders and Order Details all remain synchronized. For this to happen, all of these controls must share the same CurrencyManager, which means that they must all use the same binding object. This results in some syntactical differences from the code that I used earlier in the chapter.

For example, here's the code that sets up the data binding for the txtCustomerID control:

```
    txtCustomerID.DataBindings.Add( _
      "Text", dsMain, "Customers.CustomerID")
```

Rather than specify the DataTable as the object to bind (as did the examples earlier in the chapter), this line of code uses the entire DataSet as the object to bind. The item to bind is specified by the format *DataTable.DataColumn*—here, the CustomerID column in the Customers table.

Similarly, the DataGrid is also bound to the dsMain DataSet, specifically to the CustOrder relation within the DataSet:

```
    dgOrders.DataSource = dsMain
    dgOrders.DataMember = "Customers.CustOrder"
```

Specifying a DataRelation rather than a DataTable as the top level to bind to the DataGrid means that the form will know how to keep this DataTable synchronized with the other controls on the form. Because all the display controls are based on the Customers table at their top level, they can all be manipulated by using a CurrencyManager that specifies that table. For instance, here's the code that moves forward in the DataSet (and thus updates all the controls on the form to display data from the next row of the DataSet):

```
    Private Sub btnNext_Click(ByVal sender As System.Object, _
      ByVal e As System.EventArgs) Handles btnNext.Click
```

Part IV

```
Try
    Me.BindingContext( _
        dsMain, "Customers").Position += 1
    UpdatePosition()

Catch ex As Exception
    MsgBox("Error: " & ex.Source & ": " & ex.Message, _
        MsgBoxStyle.OKOnly, "btnNext_Click")
End Try

    End Sub
```

As you can see, the BindingContext property is overloaded to allow you to specify both the object and the path within the object that supplies the binding in which you are interested.

WHAT'S NEXT

In this chapter, you've learned about using both simple- and complex-bound controls on Windows Forms to display ADO.NET data. You saw how to hook these controls to data from the Visual Basic .NET interface (which provides rapid development capabilities) as well as from code (which provides more control over the results). You also learned how to navigate through data with bound controls and how to use bound controls to alter the data.

This chapter wraps up the section on ADO.NET. In the next section, you will learn how to use XML in your Visual Basic .NET applications. Although it may not be evident so far, XML is a core technology in .NET.

You have already had a brief exposure to how essential XML is to .NET and Visual Basic .NET through this section. In Chapter 14, you learned that XML was the core storage and transfer mechanism in ADO.NET, and Chapter 15 taught you how to use XML as a data source for your DataSet.

In the next section, you will learn to use XML in both Windows Forms and WebForm applications.

Part V
XML AND VB .NET

Chapter 18

USING XML WITH VISUAL BASIC .NET

You already know how to retrieve data from a database, update its tables using data adapters, and how to store structured, related data into DataSets. You also know that the information flows out of and into the DataSets and the database in XML format. XML is a standard that can represent all types of data as text. It's a simple standard and, because of this, it has the potential of becoming a universal standard.

XML is a very promising standard. People are using it with all types of applications, and it's permeating the computer industry. You shouldn't be surprised to see a programming language modeled after XML in the future. Actually, you can see how Microsoft uses XML to store the description of a form. Open a project, any project that happens to be on your hard disk. Click the Show All Files button on the Solution Explorer's toolbar, and you will see a few more files, which aren't displayed on the Solution Explorer by default. Among them are the RESX files of each form. These files describe the resources of each

Adapted from the forthcoming *Visual Basic .NET Developer's Handbook* by Evangelos Petroutsos and Kevin Hough

ISBN 0-7821-2879-3 $59.99

form. If you open any of the RESX files, you will see that the resources are described in XML format. Fortunately, you'll never have to create these files yourself, so it doesn't really matter whether you understand them or not. By the way, XML files are easy to understand, but they're not so easy to produce.

This is also how XML is used with ADO.NET. The data you move through the data adapters arrive to the DataSet in XML format, and this is how they're transmitted to the server. So far, you haven't had to look at the XML description of your data, and it would be nice if you could keep it that way. However, there are situations where you may have to write code to parse XML files and extract the desired data (when you receive data from a non-Windows database, for example, in XML format). In this chapter, we'll look at how XML is used in database programming. Even if you don't plan to exchange data with other databases and/or systems, you should have an idea of what XML does, and how it's used in ADO.NET. You'll also learn how to create DataSets in code by specifying their schema in XML, populate the table(s) of the DataSet, and persist them to local files.

This chapter doesn't condense an entire XML book into a single chapter; however, it will help you develop a better understanding of XML and help you recognize when you might benefit from using XML in your projects. You can find out the details as you need them. To begin, it's important to understand how XML is used and what it can do for you. To make the chapter practical, I've structured it around a few useful examples that implement common operations. I won't spend much time explaining the XML structure, and I won't show you how to create valid and well-formed XML documents. Instead, I relied on Microsoft's tools to format the desired information in XML format.

XML in ADO.NET

When you program with ADO.NET, the encoding of the data in XML format takes place behind the scenes and you need not even know that your data undergoes a transformation. With ADO, there was a different, proprietary protocol that moved data from the database into RecordSets (it was of no use outside Windows). Each database uses its own format to store data, but a Windows application using ADO (or ADO.NET) expects to find its data in RecordSets (or DataSets in ADO.NET). XML is as useful outside Windows, as it is inside Windows. A DataSet in XML format can be parsed and used on any other platform. You can actually read an XML document and figure out the information stored in it, and you can also understand how the data is structured. If you need to exchange information with an IBM or a Linux database, you can package your data in XML format and send it to the other computer. You can also receive an XML document from the other computer, parse it, extract the information you need, possibly transform it, and finally save it in a SQL Server database.

Most of us have been doing this with some form of delimited files. As far a mechanism for exchanging "dry" data, XML documents are quite similar to delimited files. In their simplest form, XML documents are simply another mechanism for exchanging data. Makes you wonder why no one thought of XML (or something similar) during the past decades, when "universal" formats appeared and disappeared like comets. However, XML is much more than a mechanism for moving data around. XML documents store more than just data; they store information about the structure of the data, which is called its *schema*. XML files have other benefits, as well. There are tools for parsing XML files, tools to transform XML files, and even tools to query XML files.

XML Tags

Let's start with a few definitions. XML stands for eXtensible Markup Language, and it's a markup language, like HTML. HTML describes the appearance of a document (how the data will be rendered on a browser) with tags; XML describes the data itself, also with tags. Another difference is that HTML consists of a fixed number of tags that all browsers understand, while XML does not use predefined tags. You can create your tags to describe your information. Of course, you can't expect other applications to understand what your tags mean. The application that will process the XML document must know what each tag means. Even if you receive an XML document and you have no idea what it describes, you can easily extract the information and place it in one or more database tables. The structure of the information is there, and that's all the matters for the computer. You can get a good idea about the information stored in an XML file (after all, it's a text file). However, an XML document with names, ages, and other related data could represent a list of customers, a baseball team, or the FBI's Most-Wanted List. The information will make sense to humans only if they're told what it represents. Only then can you write code to process the data.

To describe a list of books with XML, you could use a document like the following:

```
<books>
    <book>
        <title>All About Visual Basic .NET</title>
        <ISBN>972837559X</ISBN>
        <chapter>What's new in VB. NET</chapter>
        <chapter>The .NET Framework</chapter>
        <chapter>The new Windows Controls</chapter>
    </book>
</books>
```

The `<books>` tag describes the entire document: it's a document for storing information about books. Its name could be anything, of course. XML doesn't understand English. I've chosen this name for the tag so that the file makes sense to humans.

Each "piece" of information is described by a special tag. The `<title>` tag describes the book's title, the `<chapter>` tag describes chapter titles, and so on. Someone else might have used different tags, like `<BookTitle>`, `<Chapter>`, and so on. Notice that XML is case-sensitive.

When you parse an XML document, you can think of the elements making up the file as nodes. Each element is a node, and the nodes are nested. At any time, you can access a node's child nodes (which is a collection) or its parent node (this is a single node). If we included author information in our sample XML segment, it would look like this:

```
<books>
    <book>
        <title>All About Visual Basic .NET</title>
        <ISBN>972837559X</ISBN>
        <chapter>What's new in VB. NET</chapter>
        <chapter>The .NET Framework</chapter>
        <chapter>The new Windows Controls</chapter>
        <authors>
            <name>first author's name</name>
            <name>second author's name</name>
        </authors>
```

```
        </book>
    </books>
```

The <authors> element is a child element of the <book> element, and it has its own child elements (the <name> elements). The outmost element is the root element of the document, and all other elements are child elements. The root element in this example is <books>. Each tag has a matching closing tag, which has the same name as the opening tag, but it's prefixed by a backslash. The example you saw contains information that authors would probably share between them. A bookseller would use an XML document to store different data about the same book:

```
<books>
    <book>
        <title>All About Visual Basic .NET</title>
        <ISBN>972837559X</ISBN>
        <price>49.99</price>
        <discount>0.25</discount>
        <supplier>Books-a-Load</supplier>
        <publicationYear>2002</publicationYear>
    </book>
</books>
```

Because books are identified by their ISBNs, you can combine the two documents by matching their <ISBN> tags. If you load the last two XML sample documents into a DataSet as two tables, you can establish a relation based on the ISBN.

XML isn't limited to describing tabular data—the type of data that comes from a database or can be stored to a database table. The following is the XML description of a message:

```
<email>
    <from>evangelos@example.org</from>
    <to>Richard@example.org</to>
    <subject>Reminder</subject>
    <body>I'll be in town next week</body>
</email>
```

This document could be created by an e-mail application. I'm not implying that this information couldn't be stored to a database, but its

Part V

addresses and messages are stored in different data stores for this example. When a message is actually sent, a `<sent>` tag might be added to indicate the date and time the message was sent. When another application receives it, a `<received>` tag might be added, and so on. As long as the applications that deal with the XML-formatted messages understand what each tag means, they can use a text file to store the messages. Of course, searching through a large text file with many messages might be a problem; but as you will see later in this chapter, there are tools to automate the parsing of an XML document.

The two applications that exchange messages in this format need not be absolutely compatible. One of them might use the `<from>` tag to indicate the sender; the other one might use the `<sender>` tag. It is possible to apply a transformation that will automatically rename the tags to match the requirements of another application. One of the two systems may not even recognize all the tags. A tag like `<priority>` is not really required, and one of the applications may actually ignore it—or pass it around without processing it.

NOTE

There are a few rules you should be aware of when you are creating tag names. The most important one is that tags may not start with the letters "xml." Because XML tags are case-sensitive, no variation of these letters may be used ("XML," "Xml," and so on). Tag names may not start with a number or punctuation symbols, and they can't contain spaces.

Tags may also have attributes, which appear as name/value pairs following the name of the tag. The following tag represents a computer. Computers are classified into two categories, notebooks and desktops. Instead of creating two different tags, we can use the `<computer>` tag with a type attribute:

```
<computer type="notebook">
    { other tags }
</computer>
```

Attribute values always appear in double or single quotes, even if they're numeric. There are no hard rules regarding when you should use attributes. Most of the time we don't bother with attributes; we implement them as child tags. The last example is equivalent to the following:

```
<computer>
    <type="notebook">
```

```
{ other tags }
</computer>
```

Attributes shouldn't be used frequently with XML. If you go too far with attributes, you're actually misusing the new format.

XML versus DataSets

As you know, ADO.NET DataSets store their data in XML format. Because XML is a universal standard, we don't need to bother with proprietary formats when we can use a universal mechanism for storing data. Besides, when we are using XML incompatible application, even different operating systems, we can exchange data with one another. DataSets contain a relational view of the data: They contain multiple tables with relations between them based on the values of one or more columns, the primary and foreign key columns. The underlying XML file contains the same data, but in a hierarchical view. The DataSet object maintains a synchronized XML description of its data, and you can view the data in either relational or hierarchical view at any time.

Why abandon the relational view of the data and the tools you've learned to use so far in the book? If you're developing database applications with ADO.NET, you'll never have to switch to the XML view. However, you may receive data from a different computer in XML format, or you may create XML files from your data and send them to a non-Windows system. You can send a price list in XML format to any other application or operating system. The recipient of the data can modify the data, possibly by adding a column with quantities, and return the revised XML file to your application, which should be able to extract the quantities and create a new order. You can also create a DataSet entirely in code and never use it to update a database table; you can bind DataSets to controls, populate them, and then persist the DataSet to a disk file, from where the DataSets can be read at a later time.

The XMLData Project

Let's start with a DataSet and explore the structure of the equivalent XML file. The project we'll develop in this section is called XMLData.

Start a new project, design a form like the one shown in Figure 18.1, and then drop the Publishers and Titles tables of the Pubs database on the design surface. A Connection and two DataAdapter objects will be created automatically, and you should configure the two DataAdapters for their corresponding tables. You need not generate the SQL statements to update the database, just the SELECT statements to retrieve all the publishers and all the titles. After the DataAdapter is in place, create a new DataSet, the PublishersTitles DataSet, which contains both tables.

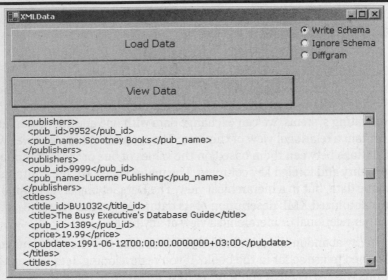

FIGURE 18.1: The XMLData application demonstrates how DataSets are persisted in XML format.

Insert the following statements into the Load Data button's Click event handler. These statements populate the DataSet with two tables, the Publishers and Titles tables:

```
Private Sub Button1_Click(ByVal sender _
 As System.Object, ByVal e As System.EventArgs) _
 Handles Button1.Click
    DAPublishers.Fill(PublisherTitles1, "Publishers")
    DATitles.Fill(PublisherTitles1, "Titles")
End Sub
```

After populating the DataSet, you can view the XML representation of the data on the TextBox control. To extract the XML description of the data from a DataSet, use the DataSet's WriteXml method, which accepts two arguments: a Stream object to the file where the XML data will be stored and a constant that specifies the exact structure of the XML data:

```
Dataset.WriteXml(stream, mode)
```

The mode argument can have one of the values of the XmlWriteMode enumeration, as shown in Table 18.1.

TABLE 18.1:   The XmlWriteMode Enumeration

MEMBER	DESCRIPTION
IgnoreSchema	Writes the data without schema information (default value).
WriteSchema	Writes the data with an inline schema.
DiffGram	Writes the data as a diffgram, which includes the original and current versions of each row. You will find more information on diffgrams later in this chapter.

After saving the XML description of the data to a file, the code reads the same file and displays it on the TextBox control. Listing 18.1 shows the code behind the View Data button.

Listing 18.1: Viewing a DataSet in XML Format

```
Private Sub Button2_Click(ByVal sender As System.Object, _
ByVal e As System.EventArgs) Handles Button2.Click
    Dim WStream As _
     New System.IO.StreamWriter("PublisherTitles.xml")
    Dim mode As XmlWriteMode
    If radioWriteSchema.Checked Then
        mode = XmlWriteMode.WriteSchema
    Else
        If radioDiffGram.Checked Then
            mode = XmlWriteMode.DiffGram
        Else
            mode = XmlWriteMode.IgnoreSchema
        End If
    End If
    PublisherTitles1.WriteXml(WStream, mode)
    WStream.Close()
    Dim RStream As
     New System.IO.StreamReader("PublisherTitles.xml")
    TextBox1.Text = RStream.ReadToEnd()
```

```
        RStream.Close()
    End Sub
```

The file in which we store the XML description of the DataSet is called
`PublishersTitles.XML`, and it's created in the Bin folder under the
project's folder. You can add a File Save dialog box to the project to make
it a little more functional. The code takes into consideration the settings
of the radio buttons on the form to save the data in the format specified
by the user. You can check out all three versions of the XML file and see
how the mode argument affects the type of output generated by the
WriteXml method.

Here are the first few publishers, followed by the first few titles. I've
omitted many lines, but they all have the same structure:

```
<publishers>
  <pub_id>0736</pub_id>
  <pub_name>New Moon Books</pub_name>
</publishers>
<publishers>
  <pub_id>0877</pub_id>
  <pub_name>Binnet &amp; Hardley</pub_name>
{ more publisher entries }
<titles>
  <title_id>BU1032</title_id>
  <title>The Busy Executive's Database Guide</title>
  <pub_id>1389</pub_id>
  <price>19.99</price>
  <pubdate>1991-06-12T00:00:00.0000000+03:00</pubdate>
</titles>
<titles>
  <title_id>BU1111</title_id>
  <title>Cooking with Computers: _
    Surreptitious Balance Sheets</title>
  <pub_id>1389</pub_id>
  <price>11.95</price>
  <pubdate>1991-06-09T00:00:00.0000000+03:00</pubdate>
</titles>
{ more titles entries }
```

You can't experiment with the DiffGram option because the DataSet can't be modified, so the current version is the same as the original version. In the next example, we'll edit the DataSet's tables and you'll see how the XML file stores the changes in the data. But first, we must relate the two tables. If you examine the XML representation of the DataSet, you'll realize that it contains the rows of the two tables, but no relation between them. Because the DataSet doesn't contain any relations, its XML representation couldn't be any different.

Let's add a relation between the two tables. You can do so in your code, or you can edit the XSD file in the Designer. In this example, I've added the relation between the two tables in the code, so that you can easily remove it (by commenting out the appropriate lines) or reinstate it by removing the comment characters in front of the same lines. The lines in Listing 18.2 add the relation between the two tables.

Listing 18.2: Adding a Relation Between the Publishers and Titles Tables

```
PublisherTitles1.Relations.Add(New _
DataRelation("PubTitles", _
PublisherTitles1.Tables("publishers").Columns("pub_id"), _
        PublisherTitles1.Tables("titles").Columns("pub_id")))
```

After adding the relation between the two tables, the resulting XML looks like the original, and only the following section was added. This section contains the description of the relation. The `<xs:unique>` tag makes the pub_id column of the Publishers table unique. The `<xs:keyref>` tag establishes a relation between the two tables based on the pub_id column.

```
<xs:unique name="Constraint1" msdata:PrimaryKey="true">
    <xs:selector xpath=".//mstns:publishers" />
    <xs:field xpath="mstns:pub_id" />
</xs:unique>
<xs:unique name="titles_Constraint1" msdata:
            ConstraintName="Constraint1"
            msdata:PrimaryKey="true">
    <xs:selector xpath=".//mstns:titles" />
    <xs:field xpath="mstns:title_id" />
</xs:unique>
<xs:keyref name="PubTitles" refer="Constraint1">
```

```
<xs:selector xpath=".//mstns:titles" />
<xs:field xpath="mstns:pub_id" />
</xs:keyref>
```

The rest of the file contains the publishers and the titles. You may have noticed that typical XML files contain nested entries: Each publisher section contains all the books of this publisher, then the next publisher with its books, and so on. To create a hierarchical XML file, you must declare that the relations between the tables are nested. To do so, set the Nested property of the relation to True (the default value of this property is False). Add the following statement to the Load Data button's Click event handler after the statement that adds the relation to the schema:

```
PublisherTitles1.Relations(0).Nested = True
```

This time the structure of the XML file reflects the hierarchy of the data. The `<title>` tags are nested within their matching `<publisher>` tags. The code in Listing 18.3 is a small section of the XML file generated by the WriteXml method when the relations between the tables of the DataSet are nested.

Listing 18.3: The XML Description of a DataSet with Nested Relations

```
<publishers>
  <pub_id>0736</pub_id>
  <pub_name>New Moon Books</pub_name>
  <titles>
    <title_id>BU2075</title_id>
    <title>You Can Combat Computer Stress!</title>
    <pub_id>0736</pub_id>
    <price>2.99</price>
    <pubdate>1991-06-30T00:00:00.0000000+03:00</pubdate>
  </titles>
  <titles>
    <title_id>PS2091</title_id>
    <title>Is Anger the Enemy?</title>
    <pub_id>0736</pub_id>
    <price>10.95</price>
    <pubdate>1991-06-15T00:00:00.0000000+03:00</pubdate>
  </titles>
</publishers>
```

```
<publishers>
  <pub_id>1389</pub_id>
  <pub_name>Algodata Infosystems</pub_name>
  <titles>
    <title_id>BU1032</title_id>
    <title>The Busy Executive's Database Guide</title>
    <pub_id>1389</pub_id>
    <price>19.99</price>
    <pubdate>1991-06-12T00:00:00.0000000+03:00</pubdate>
  </titles>
</publisher>
```

Loading XML into DataSets

In this section, we'll load the PublisherTitles.xml we created in the previous section into a DataSet. The XML file resides on the hard disk, and it could have originated anywhere. To fill a DataSet from an XML file, use the ReadXml method of the DataSet object, which reads its data from a file (or stream). The ReadXml method's arguments are the name of the file (or a Stream object) and an optional argument that determines which section of the file will be read:

```
Dataset.ReadXml(source, mode)
```

The first argument can be the name of a file, a Stream, or a TextWriter object. The value of the second argument can be one of the members of the XmlReadMode enumeration, which is shown in Table 18.2.

TABLE 18.2: The XmlReadMode Enumeration

MEMBER	DESCRIPTION
Auto	The ReadXml method examines the XML and chooses the most appropriate option. If the XML is a DiffGram, the entire DiffGram is loaded (the original and current versions of the rows). If the DataSet or the XML contains a shape, then the schema is read. If neither the DataSet nor the XML contains a shape, then the ReadXml method attempts to infer the schema from the data (see the InferSchema entry in this table). Auto is the default member.
ReadSchema	The DataSet loads the schema and the data from the XML. If the DataSet contains a schema, then the new tables are added to the existing schema. If there are common tables, an exception will be thrown. The DataSet understands XSD (XML Schema Definition language) and XDR (XML Data Reduced language) formats, but the preferred format is XSD.

TABLE 18.2 continued: The XmlReadMode Enumeration

MEMBER	DESCRIPTION
IgnoreSchema	The ReadXml method ignores any schema information in the XML and loads the data into the DataSet. Any data that doesn't match the existing schema is ignored.
DiffGram	This member causes the ReadXml method to add data to the current schema. It merges the new rows with any existing rows if their primary keys match.
InferSchema	This member causes the ReadXml method to infer the schema from the XML data. If the DataSet contains a schema already, new tables may be created for the XML tables that don't match a table in the DataSet. If incompatible columns exist in the XML data and the DataSet, then an exception will be thrown.
Fragment	This member causes the ReadXml method to read XML fragments, which must match the DataSet schema.

To load an XML file into a DataSet, call the ReadXml method as follows:

```
DS.ReadXml("c:\myContacts.xml")
```

DS is a properly declared DataSet object, and you need not create a schema for it. This DataSet isn't derived from a database; it's based on a stand-alone file. Once the data is in the DataSet, you can use any of the techniques discussed earlier in the book to process it. You can view its tables and edit them, navigate through its rows using the appropriate Relation objects, and so on. You can accept or reject changes, and you can do everything you can do with a table-based DataSet. You can bind the DataSet to DataGrid control, allow users to edit the data, and then save the data to an XML file with the WriteXml method. This is what we'll do in the following section.

The LoadXML Project

The LoadXML project demonstrates how to load a DataSet with an XML file, edit the data, and then save it back to an XML file. Create a new project and design a form with two buttons and a DataGrid control, as shown in Figure 18.2. This project's folder must reside under the same folder as the XMLData project, because it uses the PublisherTitles.xml file created by the XMLData project. If you create the folder elsewhere, you must also change the reference to the XML file (the code uses a relative reference to the XML file generated by the previous example).

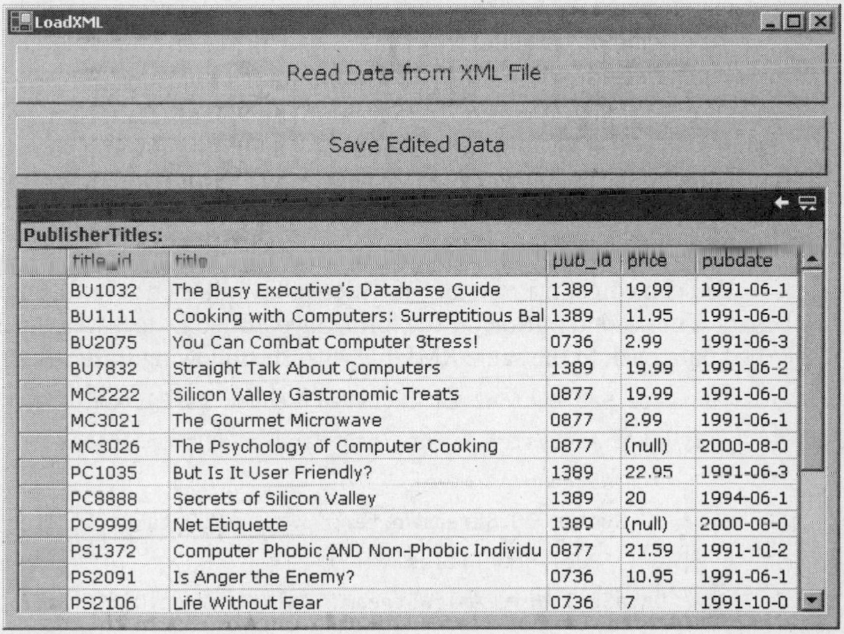
LoadXML
Read Data from XML File
Save Edited Data
PublisherTitles:
title_id title pub_id price pubdate
BU1032 The Busy Executive's Database Guide 1389 19.99 1991-06-1
BU1111 Cooking with Computers: Surreptitious Bal 1389 11.95 1991-06-0
BU2075 You Can Combat Computer Stress! 0736 2.99 1991-06-3
BU7832 Straight Talk About Computers 1389 19.99 1991-06-2
MC2222 Silicon Valley Gastronomic Treats 0877 19.99 1991-06-0
MC3021 The Gourmet Microwave 0877 2.99 1991-06-1
MC3026 The Psychology of Computer Cooking 0877 (null) 2000-08-0
PC1035 But Is It User Friendly? 1389 22.95 1991-06-3
PC8888 Secrets of Silicon Valley 1389 20 1994-06-1
PC9999 Net Etiquette 1389 (null) 2000-08-0
PS1372 Computer Phobic AND Non-Phobic Individu 0877 21.59 1991-10-2
PS2091 Is Anger the Enemy? 0736 10.95 1991-06-1
PS2106 Life Without Fear 0736 7 1991-10-0

FIGURE 18.2: The LoadXML project demonstrates how to use an XML file as a data source.

The Read Data From XML File button reads the `PublisherTitles.xml` file and loads it on a new DataSet with the statements shown in Listing 18.4. Then the DataSet is bound to the DataGrid control.

Listing 18.4: Loading XML Data on a DataGrid Control

```
Private Sub Button1_Click(ByVal sender As System.Object, _
 ByVal e As System.EventArgs) Handles Button1.Click
   Dim RStream As New _
       System.IO.StreamReader("..\..\XMLData\Bin\" & _
        "PublisherTitles.xml")
   DataSet1.Clear()
   DataSet1.ReadXml(RStream)
   DataSet1.Relations.Clear()
```

```
      DataSet1.Relations.Add(New DataRelation("Pubs2Titles", _
               DataSet1.Tables(0).Columns("pub_id"), _
               DataSet1.Tables(1).Columns("pub_id")))
      DataGrid1.DataSource = DataSet1
      RStream.Close()
   End Sub
```

The control is cleared so that you can reload the DataSet by clicking the top button on the form. If you comment out this statement, you'll be able to load the XML file on the control the first time, but if you attempt to reload the control, you'll get an exception. The DataSet has a schema already, and the ReadXml method can't add a new table with the same name.

You can edit some rows of the Titles table and then save the modified data. The second button on the form, Save Edited Data, saves the modified data back to the same XML file with the following statements:

```
   Private Sub Button2_Click(ByVal sender As System.Object, _
   ByVal e As System.EventArgs) Handles Button2.Click
      Dim WStream As New _
         System.IO.StreamWriter("..\..\XMLData\Bin\" & _
         "PublisherTitles.xml")
      DataSet1.WriteXml(WStream, XmlWriteMode.DiffGram)
      WStream.Close()
      DataSet1.Clear()
   End Sub
```

Why use the DiffGram mode? You don't have to save the changes, but I've chosen to use this mode in the example, so that we can view how changes are stored in an XML file. Typically, you accept all the changes and create a new XML file with the most recent version of the data. If you're working with your notebook, however, you may create the DataSet when you're connected to the server, persist the data to a file, and update the database when you get back to the office. In this case, you should store the changes as well, so that your application won't change rows that have been updated already.

This project also demonstrates how to use the DataGrid control as a data-entry and editing tool. All you really need is an XML that describes the schema of the data you want to display on the control—no data. You can load this schema, adjust the appearance of the DataGrid control, and allow users to enter data and edit them. You can then move the data back to the XML file and reload them at a later session. For more information on using the DataGrid control as a data entry tool, see the section "The MakeXMLFile Project," later in this chapter. But first, let's take a closer look at how changes in a DataSet are persisted in XML.

The DiffGram of the Edited DataSet

In this section, we'll develop a project very similar to the LoadXML project, but we'll replace the TextBox control at the bottom of the form with a DataGrid control. You can edit the DataSet on the DataGrid and then persist it in an XML file. If you edit the XML file you loaded in the LoadXML example and then persist it, the changes won't be recorded to the file. The row versions are a trademark of DataSets; that's why we developed a different project to demonstrate how DataSets are persisted in XML.

You can copy the folder of the XMLLoad project and rename the copied project to EditXMLData. Replace the TextBox control with a DataGrid control and bind it to the project's DataSet, PublisherTitles1 DataSet. The DataSet contains two related tables, and you can edit them both on the DataGrid control. The code of the project didn't change substantially; I simply removed the statements that displayed text on the TextBox control.

Run the project, edit a few title rows, add a few rows, and delete one of the original rows. Then click the Persist DataSet button as a DiffGram, and open the PublisherTitles.xml file that the application will create in the project's Bin folder.

The following is the element corresponding to a title that has been edited:

```
<titles diffgr:id="titles3" msdata:rowOrder="2"
        diffgr:hasChanges="modified">
    <title_id>BU2075</title_id>
    <title>You Can Combat Computer Stress!</title>
    <pub_id>0736</pub_id>
    <price>33</price>
    <pubdate>1991-06-30T00:00:00.0000000+03:00</pubdate>
</titles>
```

This section is the XML representation of the current data. Notice the attribute hasChanges, whose value is "modified." The most interesting segment of the file is at the end, and it's the `<diffgr:before>` segment. This segment contains the original version of the same title:

```
<diffgr:before>
    <titles diffgr:id="titles3" msdata:rowOrder="2"
      xmlns="http://www.tempuri.org/PublisherTitles.xsd">
        <title_id>BU2075</title_id>
        <title>You Can Combat Computer Stress!</title>
        <pub_id>0736</pub_id>
        <price>2.99</price>
        <pubdate>1991-06-30T00:00:00.0000000+03:00</pubdate>
    </titles>
</diffgr:before>
```

This section contains the original data. If you call the AcceptChanges method of the DataSet, the section with the original data will be removed from the XML representation of the DataSet. The values of the `<diffgr:before>` segment will replace the current (edited) values. As you already know, the AcceptChanges and RejectChanges methods apply to individual rows as well. If you apply these two methods to individual rows, some of the titles in the `<diffgr:before>` section will be removed (the changed rows you accept) and some of the titles in the same section will replaced the matching products in the `<diffgr:diffgram>` section.

If you delete a line, the corresponding entry in the `<diffgr:diffgram>` will be removed and the original line will be added to the `<diffgr:before>` section. This is how the DataSet knows about deleted lines, and you already know how it will handle a deleted row if you reject the changes.

If you add a row to the DataSet, a new item will be added to the section `<diffgr:diffgram>` and it will be marked as "inserted," as shown here:

```
<titles diffgr:id="titles19" msdata:rowOrder="18"
        diffgr:hasChanges="inserted">
  <title_id>TC8888</title_id>
  <title>New Title</title>
  <pub_id>0736</pub_id>
```

```
        <price>3.99</price>
        <pubdate>2001-01-01T00:00:00.0000000+02:00</pubdate>
    </titles>
```

As you can see, the XML description of the DataSet contains all the information needed to manipulate the data at the client and, yet, is able to update the underlying tables in the database. At any point you can accept and reject the changes (or selected changes) and the DataSet will be adjusted accordingly. This is also how the GetChanges method works. To retrieve the edited rows, this method looks for rows marked as "modified." Likewise, it retrieves the new rows by looking for rows marked as "inserted" and it retrieves the deleted rows by locating the rows that appear in the <diffgr:before> section that have no counterpart in the <diffgr:diffgram> segment. As you can see, XML is a very convenient method of storing DataSets and the versions of their rows. This example showed you exactly how the DataSet works and why Microsoft has chosen this format for encoding the DataSet's contents.

The DataAdapter object uses the information stored in the DataSet to figure out whether it should update the underlying tables in the database.

Creating an XML Schema

In this section, we'll create a schema from scratch. Instead of retrieving the schema from one or more database tables, we'll add an XML Schema component to our project and we'll create its schema from scratch.

Create a new Windows application, and name it MakeXMLFile. Right-click the project's name in the Solution Explorer and select Add ➢ Add New Item. In the Add New Item that will appear, select XML Schema and click OK. The name of the XML Schema that will be added is XMLSchema1.xsd by default. Double-click this file's name to open it in the Designer. There are two ways to work with an XSD file: In the Schema mode you can create a schema with visual tools, and in the XML mode you can edit the XML description of the schema. You can switch between the two views by selecting the appropriate tab at the bottom of the Designer. We'll use the visual tools exclusively, but you can switch to the XML view at any time. You can edit the schema in either view, and then see how the edits affected the other view.

So, let's create a simple schema for storing data about people (customers, contacts, any collection of people your application may require).

We'll create a table where we'll store information like names, social security numbers, addresses, phone numbers, and the like. We'll also create one more table with groups. Each group will have a name and a unique ID. It's nice to be able to classify the people into one or more groups, like customers, suppliers, press, and so on. The same person may belong to multiple groups, as well. To connect the two tables, we must introduce a third one, which will hold pairs of IDs that identify people and the groups to which they belong. If the same person belongs to two groups, then we simply add two lines to the middle table.

Let's start by building the first table, the Person table. Right-click somewhere on the Designer's surface, and select Add ≻ New Element. A new box, which represents an element, will be added to the Designer. Start typing the name of the element (Person), and then click on the first empty line of the table. Enter the name of the field (PersonID), and in the box next to it, select the datatype of the column. Because this is an ID that identifies each person, make it an integer. While this row is selected, switch to the Property Browser and you will see that the Integer datatype provides the AutoIncrement property, which is similar to the Identity property. This element's value will be set to the next integer automatically every time you add a new row to the table.

Then move to the next row, enter the name of the next attribute and select its type from the drop-down list in the next box. This attribute's name is LastName, and it's a string. The next attribute is FirstName and the last attribute's name is SSN (both are strings). To add a new element to the schema, right-click the Designer's surface and select Add ≻ Element. Name the new element **Group** (it's the table that stores the names and IDs of the various groups to which a person belongs). This element has two subelements, the GroupID (an integer with AutoIncrement set to True) and the GroupName attributes (a string). To add the subelements, just type their names and select the appropriate type from the drop-down list next to the name.

The last step is to create a third element, the Members element. This element contains relations between persons and groups. Its attributes are named PersonID and GroupID, and they're both integers. Each time you want to add a person to a group, you must add a new row to the Members table and set its columns to the ID of the person and the ID of the group to this table.

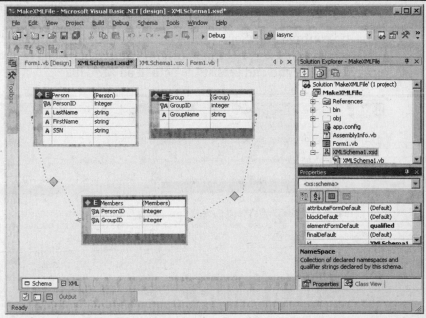

FIGURE 18.3:   The Schema of the MakeXMLFile project

To complete the schema, we must add the proper relations between the various elements. Add two Relations to the schema (double-click the Relation icon on the Toolbox), and then configure them as follows. The first relation should connect the Person table to the Members table by relating the PersonID columns in both tables. The second relation should connect the Members table to the Group table by relating the GroupID column in both tables, as shown in Figure 18.3.

Once you've created the schema, you can create a DataSet object with the identical structure. Switch to the project's form, and add a DataSet object from the Toolbox. When the Add DataSet dialog box appears, as shown in Figure 18.4, check the option Typed DataSet and in the Name box select the name of the XSD file with the XML schema you just created. Then click the OK button to close the dialog box and add the appropriate DataSet to the project.

Once the DataSet has been added to the project, we can add a Data-Grid control to the form and bind it to the DataSet just created. Set the DataGrid control's DataSource property to the name of the DataSet (XMLSchema11) and run the application. You will be able to enter and edit data on the grid and persist the data in an XML file.

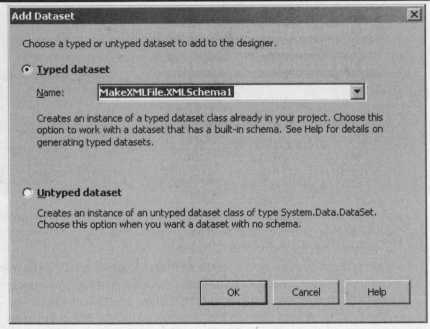

FIGURE 18.4:   Creating a DataSet based on the schema shown in Figure 18.3

In the following section, we'll take a closer look to the MakeXMLFile project.

The MakeXMLFileProject

We have created a DataSet schema with three related tables, and we can bind a DataGrid control to it. Place a DataGrid control on the application's main form along with two buttons, as shown in Figure 18.5. Then bind the DataGrid control to the project's DataSet by setting its Data-Source property to XmlSchema11 (or whatever you've named the DataSet generated by the wizard).

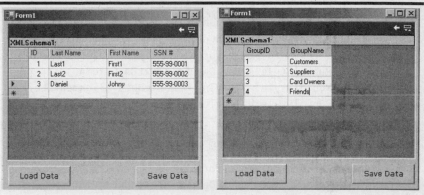

FIGURE 18.5:   The MakeXMLFile project demonstrates how to use the DataGrid control as a data-entry tool.

The default appearance of the DataGrid control is rather blunt, but you can customize it from within your code. The code that sets up the DataGrid control for the columns of the Person table is executed from within the form's Load event handler, and it's shown in Listing 18.5. You can insert additional code for the other tables.

Listing 18.5: Customizing the Appearance of the DataGrid Control

```
Private Sub Form1_Load(ByVal sender As System.Object, _
ByVal e As System.EventArgs) Handles MyBase.Load
    Dim PubTableStyle As New DataGridTableStyle()
    PubTableStyle.HeaderForeColor = Color.Blue
    PubTableStyle.MappingName = "Person"
    Dim PubColStyle As New DataGridTextBoxColumn()
    ' First column's format
    PubColStyle.Alignment = HorizontalAlignment.Center
    PubColStyle.HeaderText = "ID"
    PubColStyle.Width = 35
    PubColStyle.MappingName = "PersonID"
    PubTableStyle.GridColumnStyles.Add(PubColStyle)
    ' Second column's format
    PubColStyle = New DataGridTextBoxColumn()
    PubColStyle.Alignment = HorizontalAlignment.Left
    PubColStyle.HeaderText = "Last Name"
```

```
        PubColStyle.Width = 100
        PubColStyle.MappingName = "LastName"
        PubTableStyle.GridColumnStyles.Add(PubColStyle)
        ' Third column's format
        PubColStyle = New DataGridTextBoxColumn()
        PubColStyle.Alignment = HorizontalAlignment.Left
        PubColStyle.HeaderText = "First Name"
        PubColStyle.Width = 75
        PubColStyle.MappingName = "FirstName"
        PubTableStyle.GridColumnStyles.Add(PubColStyle)
        ' Fifth column's format
        PubColStyle = New DataGridTextBoxColumn()
        PubColStyle.Alignment = HorizontalAlignment.Left
        PubColStyle.HeaderText = "SSN #"
        PubColStyle.Width = 75
        PubColStyle.MappingName = "SSN"
        PubTableStyle.GridColumnStyles.Add(PubColStyle)
        DataGrid1.TableStyles.Add(PubTableStyle)
    End Sub
```

As a quick reminder, the DataGrid control provides a TableStyles collection, and there's one such collection for each table of the DataSet displayed on the control. Each member of the TableStyles collection is itself another collection, a GridColumnStyles collection. The Grid-ColumnStyles collection contains a member for each column of the corresponding table, and each member is of the DataGridTextBoxColumn type (or the DataGridBoolColumn type for True/False columns). You can set the properties of this object to determine the appearance of the column. You shouldn't forget to set the MappingName property of each table and column of the grid to the names of the table column you plan to map to each item. If not, the DataGrid will not be bound to the DataSet.

The code sets up a DataGridTextBoxColumn object for each element and then adds them to the GridColumnStyles collection of the DataGrid-TableStyle property of the control. Notice that you must create one DataGridTableStyle object for each table in the DataSet. If a table doesn't have its own member in the TableStyles collection, the corresponding table will have its default appearance. The code shown previously in Listing 18.5 sets up the columns of the Person table. You can insert similar statements for the remaining tables in the form's Load event handler.

Run the application, enter some data in all three tables, and check out the operation of the application. You can populate and edit all three tables in the DataSet, but in most cases you need a grid for a single table.

This table need not correspond to a database table; it can have any schema, and you can persist it to an XML file with a call to the XmlWrite method of the DataSet object.

The statements in the Save Data button's Click event handler persist the data to an XML file (see Listing 18.6). I've hard-coded the name of the file, but you can easily prompt the user with a File Open dialog box.

Listing 18.6: Persisting the Data to an XML File

```
Private Sub SaveData(ByVal sender As System.Object, _
  ByVal e As System.EventArgs) Handles bttnSave.Click
    Dim fname As String
    fname = "c:\Persons.xml"
    Dim OutStream As New System.IO.StreamWriter(fname)
    XmlSchema11.WriteXml(OutStream, _
     System.Data.XmlWriteMode.IgnoreSchema)
    OutStream.Close()
End Sub
```

In a later session, you can load the DataSet with the data in the Persons.xml file. The Click event handler of the Load Data button is shown in Listing 18.7.

Listing 18.7: Loading the DataSet with Data from an XML File

```
Private Sub LoadData(ByVal sender As System.Object, _
  ByVal e As System.EventArgs) Handles bttnLoad.Click
    Dim fname As String
    fname = "c:\Persons.xml"
    Dim InStream As New System.IO.StreamReader(fname)
    XmlSchema11.ReadXml(InStream, _
     System.Data.XmlReadMode.Auto)
    InStream.Close()
End Sub
```

So far you've seen basic examples of using XML in database applications, as well as how to persist structured, related data to XML files. As you can understand, you can use XML files as data stores for many applications that would otherwise be manipulating files. The advantage of XML is that you don't have to worry about the structure of the file, nor do you need to handle special characters, etc. XML is a text-based protocol, and it can store all types of information. Notice that you haven't had to deal directly with the structure of the XML files so far. This means that the DataSet does a fine job of abstracting the process of persisting data to XML files, as well as loading a DataSet from an XML file. However, there's more you can do with XML, and we're going to look at a few more practical XML topics.

Transforming XML Files

If you open an XML file in Internet Explorer, you will see the actual contents of the file. Internet Explorer understands XML, but it can't display it any better. However, you can apply a so-called transformation to the file and display it as you wish on the browser. We usually display XML files as tables, but you can also create a page with data-bound controls on it. To transform an XML document, you use XSL stylesheets, which process an XML file and generate another text file. XSL stylesheets are not executables; they contain instructions that will be processed by other programs, like the browser or the XML server control.

Let's look at a stylesheet for manipulating the PublisherTitles.xml file. This XML file contains publishers and titles. The stylesheet will generate an HTML page with two tables, one for the publishers and another one for the titles. This is a very simple HTML page, but it's straight HTML, and you can make it as complicated as you wish. Listing 18.8 shows the contents of the PublisherTitles.xsl file. It starts with a standard header, and it contains mostly HTML tags. This stylesheet transforms the XML document into an HTML page, so it's only natural that it's made up mostly of HTML tags. You can transform your XML data into a file of arbitrary structure. It's actually not uncommon to transform an XML file into another XML file with the identical structure and different element tags to match the description of your database. You can even create delimited text files from XML files, but if you're even considering it, you should go back to page one of the book.

Listing 18.8: The *PublisherTitles.xsl* Stylesheet

```
<xsl:stylesheet version = '1.0'
xmlns:xsl='http://www.w3.org/1999/XSL/Transform'>
<xsl:template match='/'>
<table cellspacing='3' border='2'>
<tr>
<th>PubID</th>
<th>Publisher</th>
</tr>
<xsl:for-each select='PublisherTitles/publishers'>
```

```
<tr>
<td>
<xsl:value-of select='pub_id'/>
</td>
<td>
<xsl:value-of select='pub_name'/>
</td>
</tr>
</xsl:for-each>
</table>
<br></br>
<table border='2'>
<tr>
<th>ID</th>
<th>Title</th>
<th>Price</th>
</tr>
<xsl:for-each select='PublisherTitles/titles'>
<tr>
<td>
<xsl:value-of select='title_id'/>
</td>
<td>
<xsl:value-of select='title'/>
</td>
<td>
<xsl:value-of select='price'/>
</td>
</tr>
</xsl:for-each>
</table>
</xsl:template>
</xsl:stylesheet>
```

All the HTML tags, or literals, that appear in the XSL file are copied to the output. The tags that are processed begin with the xsl prefix. The first such tag (after the header) is the following:

```
<xsl:for-each select='PublisherTitles/publishers'>
```

This tag starts a loop that iterates through the <publishers> tags of the XML file. All the statements from this tag to the matching closing tag are repeated for each <publishers> tag in the XML file. In this section, there are two columns: one for the pub_id field and another one for the pub_name field. The `value-of-select` keyword is replaced by the appropriate field. The line:

```
<xsl:value-of select='pub_id'/>
```

is replaced by the ID of the first publisher in the file during the first iteration, by the ID of the second publisher during the second iteration, and so on. The loop ends with the tag `</xsl:for-each>`. The stylesheet of Listing 18.8 will translate the `PublisherTitles.xml` file into an HTML page with two tables, one with the publishers and another one with the titles, as shown in Figure 18.6.

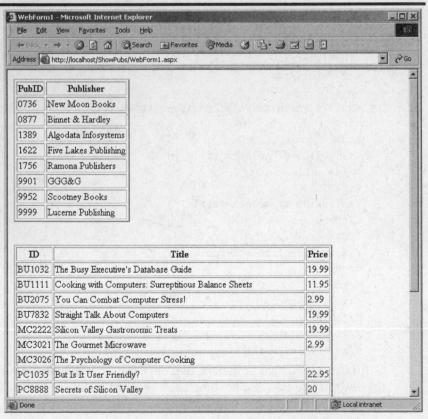

FIGURE 18.6:   Translating an XML file into an HTML page with two tables

To use the XSL file, create a new web project and place an instance of the XML control on the Web form. This is a trivial control with two properties of interest: the DocumentSource property, which is the URI of the

XML file to be translated, and the TransformSource property, which is the URI of the XSL file with the description of the transformation to be applied to the XML file. Set these two properties to the PublisherTitles.xml and PublisherTitles.xsl files, and then run the application. Internet Explorer will come up, displaying the two tables shown in Figure 18.6.

If you want to apply a transformation and save the result to a file, you must use the XslTransform object, load the stylesheet, and then call the XslTransform object's Transform method to save the transformed file. The Transform method is overloaded, and its simplest form accepts as an argument the path of the XML file to be transformed and the path of the output file, as shown in the statements in Listing 18.9.

Listing 18.9: Transforming an XML File with the XslTransform Object

```
Dim objXSLT As New XslTransform()
objXSLT.Load("PublisherTitles.xsl")
objXSLT.Transform("PublisherTitles.xml", _
  "TransformedFile.html")
Dim InStream As +
  New System.IO.StreamReader("TransformedFile.html")
TextBox1.Text = InStream.ReadToEnd
InStream.Close()
```

These statements of Listing 18.9 transform an XML file and save the transformed data into another file. The new file is then displayed on a TextBox control. Place these statements in the Click event of a button and experiment with XSL transformations.

Parsing XML Files

In addition to storing data in XML format, you should also be able to parse XML files without storing them to DataSets. Most developers will use a DataSet to store XML data that originates outside a database, but there will be occasions when you want to parse an XML file directly and extract the desired information.

The XML document is a hierarchical view of the data, and some web developers may find it simpler to work with the XML view of the data. Currently, there are no practical visual tools for working with XML files, but with the wide acceptance of the XML protocol the situation may change in the very near future. You have seen how to create an XML file's schema in the IDE. In this section, you'll learn how to process XML files from within your code.

There are two classes for accessing XML data: the XmlDocument class and the XmlDataDocument class. Both classes represent the XML file in memory and they allow you to read or modify the XML document. For very large documents, you can use the XmlReader class, which provides forward-only, read-only access. This means that you can't edit the XML file with the XmlReader class. However, you can always create a new XML document based on an existing one and save it with the help of the XmlWriter class.

The XmlDocument and XmlDataDocument objects are very similar. The XmlDataDocument class is new to .NET, and it provides a property called DataSet, which exposes the XML data as a DataSet. You can use the techniques you've learned so far to access the data. The DataSet property of the XmlDataDocument object provides a relational view of the XML data and, as a database programmer, you're more comfortable with this notation. In this chapter, we'll use the XmlDataDocument class to access XML files from within our code. The advantage of the XmlData-Class is that it provides a relational view of the loaded XML data.

There are several methods to scan an XML file, but in this section I'll show you how to go through the elements, and their child elements, by treating them as nodes. You read a node and process its child nodes, one at a time. If one of the child nodes has children of its own, you process them and continue.

To use the XmlDataDocument class, you must first create an instance of the class and load it with an XML file. The following statements create an instance of the XmlDataDocument class and load it with the data of the PublisherTitles.xml file:

```
Dim objXMLDoc As New XmlDataDocument()
objXMLDoc.Load("PublisherTitles.xml")
```

The XML document consists of nodes, and each node may have one or more child nodes. There are several ways to select group nodes. No matter which one you use, the selected nodes are returned as a collection of the XmlNodeList type. Each element of the collection is an XmlNode object, and you can use its properties to extract the node's name and value. The GetElementsByTagName method of the XmlDataDocument, for example, selects all the elements with a tag you specify and returns them as an XmlNodeList collection. The following statements will retrieve all the `<publishers>` tags in the file and store them in a collection, the oNodes collection:

```
Dim oNodes As XmlNodeList
oNodes = objXMLDoc.GetElementsByTagName("publishers")
```

How do we iterate through the oNodes collection? Since it's made up of XmlNode objects, we can use a For Each...Next loop like the following:

```
Dim oNode As XmlNode
For Each oNode In oNodes
    { statements to process the current node }
Next
```

The XmlNode object exposes a large number of properties, which we aren't going to discuss here. We'll only look at the properties you need to iterate through a collection of nodes and extract the desired information. Although it's possible to write code to iterate through the nodes of an arbitrary XML document, you should have a good idea about the structure of the document. Being able to iterate through the tables of any DataSet and the rows of any of its tables is of questionable value. The idea is to extract useful information from the XML document and process it, not just print the values. Let's write a loop to iterate through the publishers of the PublisherTitles.xml file.

First, we set up a For Each...Next loop as shown earlier. At each iteration, the *oNode* variable represents another `<publishers>` node, which in turn has two child nodes, the `<pub_id>` and `<pub_name>` elements. To retrieve the values of these nodes, use the ChildNodes collection of the current node. Each element of this collection is another XmlNode object, and its two basic properties are the Name and InnerText properties. Name is the name of the node (its tag name), and the InnerText property represents the node's value (the string between the two tags). A related property is the InnerXml property, which returns the same string in XML encoding (the "<" character is represented as <, for example).

```
Dim oNode As XmlNode
For Each oNode In oNodes
    If oNode.HasChildNodes Then
        Dim iNode, iNodes As Integer
        iNodes = oNode.ChildNodes.Count
        For iNode = 0 To iNodes - 1
            TextBox1.AppendText(oNode.ChildNodes(iNode).Name _
```

```
                & vbTab & oNode.ChildNodes(iNode).InnerText _
                & vbCrLf)
        Next
    End If
Next
```

The XmlNode object exposes a Value property, which returns the value of the node, but this value is not the same string as the InnerText property. The string returned by the Value property depends on the type of the current node, according to Table 18.3.

TABLE 18.3:   Node Types and Their Values

NODE TYPE	VALUE
Attribute	The value of the attribute
CDATASection	The content of the CDATA Section
Comment	The content of the comment
Document	A Nothing value
DocumentFragment	A Nothing value
DocumentType	A Nothing value
Element	A Nothing value
Entity	A Nothing value
EntityReference	A Nothing value
Notation	A Nothing value
ProcessingInstruction	The entire content excluding the target
Text	The content of the text node
SignificantWhitespace	The white space (spaces, carriage returns, line feeds, or tabs)
Whitespace	The white space (spaces, carriage returns, line feeds, or tabs)
XmlDeclaration	The content of the declaration (that is, everything between <?xml and ?>)

To demonstrate how to scan the nodes of an XML document, as well as how to query an XML document, we've prepared the XMLDataDoc project, whose main form is shown in Figure 18.7.

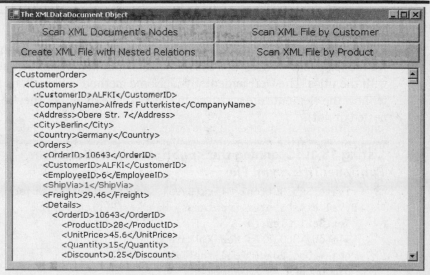

FIGURE 18.7: The XMLDataDoc project demonstrates the members of the XmlDataDocument object.

The Scan XML Document's Nodes button creates an XML document with the publishers and titles of the Pubs database and iterates through the publishers. The code shown in Listing 18.10 handles the Click event of the Scan XML Document's Nodes button. It will generate the following output (there are eight publishers in the file):

```
pub_id       0736
pub_name     New Moon Books
pub_id       0877
pub_name     Binnet & Hardley
pub_id       1389
pub_name     Algodata Infosystems
pub_id       1622
pub_name     Five Lakes Publishing
pub_id       1756
pub_name     Ramona Publishers
pub_id       9901
pub_name     GGG&G
pub_id       9952
pub_name     Scootney Books
```

```
pub_id      9999
pub_name    Lucerne Publishing
```

The PublishersTitles.xml file doesn't contain nested relations. It's made up of a section with the publishers, followed by another section with the titles. The GetElementsByTagName method will work, no matter how the elements are arranged in the XML file (whether they're nested or not).

Listing 18.10: Scanning the *<publishers>* Nodes of the *PublisherTitles.xml* File

```
Private Sub Button1_Click(ByVal sender As System.Object, _
ByVal e As System.EventArgs) Handles Button1.Click
  TextBox1.Clear()
  Dim objXMLDoc As New XmlDataDocument()
  objXMLDoc.Load("PublisherTitles.xml")
  Dim oNodes As XmlNodeList
  oNodes = objXMLDoc.GetElementsByTagName("publishers")
  TextBox1.AppendText("There are " & _
   oNodes.Count.ToString & _
   " publishers in the file" & vbCrLf)

  Dim oNode As XmlNode
  For Each oNode In oNodes
    If oNode.HasChildNodes Then
      Dim iNode, iNodes As Integer
      iNodes = oNode.ChildNodes.Count
      For iNode = 0 To iNodes - 1
        TextBox1.AppendText(oNode.ChildNodes(iNode).Name & _
          vbTab & oNode.ChildNodes(iNode).InnerText & vbCrLf)
      Next
    End If
  Next
End Sub
```

The second button on the Form, the Create XML File with Nested Relations button, creates an XML file with nested relations. This time we'll use data from the Northwind database; we'll read customers, their orders, and each order's details. In a real-world application, the resulting file would be enormous, but you can limit the number of selected rows through the SELECT statements. You can retrieve only customers in a state, or a single customer, and then only the orders that were placed within a week's or month's time span.

The statements in Listing 18.11 populate a DataSet with three tables, the Customers, Orders, and Details tables, and then they establish a nested relation between the customers and their orders, and the orders and their details. The DataSet is then loaded into an XML document, which is saved in the AllOrders.xml file.

Listing 18.11: Storing Customers, Orders, and Details in an XML File

```
Private Sub Button2_Click(ByVal sender As System.Object, _
ByVal e As System.EventArgs) Handles Button2.Click
  TextBox1.Clear()
  Dim CN As New SqlClient.SqlConnection("data source=.;" & _
              "initial catalog=northwind;user id=sa;" & _
              "workstation id=POWERTOOLKIT")
  Dim DS As New DataSet("CustomerOrder")
  CN.Open()
  Dim DACustomers As New SqlClient.SqlDataAdapter( _
      "SELECT * FROM Customers", CN)
  DACustomers.Fill(DS, "Customers")
  Dim DAOrders As New SqlClient.SqlDataAdapter( _
      "SELECT * FROM Orders", CN)
  DAOrders.Fill(DS, "Orders")
  Dim DADetails As New SqlClient.SqlDataAdapter( _
      "SELECT * FROM [Order Details]", CN)
  DADetails.Fill(DS, "Details")
  CN.Close()

  DS.Relations.Add(New DataRelation("CustomerOrders", _
      DS.Tables("Customers").Columns("CustomerID"), _
      DS.Tables("Orders").Columns("CustomerID")))
  DS.Relations.Add(New DataRelation("OrderDetails", _
      DS.Tables("Orders").Columns("OrderID"), _
      DS.Tables("Details").Columns("OrderID")))
  DS.Relations("CustomerOrders").Nested = True
  DS.Relations("OrderDetails").Nested = True

  Dim objXMLDoc As XmlDataDocument
  objXMLDoc = New XmlDataDocument(DS)
  TextBox1.Text = objXMLDoc.OuterXml
  objXMLDoc.Save("AllOrders.xml")
End Sub
```

The XML document is also displayed on the text box, and its first few elements are shown here:

```
<CustomerOrder>
  <Customers>
    <CustomerID>ALFKI</CustomerID>
    <CompanyName>Alfreds Futterkiste</CompanyName>
    <ContactName>Maria Anders</ContactName>
    <ContactTitle>Sales Representative</ContactTitle>
    <Address>Obere Str. 57</Address>
    <City>Berlin</City>
    <PostalCode>12209</PostalCode>
    <Country>Germany</Country>
    <Phone>030-0074321</Phone>
    <Fax>030-0076545</Fax>
    <Orders>
      <OrderID>10643</OrderID>
      <CustomerID>ALFKI</CustomerID>
      <EmployeeID>6</EmployeeID>
      <OrderDate>1997-08-25T00:00:00.00+03:00</OrderDate>
      <RequiredDate>1997-09-22T00:00:00+03:00</RequiredDate>
      <ShippedDate>1997-09-02T00:00:00.00+03:00</ShippedDate>
      <ShipVia>1</ShipVia>
      <Freight>29.46</Freight>
      <ShipName>Alfreds Futterkiste</ShipName>
      <ShipAddress>Obere Str. 57</ShipAddress>
      <ShipCity>Berlin</ShipCity>
      <ShipPostalCode>12209</ShipPostalCode>
      <ShipCountry>Germany</ShipCountry>
      <Details>
        <OrderID>10643</OrderID>
        <ProductID>28</ProductID>
        <UnitPrice>45.6</UnitPrice>
        <Quantity>15</Quantity>
        <Discount>0.25</Discount>
```

```
      </Details>
      <Details>
        <OrderID>10643</OrderID>
        <ProductID>39</ProductID>
        <UnitPrice>18</UnitPrice>
        <Quantity>21</Quantity>
        <Discount>0.25</Discount>
      </Details>
      <Details>
        <OrderID>10643</OrderID>
        <ProductID>46</ProductID>
        <UnitPrice>12</UnitPrice>
        <Quantity>2</Quantity>
        <Discount>0.25</Discount>
      </Details>
          ' more detail lines
    </Orders>
        ' more orders
  </Customers>
    more customers
</CustomerOrder>
```

Let's say you have received this XML file and you want to process it in its native format—without converting it to a DataSet or storing it to a local database. First, you must load it into an XmlDataDocument object, and you already know how to do this:

```
Dim objXMLDoc As New XmlDataDocument()
objXMLDoc.Load("AllOrders.xml")
```

Next, you must retrieve the nodes that interest you. You can retrieve all the customer elements, or all the orders, with the GetElementsByTag-Name method, but this time we'll use a different approach. We'll retrieve all the orders of a specific customer, and then we'll scan all their child elements, which are the detail lines of the corresponding order.

Just as you can select rows from a database table with an SQL statement, you can select rows in an XML document using the XPath language. XPath is a language for performing queries against an XML document, but it's nothing like SQL. It has a rather odd syntax and it's not nearly as powerful. The current implementation of XPath allows you to specify simple criteria for selecting elements of the document. To select the elements that correspond to orders of the customer with the ID of *ALFKI*, you must specify the element tag to which the selection applies by supplying the name of the table and the criteria in square brackets as:

```
descendant::Orders[CustomerID="ALFKI"]
```

The first part of the expression indicates that we want all the child elements of the selected element that meet the selection criteria. In other words, we want the <Orders> elements (including their child elements) in which the CustomerID field is *ALFKI*. The code actually prompts the user for the ID of the desired customer, and it creates a string similar to the one shown above. This expression must be passed to the SelectNodes method, which return an XmlNodeList collection:

```
Dim ordNodes As XmlNodeList
ordNodes = _
   objXMLDoc.SelectNodes("descendant::Orders[CustomerID=
      ""ALFKI""]")
```

Once you have retrieved the selected nodes, you can iterate through them with a For...Each loop. The <Order> elements have child nodes, some of which are <Detail> elements. Every time we run into a <Detail> element, we must set up another loop to iterate through its child nodes, which are the order's detail lines. The statements in Listing 18.12 iterate through the orders of the *ALFKI* customer and display all the related elements on the TextBox control.

Listing 18.12: Scanning the Elements of a Specific Customer

```
Private Sub Button3_Click(ByVal sender As System.Object, _
ByVal e As System.EventArgs) Handles Button3.Click

  Dim custID As String
  custID = InputBox("Please enter the desired " & _
    "customer's ID", "Search by Customer ID", "ALFKI")
  TextBox1.Clear()
  Me.Cursor = Cursors.WaitCursor
  Dim objXMLDoc As New XmlDataDocument()
  objXMLDoc.Load("AllOrders.xml")
  Dim ordNodes As XmlNodeList
```

```
ordNodes = objXMLDoc.SelectNodes( _
  "descendant::Orders[CustomerID=""" & custID & """]")
Dim ordNode As XmlNode
Dim mRow As DataRow
For Each ordNode In ordNodes
  Dim i As Integer
  For i = 0 To ordNode.ChildNodes.Count - 1
    If ordNode.ChildNodes(i).Name <> "Details" Then
      TextBox1.AppendText(ordNode.ChildNodes(i).Name & _
        vbTab & ordNode.ChildNodes(i).InnerText & vbCrLf)
    End If
    If ordNode.HasChildNodes Then
        Dim detNodes As XmlNodeList
        detNodes = ordNode.ChildNodes(i).ChildNodes
        Dim detNode As XmlNode
        For Each detNode In detNodes
          Dim j As Integer
          For j = 0 To detNode.ChildNodes.Count - 1
            TextBox1.AppendText(vbTab & detNode.Name & _
              vbTab & detNode.InnerText & vbCrLf)
          Next
        Next
    End If
  Next
Next
Me.Cursor = Cursors.Default
End Sub
```

Another important property of the XmlNode object is the ParentNode property, which returns the parent element of the current element. Let's say you want a list of all customers who have ordered a specific product, along with their matching orders. The following XPath query will return all the detail rows that contain the product with an ID of 20:

```
descendant::Details[ProductID=20]
```

Once you have all the detail lines with the specified product, you can also retrieve the order to which they belong and the customer that placed the order. The order is the parent node of each selected element, and the customer is the parent node of the corresponding order. The statements in Listing 18.13 iterate through the detail lines that contain the product with the specified ID value (20). This is what the last button on the form does. It retrieves all the elements that correspond to orders that contain the user-supplied product ID. Then it displays the parent node of the first selected detail line, which is the order number. It also displays the order's parent node, which is the ID of the customer that placed the order.

Listing 18.13: Scanning the Orders that Contain a Specific Product

```
Private Sub Button4_Click(ByVal sender +
As System.Object, ByVal e As System.EventArgs) _
Handles Button4.Click
 Dim prodID As String
 prodID = InputBox("Please enter the desired " & _
   "product's ID", "Search by Product ID", "12")
 TextBox1.Clear()
 Me.Cursor = Cursors.WaitCursor
 Dim objXMLDoc As New XmlDataDocument()
 objXMLDoc.Load("AllOrders.xml")
 Dim detailNodes As XmlNodeList
 detailNodes = objXMLDoc.SelectNodes( _
   "descendant::Details[ProductID=" & prodID & "]")
 Dim detailNode As XmlNode
 Dim mRow As DataRow
 For Each detailNode In detailNodes
   Dim i As Integer
   Dim orderNode As XmlNode
   orderNode = detailNode.ParentNode
   TextBox1.AppendText("ORDER ID  " & vbTab & _
     orderNode.Item("OrderID").InnerText & vbCrLf)
   TextBox1.AppendText("PLACED ON " & vbTab & _
     orderNode.Item("OrderDate").InnerText & vbCrLf)
   TextBox1.AppendText("FREIGHT   " & vbTab & _
     orderNode.Item("Freight").InnerText & vbCrLf)
   Dim customerNode As XmlNode
   customerNode = orderNode.ParentNode
   TextBox1.AppendText(vbTab & "PLACED BY " & _
     customerNode.Item("CompanyName").InnerText & vbCrLf)
   For i = 0 To orderNode.ChildNodes.Count - 1
     If orderNode.ChildNodes(i).ChildNodes.Count = 1 Then
       TextBox1.AppendText(vbTab & _
         orderNode.ChildNodes(i).Name & vbTab & _
         orderNode.ChildNodes(i).InnerText & vbCrLf)
     Else
```

```
            If orderNode.HasChildNodes Then
              Dim orderDetailNodes As XmlNodeList
              orderDetailNodes = _
                OrderNode.ChildNodes(i).ChildNodes
              Dim orderDetailNode As XmlNode
              For Each orderDetailNode In orderDetailNodes
                Dim j As Integer
                TextBox1.AppendText(vbTab & vbTab & _
                  orderDetailNode.Name & vbTab & _
                  orderDetailNode.InnerText & vbCrLf)
              Next
            End If
          End If
        Next
      Next
        Me.Cursor = Cursors.Default
    End Sub
```

The outer For Each...Next loop goes through the selected detail lines. At each iteration, the variable *ordNode* represents another detail element. To extract the element of the order to which the detail line belongs, we retrieve the ParentNode property of the current element, which is the *detailNode* element:

```
orderNode = detailNode.ParentNode
```

and then we print the fields of this order (who placed it, when, the ID of the employee who made the sale, and so on). To retrieve information about the customer who placed this order, we retrieve the ParentNode property of the *orderNode* element:

```
customerNode = orderNode.ParentNode
```

Once the headers of the order and the order's customer are printed, we can iterate through the child nodes of the *orderNode* element. These child nodes are the detail lines, and we print all the lines of the order:

```
For i = 0 To orderNode.ChildNodes.Count - 1
    { statements to print the current detail line }
Next
```

A segment of the output produced by the last button on the form is shown in Listing 18.14. Notice that all the selected orders contain the product with ID = 12.

Listing 18.14: The Output of the SCAN XML File by Product Button of the XMLDataDoc Project

```
ORDER ID      10633
PLACED ON     1997-08-15T00:00:00.0000000+03:00
FREIGHT       477.9
   PLACED BY Ernst Handel
   OrderID        10633
   CustomerID     ERNSH
   EmployeeID     7
   OrderDate      1997-08-15T00:00:00.0000000+03:00
   RequiredDate   1997-09-12T00:00:00.0000000+03:00
   ShippedDate    1997-08-18T00:00:00.0000000+03:00
   ShipVia        3
   Freight        477.9
   ShipName       Ernst Handel
   ShipAddress    Kirchgasse 6
   ShipCity       Graz
   ShipPostalCode 8010
   ShipCountry    Austria
      OrderID        10633
      ProductID      12
      UnitPrice      38
      Quantity       36
      Discount       0.15
      OrderID        10633
      ProductID      13
      UnitPrice      6
      Quantity       13
      Discount       0.15
      OrderID        10633
      ProductID      26
      UnitPrice      31.23
      Quantity       35
      Discount       0.15
      OrderID        10633
      ProductID      62
      UnitPrice      49.3
      Quantity       80
      Discount       0.15
```

This is the first order in the XML file that contains the specified product. The code displays all the relevant fields because it's a demo application. In a real application, you'd isolate the fields you need and use their values in your code.

As you experiment with XML, especially with scanning the nodes of an XML file, you will notice that the process is rather slow. XML is not a substitute for a database; it's a convenient method of storing limited amounts of information and sharing it with business partners. XML is a verbose, text-based format, and it can't be as efficient as a real database. However, it's the best method to exchange data with other computers.

This chapter doesn't exhaust the topic of XML or the capabilities of the XmlDataDocument object. The XmlDataDocument object provides methods to add new elements, edit elements, and even remove existing elements. These techniques are the most useful ones, especially for a database programmer. If you want to manipulate XML data, you will find it much more convenient to create a DataSet with the same structure as the XML file, and then use the members of the DataSet object, with which you're quite familiar.

SQL SERVER AND XML

So far you've learned how to extract XML data from a DataSet and how to create your own XML files from scratch. SQL Server can return the results of a query directly in XML format. In other words, it's possible to execute a query against a SQL Server database and request that the result is returned in XML format. You can look at the results of a query in XML format right in the Query Analyzer's window by executing a query and appending the FOR XML AUTO clause. The following statement will return all the rows of the Customers table in XML format:

```
SELECT * FROM Customers FOR XML AUTO
```

The output of this query looks like this:

```
XML_F52E2B61-18A1-11d1-B105-00805F49916B

------------------------------------------------

<customers CustomerID="ALFKI" CompanyName= _
 "Alfreds Futterkis ContactName="Maria Anders" _
 ContactTitle="Sales
```

```
Representative" Address="Obere Str. 57" City="Berlin" _
  PostalCode="12209" Country="Germany" Phone="030-0074321"

Fax="030-0076545"/><customers Cust
ce Lebihan" ContactTitle="Owner" Address= _
  "12, rue des Bouche City="Marseille" PostalCode="13008" _
  Country="France"

Phone="91.24.45.40" Fax="91.24.45.41"/><customers _
  CustomerID CompanyName="Bottom-Dollar Markets"

ContactName="Elizabeth Lincoln"
```

The lines are too long to be displayed on the Results pane of Query Analyzer, and they're truncated. The problem is that each row displayed by the Query Analyzer has a size limitation. You can increase the length of each line, but not beyond 8,192 characters. As you will see, this limitation doesn't exist when the results are returned to the application as an XmlDataDocument.

When you program against a local SQL Server database with ADO.NET, there's no reason to retrieve the results in XML format. The DataSet you'll retrieve will convert them to XML format anyway. However, SQL Server supports XML so that it can be accessed over the HTTP protocol. By appending the query to a URL that identifies SQL Server and the query you want to execute, it is possible to execute a query against SQL Server from within Internet Explorer. A corporation may choose to expose some of its data to the Web, not through a web application or a Web Service, but by allowing applications to execute queries against their database over HTTP. The client applications don't have access to the entire database; the owner of the database can prepare a number of queries that the clients are allowed to execute against the database, either to retrieve data or even update some tables. For example, you may allow clients to add orders to your database by submitting a query directly to SQL Server. In the next section, we'll explore selection queries. You'll learn how to contact a remote SQL Server through a URL, execute specific queries, and retrieve the results in XML format.

You can also create web pages with data by retrieving a result set from SQL Server in XML format and applying an XSL transformation on the result set. The next version of SQL Server will provide extensive support for XML. The next section is a brief introduction to the XML features of SQL Server 2000.

The SELECT statement of T-SQL supports the FOR XML clause that specifies that the statement result be returned in the form of an XML document instead of a relational result set. Complex queries, or queries that you want to make secure, can be stored as templates in an IIS virtual directory and executed by referencing the template name. The template is basically a SQL query, or stored procedure, which resides in a special folder, a *virtual folder,* as it's called. Clients have access to this folder, rather than SQL Server, and they can execute only the templates stored in the virtual folder.

Configuring a Virtual Directory for SQL Server

To enable SQL Server to interact with a client through XML, you must first create a virtual directory, as you would do for a web application. All the requests to be serviced by SQL Server must include the name of this virtual directory in their URL. To do so, start the Configure SQL XML Support in IIS utility and when the window of the IIS Virtual Directory Management for SQL Server utility comes up, select the default website, as shown in Figure 18.8.

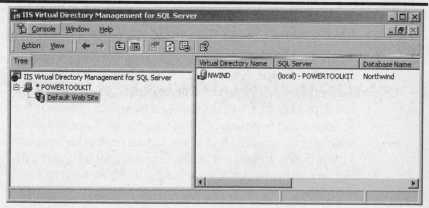

FIGURE 18.8:   The Configure SQL XML Support in an IIS Utility

Open the Action menu, and select New ➢ Virtual Directory. You will see the New Virtual Directory Properties dialog box, which is shown in

Figure 18.9. The dialog box has six tabs where you must specify the following:

General   Here you specify the name of the virtual directory and its path. The virtual directory is mapped to an existing path, which can be the path of any folder on the system. It's usually a subfolder under the web server's root folder.

Security   Here you specify how the requests made to the new virtual directory will be authenticated. You can use a SQL Server account, a Windows account, or Basic Authentication.

Data Source   On this tab, you can select the name of an instance of SQL Server that will be associated with the virtual directory and a database. Set the name of the virtual directory to **NWIND** (this is the name we'll use in the examples), and select the local server and the Northwind database.

Settings   Here you can specify the type of access you want to provide through the virtual directory. URL queries are SQL queries that can be submitted to SQL Server through a URL, as if clients were requesting a script on the server. You should disable this option and enable the Allow Template Queries option. A template is a file with a query, which can be called through a URL by name. Templates don't allow users to execute any query, just one of a number of predefined queries, which you have prepared ahead of time. The option Allow XPath Queries allows clients to execute XPath queries on SQL views.

Virtual Names   On this tab, you can specify additional virtual folders under the SQL Server's virtual folder. These folders will be used for storing specific types of items. The allowed types are database objects (like views and stored procedures), schemas, and templates. In this chapter, we'll use templates with specific queries. Add a new virtual name, the Templates virtual name, and map it to the Templates folder under SQL Server's virtual folder. This is the folder where we'll store the templates.

Advanced   This tab contains a couple of advanced settings, like the location of the SQLISAPI.DLL file. It's unlikely that you will change the default settings on this tab.

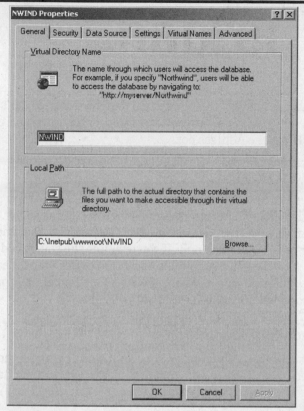

FIGURE 18.9: Specifying a new virtual directory for SQL Server

Once the new virtual directory is added to the Default Web Site, its name will appear in the right pane of the IIS Virtual Directory Management for SQL Server, as shown previously in Figure 18.8. Close the window, and you're ready to submit queries to the Northwind database over the HTTP protocol. You can think of the name of the virtual folder as the name of an application like Query Analyzer. To execute a query against the Northwind database, you must form a URL starting with the URL of the machine on which SQL Server is running, followed by the name of the virtual folder and the text of the SQL query.

Of course, the query's text must be URL encoded. The following special characters must be replaced by the indicated strings:

+ (space)   %20

/   %2F

?	%3F
%	%25
#	%23
&	%26

To test the functionality of the new virtual folder we created, let's submit a query directly to the SQL Server. Start Internet Explorer, and enter the following URL in the Address box:

```
http://localhost/nwind?sql=SELECT%20*%20FROM%20Customers
%20FOR%20XML%20AUTO
```

You don't need to use URL encoding as you type. As soon as you press the Enter key, the URL will be encoded and submitted to the server. This query will return an error message to the effect that an XML document is allowed to have one top element only. If you examine the source code of the document, you'll see that it contains one <Customers> tag for each row of the table. To avoid this problem, specify a root element by appending the root=root parameter to the end of the URL:

```
http://localhost/nwind?sql=SELECT%20*%20FROM%20Customers
%20FOR%20XML%20AUTO&root=root
```

If you request this URL, the result will be an XML file with all the rows of the Customers table. Here are the first few lines of the document:

```
<root>
  <Customers CustomerID="ALFKI"
  CompanyName="Alfreds Futterkiste"
  ContactName="Maria Anders" ContactTitle="Sales
  Representative" Address="Obere Str. 57" City="Berlin"
  PostalCode="12209" Country="Germany" Phone="030-0074321"
  Fax="030-0076545" />
  <Customers CustomerID="ANATR"
  CompanyName="Ana Trujillo Emparedados y helados"
  ContactName="Ana Trujillo" ContactTitle="Owner"
  Address="Avda. de la Constitución 2222"
  City="México D.F." PostalCode="05021"
  Country="Mexico" Phone="(5) 555-4729"
  Fax="(5) 555-3745" />
```

As you can see, each customer is represented by a single element and its fields are attributes of the <Customers> tag. The entire document is contained within a <root> element (you can use any other name for the top element). You can create an XML document with separate elements for each field by specifying the ELEMENTS modifier to the FOR XML clause. If you request the following URL:

```
http://localhost/nwind?sql=SELECT%20*%20FROM%20Customers
%20FOR%20XML%20AUTO,%20ELEMENTS&root=root
```

you'll get back an XML document with a separate element for each field, like the following:

```
<Customers>
    <CustomerID>ALFKI</CustomerID>
    <CompanyName>Alfreds Futterkiste</CompanyName>
    <ContactName>Maria Anders</ContactName>
    <ContactTitle>Sales Representative</ContactTitle>
    <Address>Obere Str. 57</Address>
    <City>Berlin</City>
    <PostalCode>12209</PostalCode>
    <Country>Germany</Country>
    <Phone>030-0074321</Phone>
    <Fax>030-0076545</Fax>
</Customers>
<Customers>
    <CustomerID>ANATR</CustomerID>
    <CompanyName>Ana Trujillo Emparedados y helados
      </CompanyName>
    <ContactName>Ana Trujillo</ContactName>
    <ContactTitle>Owner</ContactTitle>
    <Address>Avda. de la Constitución 2222</Address>
    <City>México D.F.</City>
    <PostalCode>05021</PostalCode>
    <Country>Mexico</Country>
    <Phone>(5) 555-4729</Phone>
    <Fax>(5) 555-3745</Fax>
</Customers>
```

The possible modifiers for the XML mode are the following:

XMLDATA   Specifies that the query must return an XML-Data schema, inserted at the top of the document.

ELEMENTS   This option specifies that the columns are returned as subelements. Otherwise, they are returned as elements. This option is supported in AUTO mode only.

BINARY BASE64   If the BINARY Base64 option is specified, any binary data returned by the query is represented in base64-encoded format. You must specify this modifier if you plan to retrieve binary data using the RAW and EXPLICIT modes.

Using Templates

Appending your queries to the URL is awkward, at best. It's also dangerous, because users can also specify action queries to be executed against your database. You can create queries and store them as XML files in a special folder under the SQL Server's virtual folder. As indicated earlier, the Template folder under SQL Server's virtual folder is where the templates are stored in the examples of this section.

A template is a text file that contains the text of the query to be executed against the database. However, the query must be XML formatted. This is done by embedding the text of the query in a pair of `<sql:query>` tags:

```
<sql:query>
  SELECT  Customers.CustomerID, CompanyName, ContactName,
   ContactTitle
  FROM     Customers
</sql:query>
```

To avoid the problem of multiple root elements, you can specify the root element of the document in the template file, with the statements shown here:

```
<ROOT xmlns:sql="urn:schemas-microsoft-com:xml-sql">
  <sql:query>
  SELECT  Customers.CustomerID, CompanyName, ContactName,
   ContactTitle
  FROM     Customers
  </sql:query>
</ROOT>
```

Store the statements of the last listing to the file GetCustomers.xml in the Templates folder under the SQL Server's virtual folder. Then request this file from within Internet Explorer by specifying the following URL in its Address box:

```
http://localhost/NWIND/Templates/GetCustomers.xml
```

This query will return information about all the customers in the database, which for a real database represents an enormous amount of information. A more practical query would return a set of customers. Let's modify the query so that it selects customers from a specific country. Creating a parameterized query is straightforward, but we must specify that the template accepts a parameter. This is the template file with a query that retrieves the customers from a specific country (specified with a parameter). The parameter of the query is the @*country* variable, and it's declared with the <sql:param> tag. If this query is called without a value for the parameter, then the default value USA will be used.

```
<ROOT xmlns:sql="urn:schemas-microsoft-com:xml-sql">
  <sql:header>
      <sql:param name='Country'>USA</sql:param>
  </sql:header>
  <sql:query>
    SELECT  Customers.CustomerID, CompanyName, ContactName, _
    ContactTitle
    FROM      Customers
    WHERE     Country=@country
    ORDER BY Customers.CompanyName
    FOR XML AUTO, ELEMENTS
  </sql:query>
</ROOT>
```

If you enter the following URL in the browser's Address box, you will execute the GetCustomers query in the Templates folder:

```
http://localhost/NWIND/Templates/GetCustomers.xml?
Country=Germany
```

This query will return the customers from Germany. Figure 18.10 shows a segment of the result of the query as displayed on the browser.

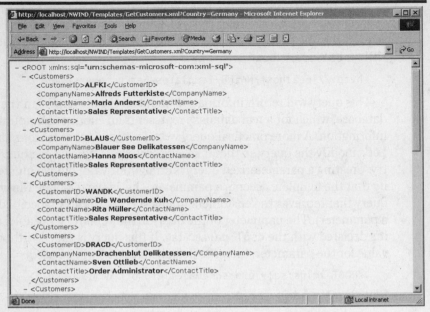

FIGURE 18.10:   Retrieving customer information in XML format

In the following section, we'll use a more interesting query, which returns nested related tables. The revised query, Listing 18.15, returns all the customers from a specific country, along with their orders, including the details of the orders.

Listing 18.15: A Template for Retrieving Customer Orders

```
<ROOT xmlns:sql="urn:schemas-microsoft-com:xml-sql">
  <sql:header>
    <sql:param name='Country'>USA</sql:param>
  </sql:header>
  <sql:query>
    SELECT  Customers.CustomerID, CompanyName,
            ContactName, ContactTitle, Orders.OrderID,
```

```
              OrderDate, Order Details].ProductID,
              [Order Details].UnitPrice, Quantity
       FROM    Customers
       JOIN Orders ON Orders.CustomerID=Customers.CustomerID
       JOIN [Order Details] ON Orders.OrderID =
              [Order Details].OrderID
       WHERE Country=@country
       ORDER BY Customers.CustomerID, Orders.OrderID
       FOR XML AUTO, ELEMENTS
    </sql:query>
  </ROOT>
```

Create a text file with the statements of Listing 18.15, name it Get-CustomerOrders.xml, and store it in the Templates folder under the virtual directory of SQL Server. As you can see, a template is basically a query embedded in a few XML tags.

The SQLServerXML Project

As you have guessed by now, it's fairly easy to connect to a remote SQL Server, extract data in XML format, and process it from within your code as usual. Let's build an application that retrieves data from a SQL Server database through a web server and uses it to create a DataSet and bind it to a DataGrid control. Figure 18.11 shows the SQLServerXML project's main form. The Load XML Button contacts the local SQL Server through the web server running on your machine. You can contact any server on your network, but this is how you can test the application on a single machine. The XML data returned by SQL Server forms a long string. This string is displayed on a TextBox control at the top of the form of the SQLServerXML project. The XML document you see in Figure 18.11 has been edited manually. If you run the project, you will see the same information in a very long string.

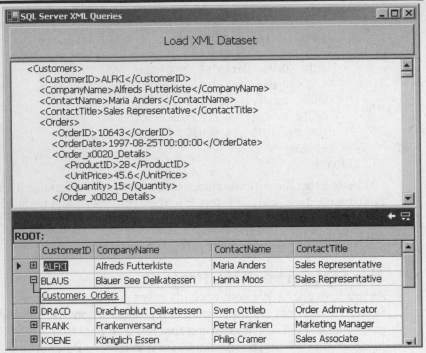

FIGURE 18.11: The SQLServerXML project demonstrates how to request the result of a query from SQL Server in XML format.

To execute the GetCustomerOrders query and retrieve the results in XML format, click the Load XML DataSet button, whose Click event handler is shown in Listing 18.16.

Listing 18.16: Retrieving the Customers and Their Orders in XML Format

```
Private Sub Button1_Click(ByVal sender As System.Object, _
    ByVal e As System.EventArgs) Handles Button1.Click
    Dim xmlDoc As New XmlDataDocument()
    xmlDoc.Load("http://localhost/NWIND/Templates/" & _
            "GetCustomerOrders.xml?Country=Germany")
    TextBox1.AppendText(xmlDoc.OuterXml)
    xmlDoc.Save("NWCustomerOrders.xml")
    SqlConnection1.Close()
    Dim DS As New DataSet()
```

```
    DS.ReadXml("NWCustomerOrders.xml")
    DataGrid1.DataSource = DS
End Sub
```

This event handler calls the Load method of the XMLDataDocument object passing a URL as an argument. The URL is the address of the `Get-CustomerOrders.xml` template, followed by the name and value of the query's argument. If the query accepts multiple arguments, they should all appear after the address and be separated by ampersand (&) characters. Then XMLDataDocument object's OuterXML property returns the entire document, which is displayed on a TextBox control. The same document is then saved to an XML file, which is read with the DataSet object's ReadXml method. Once the DataSet is populated with the customers and their orders, it's bound to the DataGrid control. The DataSet contains nested relations between its tables, and the data will be displayed hierarchically on the DataGrid control. You can view the customers, expand a customer to see their orders, and then expand an order to see its details. You can edit the SQL statement to display more or fewer fields of each table and display product names in the order detail lines instead of product IDs.

You can also submit action queries in XML format to SQL Server to update the database. The topic of SQL Server's support for XML is quite interesting, and it's worth exploring on your own.

WHAT'S NEXT

This chapter was a quick overview of XML for database developers. XML is at the core of ADO.NET, but you need not fully understand the new format in order to write data-driven applications. We've presented the basics of XML and given several examples to demonstrate how the DataSet object uses XML and how you can switch between the relational (tables, columns, and relationships) and hierarchical (XML) views of the same data. XML is also the best method to pass data between remote computers. Actually, this is how information is passed between layers of an application. XML, as SOAP, is also used to pass data from a Web Service (an application running on a web server) to a client. ADO.NET is based on a "universal" protocol, and the best part of it is that you need not write any code to manipulate XML documents. Everything is done in the background by ADO.NET for you.

In the next chapter, you will build on the skills you learned in this chapter and utilize XML in your web applications. The entire chapter will focus on using XML with your Web Forms and user controls.

As the next chapter focuses on ASP.NET, some of the content will focus on rendering the user interface using server-side web controls. Much of the material will focus on rendering a proper user interface using XML and ASP.NET.

Chapter 19

USING XML IN WEB APPLICATIONS

Despite the relative youth of the XML specification, it has rapidly become a major focus of web programming. XML is the underpinning for the newest version of HTML, called XHTML; it's the basis of Web Services, and in combination with the XSLT and XPath recommendations, it's one of the most effective ways to ensure the separation of your data from the interface that displays the data. XML is a crucial part of .NET, so it's not surprising that the framework provides some sophisticated, powerful, and flexible methods for reading, writing, and transforming XML data. You'll find the classes you need to manipulate XML in the System.Xml namespace.

Adapted from *Mastering ASP.NET with VB.NET*
by A. Russell Jones
ISBN 0-7821-2875-0 $49.99

INTRODUCTION TO THE *System.Xml* NAMESPACE

The System.Xml namespace contains all the classes you need to work with XML in .NET. At the most basic level, the XmlDocument class lets you load and save XML documents from disk files or from strings. If you've worked with XML in other systems, such as Microsoft's own msxml.dll, you'll recognize the XmlDocument as similar to the root object in those systems. An XmlDocument object uses a *parser* to read the XML document and create a *node tree* (a hierarchical representation of the elements, attributes, and text in the document). For example, to initiate the parsing process for an XML document, you create an XmlDocument instance and pass the file you want to parse to its Load method:

```
Dim xml as New XmlDocument
Xml.Load(physical filename of XML document)
Response.Write(xml.InnerXml)
```

The code fragment loads an XML document and sends the XML string contents to the client.

What Can You Do with XML?

XML documents, by themselves, are easy for humans to read but aren't that useful to the computer. By themselves, they aren't much better than any other sequential file format—just a wordier, if easier to read, text file format. To make them useful, you need to add some functionality. In addition to the basic XmlDocument, the System.Xml namespace contains "helper" classes that provide the ability to:

- Find nodes and values.
- Define the structure and data for an XML document.
- Let you traverse a document sequentially without caching the data in memory.
- Transform a document into another form.
- Move seamlessly between XML and relational data.
- Read and write XML files.

Retrieve Individual Nodes or Groups of Nodes—*System.Xml.XPath*

An XML file consists of a tree of *nodes*. Each node may be an element, an attribute, a comment, a processing instruction, or a character data (CDATA) section. An XML document contains markup that conforms to strict rules. Therefore, you can teach the parser to separate the markup from content easily. But you need to be able to retrieve individual nodes or collections of nodes to find data quickly. You do that using System.Xml.XPath. The XPath specification describes a vocabulary for navigating through the node tree.

Define the Structure and Datatypes in an XML document—*System.Xml.Schema*

Over the years, the computer industry has standardized on many file formats for various types of information. For example, each of the many types of image formats (gif, bmp, jpg, etc.) has a specific file format. Only by rigidly adhering to this file format can you create a GIF file and have applications display it correctly. There's no room for customization—the file format is fixed. For those of you who have worked with Windows since version 3 days, another common example is INI (application initialization) files, which—before the Windows Registry—were the premier way to store application-specific information. An INI file had three customizable levels—a set of *sections* enclosed in square brackets, each of which could contain *keys* and *values* separated by an equal (=) sign. For example,

```
[section1]
key1=value1
[section2]
key1=value1
key2=value2
```

Unfortunately, without performing customized manipulations on the key or value strings, there was no way to go beyond the three fixed levels. The equivalent XML document could look like Listing 19.1.

Listing 19.1: Simple XML File that Holds INI File Type Information (XML-INI.xml)

```
<?xml version="1.0"?>
<sections>
```

```
            <section name="Section1">
               <key name"key1" value="value1" />
            </section>
            <section name="Section">
               <key name"key1" value="value1" />
               <key name"key2" value="value2" />
            <section>
         </sections>
```

In this form, the section name for each section, along with the keys and values, have become *attributes*. Attributes are fast and easy to read, but not as flexible as elements. But you aren't constrained to using attributes. Listing 19.2 shows an extended version that uses elements rather than attributes. You can extend the number of levels or the number of items associated with a particular key very easily. For example, the following document adds a second value using the tag <anothervalue> to each key in the section named Section2.

Listing 19.2: The XML Document Extends the INI File Format (XML_INI2.xml)

```
<?xml version="1.0" encoding="utf-8"?>
<sections xmlns="http://tempuri.org/XML-INI2.xsd">
  <section>
    <name>Section1</name>
    <keys>
      <key>
        <name>key1</name>
        <value>value1</value>
      </key>
    </keys>
  </section>
  <section>
    <name>Section2</name>
    <keys>
      <key>
        <name>key1</name>
        <value>value1</value>
      </key>
      <key>
        <name>key2</name>
        <value>value2</value>
      </key>
```

```
    </keys>
  </section>
</sections>
```

Because XML data can appear in so many forms, you need to be able to describe exactly what any specific XML document can contain. A *schema* lets you do this. I'm not going to go into much depth about schema in this book, because you don't need to know much about them to use XML efficiently. However, it's useful to know what a schema *does*. For each element and attribute, the schema defines the name and the value type. Elements can be simple (they only contain a value) or complex (they may contain a combination of other elements and attributes, and a value). For example, in the first XML INI file example, the element <sections> is a complex element that contains one child element <section>. In turn, each <section> element is a complex element that contains one attribute called name and one complex element named key. Here's a portion of the schema for the XML-INI.xml document that shows the <section> element definition:

```
<xsd:element name="section">
  <xsd:complexType>
    <xsd:sequence>
      <xsd:element name="key" minOccurs="0"
        maxOccurs="unbounded">
        <xsd:complexType>
        <xsd:attribute name="name" form="unqualified"
          type="xsd:string" />
        <xsd:attribute name="value" form="unqualified"
          type="xsd:string" />
        <xsd:attribute name="section_Id" type="xsd:int"
          use="prohibited" />
        </xsd:complexType>
      </xsd:element>
    </xsd:sequence>
    <xsd:attribute name="section_Id"
      msdata:AutoIncrement="true"
      type="xsd:int" msdata:AllowDBNull="false"
      use="prohibited" />
```

```
        <xsd:attribute name="name" form="unqualified"
          type="xsd:string"/>
      </xsd:complexType>
    </xsd:element>
```

You can see that the `<section>` element is a complex element. Look
carefully at the attributes for the key element. There are three, even
though I only used two: `name` and `value`. The VS XML editor defined the
`section_Id` element automatically. In fact, the VS XML editor defined
the entire schema automatically by looking at the XML document elements and making a "best guess" as to the types. Letting the IDE generate schema is extremely convenient. In addition, you can use the schema
it creates to define the data in a DataSet. By creating such a schema, you
can load your XML directly into a DataSet and then bind it to controls.

Transform XML Documents—*System.Xml.Xsl*

XML data is *mutable*—you can change it from one form of XML into
another form, using an XML vocabulary called XSL (Extensible
Stylesheet Language) or XSLT (Extensible Stylesheet Language Transformations). The most popular use of XSLT has been to transform it into
HTML, or more precisely, XHTML, which is simply HTML cleaned up so
it conforms to the XML specification. The advantage of transforms is that
you cleanly separate the data from the markup, because the data is in the
XML file, while the markup is in an XSLT file, called a *stylesheet*. Using
Internet Explorer, you can view the results of a transform by simply loading an XML file. That's because IE contains a *default stylesheet* that it
applies to XML documents that don't define their own stylesheet.
Listing 19.3 shows a simple XML document called `flexible.xml`.

Listing 19.3: The *flexible.xml* XML File

```
<?xml version="1.0" encoding="utf-8" ?>
<items>
    <item>XML </item>
    <item>is </item>
    <item>an </item>
    <item>extremely </item>
    <item>flexible </item>
    <item>data </item>
    <item>format </item>
</items>
```

If you request the file `flexible.xml` in IE, it looks like Figure 19.1.

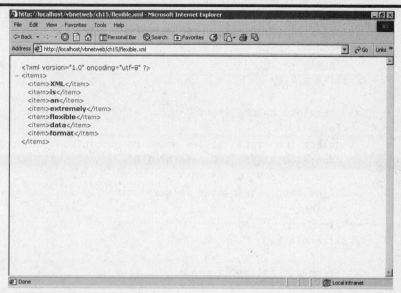

FIGURE 19.1:   The `flexible.xml` file in IE displayed with the default stylesheet

Note that the default stylesheet color-codes the various parts of the document and clearly shows the tree structure. It even lets you expand and collapse tags that contain child elements. That's nice, but fortunately, you're not limited to using the default stylesheet. By including a tag that references an XSL or XSLT stylesheet, IE will perform the transform for you and display the results.

For example, the following stylesheet displays the items in an HTML ListBox control (see Listing 19.4).

Listing 19.4: The *flexible.xsl* File Creates an HTML ListBox Containing the Items from the *flexible.xml* File (*flexible.xsl*).

```
<?xml version='1.0'?>
<xsl:stylesheet version="1.0"
    xmlns:xsl="http://www.w3.org/1999/XSL/Transform">
<xsl:output method="html" />

<xsl:template match="/">
    <html>
    <head>
```

```
      <title>Simple XSLT Stylesheet</title>
      </head>
      <body>
         <xsl:apply-templates select="items"/>
      </body>
      </html>
   </xsl:template>

   <xsl:template match="items">
      <form>
      <select id="list1" style="position:absolute;
         top: 100; left: 100; width: 150;
         height: 300" size="20">
         <xsl:apply-templates select="item" />
      </select>
      </form>
   </xsl:template>

   <xsl:template match="item">
      <option>
         <xsl:value-of select="." />
      </option>
   </xsl:template>
</xsl:stylesheet>
```

Performing Client-Side Transforms Using IE5x Client-side (in-browser) XSLT transforms work only with IE5 and higher; at this writing, no other browser supports transforms on the client side. In addition, you must have the msxml3.dll or msxml4.dll installed on the client computer. Finally, if you're using msxml3.dll, you must download and run the xmlinst.exe file for IE to recognize the XSLT namespace.

Uncomment the following highlighted line in the flexible.xml file.

```
<?xml version="1.0" ?>
<?xml-stylesheet type="text/xsl" href="flexible.xsl" ?>
<items>
   <item>XML </item>
   <item>is </item>
   <item>an </item>
   <item>extremely </item>
```

```
<item>flexible </item>
<item>data </item>
<item>format </item>
</items>
```

When you load the file `flexible.xml` into IE, it recognizes the file type and parses the document. The processing instruction you just uncommented instructs the browser to load the stylesheet `flexible.xsl`, perform the transform, and display the results of the transform rather than the XML document itself.

If you're not familiar with XSLT, this book won't help you much, but I will briefly walk you through the `flexible.xsl` stylesheet.

```
<?xml version='1.0'?>
<xsl:stylesheet version="1.0"
    xmlns:xsl="http://www.w3.org/1999/XSL/Transform">
```

You can see from the first line that XSLT is an XML vocabulary, not a separate language. You can manipulate XSLT files by loading them into an XmlDocument just as you can any other XML file.

The second line of code references the XSLT *namespace* schema URI (Universal Resource Identifier). A URI is different from a URL in that it only needs to be unique. It doesn't need to reference a real file (although it can); it only needs to be a unique identifier. For example, if you enter the XSLT namespace into a browser, you'll see a text message that states, "This is the XSLT namespace." But you won't see the XSLT namespace schema itself, because it isn't there. Instead, IE has an internal reference to the schema—you created that reference when you installed the `msxml3.dll` and ran the `xmlinst.exe` file.

The next line determines the type of output from the transform. Valid values are `html`, `xml`, and `text`. The default output type is `xml`.

```
<xsl:output method="html" />
```

The remainder of the file consists of three *templates*. A template is a block of code that handles a specific tag or group of tags. The `match` attribute in the template definition determines which tags a particular template will handle. For example, the first template matches the root node of the XML document. XSLT works from the concept of a context node. Until you select a node, there is no context. In this stylesheet, the root template creates `<html>`, `<head>`, `<title>`, and

`<body>` tags, and then tells the stylesheet to select the `<items>` node and apply a template to it.

```
<xsl:template match="/">
    <html>
    <head>
    <title>Simple XSLT Stylesheet</title>
    </head>
    <body>
        <xsl:apply-templates select="items"/>
    </body>
    </html>
</xsl:template>
```

The stylesheet searches for a template that matches the name `items` (see the next code fragment). When the stylesheet begins processing the `items` template, the `<items>` node becomes the context node, not the root node. Select queries within the `items` template work from the `<items>` node by default; in other words, changing templates is one way to change the context.

The template outputs a `<form>` tag and a `<select>` tag, and then it calls `xsl:apply-templates` again—this time selecting the `item` nodes first. Note that the `select="item"` attribute selects *all* the `<item>` elements, and the `xsl:apply-templates` method applies the matching `item` template once for each node in the list of `item` nodes.

```
<xsl:template match="items">
    <form>
    <select id="list1" style="position:absolute;
        top: 100; left: 100; width: 150;
        height: 300" size="20">
        <xsl:apply-templates select="item" />
    </select>
    </form>
</xsl:template>
```

The `item` template itself (see below) writes an `<option>` tag and outputs the value of the context node; in this case, an `<item>` element. The highlighted line in the template uses a shortcut notation to select the current node, `select=". "`. The value of a node is the text it contains.

Each <item> node in the flexible.xml file contains a single word and a space.

```
<xsl:template match="item">
   <option>
      <xsl:value-of select="." />
   </option>
</xsl:template>
</xsl:stylesheet>
```

The stylesheet "walks the tree" from the root node to the lowest-level node, applying a template at each level. Figure 19.2 shows the result.

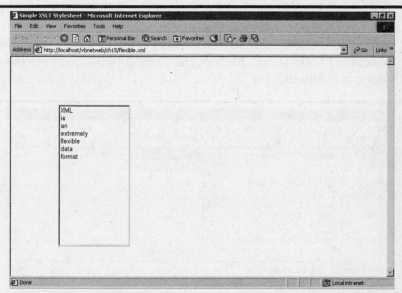

FIGURE 19.2:   Result from transforming flexible.xml using the XSLT stylesheet flexible.xsl

Interestingly, if you view the source in the browser, you'll see the XML document only. You won't see the HTML for the transform results, and you won't see the XSLT stylesheet code.

Performing Server-Side Transforms   As I mentioned at the start of the previous section, client-side automatic transforms are useful now only if all your clients use IE. Future browser versions will no doubt support more XML/XSLT operations, but right now, the only cross-browser solution is to perform the transform on the server and send the XHTML result to the browser.

NOTE

Before you continue, comment out or delete the line that defines the stylesheet reference in the `flexible.xml` file in the ch19 folder of your VBNetWeb project. Remember that XML comments are the same as HTML comments (`<!-- -->`). Save the changes, and then continue.

There are several ways to perform XSLT transforms in .NET, but the *easiest* way is to drag an XML Web Server control onto your Web Form's design surface. For example, create a new Web Form named `ch19-1.aspx` in the ch19 folder. Add an Xml Server control, and click the custom property button in the Properties dialog for the `DocumentSource` property. In the resulting dialog, select the ch19 folder in the `Projects` pane and then select the `flexible.xml` file from the Contents pane. You'll see the dialog in Figure 19.3.

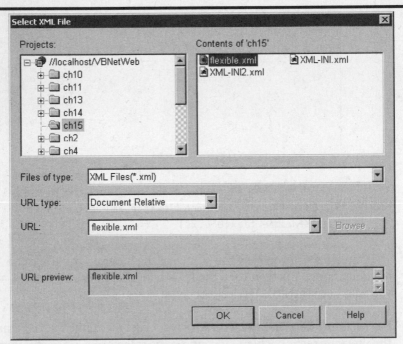

FIGURE 19.3:   The Select XML File property dialog

Accept the default settings, and click OK to close the dialog. Repeat the process to set the TransformSource property to the `flexible.xsl` file. Now run the Web Form. The result *looks* identical to performing the client-side transform, but it isn't. You can prove that to yourself by viewing the browser source. This time, rather than the XML file contents, you'll see the HTML resulting from the transform. In other words, the server performed the transform for you and automatically sent the result to the browser.

The Xml Web Server control is extremely convenient. But what if you need to process an XML document in some other way, such as extracting only some individual data items, saving all or a selected portion of a document to a database, or performing a transform and then modifying the results using VB? To do that, you need to learn a little more about how XML works in .NET, and about the classes available in the `System.Xml` namespace.

READING XML DOCUMENTS

As you've seen, the XmlDocument object provides a Read method that reads an XML document and initiates parsing, but underneath, the Read method creates an XmlReader object and uses that to read the document. Of course, underneath the XmlTextReader is a TextReader object. The XmlTextReader wraps the TextReader and implements rules for accessing the content that apply specifically to the process of reading XML. Beyond the physical process of reading the file, there are several different ways of approaching the parse problem.

DOM versus SAX

Up until .NET, there had been two primary ways to access data in an XML document. The XmlDocument object implements the node tree as I've already explained. Using an XmlDocument is very efficient when you need to update or extract data from a document multiple times and you don't know in advance *where* the data lies within the document. For example, suppose you have an XML document containing 50,000 usernames and passwords. You can load the document once and then check it repeatedly to search for matches to usernames and addresses. The big advantage of an XmlDocument is that, once loaded, it remains in memory; therefore, operations on loaded documents, especially XPath operations such as finding a matching node, are very efficient. The set of classes implemented to build an in-memory representation of an XML document is called the Document Object Model (DOM).

Unfortunately, the XmlDocument's greatest advantage is also its greatest liability. First, it takes much longer to parse an XML document into a DOM tree than it does to simply scroll through the file contents looking for a specific data item. So, when you only need to make a single pass through the file, looking for specific content, it's much faster *not* to use the DOM model. An alternative way of extracting data from XML documents, called the Simple API for XML (SAX), reads an XML document sequentially, raising events as it encounters the elements and attributes in the file. By handling only the events you need, you can find specific nodes or values very quickly. Second, as you can imagine, building a large DOM in memory takes significant memory. A rough rule of thumb is that building a DOM requires about three to five times the memory that the XML file requires on disk. In contrast, reading the document with SAX requires very little memory—just the SAX parser and the buffer space.

The SAX model is a push model—SAX always starts at the beginning of the document and reads forward, pushing out events to your application as it goes. In contrast, .NET introduces a third model for reading XML document content—the pull model, implemented by the XmlReader abstract classes and the various XmlNavigator objects. The difference lies in where you put the logic. A SAX parser doesn't know whether your application needs to respond to the content available during any individual event, so it makes the data available in string form for every event. In other words, when a SAX parser encounters an element, it reads the element, determines its type and raises an event, passing the string representation of the element as data to the event handler. Using an XmlReader, you can tell the parser in advance which elements you want to handle, and the reader can skip over all other types of content, making the XmlReader pull model much more efficient.

Using XmlReader Classes

Although the XmlReader class is an abstract class, the System.Xml namespace contains three fully implemented versions: the XmlTextReader, XmlNodeReader, and XmlValidatingReader classes. The XmlTextReader and XmlValidatingReader are similar, but the XmlValidatingReader supports document validation from a schema or DTD, whereas the XmlTextReader does not. Note that the XmlValidatingReader's validation capabilities also give it the ability to expand entities and read typed data, which can be a big advantage.

Part V

NOTE

The term *entities* as used in the preceding sentence isn't the same as the character entities already discussed. Using a DTD, you can define a substitute name for a larger block of XML data. It's the same idea as creating a named macro in a word processor that inserts a predefined block of text. Validating parsers must be able to read the DTD and *expand* or *resolve* entities whenever they find an entity name in the body of the document. The current specification for W3C XSD schema does not support entity definitions.

But don't fall into the habit of using the XmlValidatingReader just because it covers all the bases—it's not nearly as efficient as the XmlTextReader.

You use the XmlNodeReader class to iterate through the nodes of a document that's already been loaded and parsed with an XmlDocument or XslTransform object—either a complete document, the DOM itself, or just a portion of the document, called a *DOM subtree*, or *document fragment*. The XmlNodeReader has no validation capabilities, but it can expand entities. Because this reader works directly in memory only with well-formed and possibly prevalidated nodes, it doesn't have to handle IO or perform schema/DTD comparisons; therefore, it's extremely fast.

Using the XmlTextReader Class

As you might expect after having seen the set of Stream objects available for reading files, XmlTextReader can read from a file, a string, or an input stream. You provide the input type when you create an XmlTextReader instance, so it has several overloaded constructors. At the simplest level, you can pass the constructor a file name. After constructing the XmlTextReader object, you call the Read method repeatedly. The Read method reads the next sequential node. It returns True if the read is successful and False if it reaches the end of the data. Be careful. The XmlTextReader object isn't a validating parser—it doesn't ensure that a document conforms to a schema—but it does check for well-formedness. In other words, if the XML document violates the XML syntax rules, the reader raises an error. Therefore, you should treat XML documents like any other external resource, and trap for potential errors as you're reading them.

The Web Form ch19-2 shows how to read the flexible.xml file and gives you some examples of the type of information available from the XmlTextReader for each element it encounters. When the Web Form loads, it creates a new XmlTextReader object by passing it the physical path of the `flexible.xml` file, then it calls `Read` until it reaches the end, writing various available node properties and values to the browser in a table for each node the reader encountered. The properties and methods used in the Web Form `ch19-2` are as follows:

NodeType Property   An enumeration value specifying the *function* of the node in the document. By applying the `ToString` method, you can see a human-friendly version of the `NodeType` property.

IsName(name) Method   Returns True if the name is a valid XML name—meaning that it conforms to the XML naming specifications, not that the name necessarily even exists in the document. The method returns True only for named nodes. For example, Element nodes are named nodes, whereas White-Space nodes are not.

Name Property   The full string name of the node, including any namespace prefix. This is called the *qualified name*. For example, for the node `<xsl:apply-templates>`, the Name property would return `xsl:apply-templates`.

LocalName Property   When a node has a namespace prefix, such as `<xsl:apply-templates>`, the local name is the portion of the name after the prefix (`apply-templates`). If the node does not have a namespace prefix, the `LocalName` property returns the same value as the `Name` property.

HasAttributes Property   Returns True if the node has attributes; otherwise, it returns False.

AttributeCount Property   The number of attribute nodes in the current node. If the node has no attributes, the property returns 0.

MoveToAttribute (Overloaded)   You can supply a string name, a local name and a `namespaceURI`, or an Integer value (an index into the list of nodes). The XmlReader reads the specified node. Attribute nodes have a `Name` and a `Value`.

ReadString   Reads the text content of the current node. The text content consists of the text, all white space, and the contents of any child CDATA section nodes concatenated together, with no delimiting characters or white space between the values.

Listing 19.5 shows the code to read the XML file and return the properties for node type, name, attributes, and value.

Listing 19.5: The Web Form *ch19-2.aspx* Uses an XmlTextReader to Read the *flexible.xml* File (*ch19-2.aspx.vb*).

```vb
Imports System.Xml

Private Sub Page_Load(ByVal sender As System.Object, _
ByVal e As System.EventArgs) Handles MyBase.Load

' create a new XmlTextReader
Dim xr As New XmlTextReader(Server.MapPath(".") & _
 "\flexible.xml")
Dim i As Integer
Response.Write("Reading file: " & xr.BaseURI & "<br>")

' create a table
Response.Write("<table border=""1"" align=""center"">")
Response.Write("<tr>")

' set up the table headers
Response.Write("<th>NodeType String</th>" & _
  "<th>NodeType</th>" & _
  "<th>isName</th><th>Element</th><th>Name</th>" & _
  "<th>LocalName</th><th>HasAttributes</th>" *& _
  "<th>Attributes</th>" & _
  "<th>Text</td>")
Response.Write("</tr>")

' loop through the XML file
Do While xr.Read()
 Response.Write("<tr>")

 Response.Write("<td>" & xr.NodeType.ToString & "</td>")
 Response.Write("<td>" & xr.NodeType & " </td>")
 Response.Write("<td>" & xr.IsName(xr.Name).ToString & _
   " </td>")
 If xr.IsName(xr.Name) Then
```

```
            Response.Write("<td>" & Server.HtmlEncode("<" & _
               xr.Name & ">") & "</td>")
        Else
            Response.Write("<td> </td>")
        End If
        Response.Write("<td>" & xr.Name & " </td>")
        Response.Write("<td>" & xr.LocalName & " </td>")
        Response.Write("<td>" & xr.HasAttributes().ToString & _
           " </td>")

        ' Loop through the attribute list, if any
        Response.Write("<td>")
        If xr.HasAttributes Then
            For i = 0 To xr.AttributeCount - 1
                xr.MoveToAttribute(i)
                Response.Write(xr.Name & "=" & xr.Value)
                If i < xr.AttributeCount - 1 Then
                    Response.Write(", ")
                End If
            Next
        Else
            Response.Write(xr.AttributeCount.ToString)
        End If
        Response.Write("</td>")
         ' Write the node value
        If xr.NodeType = XmlNodeType.Text Then
            Response.Write("<td>" & _
               Server.HtmlEncode(xr.ReadString()) & _
               "</td>")
        Else
            Response.Write("<td> </td>")
        End If
    Loop
    Response.Write("</table>")
End Sub
```

Figure 19.4 shows how the Web Form ch19-2.aspx looks in the browser.

The XmlReader contains several other useful properties and methods not shown in the example Web Form ch19-2.aspx. I'm not going to list all the properties and methods, because they're available in the

Class Explorer, but I've listed the most important ones in the following section.

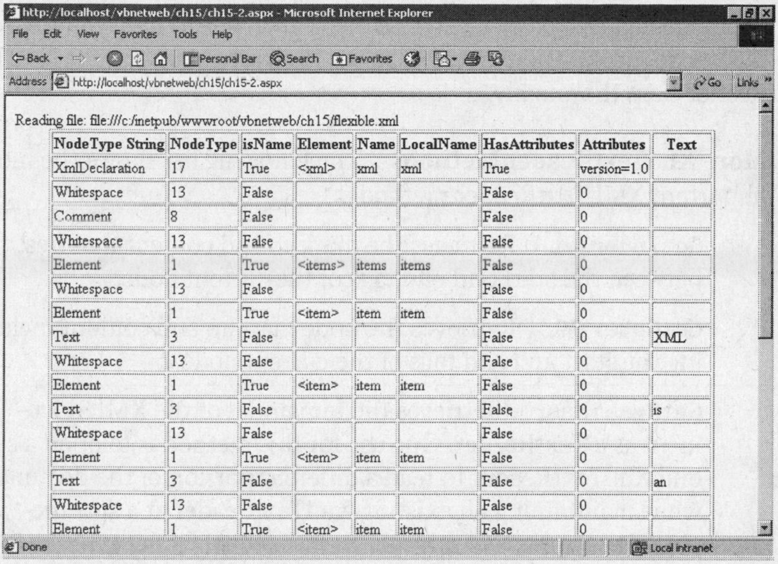

NodeType String	NodeType	isName	Element	Name	LocalName	HasAttributes	Attributes	Text
XmlDeclaration	17	True	<xml>	xml	xml	True	version=1.0	
Whitespace	13	False				False	0	
Comment	8	False				False	0	
Whitespace	13	False				False	0	
Element	1	True	<items>	items	items	False	0	
Whitespace	13	False				False	0	
Element	1	True	<item>	item	item	False	0	
Text	3	False				False	0	XML
Whitespace	13	False				False	0	
Element	1	True	<item>	item	item	False	0	
Text	3	False				False	0	is
Whitespace	13	False				False	0	
Element	1	True	<item>	item	item	False	0	
Text	3	False				False	0	an
Whitespace	13	False				False	0	
Element	1	True	<item>	item	item	False	0	

FIGURE 19.4: The Web Form `ch19-2.aspx` uses an XmlTextReader to display node values from the `flexible.xml` file.

More XmlTextReader Properties The following list shows the most important XMLTextReader properties.

`Depth` Retrieves the count of ancestor nodes for the current node. Among other things, you can use this property to create indented or "pretty-print" XML output. The property returns 0 for the root node of a document.

`LineNumber` Retrieves the line number of the line containing the current node. This property is only useful if the document lines have intrinsic meaning—for example, if the document is stored in human-readable form.

`LinePosition` Retrieves the character position of the current node in the current line. Unlike the `LineNumber` property, this property value is useful even when a document is not stored in human-readable form.

NameTable   Retrieves the NameTable object used by the reader (see the section "Using the *XmlNameTable*" for more information).

There are more properties than I've shown here. I urge you to use the MSDN documentation and the Object Browser to explore the XmlText-Reader class thoroughly.

More XmlTextReader Methods   The following list shows the most important XMLTextReader methods.

GetInnerXML   Retrieves the markup and content that lies between the start and end tags of the current node.

GetOuterXML   Retrieves the node markup and content including the start and end tags of the current node.

GetRemainder   Retrieves the remainder of the XML document as a TextReader. One use for this method is to open a second XmlTextReader to read a different portion of the document while maintaining an existing XmlTextReader at a specific position.

IsStartElement   Returns True if the current node is the start tag of an element.

MoveToNextAttribute, MoveToPreviousAttribute   Causes the reader to read the attribute after or preceding the current attribute.

MoveToLastAttribute   Causes the reader to skip to the last attribute for the current node.

MoveToElement   When reading attributes, you can move the reader *back* to the parent element. You would use this if you needed to ensure that an attribute or attribute value exists in the document before dealing with the element's contents. For example, if you had the following element structure, you could test the value of the `level` attribute and output only names of the employees at level g5.

```
<employee id="em2930" level="g3">Bob Whitehead</employee>
<employee id="em0830" level="g5">Amanda Criss</employee>
```

MoveToContent   Moves the reader to the next node that contains text content. You can use this to skip over nodes that contain only markup.

Skip   Skips the current element. By skipping elements, you can reduce the processing time for documents that contain content you don't need.

There are more methods than I've shown here. I urge you to use the MSDN documentation and the Object Browser to explore the XmlTextReader class thoroughly.

Using the XmlNameTable

The XmlNameTable class is an *abstract* class. The table stores string names in a format that provides fast lookups. The implementation of the XmlNameTable class for the XmlTextReader is called NameTable, without the Xml prefix.

As the reader progresses through the document, it can check the set of names in its NameTable against the current node name. Strings are immutable in .NET; therefore, this scheme is advantageous because as the reader progresses through the document, it doesn't have to perform string comparisons for names it already has in the table; instead, it can simply compare the two strings to see if they reference the same object. The .NET documentation states that because of the difference between string comparison and reference comparison, using an XmlNameTable is faster.

You can retrieve the NameTable object from a reader and add names to it programmatically to improve the speed of node name comparisons, or you can create a new XmlNameTable object, add names to it, and then apply that XmlNameTable object to the XmlTextReader.

For example, suppose you wanted to find a single tag in a reasonably long document. By adding the tag name to the reader's NameTable, you can improve the comparison speed. I tested the theory using a loop. To eliminate the side effects that occur when you load a file from disk, the following example creates an XML string in memory using a String-Builder, then provides that string to the overloaded XmlTextReader constructor. The overloaded constructor can take a Stream object instead of a file URL, which you can provide by opening a StringReader object on the generated XML string. For example,

```
' open an XmlTextReader on a string (sXML) containing some XML
' using a StringReader to provide the Stream argument.
xtr = New XmlTextReader(New StringReader(sXML))
```

Here's how you add names to the NameTable:

```
' create a new NameTable
Dim itemXObj as Object
xnt = New NameTable()
itemXObj = xnt.Add("itemX")
```

The XML string the example constructs is a list of 1,000 <item> tags, each of which contains a different value. The last tag in the list is named <itemX>. The code searches for that tag. The generated XML file looks like this:

```
<?xml version="1.0"?>
<items>
    <item>Item1</item>
    <item>Item2</item>
    <item>Item3</item>
    ...
    <item>Item999</item>
    <itemX>Item1000</itemX>
</items>
```

The example code creates the document and then loops through it 1,000 times, hunting for the <itemX> tag. When it finds the tag, it increments a counter, providing that the loop finds a match.

Using this test, there's about a 5 percent improvement for the version that uses the XmlNameTable. As each loop searches through 1,000,000 tags, you can see that for most web application XML documents, the improvement is unlikely to be noticeable.

```
Imports System.Xml
Imports System.IO
Imports System.Text
' auto-generated code omitted
Private Sub Page_Load(ByVal sender As System.Object, _
ByVal e As System.EventArgs) Handles MyBase.Load
  Dim xtr As XmlTextReader
  Dim sXML As String
  Dim xnt As NameTable
  Dim i As Integer
```

```
Dim counter As Integer
Dim itemObj As Object
Dim itemXObj As Object
Dim startTick As Integer
Dim endTick As Integer
Dim sb As New StringBuilder(50000)
Dim tickDuration1 As Integer
Dim tickDuration2 As Integer
sb.Append("<?xml version=""1.0""?>")
sb.Append("<items>")
For i = 1 To 1000
    If i = 1000 Then
        sb.Append("<itemX>")
        sb.Append("Item" & i.ToString)
        sb.Append("</itemX>")
    Else
        sb.Append("<item>")
        sb.Append("Item" & i.ToString)
        sb.Append("</item>")
         End If
Next
sb.Append("</items>")
sXML - sb.ToString


' output the method used and the current time
startTick = System.Environment.TickCount
Response.Write("Starting reader without NameTable" & _
    "lookup at: " & _
    System.DateTime.Now.Second & ":" & _
    System.DateTime.Now.Millisecond & "<br>")
' parse the string in a loop
counter = 0
For i = 1 To 1000
    xtr = New XmlTextReader(New StringReader(sXML))
```

```
            Do While xtr.Read
                If xtr.NodeType = XmlNodeType.Element _
                    AndAlso xtr.Name = "itemX" Then
                    counter += 1
                End If
            Loop
        Next
        endTick = System.Environment.TickCount
        ' output the method used and the current time
        Response.Write("Ending reader without NameTable " & _
         "lookup at: " & _
         System.DateTime.Now.Second & ":" & _
         System.DateTime.Now.Millisecond & "<br>" & "Found " & _
         counter.ToString & " instances." & "<br>")
        tickDuration1 = endTick - startTick
        Response.Write("Duration in milliseconds = " & _
            tickDuration1.ToString)
        Response.Write("<br>")
        ' Now repeat, using a NameTable
        Response.Write("Starting reader with NameTable " & _
            "lookup at: " & _
            System.DateTime.Now.Second & ":" & _
            System.DateTime.Now.Millisecond & "<br>")
        ' parse the string in a loop
        startTick = System.Environment.TickCount
        counter = 0

        ' create a new NameTable
        xnt = New NameTable()
        itemXObj = xnt.Add("itemX")
        itemObj = xnt.Add("item")
        For i = 1 To 1000
            xtr = New XmlTextReader(New StringReader(sXML), xnt)
```

```
                Do While xtr.Read
                   If xtr.NodeType = XmlNodeType.Element _
                      AndAlso xtr.Name Is itemXObj Then
                      counter += 1
                   End If
                Loop
             Next
             endTick = System.Environment.TickCount
             ' output the method used and the current time
             Response.Write("Ending reader with NameTable " & _
                "lookup at: " & _
                System.DateTime.Now.Second & ":" & _
                System.DateTime.Now.Millisecond & "<br>" & "Found " & _
                counter.ToString & " instances." & "<br>")
             tickDuration2 = endTick - startTick
             Response.Write("Duration in milliseconds = " & _
                tickDuration2.ToString & "<br>")
             Response.Write("<br>")
             Response.Write("The NameTable version is " & _
                (((tickDuration1 - _
                tickDuration2) / tickDuration1)).ToString("p") & _
                " faster than the " & _
                "non-NameTable version.")
          End Sub
```

Based on this test, I would recommend using the NameTable only where speed is critical. You should, of course, perform your own tests on your own documents.

If you ran the ch19-3.aspx Web Form, you can see by the timings that the XmlTextReader is extremely fast. When you need to read a document one time to extract values quickly, use an XmlTextReader. But that's not the only way to find nodes and values in a document. You saw a little about how to use XSLT and XPath in stylesheets, but you can also use XPath queries in code.

Querying XML Documents for Data

Three classes in the System.Xml namespace let you use XPath to query their contents: XmlDocument, XmlDataDocument, and XPathDocument. I'll discuss the XmlDataDocument in more detail in the upcoming section "Using the *XmlDataDocument* Class," but the only real difference between an XmlDataDocument and the other two DOM document types is that the source data for an XmlDataDocument comes from a DataSet rather than a file. However, regardless of the data source, after parsing the XML data into a DOM tree, the *concepts* for retrieving data from an XmlDataDocument are the same as the ones shown in the following section, although the methods differ slightly.

Using the SelectSingleNode and SelectNodes Methods

At the simplest level, all you need to do to retrieve a data item from an XML document is create an XmlDocument object, call its Load method, and then use the SelectSingleNode or SelectNodes method with the appropriate XPath query to retrieve the data. For example, the following code fragment writes the word *extremely* in the browser, as that word is the text content of the fourth <item> node from the flexible.xml file.

```
Dim xml As New XmlDocument()
xml.Load(Server.MapPath(".") & "\flexible.xml")
Response.Write( _
    xml.SelectSingleNode("/items/item[4]").InnerText)
```

Similarly, you can use the SelectNodes method to select multiple nodes from a loaded XmlDocument object. For example,

```
Dim xml As New XmlDocument()
Dim N As XmlNode
xml.Load(Server.MapPath(".") & "\flexible.xml")
For Each N In xml.SelectNodes("/items/item")
    Response.Write(N.InnerText)
Next
```

The preceding code fragment writes "XML is an extremely flexible data format" to the browser.

Using the XPathDocument and XPathNavigator Classes

When you're loading a document just to make a few queries, it doesn't matter which XmlDocument type you use, but when you need to query a document repeatedly, it's more efficient to load it into an XPathDocument object than to load and scroll through the document for each query.

The XPathDocument object maximizes the efficiency of XPath queries. Rather than using the SelectNodes and SelectSingleNode methods, you use an object called an XPathNavigator to perform XPath requests. For example,

```
Dim xml As New XPathDocument(Server.MapPath(".") & _
    "\flexible.xml")
Dim xpn As XPathNavigator = xml.CreateNavigator
Dim xpni As XPathNodeIterator
xpni = xpn.Select("/items/item")
Do While xpni.CurrentPosition < xpni.Count
    xpni.MoveNext()
    Response.Write(xpni.Current.Name & "=" & _
        xpni.Current.Value & "<Br>")
Loop
```

The preceding code fragment writes the following output:

```
item=XML
item=is
item=an
item=extremely
item=flexible
item=data
item=format
```

You should explore XPath in detail to make full use of these objects. Unfortunately, a thorough discussion of XPath is beyond the scope of this book, but you'll see more examples later on in this book.

USING THE XMLDATADOCUMENT CLASS

So far, you've worked exclusively with XML documents stored on disk or created as strings. But the XmlDataDocument class represents a third type of top-level DOM document. The main difference between an XmlDataDocument object and the XmlDocument or XPathDocument objects is that you populate the XmlDataDocument object via a DataSet. For example, the Web Form ch19-4.aspx uses a DataSet containing the Students table. I dragged a SqlConnection and a SqlDataAdapter from the Toolbox onto the form design surface and configured the SqlDataAdapter1 object with a SQL query to return all the fields from the Students table. When you right-click the SqlDataAdapter1 on that Web Form, you see the option to Generate Dataset. When you do that, you'll see the Generate Dataset dialog (see Figure 19.5).

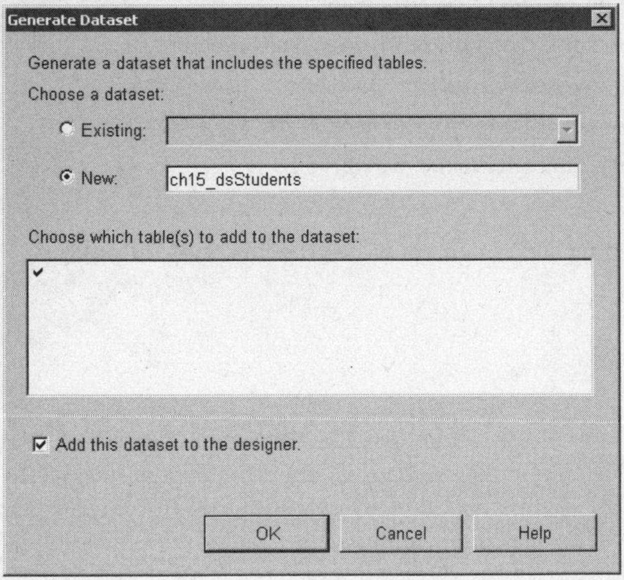

FIGURE 19.5: The Generate Dataset dialog

Click the New radio button and enter the name **ch19_dsClassRecords _Students**. Check the option titled Add This Dataset To The Designer. When you click OK, the designer generates a schema for the DataSet and a class and adds both to the current folder in the Solution Explorer. Double-click the Ch19_dsClassRecords_Students.xsd item in the Solution Explorer to open the schema in the designer. You'll see the schema in Listing 19.6.

Listing 19.6: Generated XSD Schema for the ClassRecords Students Table

```
<xsd:schema id="Ch19_dsClassRecords_Students"
targetNamespace=
 "http://www.tempuri.org/Ch19_dsClassRecords_Students.xsd"
 xmlns="http://www.tempuri.org/Ch19_dsClassRecords_Stud.xsd"
 xmlns:xsd="http://www.w3.org/2001/XMLSchema"
 xmlns:msdata="urn:schemas-microsoft-com:xml-msdata"
 attributeFormDefault="qualified"
 elementFormDefault="qualified">
 <xsd:element name="Ch19_dsClassRecords_Students"
   msdata:IsDataSet="true">
  <xsd:complexType>
    <xsd:choice maxOccurs="unbounded">
      <xsd:element name="Students">
       <xsd:complexType>
         <xsd:sequence>
          <xsd:element name="StudentID" _
            msdata:ReadOnly="true"
             msdata:AutoIncrement="true" type="xsd:int" />
          <xsd:element name="Grade" _
            type="xsd:unsignedByte" />
          <xsd:element name="LastName" type="xsd:string" />
          <xsd:element name="FirstName" type="xsd:string" />
         </xsd:sequence>
       </xsd:complexType>
      </xsd:element>
    </xsd:choice>
  </xsd:complexType>
  <xsd:unique name="Constraint1" msdata:PrimaryKey="true">
   <xsd:selector xpath=".//Students" />
   <xsd:field xpath="StudentID" />
  </xsd:unique>
 </xsd:element>
</xsd:schema>
```

The schema shows you how the XML representation of the data will look. For example, the root element will be `<Students>`; each field becomes an element in a sequence that follows the order of the fields in the SQL query for the SqlDataAdapter. Notice that the StudentID element has an attribute with the name and value `msdata:Auto Increment="true"`, meaning that the schema understands that the `StudentID` field is marked as an Identity field in SQL Server. Also, look at the constraint definition toward the end of the schema. The schema also captures the fact that the `StudentID` is a primary key as well as the XPath query to select the `<Students>` and the name of the primary key field.

WARNING

XML is case sensitive, so be careful with your SQL and XPath query names.

The generated class is interesting as well, and I urge you to look at it, although due to its size, I won't show it here. You should *not* alter the generated code manually, because the system will overwrite the code if you later regenerate or alter the DataSet.

You can now use the Fill method to fill the `ch19_dsClassRecords _Students` DataSet and print the result to the browser so you can see the XML. For example, the Form_Load method in the `ch19-4.aspx` Web Form displays the DataSet's XML document contents using very little hand-generated code. One of the reasons it uses so little code is that the `Fill` method opens and closes the associated Connection object automatically, so you don't have to do it yourself. However, as you've seen, if you write the code, you have control over what can be seen when page tracing is enabled, whereas when you rely on the designers, you don't.

```
Private Sub Page_Load(ByVal sender As System.Object, _
    ByVal e As System.EventArgs) Handles MyBase.Load
    Dim ds As DataSet = Me.Ch19_dsClassRecords_Students1
    Me.SqlDataAdapter1.Fill(ds)
    Response.Write(Server.HtmlEncode(ds.GetXml))
```

```
        Me.SqlDataAdapter1.Dispose()
    End Sub
```

You can see from the result that the DataSet does indeed contain the data from the Students table in XML form, but the results aren't very satisfying. Fortunately, the GetXml method's return value already contains line breaks and indentation. If you place the results of the DataSet.GetXml call between <pre></pre> tags, you'll get a better format. Here's another version with better output (see Figure 19.6).

```
    Private Sub Page_Load(ByVal sender As System.Object, _
        ByVal e As System.EventArgs) Handles MyBase.Load
        Dim ds As DataSet = Me.Ch19_dsClassRecords_Students1
        Me.SqlDataAdapter1.Fill(ds)
        Response.Write("<pre>" & Server.HtmlEncode(ds.GetXml) & _
            "</pre>")
        Me.SqlDataAdapter1.Dispose()
    End Sub
```

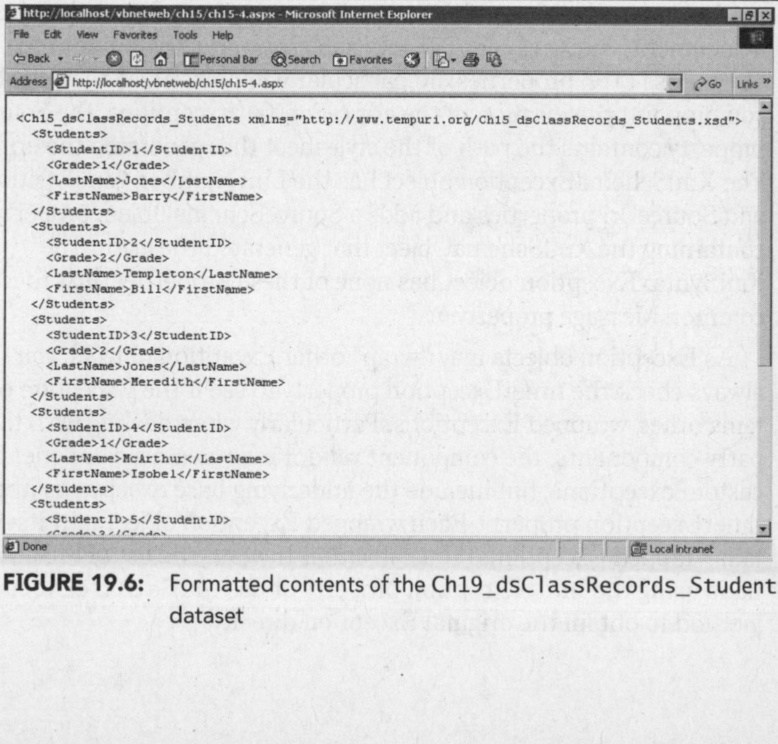

FIGURE 19.6: Formatted contents of the Ch19_dsClassRecords_Students1 dataset

THE XMLEXCEPTION CLASSES

One of the biggest flaws of the msxml.dll parser was that it allowed programmers to load an XML document without raising a COM error. Instead, the Load method returned a Boolean value that programmers all too often ignored. The System.Xml classes don't suffer from that particular malady. When you attempt to load a malformed document, compile or perform an XSLT transform, or validate against a schema, you will throw one of the following exceptions:

- ► XmlException
- ► XmlSyntaxException
- ► XmlSchemaException
- ► XsltException
- ► XsltCompileException

There's nothing particularly special about any of these exceptions compared to other Exception objects, but they do provide detailed information about the cause of the error. When an error occurs while loading a document, the XmlException.LineNumber and XmlException .LinePosition properties are particularly important, as they can help you pinpoint the location of the error. For XsltExceptions, the SourceUri property contains the path of the stylesheet that generated the error. The XmlSchemaException object has the LineNumber, LinePosition, and SourceUri properties and adds a SourceSchemaObject property containing the XmlSchemaObject that generated the error. The XmlSyntaxException object has none of these properties, just the common Message property.

As Exception objects may "wrap" other Exception objects, you should always check the InnerException property to see if the Exception contains other, wrapped Exceptions. Particularly when dealing with third-party components, the component vendor may create a component with custom exceptions, but include the underlying base exceptions in the InnerException property. Each wrapped Exception object may itself contain wrapped Exceptions. You can either traverse the list of linked exceptions using the InnerException property or use the GetBaseException method to obtain the original Exception directly.

PERFORMING XSLT TRANSFORMS PROGRAMMATICALLY

Early in this chapter, I promised to show you how to perform server-side transforms programmatically after you learned more about the System.Xml namespace. At this point, you should have at least a tenuous grasp on the various types of DOM objects, how to read XML data, how to find nodes, and how to extract XML from a database. You've also seen how to use the Xml Web Server control to perform a transform. Now it's time to use some of the objects you've seen to perform one yourself.

Here's the basic procedure:

1. Load the XML into an XmlDocument, XPathDocument, or XpathNavigator.

2. Load the stylesheet into an XslTransform instance.

3. Call the XslTransform.Transform method.

The Transform method is overloaded. It can do the following:

▶ Send the result of the transform to a TextWriter, Stream, or XmlWriter that you supply as a parameter.

▶ Write the result of the transform to a file.

▶ Return an XmlTextReader object that you can use to process the result.

TIP

The .NET documentation states that you should use an XPathDocument object when possible, as it is optimized for XSLT transformations.

The Web Form ch19-5.aspx contains an example (see Listing 19.7).

Listing 19.7: Programmatic XSLT Transform

```
Imports System.Xml
Imports System.Xml.XPath
Imports System.text
Imports System.io
' autogenerated code omitted
```

```
Private Sub Page_Load(ByVal sender As System.Object, _
ByVal e As System.EventArgs) Handles MyBase.Load
Dim xml As XPathDocument
Dim xslt As Xsl.XslTransform
Dim xmlResult As XPathDocument
Dim rd As XmlReader
Try
    xml = New XPathDocument(Server.MapPath(".") & _
            "\people.xml")
    xslt = New Xsl.XslTransform()
    xslt.Load(Server.MapPath(".") & "\people.xsl")
    xslt.Transform(xml, Nothing, Response.OutputStream)
Catch exxslt As Xsl.XsltException
    Response.Write("XsltException: " & exxslt.Message)
Catch exxml As XmlException
    Response.Write("XmlException: " & exxml.Message)
Catch ex As Exception
    Response.Write(ex.GetType.Name & ": " & ex.Message)
End Try
Response.End()
End Sub
```

MOVING TO APPLICATIONS

You've completed Part V of this book. You've seen the basic tools to build dynamic web pages using XML. In Part VI, you'll apply the knowledge you've gained in the context of building applications. The technologies you've seen—HTML, the System.Web classes, Web Forms and Web Controls, XML, and SQL Server—are sufficient to build websites. Putting these together as applications requires a different mindset—pages that work together. From planning, all the way through development and delivery, an application is different from a set of HTML files or a set of unrelated Web Forms. Applications should have a consistent look and feel, store data and metadata, abstract data into classes, and be both scalable and efficient. They should respond to user requests quickly, and protect data integrity.

If you're not yet comfortable with the ideas in the first five sections, I urge you to go back and extend the examples. There's no way that a book this size can cover all the properties and methods of even the few namespaces I've shown here; therefore, you'll need to explore those on your own.

WHAT'S NEXT

In this chapter, you've seen the rudiments of how to create, modify, search, and transform XML documents using the System.Xml classes. Because XML is so important right now, not just to .NET and web applications, but to computing in general, if you haven't worked with XML before, you should practice creating XML documents and schema, creating DataSets, searching documents using XPath, and writing XSLT transforms until you're comfortable with the basic operations.

This chapter ends the section on using XML with Visual Basic .NET. In the next section, you will put some wheels on what you have learned in this book by learning how to create real-world applications.

In the next chapter, you will learn how to plan an n-tier application using Visual Basic .NET. You will work through a project from the original vision through creating the various tiers (data, business rules, and presentation). This exercise will be largely academic, as you are learning to plan an application rather than working directly with code.

The knowledge gained from the next chapter will be expanded throughout the next section, as you learn to build different tiers and finally build an online store application.

Part VI
BUILDING REAL-WORLD
APPLICATIONS

Chapter 20

PLANNING APPLICATIONS

T he tasks of application developers run the gamut from extremely specific to extremely general. Some programmers work in shops where they're given detailed specifications for individual program functions; their job is to build functions or modules to those specifications. Others are given a general description of a task and are expected to plan and document the code they write to meet the description. Still others are given a general description of an entire application; they must design, write, and test the application, either by themselves, in which case they have final control over every facet of the application, or as part of a team, where the entire team makes decisions about the application. Finally, because they're close to the process, developers often imagine applications that could simplify or streamline a business process (often a tedious part of their own jobs). In this case, the task is to sell that application idea, taking it from conception to fruition; documenting the

Adapted from *Mastering ASP.NET with VB.NET* by A. Russell Jones
ISBN 0-7821-2875-0 $49.99

business need for the application; performing a cost/benefit analysis; creating and selling the vision, the way users would interact with the application, and the database; coding; testing; and finally, performing deployment, delivery, and maintenance.

No single situation applies to everyone. In some cases, an individual might perform all the tasks; in other cases many different individuals or teams may cooperate to perform the tasks. The point of this chapter is, don't skip steps. Even if you think that the task doesn't apply to the application you're developing, it does, to some degree—although it may not be *your* job to handle that task, someone should at least consider the relationship of the application to each of the tasks in this chapter.

IMAGINE SOMETHING

All applications begin with imagination. Somewhere, someone thinks, "Wouldn't it be great if we had an application that could do [something]." That something may be impossible, too expensive, trivial, unnecessary, impractical—or it may be the next killer app. That doesn't matter. All that matters is that the person or group imagining the application feels strongly enough about the idea to take it in hand, think about it realistically, and mold it into a finished, *presentable* idea. Ideas are legion; presentable ideas are rare. An idea is a thought that produces a reaction in the individual who has it, whereas a presentable idea is a thought communicable to others in such a way that it produces a similar reaction in them. Therefore, the first requirement for an application is the creation of a presentable idea—and that means you must consider the application from the aspects presented in the remainder of this chapter.

DETERMINE THE AUDIENCE

All applications have an intended audience, but when you initially conceive of an application, you're often unclear exactly who the audience is. For example, suppose you imagine the perfect search engine, one that not only finds relevant information, but also contains links to every piece of related information across the entire Internet. By paying a small fee, users could improve their search experience. But wait—who's the audience? Is there an audience for a pay-per-search service when there are so many free search services already available? It turns out that people *are* willing to pay for search services, but only when those services are extremely targeted.

While that may be an extreme example, you can apply the same thought process to almost any program. For example, suppose your company's salespeople fill out orders by hand when they're on the road and then enter them into a mainframe application when they return to the office. The data-entry process is error-prone, not only because the salespeople don't type very well, but also because they're removed from the customer when they actually fill out the order. You think it would be more efficient if the salespeople filled out the order interactively, when they're actually speaking with the customer. That way, when questions arise, they could ask the customer right away, rather than having to call or e-mail the customer later, when the transaction isn't fresh, and also avoid the inevitable delays caused by this. But who's the audience? Who benefits from the salespeople being able to fill out the orders immediately? The business and the customer may benefit from the reduced turnaround time between order placement and order fulfillment. The data processing department may benefit by not having to maintain as many mainframe terminals. However, giving the salespeople laptops may not benefit the IT department, because they would have to load and maintain many more computers. Finally, the program may not benefit the salespeople themselves, because they don't *want* to fill out the order in front of the customer—they want to talk, to increase the sale amount, to build a relationship so they can return and be reasonably assured of future sales. They may tell you that calling customers back with questions provides additional sales opportunities that they wouldn't have if they filled out the order immediately.

As you can see, it's not immediately obvious who the audience is in this example. It may turn out that the reduced error rate and faster sales turnaround *increases* sales and overcomes the salespeople's initial reluctance to use the program. It may turn out that the salespeople are more than willing to accept the solution once they see that filling out the order, rather than being an onerous handwritten process, has become an automated point-and-click operation that they can perform not only at the point-of-sale, but with equal ease back in the office after the sale, just as they do now.

Finally, you should recognize that this example is a rare application that affects only the direct audience. Most applications affect several groups—sometimes they end up affecting people or groups who initially had no direct interest in the application itself. For example, the hypothetical sales application obviously affects the salespeople, but it may also affect the central data operations group, because they must now acquire data in some way other than through the mainframe terminals. It may affect managers, who can use the data to track dates and times of sales appointments more closely. As you determine the audience, try to keep in mind the direct beneficiaries, but also try to anticipate how the application will affect the organization as a whole.

DETERMINE THE APPLICATION REQUIREMENTS

It's very difficult for people to describe how a computer program works. In fact, for computer programs with interfaces, as soon as the program grows beyond a few screens, it's usually very difficult for people to describe exactly what the program should look like and what it should do. That's partly because different people have different visions, partly because it's relatively rare for a single individual to know *all* the ins and outs of the business, and partly because people react to existing programs much more readily and accurately than they do to the *idea* of a program in the planning stages.

Choose a Design Methodology

Despite the numerous names for application design methodologies, there are only two basic approaches to application design: top-down and bottom-up. A top-down approach concentrates on the planning stage, ensuring the existence of a detailed plan for each portion of the application before coding begins, whereas a bottom-up approach begins coding sooner, but spends more time making changes during the debugging and testing phases.

There is no one "right" way. I prefer to mix the two, spending considerable time and effort planning the database operations, noninteractive data, and business rule components of the application. That's because it's relatively easy to determine in advance which tables and fields you'll need, how to get the data in and out, and how to massage the data to fit the business rules. In addition, these types of components are relatively easy to test, because they have well-defined inputs and outputs. Finally, if you can't get these components right, there's no point in working on the interface, because the program will never work correctly.

In contrast, for the interactive portion of the application—the user interface—I prefer to build and test it iteratively. Facets of application development that matter very little in back-end processing are critical in user interface design. For example, in a well-planned back-end system, it doesn't matter much whether you have a few hundred or a few thousand rows in a table; for most applications the difference isn't sufficient to change the program design. However, the difference between *displaying* a few hundred and a few thousand rows is significant; users don't need, don't want to scroll through, and often can't use all the data at one time.

Use Terminology Appropriately

Different users and groups prefer and understand different terminology. For example, programmers quickly become comfortable with using abbreviated field names, such as CU_ORD or ORDNUM, but end users would rather see Customer Order and Order Number. Programmers are comfortable with reading technical explanations of what a field does, but a help file containing information suitable for programmers may not be suitable for end users.

Test Often

The people who use a program may see the process very differently from the people who build it. Sometimes, especially for large programs, that's because each end user group may use a different part of the program and may not be interested in the other parts. Other times, it's because the people using the program may not use, or be able to use, all the data fields at one time. In some cases, end user comments will necessitate back-end program changes even late in the program creation cycle. You should plan to test interfaces often with a minimum of five representative end users. You should do this very early in the program cycle, so you can capture as much of the program's data requirements as possible and also iteratively as you build the user interface. People's ideas often change as they become familiar with the capabilities of a program. They almost invariably think of additional features that could be added or ways that a program should interface with other applications or systems that they're using. The more exposure you can give the target audience before the program design is complete, and the more realistic that exposure is, the more likely you are to build a successful program. For example, I've seen numerous examples of programs that violated almost every rule of good interface design but were extremely successful programs, because the people who used them had a large influence over how they looked and acted, and they chose that particular interface because it suited their business processes.

Consider All Facets of the Application

A program doesn't start and end with the program designer. I've seen numerous programs, designed and coded by a single individual, that had extreme "quirks." The programs work in their original configuration, but the designer forgot to consider several ancillary—and critical—parts of the application cycle. The most commonly missed parts are as follows:

Security   People create an application and then try to tack the security requirements on at the end of the application development cycle.

Versioning   If you think you may need to deliver multiple versions of your program (and even if you don't), think about versioning. For example, your application may acquire data from flat files. If you should ever need to change the file format, you'll want to ensure that you can differentiate between the original file format and any changed file format. Add versioning support to tables, resources, the application itself, and to any components that the application requires. Writing the version support code in the *first* release of the application will save you considerable time when you want to create the next version. For example, when you're reading a file, create a separate component to import and parse the file. To change file versions, you only need to update that component, not the entire application.

Installation   Installation programs are often forgotten until the end of the development cycle and are often the source of huge problems during the deployment phase. Several powerful installation-building programs are available; take advantage of them. Unlike a custom installation, these programs help ensure that users can uninstall the program as well, which is often just as important as installing it properly. You should develop the installation program as soon as you begin testing the application. Don't fix test installations manually by copying files and registering components; instead, add any missing components and files to the installation program and reinstall.

Deployment   Despite knowing that the application must be deployed to possibly widely differing machine configurations, developers often pay attention to deployment only when the application is ready to be deployed, often leading to problems and sometimes a reworking of the application. During the testing phase, insist that the application be deployed to a significant fragment of the intended audience so that you can uncover problems before the official rollout. There may be several different deployment tracks. For example, the desktop support group might initially install a Windows application that consumes Web Services. Subsequent installations might be delivered on a CD or DVD, via an install from a network share, delivered via an application management system such as MS SMS, or via the intranet or VPN.

Training   Even simple programs require training, but new applications are often dumped on the target audience without any training whatsoever. Begin planning the training requirements early in the development cycle, in tandem with the user interface. If the program is complicated enough to require training, you will also want to prepare overheads, handouts, and printed manuals.

Help   Help can be as simple as pop-up windows when a user hovers over a field, or it can be more complex and include online help files, paper manuals, quick reference guides, online audio and video, or offline support materials. In large organizations, you should alert the desktop support group well in advance of the program rollout, train them if necessary, and help them set up support procedures for the application. At the very least, such support procedures should include a list of possible problems and workarounds, including any unfixed problems that you uncover during testing. Find or create a procedure for the support group to follow to track or log ongoing or repeated problems so that they can be fixed for the next application release. Make sure the support group can contact the people responsible for maintaining the program. For mission-critical applications, you'll need to designate people from the maintenance group. For round-the-clock critical applications, at least one person from the support group must be available 24/7.

Maintenance   I'm using the term "maintenance" to mean everything related to keeping the application running in its current form. For example, data backups, solving problems related to network hardware or configuration changes, adding additional servers to scale the application, optimization, and solving problems experienced by end users are all part of application maintenance.

Ongoing development   Few programs are "finished" when first deployed. Sometimes, people suggest changes that everyone agrees would be useful, but they're too big or too difficult to fit into the initial budget or schedule. For most programs, you should plan for ongoing development to incorporate the best or the most critical suggestions. Don't react to every suggestion by updating the current application version; instead, save the suggestions, prioritize them, and add features to subsequent versions. If you get this far, you'll appreciate the versioning features you built into the first version of the application.

Troubleshooting   As used in this context, troubleshooting means the process of figuring out why an application isn't working *after* it's been debugged and deployed, even though it isn't causing an error. You'll find that this process is much easier if you build in a switch that lets you turn logging on and off for the application. This process goes hand-in-hand with error trapping and error logging, but isn't exactly the same. You should *always* log application errors, but you don't want to log every application action, except when you're trying to troubleshoot the application. However, you *do* want to be able to log application actions so you can pinpoint the source of problems while the application is running. With server-based ASP.NET applications, tracing can handle most of your needs, but not all of them. Consider adding a switch that logs each application action, with checks after each action to confirm the action took place. I recommend you add this switch as an administrative and maintenance-level option only. You should be able to turn logging on and off for an individual user or for the application as a whole.

CREATE AND SELL A VISION

All the planning in the world won't help you create a program unless you have a clear vision of how that program will help people accomplish a task more easily, increase their power, save them time, or give them new capabilities. Further, unless you're a one-person operation, you probably need to get other people to share your vision. So, at the beginning of the application creation cycle, you need to be a salesperson as well as an inventor. It doesn't matter how good your application is if you can't get other people to agree. Whether you're creating the next killer app or a manufacturing workflow application, you'll need to convince others that your idea is viable. The goal is to create a vision that others can share; if they can share your vision, they can help you make the application a reality. Without a shared vision, you'll be hard-pressed to co-opt others into working with you effectively.

You'll find that as you determine the audience and application requirements, you'll also build a vision of the application that you can communicate to the various people involved. Not everyone needs exactly the same vision, and not everyone wants or needs to know about the application in its entirety. You'll probably want to articulate the vision differently to different individuals depending on their interests. For example, describing to a senior manager how the network architecture of your application will reduce resource contention doesn't constitute a shared vision, but the same language may greatly interest a network administrator. Discussions of database relationships with a database administrator may win you friends, but the same vision, when shared with a salesperson or data-entry clerk, may only tag you as a consummate bore.

In some cases, you may be competing with other application vendors; these may be in-house vendors, commercial vendors, or consultants. Your job during this stage is to make sure you have a clear idea of how to describe the application—not a screen-by-screen slideshow, an object diagram, or a flowchart, but a way to make sure that the people who can approve and fund the project understand the intent of the program and how it will help the company, the audience, and in some cases, the bottom line. You need a reasonable estimate of what the program will cost or, at minimum, how long it will take and what human resources it will require. But just as a good salesperson doesn't list the price of every possible feature, you should try not to get dragged into a financial or resources discussion at this time. Also, try to stay away from any implementation details. At this stage, it's not important exactly how the program will work, what technology you're planning to use, or whether the application will require one server or many. Instead, try to maintain focus on the *purpose* of the application and to build excitement, enthusiasm, or at least a reasonable level of support.

While you should aim to avoid detailed discussions of program implementation at this stage, you must *personally* have a clear idea of how the application will work, so that if you do find yourself drawn into a discussion of hardware or technology requirements, you'll be able to provide reasonably specific answers. Most applications require buy-in from one or more people or groups; you have to convince them that your idea is the best, or that you're the best person to build the application— one or the other, preferably both.

With each group, you should share the portion of your application's vision that will gain a champion for the application. Champions are people in each area who can influence others. Focus on the people who *can* help or authorize your application, then communicate your vision so they'll *want* to help. They'll only want to help if it solves a problem. Perhaps the application saves money or time. Perhaps it simplifies a task through automation. Perhaps it does none of these things, but it provides integration with other applications they already have, or grafts an aesthetic face onto an existing unappealing application. The point is that each group has different interests, and it's your task to create a vision that appeals to each group.

PLAN THE USER INTERFACE

Although many application-planning methodologies start with the data and work forward from there, I usually start with the interface, because that's the public persona of your application. Also, at this stage, you can often uncover requirements that aren't part of the back-end program data. For example, a few minutes with paper and pencil drawing screens will let you see immediately that the order form you want to put online can't be directly transferred from the paper form; it will have to be broken into several parts. Also, you may discover that some data repeats on almost every screen. While people may be *used* to writing or typing the data for paper versions, there's no reason that they have to do the same in an online version. By saving a unique set of past entries, you can probably give them a drop-down list or a set of preferences or....
You probably get the picture.

Some applications have no interface requirements—in fact, parts of your VB .NET web applications, as you begin writing data-access components, business components, and Web Services, won't need an interface. However, those portions that do require an interface are the ones that people see. You need to groom and plan them artistically and aesthetically, because if people don't like the interface, they're unlikely to use the application.

You shouldn't try to plan every detail of the user interface at this point—you probably can't, because you're unlikely to *know* all the details yet—but you should be able to gain a good sense of how you want the end users to interact with the program. If you're not intimately familiar with the end-user audience, you should take the time to find out *now* what they do and don't like about a current program, or how they'd prefer to work with a new one. You don't have to translate every suggestion that end users make into a program requirement. Often, the process of getting a good picture of the user interface is a learning process on both sides; you learn what end users want and need, and they learn what's possible, what's expensive, and what they can reasonably expect given the time and budget constraints of the project.

Goals for User Interface Planning

The output from this stage should be a rough mental picture of how the screens that make up the application should look, a basic set of features, and a sense of how users reach those features, for example, via a button, a menu, a keystroke combination, or all three. You should understand the various paths a user might take through the application, and you need to envision what happens when a user quits the application, and how or if the application lets them go "backward." As you've seen, controlling the sequence is a critical part of web interface design. In addition, you need to have a good idea of security and how the various security levels (if any) affect the screens and features of the application. Try to keep these goals in mind as you design the user interface:

▶ Make the application time-sensitive. By that, I mean make the most common actions both easy to perform and as responsive as possible.

▶ Spend your efforts on the 30 percent of the application that people use every day.

Part VI

- ▶ Minimize difficult input. Gather the information you'll need for pick lists and consider ways to program intelligence into the application. A program that responds rapidly and consistently is much more pleasant to learn and use.

- ▶ Remember that many people don't like computers. Try to make the computer adjust to suit the humans. If people want to see spreadsheet-like applications and reports, provide them. If some people would rather fill out forms, provide an alternative interface.

- ▶ Have the application remember its state from one session to another. Little is more irritating to users than having to reset preferences because a program designer forgot to save them.

In short, before you begin writing code, you must refine your vision of the end product until it begins to take a clear shape. Write down what you decide upon or agree to. You don't have to make professional-quality screen-design documents; rough sketches will suffice, but try to capture the main features and get a sense of how a person will use the program, what tools they need, and how you'll build those into the final screens.

Building Prototypes

If you want to build a prototype to see how the application will work, this is a good time to do that, but don't let the prototype mutate into the first release of the application. Negotiate the time and budget to build a minimal prototype, show it off to management, and use it to demonstrate the application to the target audience if you like, but remember that it's a prototype and not production code. Plan to throw the entire program away before you continue. Prototypes can be dangerous, because they set expectations that you may not be able to meet. Showing a prototype is analogous to agreeing to an unwritten contract. You're stating that the application actually *will* look and act exactly like the prototype. After a prototype has been approved, it's that much more difficult to explain to management and the potential audience why changes are needed. Also, because the user interface is all that most people ever see of your application, if you show them a prototype, they immediately jump to the conclusion that the application's almost finished—even when the prototype consists of only the interface and doesn't deal with real data.

PLAN DATA STORAGE AND RETRIEVAL

Now that you know how the program looks and how you want it to act, you can design how the program should store and retrieve data. If you intend to use a database, plan the tables, relationships, and indexes. I typically do this twice, once to "play" with the data model, and then later to build a final database. For example, your application may get data in XML form, from a mainframe in a flat file, from user input as large text strings, or from uploaded binary files. You need to decide *how* you're going to handle the various data requirements, but not necessarily create the details. For example, it's overkill to begin writing every stored procedure at this point, but it's perfectly logical to create some tables and experiment with the relative efficiency of storing XML as complete documents (long text strings or blobs), separated into individual fields, translated into the appropriate datatypes or left as text, or some combination. For binary files, you must decide if you want to store the data itself in the database or store the data as files and have the database reference the file location.

If you're not using a database, you need to plan the file structures and folder hierarchy; select names and locations; and consider security, backup plans, and how you can avoid contention for resources.

If you get data from other sources, such as mainframe flat files, decide how you want to get the data into a form (such as XML) usable by your application. Decide when that should occur. For example, mainframes often send text files to a specific directory at intervals. You need a scheduled process to read those files and get them into a form appropriate for your application.

Plan to Archive or Delete Unwanted Data

Consider how you plan to eliminate or archive unwanted data. For example, if you're saving user preferences, or intermediate form data, what do you plan to do with preferences when a user quits or never returns to your application? How long should you maintain intermediate form data? If you never purge obsolete data, you'll most definitely want to take your application down at some point to archive unneeded records. Most (but not all) data has a reasonably useful lifetime, after which you can discard it without problems. Some types of data can't ever be discarded, but can

Part VI

be moved to a place where they don't hinder operations on current data but can be retrieved if needed. For example, people working with a medical records application need fast access to current patient data, in addition to recent patient data, such as last quarter's patients and next week's appointments, but they don't need immediate access to non-current patients or data from five years ago. However, you can't ever delete the information altogether. In contrast, if you have an application that provides online registration services for a conference, you might elect to keep incomplete registrations until the start of the conference, after which you can safely delete them, or you may decide not to store incomplete registrations at all.

Just as with the preceding user interface section, by the end of this stage, you should have a clear idea of each major data input, output, and transfer required by your application, but not necessarily the details, such as individual field names or filenames. Whatever you decide, write it all down.

Plan Object Responsibilities and Interfaces

VB .NET is an object-oriented language, so you should build an object model for your application. Because you've been working with the user interface and the data requirements, by this time you will have a fair idea of the *things* that your users and application must manipulate. You don't have to match these up exactly with either the user's expectations or the back-end data model. For example, despite the fact that a given application works with sales data from a mainframe and stores each order in a table row, it may or may not be useful to have an Order object—you might not care about individual orders because the application identifies sales trends. The goal is to discover—and that's the watchword here, *discover*—the discrete parts of the application and the data. Find the discrete parts, and differentiate between the *attributes* of those parts and the *variations* on the parts. That's often difficult and is the subject of much discussion and argument among even the best OOP application designers. For example, is it better to have a User object that has a PermissionLevel property, or to have an abstract User object and subclasses for the various permission levels, such as Administrator, Manager, and Employee? Only you can decide, and now is the time to do that, *before* you start writing code.

PLAN ADMINISTRATIVE FUNCTIONS

Even for programs with no built-in differentiation among various security levels, you need to plan administrative functionality. For example, suppose you want to be able to shut your application down for maintenance at odd intervals. Certainly, you can just shut down the server, but that may not be the best method. Instead, you might want to create a warning message that would begin displaying a warning—perhaps 24 hours in advance—that the site is unavailable. You might be able to leave one server running and redirect users to another site or to a message page that states why the application is unavailable and when it will become available again. To do this, you'll need a way to intercept all requests and redirect them to some new location—and unless you want to write custom code each time, you need a way for an application administrator to create the messages and specify times. In other words, you need an administrative interface into the application itself, one or more Web Forms that are not part of the normal user interface.

Similarly, you may want to build in ways to switch detailed logging or state message levels on or off, for debugging purposes. You may want a way to purge obsolete or expired data, to archive data, or to change values in static tables. If your application doesn't use integrated Windows security but requires users to log in, you'll definitely want a way to clear passwords and fix misspelled usernames. If you collect metadata, such as page counts, application usage times, or user paths through your site, you'll want to be able to analyze the data and create reports.

No general statement fits all applications, but I would venture to say that if you read this section and *don't* find ideas applicable to your situation, you should probably rethink your application. I cannot imagine a web application that couldn't benefit from some type of administrative interface. At the very least, you should be able to track application usage, because collecting metadata about an application is one of the best ways to discover whether the money required to create it was well spent.

CREATE THE DATABASE

Finally, you're ready to code something. Armed with the results of all the interface planning, data requirements, object modeling, and administrative planning, you should have enough requirements to build the database. At this stage, you *do* create the tables, relationships, indexes, triggers, stored procedures, and functions. You build the database before writing the program, because you can (and should) test it exhaustively without writing any interface code. Populate the tables with sample data. When you're done, make sure you can re-create the database in its entirety by saving the SQL DDL statements that create the database objects.

The database is the backbone of your application; therefore, it should be bulletproof. That means it should not accept information that doesn't meet requirements. It's easy to write code that tests for information validity, but you can't be sure everyone will write bulletproof code. While *you* would never allow an invalid value to slip through, you can be sure that eventually one will slip through someone else's code.

Databases on the Web must service all the application's users, and because of the stateless nature of the Web, they must provide more information more often than in a standard client-server situation. Because database operations are inherently machine- and network-intensive, it's your job to minimize the volume of data that must traverse the network for any given request. That means you must take advantage of SQL's ability to select only the required data. But that's only the beginning.

Plan Data Relationships Carefully

The relationships you build into your database during this stage will grow deep roots. For example, the way you plan to store something as simple as a phone number has major ramifications. Not all phone numbers are alike. Some phone numbers require area codes. Some have extensions. Foreign phone numbers are completely different from U.S. phone numbers. In addition, many people would prefer to dial numbers using their phone card PIN to transfer charges. Consider the total phone numbers a person may have. You might put the phone numbers in a Contacts table using fields like HomePhone, WorkPhone, FaxPhone, and CellPhone. But how many fields are sufficient? Those four may meet your application's needs today, but it's almost certain that someone will require more eventually. You can circumvent this problem by normalizing the database. Put the telephone numbers in a separate table with ContactID as a foreign key and use JOIN operations to retrieve the telephone numbers associated with an individual. Add a field such as TelephoneType to the telephone table. Index the ContactID field and the TelephoneType field, because you're most likely to use these fields to look up values. After a database enters production—and especially after other programs (other than this application) begin using the database—it becomes much more difficult, if not impossible, to change the database structure.

Plan a Data Programming Interface

Plan the interface to the database as carefully as you plan the names and arguments of your class methods and properties. You can control *access* to the database through security, but your primary methods for controlling *content* are through stored procedures, triggers, and views. You can (and often should) deny direct access to any database table. Instead, you provide SELECT access through views and stored procedures, and INSERT and UPDATE operations through stored procedures, defaults, and triggers. For example, if you have a CreatedOn field, you don't have to trust programmers to update the field. Write a default value or a trigger to insert the value. Create a rule or constraint that protects the field from invalid or out-of-range values. Don't expose the field for direct update. If other database values depend on the field, write a trigger to update them when the field value changes—don't rely on programming to do that for you. Maintain relationships between data values within the database automatically, if possible.

Consider Database Administration

Plan time for administrative pages. The rule of thumb is that you need to create at least four procedures for each top-level database table for administration purposes. These are as follows:

- ▶ A way for the administrator to select records to modify
- ▶ A way to add new records
- ▶ A form for editing existing records
- ▶ A script to delete records

If you have username and password fields in your database, the administrator will need to be able to clear passwords and modify usernames. You'll need a form where administrators can select an individual and a ClearPassword stored procedure. If any database processes must be run on a schedule, such as archiving or deleting obsolete records, you need to create a mechanism that will launch the processes. You also need a way to let the appropriate people know whether the process completed successfully.

Data Size Matters

Plan your data size requirements. Databases tend to grow over time. A SELECT query on an unindexed field may perform adequately when the database has a few hundred records. But when the database grows to hundreds of thousands of records, that same query will bog down the application. You need to plan for the future. Does the data expire or become obsolete? How will you remove obsolete data from the database? Manually? Automatically? What will you do with the records you remove? Discard them? Archive them?

The size of the data at any given time may also affect the application code. You should cringe whenever you see a query like SELECT * FROM <Tablename>. Unless you know the table contains a fixed number of rows, such queries are an invitation to disaster. The first few hundred rows won't matter, but when the code needs to display or winnow through thousands of records, it will make a huge difference in the responsiveness of your code.

How many servers will it take to service the total anticipated number of users? If it takes more than one, how will you split up or replicate the data? Test the queries using the database server's analysis tools. If the database doesn't have such tools built in, obtain them. Database design and analysis tools can help you find and anticipate problems. For example, the SQL Server Query Analyzer tool can show you the query plan for any query—the SQL, the indexes used, any other columns used in the query, the output, and the time required. When using the Query Analyzer, you should particularly look for table scans, because those indicate columns for which the database was unable to find an appropriate index to use for the query and therefore has to read the entire column.

CREATE DATA-ACCESS COMPONENTS

As part of the database testing, you create the components and objects you'll use to get data into and out of the database. The goal is to be able to SELECT, INSERT, UPDATE, and DELETE every table in the database. There are two major approaches. One approach is to write just a few stored procedures that perform those operations on entire rows. The other approach is to write many smaller stored procedures that return or update just the data you want. While I believe the second approach is better because you have pinpoint control and can write stored procedures with names appropriate to their individual functions, there's little difference in speed between the two approaches. While there is an efficiency gain using small specific procedures, especially for wide tables or for those that store long text or binary values, there's a corresponding increase in the amount of time you spend testing the procedures, and there's a larger penalty for changing the database because you have more procedures to update and retest. With larger row-oriented procedures, you retrieve and maintain extra data—either on the server or by maintaining the values through cookies, hidden form variables, or ViewState

To minimize the problem, you can create "business objects" that handle calling the queries. But don't make the mistake of combining the business object functionality and the pure database operations. You can often create just one data-access component that accepts a stored procedure name, an optional list of parameter values, and some optional transaction information. The component should either return data (SELECT) or perform an operation that alters data.

CREATE BUSINESS COMPONENTS

A business component contains the business rules for manipulating the data you retrieve from and insert into the database. You should build the business components as classes—usually a single class and often a collection class for each type of object in your application. Sometimes, the objects' properties mirror a database table, but often they don't. You want to isolate the business rules in a separate layer, or application tier, because the rules often change more often than either the user interface or the database itself. The usual example is a tax-calculating application. There are many rules for calculating taxes, and they change often; however, neither the interface for entering the data nor the data storage needs to change often.

Another example might be an application that arranges route patterns for salespeople. The route data—the customer lists and locations—resides in a database. Although the data changes constantly, the format of the data does not. On the other hand, the rules for calculating the routes change constantly, depending on pricing, product availability, the potential size of orders from different customers, and many other business factors.

The application must be able to adapt to the changing route rules. You do that by adding or changing the business components. For example, one rule might be that salespeople must visit each customer a minimum of once each month unless the customer has been inactive for three or more consecutive months. Another might be that customers with total orders exceeding $1,000,000 per year receive a discount of 15 percent on all orders over $10,000, whereas customers with total orders between $500,000 and $999,999 receive a 10 percent discount. Customers with yearly orders totaling less than $500,000 get discounts on a sliding scale, depending on the size of each individual order.

If (or rather, when) these rules change—perhaps the business focus changes to acquire new customers, so discounts to smaller customers increase—the business logic must also change. Therefore, the main purpose of a business component is to isolate business rules so you can replace the logic inside the component without disturbing any other parts of the application.

This isn't as simple as it sounds, although it is much simpler with VB .NET than it ever was with classic VB. The challenge is to design the components so you can change the logic *inside* the components without changing the external programmatic interface.

In classic VB, changing the interface also required you to recompile any parts of the application that used the component. To work around this, people often created "generic" methods that accepted Variant arrays. You no longer need to do this. You can use overloading to add new methods that accept additional parameters, or you can subclass existing components and add new methods to those. And replacing the component no longer breaks the application. The .NET runtime recognizes that the class has been changed, and it handles JIT recompilation of other parts of the application that use the updated class. Another common workaround was to create data access methods that could accept any ad-hoc SQL statement and a command type. Doing that "covers" for missing stored procedures. Unfortunately, unless people were very careful, such workarounds quickly led to errors and unmaintainable code.

Although .NET makes it much easier to update the components of an application, try to anticipate the kinds of changes that are likely to occur, and plan for them in advance. For example, you may have started the application with browser clients in mind, but maybe it's worthwhile to expose some of the data as Web Services, or to ensure that you can deliver in multiple languages or to other client types. Don't forget to build in security as you create the application—it's much harder to add it later.

Finally, test everything thoroughly. You should be able to perform all the data manipulation *without* building the user interface (not without *planning* the interface, though). I know it's tempting because it's very satisfying to put controls on the screen and work backward from the user interface—and you can often change the way you think about the application by doing that. Unfortunately, I've seen several projects fail because the people coding them began mixing up the business rules and data access with the user interface. Later, after the original development group left, the maintenance programmers, not understanding the ramifications of their actions, were unable to make even simple changes quickly without causing other problems. In addition, the development time went way up, because the programmers concentrated on the quirks and problems of the user interface rather than testing the back-end code, leading to cascading change lists and lots of bugs. If you're the kind of developer who *must* see and "feel" the user interface first, build a prototype project. When you're satisfied with that, throw away all the code and start over, following the steps listed here. The prototype project will uncover most of the big problems you'll face, so you won't lose much time by building it, as long as you recognize that almost all the code you write during the prototype phase is throwaway code.

BUILD THE USER INTERFACE

After you can manipulate the data and you have a well-defined interface to the business objects, putting the user interface together is often very straightforward. Even if you do find additional data requirements because of changes during the user interface development, they're often much easier to implement, because you can add items to a well-tested back-end model with fewer problems than if you were trying to make changes to both tiers simultaneously.

As you build the user interface, keep these points in mind:

- ▶ Try to keep the interface uncluttered.
- ▶ Use applications that you and the potential audience admire as models.
- ▶ Use controls appropriately.
- ▶ Make the application functional first, and then make it aesthetically pleasing as well.

- ▶ Use graphics effectively, as aids to help people locate and place information rather than as pure decoration.

- ▶ Use high-contrast color schemes.

- ▶ Avoid small font sizes.

- ▶ Try to minimize the interdependence of controls.

- ▶ Consider the state of the application at all times. Hide or disable controls that people shouldn't use during that state. For example, you've probably seen numerous forms on the Internet that have required fields—and also have an enabled Submit button before those fields contain data.

- ▶ For browser-based applications, use client-side script when possible to avoid server round-trips.

- ▶ Use directions liberally, and word them carefully.

- ▶ If you plan to internationalize your application, create database tables and resource files containing the text, and test the application in the languages you'll support. Different languages require differing amounts of space for equivalent meanings. Try to avoid embedding text within graphics; otherwise, you'll need to change the graphics whenever you change languages.

- ▶ Keep control placement consistent. If you have navigation controls that appear on most pages, consider putting them on every page and disabling the ones that aren't applicable.

- ▶ Try to avoid scrolling forms (it's OK to deliver content pages that scroll). Unless you have an extremely homogenous client base, you'll probably need to consider the client's screen resolution. If you have many downlevel clients, you may also need to consider the color depth, although that restriction has largely disappeared over the past few years, as most modern computers support "true" color.

Although you can't test a user interface in the same way that you can test back-end components, there are test suites that let you program in action patterns; if you have the resources, it's probably a good idea. If you can borrow members of the target audience, they will give you useful feedback. Try to plan for at least two tests with potential end users.

For other testing, consider dedicating one or more people to a quality assurance (QA) process. It's very difficult to test an event-driven interface exhaustively, but a good rule of thumb is that it takes five individuals to find 95 percent of the problems. Don't be complacent—test thoroughly and find and fix bugs during development.

WHAT'S NEXT

In this chapter, you've seen that web application development goes far beyond learning the ASP.NET framework and writing code. Sure, you can build an application and hope that it gets adopted solely because it's useful, but most successful applications require more planning than that. Not every application needs such elaborate planning, but by following the guidelines in this chapter, you can ensure that your applications won't be ignored—they'll be eagerly anticipated. More than that, management, the help desk, network and database administrators, and maintenance programmers will welcome and support them. Finally, and perhaps most important, the applications themselves will work better and last longer than if you just sit down and start coding.

As you're planning applications and thinking about efficiency and the user interface, consider how you might improve the interface and responsiveness of your web applications. Writing client-side code lets you minimize the number of server round-trips. In addition, by manipulating content dynamically with script using the Document Object Model (DOM) built into modern browsers, you can create smooth, easy-to-use interfaces. In the next chapter, you'll see how to take advantage of client-side script in your ASP.NET applications.

In the next chapter, you will examine important issues in deploying Visual Basic .NET applications. By the end of the chapter, you should have a decent idea of how to deploy your own .NET applications and be prepared for some of the issues that might hinder your deployment.

The next chapter takes a two-pronged approach to deployment. First, you will learn the strategies necessary for a successful deployment of a .NET application. This section deals with important questions to ask yourself about your deployment to ensure you include everything to make your software release a success. Second, you will learn about the deployment tools included in Visual Studio .NET that will help you deploy your application.

Chapter 21
VS .NET Deployment Considerations

Did anyone ever tell you that Buddhism is not a religion, but a way of life? Well, the same applies for .NET—it's not just a language or a platform, but a way of programming. You have to completely rethink how you do the most basic things in programming such as object model design, debugging, testing, and, yes, deployment. Which bring us to why we are here—how does deployment work under the .NET paradigm?

Clearly, deployment with VS .NET has made much progress since previous versions of Visual Studio. Many of these changes are tactical changes, such as improved file packaging, Registry management, and virtual root installations. However, more importantly, many strategic changes have emerged with the release of the .NET Framework. The distribution of Microsoft Web Services enables organizations and businesses to strategically reuse functionality and content from one another, without going through the pains of local installation. The strategy of

Adapted from *Mastering Visual Basic .NET Database Programming* by Evangelos Petroutsos and Asli Bilgin

ISBN 0-7821-2878-5 $49.99

leveraging the Internet as a distribution platform enables applications to mesh together organically. Both these technical and strategic advances should give you pause on how you design your deployment approach.

In this chapter, we take a two-pronged approach. In the first part of the chapter, you'll review the considerations that go into a well-thought-out .NET deployment strategy. You'll review the various angles from which you should examine your project in order to prepare for deployment. You'll learn to ask important questions: Will your components be shared with other applications? How will uninstallations and upgrades work?

In the second half of this chapter, we take a tactical approach. You will focus on the deployment tools available in with VS .NET. You'll examine the deployment options available with a web application, as well as a Windows application. This chapter is not intended to be a thorough exploration of every single deployment configuration setting; instead, it should give you a firm foundation from which to begin packaging your application. You will begin by exploring the importance of deployment design.

IMPORTANCE OF DEPLOYMENT DESIGN

Like any other process of the software development cycle, deployment should be designed before it is implemented. You can't just package up an application and install it on another machine, without understanding how you want your application to work now, and how you want it to scale in the future. You need to envision how it will work with existing applications and how reinstallation and upgrades will be done.

There are certain considerations that you should take into account during each of the phases of your project. All play a part in how your application is deployed. The traditional phases of the software development cycle are shown in Figure 21.1. As you step through each phase, you can ask yourself questions that pertain to how the application will be deployed.

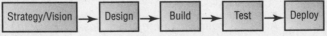

FIGURE 21.1:   Software development phases

In the Strategy/Vision phase, you discover and identify such things as business requirements and the features which belong in each release. This is a good time to identify scalability and integration issues. Will you need to connect to external systems? Do you plan for incremental versioning? If so, how will your upgrade policy work? All these considerations need to go into your deployment strategy.

During the Design phase, you create the system architecture. At this point, you incorporate the scope of your components into your design. Will there ever be a reason for your components and services to be shared in the future? If so, will there be a need to design your components as Web Services or as shared components? You'll need to identify which components should be grouped together in a single assembly or namespace. What is the physical architecture of the servers? Will you have a web farm with multiple servers? If so, you'll need to identify how you want to install your virtual root onto the web server. Most likely, you'll want to simply things by using a Windows Installer package, which you will learn how to build in this chapter.

During the Build phase, you begin the tactical implementation of your deployment strategy. You'll need to identify how often you want to do your builds and begin testing the deployment process onto your development environment.

The Test phase will further solidify deployment implementation. More than likely, you will have a Quality Assurance (QA) environment which mimics the production environment. Here you can address issues such as remote debugging, communication through firewalls, and system integration.

After you've been though all these phases of the software development life-cycle, you finally arrive at the Deployment stage. By this time, you should have fully designed, tested, and finalized your delivery strategy. This way, you can eliminate all foreseeable risks, so that you ensure a more successful and timely rollout. As you can see, proper deployment planning takes place in every stage of the software development process. Once you understand the importance of deployment design, you can create a deployment strategy that best meets the needs of your system.

DESIGNING YOUR DEPLOYMENT STRATEGY

Before a single file is deployed, you must first design how you want the deployment process to occur. For example, you must determine such things as which components you want to keep local to the application and which you want to share. You should examine whether you want your installation to be formalized with a package file, rather than simply using the lazy XCOPY distribution that's possible with .NET applications.

In this section, we will examine the different questions that you should consider before you prepare your deployment package.

What Type of Project Are You Deploying?

VB .NET has advanced the concept of deployment by treating deployment packages as projects in their own right. Before you actually deploy your system, you must first determine which of these projects is applicable to your needs. You can find them by selecting File ≻ New ≻ Project from the VS .NET menu and selecting the Setup and Deployment Projects folder, as shown in Figure 21.2.

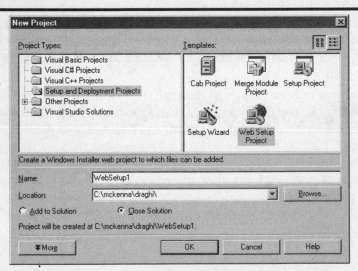

FIGURE 21.2:   Setup and Deployment Projects folder

Table 21.1 briefly outlines the different deployment packages. Later, in the implementation section, we'll review the specifics of where and when to implement each type of deployment package.

TABLE 21.1:   Deployment Projects

DEPLOYMENT PROJECT TYPE	DESCRIPTION
Cab Project	Creates a cabinet file (best for when your user base is using old browser versions).
Merge Module Project	Packages shared components as subsets of a single application.
Setup Project	Windows-based application—installs files to the Program Files directory on a local computer.
Web Setup Project	Builds an installer for a web application—installs files onto a virtual root on a web server.

Part VI

There is one last type of deployment project. The Setup Wizard is not really a project, but an overarching guide to help you determine the appropriate deployment project options to meet your needs. It can direct you through the setup options of the four project templates mentioned in the table. We aren't going to focus on this wizard in this chapter. When you learn about the four deployment projects, you'll be able to work with the wizard, which really just helps you identify which project best meets your needs. It's fairly intuitive, and you should have no trouble using it.

What Is the Scope of Your Application Components?

One of the main benefits of the .NET platform is the ability to isolate components between applications, thus preventing the pains of DLL Hell. This way, you can guarantee that your application runs with the appropriate version of your component. This enables side-by-side execution of multiple versions of the same component. Granted, this means that there might be redundancy with the components on any given system; however, the opportunity cost of disk space seems trivial compared with the debugging and maintenance costs of ensuring version compatibility between shared components.

However, this isn't to say that shared components have no place in the .NET Framework. It just means that you have to make an explicit decision to implement component sharing. Component sharing is not the default behavior with the .NET platform.

Component sharing works differently than it did with previous versions of VB. Rather than cataloging shared components in the Windows Registry, they maintain their self-describing nature. The difference is in the deployment. Local components are stored within the application directory. Shared components are deployed to the global assembly store, which is generally found in the C:\WINNT\Assembly directory.

Before you begin coding your application, you should first determine the scope of your components. That way, you can ascertain where they will be deployed and mitigate any risks caused by sharing components.

What Are Your Dependencies?

More often than not, your system will rely on external utilities or systems to provide additional functionality or content. This makes sense because you don't want to reinvent the wheel when you can leverage an existing technology. However, you should consider how you will manage your dependencies to external systems. For example, what will you do when new versions of external assemblies emerge? What if they are not compatible with the version that you use?

Fortunately, the .NET Framework helps alleviate the management of dependencies by ensuring that your application will always work with the right version of any dependent component. When you package your files, the dependencies are also packaged along with it and stored into the local application directory. Should your user upgrade that assembly within their system directory, your application will remain unscathed.

This doesn't mean that you can forget about dependencies altogether. The .NET Framework opens up the doors to tighter integration between systems, especially with Web Services. You'll need to build exception-trapping code to handle any incompatibility issues in case an external system does not upgrade gracefully. Additionally, you should take care to ensure that your own shared components abide by proper versioning and compatibility standards, so that external systems can continue to leverage your systems.

Where Should You Deploy the Files?

Where to deploy files? This seems like a silly consideration. Of course, you are going to deploy the files onto the machine that they are going to be used. Obviously, ASP.NET files are distributed on the web server, and SQL stored procedures are loaded onto the database server. This is logical enough; however, there is a deeper level of granularity that you should consider when determining the physical distribution of your files.

Keeping all your files within a single directory is a good practice to follow when deploying your application. That way, uninstallation is quick and painless, requiring only the deletion of the parent directory. Within the parent directory, you can choose to distribute your ASP.NET files and your VB .NET files into two subdirectories.

The best way to make sure your files are distributed properly lies with the packaging. A good practice is to split your application into multiple-package files that match the number of logical servers that are hosting your application. For example, if you have four servers, two web servers and two application servers, then logically you have two different server roles. In this scenario, you would have two package files: one containing the assembly components for your middle tier, the other containing the ASP.NET files.

Part VI

How Will You Distribute Your Files?

All you really have to decide is how you plan on distributing your files. You have several options for this: FTP, cabinet files, Windows Installer package, or a third-party packaging software.

Sometimes, to save time, you may choose to copy your ASP.NET and web files onto the web server using Windows Explorer. This may suit your needs for a one-time demo, but what if you are preparing for a production installation onto multiple web servers? In this case, it might make sense to use a Windows Installer package to deploy your files, as well as configure installation settings. In this chapter, you will explore the options you have with VS .NET. This information will help you gauge which delivery mechanism is best for you.

XCOPY DEPLOYMENT

You may have heard the term *XCOPY deployment*. This is a term that symbolizes the nirvana of deployment scenarios where nothing beyond simply copying the files needs to be done. No registration, no fuss, no mess. No coupling between the file and the Registry—the end of DLL Hell. You get closer to this nirvana with the .NET platform, where some of the simpler applications can be deployed by simply copying a file directory. However, it may not be that easy for more advanced applications that have external dependencies or shared components.

.NET certainly doesn't solve all your deployment woes; in fact, some argue the reliance on the Common Language Runtime (CLR) prevents an ideal deployment scenario. However, the .NET Framework makes XCOPY deployment more feasible by eliminating the centralized cataloging of components in the Windows Registry, as well as advocating self-describing components.

Deploying a .NET Framework application is very simple. Once you determine your method of distribution, all that remains is copying the files into the appropriate application directory.

There are many ways to copy your application files to the destination directory. You can copy the directory contents using Windows Explorer, browsing to the appropriate machines. You can copy the files directly from the source directory to the target directory using FTP. You can zip up all the files, using a compression utility, and unzip them onto the target server. Or you can use the DOS command XCOPY, from which the term XCOPY deployment originates. You can leverage the XCOPY syntax to copy entire directory trees:

```
XCOPY source_directory destination_directory
```

What type of files can you copy? HTML, XML, local assemblies (DLLs and EXEs), and ASP.NET files can all be directly copied into the file system. All of these file types can be copied using any of the techniques mention above. In fact, VS .NET provides you with native copying functionality within its IDE. For example, you can deploy the project right from Visual Studio .NET. To do so, select the Project ➤ Copy Project option from the VS .NET menu. Alternatively, you can use the Windows Explorer to Copy/Paste the files from the source directory to the web server.

IMPLEMENTING DEPLOYMENT SETTINGS

Once you've determined your deployment design, it's time to turn to how you are going to implement your application's installation package. Deployment in VS .NET is very powerful and flexible. By the end of this chapter, you may even call it easy and painless. Painless was not the word to describe deployment in previous versions of Visual Studio. More often than not, you had to revert to manually installing the application, especially for server-side components. When you are a deploying onto a COM+ server, manually copying and registering files and manually setting up packages and connections is a lot faster than building a custom installer to distribute your application. The Package and Deployment Wizard, which comes with VB6, was always an option, but oftentimes, you would still need to do some manual tweaking. VS .NET has tried to simplify this installation packaging by providing some deployment project templates, which may absolve you from some of the custom scripting you had to do with previous versions of Visual Studio.

Working with the VS .NET Deployment Project Templates

As you remember from Figure 21.2, a deployment project template can be created by choosing File ➤ New ➤ Project from the VS .NET menu and selecting the Setup and Deployment Projects folder. Alternatively, you can add a deployment project to an existing solution, by selecting File ➤ Add Project ➤ New Project.

In Table 21.1, we briefly outlined the different deployment templates that are available with VS .NET. Now you are going to see when and where they should be used.

Using a Cab Project Template

The Cab Project template is the most straightforward deployment choice. It simply compresses your application files into a single file with a .cab extension. If you have built web applications in the past, you should know that the .cab files can then consequently be downloaded via a web browser for installation on the client machine.

Most often, you use this deployment option for intranet sites where the network administrators permit you to download local application files and when you are dealing with an environment that supports only legacy browsers.

Using a Merge Module Project Template

The Merge Module project is a very interesting deployment template, introducing a new technology to the way you deliver applications. It enables you to easily distribute shared components. This promotes the reuse of your component-specific installation scripts. That way, other systems synchronize their delivery mechanism for a shared component.

The Merge Module project hinges upon the creation of *merge module,* which logically packages a component and its related files. This logical grouping creates a stand-alone module, which can be reused from other deployment projects.

Merge Module projects enable you to share setup code between applications. You can think of them as templates for deployment projects. A Merge Module is a single file with an `.msm` extension. Merge Modules are used with the Windows Installer in conjunction with an `.msi` file. The best time to use Merge Modules is when you want to package a shared component. This way, multiple installation programs can share the Merge Module, allowing each application to be consistent with the way it deploys the same shared component. We aren't going to get into much detail with Merge Modules in this chapter, but feel free to explore this topic in more detail by reading the VS .NET documentation.

Using a Setup Project Template

The Setup Project template works much like the Packaging and Deployment Wizard in VS6, and it creates a setup package. It leverages the Windows Installer as its delivery mechanism. You should use this option when you want to deploy a standard Windows forms-based application onto a client machine. Generally, when you create a Windows application project type, you would use this deployment template to package your application. The default installation for this type of project is to install it into the Program Files directory. You will be exploring this project later in this chapter.

Using a Web Setup Project Template

The Web Setup Project template is designed to be the obvious choice for installing VS .NET web applications. You should choose this template when you want to install a web application into a virtual root on a web server. This deployment option is most appropriate when you are working with a web application that contains files such as ASP.NET, XML, and HTML files. Like the Setup Project template, the Web Setup Project templates leverages the Windows Installer as its delivery mechanism.

In the next section, you will experiment with the various tools and editors available when working with a deployment project. Additionally, you'll learn more about the Web Setup Project template.

VS .NET Deployment Tools Walkthrough

In this section, you will explore the various options available to you within deployment projects. You will review the tools by using both a Windows and a web application. This way, you can familiarize yourself with the various tools and options that you have with a deployment project.

Deploying a Windows Application

Begin by creating a Windows application project, and then add a Setup project to it. Keep the default project names, WindowsApplication1 and Setup1, respectively. After this, your Solution Explorer should look similar to Figure 21.3.

NOTE
To keep things simple, instead of using one of the applications we built earlier in this book, we are going to use a new Windows application.

Part VI

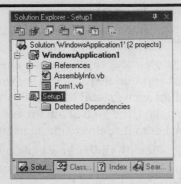

FIGURE 21.3: Adding a deployment project to an existing solution

There are many deployment tools and utilities that come with a deployment project. Right-click on the Setup1 project, and select the View option from the shortcut menu. You will see a list of all the available deployment editors, as shown in Figure 21.4. Alternatively, you can launch these editors from the View ➤ Editor menu in VS .NET.

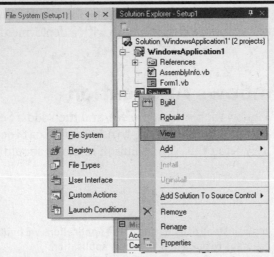

FIGURE 21.4: Deployment editors

The File System Editor enables you to work with a virtual representation of the file directory on the target machine. The Registry Editor enables you to work with a virtual representation of the Windows Registry on the target machine. The File Types Editor enables you to associate different file extensions with specific actions. The User

Interface gives you the ability to tweak the installation dialog boxes that present the steps in the Installation Wizard. The Custom Actions Editor is for advanced installs, and it enables you to specify the execution of scripts, actions, or programs upon various installation events (such as Install or Uninstall). The Launch Conditions Editor enables you to specify criteria that must be met before your application can be successfully deployed onto the target machine. For example, you can use this editor to define searches for certain files or Registry keys on the target machine.

In this section, you will take a closer look at many of these tools. This chapter focuses on more common deployment practices, so we won't be reviewing the Custom Actions Editor or the Launch Conditions Editor; however, you can find more information about these tools in the help documentation that ships with VS .NET. Now, let's go back to the Setup1 project that you have just created, and review how the Windows Installer packages your application.

Windows Installer

The Setup1 project represents the .msi file that will be generated once your deployment project is compiled. What kind of file is an .msi file? A file with an .msi extension is a Windows Installer file. It contains the necessary files and instructions for deploying files onto a target machine.

The Windows Installer is a service that is part of Windows 2000 and ships with some software packages, such as Office 2000. The Windows Installer is not a traditional packaging program that enables you to install your system files. Instead, it serves more as a tracking system. It works with the operating system as a centralized repository for application information, such as file locations, Registry keys, and dependencies. It's capable of detecting if a dependency or file is missing, automatically repairing the installation on the fly, or ensuring that a system file is not overwritten with an older version.

You can use the Windows Installer to build your application deployment package. All you need to do is create a Windows Installer Package file, which has an .msi extension. Inside this file, you specify the instructions for your application installation. When you distribute this file, all the user needs to do is double-click the .msi file to install the application.

The installation instructions for an application should be split into three different logical subsets: features, components, and products. This enables the installer to group functional subsets to provide customizable granularity in the install.

Products consist of one or many features and components. One or many components can make up a feature. Components are the most granular level of the installation. Within each of these hierarchies, you can select what you want to install. For example, you can elect to install only certain components within a feature. You've probably seen this yourself when installing products. When you install Excel, you can select specific features, as shown in Figure 21.5.

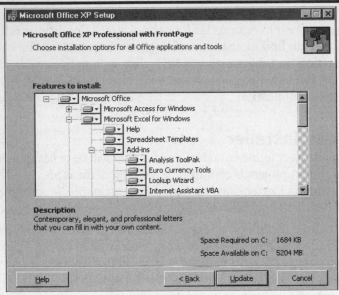

FIGURE 21.5:   Installing features

Within the Microsoft Excel for Windows product, you can choose the Help component. This is the lowest level of granularity and consists of one or many files that must be installed together to install the Help component. The Add-ins feature contains many components, such as the Euro Currency Tools, which you can select for your custom installation.

You have this option with VB6, using the Visual Studio Installer, which was released as an add-on for Visual Studio 6. What about .NET applications? VS .NET heavily leverages the Windows Installer, which is different than the VS Installer, for almost all its deployment packages. As we mentioned earlier, the Windows Installer enables you to build packages to distribute application files.

WARNING

Keep in mind that the VS .NET Windows Installer is not compatible with previous versions of the Visual Studio installer.

Now let's examine the different type of output files that can be generated for your deployment project.

Deployment Project Outputs

When you examine the Setup1 deployment project, you will see that it doesn't contain any files, by default. You will have to add the necessary external assemblies, merge modules, and other application files by choosing the Add option from the shortcut menu for the deployment application. From the submenu of the Add selection, you will see four choices: Project Output, File, Merge Module, and Assembly. The latter three are quite obvious in what they do, but what about Project Output? What does that add to your deployment project?

By default, the deployment package doesn't know that it needs to reference the existing Windows application. Select the Add ➣ Project option to add the output of your Windows application to the deployment package. This launches the Add Project Output Group dialog box, as illustrated in Figure 21.6.

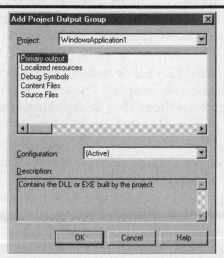

FIGURE 21.6:   The Add Project Output Group dialog box

The Add Project Output Group dialog box enables you to select different files to add to the deployment project. The drop-down list at the top of this dialog box lists the various projects that are available for packaging. Of course, it will only list those projects that are not deployment projects. You only have a single project in this solution, WindowsApplication1, so this is what you see listed.

Below the ComboBox is an Outputs List, containing several packaging options. Technically, this dialog box serves as a wizard, with these options serving as the various paths you can take in the wizard. Oddly, the dialog box doesn't take the form of a traditional wizard, so it may be a bit confusing to understand what happens once you hit the OK button. Depending on the option you select in the box below the project name, different files will be added to your deployment project. You can select more than one output from the Outputs List.

The Primary Output choice specifies the project DLL or EXE, as well as its dependency tree. In order to avoid DLL Hell, copies of all the dependencies and children dependencies are deployed along with the application. This way, the application doesn't have to depend on the presence or reliability of external DLLs on the target machine.

The Localized Resources option is used for specifying country, language, or culture-specific files. The Debug Symbols option enables you to specify that the project should be compiled with debugging information. The Content Files option pertains to web applications, where you can specify the resource files such as HTML and graphic files. The Source Files option enables you to add all the source code for a project, not including the solution file.

Finally, the Configuration setting ComboBox enables you to specify whether you want debug or release code compiled. Choosing the (Active) option indicates that you want to use the existing configuration specified within that project.

Choose the Primary Output choice, and click OK. You will see that the Detected Dependencies folder in the Solution Explorer now contains two references, as shown in Figure 21.7.

The first reference is a merge module, called `dotnetfxredist_x86_enu.msm`. You can see that it's a merge module based on its extension, `.msm`. We discussed merge modules earlier and, as you remember, merge modules contain independently distributable components. In this case, the `dotnetfxredist_x86_enu.msm` contains the .NET Framework's CLR. The second dependency is the `mscorlib.dll`, which contains the type definitions used within the .NET Framework.

FIGURE 21.7: The Detected Dependencies folder

File System Editor

After VS .NET adds your deployment project to your solution, VS .NET launches the File System Editor tab within your designer pane, as shown in Figure 21.8. Alternatively, you can launch the File System Editor by right-clicking on the Setup1 project and choosing View ➤ File System from the shortcut menu.

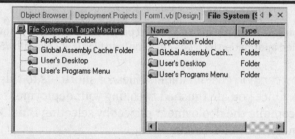

FIGURE 21.8: The File System tab

You can use this tool to determine where you want your application files distributed. The File System Editor is a virtual representation of the file directory on the target installation machine. For example, by default the Application Folder is within the Program Files subdirectory for your specific Windows application. The application will be installed in sub-directories named after the manufacturer and project name. You can set these from the properties for the project. Based on the settings shown in Figure 21.9, the application will be stored within the C:\Program Files\ Neslihan\Setup1 directory.

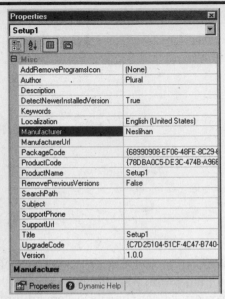

FIGURE 21.9: Project Properties window

NOTE

We are not going to review all of these project properties individually; however, there is detailed information located within the help files that ship with VS .NET.

If you'd like, you can add custom folders, files, or shortcuts to this virtual file system. Once you are finished tweaking your deployment settings, you can compile the deployment project by selecting Build ➤ Build Setup1 from the VS .NET menu.

Deploying a Web Application

Let's continue our exploration of the deployment tools. This time you will use a web application. Create a new project using the ASP.NET Web Application project template. Name your project **WebDeployment**. Add a new project using the Web Setup deployment project template. Use the default name **WebSetup1**. In the end, you should have a solution file containing two projects, as shown in Figure 21.10.

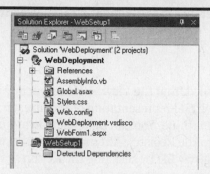

FIGURE 21.10: Deploying a web application

Although web applications also use an `.msi` file for deployment, the installation works a bit differently than Windows applications. Web applications install via a virtual root, rather than within a Program Files directory. Regardless, you can still specify how you would like the files packaged. In the Project Properties for the deployment, under the Build page, you can specify if you would like the files to be compressed in a cabinet file or within a Windows Installer package (`.msi`) file.

Aside from the fact that the files are installed into a virtual root, the deployment packaging of a web application works much the same was as a Windows application. The deployment tools, such as the File System Editor and the Registry Editor, are used almost the same way.

After your deployment project is created, there will be no files or dependencies. As with Windows applications, you have to add the Project Output for your web application to the deployment project. You can do this the same way you did earlier with the Windows application. Right-click on the WebSetup1 file in the Solution Explorer, and choose the Add ➤ Project Output from the shortcut menu. From the Add Project Output Group dialog box, select the WebDeployment1 application and choose the Primary Output option to add the WebDeployment1 to the deployment project.

Unlike the Windows application project, we couldn't compile and distribute our deployment project as it stands now. Web applications contain content files, such as HTML and graphics, which also need to be packaged with the deployment application. Repeat the same steps to add another project output to the deployment project. This time, choose the Content Files option from the Outputs list. If you examine your File

System Editor, you will see a reference to the content files listed within the Web Application folder.

The Registry Editor

The Registry Editor can be accessed from the View ➤ Editor menu. This editor presents you with a virtual representation of the hives in the Windows Registry of the target machine. You can right-click on any of these hives to add custom keys to the Registry. Alternatively, you can choose to import an existing Registry file by selecting the Action ➤ Import menu from VS .NET.

The File Types Editor

The File Types Editor enables you to associate actions to specific file types. You identify these file types by specifying the extension using the Extensions property. Experiment with this editor by adding a file type called Special File. You can add this file type by choosing Add File Type from the Action menu of VS .NET. In the Properties window for this file type, you can set the Extension property to what you would like, such as .spc. This is an arbitrary extension we chose for the purposes of illustrating the point. By default, the Open action will be associated with this file type. You can choose to associate a specific application that will be opened when the file system encounters a file with the extension you specified.

The User Interface Editor

The User Interface Editor enables you to modify the installation steps for your application. As you know, most installations programs follow a wizard metaphor, and the VS .NET deployment project is no different. The steps within the wizard are displayed in a hierarchical format, as shown in Figure 21.11.

The TreeView is broken into two installation options: the regular user installation and the administrative installation. The former is intended for the typical end user. The latter is for a network installation by a system administrator, and it can be executed appending the /a parameter to the command-line call for msiexec.exe, as such:

```
Msiexec.exe /a package_name.msi
```

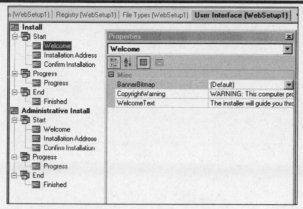

FIGURE 21.11: The User Interface Editor

You can click on any of these nodes and modify its properties. You can drag-and-drop the nodes to change the order of the steps. If you'd like, you can add additional steps to the wizard. To add another dialog box, you select the Action ➢ Add Dialog option from the VS .NET menu. Fortunately, VS .NET provides some predefined dialog box templates from which you can choose.

WHAT'S NEXT

By the end of this chapter you should understand how to plan your deployment strategy. You should be aware of issues such as the scope of your components, your delivery mechanism, and how you want your application to scale and grow. Additionally, this chapter provides you with a high-level overview of the various editors and tools you have available with deployment projects in VS .NET.

In the next chapter, you will learn to create a three-tiered application using Visual Basic .NET. The application in this chapter is a Windows Forms application, with a simple user interface. All of the code working with both data and business rules will be moved out of the form into class libraries (ActiveX DLLs in Visual Basic 6).

In the application built in the next chapter, you are going to create two projects, one for the user services tier and another for the business services tier. The data services tier is primarily composed of stored procedures in SQL Server. The knowledge gained in the next chapter is crucial to building scalable Enterprise-level applications.

Part VI

Chapter 22

THREE-TIERED APPLICATIONS

In this chapter, we will build an example three-tiered application based on the Pubs database and use SQL Server 2000 as the database engine.

Three-tiered architecture partitions an application into three logical tiers, or services:

- ▶ User services (the front-end)
- ▶ Business services (the middle)
- ▶ Data services (the back-end)

By using three-tiered architecture, you can develop applications that separate user access, business rules, and data access into separate modules. VB .NET and the .NET Framework are well suited for developing multi-tiered applications because of the rich graphical user interface tools and the power of the database tools.

Adapted from the forthcoming *Visual Basic .NET Developer's Handbook* by Evangelos Petroutsos and Kevin Hough

ISBN 0-7821-2879-3 $59.99

The secret to three-tiered projects is building and using reusable components. In this chapter, we will discuss the process of building a Class project that performs database manipulation, for use by programs that need to access and maintain a database. You could just as easily build a class that performs some other type of processing, such as mathematical calculations, inventory control, or data presentation, for use in one or many applications. That is the beauty of a multi-tiered architecture; build it once and use it over and over again.

UNDERSTANDING THE THREE TIERS

The sample application presented in this chapter relies on three-tiered architecture to keep the services separate. This allows you to build a very flexible, scaleable solution that can be used by any project that needs access to the data. In this section, we will discuss some background on each of the three tiers used in this sample.

NOTE
You will often see three-tiered programming called n-tier programming. This is due to the fact that a single tier can be broken into multiple tiers for reusability.

Defining TierOne

In our sample application, TierOne, or user services, consists of one form (shown in Figure 22.1) with the fields from the Authors table in the Pubs database that will allow the user to do the following:

▶ Add new records to the Authors table

▶ Delete records from the Authors table

▶ Find records based on an author's ID number that is actually a Social Security number

▶ Update records and change the current values

The user interface for TierOne incorporates components that we discussed in many previous chapters, including:

▶ Menus

▶ Toolbars

▶ Status bars

▶ Advanced .NET controls

Three-Tiered Application

File   Edit

Author ID :	172-32-1176
First Name :	Johnson
Last Name :	White
Phone :	408 496-7223
Address :	10932 Bigge Rd.
City :	Menlo Park
State :	CA
Zip :	94025
Contract :	☑

11/18/2001

FIGURE 22.1:   The TierOne Form

Part VI

Examining TierTwo

TierTwo, business services, is a separate application compiled into a
DLL. There is no interface for TierTwo because it receives requests from
TierOne and passes them on to the database through ADO.NET. TierTwo
encapsulates all of the data access into a VB .NET Class project that provides access to the database and processes the requests that are initiated
in TierOne.

NOTE

See Part IV of this book for a complete discussion of ADO.NET.

Investigating TierThree

TierThree, data services, consists of the Pubs database, which we use
throughout this book. It is the same sample database that comes with
SQL Server 2000 and is created when SQL Server is installed. In order to
run the examples in this chapter, you must have access to the database.

If the Pubs database is not installed on your server or if it has been altered, install it by running the `Instpubs.sql` script included on the Sybex website.

THE THREE-TIERED PROJECT

The Three-Tiered project in this book is composed of two applications and the database. The front-end, or TierOne (as shown in Figure 22.1), provides the user interface for presenting information and gathering data. It gathers requirements from the user and presents data in response to a question or a query. The user can add, delete, update, and search records in the Pubs database.

In this project, we have used a DataSet and DataRow. Bound objects could have been used, but they would not have afforded as much flexibility. By using the approach of DataSets and DataRows, you are free to use the values for any type of data presentation and are not confined to bound controls.

NOTE
You will find the TierOne and TierTwo projects, as well as the `instpubs.sql` script, on the Sybex website.

Processing Toolbar Requests

Our application provides a toolbar (shown in Figure 22.2) with which users can interact with the program. The toolbar has four buttons that perform the following actions:

▶ New Record sends a request to add a new record to the database using the current field values.

▶ Delete Record sends a request to delete the current record.

▶ Find sends a request to find the record that has the current AuthorID.

▶ Save Record sends a request to the TierTwo application to save changes to the current record.

FIGURE 22.2:   The TierOne toolbar

The code used to respond to the user's toolbar selection is shown in Listing 22.1.

Listing 22.1: The Three-Tiered Application Toolbar

```
Private Sub ToolBar1_ButtonClick _
  (ByVal sender As System.Object, _
  ByVal e As _
    System.Windows.Forms.ToolBarButtonClickEventArgs) _
  Handles ToolBar1.ButtonClick

    Select Case ToolBar1.Buttons.IndexOf(e.Button)
    Case 0 'Save
      Call mnuSave_Click(mnuSave, New System.EventArgs())
    Case 1 'Find
      Call mnuFind_Click(mnuFind, New System.EventArgs())
    Case 3 'New
      Call mnuNew_Click(mnuNew, New System.EventArgs())
    Case 4 'Delete
      Call mnuDelete_Click(mnuDelete, _
        New System.EventArgs())
    End Select
  End Sub
```

As you can see, the toolbar simply calls the associated code in the menu to perform the request. This alleviates the need to duplicate the code.

Part VI

Adding Records

To add a new author's record to the database, you simply click the New Record button on the toolbar, as shown in Figure 22.2, or choose Edit ➤ New Record. This will call the mnuNew_click code, as shown in Listing 22.2.

NOTE
Remember: TierOne does not actually have any SQL statements or database code. It simply passes requests to TierTwo.

If all goes well, the record is added to the database, and the status bar is updated to display Record Added, as shown in Listing 22.2.

Listing 22.2: Sending a Request to TierTwo to Add a Record

```
Private Sub mnuNew_Click(ByVal sender As System.Object, _
    ByVal e As System.EventArgs) Handles mnuNew.Click

    Dim objE As Exception

    Try
        'Get the Authors ID
        clsAuthor.AuthorID = txtAuthorID.Text
        'Assign the class values
        Call AssignValues()

        'Add the new record
        clsAuthor.Add()
    Catch objE
        MsgBox(objE.Message)
    End Try
End Sub
```

NOTE
Notice the use of the Try...Catch error-trapping code. Error-trapping code is always important, but here it is essential. You are calling a DLL, and if an error occurs, it is important for you to know where and why.

This code calls the Add subroutine in the TierTwo application, where all the work is performed. TierOne simply gathers requirements from the user and processes requests. It should not know or care how the data is processed.

When a request is processed, one of three things happens:

▶ The request is processed without any errors.

▶ A noncritical error occurs (for example, the record is not found).

▶ A database error occurs.

If the request is successful or if a noncritical error occurs, the TierTwo application raises the Action event in the TierOne application, and the status bar is updated, as demonstrated in Listing 22.3.

Listing 22.3: Raising the Action Event in Tier One

```
Private Sub clsAuthor_Action(ByVal Status As Short) _
    Handles clsAuthor.Action
    'This event is raised by TierTwo.dll
    'in the event of an error

        'Define variables
    Dim msg As String
    Dim title As String
    Dim style As MsgBoxStyle
    Dim response As MsgBoxResult

    'Clear the status
    Me.StatusBarPanel2.Text = ""

    Select Case Status
        Case 2
            'No record found
            msg = _
            "No Authors record was located with" &
            " the AuthorID: " & txtAuthorID.Text
            title = "No Records Found"
            Me.StatusBarPanel2.Text = "Record Not Found"
        Case 3
            'Record not deleted
            msg = _
            "No Authors record was located " &
            "with the AuthorID: " _
            & txtAuthorID.Text & Chr(10) & _
            "No record was deleted"
            title = "Delete Error"
            Me.StatusBarPanel2.Text = "Record Not Deleted"
```

Part VI

```
Case 4
    'Record not updated
    msg = _
    "No Authors record was located "
    "with the AuthorID: " _
    & txtAuthorID.Text & Chr(10) & _
    "No record was updated"
    title = "Update Error"
    Me.StatusBarPanel2.Text = "Record Not Updated"
Case 5
    'Duplicate record
    msg = _
    "Record already exists:" & txtAuthorID.Text & _
    Chr(10) & "No record was updated"
    title = "Add Error"
    Me.StatusBarPanel2.Text = _
        "Duplicate Record Not Added"
Case 100
    'Record Deleted
    Me.StatusBarPanel2.Text = "Record Deleted"
    Exit Sub
Case 200
    'Record Found
    Me.StatusBarPanel2.Text = "Record Found"
    Exit Sub
Case 300
    'record Added
    Me.StatusBarPanel2.Text = "Record Added"
    Exit Sub
Case 400
    'Record Updated
    Me.StatusBarPanel2.Text = "Record Saved"
    Exit Sub
Case 500
    'Duplicate Record
    msg = "A record already exists " & _
    "with this AuthorID: " & txtAuthorID.Text _
    & Chr(10) & "No record was updated"
    title = "Add Error"
    Me.StatusBarPanel2.Text = _
    "Duplicate Record Not Added"
End Select
```

```
                'Display the msgbox
                response = MsgBox(msg, style, title)

        End Sub
```

The code in the Action subroutine is passed an Integer value from the TierTwo application in response to an action request. If no errors were found, a value of 100, 200, 300, or 400 is passed. The Action code interprets this value and constructs the proper status bar response.

If a record was not found, a value of 2, 3, or 4 is passed back. In this case, in addition to the status bar response, a message box is displayed, notifying the user of the error.

If a database error occurs while the record is being processed, the TierTwo application raises the Errors event in the TierOne application and calls the code in Listing 22.4. This code displays a message box, notifying you that an error has occurred. (See Figure 22.3.)

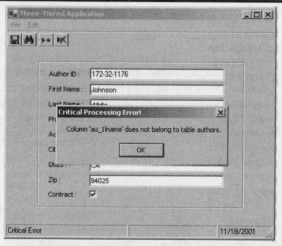

FIGURE 22.3:   The Three-Tiered application displaying error messages

Listing 22.4: Raising an Error

```
    Private Sub clsAuthor_Errors(ByVal ErrorStr As String) _
        Handles clsAuthor.Errors
        'This event is raised by TierTwo.dll in the event
        'of a critical error
```

Part VI

```
'Define variables
Dim msg As String
Dim title As String
Dim style As MsgBoxStyle
Dim response As MsgBoxResult

'Clear the status
Me.StatusBarPanel1.Text = ""
msg = ErrorStr
title = "No Records Found"
Me.StatusBarPanel1.Text = "Critical Error"

'Display the msgbox
response = MsgBox(msg, style, title)

End Sub
```

This generic error-handling code module is raised, or called, from the TierTwo application in the event of a critical database error.

Deleting Records

Deleting records is easy in our application. With a valid AuthorID present, choose Edit ➤ Delete Record or simply click the Delete button, as shown in Figure 22.2, earlier in this chapter. A message box will ask you to confirm the delete request. If you select Yes, the record is deleted. Select No to cancel the request. When you delete the record, the status bar is updated to display Record Deleted to let you know that the delete was successful.

If an error occurs while the record is being processed, a message box notifies you that an error has occurred, and a RichTextBox control becomes visible between the author fields and the status bar. The rdoErrors is written to the RichTextBox control, and the status bar displays Processing Error.

The TierOne application uses the following code, shown in Listing 22.5, to request a delete from the TierTwo application.

Listing 22.5: Sending a Delete Request

```
Private Sub mnuDelete_Click(ByVal sender As System.Object, _
ByVal e As System.EventArgs) Handles mnuDelete.Click
    'Declare variables
```

```
Dim msg As String
Dim title As String
Dim style As MsgBoxStyle
Dim response As MsgBoxResult

'Get the Authors ID
clsAuthor.AuthorID = txtAuthorID.Text

msg = "Delete the current Author's record?"
style = MsgBoxStyle.YesNo + MsgBoxStyle.Question _
+ MsgBoxStyle.DefaultButton1
title = "Confirm Delete"
response = MsgBox(msg, style, title)
If response = MsgBoxResult.Yes Then
    'Delete the record
    clsAuthor.Delete()

    'instantiate object
    clsAuthor = New TierTwo.Authors()

    Call PopulateTextBoxes()
Else
    'no action
    Me.StatusBarPanel2.Text = "Delete Aborted"
End If
End Sub
```

This code gets the author's ID from the AuthorID field, which is used to actually locate the record for deletion. Next, a message box is constructed and displayed; it asks you to confirm the delete request. If you select Yes, the request is sent to the DLL; if you select No, the status bar is updated with Delete Aborted, and no action is taken.

Finding an Author's Record

Our application also makes easy work of searching for a particular author; you simply enter the author's ID number in the AuthorID field and click the Find icon, as shown in Figure 22.2 earlier in this chapter. The application gets the AuthorID number from the TierTwo application and then sends a request to the application to create a RecordSet with the AuthorID number.

If the process is completed successfully and the record is found, the fields are filled in with the record, and the status bar is updated to display Record Found. As in the other cases, if an error occurs, the text box at the bottom of the screen displays the error messages. The following code, shown in Listing 22.6, sends the Find request to the DLL.

Listing 22.6: Sending a Request to Find a Record

```
Private Sub mnuFind_Click(ByVal sender As System.Object, _
ByVal e As System.EventArgs) Handles mnuFind.Click
    'Search for an author's record
    'AuthorID to find
    clsAuthor.AuthorID = txtAuthorID.Text

    'Lookup
    clsAuthor.Search()
    Call PopulateTextBoxes()
End Sub
```

This code is straightforward. First, the AuthorID number is retrieved from the AuthorID text box; then, a request is sent to the TierTwo application to perform a search; and finally, the new records populate the text boxes.

Updating a Current Record

From time to time, you will find it necessary to make changes to current records. Our application supports changes by sending an update request to the TierTwo application. To change a record, you simply locate a current record with the Find method, or add a new record and change one or more fields. Click the Save Record icon, as shown in Figure 22.2 earlier in this chapter, to send an Update request to the TierTwo application. If the record is successfully changed, the status bar displays Record Updated, notifying you that the change was successful. If an error occurs, the text box at the bottom of the screen displays the error message. The code shown in Listing 22.7 sends an update request to TierTwo.

Listing 22.7: Sending an Update Request to TierTwo

```
Private Sub mnuSave_Click()
    On Error GoTo ErrorRoutineErr
    'Get the Authors ID
    clsAuthor.AuthorID = txtAuthorID
    'Assign the class values
    Call AssignValues
    'Add the new record
```

```
     clsAuthor.Update
ErrorRoutineResume:
   Exit Sub
ErrorRoutineErr:
   MsgBox "TierOne.Form1.mnuSave_Click" & Err & Error
   Resume Next
End Sub
```

This code looks a lot like the code used to add or delete a record. First, the AuthorID number is retrieved from the AuthorID text box, and then the update request is sent. If the update is successful, the status bar displays Record Updated.

The user interface, or TierOne, of a three-tiered application simply gathers requests and passes them to the business services, or the second tier. No SQL statements or records are processed. In the next section, we will explore the TierTwo application where the records are processed.

THE TIERTWO APPLICATION

In our sample application, the business services or middle tier is made up of a Class project that is compiled into a Dynamic Link Library program, or DLL.

The TierTwo application does not have a user interface; in fact, the user really should not even know or care about this application. Its purpose is to receive requests from the front-end application, in our case the TierOne program, to process the requests and to notify the calling application of the status. In our case, this is accomplished with one class module.

Creating Properties, Methods, and Events

We have created the class module in our TierTwo application as a Class project that includes a class module consisting of properties, methods, and events.

Defining the Class Properties

The properties in our class are the fields from the Authors table in the Pubs database. Table 22.1 lists and describes them.

Part VI

TABLE 22.1: The Class Properties

PROPERTY	DESCRIPTION
Address	The author's address
AuthorID	The author's Social Security number, which is the key to the table
City	The author's city
Contract	Signifies whether the author is under contract
FirstName	The author's first name
LastName	The author's last name
Phone	The author's phone number
State	The author's state
Zip	The author's zip code

Defining the Class Methods

The methods for our class module are the actions that can be performed from the front-end, or the TierOne application. Table 22.2 lists and describes them.

TABLE 22.2: Methods Supported by the TierTwo Application

METHOD	DESCRIPTION
Add	Adds a new record to the Authors table
Delete	Deletes the current record from the Authors table
Search	Locates a record matching the current AuthorID field
Update	Saves changes to the current author's record

Defining the Class Events

The events in our class module are raised and are available in the TierOne application. Table 22.3 lists and describes these events.

TABLE 22.3: Events Raised by the TierTwo Application

EVENT	DESCRIPTION
Action	Called in response to a method. If the method completes without a critical database error, the Action event is raised.
Errors	Raised if a critical database error occurs.

In the next sections, we will discuss the TierTwo application flow and examine some of the code modules.

Writing the Code for TierTwo

As we discussed earlier in this chapter, the business services, or second tier, in a three-tiered application does not include a user interface. It is composed of a class module that is comprised of properties, methods, and events. In this section, we will examine the major code required for our project's class module.

Creating the Properties

In a class module, you must define a property for all of the fields that you want to access in your program. For the TierTwo project, you must define all of the properties that are listed in Table 22.1, shown earlier in this section. A property must have a section for Get and a section for Set. The Get property procedure is used to assign a value to a property. The Set property procedure is used to assign a value to a property. Both of these statements work in concert with each other to supply values to the TierOne application as needed.

Listing 22.8 demonstrates how to define the property for the AuthorID field in the database. A property statement must be defined for all of the properties that your application will access. In the next section, we will discuss the Events that are raised from TierTwo.

Listing 22.8: The AuthorID Property

```
Public Property AuthorID() As String
      Get
            AuthorID = mvarAuthorID
      End Get
```

```
         Set(ByVal Value As String)
             mvarAuthorID = Value
         End Set
    End Property
```

Defining the Events

An event is a signal that informs an application that something important has happened. In our application, we use events to signal the completion of a task, such as adding a record or informing the user of an error. The code shown in Listing 22.10 is used to define the events in the Authors Class module.

Listing 22.10: Code Added for Events

```
'To fire this event, use RaiseEvent
'with the following syntax:
'RaiseEvent Action[(arg1, arg2, ... , argn)]
Public Event Action(ByVal Status As Integer)
'To fire this event, use RaiseEvent
'with the following syntax:
'RaiseEvent rdoe[(arg1, arg2, ... , argn)]
Public Event Errors(ErrMessages As Object)
```

This code defines the events that can be raised for the calling application or, in our example, the TierOne application.

In the next section, we will add code to each of the methods to make them actually perform a function for us.

Coding the Methods

The methods of a class are simply the public Sub or Function procedures declared within the class. In a multi-tiered application like our sample, TierOne calls methods in TierTwo to perform actions. In this section, we will take a look at the code necessary to construct these methods.

Adding Code to the Add Method

In our application, the Add method adds a new record to the Authors table in the Pubs database. The following subroutine, shown in Listing 22.11, makes a connection to the database, creates a data adapter, and defines a table and row object. Next, values are added to a new row based on the value from the text boxes on the TierOne application Form and the row is added to the Authors table. The values are retrieved by the Property Get procedures in the TierTwo application.

If an error occurs, the Errors event is raised in the TierOne application. If no errors are encountered, the Action event is raised to notify the user that the record was added.

NOTE
See Listing 22.3 earlier in this chapter for an explanation of the Action event, and see Listing 22.4 for an explanation of the Errors event.

Listing 22.11: Adding a New Record

```
Public Sub Add()

    Dim objE As Exception
    Dim SqlCon As New SqlConnection _
    ("server=localhost;uid=sa;pwd=sql;database=pubs")
    Dim SqlDA As New SqlDataAdapter _
    ("SELECT * FROM authors", SqlCon)
    Dim SCB As New SqlCommandBuilder(SqlDA)
    Dim ds As New DataSet()

    SqlDA.Fill(ds, "authors")

    Dim dt As DataTable = ds.Tables(0)
    Dim dr As DataRow = dt.NewRow()
    Try
        'Add the values to the fields
        dr("au_id") = mvarAuthorID
        dr("au_lname") = mvarLastName
        dr("au_fname") = mvarFirstName
        dr("address") = mvarAddress
        dr("phone") = mvarPhone
        dr("city") = mvarCity
        dr("state") = mvarState
        dr("zip") = mvarZip
        If mvarContract = 1 Then
            dr("contract") = True
        Else
            dr("contract") = False
        End If
```

```
                    'Add the new row
                    dt.Rows.Add(dr)
                    'Update the table
                    SqlDA.Update(ds, "authors")

                    'All is well, inform the user
                    RaiseEvent Action(300)

            Catch objE
                'Display the errors
                'Duplicate record
                If Left(objE.Message, 35) = _
                    "Violation of PRIMARY KEY constraint" Then
                    RaiseEvent Action(5)
                Else
                    RaiseEvent Errors(objE.Message)
                End If
            End Try
        End Sub
```

The code in Listing 22.11 creates a connection, adds values to the properties, and adds a new row to the database. Notice the Try and Catch statements. We included them because we want the errors to be raised in the Error event of the calling program.

Adding Code to the Delete Method

The Delete method, shown in Listing 22.12, deletes a record from the Authors table in the Pubs database. In the Delete subroutine, a connection is established with the database and a DataAdapter, DataSet, table, and row object are defined. Next, the row is marked for deletion and, finally, deleted from the Authors table based on the value from the AuthorID text box on the TierOne applications form. The value is retrieved with the Property Get AuthorID procedure in the TierTwo application.

If an error occurs during the delete attempt, the Errors event is raised in the TierOne application. In addition to checking for errors, the message property of the Exception Object is checked to see if a row was actually deleted. If not, the Action event is raised with a value of 3. In the Action event in the TierOne application, the return value of 3 is interpreted, and a message notifies the user that the record was not found and was not deleted.

The code in Listing 22.12 creates a database connection and attempts to delete the selected author's record.

Listing 22.12: Deleting a Record

```
Public Sub Delete()

    Dim objE As Exception
    Dim SqlCon As New SqlConnection _
        ("server=localhost;uid=sa;pwd=sql;database=pubs")
    Dim SqlDA As New SqlDataAdapter _
    ("SELECT * FROM authors", SqlCon)
    Dim SCB As New SqlCommandBuilder(SqlDA)
    Dim ds As New DataSet()

    SqlDA.Fill(ds, "authors")

    Dim dt As DataTable = ds.Tables(0)

    Dim dr() As DataRow = dt.Select _
    ("au_id = '" & mvarAuthorID & "'")
    Try

        'Mark the row for deletion
        dr(0).Delete()

        'Update the database
        SqlDA.Update(ds, "authors")
        ''Accept the changes
        dt.AcceptChanges()

        'All is well with the delete, inform the user
        RaiseEvent Action(100)

    Catch obje
        If objE.Message = _
          "Index was outside the bounds of the array." Then
            'Record does not exist
            RaiseEvent Action(3)
        Else
            RaiseEvent Errors(objE.Message)
        End If
    End Try
End Sub
```

Adding Code to the Search Method

The Search method, shown in Listing 22.13, locates a record from the Authors table in the Pubs database by searching for the AuthorID. In the Search subroutine, the Search method of the DataRow is used to filter the Authors table based on the value from the Author text boxes on the TierOne application Form. The value is retrieved with the Property Get AuthorID procedures in the TierTwo application.

The Catch portion of the Try...Catch statement is examined to verify if a record was found. If no record was found, the Action event is passed back with a value of 2, signifying that no record was found. If a record was found, the class properties are filled with the values from the current record in the RecordSet, and the Action event is raised with a value of 200, signifying that the record was found.

Listing 22.13: Searching for a Record

```
Public Sub Search()
    Try

        Dim SqlCon As New SqlConnection _
          ("server=localhost;uid=sa;pwd=sql;database=pubs")
        Dim SqlDA As New SqlDataAdapter _
          ("SELECT * FROM authors", SqlCon)
        Dim ds As New DataSet()

        SqlDA.Fill(ds, "authors")

        Dim DR() As DataRow = ds.Tables("authors").Select _
        ("au_id = '" & AuthorID & "'")

        'Fill the textboxes in the form
        mvarAuthorID = (DR(0)("au_id").ToString())
        mvarLastName = (DR(0)("au_lname").ToString())
        mvarFirstName = (DR(0)("au_fname").ToString())
        mvarPhone = (DR(0)("phone").ToString())
        mvarAddress = (DR(0)("address").ToString())
        mvarCity = (DR(0)("city").ToString())
        mvarState = (DR(0)("state").ToString())
        mvarZip = (DR(0)("zip").ToString())
        mvarContract = (DR(0)("contract").ToString())
        'Action 200, record found
        RaiseEvent Action(200)
```

```
        Catch ex As Exception
            If ex.Message = _
                "Index was outside the bounds of the array." Then
                'The record was not found
                mvarLastName = ""
                mvarFirstName = ""
                mvarPhone = ""
                mvarAddress = ""
                mvarCity = ""
                mvarZip = ""
                mvarState = ""
                mvarContract = ""
                'action 2, record not found
                RaiseEvent Action(2)
            End If
        End Try
    End Sub
```

The code in Listing 22.13 attempts to filter the Authors records by using the value obtained from the AuthorID property.

Adding Code to the Update Method

The Update method, shown in Listing 22.14, changes a record in the Authors table. In the Update subroutine, a connection is made to the database and a SqlDataAdapter and a DataSet are declared. Next, the DataRow is updated and the current record in the Authors table based on the values from the text boxes on the TierOne application Form.

If an error occurs during the update process, the Errors event is raised in the TierOne application. If not, the Action event is raised with a value of 4. In the Action event in the TierOne application, the return value of 4 is interpreted, and a message notifies the user that the record was not found and was not updated.

Listing 22.14: Updating a Record

```
    Public Sub Update()

        Dim objE As Exception
        Dim SqlCon As New SqlConnection _
        ("server=localhost;uid=sa;pwd=sql;database=pubs")
        Dim SqlDA As New SqlDataAdapter _
            ("SELECT * FROM authors", SqlCon)
        Dim SCB As New SqlCommandBuilder(SqlDA)
```

```vbnet
        Dim ds As New DataSet()

        SqlDA.Fill(ds, "authors")

        Dim dt As DataTable = ds.Tables(0)
        Dim dr() As DataRow = _
        dt.Select("au_id = '" & mvarAuthorID & "'")

        Try
            dr(0).BeginEdit()
            dr(0)("au_lname") = mvarLastName
            dr(0)("au_fname") = mvarFirstName
            dr(0)("address") = mvarLastName
            dr(0)("phone") = mvarPhone
            dr(0)("city") = mvarCity
            dr(0)("state") = mvarState
            dr(0)("zip") = mvarZip
            If mvarContract = 1 Then
                dr(0)("contract") = True
            Else
                dr(0)("contract") = False
            End If
            dr(0).EndEdit()

            'Update the table
            SqlDA.Update(ds, "authors")
            dt.AcceptChanges()
            'Record updated, inform the user
            RaiseEvent Action(400)

    Catch objE
        'Inform the user of errors
        RaiseEvent Errors(objE.Message)
    End Try
End Sub
```

The Update code is similar to the Add and Delete code. Now that we have analyzed the program flow and discussed the major code, it's time to test the Three-Tiered application.

Testing the Applications

As we have already discussed, the TierTwo application is a DLL that must be referenced in the TierOne application during production, but

VB .NET allows you to open multiple projects and reference a project from another project.

Follow these steps to test the applications:

1. Start VB .NET and open the TierTwo application.

2. Add the TierOne project to the solution.

3. Right-click References in the TierOne project, and select TierTwo from the Projects dialog box.

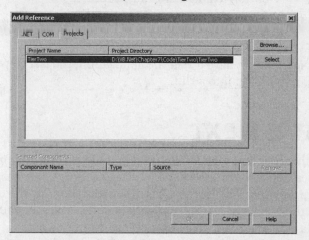

4. Set TierOne as the Startup project by right-clicking on the TierOne project, and choose Set As StartUp Project from the pop-up menu.

5. Press F5 to run the TierOne application. The first record is retrieved from the database and displayed on the form.

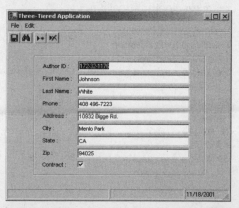

6. In the Author ID field, enter **213-46-8915,** and click the Find button to retrieve the second author's record.

7. Change the Last Name field to **Johnston**, and click the Save button. The record is saved, and the status bar shows Record Saved.

8. Change the Author ID field to **172-32-5555,** change the data in some of the other fields, and click the New Record button to add this as a new record.

9. With the record 172-32-5555 displayed from Step 8, click the Delete Record button to delete the record.

Now that we have tested the application, the last step is to compile the TierTwo project into a DLL.

WHAT'S NEXT

In this chapter, you learned the essentials of three-tier programming. The three tiers used in this chapter are user services, business services, and data services. The user services deal with rendering the user interface, or UI; the business services deal with business rules for your enterprise; and data services deal with accessing your data sources.

The remainder of the chapter dealt with putting wheels on the theory. Each of the tiers was examined and code was added to complete the tier. The theory behind the simple application in this chapter will take you far in creating scaleable enterprise applications with .NET.

The final chapter in this book covers how to use Visual Basic .NET to create an online store. This chapter will utilize ASP.NET to create Web Forms to create an e-commerce site.

Chapter 23
SAMPLE PROJECTS

This chapter contains two projects that demonstrate several of the topics discussed in this book. These projects also show how to combine some techniques discussed already to build a complete application, like the ones you'll be paid to write. We've selected two typical types of applications for this chapter: an invoicing application and an online store. We've written similar applications with several of the earlier versions of Visual Basic (and ADO), and they incorporate design features that make them almost intuitive to use.

The invoicing application consists of a single form that enables the user to enter product IDs and adds the invoices to the database. It's the type of application that runs all day long at a cash register of a retail store. If you allow users to select a customer name, shipping address, and discount (either for all items, or individual discounts for each item), you have a complete invoicing application.

• •

Adapted from *Mastering Visual Basic .NET Database Programming* by Evangelos Petroutsos and Asli Bilgin
ISBN 0-7821-2878-5 $49.99

The second application is the core of a web application for selling the items of the Northwind database on the Internet. It enables users to specify the products they're interested in, view them, and add individual items to their baskets. Users can view their baskets at any time and edit the quantities. When they're ready, they can place the order. As with the invoicing application, the order is registered to the same customer. If you add a form for users to specify a shipping address and a payment method, the form can be converted to a flexible invoicing application. The most interesting segment of the application is the part that indicates how to maintain a shopping basket, edit it, and update it anytime.

THE INVOICE PROJECT

The Invoice project consists of a single form, which is shown in Figure 23.1. Users can enter detail lines on the TextBox controls at the top of the form. Each detail line is automatically added to the DataGrid control that takes up most of the form when the user presses the Enter key in the last TextBox, which corresponds to the Quantity field. The focus on the design of the interface of the Invoice project is to enable keyboard operations, without requiring the user to reach for the mouse. Users should be able to simply type the ID of the selected product in the first TextBox, press Enter to see the product's description and price in the next two TextBoxes, and then type its quantity (or accept the default). There's no reason for the pointer to ever stop at the description or price of the product. The corresponding TextBoxes are read-only, and they don't belong to the form's tab order (in other words, their TabStop property is False).

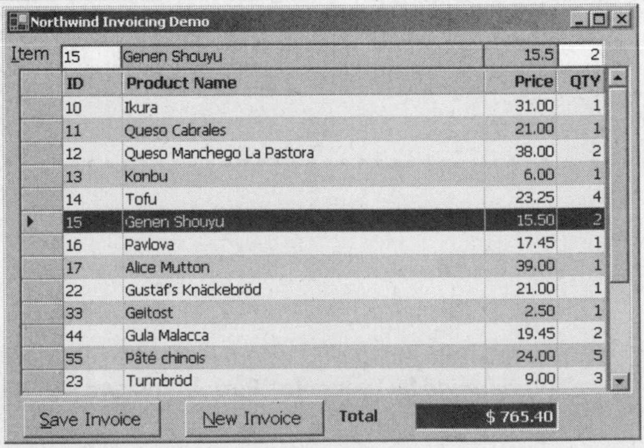

FIGURE 23.1:   Preparing an invoice

You need a data structure to store the invoice as it's being edited. This structure is a DataSet, which you must create from scratch. The simplest method to create a new DataSet in code is to add an XML schema component to the project and then add one or more elements with the designer's visual tools. The XML schema in the project is called Details.xsd, and its XML description is shown in Listing 23.1.

Listing 23.1: The *Details.xsd* **Schema**

```xml
<?xml version="1.0" encoding="utf-8" ?>
<xs:schema id="Details" targetNamespace= _
    "http://tempuri.org/Invoice.xsd"
  elementFormDefault="qualified" xmlns= _
    "http://tempuri.org/Invoice.xsd"
  xmlns:mstns="http://tempuri.org/Invoice.xsd"
  xmlns:xs="http://www.w3.org/2001/XMLSchema">
  <xs:element name="DetailLine">
   <xs:complexType>
    <xs:sequence>
      <xs:element name="ID" type="xs:integer" />
      <xs:element name="Description" type="xs:string" />
      <xs:element name="Price" type="xs:decimal" />
      <xs:element name="Quantity" type="xs:integer" />
    </xs:sequence>
   </xs:complexType>
  </xs:element>
</xs:schema>
```

To create this schema, drop an Element object from the Toolbox onto the designer's surface, call it **DetailLine**, and then add an element for each field of the detail lines, as indicated in Table 23.1.

TABLE 23.1: Elements for the Detail Lines Complex Type

ELEMENT	TYPE
ID	Integer
Description	String
Price	Decimal
Quantity	Integer

Part VI

After completing the design of the schema, right-click somewhere on the designer's surface and select Generate DataSet to create a DataSet based on this schema. This is a very simple DataSet with a single table, the DetailLine table, which in turn holds the detail lines of an invoice.

Return to the project's form and add the controls you saw previously in Figure 23.1. The boxes at the top of the form are TextBoxes, in which the user can enter (or view) the fields of the current detail line. Place a DataGrid control on the form and bind it to the newly created DataSet. Its DataSource property should be set to the name of the DataSet, **Details1**, and its DataMember property to the name of the single table in the DataSet, the DetailLine table.

To configure the DataGrid control, open the TableStyles collection and add a new table. The new table's MappingName property should be **DetailLine**. Then add a GridColumnStyle for each field and set their MappingName properties to the names of the columns of the DetailLine table, as shown in Figure 23.2. Don't forget to set the width and header of each column in the DataGrid, as shown in Figure 23.3. Depending on your monitor's resolution, the controls on the project's form might not be perfectly aligned when you open the project. Notice that the Anchor and Dock properties aren't going to help you in designing the form shown previously in Figure 23.1. This form requires that you align the controls to the columns of the DataGrid control. We have done it manually, but you can insert the appropriate code in the form's Load event handler.

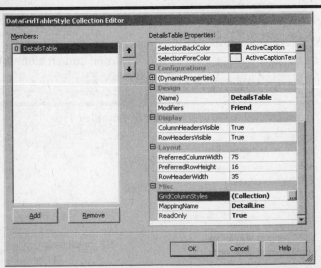

FIGURE 23.2: Setting the style of the DetailLine table in the DataGridTableStyle Collection Editor of the DataGrid control

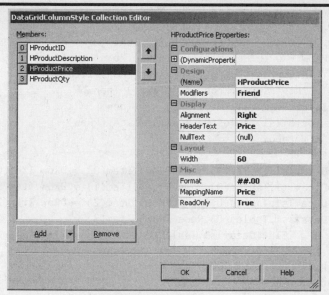

FIGURE 23.3:   Setting the styles of the DetailLine table's columns in the Data-
GridColumnStyle Collection Editor of the DataGrid control

So far, you've created the visual interface of the application. The
DataSet is bound to the DataGrid control, and every time you add/remove
or edit a row in the DataSet, the result will be reflected on the control.
Your code will manipulate the DataSet, rather than the DataGrid control.
In the following section, we'll discuss the code behind the various con-
trols of the form.

Let's assume a detail line has been filled—all TextBoxes at the top of
the form have been set to some values. The product's description and
unit price are read from the database, and you shouldn't allow users to
edit these boxes. Later in this section, you'll see the code that enables
users to supply the appropriate data. The subroutine in Listing 23.2
adds a new detail line to the DataGrid control on the form.

Listing 23.2: Adding a Detail Line to the Current Invoice

```
Sub InsertDetailLine()
  Dim PRow As Integer
  Dim DRow As Details.DetailLineRow
  DRow = CType(Details1.Tables(0).NewRow, _
              Details.DetailLineRow)
  DRow.ID = CInt(txtProductID.Text)
```

```
                   DRow.Description = txtProductName.Text
                   DRow.Price = CDec(txtProductPrice.Text)
                   DRow.Quantity = CInt(txtQuantity.Text)
                   For PRow = 0 To Details1.Tables(0).Rows.Count - 1
                     If CInt(Details1.Tables(0).Rows(PRow).Item(0)) = _
                       CInt(Trim(txtProductID.Text)) Then
                       If CInt(txtQuantity.Text) = 0 Then
                         Details1.Tables(0).Rows.RemoveAt(PRow)
                         Exit For
                       End If
                       Details1.Tables(0).Rows(PRow).Item(0) = DRow.Item(0)
                       Details1.Tables(0).Rows(PRow).Item(1) = DRow.Item(1)
                       Details1.Tables(0).Rows(PRow).Item(2) = DRow.Item(2)
                       Details1.Tables(0).Rows(PRow).Item(3) = _
                               CInt(Details1.Tables(0).Rows(PRow).Item(3)) + _
                               CInt(txtQuantity.Text)
                       Exit For
                     End If
                   Next
                   If PRow = Details1.Tables(0).Rows.Count Then
                     Details1.Tables(0).Rows.Add(DRow)
                   End If
                   ClearFields()
                   ShowTotal()
                 End Sub
```

The program creates a new row for the first (and single) table of the
Details DataSet and assigns the values entered by the user in the
TextBoxes at the top of the form to the fields of the new row. This row
isn't added immediately to the DataSet's table. The code is "intelligent"
enough to increase the quantity of an item if it's already in the invoice. It
does so by scanning all the rows of the DataGrid control and comparing
their IDs to the new ID. If a match is found, then it increases the quantity
of the existing row instead of adding a new one. If the new ID isn't found
in the existing detail lines, the new row is added to the table Details1
.Tables(0).

The ClearFields subroutine clears the TextBoxes at the top of the
form, in anticipation of the next detail line, while the ShowTotal subroutine updates the total displayed at the bottom of the form. The
ClearFields subroutine is shown in Listing 23.3.

Listing 23.3: The *ClearFields* Subroutine

```
Sub ClearFields()
    txtProductID.Clear()
    txtProductName.Clear()
    txtProductPrice.Clear()
    txtQuantity.Text = "1"
    txtTotal.Text = "$ 0.00"
End Sub
```

The subroutine that displays the order's current total at the bottom of the form iterates through the rows of the DetailLine table of the DataSet and sums the products of quantities and prices for each row. See Listing 23.4.

Listing 23.4: The *ShowTotal* Subroutine

```
Sub ShowTotal()
    Dim R As Integer
    Dim total As Decimal
    For R = 0 To Details1.Tables(0).Rows.Count - 1

        total = total + CDec(DataGrid1.Item(R, 2)) * _
            CDec(DataGrid1.Item(R, 3))
    Next
    txtTotal.Text = total.ToString("$ ##.00")
End Sub
```

Let's look now at how the application handles user input. The user must provide the ID of an item and its quantity. As soon as the user enters an ID in the first TextBox, the program should look it up in the Products database and return the matching product's description and price. These two fields are displayed in two of the TextBoxes at the top of the form, and the focus is moved to the last TextBox, where the user can enter the quantity for the item. Listing 23.5 shows what happens as soon as the user presses Enter in the first TextBox.

NOTE

Keep in mind that the setting for the Connection object should be altered to suit your environment. You will need to change the name of the database server as well as the security credentials. Realize that you should never deploy a database into production with the default sa username and password.

Part VI

Listing 23.5: Retrieving the Description and Price of a Product

```
Private Sub txtProductID_KeyPress(ByVal sender As Object, _
ByVal e As System.Windows.Forms.KeyPressEventArgs) _
Handles txtProductID.KeyPress
  If e.KeyChar <> vbCr Then Exit Sub
  If Not IsNumeric(txtProductID.Text) Then
    MsgBox("Invalid Product ID!")
    Exit Sub
  End If
  SqlConnection1.ConnectionString = _
   "initial catalog=Northwind;user id=sa;workstation " & _
   "id=POWERTOOLKIT"
  SqlConnection1.Open()
  SqlCommand1.CommandText = "SELECT ProductID, " & _
    "ProductName, UnitPrice FROM Products " & _
    "WHERE ProductID=" & txtProductID.Text
  SqlCommand1.Connection = SqlConnection1
  Dim SReader As SqlClient.SqlDataReader
  SReader = SqlCommand1.ExecuteReader()
  If Not SReader.Read Then
    MsgBox("Invalid Product ID")
    SReader.Close()
    SqlConnection1.Close()
    Exit Sub
  End If

  txtProductName.Text = _
     SReader.Item("ProductName").ToString()
  txtProductPrice.Text = _
     SReader.Item("UnitPrice").ToString()
  SReader.Close()
  SqlConnection1.Close()
  txtQuantity.Focus()
End Sub
```

To retrieve the row of the product with the ID specified by the user in the first TextBox, the program executes the following SQL statement:

```
SELECT ProductID, ProductName, UnitPrice
FROM   Products
WHERE  ProductID= xxx
```

where *xxx* is the specified ID. The corresponding row is returned to the application through an SqlDataReader object. If no matching ID is found in the database, the Read() method of the SqlDataReader returns False and the program displays an error message and exits. If the ID is found, the fields of the matching row are displayed in the appropriate TextBoxes on the form and the focus is moved to the last TextBox, where the user can enter the quantity of the current item—or press Enter to accept the default quantity of 1.

You can use this application with a bar code reader as well. The bar code reader scans the bar code and returns the characters read, followed by one or more Enters. If you configure your bar code reader to emit a single Enter, the pointer will wait at the last TextBox for the quantity. If all the items have a bar code, you need not supply a quantity; it's quicker to scan all the items. In this case, you should configure the bar code reader to emit two Enter characters. The program will bring in the description and the price of the item after the first Enter and then accept the default quantity of 1 with the second Enter. Users will be entering new detail lines by simply scanning the bar code of the item.

When the Enter key is pressed in the Quantity TextBox, the program calls the InsertDetailLine subroutine, as shown in Listing 23.6.

Listing 23.6: Accepting the Quantity and Inserting a New Detail Line

```
Private Sub txtQuantity_KeyPress(ByVal sender As Object, _
 ByVal e As System.Windows.Forms.KeyPressEventArgs) _
 Handles txtQuantity.KeyPress
  If e.KeyChar <> vbCr Then Exit Sub
  If Not (IsNumeric(txtQuantity.Text) _
      And Val(txtQuantity.Text) >= 0) Then
    MsgBox("Quantity must be a numeric value" & _
          " greater than zero!")
    Exit Sub
  End If
  InsertDetailLine()
  txtProductID.Focus()
End Sub
```

The InsertDetailLine subroutine adds the new line to the Details DataSet and then moves the focus to the first TextBox, to accept the ID of the next item.

Part VI

The New Invoice button clears the DataSet and prepares the TextBoxes for a new detail line. Here's the code behind this button:

```
Private Sub bttnClear_Click(ByVal sender As System.Object, _
    ByVal e As System.EventArgs) Handles bttnClear.Click
        Details1.Tables(0).Rows.Clear()
        ClearFields()
        txtProductID.Focus()
End Sub
```

The last button on the form, the Save Invoice button, commits the new order to the database in a transaction. First, it adds a new order to the Orders table by calling the NewOrder stored procedure. To test the application, you must add the following stored procedure to the database (see Listing 23.7).

Listing 23.7: The *NewOrder* Stored Procedure

```
CREATE PROCEDURE NewOrder
    @custID nchar(5)
AS
INSERT INTO Orders
    (CustomerID, OrderDate)
    VALUES(@custID, GetDate())
RETURN (@@IDENTITY)
GO
```

This stored procedure adds a new row to the Orders table and returns the ID of the new order. After that, you must add the detail lines to the Order Details table. Each detail line includes the ID of the order to which it belongs (the value returned by the NewOrder stored procedure). Listing 23.8 shows the NewOrderLine stored procedure, which adds a new row to the Order Details table for each detail in the invoice.

Listing 23.8: The *NewOrderLine* Stored Procedure

```
CREATE PROCEDURE NewOrderLine
    @OrderID integer,
    @ProductID integer,
    @quantity integer
AS
DECLARE @ProductPrice money
SET @ProductPrice=(SELECT UnitPrice
    FROM Products WHERE ProductID=@ProductID)
```

```
INSERT INTO [Order Details]
(OrderID, ProductID, Quantity, UnitPrice)
VALUES (@OrderID, @ProductID, @Quantity, @ProductPrice)
GO
```

After adding the two stored procedures to the Northwind database, you're ready to commit the invoices. The code behind the Save Invoice button starts a new transaction and adds the appropriate lines to the Orders and Order Details tables. The value returned by the NewOrder stored procedure is the ID of the new order (a value generated by the database), and it's used to identify this order's details. Each row in the Order Details table that belongs to this order has its OrderID field set to the ID of the order.

If all actions complete successfully, the transaction is committed. If one of them fails, then the entire transaction is aborted. Not much can go wrong in this application, because the data is validated as it's entered. You can't enter negative quantities or change the prices of the products. To force the transaction to abort, you must enter a line, switch to the database and delete from the Products table the item you just added to the invoice, and then attempt to commit the invoice. This is a highly unlikely situation in a production environment (items might go out of stock, but you rarely remove rows from a table). Listing 23.9 shows the code of the Save Invoice button.

Part VI

Listing 23.9: Committing an Invoice

```
Private Sub bttnSave_Click(ByVal sender As System.Object, _
    ByVal e As System.EventArgs) Handles bttnSave.Click
    SqlCommand1.Parameters.Clear()
    SqlCommand1.CommandText = "NewOrder"
    SqlCommand1.CommandType = CommandType.StoredProcedure
    Dim sqlParam As New SqlClient.SqlParameter()
    sqlParam.SqlDbType = SqlDbType.Char
    sqlParam.Size = 5
    sqlParam.ParameterName = "@CustID"
    sqlParam.Direction = ParameterDirection.Input
    SqlCommand1.Parameters.Add(sqlParam)

    sqlParam = New SqlClient.SqlParameter()
    sqlParam.ParameterName = "RETURN"
    sqlParam.SqlDbType = SqlDbType.Int
    sqlParam.Direction = ParameterDirection.ReturnValue
```

```
SqlCommand1.Parameters.Add(sqlParam)
' Replace this customer ID with the ID of the
' <retail> customer or prompt user for the ID
' of an existing customer
SqlCommand1.Parameters("@custID").Value = "ALFKI"


SqlConnection1.Open()
Dim DetailTrans As SqlClient.SqlTransaction
DetailTrans = SqlConnection1.BeginTransaction()
SqlCommand1.Connection = SqlConnection1
SqlCommand1.Transaction = DetailTrans
Dim orderID As Integer
Dim totalItems As Integer
Dim retValue As Integer
Try
   SqlCommand1.ExecuteNonQuery()
   ' STORE THE ID OF THE NEW ORDER

   orderID = CInt(SqlCommand1.Parameters("RETURN").Value)
   SqlCommand1.CommandText = "NewOrderLine"
   SqlCommand1.CommandType = CommandType.StoredProcedure
   ' SET UP THE PARAMETERS COLLECTION
   ' OF THE SQLCOMMAND OBJECT
   SqlCommand1.Parameters.Clear()
   sqlParam = New SqlClient.SqlParameter()
   sqlParam.SqlDbType = SqlDbType.Int
   sqlParam.ParameterName = "@OrderID"
   sqlParam.Direction = ParameterDirection.Input
   SqlCommand1.Parameters.Add(sqlParam)
   ' SET UP THE PRODUCT-ID PARAMETER
   sqlParam = New SqlClient.SqlParameter()
   sqlParam.SqlDbType = SqlDbType.Int
   sqlParam.ParameterName = "@ProductID"
   sqlParam.Direction = ParameterDirection.Input
   SqlCommand1.Parameters.Add(sqlParam)
   ' SET UP THE QUANTITY PARAMETER
   sqlParam = New SqlClient.SqlParameter()
   sqlParam.SqlDbType = SqlDbType.Int
   sqlParam.ParameterName = "@quantity"
   sqlParam.Direction = ParameterDirection.Input
```

```
        SqlCommand1.Parameters.Add(sqlParam)
        ' SET UP THE RETURN_VALUE PARAMETER
        sqlParam = New SqlClient.SqlParameter()
        sqlParam.ParameterName = "RETURN"
        sqlParam.SqlDbType = SqlDbType.Int
        sqlParam.Direction = ParameterDirection.ReturnValue
        SqlCommand1.Parameters.Add(sqlParam)

        Dim row As DataRow
        For Each row In Details1.Tables(0).Rows
            ' ASSIGN VALUES TO ALL PARAMETERS
            ' AND EXECUTE THE QUERY
            SqlCommand1.Parameters("@OrderID").Value = _
                orderID
            SqlCommand1.Parameters("@ProductID").Value = _
                row.Item(0)
            SqlCommand1.Parameters("@quantity").Value = _
                row.Item(3)
            totalItems = totalItems + CInt(row.Item(3))
            SqlCommand1.ExecuteNonQuery()
        Next
        DetailTrans.Commit()
        retValue = orderID
    Catch exc As Exception
        DetailTrans.Rollback()
        MsgBox(exc.Message)
    Finally
        SqlConnection1.Close()
    End Try
    bttnClear_Click(sender, e)
End Sub
```

All invoices are registered to the same customer. The application uses the customer ID of "ALFKI" (the first row in the Customers table). You should add a new customer to the table, a customer with a name such as "RetailCustomer," and use this customer's ID for all orders. Or, you can design another form, where users can locate the desired customer, or specify a new one, enter the shipping address, and so on.

Before ending this example, we should point out a few of the editing features of the application. The most important feature is that the data entry takes place with the help of the keyboard. You can use the mouse, but this is optional. Because this is the type of application you'll deploy in a production environment, it can also be used with a bar code reader, as we noted earlier. Configure your device to read the product's ID and then produce two Enter keystrokes. Users won't have to press a single key to enter the details of an invoice. When done, they can press Control+S to save the invoice. Of course, you must add the code to print the invoice.

To edit a line, just select it. Switch to the DataGrid control by pressing Tab a few times and then use the arrow keys to select the desired line. The fields of the current line in the DataGrid are displayed on the TextBox controls at the top of the form, and you can edit them at will. To delete the current detail line, enter the value **0** in the quantity box.

Notice that when you edit a line, the new quantity is added to the existing quantity. The application is programmed to facilitate entering single items, not for editing invoices. You can also remove the section of the code that goes through the current lines of the invoice to locate a line with the same item. Depending on the type of products sold, you could have multiple lines with the same product ID. The simplest way to use this application is to delete an item and then enter a new line.

You can also customize the application. For example, you can add some code to intercept certain keystroke that removes the most recently added item. To remove an item, the user would enter its ID (or scan its bar code) and then press a function key. Your code should keep track of the most recently added item and then delete the corresponding line from the invoice. Usually, this is how a program at the cash register works: You scan the item you want to remove from the invoice and press a key to indicate that the item should be removed from the invoice.

THE ONLINESTORE PROJECT

The second example of this chapter is a web application. The OnlineStore project consists of two forms: a form on which you can select products and place them in your basket, and another form that displays the current contents of the basket and enables you to edit the quantities. Entering zero as the quantity effectively removes the item from the basket. Figures 23.4 and 23.5 show the two forms of the application.

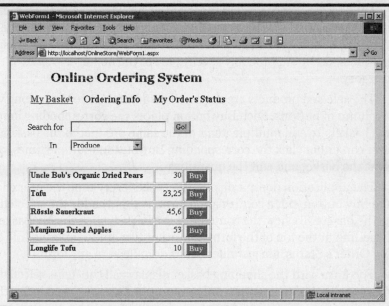

FIGURE 23.4: Selecting products by name or category

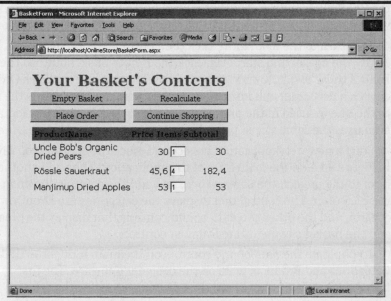

FIGURE 23.5: Editing the basket's contents

Part VI

Let's review the basic operations of the application. On the first form of the application, the user can select items by specifying part of their name, by selecting a category, or both. If your database contains many products, users will probably specify part of the name, as well as a category.

The selected products are displayed on a DataList control, along with a column of buttons. Each Buy button places the corresponding item into the basket. To add multiple items of the same product to the basket, the user can either click the corresponding Buy button multiple times, or view the basket and edit the quantities.

The application doesn't display the basket every time the user clicks the Buy button, nor a confirmation form. It simply adds the selected item to the basket. To view the contents of the basket, click the My Basket hyperlink at the top of the form. The other two links, Ordering Info and My Order's Status, are just fillers; they don't lead to any form.

The form with the shopping basket displays all the items selected so far, along with their quantities. The quantities are displayed in TextBoxes so the user can edit them. After changing the quantities, the user must click the Recalculate button. The editing of the quantities takes place at the client, and they won't be stored to the basket unless the user clicks the Recalculate button. This button will post the page to the server, where the basket's contents are updated through the appropriate code.

To return to the main form, click the Continue Shopping button. To empty the basket and start over, click the Empty Basket button. The code behind these two buttons is rather trivial. The last button, Place Order, creates a new order and inserts it into the database. The code is the same as the one we used in the previous example to create a new invoice, and it even uses the same stored procedures: `NewOrder` and `NewOrderLine`.

Start a new web application project and place the controls you saw in Figure 23.4 on the main form of the application. Then add another form to the project, the `BasketForm`, and add the controls shown in Figure 23.5 on it. The control that displays the categories is a DropDownList control, and the other two data-bound controls that display the products and the basket's contents are DataList controls.

To populate the data-bound controls on the main form, drop the Categories and Products table on the designer's surface. The first DataAdapter object should use the following query to select the categories:

```
SELECT  CategoryID, CategoryName FROM Categories
```

You should also disable the generation of the Update, Insert, and Delete commands. The second DataAdapter, which retrieves the qualifying products, is another simple query that retrieves the products of a category:

```
SELECT  ProductID, ProductName, QuantityPerUnit, UnitPrice
FROM    Products
WHERE   (CategoryID = @categoryID)
```

As you will see, this query will never be used in the code. We specified it here so that you can bind the DataList control to a DataSet with the desired fields. In your code, you will generate a query that will take into consideration the data supplied by the user on the two controls (the TextBox and the DropDownList controls).

Now generate a DataSet for each DataAdapter and name them **DSCategories** and **SelectedProducts**. Bind the DropDownList control to the instance of the DSCategories DataSet and the DataList control to the instance of the SelectedProducts DataSet.

The next step is to configure the DataList control on the main form. Each row of the DataList is formatted as a table. The cells of the table have the same width, so that the columns will be aligned. Notice how you retrieve the current row's field values through the DataBinder.Eval() method. This method accepts two arguments, the current row (Container .DataItem) and the name of the field whose value you want to read, as shown in Listing 23.10.

Part VI

Listing 23.10: The DataList Control's ItemTemplate Definition

```
<ItemTemplate>
  <TABLE border="all">
    <TR>
      <TD vAlign="top" width="240"><B>
<%# databinder.Eval(Container.DataItem, "ProductName") %>
        </B></TD>
      <TD vAlign="top" align="right" width="50">
<%# databinder.Eval(Container.DataItem, "UnitPrice") %>
      </TD>
      <TD vAlign="center" align="middle" width="50">
<asp:Button id=bttnBuy runat="server" Font-Bold="True"
Text="Buy" Font-Name="Georgia" ForeColor="#ffffcc"
BackColor="#cc6666" CommandArgument=
```

```
'<%# databinder.Eval(Container.DataItem, "ProductID") %>'>
                </asp:Button></TD>
      </TR>
    </TABLE>
  </ItemTemplate>
```

The last column contains a button. It is placed there with the `<asp:Button>` tag, which includes the CommandArgument attribute. The CommandArgument attribute is set to the ID of the product displayed on the current row. Here's the definition of the `<asp:Button>` tag:

```
<asp:Button id=bttnBuy runat="server" Font-Bold="True"
Text="Buy" Font-Name="Georgia" ForeColor="#ffffcc"
BackColor="#cc6666" CommandArgument='<%# _
   databinder.Eval(Container.DataItem, "ProductID") %>'>
</asp:Button></TD>
```

Note how the value of the CommandArgument is specified, and that the entire expression is delimited by single quotes. When this button is clicked, it invokes the OrderItem subroutine in your code. This must be specified in the declaration of the DataList control, which is as follows:

```
<asp:datalist id=DataList1
style="Z-INDEX: 106; LEFT: 34px; POSITION: absolute;
TOP: 206px" runat="server" Width="394px" DataSource="<%# _
   SelectedProducts1 %>"
DataMember="Products" DataKeyField="ProductID"
Height="128px" OnItemCommand="OrderItem">
```

The OnItemCommand attribute must be added manually, and it must be set to the name of a subroutine, which will be invoked automatically when an item is selected on the DataList control. The OrderItem subroutine adds the current row's item to the shopping basket. Listing 23.11 shows its implementation.

Listing 23.11: Adding the Selected Item to the Basket

```
Public Sub OrderItem(ByVal sender As Object, _
ByVal e As _
System.Web.UI.WebControls.DataListCommandEventArgs)
   Dim productID As Integer = e.CommandArgument
   ShoppingBasket = Session("UserBasket")
   If ShoppingBasket.ContainsKey(productID) Then
      ShoppingBasket(productID) = _
```

```
            Val(ShoppingBasket(productID) + 1)
    Else
        ShoppingBasket.Add(productID, 1)
    End If
    Session("Basket") = ShoppingBasket
End Sub
```

The selected product's ID is passed to the subroutine through the e argument, and it's the value of the CommandArgument property. If the product's ID exists in the basket, the corresponding quantity is increased by one. If not, it's added to the basket and the corresponding quantity is set to 1.

When the application is first loaded, the main form's Load event handler is executed, as shown in Listing 23.12.

Listing 23.12: Displaying the Categories

```
Private Sub Page_Load(ByVal sender As System.Object, _
  ByVal e As System.EventArgs) Handles MyBase.Load
    'Put user code to initialize the page here
    If Not Page.IsPostBack Then
        If Session("UserBasket") Is Nothing Then
            ShoppingBasket = New Hashtable()
            Session("UserBasket") = ShoppingBasket
        End If
        DACategories.Fill(DsCategories1)
        Dim newRow As DSCategories.CategoriesRow
        newRow = DsCategories1.Tables(0).NewRow
        newRow.CategoryID = "999"
        newRow.CategoryName = "All"
        DsCategories1.Tables(0).Rows.InsertAt(newRow, 0)
        DropDownList1.DataSource = DsCategories1
        DropDownList1.DataMember = "Categories"
        DropDownList1.DataTextField = "CategoryName"
        DropDownList1.DataValueField = "CategoryID"
        DropDownList1.DataBind()
    End If
End Sub
```

The code creates a new HashTable, where the basket's contents will be stored. The shopping basket is stored in the *UserBasket* Session variable. This variable is a HashTable, and each item is stored as two numeric values. The product's ID is the key, and the quantity is the value.

Then the code fills the `DSCategories` DataSet with the rows of the Categories table and binds the DropDownList control to the Categories table of the `DSCategories` DataSet. It also adds a new row to the table, the "All" category, which includes all the categories. The ID of this category is 999, and you'll soon see how it's used in the code.

The Go button retrieves the qualifying products from the database and populates the `SelectedProducts` DataSet. The code behind this button, which is shown in Listing 23.13, takes into consideration the values entered on the form by the user, and it executes the appropriate SELECT statement against the database.

Listing 23.13: Displaying the Selected Products on a DataList Control

```
Private Sub bttnGO_Click(ByVal sender As System.Object, _
  ByVal e As System.EventArgs) Handles bttnGO.Click
  If DropDownList1.SelectedItem.Value = 999 Then
    DAProducts.SelectCommand.CommandText = _
      "SELECT ProductID, ProductName, UnitPrice " & _
      "FROM Products WHERE ProductName LIKE '%" & _
      txtProductName.Text & "%'"
  Else
    DAProducts.SelectCommand.CommandText = _
      "SELECT ProductID, ProductName, UnitPrice " & _
      "FROM Products WHERE CategoryID=" & _
      DropDownList1.SelectedItem.Value & _
      " AND ProductName LIKE '%" & _
      txtProductName.Text & "%'"
  End If

  DAProducts.SelectCommand.Parameters("@categoryID").Value _
    = DropDownList1.SelectedItem.Value
  DAProducts.SelectCommand.Parameters("@productName").Value _
    = txtProductName.Text
  DAProducts.Fill(SelectedProducts1, "Products")
  DataList1.DataBind()
End Sub
```

The `ShowBasket` subroutine displays the basket's contents on a Data-List control. The code, shown in Listing 23.14, creates a new DataSet, the `DSBasket` DataSet, and adds five columns to it: ProductID, ProductName, ProductPrice, Quantity, and Subtotal. These are the items shown in the DataList control that displays the contents of the basket, except for the

ProductID column. This column isn't displayed, but you need to know each product's ID to update the basket.

Then the code iterates through the contents of the basket, collects their IDs, and retrieves the related information from the Products table. The results are returned to the application through an SqlDataReader object, and then the DSBasket DataSet is populated. After the DataList control is bound to the DataSet, the basket's contents are displayed on the control.

Listing 23.11: Displaying the Basket's Contents on a DataList Control

```
Sub ShowBasket()
    'Put user code to initialize the page here
    Dim DSBasket As New DataSet()
    DSBasket.Tables.Add("BASKET")
    DSBasket.Tables("BASKET").Columns.Add("ProductID")
    DSBasket.Tables("BASKET").Columns.Add("ProductName")
    DSBasket.Tables("BASKET").Columns.Add("ProductPrice")
    DSBasket.Tables("BASKET").Columns.Add("Quantity")
    DSBasket.Tables("BASKET").Columns.Add("Subtotal")
    Dim prodRow As DataRow
    Dim UserBasket As New Hashtable()
    UserBasket = Session("UserBasket")

    Dim itm As Integer
    Dim SelIDs As String
    If UserBasket.Count = 0 Then
        Label1.Text = "Your basket is empty"
        Exit Sub
    End If
    For Each itm In UserBasket.Keys
        SelIDs = SelIDs & itm.ToString & ", "
    Next
    SelIDs = Left(SelIDs, Len(SelIDs) - 2)
    Dim sql As String
    sql = "SELECT ProductID, ProductName, UnitPrice " & _
          "FROM Products " & _
          "WHERE ProductID IN (" & SelIDs & ")"
    Dim conn As New SqlClient.SqlConnection()
    conn.ConnectionString = "initial catalog=Northwind; " & _
        "persist security info=False;user id=sa; " & _
        "workstation id=POWERTOOLKIT;packet size=4096"
```

Part VI

```
            conn.Open()
            Dim sqlCMD As New SqlClient.SqlCommand()
            sqlCMD.Connection = conn
            sqlCMD.CommandText = sql
            sqlCMD.CommandType = CommandType.Text
            Dim DataIn As SqlClient.SqlDataReader
            DataIn = sqlCMD.ExecuteReader()
            While DataIn.Read
              prodRow = DSBasket.Tables("BASKET").NewRow
              prodRow.Item(0) = DataIn.Item(0)
              prodRow.Item(1) = DataIn.Item(1)
              prodRow.Item(2) = DataIn.Item(2)
              prodRow.Item(3) = UserBasket(DataIn.Item(0))
              prodRow.Item(4) = CDec(prodRow.Item(2)) * _
                  CDec(prodRow.Item(3))
              DSBasket.Tables("BASKET").Rows.Add(prodRow)
            End While
            DataList1.DataSource = DSBasket
            DataList1.DataMember = "BASKET"
            DataList1.DataKeyField = "ProductID"
            DataList1.DataBind()
        End Sub
```

You must also configure the DataList control. The control's
ItemTemplate and HeaderTemplate sections are shown here:

```
    <HeaderTemplate>
        <TABLE>
        <TR>
          <TD width="180"><b>ProductName</b>
          </TD>
          <TD align="right" width="50"><b>Price</b>
          </TD>
          <TD align="right" width="50"><b>Items</b>
          </TD>
          <TD align="right" width="70"><b>Subtotal</b>
          </TD>
        </TR>
        </TABLE>
    </HeaderTemplate>
```

```
<ItemTemplate>
   <TABLE>
   <TR>
     <TD width="200">
             <%# databinder.Eval(Container.DataItem, _
                "ProductName") %></TD>
     <TD align="right" width="70">
             <%# databinder.Eval(Container.DataItem, _
                "ProductPrice") %></TD>
     <TD align="right">
             <asp:TextBox id="txtQuantity" Width="30" _
             runat="server" text='<%# _
             databinder.Eval(Container.DataItem, _
             "Quantity") %>'></asp:TextBox></TD>
     <TD align="right" width="80">
             <%# databinder.Eval(Container.DataItem, _
                "Subtotal") %></TD>
   </TR>
   </TABLE>
</ItemTemplate>
```

The TextBox control that enables users to edit the quantities was inserted with the <asp:TextBox> tag, and its value is the current product's quantity. To retrieve this value from the control's DataSet, you use the DataBinder.Eval() method, as before.

The user can edit all the quantities on the form, or remove a product from the basket by setting its quantity to zero. Then, the Recalculate button must be clicked to update the contents of the basket (see Listing 23.15).

Listing 23.15: Recalculating the Basket's Total

```
Private Sub bttnRecalc_Click(ByVal sender _
 As System.Object, ByVal e As System.EventArgs) _
 Handles bttnRecal.Click
   Dim UserBasket As New Hashtable()
   Dim newUserBasket As New Hashtable()
   UserBasket = Session("UserBasket")
```

```
Dim currentRow As Integer
Dim qty As Integer
Dim key As IEnumerator
Dim keys As ICollection
keys = DataList1.DataKeys
key = keys.GetEnumerator
Dim itm As Integer
While key.MoveNext
    itm = key.Current
    qty = _
        CType(DataList1.Items( _
        currentRow).FindControl("txtQuantity"), _
        TextBox).Text
    If qty > 0 Then
        newUserBasket.Add(itm, qty)
    End If
    currentRow = currentRow + 1
End While
Session("UserBasket") = newUserBasket
ShowBasket()
End Sub
```

This is an interesting section of the application. The code goes through the IDs in the basket with the `While` loop. At each iteration, it extracts a product ID from the basket and stores it in the *itm* variable. To find the quantity of this product on the control, it calls the current item's `FindControl()` method. The current item on the control is given by the expression `DataList1.Items(`*currentRow*`)`, where *currentRow* is an index that is increased by one at each iteration. This expression returns one of the control's items. If the item contains one or more controls, you can retrieve a reference to these controls through the `FindControl()` method, which accepts as an argument the control's name. After you have a reference to the TextBox control with the revised quantity, you can cast it to the TextBox type and request its Text property. The product IDs and the matching quantities are added to a new HashTable, which is then assigned to the *UserBasket* Session variable.

Why did we have to introduce a second HashTable and not manipulate the original HashTable directly? If you remove an item from a collection while you iterate it with its Enumerator, the results are unpredictable. The safest approach is to copy the elements with positive quantities to another HashTable and then use the new HashTable as the shopping basket.

To store the order to the database, the Place Order button initiates a transaction, calls the NewOrder and the NewOrderLine stored procedures, and then either commits or aborts the transaction. The key portion of the code behind the Place Order button goes through each item in the HashTable that stores the items of the shopping basket. The code calls the NewOrderLine stored procedure for each item, passing the product's ID and its quantity as arguments. It also passes a third argument, which contains the ID of the order to which the detail line belongs (this is the value returned by the NewOrder stored procedure).

As with the invoicing demo, the web application doesn't prompt the user for additional information, such as the shipping address and payment method. For this, you'll need to display yet another form and display it before committing the order to the database. Listing 23.16 shows the code behind the Place Order button.

Listing 23.16: Storing an Order to the Database

```
Private Sub bttnCommit_Click(ByVal sender _
  As System.Object, ByVal e As System.EventArgs) _
  Handles bttnCommit.Click
  Dim UserBasket As New Hashtable()
  UserBasket = Session("UserBasket")
  Dim CMD As New SqlClient.SqlCommand()
  CMD.CommandText = "NewOrder"
  CMD.CommandType = CommandType.StoredProcedure
  Dim sqlParam As New SqlClient.SqlParameter()
  sqlParam.SqlDbType = SqlDbType.Char
  sqlParam.Size = 5
  sqlParam.ParameterName = "@CustID"
  sqlParam.Direction = ParameterDirection.Input
  CMD.Parameters.Add(sqlParam)

  sqlParam = New SqlClient.SqlParameter()
  sqlParam.ParameterName = "RETURN"
  sqlParam.SqlDbType = SqlDbType.Int
  sqlParam.Direction = ParameterDirection.ReturnValue
  CMD.Parameters.Add(sqlParam)
  CMD.Parameters("@custID").Value = "ALFKI"

  SqlConnection1.Open()
  Dim DetailTrans As SqlClient.SqlTransaction
  DetailTrans = SqlConnection1.BeginTransaction()
```

```
CMD.Connection = SqlConnection1
CMD.Transaction = DetailTrans
Dim orderID As Integer
Dim totalItems As Integer
Dim key As IEnumerator
Dim keys As ICollection
keys = DataList1.DataKeys
key = keys.GetEnumerator
Dim itm, qty As Integer
Try
  CMD.ExecuteNonQuery()
  orderID = CMD.Parameters("RETURN").Value
  While key.MoveNext
    itm = key.Current
    qty = UserBasket(itm)
    If qty > 0 Then
      CMD.CommandText = "NewOrderLine"
      CMD.CommandType = CommandType.StoredProcedure
      CMD.Parameters.Clear()

      sqlParam = New SqlClient.SqlParameter()
      sqlParam.SqlDbType = SqlDbType.Int
      sqlParam.ParameterName = "@OrderID"
      sqlParam.Direction = ParameterDirection.Input
      CMD.Parameters.Add(sqlParam)

      sqlParam = New SqlClient.SqlParameter()
      sqlParam.SqlDbType = SqlDbType.Int
      sqlParam.ParameterName = "@ProductID"
      sqlParam.Direction = ParameterDirection.Input
      CMD.Parameters.Add(sqlParam)

      sqlParam = New SqlClient.SqlParameter()
      sqlParam.SqlDbType = SqlDbType.Int
      sqlParam.ParameterName = "@quantity"
      sqlParam.Direction = ParameterDirection.Input
      CMD.Parameters.Add(sqlParam)

      sqlParam = New SqlClient.SqlParameter()
      sqlParam.ParameterName = "RETURN"
      sqlParam.SqlDbType = SqlDbType.Int
```

```
        sqlParam.Direction = ParameterDirection.ReturnValue
        CMD.Parameters.Add(sqlParam)

        CMD.Parameters("@OrderID").Value = orderID
        CMD.Parameters("@ProductID").Value = itm
        CMD.Parameters("@quantity").Value = qty
        CMD.ExecuteNonQuery()
      End If
    End While
    DetailTrans.Commit()
  Catch exc As Exception
  Finally
    SqlConnection1.Close()
  End Try
End Sub
```

Finally, there's a little bit of code behind the other two buttons. The Continue Shopping button redirects the user to the main form of the application with the following statement:

```
Response.Redirect("WebForm1.aspx")
```

The Empty Basket button empties the basket with the following statements:

```
        Dim Basket As New Hashtable()
        Basket = Session("UserBasket")
        Basket.Clear()
        Session("UserBasket") = Basket
```

WHAT'S NEXT

This book has introduced you to many Sybex authors and titles, and it has covered a variety of subjects. Although this book seeks to be an introduction to the concepts of Visual Basic .NET, each concept is covered in even greater detail in many of the source books listed at the beginning of each chapter. For more information on additional Sybex books, refer to www.sybex.com.

Part VI

INDEX

Note to the Reader: Throughout this index **boldfaced** page numbers indicate primary discussions of a topic. *Italicized* page numbers indicate illustrations.

H

ABOUT THE CONTRIBUTORS

S ome of the best—and best-selling—Sybex authors have contributed chapters from their books to *Visual Basic .NET Complete*.

Asli Bilgin is a .NET Technical Evangelist for Plural, where she consults for Fortune 500 companies on enterprise development using Microsoft technologies. She is a contributing editor to *Inside Visual Basic* and has written many articles on ASP.NET and ADO.NET.

Mike Gunderloy, MCSE, MCSD, MCDBA, and MCT, is a senior consultant with MCW Technologies, where he specializes in Microsoft Visual Basic and SQL Server. He is the author of *Visual Basic Developer's Guide to ADO* and *VB/VBA Developer's Guide to the Windows Installer*, both from Sybex.

Kevin Hough is a senior developer and consultant for Fortune 500 companies and specializes in high-level client server applications written in VB and SQL Server. He wrote Sybex's *MCSE/MCSD: SQL Server 7 Database Design Study Guide*.

A. Russell Jones, Ph.D., a confessed former zookeeper and professional musician, now composes computer applications. He is a consultant and the Managing Web Development Editor for the leading website for professional developers, www.devx.com. He is a regular contributor to *Visual Basic Programmer's Journal* and wrote Sybex's *Mastering Active Server Pages 3* and *Visual Basic Developer's Guide to ASP and IIS*.

Evangelos Petroutsos is a computer engineer who has worked for the California Institute of Technology and MCI. Currently, he writes computer books and articles, teaches networking and programming courses, and works as a computer communications consultant. Recently he has consulted on a number of major e-commerce projects. He wrote the best-selling *Mastering Visual Basic 6*, *Visual Basic 6 Developer's Handbook*, and *Mastering Database Programming with Visual Basic 6*, all from Sybex. A Visual Basic programmer since version 1, Evangelos has taught numerous VB courses and worked as a consultant on many VB projects.